New Perspectives on

Microsoft®

Excel 97

COMPREHENSIVE

The New Perspectives Series

The New Perspectives Series consists of texts and technology that teach computer concepts and microcomputer applications (listed below). You can order these New Perspectives texts in many different lengths, software releases, custom-bound combinations, CourseKits™ and Custom Editions®. Contact your Course Technology sales representative or customer service representative for the most up-to-date details.

The New Perspectives Series

Computer Concepts

Borland® dBASE®

Borland® Paradox®

Corel® Presentations™

Corel® Quattro Pro®

Corel® WordPerfect®

DOS

HTML

Lotus® 1-2-3®

Microsoft® Access

Microsoft® Excel

Microsoft® Internet Explorer

Microsoft® Office Professional

Microsoft® PowerPoint®

Microsoft® Windows® 3.1

Microsoft® Windows® 95

Microsoft® Windows NT® Server 4.0

Microsoft® Windows NT® Workstation 4.0

Microsoft® Word

Microsoft® Works

Netscape Navigator™

Netscape Navigator™ Gold

Microsoft® Visual Basic® 4 and 5

New Perspectives on
Microsoft®
Excel 97

COMPREHENSIVE

June Jamrich Parsons
University of the Virgin Islands

Dan Oja
Guildware, Inc.

Roy Ageloff
University of Rhode Island

Patrick Carey

COURSE
TECHNOLOGY

ONE MAIN STREET, CAMBRIDGE, MA 02142

an International Thomson Publishing company I⊤P®

Cambridge • Albany • Bonn • Boston • Cincinnati • London • Madrid • Melbourne • Mexico City
New York • Paris • San Francisco • Singapore • Tokyo • Toronto • Washington

New Perspectives on Microsoft® Excel 97 — Comprehensive is published by Course Technology.

Associate Publisher	Mac Mendelsohn
Series Consulting Editor	Susan Solomon
Product Manager	Donna Gridley
Developmental Editor	Barbara Clemens
Production Editor	Nancy Ray
Text and Cover Designer	Ella Hanna
Cover Illustrator	Douglas Goodman

© 1997 by Course Technology
A Division of International Thomson Publishing Inc. — IⓣP®
For more information contact:

Course Technology
One Main Street
Cambridge, MA 02142

International Thomson Publishing Europe
Berkshire House 168-173
High Holborn
London WCIV 7AA
England

Thomas Nelson Australia
102 Dodds Street
South Melbourne, 3205
Victoria, Australia

Nelson Canada
1120 Birchmount Road
Scarborough, Ontario
Canada M1K 5G4

International Thomson Editores
Campos Eliseos 385, Piso 7
Col. Polanco
11560 Mexico D.F. Mexico

International Thomson Publishing GmbH
Königswinterer Strasse 418
53227 Bonn
Germany

International Thomson Publishing Asia
211 Henderson Road
#05-10 Henderson Building
Singapore 0315

International Thomson Publishing Japan
Hirakawacho Kyowa Building, 3F
2-2-1 Hirakawacho
Chiyoda-ku, Tokyo 102
Japan

Trademarks
Course Technology and the Open Book logo are registered trademarks and CourseKits is a trademark of Course Technology. Custom Editions and the ITP logo are registered trademarks of International Thomson Publishing Inc.

Microsoft and the Office logo are either registered trademarks or trademarks of Microsoft Corporation in the United States and/or other countries. Course Technology is an independent entity from Microsoft Corporation, and not affiliated with Microsoft Corporation in any manner. This text may be used in assisting students to prepare for a Certified Microsoft Office User Exam. Neither Microsoft Corporation, its designated review company, nor Course Technology warrants that use of this text will ensure passing the relevant CMOU Exam.

Some of the product names and company names used in this book have been used for identification purposes only and may be trademarks or registered trademarks of their respective manufacturers and sellers.

Disclaimer
Course Technology reserves the right to revise this publication and make changes from time to time in its content without notice.

ISBN 0-7600-5261-1

Printed in the United States of America

10 9 8 7 6 5 4 3 2

From the **New Perspectives Series Team**

At **Course Technology** we have one foot in education and the other in technology. We believe that technology is transforming the way people teach and learn, and we are excited about providing instructors and students with materials that use technology to teach about technology.

Our development process is unparalleled in the higher education publishing industry. Every product we create goes through an exacting process of design, development, review, and testing.

Reviewers give us direction and insight that shape our manuscripts and bring them up to the latest standards. Every manuscript is quality tested. Students whose backgrounds match the intended audience work through every keystroke, carefully checking for clarity and pointing out errors in logic and sequence. Together with our own technical reviewers, these testers help us ensure that everything that carries our name is error-free and easy to use.

We show both how and why technology is critical to solving problems in college and in whatever field you choose to teach or pursue. Our time-tested, step-by-step instructions provide unparalleled clarity. Examples and applications are chosen and crafted to motivate students.

As the New Perspectives Series team at Course Technology, our goal is to produce the most timely, accurate, creative, and technologically sound product in the entire college publishing industry. We strive for consistent high quality. This takes a lot of communication, coordination, and hard work. But we love what we do. We are determined to be the best. Write to us and let us know what you think. You can also e-mail us at *NewPerspectives@course.com*.

The New Perspectives Series Team

Joseph J. Adamski	Jessica Evans	Dan Oja
Judy Adamski	Marilyn Freedman	David Paradice
Roy Ageloff	Kathy Finnegan	June Parsons
David Auer	Robin Geller	Harry Phillips
Dirk Baldwin	Donna Gridley	Sandra Poindexter
Daphne Barbas	Roger Hayen	Mark Reimold
Rachel Bunin	Charles Hommel	Ann Shaffer
Joan Carey	Janice Jutras	Susan Solomon
Patrick Carey	Chris Kelly	Susanne Walker
Sharon Caswell	Mary Kemper	John Zeanchock
Barbara Clemens	Terry Ann Kremer	Beverly Zimmerman
Rachel Crapser	John Leschke	Scott Zimmerman
Kim Crowley	Mac Mendelsohn	
Michael Ekedahl	William Newman	

What is the New Perspectives Series?

Course Technology's **New Perspectives Series** is an integrated system of instruction that combines text and technology products to teach computer concepts and microcomputer applications. Users consistently praise this series for innovative pedagogy, creativity, supportive and engaging style, accuracy, and use of interactive technology. The first New Perspectives text was published in January of 1993. Since then, the series has grown to more than 100 titles and has become the best-selling series on computer concepts and microcomputer applications. Others have imitated the New Perspectives features, design, and technologies, but none have replicated its quality and its ability to consistently anticipate and meet the needs of instructors and students.

What is the Integrated System of Instruction?

New Perspectives textbooks are part of a truly Integrated System of Instruction: text, graphics, video, sound, animation, and simulations that are linked and that provide a flexible, unified, and interactive system to help you teach and help your students learn. Specifically, the *New Perspectives Integrated System of Instruction* includes a Course Technology textbook in addition to some or all of the following items: Course Labs, Course Test Manager, Online Companions, and Course Presenter. These components—shown in the graphic on the back cover of this book—have been developed to work together to provide a complete, integrative teaching and learning experience.

How is the New Perspectives Series different from other microcomputer concepts and applications series?

The **New Perspectives Series** distinguishes itself from other series in at least four substantial ways: sound instructional design, consistent quality, innovative technology, and proven pedagogy. The applications texts in this series consist of two or more tutorials, which are based on sound instructional design. Each tutorial is motivated by a realistic case that is meaningful to students. Rather than learn a laundry list of features, students learn the features in the context of solving a problem. This process motivates all concepts and skills by demonstrating to students *why* they would want to know them.

Instructors and students have come to rely on the high quality of the **New Perspectives Series** and to consistently praise its accuracy. This accuracy is a result of Course Technology's unique multi-step quality assurance process that incorporates student testing at at least two stages of development, using hardware and software configurations appropriate to the product. All solutions, test questions, and other supplements are tested using similar procedures. Instructors who adopt this series report that students can work through the tutorials independently with minimum intervention or "damage control" by instructors or staff. This consistent quality has meant that if instructors are pleased with one product from the series, they can rely on the same quality with any other New Perspectives product.

The **New Perspectives Series** also distinguishes itself by its innovative technology. This series innovated Course Labs, truly *interactive* learning applications. These have set the standard for interactive learning.

How do I know that the New Perspectives Series will work?

Some instructors who use this series report a significant difference between how much their students learn and retain with this series as compared to other series. With other series, instructors often find that students can work through the book and do well on homework and tests, but still not demonstrate competency when asked to perform particular tasks outside the context of the text's sample case or project. With the **New Perspectives Series**, however, instructors report that students have a complete, integrative learning experience that stays with them. They credit this high retention and competency to the fact that this series incorporates critical thinking and problem-solving with computer skills mastery.

How does this book I'm holding fit into the New Perspectives Series?

New Perspectives applications books are available in the following categories:

Brief books are typically about 150 pages long, contain two to four tutorials, and are intended to teach the basics of an application.

Introductory books are typically about 300 pages long and consist of four to seven tutorials that go beyond the basics. These books often build out of the Brief editions by providing two or three additional tutorials.

Comprehensive books are typically about 600 pages long and consist of all of the tutorials in the Introductory books, plus four or five more tutorials covering higher-level topics. Comprehensive books also include two Windows tutorials and three or four Additional Cases. The book you are holding is a Comprehensive book.

Advanced books cover topics similar to those in the Comprehensive books, but go into more depth. Advanced books present the most high-level coverage in the series.

Custom Books The New Perspectives Series offers you two ways to customize a New Perspectives text to fit your course exactly: *CourseKits*™, two or more texts packaged together in a box, and *Custom Editions*®, your choice of books bound together. Custom Editions offer you unparalleled flexibility in designing your concepts and applications courses. You can build your own book by ordering a combination of titles bound together to cover only the topics you want. Your students save because they buy only the materials they need. There is no minimum order, and books are spiral bound. Both CourseKits and Custom Editions offer significant price discounts. Contact your Course Technology sales representative for more information.

New Perspectives Series Microcomputer Applications

■ **Brief Titles or Modules**   ■ **Introductory Titles or Modules**   ■ **Intermediate Tutorials**   ■ **Advanced Titles or Modules**   □ **Other Modules**

Brief	Introductory	Comprehensive	Advanced	Custom Editions
2 to 4 tutorials	6 or 7 tutorials, or Brief + 2 or 3 more tutorials	Introductory + 4 or 5 more tutorials. Includes Brief Windows tutorials and Additional Cases	Quick Review of basics + in-depth, high-level coverage	Choose from any of the above to build your own Custom Editions® or CourseKits™

In what kind of course could I use this book?

This book can be used in any course in which you want students to learn all the most important topics of Microsoft Excel 97, including creating, editing, and formatting spreadsheets, charts, lists, and integrating Excel with other applications; working with multiple worksheets, one- and two-variable input tables, and Solver; importing data, and creating applications using Visual Basic. It is particularly recommended for a full-semester course on Microsoft Excel 97. This book assumes that students have learned basic Windows 95 navigation and file management skills from Course Technology's *New Perspectives on Microsoft Windows 95—Brief* or an *equivalent* book.

This book has been approved by Microsoft as courseware for the Certified Microsoft Office User (CMOU) program. After completing the tutorials and exercises in this book, you will be prepared to take the Proficient level CMOU Exam for Microsoft Excel 97. By passing the certification exam for a Microsoft software program you demonstrate your proficiency in that program to employers. CMOU exams are offered at participating test centers, participating corporations, and participating employment agencies. For more information about certification, please visit the CMOU program World Wide Web site at http://www.microsoft.com/office/train_cert/.

How do the Windows 95 editions differ from the Windows 3.1 editions?

Sessions We've divided the tutorials into sessions. Each session is designed to be completed in about 45 minutes to an hour (depending, of course, upon student needs and the speed of your lab equipment). With sessions, learning is broken up into more easily assimilated portions. You can more accurately allocate time in your syllabus, and students can better manage the available lab time. Each session begins with a "session box," which quickly describes the skills students will learn in the session. Furthermore, each session is numbered, which makes it easier for you and your students to navigate and communicate about the tutorial. Look on page E 4.21 for the session box that opens Session 4.2.

Quick Check

Quick Checks Each session concludes with meaningful, conceptual Quick Check questions that test students' understanding of what they learned in the session. Answers to the Quick Check questions in this book are provided on pages E 4.38 through E 4.40, E 7.51 through E 7.52, and E 12.53 through E 12.58.

New Design We have retained the best of the old design to help students differentiate between what they are to *do* and what they are to *read*. The steps are clearly identified by their shaded background and numbered steps. Furthermore, this new design presents steps and screen shots in a larger, easier to read format. Some good examples of our new design are pages E 3.19 and E 10.24.

What features are retained in the Windows 95 editions of the New Perspectives Series?

"Read This Before You Begin" Page This page is consistent with Course Technology's unequaled commitment to helping instructors introduce technology into the classroom. Technical considerations and assumptions about software are listed to help instructors save time and eliminate unnecessary aggravation. See pages E 1.2, E 5.2, and E 8.2 for the "Read This Before You Begin" pages in this book.

Tutorial Case Each tutorial begins with a problem presented in a case that is meaningful to students. The problem turns the task of learning how to use an application into a problem-solving process. The problems increase in complexity with each tutorial. These cases touch on multicultural, international, and ethical issues—so important to today's business curriculum. See page E 1.3 for the case that begins Tutorial 1.

Step-by-Step Methodology This unique Course Technology methodology keeps students on track. They enter data, click buttons, or press keys always within the context of solving the problem posed in the tutorial case. The text constantly guides students, letting them know where they are in the course of solving the problem. In addition, the numerous screen shots include labels that direct students' attention to what they should look at on the screen. On almost every page in this book, you can find an example of how steps, screen shots, and labels work together.

TROUBLE?

TROUBLE? Paragraphs These paragraphs anticipate the mistakes or problems that students are likely to have and help them recover and continue with the tutorial. By putting these paragraphs in the book, rather than in the Instructor's Manual, we facilitate independent learning and free the instructor to focus on substantive conceptual issues rather than on common procedural errors. Some representative examples of TROUBLE? paragraphs appear on page E 2.34.

Reference Windows Reference Windows appear throughout the text. They are succinct summaries of the most important tasks covered in the tutorials. Reference Windows are specially designed and written so students can refer to them when doing the Tutorial Assignments and Case Problems, and after completing the course. Page E 2.11 contains the Reference Window for Copying Cell Contents with the Fill Handle.

Task Reference The Task Reference contains a summary of how to perform common tasks using the most efficient method, as well as references to pages where the task is discussed in more detail. It appears as a table at the end of the book.

Tutorial Assignments, Case Problems, and Lab Assignments Each tutorial concludes with Tutorial Assignments, which provide students with additional hands-on practice of the skills they learned in the tutorial. See page E 4.34 for examples of Tutorial Assignments. The Tutorial Assignments are followed by four Case Problems that have approximately the same scope as the tutorial case. In the Windows 95 applications texts, the last Case Problem of each tutorial typically requires students to solve the problem independently, either "from scratch" or with minimum guidance. See page E 10.29 for examples of Case Problems. Finally, if a Course Lab accompanies a tutorial, Lab Assignments are included after the Case Problems. See page E 1.35 for examples of Lab Assignments.

Exploration Exercises The Windows environment allows students to learn by exploring and discovering what they can do. Exploration Exercises can be Tutorial Assignments or Case Problems that challenge students, encourage them to explore the capabilities of the program they are using, and extend their knowledge using the Help facility and other reference materials. Page E 3.39 contains Exploration Exercises for Tutorial 3.

What supplements are available with this textbook?

Course Labs: Now, Concepts Come to Life Computer skills and concepts come to life with the New Perspectives Course Labs—highly-interactive tutorials that combine illustrations, animations, digital images, and simulations. The Labs guide students step-by-step, present them with Quick Check questions, let them explore on their own, test their comprehension, and provide printed feedback. Lab icons at the beginning of the tutorial and in the tutorial margins indicate when a topic has a corresponding Lab. Lab Assignments are included at the end of each relevant tutorial. The Labs available with this book and the tutorials in which they appear are:

TUTORIAL 1
WINDOWS 95

Using a
Keyboard

TUTORIAL 1
WINDOWS 95

Using a
Mouse

TUTORIAL 2
WINDOWS 95

Using Files

TUTORIAL 1
EXCEL 97

Spreadsheets

TUTORIAL 11
EXCEL 97

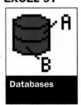

Databases

Course Test Manager: Testing and Practice at the Computer or on Paper
Course Test Manager is cutting-edge, Windows-based testing software that helps instructors design and administer practice tests and actual examinations. This full-featured program allows students to randomly generate practice tests that provide immediate on-screen feedback and detailed study guides. Instructors can also use Course Test Manager to produce printed tests. Course Test Manager can automatically grade the tests students take at the computer and can generate statistical information on individual as well as group performance.

Course Presenter: This lecture presentation tool allows instructors to create electronic slide shows or traditional overhead transparencies using the figure files from the book. Instructors can customize, edit, save, and display the figures from the text in order to illustrate key topics or concepts in class.

Online Companions: Dedicated to Keeping You and Your Students Up-To-Date When you use a New Perspectives product, you can access Course Technology's faculty sites and student sites on the World Wide Web. You can browse the password-protected Faculty Online Companions to obtain online Instructor's Manuals, Solution Files, Student Files, and more. Please see your Instructor's Manual or call your Course Technology customer service representative for more information. Student and Faculty Online Companions are accessible by clicking the appropriate links on the Course Technology home page at **http://www.course.com.**

Student Files Student Files contain all of the data that students will use to complete the tutorials, Tutorial Assignments, Case Problems, and Additional Cases. A Readme file includes technical tips for lab management. See the inside covers of this book and the "Read This Before You Begin" pages for more information on Student Files.

Instructor's Manual New Perspectives Series Instructor's Manuals contain instructor's notes and printed solutions for each tutorial. Instructor's notes provide tutorial overviews and outlines, technical notes, lecture notes, and extra Case Problems. Printed solutions include solutions to Tutorial Assignments, Case Problems, Additional Cases, and Lab Assignments.

Solution Files Solution Files contain every file students are asked to create or modify in the tutorials, Tutorial Assignments, Case Problems, and Additional Cases.

The following supplements are included in the Instructor's Resource Kit that accompanies this textbook:

- Instructor's Manual
- Solution Files
- Student Files
- The following Course Labs: Using a Keyboard, Using a Mouse, Using Files, Spreadsheets, Databases
- Course Test Manager Release 1.1 Test Bank
- Course Test Manager Release 1.1 Engine
- Course Presenter

Some of the supplements listed above are also available over the World Wide Web through Course Technology's password-protected Faculty Online Companions. Please see your Instructor's Manual or call your Course Technology customer service representative for more information.

Acknowledgments

We would like to thank the many people whose invaluable contributions made this book possible. Our reviewers Calleen Coorough, Skafit Valley College, Nancy Alderice, Murray State University, Jean Smelewicz, Quinsigamond Community College, William O. Hogbin, Northern Virginia Community College, Stephanie Bryant, James Madison University, and Mary Beth Cote, Goldey Beacom College; at Course Technology, we would like to thank Mac Mendelsohn, Associate Publisher; Susan Solomon, Series Consulting Editor; Mark Reimold, Acquisitions Editor; Donna Gridley, Product Manager; Quality Assurance Project Leader Greg Bigelow; quality assurance manuscript reviewers Brian McCooey and John McCarthy, developmental editors Kim Crowley and Barbara Clemens; production editor Nancy Ray and copy editor Jane Pedicini; our appreciation also to Gex, Inc.

June Jamrich Parsons
Dan Oja
Roy Ageloff
Patrick Carey

Brief Contents

Table of **Contents**

New Perspectives on

Microsoft® Windows® 95

BRIEF

TUTORIALS

Read This **Before You Begin**

STUDENT DISKS

To complete the tutorials and Tutorial Assignments, you need a Student Disk. Your instructor will either provide you with a Student Disk or ask you to make your own.

If you are supposed to make your own Student Disk, you will need a blank, formatted high-density disk. Follow the instructions in the section called "Creating Your Student Disk" in Tutorial 2 to use the Make Student Disk program to create your own Student Disk. See the inside front or inside back cover of this book for more information on Student Disk files, or ask your instructor or technical support person for assistance.

COURSE LABS

This book features three interactive Course Labs to help you understand Windows concepts. There are Lab Assignments at the end of each tutorial that relate to these Labs. To start a Lab, click the Start button on the Windows 95 taskbar, point to Programs, point to CTI Windows 95 Applications, point to Windows 95 New Perspectives Brief, and click the name of the Lab you want to use.

USING YOUR OWN COMPUTER

If you are going to work through this book using your own computer, you need:

■ **Computer System** Windows 95 must be installed on your computer. This book assumes a complete installation of Windows 95.

■ **Student Disk** Ask your instructor or lab manager for details on how to get the Student Disk. You will not be able to complete the tutorials or exercises in this book using your own computer until you have the Student Disk. The student files may also be obtained electronically over the Internet. See the inside front or inside back cover of this book for more details.

■ **Course Labs** See your instructor or technical support person to obtain the Course Lab software for use on your own computer.

To complete the tutorials and Tutorial Assignments in this book, your students must use a set of files on a Student Disk. The Instructor's Resource Kit for this book includes either two Student Files Setup Disks or a CD-ROM containing the student disk setup program. Follow the instructions on the disk label or in the Readme file to install the Make Student Disk program onto your server or standalone computers. Your students can then use the Windows 95 Start menu to run the program that will create their Student Disk. Tutorial 2 contains steps that instruct your students on how to generate student disks.

If you prefer to provide Student Disks rather than letting students generate them, you can run the Make Student Disk program yourself following the instructions in Tutorial 2.

COURSE LAB SOFTWARE

This book features three online, interactive Course Labs that introduce basic Windows concepts. The Instructor's Resource Kit for this book contains the Lab software either on four Course Labs Setup Disks or on a CD-ROM. Follow the instructions on the disk label or in the Readme file to install the Lab software on your server or standalone computers. Refer also to the Readme file for essential technical notes related to running the labs in a multiuser environment.

Once you have installed the Course Lab software, your students can start the Labs from the Windows 95 desktop by clicking the Start button on the Windows 95 taskbar, pointing to Programs, pointing to CTI Windows 95 Applications, pointing to Windows 95 New Perspectives Brief, and then clicking the name of the Lab they want to use.

CT LAB SOFTWARE AND STUDENT FILES

You are granted a license to copy the Student Files and Course Labs to any computer or computer network used by students who have purchased this book.

Exploring the Basics

Investigating the Windows 95 Operating System in the Computer Lab

LABS

Using a Mouse

Using a Keyboard

CASE

Your First Day in the Lab

You walk into the computer lab and sit down at a desk. There's a computer in front of you, and you find yourself staring dubiously at the stack of software manuals. Where to start? As if in answer to your question, your friend Steve Laslow appears.

Gesturing to the stack of manuals, you tell Steve that you were just wondering where to start.

"You start with the operating system," says Steve. Noticing your slightly puzzled look, Steve explains that the **operating system** is software that helps the computer carry out basic operating tasks such as displaying information on the computer screen and saving data on your disks. Your computer uses the **Microsoft Windows 95** operating system—Windows 95, for short.

Steve tells you that Windows 95 has a "gooey" or **graphical user interface (GUI)**, which uses pictures of familiar objects, such as file folders and documents, to represent a desktop on your screen. Microsoft Windows 95 gets its name from the rectangular-shaped work areas, called "windows," that appear on your screen.

Steve continues to talk as he sorts through the stack of manuals on your desk. He says there are two things he really likes about Windows 95. First, lots of software is available for computers that have the Windows 95 operating system and all this software has a standard graphical user interface. That means once you have learned how to use one Windows software package, such as word-processing software, you are well on your way to understanding how to use other Windows software. Second, Windows 95 lets you use more than one software package at a time, so you can easily switch between your word-processing software and your appointment book software, for example. All in all, Windows 95 makes your computer an effective and easy-to-use productivity tool.

Steve recommends that you get started right away by using some tutorials that will teach you the skills essential for using Microsoft Windows 95. He hands you a book and assures you that everything on your computer system is set up and ready to go.

You mention that last summer you worked in an advertising agency where the employees used something called Windows 3.1. Steve explains that Windows 3.1 is an earlier version of the Windows operating system. Windows 95 and Windows 3.1 are similar, but Windows 95 is more powerful and easier to use. Steve says that as you work through the tutorials you will see notes that point out the important differences between Windows 95 and Windows 3.1.

Steve has a class, but he says he'll check back later to see how you are doing.

Using the Tutorials Effectively

These tutorials will help you learn about Windows 95. The tutorials are designed to be used at a computer. Each tutorial is divided into sessions. Watch for the session headings, such as Session 1.1 and Session 1.2. Each session is designed to be completed in about 45 minutes, but take as much time as you need. It's also a good idea to take a break between sessions.

Before you begin, read the following questions and answers. They are designed to help you use the tutorials effectively.

Where do I start?

Each tutorial begins with a case, which sets the scene for the tutorial and gives you background information to help you understand what you will be doing in the tutorial. Read the case before you go to the lab. In the lab, begin with the first session of the tutorial.

How do I know what to do on the computer?

Each session contains steps that you will perform on the computer to learn how to use Windows 95. Read the text that introduces each series of steps. The steps you need to do at a computer are numbered and are set against a color background. Read each step carefully and completely before you try it.

How do I know if I did the step correctly?

As you work, compare your computer screen with the corresponding figure in the tutorial. Don't worry if your screen display is somewhat different from the figure. The important parts of the screen display are labeled in each figure. Check to make sure these parts are on your screen.

What if I make a mistake?

Don't worry about making mistakes—they are part of the learning process. Paragraphs labeled "TROUBLE?" identify common problems and explain how to get back on track. Follow the steps in a TROUBLE? paragraph *only* if you are having the problem described. If you run into other problems:

- Carefully consider the current state of your system, the position of the pointer, and any messages on the screen.

- Complete the sentence, "Now I want to...." Be specific, because you are identifying your goal.

- Develop a plan for accomplishing your goal, and put your plan into action.

How do I use the Reference Windows?

Reference Windows summarize the procedures you learn in the tutorial steps. Do not complete the actions in the Reference Windows when you are working through the tutorial. Instead, refer to the Reference Windows while you are working on the assignments at the end of the tutorial.

How can I test my understanding of the material I learned in the tutorial?

At the end of each session, you can answer the Quick Check questions. The answers for the Quick Checks are at the end of the book.

After you have completed the entire tutorial, you should complete the Tutorial Assignments. The Tutorial Assignments are carefully structured so you will review what you have learned and then apply your knowledge to new situations.

What if I can't remember how to do something?

You should refer to the Task Reference at the end of the book; it summarizes how to accomplish commonly performed tasks.

What are the 3.1 Notes?

The 3.1 Notes are helpful if you have used Windows 3.1. The notes point out the key similarities and differences between Windows 3.1 and Windows 95.

What are the Interactive Labs, and how should I use them?

Interactive Labs help you review concepts and practice skills that you learn in the tutorial. Lab icons at the beginning of each tutorial and in the margins of the tutorials indicate topics that have corresponding Labs. The Lab Assignments section includes instructions for how to use each Lab.

Now that you understand how to use the tutorials effectively, you are ready to begin.

SESSION

1.1

In this session, in addition to learning basic Windows terminology, you will learn how to use a mouse, to start and stop a program, and to use more than one program at a time. With the skills you learn in this session, you will be able to use Windows 95 to start software programs.

Using a Keyboard

Starting Windows 95

Windows 95 automatically starts when you turn on the computer. Depending on the way your computer is set up, you might be asked to enter your user name and password. If prompted to do so, type your assigned user name and press the Enter key. Then type your password and press the Enter key to continue.

To start Windows 95:

1. Turn on your computer.

TROUBLE? If the Welcome to Windows 95 box appears on your screen, press the Enter key to close it.

The Windows 95 Desktop

In Windows terminology, the screen represents a **desktop**—a workspace for projects and the tools needed to manipulate those projects. Look at your screen display and locate the objects labeled in Figure 1-1 on the following page.

Because it is easy to customize the Windows environment, your screen might not look exactly the same as Figure 1-1. You should, however, be able to locate objects on your screen similar to those in Figure 1-1.

Icons are small pictures that represent objects such as your computer, your computer network, a specific computer program, or a document. Your desktop probably contains several icons, such as My Computer, Network Neighborhood, and the Recycle Bin. You'll use these icons in later tutorials to work with files stored on your computer or on other computers on the network.

Figure 1-1 ◄
The Windows
95 desktop

The **desktop** is
your workspace
on the screen.

The **Start** button
is one of the
most important
controls in
Windows 95.
You use the
Start button
to access essential
Windows 95
functions, programs,
and documents.

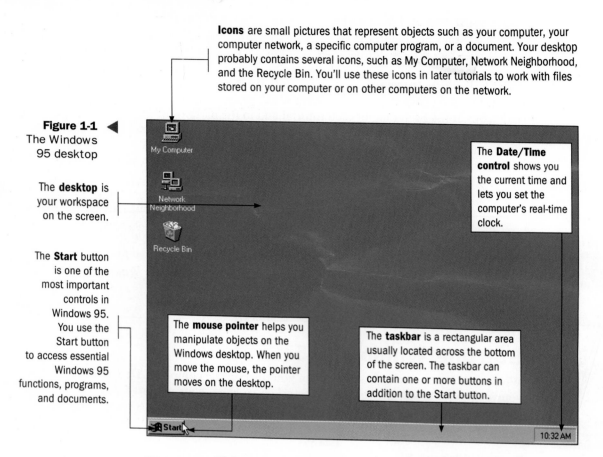

The **Date/Time control** shows you the current time and lets you set the computer's real-time clock.

The **mouse pointer** helps you manipulate objects on the Windows desktop. When you move the mouse, the pointer moves on the desktop.

The **taskbar** is a rectangular area usually located across the bottom of the screen. The taskbar can contain one or more buttons in addition to the Start button.

TROUBLE? If the screen goes blank or starts to display a moving design, press any key to restore the image.

Using the Mouse

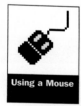

Using a Mouse

A **mouse**, like those shown in Figure 1-2, is a pointing device that helps you interact with objects on the screen. In Windows 95 you need to know how to use the mouse to point, click, and drag. In this session you will learn about pointing and clicking. In Session 1 you will learn how to use the mouse to drag objects.

You can also interact with objects by using the keyboard; however, the mouse is more convenient for most tasks, so the tutorials in this book assume you are using

Pointing

The **pointer**, or **mouse pointer**, is a small object that moves on the screen when the mouse. The pointer is usually shaped like an arrow. As you move the mo surface, the pointer on the screen moves in the direction corresponding to th of the mouse. The pointer sometimes changes shape depending on wher screen or the action the computer is completing.

Find the arrow-shaped pointer on your screen. If you do not see the po mouse until the pointer comes into view.

Figure 1-2 ◀
The mouse

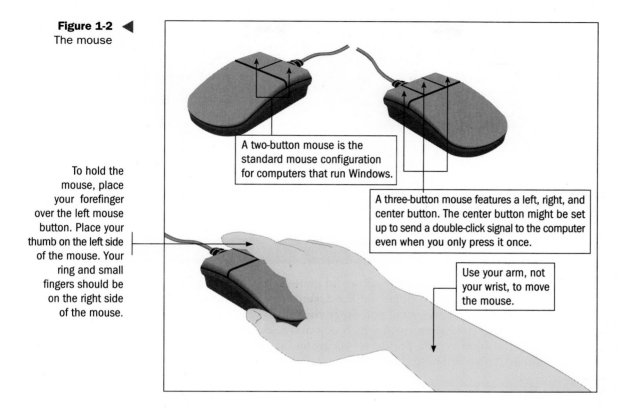

To hold the mouse, place your forefinger over the left mouse button. Place your thumb on the left side of the mouse. Your ring and small fingers should be on the right side of the mouse.

A two-button mouse is the standard mouse configuration for computers that run Windows.

A three-button mouse features a left, right, and center button. The center button might be set up to send a double-click signal to the computer even when you only press it once.

Use your arm, not your wrist, to move the mouse.

Basic "mousing" skills depend on your ability to position the pointer. You begin most Windows operations by positioning the pointer over a specific part of the screen. This is called **pointing**.

To move the pointer:

1. Position your right index finger over the left mouse button, as shown in Figure 1-2. Lightly grasp the sides of the mouse with your thumb and little finger.

   TROUBLE? If you want to use the mouse with your left hand, ask your instructor or technical support person to help you use the Control Panel to change the mouse settings to swap the left and right mouse buttons. Be sure you find out how to change back to the right-handed mouse setting, so you can reset the mouse each time you are finished in the lab.

2. Locate the arrow-shaped pointer on the screen.

3. Move the mouse and watch the movement of the pointer.

If you run out of room to move your mouse, lift the mouse and move it to a clear area on your desk, then place the mouse back on the desk. Notice that the pointer does not move when the mouse is not in contact with the desk.

When you position the mouse pointer over certain objects, such as the objects on the taskbar, a "tip" appears. These "tips" are called **ToolTips**, and they tell you the purpose or function of an object.

To view ToolTips:

1. Use the mouse to point to the **Start** button 🔲Start. After a few seconds, you see the tip "Click here to begin" as shown in Figure 1-3 on the following page.

Figure 1-3 ◀
Viewing ToolTips

Start button ─────

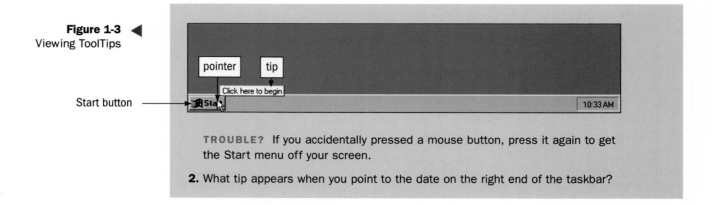

TROUBLE? If you accidentally pressed a mouse button, press it again to get the Start menu off your screen.

2. What tip appears when you point to the date on the right end of the taskbar?

Clicking

When you press a mouse button and immediately release it, it is called **clicking**. Clicking the mouse selects an object on the desktop. *You usually click the left mouse button, so* unless the instructions tell you otherwise, always click the left mouse button.

Windows 95 shows you which object is selected by highlighting it, usually by changing the object's color, putting a box around it, or making the object appear to be pushed in, as shown in Figure 1-4.

Figure 1-4 ◀
Selected objects

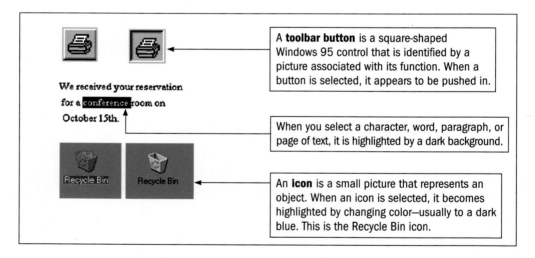

A **toolbar button** is a square-shaped Windows 95 control that is identified by a picture associated with its function. When a button is selected, it appears to be pushed in.

We received your reservation for a conference room on October 15th.

When you select a character, word, paragraph, or page of text, it is highlighted by a dark background.

An **icon** is a small picture that represents an object. When an icon is selected, it becomes highlighted by changing color—usually to a dark blue. This is the Recycle Bin icon.

To select the Recycle Bin icon:

1. Position the pointer over the **Recycle Bin** icon.

2. Click the mouse button and notice how the color of the icon changes to show that it is selected.

Starting and Closing a Program

The software you use is sometimes referred to as a program or an application. To use a program, such as a word-processing program, you must first start it. With Windows 95 you start a program by clicking the Start button. The Start button displays a menu.

A **menu** is a list of options. Windows 95 has a **Start menu** that provides you with access to programs, data, and configuration options. One of the Start menu's most important functions is to let you start a program.

The Reference Window below explains how to start a program. Don't do the steps in the Reference Window now; they are for your later reference.

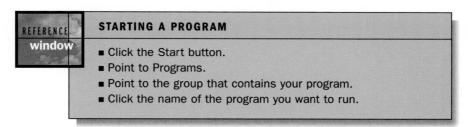

REFERENCE | **STARTING A PROGRAM**
window |
| ■ Click the Start button.
| ■ Point to Programs.
| ■ Point to the group that contains your program.
| ■ Click the name of the program you want to run.

3.1 NOTE

WordPad is similar to Write in Windows 3.1.

Windows 95 includes an easy-to-use word-processing program called WordPad. Suppose you want to start the WordPad program and use it to write a letter or report.

To start the WordPad program from the Start menu:

1. Click the **Start** button ⊞Start as shown in Figure 1-5. A menu appears.

Figure 1-5 ◀
Starting the
WordPad program

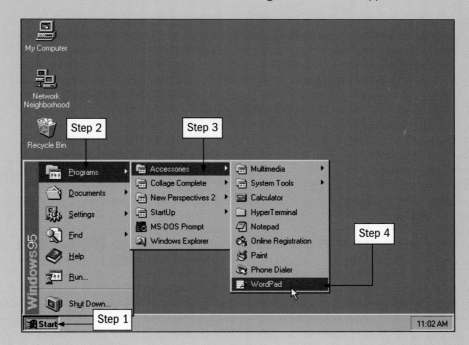

2. Point to **Programs**. After a short pause, the next menu appears.

TROUBLE? If you don't get the correct menu, go back and point to the correct menu option.

3. Point to **Accessories**. Another menu appears.

4. Click **WordPad**. Make sure you can see the WordPad program as shown in Figure 1-6 on the following page.

Figure 1-6 ◄
The WordPad
program

WordPad program
window

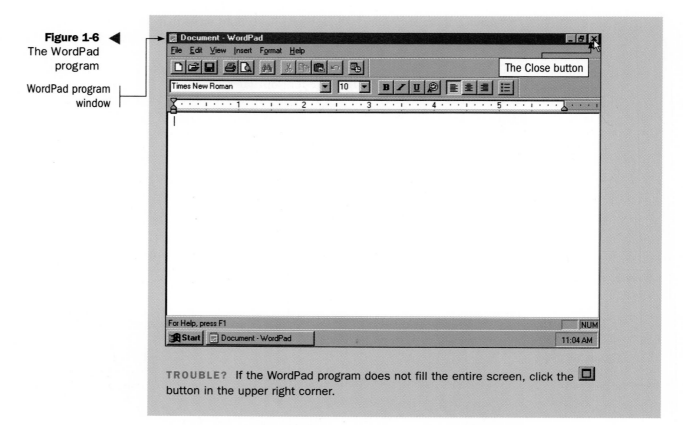

TROUBLE? If the WordPad program does not fill the entire screen, click the ▢ button in the upper right corner.

3.1 NOTE

As with Windows 3.1,
in Windows 95 you
can also exit a
program using the
Exit option from the
File menu.

When you are finished using a program, the easiest way to return to the Windows 95 desktop is to click the Close button ☒.

To exit the WordPad program:

1. Click the **Close** button ☒. See Figure 1-6. You will be returned to the Windows 95 desktop.

Running More than One Program at the Same Time

3.1 NOTE

Paint in Windows 95
is similar to
Paintbrush in
Windows 3.1.

One of the most useful features of Windows 95 is its ability to run multiple programs at the same time. This feature, known as **multi-tasking**, allows you to work on more than one task at a time and to quickly switch between tasks. For example, you can start WordPad and leave it running while you then start the Paint program.

To run WordPad and Paint at the same time:

1. Start WordPad.

TROUBLE? You learned how to start WordPad earlier in the tutorial: Click the Start button, point to Programs, point to Accessories, and then click WordPad.

2. Now you can start the Paint program. Click the **Start** button 🔲Start again.

3. Point to **Programs**.

4. Point to **Accessories**.

5. Click **Paint**. The Paint program appears as shown in Figure 1-7. Now two programs are running at the same time.

TROUBLE? If the Paint program does not fill the entire screen, click the ☐ button in the upper right corner.

Figure 1-7 ◀
The Paint
Program

Paint program
window

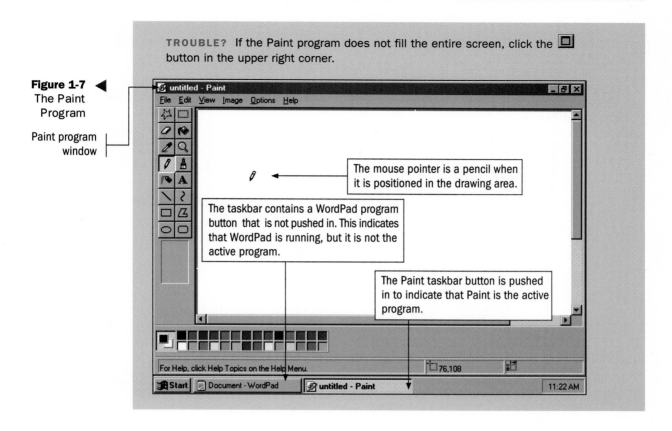

The mouse pointer is a pencil when it is positioned in the drawing area.

The taskbar contains a WordPad program button that is not pushed in. This indicates that WordPad is running, but it is not the active program.

The Paint taskbar button is pushed in to indicate that Paint is the active program.

3.1 NOTE

With Windows 3.1, some users had difficulty finding program windows on the desktop. The buttons on the Windows 95 taskbar make it much easier to keep track of which programs are running.

What happened to WordPad? The WordPad button is still on the taskbar, so even if you can't see it, WordPad is still running. You can imagine that it is stacked behind the Paint program, as shown in Figure 1-8.

Other projects might be hidden under the project you are working on. For example, you might have worked on a letter earlier, but it is now under the picture you are currently drawing.

You might keep other projects handy on your desk. Anytime you want to work with one of them, you bring it to the center of your desk.

Figure 1-8 ◀
Programs
stacked on top
of a desk

Think of your screen
as the main work
area of your desk.

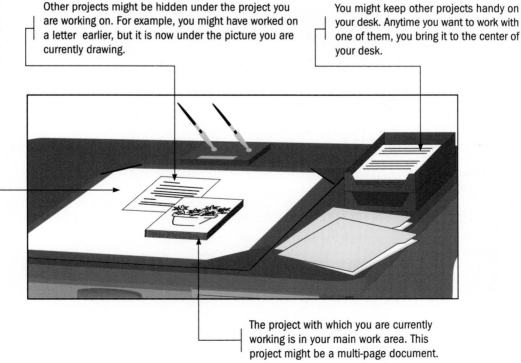

The project with which you are currently working is in your main work area. This project might be a multi-page document.

Switching Between Programs

3.I NOTE

In Windows 95, you can still use Alt-Tab to switch between programs. You can also click any open window to switch to it.

Although Windows 95 allows you to run more than one program, only one program at a time is active. The **active** program is the program with which you are currently working. The easiest way to switch between programs is to use the buttons on the taskbar.

REFERENCE window

SWITCHING BETWEEN PROGRAMS

■ Click the taskbar button that contains the name of the program to which you want to switch.

To switch between WordPad and Paint:

1. Click the button labeled **Document - WordPad** on the taskbar. The Document - WordPad button now looks like it has been pushed in to indicate it is the active program.

2. Next, click the button labeled **untitled - Paint** on the taskbar to switch to the Paint program.

Closing WordPad and Paint

It is good practice to close each program when you are finished using it. Each program uses computer resources such as memory, so Windows 95 works more efficiently when only the programs you need are open.

To close WordPad and Paint:

1. Click the **Close** button for the Paint program. The button labeled "untitled - Paint" disappears from the taskbar.

2. Click the **Close** button for the WordPad program. The WordPad button disappears from the taskbar, and you return to the Windows 95 desktop.

Shutting Down Windows 95

It is very important to shut down Windows 95 before you turn off the computer. If you turn off your computer without correctly shutting down, you might lose data and damage your files.

To shut down Windows 95:

1. Click the **Start** button 🏁Start on the taskbar to display the Start menu.

2. Click the **Shut Down** menu option to display the Shut Down Windows dialog box.

3. Make sure the **Shut down the computer?** option is selected.

4. Click the **Yes** button.

5. Wait until you see a message indicating it is safe to turn off your computer, then switch off your computer.

You should typically use the option "Shut down the computer?" when you want to turn off your computer. However, other shut-down options are available. For example, your school might prefer that you select the option to "Close all programs and log on as a different user." This option logs you out of Windows 95, leaves the computer turned on, and allows another user to log on without restarting the computer. Check with your instructor or technical support person for the preferred method for your school's computer lab.

Quick Check

1 Label the components of the Windows 95 desktop in the figure below:

Figure 1-9 ◀

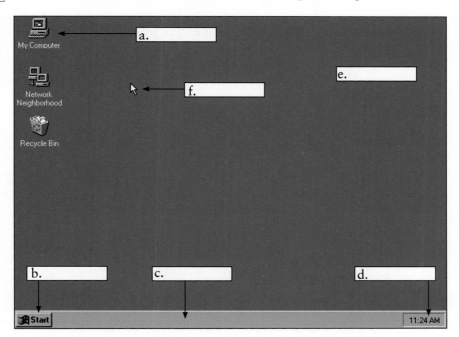

2 The _____ feature of Windows 95 allows you to run more than one program at a time.

3 The _____ is a list of options that provides you with access to programs, data, and configuration options.

4 What should you do if you are trying to move the pointer to the left edge of your screen, but your mouse runs into the keyboard?

5 Windows 95 shows you that an icon is selected by _____ it.

6 Even if you can't see a program, it might be running. How can you tell if a program is running?

7 Why is it good practice to close each program when you are finished using it?

8 Why do you need to shut down Windows 95 before you turn off your computer?

SESSION
1.2

In this session you will learn how to use many of the Windows 95 controls to manipulate windows and programs. You will learn how to change the size and shape of a window and to move a window so that you can customize your screen-based workspace. You will also learn how to use menus, dialog boxes, tabs, buttons, and lists to specify how you want a program to carry out a task.

Anatomy of a Window

When you run a program in Windows 95, it appears in a window. A **window** is a rectangular area of the screen that contains a program or data. A window also contains controls for manipulating the window and using the program. WordPad is a good example of how a window works.

Windows, spelled with an uppercase "W," is the name of the Microsoft operating system. The word "window" with a lowercase "w" refers to one of the rectangular windows on the screen.

To look at window controls:

1. Make sure Windows 95 is running and you are at the Windows 95 desktop screen.

2. Start WordPad.

   TROUBLE? To start WordPad, click the Start button, point to Programs, point to Accessories, and then click WordPad.

3. Make sure WordPad takes up the entire screen.

   TROUBLE? If WordPad does not take up the entire screen, click the ▣ button in the upper right corner.

4. On your screen, identify the controls labeled in Figure 1-10.

Figure 1-10 ◀
Window
controls

The **menu bar** contains the titles of menus, such as File, Edit, and Help.

The **toolbar** contains buttons that provide you with a shortcut to the commands listed on the menus.

The **status bar** provides you with abbreviated help relevant to the task you are doing.

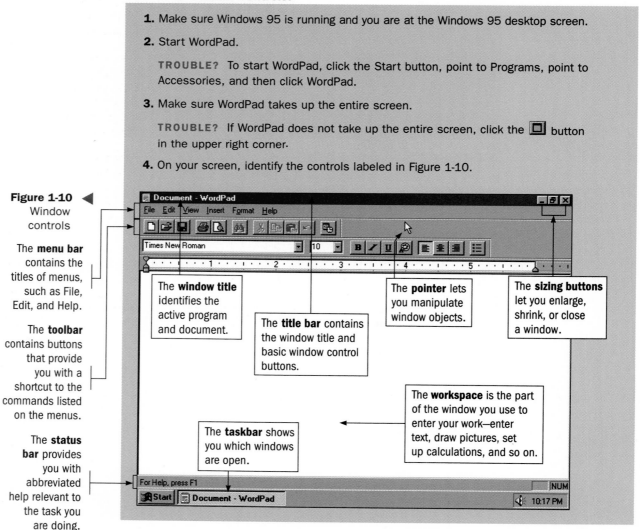

The **window title** identifies the active program and document.

The **title bar** contains the window title and basic window control buttons.

The **pointer** lets you manipulate window objects.

The **sizing buttons** let you enlarge, shrink, or close a window.

The **workspace** is the part of the window you use to enter your work—enter text, draw pictures, set up calculations, and so on.

The **taskbar** shows you which windows are open.

Manipulating a Window

There are three buttons located on the right side of the title bar. You are already familiar with the Close button. The Minimize button hides the window. The other button either maximizes the window or restores it to a predefined size. Figure 1-11 shows how these buttons work.

Figure 1-11 ◄
Minimize,
Maximize and
Restore buttons

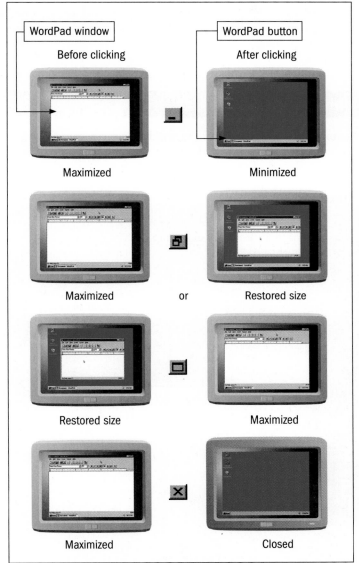

WordPad window — Before clicking

WordPad button — After clicking

Maximized — Minimized

The **Minimize button** 🔲 shrinks the window, so you only see its button on the taskbar.

Maximized — or — Restored size

The middle button appears as a **Restore button** 🔲 or a **Maximize button.** 🔲 When the window is maximized, the Restore button appears. It can be used to reduce the size of the window to a predetermined or "normal" size. When the window does not fill the entire screen, the Maximize button appears. Clicking the Maximize button enlarges the window to fill the screen.

Restored size — Maximized

Maximized — Closed

The **Close button** ⊠ closes the window and removes its button from the taskbar at the bottom of the screen.

Minimizing a Window

The **Minimize button** 🔲 shrinks the current window so that only the button on the taskbar remains visible. You can use the Minimize button when you want to temporarily hide a window but keep the program running.

To minimize the WordPad window:

1. Click the **Minimize** button 🔲. The WordPad window shrinks so only the Document - WordPad button on the taskbar is visible.

   TROUBLE? If you accidentally clicked the Close button and closed the window, use the Start button to start WordPad again.

Redisplaying a Window

You can redisplay a minimized window by clicking the program's button on the taskbar. When you redisplay a window, it becomes the active window.

To redisplay the WordPad window:

1. Click the **Document - WordPad** button on the taskbar. The WordPad window is restored to its previous size. The Document - WordPad button looks pushed in as a visual clue that it is now the active window.

Restoring a Window

The **Restore** button 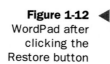 reduces the window so it is smaller than the entire screen. This is useful if you want to see more than one window at a time. Also, because of its small size, you can drag the window to another location on the screen or change its dimensions.

To restore a window:

1. Click the **Restore** button on the WordPad title bar. The WordPad window will look similar to Figure 1-12, but the exact size of the window on your screen might be slightly different.

Figure 1-12 ◀
WordPad after
clicking the
Restore button

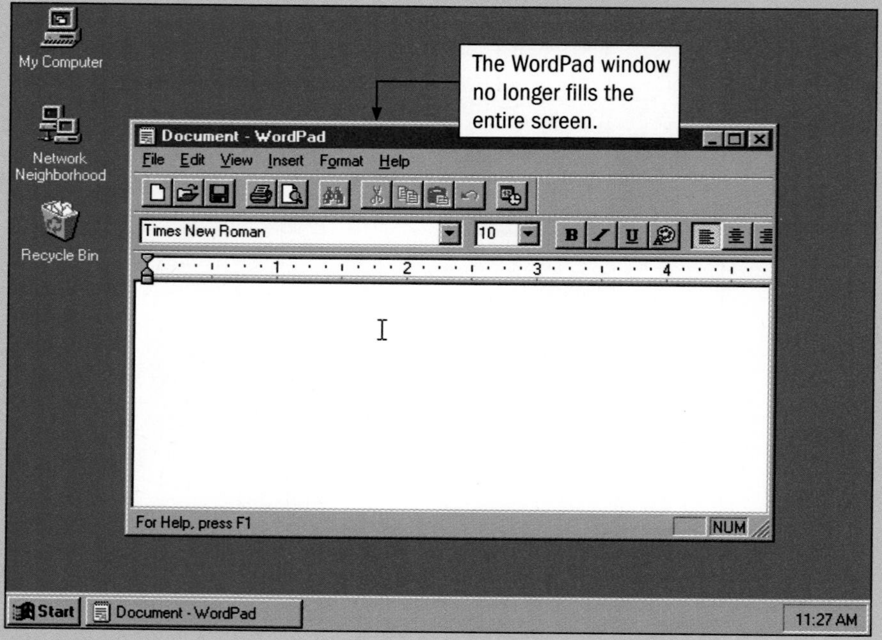

The WordPad window no longer fills the entire screen.

Moving a Window

You can use the mouse to **move** a window to a new position on the screen. When you hold down the mouse button while moving the mouse, it is called **dragging**. You can move objects on the screen by dragging them to a new location. If you want to move a window, you drag its title bar.

To drag the WordPad window to a new location:

1. Position the mouse pointer on the WordPad window title bar.

2. While you hold down the left mouse button, move the mouse to drag the window. A rectangle representing the window moves as you move the mouse.

3. Position the rectangle anywhere on the screen, then release the left mouse button. The WordPad window appears in the new location.

4. Now drag the WordPad window to the upper-left corner of the screen.

Changing the Size of a Window

3.1 NOTE

You can also change the size of a window by dragging the top, bottom, sides, and corners of the window, as you did in Windows 3.1.

You can also use the mouse to change the size of a window. Notice the sizing handle at the lower right corner of the window. The **sizing handle** provides a visible control for changing the size of a current window.

To change the size of the WordPad window:

1. Position the pointer over the sizing handle . The pointer changes to a diagonal arrow .

2. While holding down the mouse button, drag the sizing handle down and to the right.

3. Release the mouse button. Now the window is larger.

4. Practice using the sizing handle to make the WordPad window larger or smaller.

Maximizing a Window

The **Maximize button** enlarges a window so that it fills the entire screen. You will probably do most of your work using maximized windows because you can see more of your program and data.

To maximize the WordPad window:

1. Click the **Maximize** button on the WordPad title bar.

Using Program Menus

Most Windows programs use menus to provide an easy way for you to select program commands. The **menu bar** is typically located at the top of the program window and shows the titles of menus such as File, Edit, and Help.

Windows menus are relatively standardized—most Windows programs include similar menu options. It's easy to learn new programs, because you can make a pretty good guess about which menu contains the command you want.

Selecting Commands from a Menu

When you click any menu title, choices for that menu appear below the menu bar. These choices are referred to as **menu options**. To select a menu option, you click it. For example, the File menu is a standard feature in most Windows programs and contains the options related to working with a file: creating, opening, saving, and printing a file or document.

To select Print Preview from the File menu:

1. Click **File** in the WordPad menu bar to display the File menu.

   TROUBLE? If you open a menu but decide not to select any of the menu options, you can close the menu by clicking its title again.

2. Click **Print Preview** to open the preview screen and view your document as it will appear when printed. This document is blank because you didn't enter any text.

3. After examining the screen, click the button labeled "Close" to return to your document.

Not all menu options immediately carry out an action—some show submenus or ask you for more information about what you want to do. The menu gives you hints about what to expect when you select an option. These hints are sometimes referred to as **menu conventions**. Study Figures 1-13a and 1-13b so you will recognize the Windows 95 menu conventions.

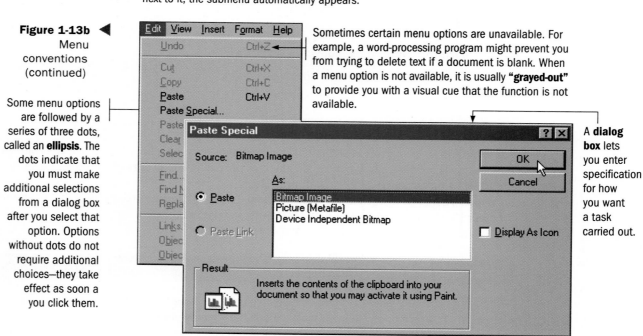

Figure 1-13a ◄
Menu Conventions

Some menu options are toggle switches that can be either "on" or "off." When a feature is turned on, a **check mark** appears next to the menu option. When the feature is turned off, there is no check mark.

Certain menu selections lead you to an additional menu, called a **submenu**. A triangle on the right side of the menu choice indicates menu options that lead to submenus. When you move the pointer to a menu option with a triangle next to it, the submenu automatically appears.

Figure 1-13b ◄
Menu conventions (continued)

Some menu options are followed by a series of three dots, called an **ellipsis**. The dots indicate that you must make additional selections from a dialog box after you select that option. Options without dots do not require additional choices—they take effect as soon a you click them.

Sometimes certain menu options are unavailable. For example, a word-processing program might prevent you from trying to delete text if a document is blank. When a menu option is not available, it is usually **"grayed-out"** to provide you with a visual cue that the function is not available.

A **dialog box** lets you enter specification for how you want a task carried out.

Using Toolbars

A **toolbar** contains buttons that provide quick access to important program commands. Although you can usually perform all program commands using the menus, the toolbar provides convenient one-click access to frequently-used commands. For most Windows 95 functions, there is usually more than one way to accomplish a task. To simplify your introduction to Windows 95 in this tutorial, you will learn only one method for performing a task. As you become more accomplished using Windows 95, you can explore alternative methods.

In Session 1.1 you learned that Windows 95 programs include ToolTips that indicate the purpose and function of a tool. Now is a good time to explore the WordPad toolbar buttons by looking at their ToolTips.

To find out a toolbar button's function:

1. Position the pointer over any button on the toolbar, such as the Print Preview icon. After a short pause, the name of the button appears in a box and a description of the button appears in the status bar just above the Start button.

2. Move the pointer to each button on the toolbar to see its name and purpose.

You select a toolbar button by clicking it.

To select the Print Preview toolbar button:

1. Click the **Print Preview** button. The Print Preview dialog box appears. This is the same dialog box that appeared when you selected File, Print Preview from the menu bar.

2. Click Close to close the Print Preview dialog box.

Using List Boxes and Scroll Bars

As you might guess from the name, a **list box** displays a list of choices. In WordPad, date and time formats are shown in the Date/Time list box. List box controls include arrow buttons, a scroll bar, and a scroll box, as shown in Figure 1-14.

Figure 1-14 ◀
List box

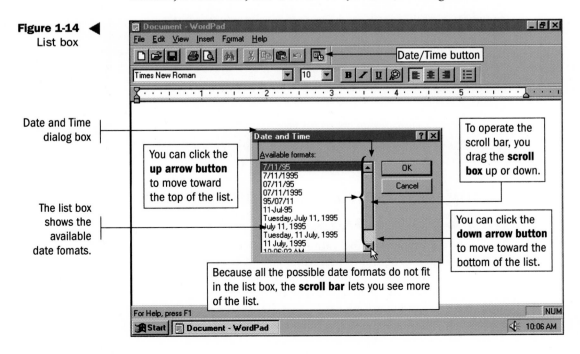

Date and Time dialog box

You can click the **up arrow button** to move toward the top of the list.

The list box shows the available date formats.

To operate the scroll bar, you drag the **scroll box** up or down.

You can click the **down arrow button** to move toward the bottom of the list.

Because all the possible date formats do not fit in the list box, the **scroll bar** lets you see more of the list.

To use the Date/Time list box:

1. Click the **Date/Time** button 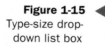 to display the Date and Time dialog box. See Figure 1-14.

2. To scroll down the list, click the **down arrow** button ▼. See Figure 1-14.

3. Find the scroll box on your screen. See Figure 1-14.

4. Drag the **scroll box** to the top of the scroll bar. Notice how the list scrolls back to the beginning.

5. Find a date format similar to "October 2, 1997." Click that date format to select it.

6. Click the **OK** button to close the Date and Time list box. This inserts the current date in your document.

A variation of the list box, called a **drop-down list box**, usually shows only one choice, but can expand down to display additional choices on the list.

To use the Font Size drop-down list:

1. Click the **down arrow** button ▼ shown in Figure 1-15.

Figure 1-15 ◀
Type-size drop-down list box

Click this down arrow button to display the list

2. Click **18**. The drop-down list disappears and the font size you selected appears at the top of the pull-down list.

3. Type a few characters to test the new font size.

4. Click the **down arrow** button ▼ in the Font Size drop-down list box again.

5. Click **12**.

6. Type a few characters to test this type size.

7. Click the **Close** button ☒ to close WordPad.

8. When you see the message "Save changes to Document?" click the **No** button.

Using Tab Controls, Radio Buttons, and Check Boxes

Dialog boxes often use tabs, radio buttons, or check boxes to collect information about how you want a program to perform a task. A **tab control** is patterned after the tabs on file folders. You click the appropriate tab to view different pages of information or choices. Tab controls are often used as containers for other Windows 95 controls such as list boxes, radio buttons, and check boxes.

Radio buttons, also called **option buttons,** allow you to select a single option from among one or more options. **Check boxes** allow you to select many options at the same time. Figure 1-16 explains how to use these controls.

Figure 1-16 ◀
Tabs, radio buttons, and check boxes

A **tab** indicates an "index card" that contains information or a group of controls, usually with related functions. To look at the functions on an index card, click the tab.

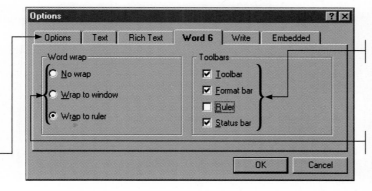

Check boxes allow you to select one or more options from a group. When you click a check box, a check mark appears in it. To remove a check mark from a box, click it again.

Radio buttons are round and usually come in groups of two or more. You can select only one radio button from a group. Your selection is indicated by a black dot.

Using Help

Windows 95 **Help** provides on-screen information about the program you are using. Help for the Windows 95 operating system is available by clicking the Start button on the taskbar, then selecting Help from the Start menu. If you want Help for a program, such as WordPad, you must first start the program, then use the Help menu at the top of the screen.

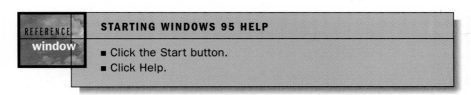

REFERENCE
window

STARTING WINDOWS 95 HELP

■ Click the Start button.
■ Click Help.

To start Windows 95 Help:

1. Click the **Start** button.

2. Click **Help.**

Help uses tabs for each section of Help. Windows 95 Help tabs include Contents, Index, and Find as shown in Figure 1-17 on the following page.

Figure 1-17 ◄
Windows 95
Help

Each section of
Help is divided
into "books."
To open a book,
you click the
book, then click
the Open button.

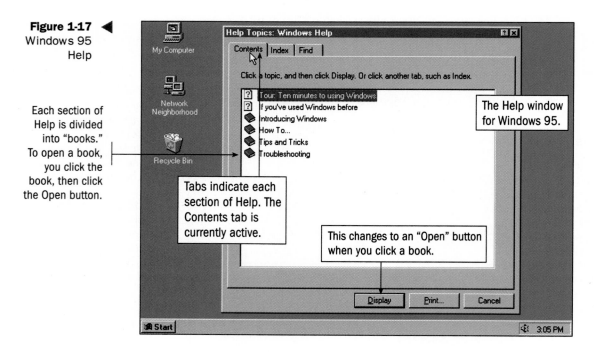

The Contents **tab** groups Help topics into a series of books. You select a book, which then provides you with a list of related topics from which you can choose. The **Index tab** displays an alphabetical list of all the Help topics from which you can choose. The **Find tab** lets you search for any word or phrase in Help.

Suppose you're wondering if there is an alternative way to start programs. You can use the Contents tab to find the answer to your question.

3.1 NOTE

You can also double-click to select and open a topic in a single step.

To use the Contents tab:

1. Click the **Contents** tab to display the Contents window.

2. Click the **How To...** book title, then click the **Open** button. A list of related books appears below the book title. See. Figure 1-18.

Figure 1-18 ◄
Help window

Click this book,
then click the
Open button to
display a list of
related books.

Books related to
the "How To" topic.

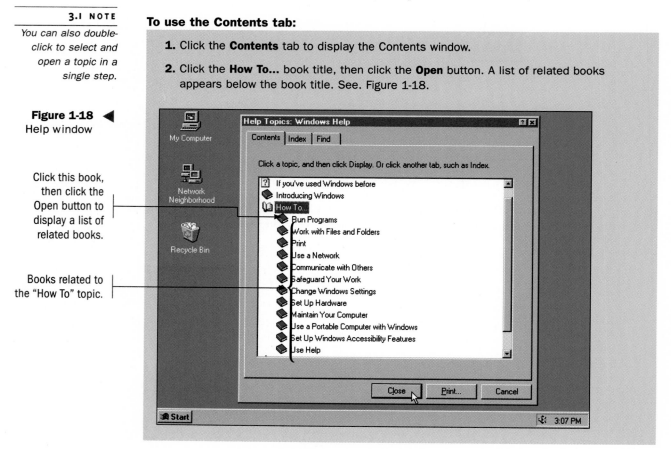

3. Click the **Run Programs** book, then click the **Open** button. The table of contents for this Help book is displayed.

4. Click the topic **Starting a Program**, then click the **Display** button. A Help window appears and explains how to start a program.

Help also provides you with definitions of technical terms. You can click any under-lined term to see its definition.

To see a definition of the term "taskbar":

1. Point to the underlined term, **taskbar** until the pointer changes to a hand. Then click.

2. After you have read the definition, click the definition to deselect it.

3. Click the **Close** button ☒ on the Help window.

The **Index tab** allows you to jump to a Help topic by selecting a topic from an indexed list. For example, you can use the Index tab to learn how to arrange the open windows on your desktop.

To find a Help topic using the Index tab:

1. Click the **Start** button.

2. Click **Help**.

3. Click the **Index** tab.

4. A long list of indexed Help topics appears. Drag the scroll box down to view additional topics.

5. You can quickly jump to any part of the list by typing the first few characters of a word or phrase in the line above the Index list. Type **desktop** to display topics related to the Windows 95 desktop.

6. Click the topic **arranging open windows on** in the bottom window.

7. Click the **Display** button as shown in Figure 1-19.

Figure 1-19 ◀
Displaying a
Help Topic

Click here to type
words or phrases.

Index topics are
displayed here.
Click the topic to
select it.

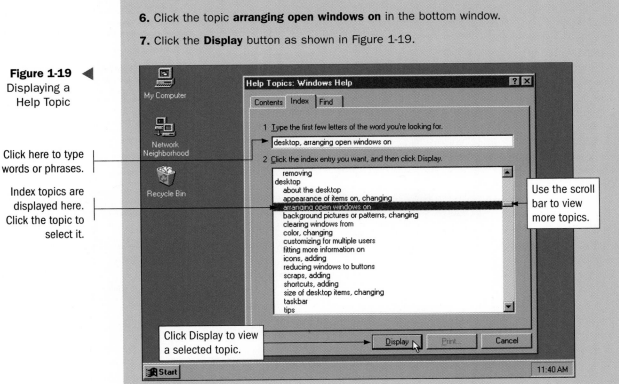

Use the scroll
bar to view
more topics.

Click Display to view
a selected topic.

8. Click the **Close** button ⊠ to close the Windows Help window.

The **Find tab** contains an index of all words in Windows 95 Help. You can use it to search for Help pages that contain a particular word or phrase. For example, suppose you heard that a screen saver blanks out your screen when you are not using it. You could use the Find tab to find out more about screen savers.

To find a Help topic using the Find tab:

1. Click the **Start** button ▥Start .

2. Click **Help**.

3. Click the **Find** tab.

   TROUBLE? If the Find index has not yet been created on your computer, the computer will prompt you through several steps to create the index. Continue with Step 4 below after the Find index is created.

4. Type **screen** to display a list of all topics that start with the letters "screen."

5. Click **screen-saver** in the middle window to display the topics that contain the word "screen-saver."

6. Click **Having your monitor automatically turn off**, then click the **Display** button.

7. Click the **Help window** button shown in Figure 1-20. The screen saver is shown on a simulated monitor.

   TROUBLE? If you see an error message, your lab does not allow students to modify screen savers. Click the OK button and go to Step 9.

Figure 1-20 ◀
Clicking a
Button in Help

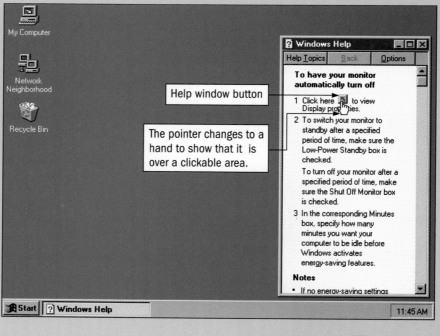

8. To close the Display properties window, click the **Close** button ⊠ in the Display Properties window.

9. Click the **Close** button ⊠ to close the Help window.

Now that you know how Windows 95 Help works, don't forget to use it! Use Help when you need to perform a new task or when you forget how to complete a procedure.

Quick Check

1 Label the parts of the window shown in Figure 1-21.

Figure 1-21 ◀

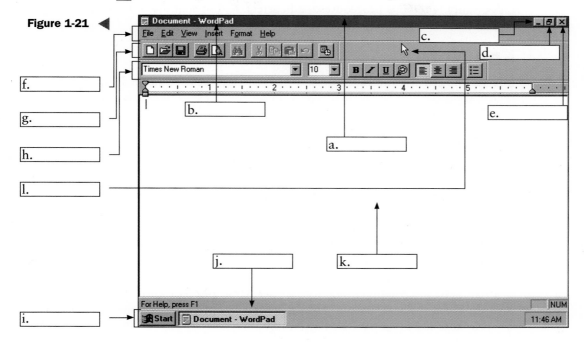

2 Provide the name and purpose of each button:
a. ▬
b. ▢
c. ▣
d. ✕

3 Explain each of the following menu conventions:
a. Ellipsis...
b. Grayed out
c. ▶
d. ✔

4 A(n) _____ consists of a group of buttons, each of which provides one-click access to important program functions.

5 Label each part of the dialog box below:

Figure 1-22 ◀

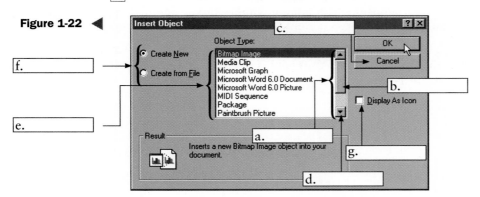

[6] Radio buttons allow you to select _____ option(s) at a time, but _____ allow you to select one or more options.

[7] It is a good idea to use _____ when you need to learn how to perform new tasks, simplify tedious procedures, and correct actions that did not turn out as you expected.

End Note

You've finished the tutorial, but Steve Laslow still hasn't returned. Take a moment to review what you have learned. You now know how to start a program using the Start button. You can run more than one program at a time and switch between programs using the buttons on the taskbar. You have learned the names and functions of window controls and Windows 95 menu conventions. You can now use toolbar buttons, list boxes, drop-down lists, radio buttons, check boxes, and scroll bars. Finally, you can use the Contents, Index, and Find tabs in Help to extend your knowledge of how to use Windows 95.

Tutorial Assignments

1. Running Two Programs and Switching Between Them In this tutorial you learned how to run more than one program at a time using WordPad and Paint. You can run other programs at the same time, too. Complete the following steps and write out your answers to questions b through f:

  a. Start the computer. Enter your user name and password if prompted to do so.
  b. Click the Start button. How many menu options are on the Start menu?
  c. Run the program Calculator program located on the Programs, Accessories menu. How many buttons are now on the taskbar?
  d. Run the Paint program and maximize the Paint window. How many application programs are running now?
  e. Switch to Calculator. What are the two visual clues that tell you that Calculator is the active program?
  f. Multiply 576 by 1457. What is the result?
  g. Close Calculator, then close Paint.

2. WordPad Help In Tutorial 1 you learned how to use Windows 95 Help. Just about every Windows 95 program has a help feature. Many computer users can learn to use a program just by using Help. To use Help, you would start the program, then click the Help menu at the top of the screen. Try using WordPad Help:

  a. Start WordPad.
  b. Click Help on the WordPad menu bar, then click Help Topics.
  c. Using WordPad help, write out your answers to questions 1 through 3.
    1. How do you create a bulleted list?
    2. How do you set the margins in a document?
    3. What happens if you hold down the Alt key and press the Print Screen key?
  d. Close WordPad.

3. Using Help to Explore Paint In this assignment, you will use the Paint Help to learn how to use the Paint program. Your goal is to create and print a picture that looks like the one in Figure 1-23.

Figure 1-23 ◄

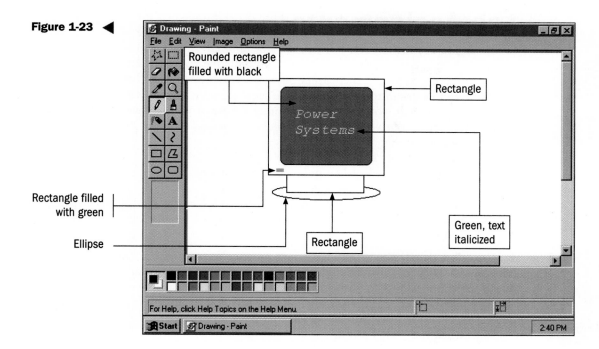

Rounded rectangle filled with black

Rectangle

Power Systems

Rectangle filled with green

Ellipse

Rectangle

Green, text italicized

a. Start Paint.
b. Click Help, then click Help Topics.
c. Use Paint Help to learn how to put text in a picture and how to draw rectangles and circles.
d. Draw a picture of a monitor using rectangles, circles, and text as shown in Figure 1-23.
e. Print your picture.
f. Close Paint.

4. The Windows 95 Tutorial Windows 95 includes a five part on-line tutorial. In Tutorial 1 you learned about starting programs, switching windows, and using Help. You can use the on-line Windows 95 Tutorial to review what you learned and pick up some new tips for using Windows 95. Complete the following steps and write out your answers to questions f, g, and h:

a. Click the Start button to display the Start menu.
b. Click Help to display Windows help.
c. Click the Contents tab.
d. From the Contents screen, click Tour: Ten minutes to using Windows.
e. Click the Display button. If an error message appears, the Tour is probably not loaded on your computer. You will not be able to complete this assignment. Click Cancel, then click OK to cancel and check with your instructor or technical support person.
f. Click Starting a Program and complete the tutorial. What are the names of the seven programs on the Accessories menu in the tutorial?
g. Click Switching Windows and complete the on-line tutorial. What does the Minimize button do?
h. Click Using Help and complete the tutorial. What is the purpose of the [?] button?
i. Click the Exit button to close the Tour window.
j. Click the Exit Tour button to exit the Tour and return to the Windows 95 desktop.

Lab Assignments

Using a Keyboard

1. Learning to Use the Keyboard If you are not familiar with computer keyboards, you will find the Keyboard Lab helpful. This Lab will give you a structured introduction to special computer keys and their function in Windows 95. As you work through the Lab, you will be asked to answer Quick Check questions about what you have learned. At the end of the lab, you will see a summary report of your answers. If your instructor wants you to print out your answers to these questions, click the Print button on the summary report screen.

    a. Click the Start button.

    b. Point to Programs, then point to CTI Windows 95 Applications.

    c. Click Windows 95 New Perspectives Brief.

    d. Click Using a Keyboard. If you cannot find Windows 95 New Perspectives Brief or Using a Keyboard, ask for help from your instructor or technical support person.

Using a Mouse

2. Mouse Practice If you would like more practice using a mouse, you can complete the Mouse Lab. As you work through the Lab, you will be asked to answer Quick Check questions about what you have learned. At the end of the lab, the Quick Check Report shows you how you did. If your instructor wants you to print out your answers to these questions, click the Print button on the summary report screen.

    a. Click the Start button.

    b. Point to Programs, then point to CTI Windows 95.

    c. Point to Windows 95 New Perspectives Brief.

    d. Click Using a Mouse. If you cannot find Windows 95 New Perspectives Brief or Using a Mouse, ask for help from your instructor or technical support person.

Working with Files

LABS

Using Files

Your First Day in the Lab—Continued

CASE Steve Laslow is back from class, grinning. "I see you're making progress!"

"That's right," you reply. "I know how to run programs, control windows, and use Help. I guess I'm ready to work with my word-processing and spreadsheet software now."

Steve hesitates before he continues, "You could, but there are a few more things about Windows 95 that you should learn first."

Steve explains that most of the software you have on your computer—your word-processing, spreadsheet, scheduling, and graphing software—was created especially for the Windows 95 operating system. This software is referred to as **Windows 95 applications** or **Windows 95 programs**. You can also use software designed for Windows 3.1, but Windows 95 applications give you more flexibility. For example, when you name a document in a Windows 95 application, you can use descriptive filenames with up to 255 characters, whereas in Windows 3.1 you are limited to eight-character names.

You typically use Windows 95 applications to create files. A **file** is a collection of data that has a name and is stored in a computer. You typically create files that contain documents, pictures, and graphs when you use software packages. For example, you might use word-processing software to create a file containing a document. Once you create a file, you can open it, edit its contents, print it, and save it again—usually using the same application program you used to create it.

Another advantage of Windows 95 is that once you know how to save, open, and print files with one Windows 95 application, you can perform those same functions in *any* Windows 95 application. This is because Windows 95 applications have similar controls. For example, your word-processing and spreadsheet software will have identical menu commands to save, open, and print documents. Steve suggests that it would be worth a few minutes of your time to become familiar with these menus in Windows 95 applications.

You agree, but before you can get to work, Steve gives you one final suggestion: you should also learn how to keep track of the files on your disk. For instance, you might need to find a file you have not used for a while or you might want to delete a file if your disk is getting full. You will definitely want to make a backup copy of your disk in case something happens to the original. Steve's advice seems practical, and you're eager to explore these functions so you can get to work!

Tutorial 2 will help you learn how to work with Windows 95 applications and keep track of the files on your disk. When you've completed this tutorial, you'll be ready to tackle all kinds of Windows 95 software!

In Session 2.1 you will learn how to format a disk so it can store files. You will create, save, open, and print a file. You will find out how the insertion point is different from the mouse pointer, and you will learn the basic skills for Windows 95 text entry, such as inserting, deleting, and selecting.
For this tutorial you will need two blank 3 ½-inch disks.

Formatting a Disk

Before you can save files on a disk, the disk must be formatted. When the computer **formats** a disk, the magnetic particles on the disk surface are arranged so data can be stored on the disk. Today, many disks are sold preformatted and can be used right out of the box. However, if you purchase an unformatted disk, or if you have an old disk that you want to completely erase and reuse, you can format the disk using the Windows 95 Format command.

The following steps tell you how to format a 3 ½-inch high-density disk using drive A. Your instructor will tell you how to revise the instructions given in these steps if the procedure is different for your lab equipment.

All data on the disk you format will be erased, so don't perform these steps using a disk that contains important files.

To format a disk:

1. Start Windows 95, if necessary.

2. Write your name on the label of a 3 ½-inch disk.

3. Insert your disk in drive A. See Figure 2-1.

Figure 2-1 ◀
Inserting a
disk into the
disk drive

floppy disk drive

edge with the
notch goes into
the drive first

edge with the
label goes
in last

TROUBLE? If your disk does not fit in drive A, put it in drive B and substitute drive B for drive A in all of the steps for the rest of the tutorial.

4. Click the **My Computer** icon to select it, then press the **Enter** key. Make sure you can see the My Computer window. See Figure 2-2.

TROUBLE? If you see a list instead of icons like those in Figure 2-2, click View. Then click Large Icon.

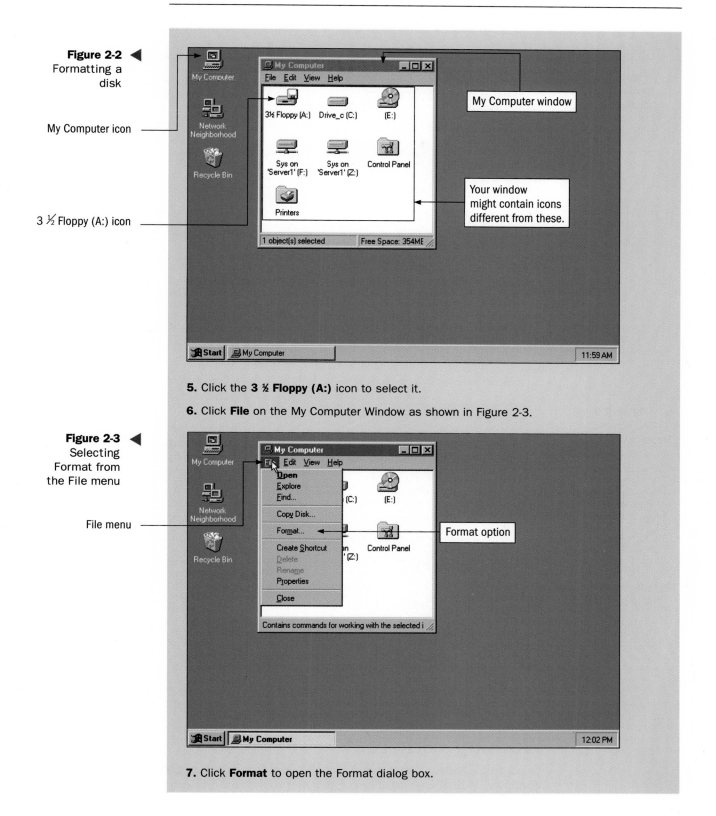

Figure 2-2
Formatting a
disk

My Computer icon

3 ½ Floppy (A:) icon

5. Click the **3 ½ Floppy (A:)** icon to select it.

6. Click **File** on the My Computer Window as shown in Figure 2-3.

Figure 2-3
Selecting
Format from
the File menu

File menu

7. Click **Format** to open the Format dialog box.

8. Make sure the dialog box settings on your screen match those in Figure 2-4.

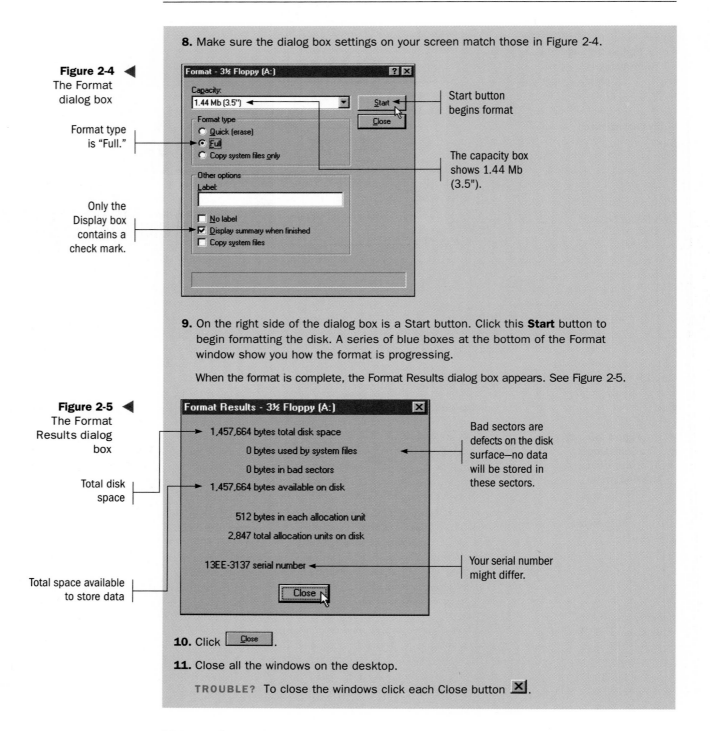

Figure 2-4
The Format dialog box

Format type is "Full."

Only the Display box contains a check mark.

Start button begins format

The capacity box shows 1.44 Mb (3.5").

9. On the right side of the dialog box is a Start button. Click this **Start** button to begin formatting the disk. A series of blue boxes at the bottom of the Format window show you how the format is progressing.

When the format is complete, the Format Results dialog box appears. See Figure 2-5.

Figure 2-5
The Format Results dialog box

Total disk space

Total space available to store data

Bad sectors are defects on the disk surface—no data will be stored in these sectors.

Your serial number might differ.

10. Click Close.

11. Close all the windows on the desktop.

TROUBLE? To close the windows click each Close button.

Working with Text

To accomplish many computing tasks, you need to type text in documents and text boxes. Windows 95 facilitates basic text entry by providing a text-entry area, by showing you where your text will appear on the screen, by helping you move around on the screen, and by providing insert and delete functions.

When you type sentences and paragraphs of text, do *not* press the Enter key when you reach the right margin. The software contains a feature called **word wrap** that automatically continues your text on the next line. Therefore, you should press Enter only when you have completed a paragraph.

If you type the wrong character, press the Backspace key to backup and delete the character. You can also use the Delete key. What's the difference between the Backspace and the Delete keys? The Backspace key deletes the character to left. The Delete key deletes the character to the right.

Now you will type some text using WordPad to learn about text entry.

To type text in WordPad:

1. Start WordPad.

   TROUBLE? If the WordPad window does not fill the screen, click the Maximize button 🔲.

2. Notice the flashing vertical bar, called the **insertion point**, in the upper-left corner of the document window. The insertion point indicates where the characters you type will appear.

3. Type your name, using the Shift key to type uppercase letters and using the spacebar to type spaces, just like on a typewriter.

4. Press the **Enter** key to end the current paragraph and move the insertion point down to the next line.

5. As you type the following sentences, watch what happens when the insertion point reaches the right edge of the screen:

   This is a sample typed in WordPad. See what happens when the insertion point reaches the right edge of the screen.

   TROUBLE? If you make a mistake, delete the incorrect character(s) by pressing the Backspace key on your keyboard. Then type the correct character(s).

The Insertion Point versus the Pointer

The insertion point is not the same as the mouse pointer. When the mouse pointer is in the text-entry area, it is called the **I-beam pointer** and looks like I. Figure 2-6 explains the difference between the insertion point and the I-beam pointer.

Figure 2-6 ◀
The insertion point vs. the pointer

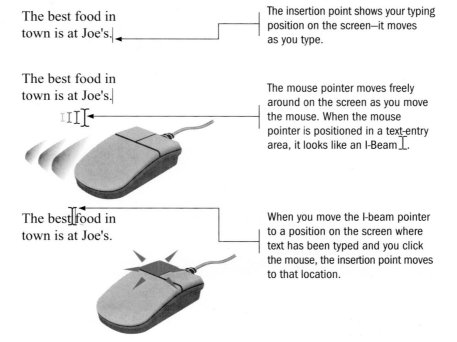

The best food in town is at Joe's.|

The insertion point shows your typing position on the screen—it moves as you type.

The best food in town is at Joe's.|

The mouse pointer moves freely around on the screen as you move the mouse. When the mouse pointer is positioned in a text-entry area, it looks like an I-Beam I.

The best food in town is at Joe's.

When you move the I-beam pointer to a position on the screen where text has been typed and you click the mouse, the insertion point moves to that location.

To move the insertion point:

1. Check the location of the insertion point and the I-beam pointer. The insertion point should be at the end of the sentence you typed in the last set of steps.

   TROUBLE? If you don't see the I-beam pointer, move your mouse until you see it.

2. Use the mouse to move the I-beam pointer to the word "sample," then click the left mouse button. The insertion point jumps to the location of the I-beam pointer.

3. Move the I-beam pointer to a blank area near the bottom of the work space and click the left mouse button. *Notice that the insertion point does not jump to the location of the I-beam pointer.* Instead the insertion point jumps to the end of the last sentence. The insertion point can move only within existing text. It cannot be moved out of the existing text area.

Selecting Text

Many text operations are performed on a **block** of text, which is one or more consecutive words, sentences, or paragraphs. Once you select a block of text, you can delete it, move it, replace it, underline it, and so on. As you select a block of text, the computer highlights it. If you want to remove the highlighting, just click in the margin of your document.

Suppose you want to replace the phrase "See what happens" with "You can watch word wrap in action." You do not have to delete the text one character at a time. Instead you can highlight the entire phrase and begin to type the replacement text.

To select and replace a block of text:

1. Move the I-beam pointer just to the left of the word "See."

2. While holding down the left mouse button, drag the I-beam pointer over the text to the end of the word "happens." The phrase "See what happens" should now be highlighted. See Figure 2-7.

Figure 2-7 ◀
Highlighting
text

Position the
I-beam pointer here.

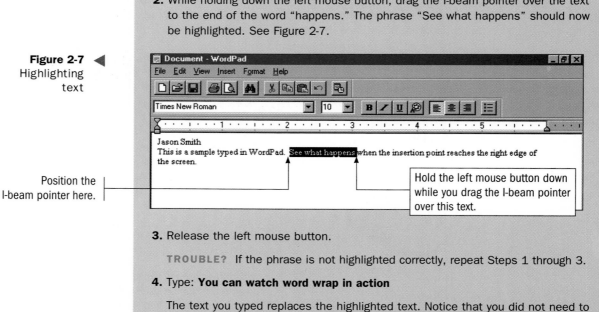

Hold the left mouse button down while you drag the I-beam pointer over this text.

3. Release the left mouse button.

   TROUBLE? If the phrase is not highlighted correctly, repeat Steps 1 through 3.

4. Type: **You can watch word wrap in action**

   The text you typed replaces the highlighted text. Notice that you did not need to delete the highlighted text before you typed the replacement text.

Inserting a Character

Windows 95 programs usually operate in **insert mode**—when you type a new character, all characters to the right of the cursor are pushed over to make room.

Suppose you want to insert the word "sentence" before the word "typed."

To insert characters:

1. Position the I-beam pointer just before the word "typed," then click.

2. Type: **sentence**.

3. Press the **spacebar**.

Notice how the letters in the first line are pushed to the right to make room for the new characters. When a word gets pushed past the right margin, the word-wrap feature pushes it down to the beginning of the next line.

3.1 NOTE

When you save a file with a long filename, Windows 95 also creates an eight-character filename that can be used by Windows 3.1 applications. The eight-character filename is created by using the first six non-space characters from the long filename, then adding a tilde (~) and a number. For example, the filename Car Sales for 1997 would be converted to Carsal~1.

Figure 2-8 ◀
Filename and extension

Saving a File

As you type text, it is held temporarily in the computer's memory. For permanent storage, you need to save your work on a disk. In the computer lab, you will probably save your work on a floppy disk in drive A.

When you save a file, you must give it a name. Windows 95 allows you to use filenames containing up to 255 characters, and you may use spaces and punctuation symbols. You cannot use the symbols \ ? : * " < > | in a filename, but other symbols such as &, -, and $ are allowed.

Most filenames have an extension. An **extension** is a suffix of up to three characters that is separated from the filename by a period, as shown in Figure 2-8.

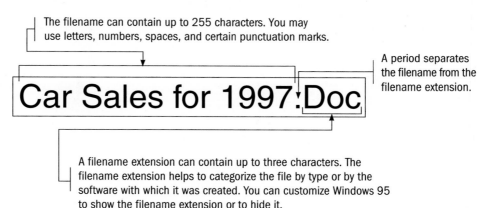

The filename can contain up to 255 characters. You may use letters, numbers, spaces, and certain punctuation marks.

A period separates the filename from the filename extension.

Car Sales for 1997.Doc

A filename extension can contain up to three characters. The filename extension helps to categorize the file by type or by the software with which it was created. You can customize Windows 95 to show the filename extension or to hide it.

The file extension indicates which application you used to create the file. For example, files created with Microsoft Word software have a .Doc extension. In general, you will not add an extension to your filenames, because the application software automatically does this for you.

Windows 95 keeps track of file extensions, but does not always display them. The steps in these tutorials refer to files using the filename, but not its extension. So if you see the filename Sample Text in the steps, but "Sample Text.Doc" on your screen, don't worry—these are the same files.

Now you can save the document you typed.

To save a document:

1. Click the **Save** button 🖫 on the toolbar. Figure 2-9 shows the location of this button and the Save As dialog box that appears after you click it.

Figure 2-9 ◀
The Save button

Save button

Save As
dialog box
appears after
you click the
Save button

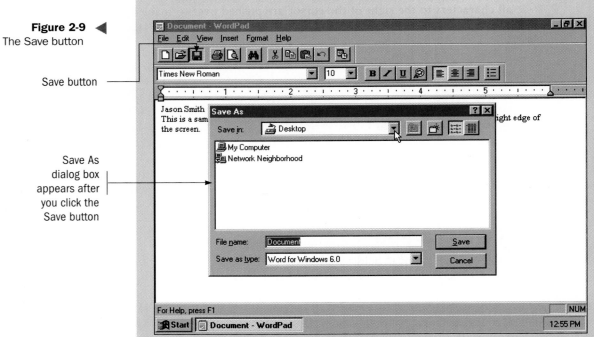

2. Click ▼ on the side of the Save in: box to display a list of drives. See Figure 2-10.

Figure 2-10 ◀
Selecting the
drive

3 ½ Floppy (A:)
drive menu
option

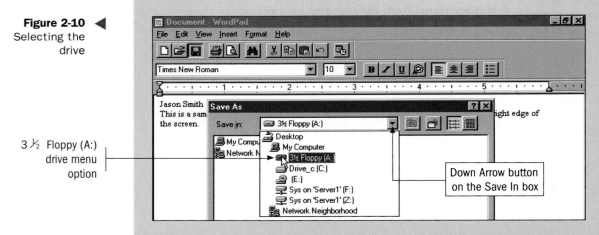

3. Click **3½ Floppy (A:)**.

4. Select the text in the File Name box.

   TROUBLE? To select the text, position the I-beam pointer at the beginning of the word "Document." While you hold down the mouse button, drag the I-beam pointer to the end of the word.

5. Type **Sample Text** in the File Name box.

6. Click the **Save** button. Your file is saved on your Student Disk and the document title, "Sample Text," appears on the WordPad title bar.

What if you tried to close WordPad *before* you saved your file? Windows 95 would display a message—"Save changes to Document?" If you answer "Yes," Windows displays the Save As dialog box so you can give the document a name. If you answer "No," Windows 95 closes WordPad without saving the document.

After you save a file, you can work on another document or close WordPad. Since you have already saved your Sample Text document, you should continue this tutorial by closing WordPad.

To close WordPad:

> **1.** Click the **Close** button ☒ to close the WordPad window.

Opening a File

Suppose you save and close the Sample Text file, then later you want to revise it. To revise a file you must first open it. When you **open** a file, its contents are copied into the computer's memory. If you revise the file, you need to save the changes before you close the application or work on a different file. If you close a revised file without saving your changes, you will lose the revisions.

Typically, you would use one of two methods to open a file. You could select the file from the Documents list or the My Computer window, or you could start an application program and then use the Open button to open the file. Each method has advantages and disadvantages. You will have an opportunity to try both methods.

The first method for opening the Sample Text file simply requires you to select the file from the Documents list or the My Computer window. With this method the document, not the application program, is central to the task; hence this method is sometimes referred to as *document-centric*. You only need to remember the name of your document or file—you do not need to remember which application you used to create the document.

The Documents list contains the names of the last 15 documents used. You access this list from the Start menu. When you have your own computer, the Documents list is very handy. In a computer lab, however, the files other students use quickly replace yours on the list.

If your file is not in the Documents list, you can open the file by selecting it from the My Computer window. Windows 95 starts an application program that you can use to revise the file, then automatically opens the file. The advantage of this method is its simplicity. The disadvantage is that Windows 95 might not start the application you expect. For example, when you select Sample Text, you might expect Windows 95 to start WordPad because you used WordPad to type the text of the document. Depending on the software installed on your computer system, however, Windows 95 might start the Microsoft Word application instead. Usually this is not a problem. Although the application might not be the one you expect, you can still use it to revise your file.

3.I NOTE

Document-centric features are advertised as an advantage of Windows 95. But you can still successfully use the application-centric approach you used with Windows 3.1 by opening your application, then opening your document.

To open the Sample Text file by selecting it from My Computer:

> **1.** Click the **My Computer** icon. Press the **Enter** key. The My Computer window opens.
>
> **2.** Click the **3½ Floppy (A:)** icon, then press the **Enter** key. The 3½ Floppy (A:) window opens.
>
> TROUBLE? If the My Computer window disappears when you open the 3½ floppy (A:) window, click View, click Options, then click the Folder tab, if necessary. Click the radio button labelled "Browse Folders using a separate window for each folder." Then click the OK button.
>
> **3.** Click the **Sample Text** file icon, then press the **Enter** key. Windows 95 starts an application program, then automatically opens the Sample Text file.
>
> TROUBLE? If Windows 95 starts Microsoft Word instead of WordPad, don't worry. You can use Microsoft Word to revise the Sample Text document.

Now that Windows 95 has started an application and opened the Sample Text file, you could make revisions to the document. Instead, you should close all the windows on your desktop so you can try the other method for opening files.

To close all the windows on the desktop:

1. Click ☒ on each of the windows.

   TROUBLE? If you see a message, "Save changes to Document?" click the No button.

The second method for opening the Sample Text file requires you to open WordPad, then use the Open button to select the Sample Text file. The advantage of this method is that you can specify the application program you want to use—WordPad in this case. This method, however, involves more steps than the method you tried previously.

To start WordPad and open the Sample Text file using the Open button:

1. Start WordPad.

2. Click the **Open** button 🖻 on the toolbar. Figure 2-11 shows the location of this button and the dialog box that appears after you click it.

Figure 2-11 ◀
The Open button and dialog box

Open button

Open dialog box

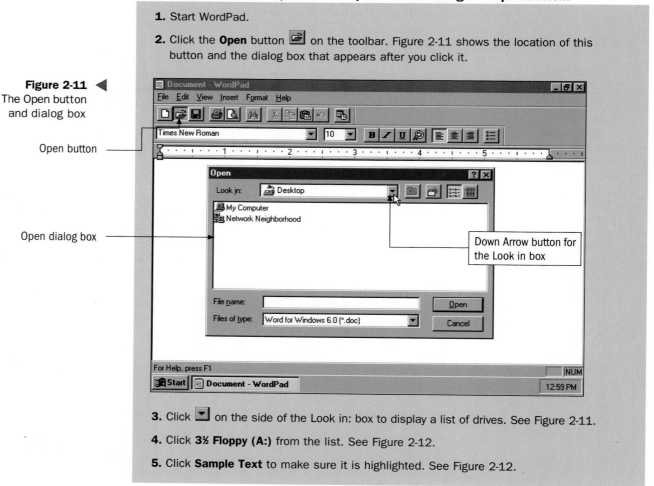

Down Arrow button for the Look in box

3. Click ▾ on the side of the Look in: box to display a list of drives. See Figure 2-11.

4. Click **3½ Floppy (A:)** from the list. See Figure 2-12.

5. Click **Sample Text** to make sure it is highlighted. See Figure 2-12.

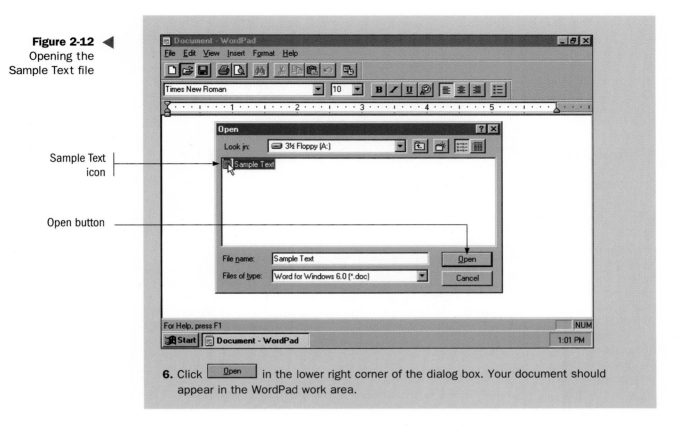

Figure 2-12 ◀
Opening the
Sample Text file

Sample Text
icon

Open button

6. Click ⬚ Open ⬚ in the lower right corner of the dialog box. Your document should appear in the WordPad work area.

Printing a File

Now that the Sample Text file is open, you can print it. It is a good idea to use Print Preview before you send your document to the printer. **Print Preview** shows on screen exactly how your document will appear on paper. You can check your page layout so you don't waste paper printing a document that is not quite the way you want it. Your instructor or technical support person might supply you with additional instructions for printing in your school's computer lab.

To preview, then print the Sample Text file:

1. Click the **Print Preview** button 🔲 on the toolbar.

2. Look at your print preview. Before you print the document and use paper, you should make sure that the font, margins, and other document features look the way you want them to.

   TROUBLE? If you can't read the document text on screen, click the Zoom In button.

3. Click the **Print** button. A Print dialog box appears.

4. Study Figure 2-13 to familiarize yourself with the controls in the Print dialog box.

This is the name of the printer that Windows 95 will use for this printout. If you are using a network, you might have a choice of printers. If you need to select a different printer, ask your instructor or your technical support person for help.

Figure 2-13 ◄
The Print
dialog box

In the Print range box, you specify how much of the document you want to print. If you want to print only part of a document, click the Pages radio button and then enter the starting and ending pages for the printout.

The Properties button lets you modify the way your printer is set up. Do not change any of the settings on your school printer without the consent of your instructor or technical support person.

When you click this check box, your printout will go on your disk instead of to the printer.

You can specify how many copies you want by typing the number in this box. Alternatively, you can use the arrow buttons to increase or decrease the number in the box.

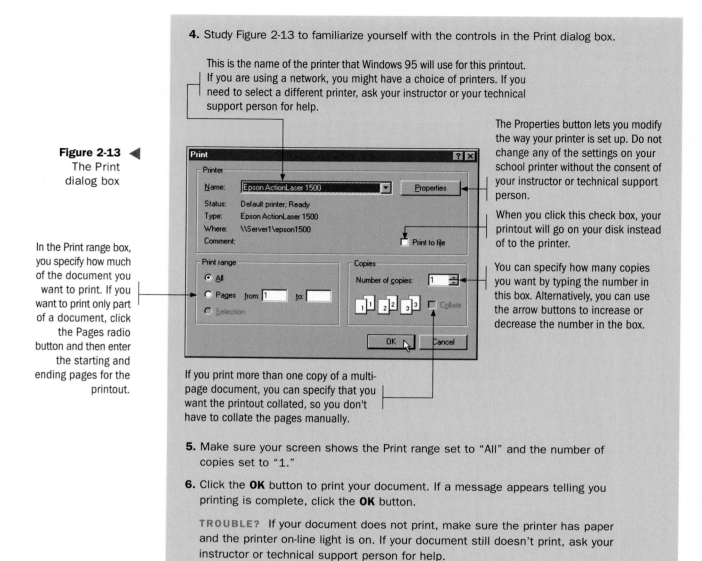

If you print more than one copy of a multi-page document, you can specify that you want the printout collated, so you don't have to collate the pages manually.

5. Make sure your screen shows the Print range set to "All" and the number of copies set to "1."

6. Click the **OK** button to print your document. If a message appears telling you printing is complete, click the **OK** button.

TROUBLE? If your document does not print, make sure the printer has paper and the printer on-line light is on. If your document still doesn't print, ask your instructor or technical support person for help.

7. Close WordPad.

TROUBLE? If you see the message "Save changes to Document?" click the "No" button.

Quick Check

1 A(n) _____ is a collection of data that has a name and is stored on a disk or other storage medium.

2 _____ erases all the data on a disk and arranges the magnetic particles on the disk surface so the disk can store data.

3 When you are working in a text box, the pointer shape changes to a(n) _____.

4 The _____ shows you where each character you type will appear.

5 _____ automatically moves text down to the beginning of the next line when you reach the right margin.

6 Explain how you select a block of text: _____.

7 Which of these characters are not allowed in Windows 95 file names: \ ? : * " < > | ! @ # $ % ^ & ; + - ( ) /

8 In the filename New Equipment.Doc, .Doc is a(n) _____.

9 Suppose you created a graph using the Harvard Graphics software and then you stored the graph on your floppy disk under the name Projected 1997 Sales - Graph. The next day, you use Harvard Graphics to open the file and change the graph. If you want the new version of the file on your disk, you need to _____.

10 You can save _____ by using the Print Preview feature.

SESSION

2.2

In this session, you will learn how to manage the files on your disk—a skill that can prevent you from losing important documents. You will learn how to list information about the files on your disk; organize the files into folders; and move, delete, copy, and rename files.

Creating Your Student Disk

For this session of the tutorial, you must create a Student Disk that contains some sample files. *You can use the disk you formatted in the previous session.*

If you are using your own computer, the CTI Windows 95 Applications menu selection will not be available. Before you proceed, you must go to your school's computer lab and find a computer that has the CTI Windows 95 Applications installed. Once you have made your own Student Disk, you can use it to complete this tutorial on any computer you choose.

To add the sample files to your Student Disk:

1. Write "Windows 95 Student Disk" on the label of your formatted disk.

2. Place the disk in Drive A.

> **TROUBLE?** If your 3½-inch disk drive is B, place your formatted disk in that drive instead, and for the rest of this session substitute Drive B where ever you see Drive A.

3. Click the **Start** button 🔲 Start . See Figure 2-14.

Figure 2-14 ◄
Making your
Student Disk

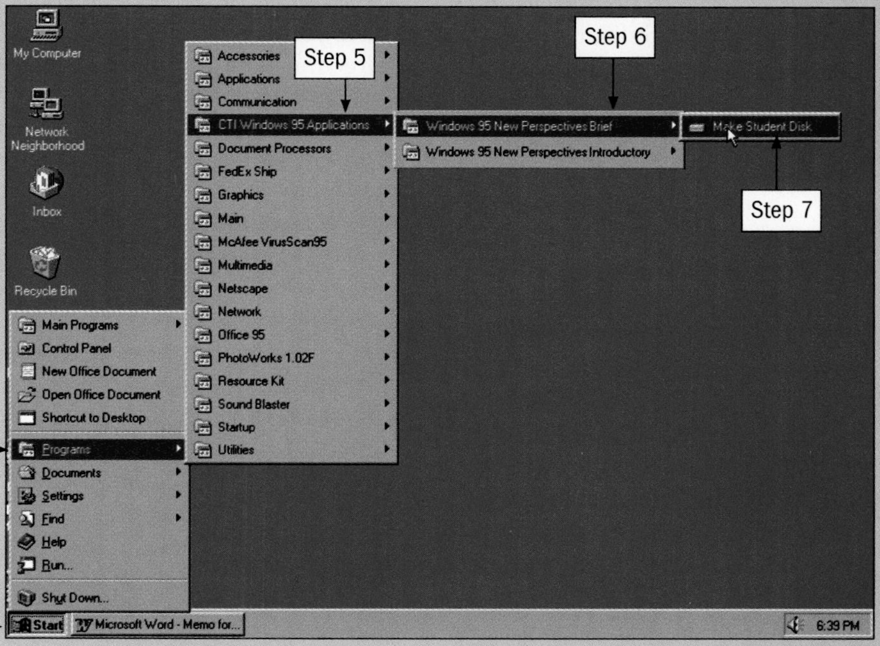

4. Point to **Programs.**

5. Point to **CTI Windows 95 Applications.**

TROUBLE? If CTI Windows 95 Applications is not listed, contact your instructor or technical support person.

6. Point to **Windows 95 New Perspectives Brief.**

7. Select **Make Student Disk.**

A dialog box opens, asking you to indicate the drive that contains your formatted disk.

8. If it is not already selected, click the Drive radio button that corresponds to the drive containing your student disk.

9. Click the **OK** button.

The sample files are copied to your formatted disk. A message tells you when all the files have been copied.

10. Click **OK.**

11. If necessary, close all the open windows on your screen.

Your Student Disk now contains sample files that you will use throughout the rest of this tutorial.

My Computer

The **My Computer** icon represents your computer, its storage devices, and its printers. The My Computer icon opens into the My Computer window, which contains an icon for each of the storage devices on your computer. On most computer systems the My Computer window also contains Control Panel and Printers folders, which help you add printers, control peripheral devices, and customize your Windows 95 work environment. Figure 2-15 on the following page explains more about the My Computer window.

You can use the My Computer window to keep track of where your files are stored and to organize your files. In this section of the tutorial you will move and delete files on your Student Disk in drive A. If you use your own computer at home or computer at work, you would probably store your files on drive C, instead of drive A. However, in a school lab environment you usually don't know which computer you will use, so you need to carry your files with you on a floppy disk that you use in drive A. In this session, therefore, you will learn how to work with the files on drive A. Most of what you learn will also work on your home or work computer when you use drive C.

In this session you will work with several icons, including My Computer. As a general procedure, when you want to open an icon, you click it and then press the Enter key.

Figure 2-15 ◀
Information
about My
Computer

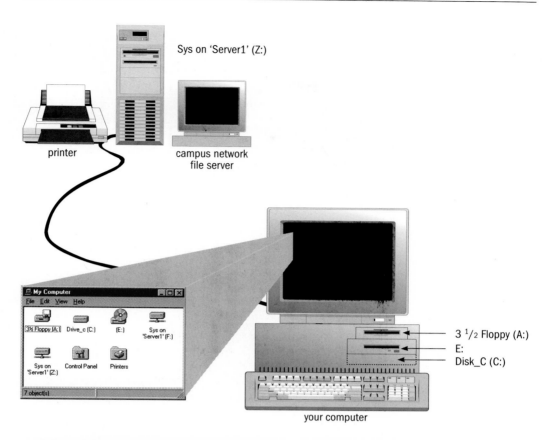

Sys on 'Server1' (Z:)

printer

campus network
file server

3 ¹/₂ Floppy (A:)

E:

Disk_C (C:)

your computer

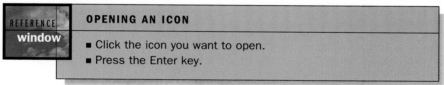

REFERENCE
window

OPENING AN ICON

- Click the icon you want to open.
- Press the Enter key.

Now you should open the My Computer icon.

To open the My Computer icon:

1. Click the **My Computer** icon to select it.

2. Press the **Enter** key. The My Computer window opens.

Now that you have opened the My Computer window, you can find out what is on your Student Disk in drive A.

To find out what is on your Student Disk:

1. Open the **3½ Floppy (A:)** icon by clicking it, then pressing the **Enter** key. A window appears showing the contents of drive A:. See Figure 2-16.

Figure 2-16 ◄
Contents of
Student Disk

Icons show contents
of drive A

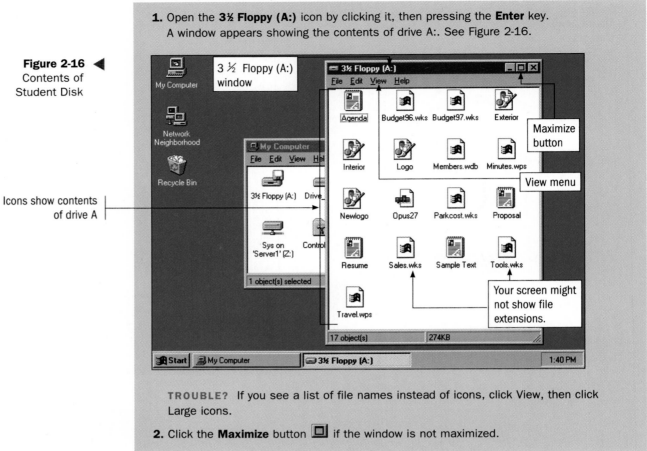

TROUBLE? If you see a list of file names instead of icons, click View, then click Large icons.

2. Click the **Maximize** button 🗖 if the window is not maximized.

Windows 95 provides four ways to view the contents of a disk—large icons, small icons, list, or details. The standard view, shown on your screen, displays a large icon and title for each file. The icon provides a visual cue to the type and contents of the file, as Figure 2-17 illustrates.

Figure 2-17 ◄
Program and
file icons

| Text files that you can open and read using the WordPad or NotePad software are represented by notepad icons. | WordPad Document | Netlog | Exchng32 |

| The icons for Windows programs usually depict an object related to the function of the program. For example, an icon that looks like a calculator signifies the Windows Calc program; an icon that looks like a computer signifies the Windows Explorer program. | Explorer | Calc |

| Many of the files you create are represented by page icons. Here the page icon for the Circles file shows some graphics tools to indicate the file contains a graphic. The Page icon for the Access file contains the Windows logo, indicating that Windows does not know if the file contains a document, graphics, or data base. | Access.mdb | Circles |

| Folders provide a way to group and organize files. A folder icon contains other icons for folders and files. Here, the System folder contains files used by the Windows operating system. | System |

| Non-Windows programs are represented by this icon of a blank window. | Command |

The **Details** view shows more information than the large icon, small icon, and list views. Details view shows the file icon, the filename, the file size, the application you used to create the file, and the date/time the file was created or last modified.

To view a detailed list of files:

1. Click **View** then click **Details** to display details for the files on your disk as shown in Figure 2-18.

Figure 2-18 ◀
Detailed file list

File icon —

Filename —

Your screen might not
show file extensions

Total number of
files and folders
in the window

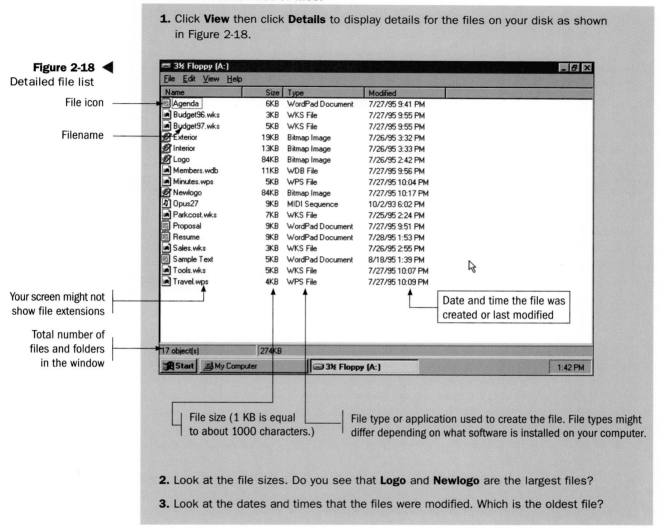

File size (1 KB is equal
to about 1000 characters.)

File type or application used to create the file. File types might differ depending on what software is installed on your computer.

Date and time the file was
created or last modified

2. Look at the file sizes. Do you see that **Logo** and **Newlogo** are the largest files?

3. Look at the dates and times that the files were modified. Which is the oldest file?

Now that you have looked at the file details, switch back to the large icon view.

To switch to the large icon view:

1. Click **View** then click **Large Icons** to return to the large icon display.

Folders and Directories

A list of files is referred to as a **directory**. The main directory of a disk is sometimes called the **root directory**. The root directory is created when you format a disk and is shown in parentheses at the top of the window. For example, at the top of your screen you should see "3 ½ Floppy (A:)." The root directory is A:. In some situations, the root directory is indicated by a backslash after the drive letter and colon, such as A:\. All of the files on your Student Disk are currently in the root directory.

If too many files are stored in a directory, the directory list becomes very long and difficult to manage. A directory can be divided into **folders** (also called **subdirectories**), into which you group similar files. The directory of files for each folder then becomes much shorter and easier to manage. For example, you might create a folder for all the papers you write for an English 111 class as shown in Figure 2-19.

A folder appears on the screen as a folder icon. When you open the folder icon, the folder is represented by a window. The ENG111 folder appears as the ENG111 window on the screen. The contents of the folder are represented by icons in the window.

Figure 2-19 ◀
Folders and
directories

You create folders
to hold groups
of similar objects,
such as documents,
programs, and
other folders.

A folder can contain
other folders. Here,
the ENG111 folder
contains a folder
called TERM PAPER.

If you open a folder that is contained
in a window, it opens to its own window
and displays the objects it contains.

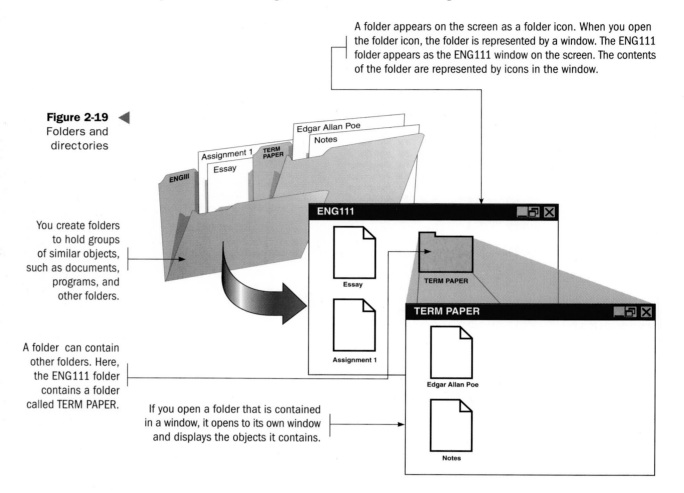

Now, you'll create a folder called My Documents to hold your document files.

To create a My Documents folder:

1. Click **File** then point to **New** to display the submenu.

2. Click **Folder**. A folder icon with the label "New Folder" appears.

3. Type **My Documents** as the name of the folder.

4. Press the **Enter** key.

When you first create a folder, it doesn't contain any files. In the next set of steps you will move a file from the root directory to the My Documents folder.

CREATING A NEW FOLDER

- Open the My Computer icon to display the My Computer window.
- Open the icon for the drive on which you want to create the folder.
- Click File then point to New.
- From the submenu click Folder.
- Type the name for the new folder.
- Press the Enter key.

Moving and Copying a File

You can move a file from one directory to another or from one disk to another. When you move a file it is copied to the new location you specify, then the version in the old location is erased. The move feature is handy for organizing or reorganizing the files on your disk by moving them into appropriate folders. The easiest way to move a file is to hold down the *right* mouse button and drag the file from the old location to the new location. A menu appears and you select Move Here.

You can also copy a file from one directory to another, or from one disk to another. When you copy a file, you create an exact duplicate of an existing file in whatever disk or folder you specify. To copy a file from one folder to another on your floppy disk, you use the same procedure as for moving a file, except that you select Copy Here from the menu.

Suppose you want to move the Minutes file from the root directory to the My Documents folder. Depending on the software applications installed on your computer, this file is either called Minutes or Minutes.wps. In the steps it is referred to simply as Minutes.

To move the Minutes file to the My Documents folder:

1. Click the **Minutes** icon to select it.

2. Press and hold the right mouse button while you drag the **Minutes** icon to the My Documents folder. See Figure 2-20.

Figure 2-20 ◀
Moving a file

Minutes file ——

My Documents folder ——

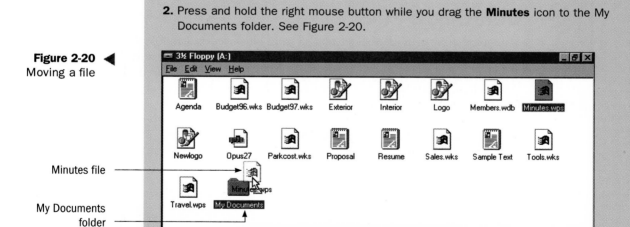

3. Release the right mouse button. A menu appears.

4. Click **Move Here**. A short animation shows the Minutes file being moved to My Documents. The Minutes icon disappears from the window showing the files in the root directory.

MOVING A FILE

- Open the My Computer icon to display the My Computer window.
- If the document you want to move is in a folder, open the folder.
- Hold down the *right* mouse button while you drag the file icon to its new folder or disk location.
- Click Move Here.
- If you want to move more than one file at a time, hold down the Ctrl key while you click the icons for all the files you want to move.

3.1 NOTE

Windows 3.1 users be careful! When you delete or move an icon in the Windows 95 My Computer window you are actually deleting or moving the file. This is quite different from the way the Windows 3.1 Program Manager worked.

Anything you do to an icon in the My Computer window is actually done to the file represented by that icon. If you move an icon, the file is moved; if you delete an icon, the file is deleted.

After you move a file, it is a good idea to make sure it was moved to the correct location. You can easily verify that a file is in its new folder by displaying the folder contents.

To verify that the Minutes file was moved to My Documents:

1. Click the **My Documents** folder, then press **Enter**. The My Documents window appears and it contains one file—Minutes.

2. Click the My Documents window **Close** button ![X].

   TROUBLE? If the My Computer window is no longer visible, click the My Computer icon, then press Enter. You might also need to open the 3 ½ Floppy (A:) icon.

Deleting a File

You delete a file or folder by deleting its icon. However, be careful when you delete a *folder*, because you also delete all the files it contains! When you delete a file from the hard drive, the filename is deleted from the directory but the file contents are held in the Recycle Bin. If you change your mind and want to retrieve the deleted file, you can recover it by clicking the Recycle Bin.

When you delete a file from a floppy disk, it does not go into the Recycle Bin. Instead it is deleted as soon as its icon disappears. Try deleting the file named Agenda from your Student Disk. Because this file is on the floppy disk and not on the hard disk, it will not go into the Recycle Bin.

To delete the file Agenda:

1. Click the icon for the file **Agenda**.

2. Press the **Delete** key.

3. If a message appears asking, "Are sure you want to delete Agenda?", click **Yes**. An animation, which might play too quickly to be seen, shows the file being deleted.

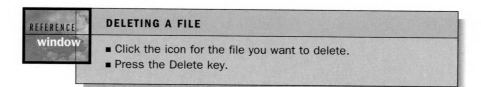

DELETING A FILE

- Click the icon for the file you want to delete.
- Press the Delete key.

Renaming a File

You can easily change the name of a file using the Rename option on the File menu or by using the file's label. Remember that when you choose a filename it can contain up to 255 characters, including spaces, but it cannot contain \ ? : " < > | characters.

Practice using this feature by renaming the Sales file to give it a more descriptive filename.

To rename Sales:

1. Click the **Sales** file to select it.

2. Click the label "Sales". After a short pause a solid box outlines the label and an insertion point appears.

3. Type **Preliminary Sales Summary** as the new filename.

4. Press the **Enter key**.

5. Click the **Close** button ☒ to close the 3 ½-inch Floppy (A:) window.

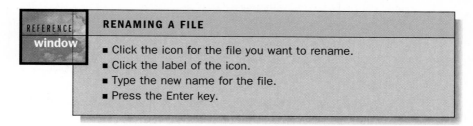

RENAMING A FILE

- Click the icon for the file you want to rename.
- Click the label of the icon.
- Type the new name for the file.
- Press the Enter key.

Copying an Entire Floppy Disk

You can have trouble accessing the data on your floppy disk if the disk gets damaged, exposed to magnetic fields, or picks up a computer virus. If the damaged disk contains important files, you will have to spend many hours to try to reconstruct those files. To avoid losing all your data, it is a good idea to make a copy of your floppy disk. This copy is called a **backup** copy.

If you wanted to make a copy of an audio cassette, your cassette player would need two cassette drives. You might wonder, therefore, how your computer can make a copy of your disk if you have only one disk drive. Figure 2-21 illustrates how the computer uses only one disk drive to make a copy of a disk.

Figure 2-21 ◀
Using one disk
drive to make a
copy of a disk

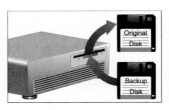

1. First, the computer
copies the data from your
original disk into memory.

2. Once the data is in
memory, you remove your
original disk from the drive
and replace it with your
backup disk.

3. The computer moves the
data from memory onto
your backup disk.

REFERENCE
window

MAKING A BACKUP OF YOUR FLOPPY DISK

- Click My Computer then press the Enter key.
- Insert the disk you want to copy in drive A.
- Click the 3 ½ Floppy (A:) icon ▭ to select it.
  3½ Floppy (A:)
- Click File then click Copy Disk to display the Copy Disk dialog
  box.
- Click Start to begin the copy process.
- When prompted, remove the disk you want to copy. Place your
  backup disk in drive A.
- Click OK.
- When the copy is complete, close the Copy Disk dialog box.
- Close the My Computer dialog box.

If you have two floppy disks, you can make a backup of your Student Disk now. Make
sure you periodically follow the backup procedure, so your backup is up-to-date.

To back up your Student Disk:

1. Write your name and "Backup" on the label of your second disk. This will be your
   backup disk.

2. Make sure your Student Disk is in drive A.

3. Make sure the My Computer window is open. See Figure 2-22.

Figure 2-22 ◀
The My
Computer
window

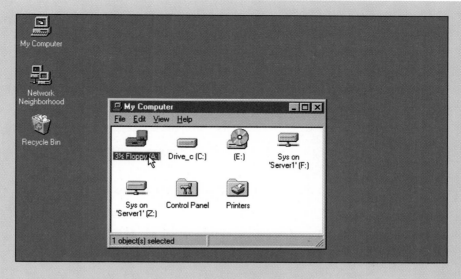

4. Click the **3 ½ Floppy (A:)** icon ![floppy icon] 3½ Floppy (A:) to select it.

> **TROUBLE?** If you mistakenly open the 3½ Floppy (A:) *window*, click ![X].

5. Click **File**.

6. Click **Copy Disk** to display the Copy Disk dialog box as shown in Figure 2-23.

Figure 2-23 ◀
The Copy Disk
dialog box

7. On the lower right side of the dialog box, you'll see a Start button. Click this **Start** button to begin the copy process.

8. When the message, "Insert the disk you want to copy from (source disk)..." appears, click the **OK** button.

9. When the message, "Insert the disk you want to copy to (destination disk)..." appears, insert your backup disk in drive A.

10. Click the **OK** button. When the copy is complete, you will see the message "Copy completed successfully."

11. After the data is copied to your backup disk, click ![X] on the blue title bar of the Copy Disk dialog box.

12. Click ![X] on the My Computer window to close the My Computer window.

13. Remove your disk from the drive.

Each time you make a backup, the data on your backup disk is erased, and replaced with the data from your updated Student Disk. Now that you know how to copy an entire disk, make a backup whenever you have completed a tutorial or you have spent a long time working on a file.

Quick Check

1. If you want to find out about the storage devices and printers connected to your computer, click the _____ icon.

2. If you have only one floppy disk drive on your computer, it is identified by the letter _____.

3. The letter C: is typically used for the _____ drive of a computer.

4. What are the five pieces of information that the Details view supplies about each of your files?

5. The main directory of a disk is referred to as the _____ directory.

6. You can divide a directory into _____.

7. If you delete the icon for a file, what happens to the file?

8. If you have one floppy disk drive, but you have two disks, can you copy a file from one floppy disk to another?

End Note

Just as you complete the Quick Check for Session 2.2, Steve appears. He asks how you are doing. You summarize what you remember from the tutorial, telling him that you learned how to insert, delete, and select text. You also learned how to work with files using Windows 95 software—you now know how to save, open, revise, and print a document. You tell him that you like the idea that these file operations are the same for almost all Windows 95 software. Steve agrees that this makes work a lot easier.

When Steve asks you if you have a supply of disks, you tell him you do, and that you just learned how to format a disk and view a list of files on your disk. Steve wants you to remember that you can use the Details view to see the filename, size, date, and time. You assure him that you remember that feature—and also how to move, delete, and rename a file.

Steve seems pleased with your progress and agrees that you're now ready to use software applications. But he can't resist giving you one last warning—don't forget to back up your files frequently!

Tutorial Assignments

1. Opening, Editing, and Printing a Document In this tutorial you learned how to create a document using WordPad. You also learned how to save, open, and print a document. Practice these skills by opening the document on your Student Disk called Resume, which is a résumé for Jamie Woods. Make the changes shown in Figure 2-24, and then print the document. After you print, save your revisions.

Figure 2-24 ◄

Change this to your name, address, and phone number. If you don't have an office number delete this.

Change this to the name of your university or college.

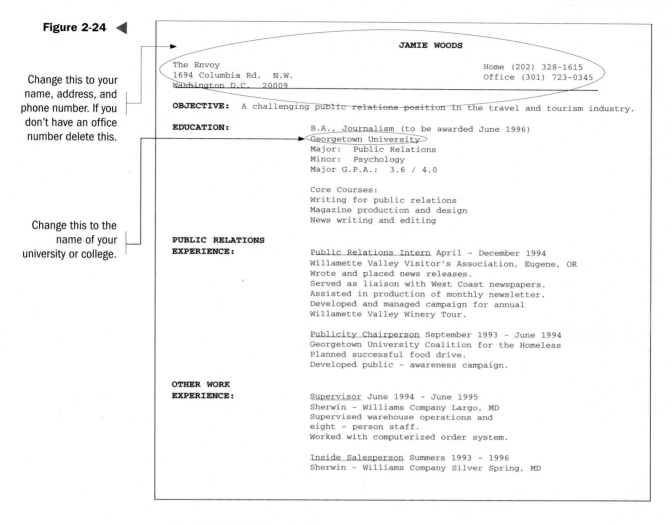

JAMIE WOODS

The Envoy
1694 Columbia Rd. N.W.   Home (202) 328-1615
Washington D.C. 20009   Office (301) 723-0345

OBJECTIVE: A challenging public relations position in the travel and tourism industry.

EDUCATION: B.A., Journalism (to be awarded June 1996)
                                  Georgetown University
                                  Major: Public Relations
                                  Minor: Psychology
                                  Major G.P.A.: 3.6 / 4.0

                                  Core Courses:
                                  Writing for public relations
                                  Magazine production and design
                                  News writing and editing

**PUBLIC RELATIONS
EXPERIENCE:**   Public Relations Intern April - December 1994
                                  Willamette Valley Visitor's Association, Eugene, OR
                                  Wrote and placed news releases.
                                  Served as liaison with West Coast newspapers.
                                  Assisted in production of monthly newsletter.
                                  Developed and managed campaign for annual
                                  Willamette Valley Winery Tour.

                                  Publicity Chairperson September 1993 - June 1994
                                  Georgetown University Coalition for the Homeless
                                  Planned successful food drive.
                                  Developed public - awareness campaign.

**OTHER WORK
EXPERIENCE:**   Supervisor June 1994 - June 1995
                                  Sherwin - Williams Company Largo, MD
                                  Supervised warehouse operations and
                                  eight - person staff.
                                  Worked with computerized order system.

                                  Inside Salesperson Summers 1993 - 1996
                                  Sherwin - Williams Company Silver Spring, MD

2. Creating, Saving, and Printing a Letter Use WordPad to write a one-page letter to a relative or a friend. Save the document in the My Documents folder with the name "Letter." Use the Print Preview feature to look at the format of your finished letter, then print it, and be sure you sign it.

3. Managing Files and Folders Earlier in this tutorial you created a folder and moved the file called Minutes into it. Now complete a through g below to practice your file management skills.

    a. Create a folder called Spreadsheets on your Student Disk.

    b. Move the files ParkCost, Budget96, Budget97, and Sales into the Spreadsheets folder.

    c. Create a folder called Park Project.

    d. Move the files Proposal, Members, Tools, Logo, and Newlogo into the Park Project folder.

    e. Move the ParkCost file from the Spreadsheets folder to the Park Project folder.

    f. Delete the file called Travel.

    g. Switch to the Details view and answer the following questions:

Write out your answers to questions a through e.

    a. What is the largest file in the Park Project folder?

    b. What is the newest file in the Spreadsheets folder?

    c. How many files are in the root directory?

    d. How are the Members and Resume icons different?

    e. What is the file with the most recent date on the entire disk?

4. More Practice with Files and Folders For this assignment, you will format your disk again and put a fresh version of the Student Disk files on it. Complete a through h below to practice your file management skills.

    a. Format a disk.
    b. Create a Student Disk. Refer to the section "Creating Your Student Disk" in Session 2.2.
    c. Create three folders on your new Student Disk: Documents, Budgets, and Graphics.
    d. Move the files Interior, Exterior, Logo, and Newlogo to the Graphics folder.
    e. Move the files Travel, Members and Minutes to the Documents folder.
    f. Move Budget96 and Budget97 to the Budgets folder.
    g. Switch to the Details view.

Answer questions a through f.

    a. What is the largest file in the Graphics folder?
    b. How many WordPad documents are in the root directory?
    c. What is the newest file in the root directory?
    d. How many files in all folders are 5KB in size?
    e. How many files in the Documents folder are WKS files?
    f. Do all the files in the Graphics folder have the same icon?

5. Finding a File Microsoft Windows 95 contains an on-line Tour that explains how to find files on a disk without looking through all the folders. Start the Windows 95 Tour (if you don't remember how, look at the instructions for Tutorial Assignment 1 in Tutorial 1), then click Finding a File, and answer the following questions:

    a. To display the Find dialog box, you must click the _____ button, then select _____ from the menu, and finally click _____ from the submenu.
    b. Do you need to type in the entire filename to find the file?
    c. When the computer has found your file, what are the steps you have to follow if you want to display the contents of the file?

6. Help with Files and Folders In Tutorial 2 you learned how to work with Windows 95 files and folders. What additional information on this topic does Windows 95 Help provide? Use the Start button to access Help. Use the Index tab to locate topics related to files and folders. Find at least two tips or procedures for working with files and folders that were not covered in the tutorial. Write out the tip in your own words and indicate the title of the Help screen that contains the information.

Lab Assignments

1. Using Files Lab In Tutorial 2 you learned how to create, save, open, and print files. The Using Files Lab will help you review what happens in the computer when you perform these file tasks. To start the Lab, follow these steps:

    a. Click the Start button.
    b. Point to Programs, then point to CTI Windows 95 Applications.
    c. Point to Windows 95 New Perspectives Brief.
    d. Click Using Files. If you can't find Windows 95 New Perspectives Brief or Using Files, ask for help from your instructor or technical support person.

Answer the Quick Check questions that appear as you work through the Lab. You can print your answers at the end of the Lab.

Answers to Quick Check Questions

SESSION 1.1

1 a. icon b. Start button c. taskbar d. Date/Time control e. desktop f. pointer

2 Multitasking

3 Start menu

4 Lift up the mouse, move it to the right, then put it down, and slide it left until the pointer reaches the left edge of the screen.

5 Highlighting

6 If a program is running, its button is displayed on the taskbar.

7 Each program that is running uses system resources, so Windows 95 runs more efficiently when only the programs you are using are open.

8 Answer: If you do not perform the shut down procedure, you might lose data.

SESSION 1.2

1 a. title bar b. program title c. Minimize button d. Restore button e. Close button f. menu bar g. toolbar h. formatting bar i. status bar j. taskbar k. workspace l. pointer

2 a. Minimize button—hides the program so only its button is showing on the taskbar.
b. Maximize button—enlarges the program to fill the entire screen.
c. Restore button—sets the program to a pre-defined size.
d. Close button—stops the program and removes its button from the taskbar.

3 a. Ellipses—indicate a dialog box will appear.
b. Grayed out—the menu option is not currently available.
c. Submenu—indicates a submenu will appear.
d. Check mark—indicates a menu option is currently in effect.

4 Toolbar

5 a. scroll bar b. scroll box c. Cancel button d. down arrow button e. list box f. radio button g. check box

6 one, check boxes

7 On-line Help

SESSION 2.1

1 file

2 formatting

3 I-beam

4 insertion point

5 word wrap

6 You drag the I-beam pointer over the text to highlight it.

7 \ ? : * < > | "

8 extension

9 save the file again

10 paper

SESSION 2.2

1 My Computer

2 A (or A:)

3 Hard (or hard disk)

4 Filename, file type, file size, date, time

5 Root

6 Folders (or subdirectories)

7 It is deleted from the disk.

8 Yes

NEW
PERSPECTIVES
SERIES

Microsoft®
Excel 97

LEVEL I

TUTORIALS

Read This **Before You Begin**

STUDENT DISK

To complete Excel 97 Tutorials 1-4, you need two Student Disks. Your instructor will either provide you with Student Disks or ask you to make your own.

If you are supposed to make your own Student Disks, you will need **two** blank, formatted high-density disks. You will need to copy a set of folders from a file server or standalone computer onto your disks. Your instructor will tell you which computer, drive letter, and folders contain the files you need. The following table shows you which folders go on your disks:

Student Disk	Write this on the disk label	Put these folders on the disk
1	Student Disk 1: Excel 97 Tutorials 1-3	Tutorial.01, Tutorial.02, Tutorial.03
2	Student Disk 2: Excel 97 Tutorial 4	Tutorial.04

See the inside front or inside back cover of this book for more information on Student Disk files, or ask your instructor or technical support person for assistance.

COURSE LAB

Tutorial 1 features an interactive Course Lab to help you understand spreadsheet concepts. There are Lab Assignments at the end of the tutorial that relate to this Lab. To start the Lab, click the Start button on the Windows 95 Taskbar, point to Programs, point to Course Labs, point to New Perspectives Applications, and click Spreadsheets.

USING YOUR OWN COMPUTER

If you are going to work through this book using your own computer, you need:

■ **Computer System** Microsoft Excel 97 and Windows 95 or Windows NT Workstation 4.0 must be installed on your computer. This book assumes a typical installation of Microsoft Excel 97.

■ **Student Disks** Ask your instructor or technical support person for details on how to get the Student Disks. You will not be able to complete the tutorials or exercises in this book using your own computer until you have Student Disks. The Student Files may also be obtained electronically over the Internet. See the inside front or inside back cover of this book for more details.

■ **Course Lab** See your instructor or technical support person to obtain the Course Lab software for use on your own computer.

To complete Excel 97 Tutorials 1-4, your students must use a set of student files on two Student Disks. These files are included in the Instructor's Resource Kit, and they may also be obtained electronically over the Internet. See the inside front or inside back cover of this book for more details. Follow the instructions in the Readme file to copy the files to your server or standalone computer. You can view the Readme file using WordPad. Once the files are copied, you can make Student Disks for the students yourself, or you can tell students where to find the files so they can make their own Student Disks.

COURSE LAB SOFTWARE

The Course Lab software is distributed on a CD-ROM included in the Instructor's Resource Kit. To install the Course Lab software, follow the setup instructions in the Readme file on the CD-ROM. Refer also to the Readme file for essential technical notes related to running the Lab in a multi-user environment. Once you have installed the Course Lab software, your students can start the Lab from the Windows 95 desktop by following the instructions in the Course Lab section above.

COURSE TECHNOLOGY STUDENT FILES AND COURSE LAB SOFTWARE

You are granted a license to copy the Student Files and Lab software to any computer or computer network used by students who have purchased this book.

Using Worksheets to Make Business Decisions

Evaluating Sites for an Inwood Design Group Golf Course

Excel

OBJECTIVES

In this tutorial you will:

- Start and exit Excel

- Discover how Excel is used in business

- Identify the major components of the Excel window

- Navigate an Excel workbook and worksheet

- Open, save, print, and close a worksheet

- Enter text, numbers, formulas, and functions

- Correct mistakes

- Perform what-if analysis

- Clear contents of cells

- Use the Excel Help system

LAB

Spreadsheets

CASE

Inwood Design Group

In Japan, golf is big business. Spurred by the Japanese passion for the sport, golf enjoys unprecedented popularity. But because Japan is a small, mountainous country, the 12 million golfers have fewer than 2,000 courses from which to choose. Fees for 18 holes on a public course average between $200 and $300; golf club memberships are bought and sold like stock shares. The market potential is phenomenal, but building a golf course in Japan is expensive because of inflated property values, difficult terrain, and strict environmental regulations.

Inwood Design Group plans to build a world-class golf course, and one of the four sites under consideration is Chiba Prefecture, Japan. Other possible sites are Kauai, Hawaii; Edmonton, Canada; and Scottsdale, Arizona. You and Mike Nagochi are members of the site selection team for Inwood Design Group. The team is responsible for collecting information on the sites, evaluating that information, and recommending the best site for the new golf course.

Your team identified five factors likely to determine the success of a golf course: climate, competition, market size, topography, and transportation. The team has already collected information on these factors for three of the four potential golf course sites. Mike has just returned from visiting the last site in Scottsdale, Arizona.

Using Microsoft Excel 97 for Windows 95, Mike has created a worksheet that the team can use to evaluate the four sites. He needs to complete the worksheet by entering the data for the Scottsdale site. He then plans to bring the worksheet to the group's next meeting so that the team can analyze the information and recommend a site to management.

In this tutorial you will learn how to use Excel as you work with Mike to complete the Inwood site selection worksheet and work with the Inwood team to select the best site for the golf course.

Using the Tutorials Effectively

These tutorials are designed to be used at a computer. Each tutorial is divided into sessions. Watch for the session headings, such as "Session 1.1" and "Session 1.2." Each session is designed to be completed in about 45 minutes, but take as much time as you need. When you've completed a session, it's a good idea to exit the program and take a break. You can exit Microsoft Excel by clicking the Close button in the top-right corner of the program window.

Before you begin, read the following questions and answers. They are designed to help you use the tutorials effectively.

Where do I start?

Each tutorial begins with a case, which sets the scene for the tutorial and gives you background information to help you understand what you will be doing in the tutorial. Read the case before you go to the lab. In the lab, begin with the first session of the tutorial.

How do I know what to do on the computer?

Each session contains steps that you will perform on the computer to learn how to use Microsoft Excel. The steps are numbered and are set against a colored background. Read the text that introduces each series of steps, and read each step carefully and completely before you try it.

How do I know if I did the step correctly?

As you work, compare your computer screen with the corresponding figure in the tutorial. Don't worry if your screen display is somewhat different from the figure. The important parts of the screen display are labeled in each figure. Check to make sure these parts are on your screen.

What if I make a mistake?

Don't worry about making mistakes—they are part of the learning process. Paragraphs labeled TROUBLE? identify common problems and explain how to get back on track. Follow the steps in a TROUBLE? paragraph *only* if you are having the problem described. If you run into other problems, carefully consider the current state of your system, the position of the pointer, and any messages on the screen.

How do I use the Reference Windows?

Reference Windows summarize the procedures you learn in the tutorial steps. Do not complete the actions in the Reference Windows when you are working through the tutorial. Instead, refer to the Reference Windows while you are working on the assignments at the end of the tutorial.

How can I test my understanding of the material I learned in the tutorial?

At the end of each session, you can answer the Quick Check Questions. If necessary, refer to the Answers to Quick Check Questions to check your work.

After you have completed the entire tutorial, you should complete the Tutorial Assignments and Case Problems. These exercises are carefully structured so you will review what you have learned and then apply your knowledge to new situations.

What if I can't remember how to do something?

You should refer to the Task Reference at the end of the book; it summarizes how to accomplish commonly performed tasks.

What is the Spreadsheets Course Lab, and how should I use it?

This interactive Lab helps you review spreadsheet concepts and practice skills that you learn in Tutorial 1. The Lab Assignments section at the end of Tutorial 1 includes instructions for using the Lab.

Now that you've seen how to use the tutorials effectively, you are ready to begin.

SESSION

1.1

In this session you will learn what a spreadsheet is and how it is used in business. You will learn what Excel is and about the Excel window and its elements, how to move around a worksheet using the keyboard and the mouse, and how to open a workbook.

Spreadsheets

What Is Excel?

Excel is a computerized spreadsheet. A **spreadsheet** is an important business tool that helps you analyze and evaluate information. Spreadsheets are often used for cash flow analysis, budgeting, decision making, cost estimating, inventory management, and financial reporting. For example, an accountant might use a spreadsheet like the one in Figure 1-1 for a budget.

Figure 1-1 ◀
Budget
spreadsheet

Cash Budget Forecast

	January Estimated	January Actual
Cash in Bank (Start of Month)	$1,400.00	$1,400.00
Cash in Register (Start of Month)	100.00	100.00
Total Cash	$1,500.00	$1,500.00
Expected Cash Sales	$1,200.00	$1,420.00
Expected Collections	400.00	380.00
Other Money Expected	100.00	52.00
Total Income	$1,700.00	$1,852.00
Total Cash and Income	$3,200.00	$3,352.00
All Expenses (for Month)	$1,200.00	$1,192.00
Cash Balance at End of Month	$2,000.00	$2,160.00

To produce the spreadsheet in Figure 1-1, you could manually calculate the totals and then type your results, or you could use a computer and spreadsheet program to perform the calculations and print the results. Spreadsheet programs are also referred to as electronic spreadsheets, computerized spreadsheets, or just spreadsheets.

In Excel 97, the document you create is called a **workbook**. Each workbook is made up of individual worksheets, or **sheets**, just as a spiral-bound notebook is made up of sheets of paper. You will learn more about using multiple sheets later in this tutorial. For now, just keep in mind that the terms *worksheet* and *sheet* are often used interchangeably.

Starting Excel

Mike arrives at his office early because he needs to work with you to finish the worksheet and get ready for your meeting with the design team.

Start Excel and complete the worksheet that Mike will use to help the design team decide about the golf course site.

To start Microsoft Excel:

1. Make sure Windows 95 is running on your computer and the Windows 95 desktop appears on your screen.

TROUBLE? If you're running Windows NT Workstation 4.0 (or a later version) on your computer or network, don't worry. Although the figures in this book were created while running Windows 95, Windows NT 4.0 and Windows 95 share the same interface, and Microsoft Excel 97 runs equally well under either systems.

2. Click the **Start** button on the taskbar to display the Start menu, and then point to **Programs** to display the Programs menu.

3. Point to **Microsoft Excel** on the Programs menu. See Figure 1-2.

Figure 1-2 ◄
Starting
Microsoft Excel

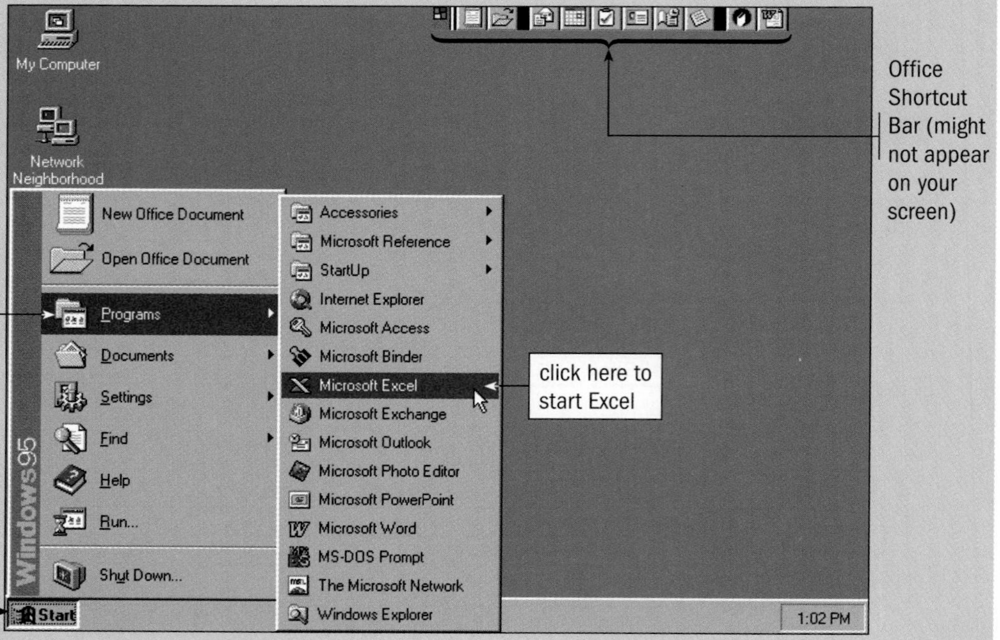

position mouse
pointer here
to display
Programs menu

Start button

Office
Shortcut
Bar (might
not appear
on your
screen)

click here to
start Excel

TROUBLE? If you don't see the Microsoft Excel option on the Programs menu, ask your instructor or technical support person for assistance.

TROUBLE? The Office Shortcut Bar, which appears along the top border of the desktop in Figure 1-2, might look different on your screen or it might not appear at all, depending on how your system is set up. The steps in these tutorials do not require that you use the Office Shortcut Bar; therefore, the remaining figures do not display the Office Shortcut Bar.

4. Click **Microsoft Excel**. After a short pause, the Microsoft Excel copyright information appears in a message box and remains on the screen until the Excel program window and a blank worksheet are displayed. See Figure 1-3.

TROUBLE? Depending on how your system is set up, the Office Assistant (see Figure 1-3) window might open when you start Excel. For now, click the Close button **X** on the Office Assistant window to close it; you'll learn more about this feature later in this tutorial. If you've started Microsoft Excel immediately after installing it, you'll need to click the Start Using Microsoft Excel option, which the Office Assistant displays, before closing the Office Assistant window.

Figure 1-3
Excel Program
window
with blank
worksheet

title bar

Name box

active cell

mouse pointer

row headings

active sheet

status bar

sheet tab
scroll buttons

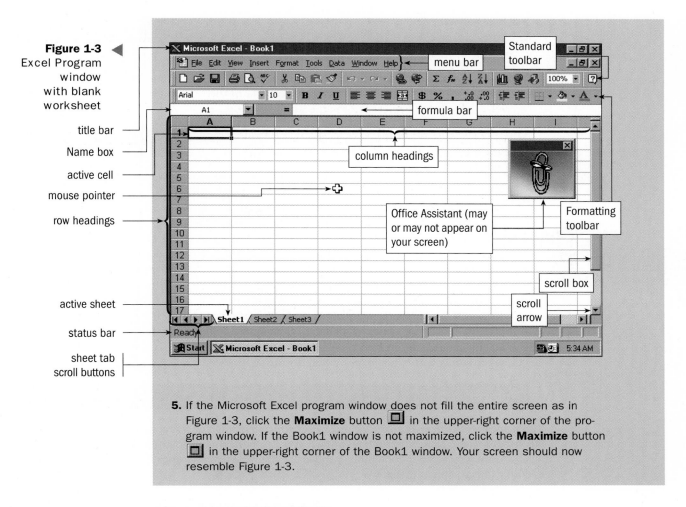

5. If the Microsoft Excel program window does not fill the entire screen as in
   Figure 1-3, click the **Maximize** button in the upper-right corner of the program window. If the Book1 window is not maximized, click the **Maximize** button
   in the upper-right corner of the Book1 window. Your screen should now
   resemble Figure 1-3.

The Excel Window

The Excel window layout is consistent with the layout of other Windows programs. It
contains many common features, such as the title bar, menu bar, scroll bars, and taskbar.
Figure 1-3 shows these elements as well as the main components of the Excel window.
Take a look at each of these Excel components so you know their location and purpose.

Toolbars

Toolbars allow you to organize the commands in Excel. The menu bar is a special toolbar
at the top of the window that contains menus such as File, Edit, and View. The Standard
toolbar and the Formatting toolbar are located below the menu bar. The **Standard** toolbar
contains buttons corresponding to the most frequently used commands in Excel. The
Formatting toolbar contains buttons corresponding to the commands most frequently used
to improve the appearance of a worksheet.

Formula Bar

The **formula bar**, located immediately below the toolbars, displays the contents of the active cell. A **cell's contents** is the data you enter into it. As you type or edit data, the changes appear in the formula bar. At the left end of the formula bar is the **Name box.** This area displays the cell reference for the active cell.

Worksheet Window

The document window, usually called the **worksheet window** or **workbook window**, contains the sheet you are creating, editing, or using. Each worksheet consists of a series of columns identified by lettered column headings and a series of rows identified by numbered row headings. Columns are assigned alphabetic labels from A to IV (256 columns). Rows are assigned numeric labels from 1 to 65,536 (65,536 rows).

A **cell** is the rectangular area where a column and a row intersect. Each cell is identified by a **cell reference**, which is its column and row location. For example, the cell reference B6 indicates the cell where column B and row 6 intersect. The column letter is always first in the cell reference. B6 is a correct cell reference; 6B is not. The **active cell** is the cell in which you are currently working. Excel identifies the active cell with a dark border that outlines one cell. In Figure 1-3, cell A1 is the active cell. Notice that the cell reference for the active cell appears in the reference area of the formula bar. You can change the active cell when you want to work elsewhere in the worksheet.

Pointer

The **pointer** is the indicator that moves on your screen as you move your mouse. The pointer changes shape to reflect the type of task you can perform at a particular location. When you click a mouse button, something happens at the pointer's location. In Figure 1-3 the pointer looks like a white plus sign ✛ .

Sheet Tabs

The **sheet tabs** let you move quickly between the sheets in a workbook; you can simply check the sheet tab of the sheet you want to move to. By default, a new workbook consists of three worksheets. If your workbook contains many worksheets, you can use the **sheet tab scroll buttons** to scroll through the sheet tabs that are not currently visible to find the sheet you want.

Moving Around a Worksheet

Before entering or editing the contents of a cell, you need to select that cell to make it the active cell. You can select a cell using either the keyboard or the mouse.

Using the Mouse

Using the mouse, you can quickly select a cell by placing the mouse pointer on the cell and clicking the mouse button. If you need to move to a cell that's not currently on the screen, use the vertical and horizontal scroll bars to display the area of the worksheet containing the cell you are interested in, and then select the cell.

Using the Keyboard

In addition to the mouse, Excel provides you with many keyboard options for moving to different cell locations within your worksheet. Figure 1-4 shows some of the keys you can use to select a cell within your worksheet.

Excel

Figure 1-4 ◀
Keys to move
around the
worksheet

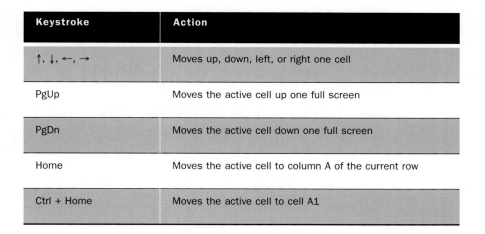

Keystroke	Action
↑, ↓, ←, →	Moves up, down, left, or right one cell
PgUp	Moves the active cell up one full screen
PgDn	Moves the active cell down one full screen
Home	Moves the active cell to column A of the current row
Ctrl + Home	Moves the active cell to cell A1

Now, try moving around the worksheet using your keyboard and mouse.

To move around the worksheet:

1. Position the mouse pointer � over cell E8, then click the **left mouse** button to make it the active cell. Notice that the cell is surrounded by a black border to indicate that it is the active cell and that the Name box on the formula bar displays E8.

2. Click cell **B4** to make it the active cell.

3. Press the → key to make cell C4 the active cell.

4. Press the ↓ key to make cell C5 the active cell. See Figure 1-5.

Figure 1-5 ◀
Cell C5 as
active cell

active cell ————

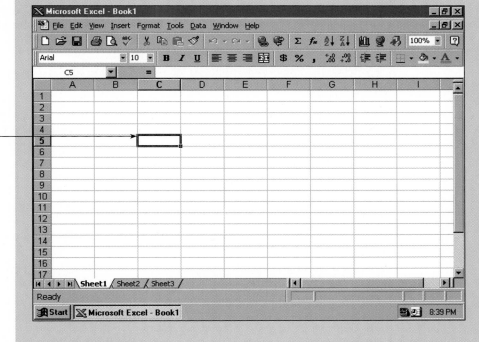

5. Press the **Home** key to move to cell A5, the first cell in the current row.

6. Press **Ctrl + Home** to make cell A1 the active cell.

So far you've moved around the portion of the worksheet you can see. Many worksheets can't be viewed entirely on one screen. Next, you'll use the keyboard and mouse to move beyond the worksheet window.

To move beyond the worksheet window:

1. Press the **Page Down** key to move the display down one screen. The active cell is now cell A17 (the active cell on your screen may be different). Notice that the row numbers on the left side of the worksheet indicate you have moved to a different area of the worksheet. See Figure 1-6.

Figure 1-6 ◄
Worksheet
screen after
moving to
different area
of worksheet

row headings
changed

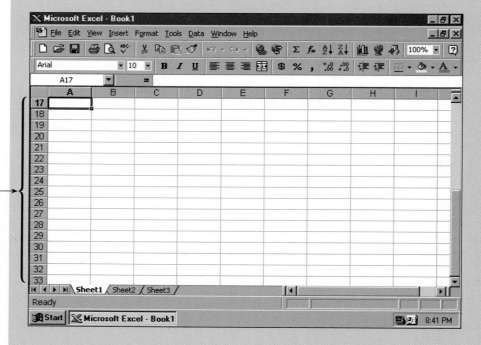

2. Press the **Page Down** key again to move the display down one screen. Notice that the row numbers indicate that you have moved to a different area of the worksheet.

3. Press the **Page Up** key to move the display up one screen. The active cell is now cell A17 (the active cell on your screen may be different).

4. Click the **vertical scroll bar arrow** until row 12 is visible. Notice that the active cell is still A17 (the active cell on your screen may be different). Using the scroll bar changes the portion of the screen you can view without changing the active cell.

5. Click cell **C12** to make it the active cell.

6. Click the blank area above the vertical scroll box to move up a full screen.

7. Click the blank area below the vertical scroll box to move down a full screen.

8. Click the **scroll box** and drag it to the top of the scroll area to again change the area of the screen you're viewing. Notice that the ScrollTip appears telling you where you will scroll to.

9. Click cell **E6** to make it the active cell.

As you know, a workbook can consist of one or more worksheets. Excel makes it easy to switch between them. Next, try moving from worksheet to worksheet.

Navigating in a Workbook

The sheet tabs let you move quickly between the different sheets in a workbook. If you can see the tab of the sheet you want, click the tab to activate the worksheet. You can also use the sheet tab scroll buttons to see sheet tabs hidden from view. Figure 1-7 describes the four tab scrolling buttons and their effects.

Figure 1-7 ◀
Sheet tab
scrolling
buttons

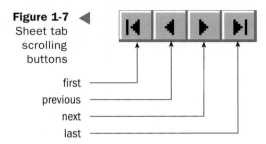

first
previous
next
last

Next, try moving to a new sheet.

To move to Sheet2:

1. Click the **Sheet2** tab. Sheet2, which is blank, appears in the worksheet window. Notice that the Sheet2 sheet tab is white and the name is bold, which means that Sheet2 is now the active sheet. Cell A1 is the active cell in Sheet2.

2. Click the **Sheet3** tab to make it the active sheet.

3. Click the **Sheet1** tab to make it the active sheet. Notice that cell E6 is the active cell.

Now that you have some basic skills navigating a worksheet and workbook, you can begin working with Mike to complete the golf site selection worksheet.

Opening a Workbook

When you want to use a workbook that you previously created, you must first open it. Opening a workbook transfers a copy of the workbook file from the hard drive or 3½-inch disk to the random access memory (RAM) of your computer and displays it on your screen. When the workbook is open, the file is both in RAM and on the disk.

After you open a workbook, you can view, edit, print, or save it again on your disk.

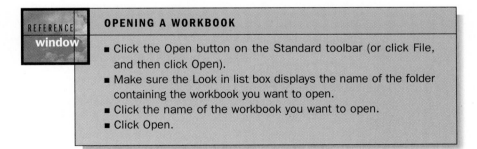

REFERENCE
window

OPENING A WORKBOOK

- Click the Open button on the Standard toolbar (or click File, and then click Open).
- Make sure the Look in list box displays the name of the folder containing the workbook you want to open.
- Click the name of the workbook you want to open.
- Click Open.

Mike created a workbook to help the site selection team evaluate the four potential locations for the golf course. The workbook, Inwood, is on your Student Disk.

To open an existing workbook:

1. Place your Excel Student Disk in the appropriate drive.

   TROUBLE? If you don't have a Student Disk, you need to get one before you can proceed. Your instructor or technical support person will either give you one or ask you to make your own by following the instructions on the "Read This Before You Begin" page before this tutorial. See your instructor or technical support person for information.

2. Click the **Open** button 🖼 on the Standard toolbar. The Open File dialog box opens. See Figure 1-8.

Figure 1-8 ◀
Open dialog
box

names and files
specified here
(yours may differ)

click here to
specify drive

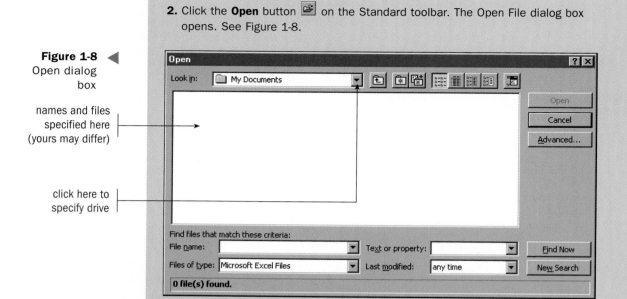

3. Click the **Look in** list arrow to display the list of available drives. Locate the drive containing your Student Disk. In this text, we assume your Student Disk is a 3½-inch floppy in drive A.

4. Click the drive that contains your Student Disk. A list of documents and folders on your Student Disk appears in the list box.

5. In the list of document and folder names, double-click **Tutorial.01** to display that folder in the Look in list box, then click **Inwood**.

6. Click the **Open** button. (You could also double-click the filename to open the file.) The Inwood workbook opens and the first sheet in the workbook, Title Sheet, appears. See Figure 1-9.

TROUBLE? If you do not see Inwood listed, use the scroll bar to see additional names.

Figure 1-9 ◀
Title Sheet
sheet in Inwood
workbook

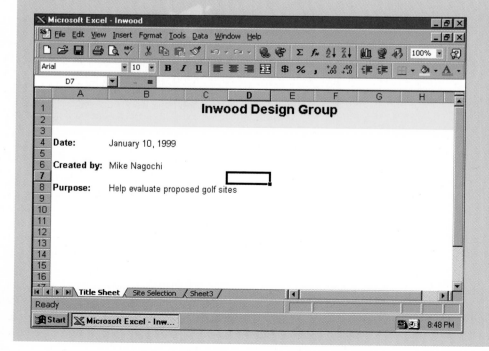

Layout of the Inwood Workbook

The first worksheet, Title Sheet, contains information about the workbook. The Title Sheet shows who created the workbook, the date when it was created, and its purpose.

Mike explains that whenever he creates a new workbook he makes sure he documents it carefully. This information is especially useful if he returns to a workbook after a long period of time (or if a new user opens it) because it provides a quick review of the workbook's purpose.

After reviewing the Title Sheet, Mike moves to the Site Selection worksheet.

To move to the Site Selection worksheet:

1. Click the **Site Selection** sheet tab to display the worksheet Mike is preparing for the site selection team. See Figure 1-10.

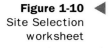

Figure 1-10
Site Selection worksheet

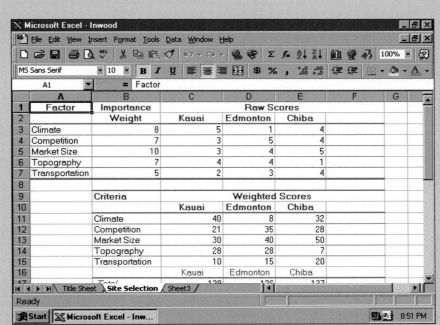

Mike explains the general layout of the Site Selection worksheet to you. He reminds you that to this point he has only entered data for three of the four sites. He will provide the missing Scottsdale information to you. Cells C2 through E2 list three of the four sites under consideration for which he has data. Cells A3 through A7 contain the five factors on which the team's decision will be based: Climate, Competition, Market Size, Topography, and Transportation. They assign scores for climate, competition, market size, topography, and transportation to each location. The team uses a scale of 1 to 5 to assign a raw score for each factor. Higher raw scores indicate strength; lower raw scores indicate weakness. Cells C3 through E7 contain the raw scores for the first three locations. For example, the raw score for Kauai's climate is 5; the two other locations have scores of 1 and 4, so Kauai, with its warm, sunny days all year, has the best climate for the golf course of the three sites visited so far. Edmonton, on the other hand, has cold weather and only received a climate raw score of 1.

The raw scores, however, do not provide enough information for the team to make a decision. Some factors are more important to the success of the golf course than others. The team members assigned an *importance weight* to each factor according to their knowledge of what factors contribute most to the success of a golf course. The importance weights are on a scale from 1 to 10, with 10 being most important. Mike entered the weights in cells B3 through B7. Market size, weighted 10, is the most important factor. The team believes the least important factor is transportation, so transportation is assigned a lower weight. Climate is important but the team considers market size most important. Therefore, they do not use the raw scores to make a final decision. Instead, they multiply each raw score by its importance weight to produce a weighted score. Which of the three sites already visited has the highest weighted score for any factor? If you look at the scores in cells C11 through E15, you see that Chiba's score of 50 for market size is the highest weighted score for any factor.

Cells C17 through E17 contain the total weighted scores for the three locations. With the current weighting and raw scores, Chiba is the most promising site, with a total score of 137.

Quick Check

1 A(n) _____ is the rectangular area where a column and a row intersect.

2 When you _____ a workbook, the computer copies it from your disk into RAM.

3 The cell reference _____ refers to the intersection of the fourth column and the second row.

4 To move the worksheet to the right one column:
   a. Press the Enter key
   b. Click the right arrow on the horizontal scroll bar
   c. Press the Escape key
   d. Press Ctrl + Home

5 To make Sheet2 the active worksheet, you would _____.

6 What key or keys do you press to make cell A1 the active cell?

You have now reviewed the layout of the worksheet. Now, Mike wants you to enter the data on Scottsdale. Based on his meeting with local investors and a visit to the Scottsdale site, he has assigned the following raw scores: Climate 5, Competition 2, Market Size 4, Topography 3, and Transportation 3. To complete the worksheet, you must enter the raw scores he has assigned to the Scottsdale site. You will do this in the next session.

SESSION

1.2

In this session you will learn how to enter text, values, formulas, and functions into a worksheet. You will use this data to perform what-if analysis using a worksheet. You'll also correct mistakes, and use the online Help system to determine how to clear the contents of cells. Finally, you'll learn how to print a worksheet, and how to close a worksheet and exit Excel.

Text, Values, Formulas, and Functions

As you have now observed, an Excel workbook can hold one or more worksheets, each containing a grid of 256 columns and 65,536 rows. The rectangular areas at the intersections of each column and row are called cells. A cell can contain a value, text, or a formula. To understand how the spreadsheet program works, you need to understand how Excel manipulates text, values, formulas, and functions.

Text

Text entries include any combination of letters, symbols, numbers, and spaces. Although text is sometimes used as data, it is more often used to describe the data contained in a worksheet. Text is often used to label columns and rows in a worksheet. For example, a projected monthly income statement contains the months of the year as column headings and income and expense categories as row labels. To enter text in a worksheet, you select the cell in which you want to enter the text by clicking the cell to select it, then typing the text. Excel automatically aligns the text on the left when it is displayed in a cell.

Mike's Site Selection worksheet contains a number of column heading labels. You need to enter the label for Scottsdale in the Raw Scores and Weighted Scores sections of the worksheet.

To enter a text label:

1. If you took a break after the last session, make sure Excel is running and make sure the Site Selection worksheet of the Inwood workbook is displayed.

2. Click cell **F2** to make it the active cell.

3. Type **Scottsdale**, then press the **Enter** key.

TROUBLE? If you make a mistake while typing, you can correct the error with the Backspace key. If you realize you made an error after you press the Enter key, retype the entry by repeating Steps 2 and 3.

4. Click cell **F10** and type **S.** Excel completes the entry for you based on the entries already in the column. If your data involves repetitious text, this feature, known as **AutoComplete,** can make your data entry go more quickly.

5. Press the **Enter** key to complete the entry.

6. Click cell **F16**, type **S,** and press the **Enter** key to accept Scottsdale as the entry in the cell. See Figure 1-11.

Figure 1-11
Worksheet
after text
entered

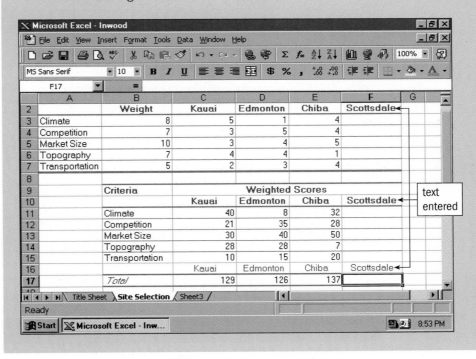

Next, you need to enter the raw scores Mike assigned to Scottsdale.

Values

Values are numbers that represent a quantity of some type: the number of units in inventory, stock price, an exam score, and so on. Examples of values are 378, 25.2, and -55. Values can also be dates (11/29/99) and times (4:40:31). As you type information in a cell, Excel determines whether the characters you're typing can be used as values. For example, if you type 456, Excel recognizes it as a value and it is right-justified when displayed in the cell. On the other hand, Excel treats some data commonly referred to as "numbers" as text. For example, Excel treats a telephone number (1-800-227-1240) or a social security number (372-70-9654) as text that cannot be used for calculations.

You need to enter the raw scores for Scottsdale.

To enter a value:

1. If necessary, click the scroll arrow so row 2 is visible. Click cell **F3**, type **5** and then press the **Enter** key. The cell pointer moves to cell F4.
2. With the cell pointer in cell F4, type **2** and press the **Enter** key.
3. Enter the value **4** for Market Size in cell F5, the value **3** for Topography in cell F6, and the value **3** for Transportation in cell F7. See Figure 1-12.

Figure 1-12 Worksheet after numbers entered

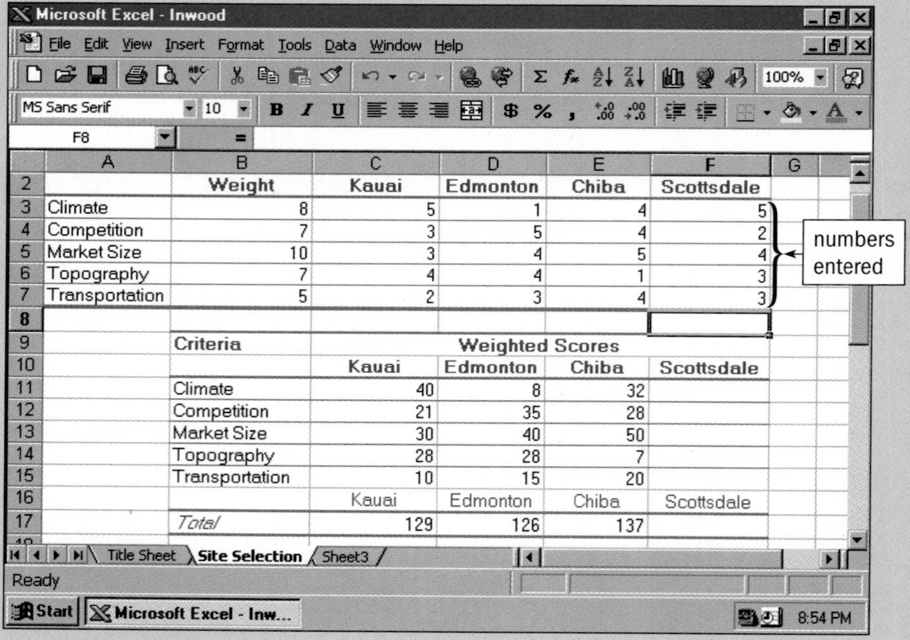

	A	B	C	D	E	F
2		Weight	Kauai	Edmonton	Chiba	Scottsdale
3	Climate	8	5	1	4	5
4	Competition	7	3	5	4	2
5	Market Size	10	3	4	5	4
6	Topography	7	4	4	1	3
7	Transportation	5	2	3	4	3
8						
9		Criteria		Weighted Scores		
10			Kauai	Edmonton	Chiba	Scottsdale
11		Climate	40	8	32	
12		Competition	21	35	28	
13		Market Size	30	40	50	
14		Topography	28	28	7	
15		Transportation	10	15	20	
16			Kauai	Edmonton	Chiba	Scottsdale
17		*Total*	129	126	137	

Next, you enter the formulas to calculate Scottsdale's weighted score in each category.

Formulas

When you need to perform a calculation in Excel you use a formula. A **formula** is the arithmetic used to calculate values displayed in a worksheet. You can take advantage of the power of Excel by using formulas in worksheets. If you change one number in a worksheet, Excel recalculates any formula affected by the change.

An Excel formula always begins with an equal sign (=). Formulas are created by combining numbers, cell references, arithmetic operators, and/or functions. An **arithmetic operator** indicates the desired arithmetic operations. Figure 1-13 shows the arithmetic operators used in Excel.

Figure 1-13
Arithmetic
operators used
in formulas

Arithmetic Operation	Arithmetic Operator	Example	Description
Addition	+	=10+A5	Adds 10 to the value in cell A5
Subtraction	–	=C9–B9	Subtracts the value in cell B9 from the value in cell C9
Multiplication	*	=C9*B9	Multiplies the value in cell B9 by the value in cell C9
Division	/	=C9/B9	Divides the value in cell C9 by the value in cell B9
Exponentiation	^	=10^B5	Raises 10 to the value stored in cell B5

The result of the formula is displayed in the cell where you entered the formula. To view the formula that has been entered in a cell, you must first select the cell, then look at the formula bar.

REFERENCE
window

ENTERING A FORMULA

- Click the cell where you want the result to appear.
- Type = and then type the rest of the formula.
- For formulas that include cell references, such as B2 or D78, you can type the cell reference or you can use the mouse or arrow keys to select each cell.
- When the formula is complete, press the Enter key.

You need to enter the formulas to compute the weighted scores for the Scottsdale site. The formula multiples the raw score for a factor by the importance weight assigned to the factor. Figure 1-14 displays the formulas you need to enter into the worksheet.

Figure 1-14
Formula to
calculate
Scottsdale's
weighted score

Cell	Formula	Explanation
F11	=B3*F3	Multiplies importance weight by raw score for climate
F12	=B4*F4	Multiplies importance weight by raw score for competition
F13	=B5*F5	Multiplies importance weight by raw score for market size
F14	=B6*F6	Multiplies importance weight by raw score for topography
F15	=B7*F7	Multiplies importance weight by raw score for transportation

Excel

To enter the formula to calculate each weighted score for the Scottsdale site:

1. Click cell **F11** to make it the active cell. Type **=B3*F3** to multiply the weight assigned to the climate category by the raw score assigned to Scottsdale for the climate category. Press the **Enter** key. The value 40 is displayed in cell F11.

   TROUBLE? If you make a mistake while typing, you can correct the error with the Backspace key. If you realize you made an error after you press the Enter key, repeat Step 1 to retype the entry.

2. Click cell **F12**, type **=B4*F4**, and then press the **Enter** key. This formula multiplies the weight assigned to competition (the contents of cell B4) by Scottsdale's raw score for competition (cell F4). The value 14 is displayed.

3. Enter the remaining formulas from Figure 1-14 into cells F13, F14, and F15. When completed, your worksheet will look like Figure 1-15.

Figure 1-15 ◄
Worksheet after entering formulas to calculate weighted score

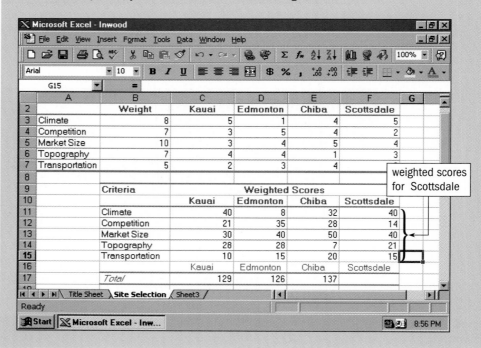

You now have to enter the formula to calculate the total weighted score for Scottsdale into the worksheet. You can use the formula *=F11+F12+F13+F14+F15* to calculate the total score for the Scottsdale site. As an alternative, you can use a function to streamline this long formula.

Functions

A **function** is a special prewritten formula that's a shortcut for commonly used calculations. For example, the SUM function is a shortcut for entering formulas that total values in rows or columns. You can use the SUM function to create the formula =SUM(F11:F15) instead of typing the longer =F11+F12+F13+F14+F15. The SUM function in this example adds the range F11 through F15. A **range** can be a single cell or a rectangular block of cells, often rows or columns. The range reference in the function SUM(F11:F15) refers to the rectangular block of cells beginning at F11 and ending at F15. Figure 1-16 shows several examples of ranges.

Figure 1-16
Examples of
ranges

range D4:I4

range B3:B9

range D14:D14

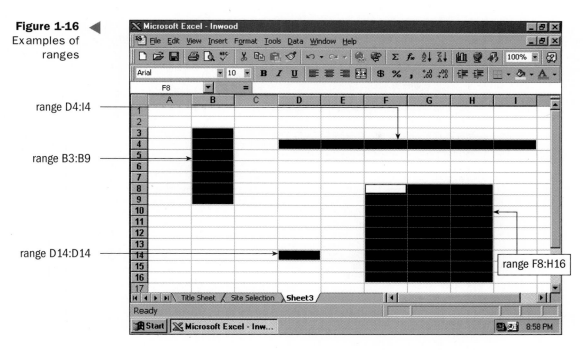

range F8:H16

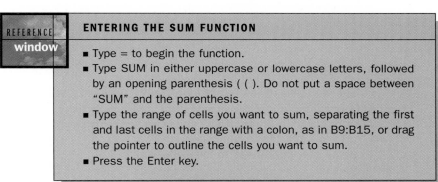

REFERENCE window

ENTERING THE SUM FUNCTION

- Type = to begin the function.
- Type SUM in either uppercase or lowercase letters, followed by an opening parenthesis (( ). Do not put a space between "SUM" and the parenthesis.
- Type the range of cells you want to sum, separating the first and last cells in the range with a colon, as in B9:B15, or drag the pointer to outline the cells you want to sum.
- Press the Enter key.

You use the SUM function to compute the total score for the Scottsdale site.

To enter the formula using a function:

1. Click cell **F17** to make it the active cell.

2. Type **=SUM(F11:F15)**. Notice that the formula appears in the cell and the formula bar as you enter it. See Figure 1-17.

Figure 1-17
Viewing
the SUM
function before
completing
the entry

SUM function
appears in
formula bar

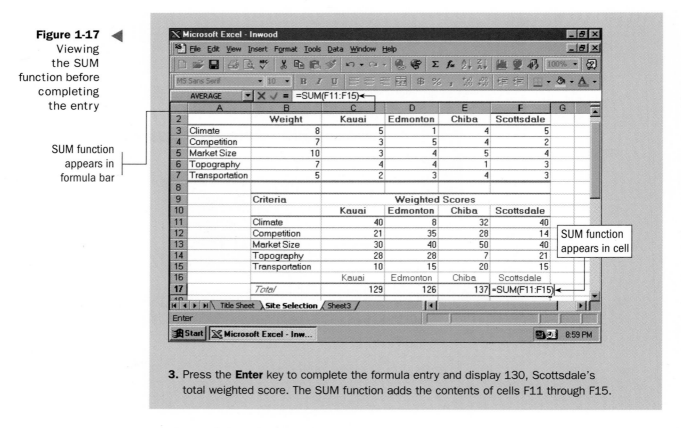

3. Press the **Enter** key to complete the formula entry and display 130, Scottsdale's total weighted score. The SUM function adds the contents of cells F11 through F15.

The worksheet for site selection is now complete. Mike's worksheet contains columns of information about the site selection and a chart displaying the weighted scores for each potential site. To see the chart you must scroll the worksheet.

To scroll the worksheet to view the chart:

1. Click the **scroll arrow** button on the vertical scroll bar until the section of the worksheet containing the chart is displayed. See Figure 1-18.

Figure 1-18
Scrolling the
worksheet to
view the chart

Chiba is leading site

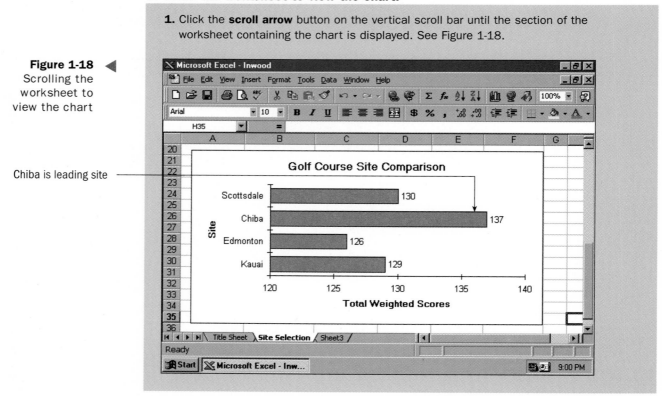

2. After you look at the chart, click and drag the **scroll box** to the top of the vertical scroll bar.

You have completed the worksheet; Mike decides to save it before showing it to the site selection team.

Saving the Workbook

To store a workbook permanently, so you can use it again without having to reenter the data and formulas, you must save it as a file on a disk. When you save a workbook, you copy it from RAM onto your disk. You'll use either the Save or the Save As command. The Save command copies the workbook onto a disk using its current filename. If a version of the file already exists, the new version replaces the old one. The Save As command asks for a filename before copying the workbook onto a disk. When you enter a new filename, you save the current file under that new name. The previous version of the file remains on the disk under its original name.

As a general rule, use the Save As command the first time you save a file or whenever you modify a file and want to save both the old and new versions. Use the Save command when you modify a file and want to save only the current version.

It is a good idea to save your file often. That way, if the power goes out or the computer stops working, you're less likely to lose your work. Because you use the Save command frequently, the Standard toolbar has a Save button , a single mouse-click shortcut for saving your workbook.

REFERENCE
window

SAVING A WORKBOOK WITH A NEW FILENAME

- Click File and then click Save As.
- Change the workbook name as necessary.
- Make sure the Save in box displays the folder in which you want to save your workbook.
- Click the Save button.

Mike's workbook is named Inwood. On your screen is a version of Inwood that you modified during this work session. Save the modified workbook under the new name Inwood 2. This way if you want to start the tutorial from the beginning, you can open the Inwood file and start over.

To save the modified workbook under a new name:

1. Click **File** on the menu bar, and then click **Save As**. The Save As dialog box opens with the current workbook name in the File name text box.

2. Click at the end of the current workbook name, press the **spacebar**, and then type **2**. *(Do not press the Enter key.)*

Before you proceed, check the other dialog box specifications to ensure that you save the workbook on your Student Disk.

3. If necessary, click the **Save in** list arrow to display the list of available drives and folders. Click **Tutorial.01**.

4. Confirm that the Save as type text box specifies "Microsoft Excel Workbook."

5. When your Save As dialog box looks like the one in Figure 1-19, click the **Save** button to close the dialog box and save the workbook. Notice that the new workbook name, Inwood 2, now appears in the title bar.

Figure 1-19 ◄
Saving the
worksheet with
a new filename

new filename

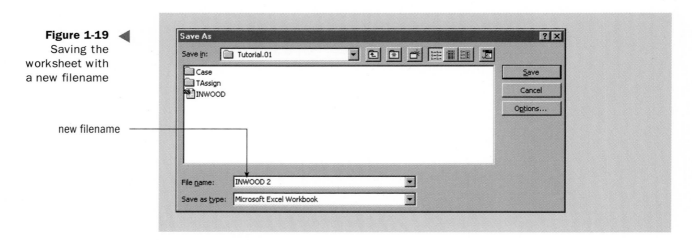

You now have two versions of the workbook: the original file—Inwood—and the modified workbook—Inwood 2.

Changing Values and Observing Results

The worksheet for site selection is now complete. Mike is ready to show it to the group. As the team examines the worksheet, you ask if the raw scores take into account recent news that a competing design group has announced plans to build a $325-million golf resort just 10 miles away from Inwood's proposed site in Chiba. Mike admits that he assigned the values before the announcement, so the raw scores do not reflect the increased competition in the Chiba market. You suggest revising the raw score for the competition factor to reflect this market change in Chiba.

When you change a value in a worksheet, Excel recalculates the worksheet and displays updated results. The recalculation feature makes Excel an extremely useful decision-making tool because it lets you quickly and easily factor in changing conditions. When you revise the contents of one or more cells in a worksheet and observe the effect this change has on all the other cells, you are performing a **what-if analysis**. In effect, you are saying, what if I change the value assigned to this factor? What effect will it have on the outcomes in the worksheet?

Since another development group has announced plans to construct a new golf course in the Chiba area, the team decides to lower Chiba's competition raw score from 4 to 2.

To change Chiba's competition raw score from 4 to 2:

1. Click cell **E4**. The black border around cell E4 indicates that it is the active cell. The current value of cell E4 is 4.

2. Type **2**. Notice that 2 appears in the cell and in the formula bar, along with a formula palette of three new buttons. The buttons shown in Figure 1-20—the Cancel button ⊠, the Enter button ☑, and the Edit Formula button ▣—offer alternatives for canceling, entering, and editing data and formulas.

Figure 1-20
Changing a
cell's contents

edit formula

cancel typing

same as pressing
the Enter key

new competition
raw score

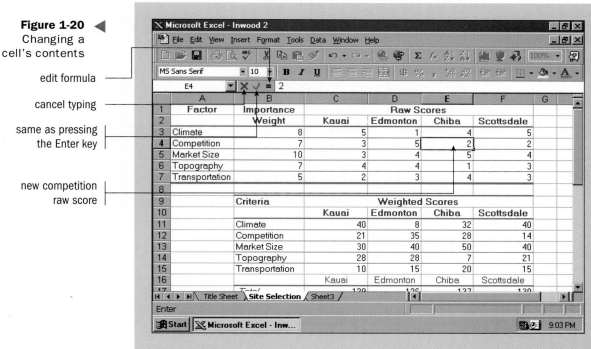

3. Click the **Enter** button. Excel recalculates Chiba's weighted score for the competition factor (cell E12) and the total score for Chiba (cell E17). If necessary, click the **vertical scroll** arrow until row 17 is visible on your screen. The recalculated values are 14 and 123. See Figure 1-21.

Figure 1-21
Worksheet
after formulas
are
recalculated

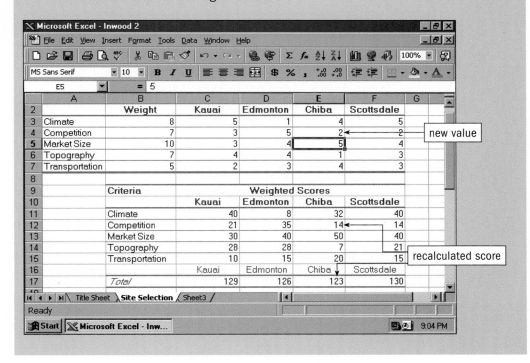

new value

recalculated score

The team takes another look at the total weighted scores in row 17. Scottsdale is now the top-ranking site, with a total weighted score of 130. Chiba's total weighted score is now 123.

As the team continues to discuss the worksheet, several members express concern over the importance weight used for transportation. In the current worksheet, transportation is weighted 5 (cell B7). You remember that the group agreed to use an importance weight of 2 at a previous meeting. You ask Mike to change the importance weight for transportation.

To change the importance weight for transportation:

1. Click cell **B7** to make it the active cell.

2. Type **2** and press the **Enter** key. Cell B7 now contains the value 2 instead of 5. Cell B8 becomes the active cell. See Figure 1-22. Notice that the weighted scores for transportation (row 15) and the total weighted scores for each site (row 17) have all changed.

Figure 1-22 ◀
Worksheet after change made to the transportation importance weight

new value

all transportation scores recalculated

all total scores recalculated

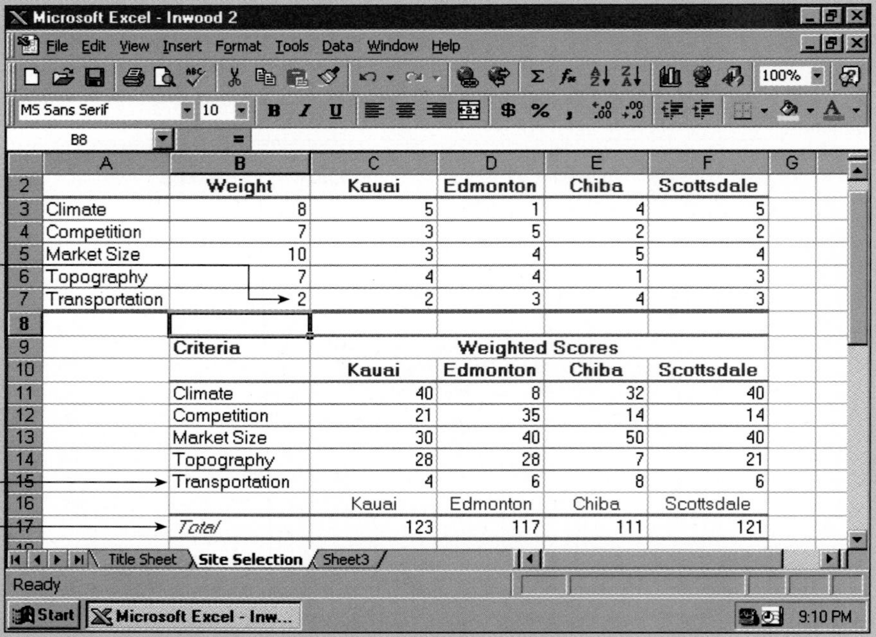

The change in the transportation importance weight puts Kauai ahead as the most favorable site, with a total weighted score of 123.

As you enter and edit a worksheet, there are many data entry errors that can occur. The most commonly made mistake on a worksheet is a typing error. Typing mistakes are easy to correct.

Correcting Mistakes

It is easy to correct a mistake as you are typing information in a cell, before you press the Enter key. If you need to correct a mistake as you are typing information in a cell, press the Backspace key to back up and delete one or more characters. When you are typing information in a cell, don't use the cursor arrow keys to edit because they move the cell pointer to another cell. One of the team members suggests changing the label "Criteria" in cell B9 to "Factors." The team members agree and you make the change to the cell.

To correct a mistake as you type:

1. Click cell **B9** to make it the active cell.

2. Type **Fak**, intentionally making an error, but don't press the Enter key.

3. Press the **Backspace** key to delete "k."

4. Type **ctors** and press the **Enter** key.

Now the word "Factors" is in cell B9. Mike suggests changing "Factors" to "Factor." The team agrees. To change a cell's contents after you press the Enter key, you use a different method. Double-clicking a cell or pressing the F2 key puts Excel into Edit mode, which lets you use the Backspace key, the ← and → keys, and the mouse to change the text in the formula bar.

REFERENCE window

CORRECTING MISTAKES USING EDIT MODE

- Double-click the cell you want to edit to begin Edit mode and display the contents of the cell in the formula bar (or click the cell you want to edit, then press F2).
- Use Backspace, Delete, ←, →, or the mouse to edit the cell's contents either in the cell or in the formula bar.
- Press the Enter key when you finish editing.

You use Edit mode to change "Factors" to "Factor" in cell B9.

To change the word "Factors" to "Factor" in cell B9:

1. Double-click cell **B9** to begin Edit mode. Note that "Edit" appears in the status bar, reminding you that Excel is currently in Edit mode.

2. Press the **End** key if necessary to move the cursor to the right of the word "Factors," then press the **Backspace** key to delete the "s."

3. Press the **Enter** key to complete the edit.

You ask if the team is ready to recommend a site. Mike believes that based on the best information they have, Kauai should be the recommended site and Scottsdale the alternative site. You ask for a vote, and the team unanimously agrees with Mike's recommendation.

Mike wants to have complete documentation to accompany the team's written recommendation to management, so he wants to print the worksheet.

As he reviews the worksheet one last time, he thinks that the labels in cells C16 through F16 (Kauai, Edmonton, Chiba, Scottsdale) are unnecessary and decides he wants you to delete them before printing the worksheet. You ask how you delete the contents of a cell or a group of cells. Mike is not sure, so he suggests using the Excel Help system to find the answer.

Getting Help

If you don't know how to perform a task or forget how to carry out a particular task, Excel provides an extensive Help system. The Excel Help system provides the same options as the Help system in other Windows programs—the Help Contents, the Help Index, and the Find feature. The Excel Help system also provides additional ways to get help as you work. One way to get help is to use the Office Assistant, which you may have seen on your screen when you first started Excel, and which you hid earlier in this tutorial. The Office Assistant, an animated object, pops up on the screen when you click the Office Assistant button on the Standard toolbar. The Office Assistant answers questions, offers tips, and provides help for a variety of Excel features. In addition to the Office Assistant, Figure 1-23 identifies several other ways you can get help.

Figure 1-23 ◀
Alternative ways
to get help

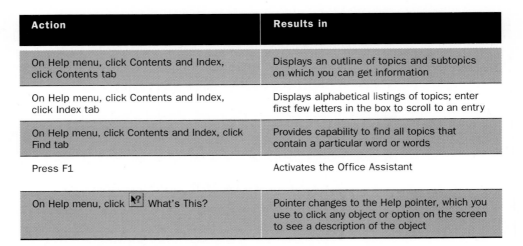

Action	Results in
On Help menu, click Contents and Index, click Contents tab	Displays an outline of topics and subtopics on which you can get information
On Help menu, click Contents and Index, click Index tab	Displays alphabetical listings of topics; enter first few letters in the box to scroll to an entry
On Help menu, click Contents and Index, click Find tab	Provides capability to find all topics that contain a particular word or words
Press F1	Activates the Office Assistant
On Help menu, click [?] What's This?	Pointer changes to the Help pointer, which you use to click any object or option on the screen to see a description of the object

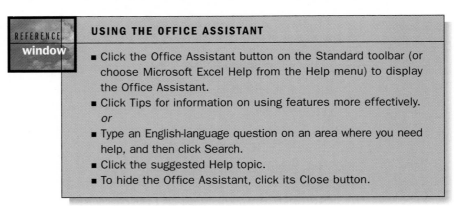

REFERENCE
window

USING THE OFFICE ASSISTANT

- Click the Office Assistant button on the Standard toolbar (or choose Microsoft Excel Help from the Help menu) to display the Office Assistant.
- Click Tips for information on using features more effectively.
  or
- Type an English-language question on an area where you need help, and then click Search.
- Click the suggested Help topic.
- To hide the Office Assistant, click its Close button.

Use the Office Assistant to get information on how to clear the contents of cells.

To get Help using the Office Assistant:

1. Click the Office Assistant [icon] button to display an animated object and an information box. See Figure 1-24.

Figure 1-24 ◀
Office
Assistant with
information box

enter question here ──

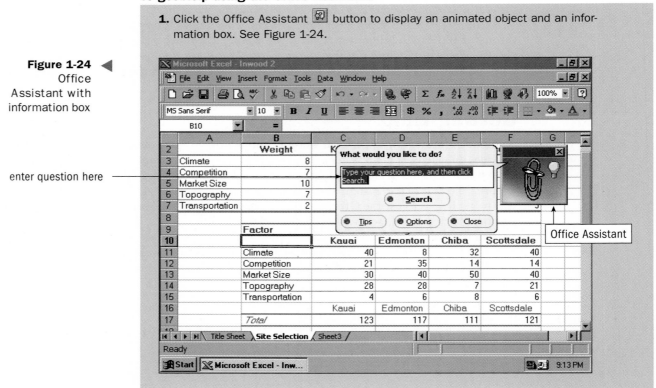

Office Assistant

Excel

The Office Assistant can respond to an English-language question.

2. Type **how do I clear cells**, and then click **Search** to display several possible Help topics. See Figure 1-25.

Figure 1-25 ◀
Office Assistant with several suggested Help topics

click this topic

suggested Help topics

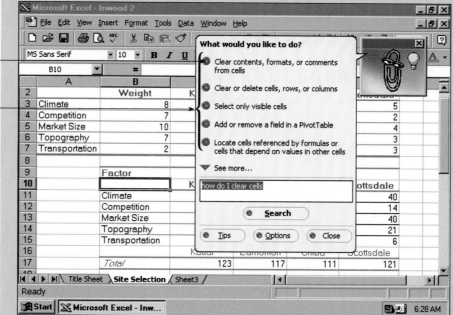

3. Click the first suggestion, **Clear contents, formats, or comments from cells**, to open a How To window on this topic. See Figure 1-26.

Figure 1-26 ◀
How To window on Clear contents, formats, or comments from cells

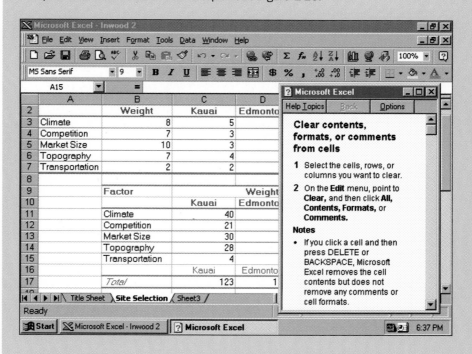

You can print the contents of the How To window, or you can click the Keep Help On Top command from the Options menu to keep the How To window on the screen where you can refer to it as you go through each step.

4. After reviewing the information, click the **Close** button ☒ on the How To window.

5. Click the **Close** button ☒ in the upper-right corner of the Office Assistant to hide the Assistant.

After reviewing the information from the Office Assistant, you are ready to remove the labels from the worksheet.

Clearing Cell Contents

As you are building or modifying your worksheet, you may occasionally find that you have entered a label, number, or formula in a cell that you want to be empty. To erase the contents of a cell, you use either the Delete key or the Clear command on the Edit menu. Removing the contents of a cell is known as clearing a cell. Do not press the spacebar to enter a blank character in an attempt to clear a cell's content. Excel treats a blank character as text, so even though the cell appears to be empty, it is not.

REFERENCE window	**CLEARING CELL CONTENTS**
	■ Click the cell you want to clear, or select a range of cells you want to clear. ■ Press the Delete key. *or* ■ Click Edit, point to Clear, and then click Contents to erase only the contents of a cell, or click All to completely clear the cell contents, formatting, and notes.

You are ready to clear the labels from cells C16 through F16.

To clear the labels from cells C16 through F16:

1. Click cell **C16**. This will be the upper-left corner of the range to clear.

2. Position the cell pointer over cell C16. With the cell pointer the shape of ✛, click and drag the cell pointer to F16 to select the range C16:F16.
If your pointer changes to a crosshair ✛ *, or an arrow* ↖ *, do not drag the cell pointer to F16, until pointer changes to* ✛ *. Note that when you select a range, the first cell in that range, cell C16 in this example, remains white and the other cells in the range are highlighted. See Figure 1-27.

Figure 1-27 ◀
Highlighted cell
range

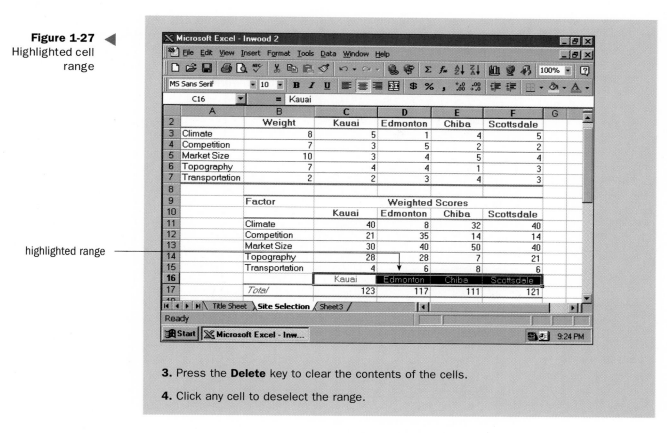

highlighted range ——

3. Press the **Delete** key to clear the contents of the cells.

4. Click any cell to deselect the range.

Now that you have cleared the unwanted labels from the cells, Mike wants you to print the site selection worksheet.

Printing the Worksheet

You can print an Excel worksheet using either the Print command on the File menu or the Print button on the Standard toolbar. If you use the Print command, Excel displays a dialog box where you can specify which worksheet pages you want to print, the number of copies you want to print, and the print quality (resolution). If you use the Print button, you do not have these options; Excel prints one copy of the entire worksheet using the current print settings.

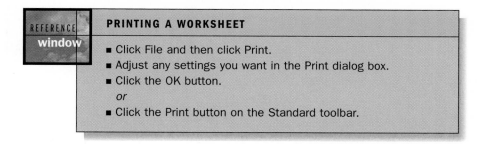

REFERENCE window

PRINTING A WORKSHEET

- Click File and then click Print.
- Adjust any settings you want in the Print dialog box.
- Click the OK button.
  or
- Click the Print button on the Standard toolbar.

Mike wants a printout of the entire Site Selection worksheet. You decide to select the Print command from the File menu instead of using the Print button so you can check the Print dialog box settings.

To check the print settings and then print the worksheet:

1. Make sure your printer is turned on and contains paper.

2. Click **File** on the menu bar, and then click **Print** to display the Print dialog box. See Figure 1-28.

Figure 1-28 ◀
Print dialog box

identifies printer (your entry may be different)

prints selected range in worksheet

prints active sheet

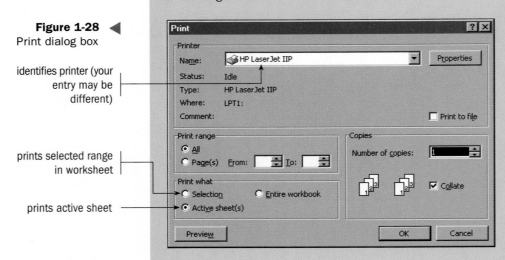

Now you need to select what to print. You could print the complete workbook, which would be the Title Sheet and the Site Selection sheet. To do this, you would click the Entire workbook option button. You could also choose to print just a portion of a worksheet. For example, to print only the weighted scores data of the Site Selection worksheet, first select this range with your mouse pointer, and then select the Selection option button in the Print dialog box. In this case, Mike needs just the Site Selection worksheet.

3. If necessary, click the **Active sheet(s)** option button in the Print what section of the dialog box to print just the Site Selection worksheet, and not the Title Sheet.

4. Make sure "1" appears in the Number of copies text box, as Mike only needs to print one copy of the worksheet.

5. Click the **OK** button to print the worksheet. See Figure 1-29.

   TROUBLE? If the worksheet does not print, see your technical support person for help.

Figure 1-29 ◀
Printed
worksheet

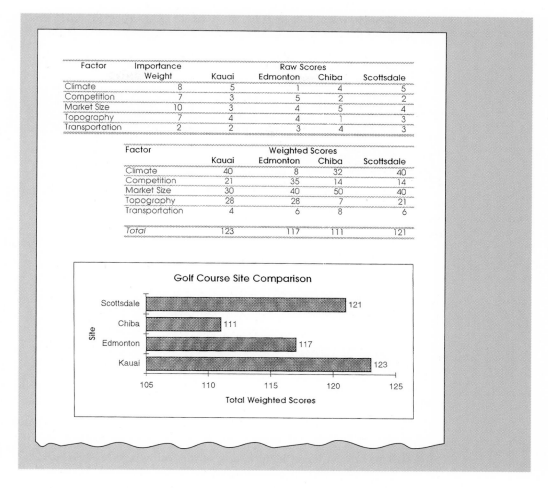

Mike volunteers to put together the report with the team's final recommendation, and the meeting adjourns. You and Mike are finished working with the worksheet and are ready to close the workbook.

Closing the Workbook

Closing a workbook removes it from the screen. If a workbook contains changes that have not been saved, Excel asks if you want to save your modified worksheet before closing the workbook. You can now close the workbook.

To close the Inwood 2 workbook:

1. Click **File** on the menu bar, and then click **Close**. A dialog box displays the message "Do you want to save the changes you made to 'INWOOD 2'?"

2. Click the **Yes** button to save the Inwood 2 workbook before closing it.

The Excel window stays open so you can open or create another workbook. You do not want to, so your next step is to exit Excel.

Exiting Excel

To exit Excel, you can click the Close button on the title bar, or you can use the Exit command on the File menu.

To exit Excel:

1. Click the Close button ☒ on the title bar. Excel closes and you return to the Windows desktop.

Quick Check

1. The formula =SUM(D1:K1) adds how many cells? Write an equivalent formula without using the SUM function.
2. What cells are included in the range B4:D6?
3. Indicate whether Excel treats the following cell entries as a value, text, or a formula:
   a. Profit
   b. 11/09/95
   c. 123
   d. =B9*225
   e. 1-800-227-1240
   f. =SUM(C1:C10)
   g. 123 N. First St.
4. To print the entire worksheet, you select the _____ option button from the _____ dialog box.
5. To print a copy of your worksheet, you use the _____ command on the _____ menu.
6. You can get Excel Help in any of the following ways except:
   a. clicking Help on the menu bar
   b. clicking the Help button on the Standard toolbar
   c. closing the program window
   d. pressing the F1 key
7. Why do you need to save a worksheet? What command do you use to save the worksheet?
8. What key do you press to clear the contents of a cell from a worksheet?
9. Explain the term *what-if analysis*.

The Inwood site selection team has completed its work. Mike's worksheet helped the team analyze the data and recommend Kauai as the best site for Inwood's next golf course. Although the Japanese market was a strong factor in favor of locating the course in Japan's Chiba Prefecture, the mountainous terrain and competition from nearby courses reduced the site's desirability.

Tutorial Assignments

The other company that had planned a golf course in Chiba, Japan, has run into financial difficulties. Rumors are that the project may be canceled. A copy of the final Inwood Design team workbook is on your Student Disk. Do the Tutorial Assignments to change this worksheet to show the effect of the other project's cancellation on your site selection.

1. If necessary, start Excel and make sure your Student Disk is in the appropriate disk drive.
   Open the Inwood 3 file in the TAssign folder for Tutorial 1 on your Student Disk.
2. Use the Save As command to save the workbook as Inwood4 in the TAssign folder for Tutorial 1. That way you won't change the original workbook.
3. In the Inwood4 worksheet, change the competition raw score for Chiba from 2 to 3. What site is ranked first?

4. The label "Transportation" in cell A9 was entered incorrectly as "Transportion." Use Edit mode to insert "ta" into the label.
5. Save the worksheet.
6. Print the worksheet.

7. Use the Contents and Index command on the Help menu to access the Help Topics dialog box. From the Contents tab, learn how to insert an additional worksheet into your workbook. (*Hint*: Choose Working with workbook and worksheets topic, then managing worksheets.) Write the steps to insert a worksheet.
8. Use the Office Assistant to learn how to delete a sheet from a workbook. Write the steps to delete a sheet.
9. Enter the text "Scores if the competing project in Chiba, Japan, is canceled" in cell A1.
10. Remove the raw scores for Chiba, cells E5 through E9. Print the worksheet.

11. Use the Index command on the Help menu to learn about the AutoCalculate feature. Write a brief explanation of this feature.

12. You are considering dropping transportation as a factor in the site selection decision. Use AutoCalculate to arrive at a revised total weighted score for each of the three remaining sites. Write the response.
13. Print the worksheet data without the chart. (*Hint*: Select the worksheet data before checking out the options in the Print dialog box.)
14. Use the What's This button ▶?. Learn more about the following Excel window components:
    a. Name box
    b. Sheet tabs
    c. Tip Wizard
    (*Hint*: Click ▶?, then click each item with the Help pointer.)
15. Close the workbook and exit Excel without saving the changes.

Case Problems

1. Market Share Analysis at Aldon Industries Helen Shalala is assistant to the regional director for Aldon Industries, a manufacturer of corporate voice mail systems. Helen has analyzed the market share of the top vendors with installations in the region. She's on her way to a meeting with the marketing staff where she will use her worksheet to plan a new marketing campaign. Help Helen and her team evaluate the options and plan the best advertising campaign for Aldon Industries. Write your responses to questions 4 through 10.

1. If necessary, start Excel and make sure your Student Disk is in the appropriate disk drive.
2. Open the workbook Aldon in the Case folder for Tutorial 1.
3. Use the Save As command to save the workbook as Aldon 2 in the Case folder for Tutorial 1. That way you won't change the original workbook for this case.
4. Take a moment to look over the Market Share worksheet. Do the following ranges contain text, values, or formulas?
   a. B13:G13
   b. C3:C10
   c. A3:A10
   d. G3:G10
5. What is Aldon Industries' overall market share?
6. Examine the worksheet to determine in which state Aldon Industries has the highest market share.
7. Which company leads the overall market?
8. What is Aldon Industries' overall ranking in total market share (1st, 2nd, 3rd, etc.)?
9. Which companies rank ahead of Aldon Industries in total market share?

10. What formula was used to calculate Total Installations in Illinois? Develop an alternative formula to calculate Total Installations in Illinois without using the SUM function.

11. Save and print the worksheet.

2. Selecting a Hospital Laboratory Computer System for Bridgeport Medical Center David Choi is on the Laboratory Computer Selection Committee for the Bridgeport Medical Center. After an extensive search, the committee has identified three vendors whose products appear to meet its needs. The Selection Committee has prepared an Excel worksheet to help evaluate the three potential vendors' strengths and weaknesses. The raw scores for two of the vendors, LabStar and Health Systems, have already been entered. Now raw scores must be entered for the third vendor, MedTech. Which vendor's system is best for the Bridgeport Medical Center? Complete these steps to find out:

1. If necessary, start Excel and make sure your Student Disk is in the appropriate disk drive.

2. Open the workbook Medical in the Case folder for Tutorial 1.

3. Use the Save As command to save the workbook as Medical 2 in the Case folder for Tutorial 1. That way you won't change the original workbook for this case.

4. Examine the Evaluation Scores worksheet, and type the following raw scores for MedTech: Cost = 6, Compatibility = 5, Vendor Reliability = 5, Size of Installed Base = 4, User Satisfaction = 5, Critical Functionality = 9, Additional Functionality = 8.

5. Use the Save command to save the modified worksheet.

6. Print the worksheet.

7. Based on the data in the worksheet, which vendor would you recommend? Why?

8. Assume you can adjust the value for only one importance weight (cells B6 through B12). Which factor would you change and what would its new weight be in order for LabStar to have the highest weighted score? (*Hint*: Remember that the value assigned to any importance weight cannot be higher then 10.)

9. Save and print the modified worksheet.

3. Enrollments in the College of Business You work 10 hours a week in the Dean's office at your college. The Assistant Dean has a number of meetings today and has asked you to complete a worksheet she needs for a meeting with Department Chairs this afternoon.

1. Open the workbook Enroll in the Case folder for Tutorial 1 on your Student Disk.

2. Use the Save As command to save the workbook as Enrollment.

3. Complete the workbook by performing the following tasks:

a. Enter the title "Enrollment Data for College of Business" in cell A1.

b. Enter the label "Total" in cell A8.

c. Calculate the total enrollment in the College of Business for 1999 in cell B8.

d. Calculate the total enrollment in the College of Business for 1998 in cell C8.

e. Calculate the change in enrollments from 1998 to 1999. Place the results in column D. Label the column heading "Change" and use the following formula:
Change = 1999 enrollment – 1998 enrollment

4. Save the workbook.

5. Print the worksheet.

4. Krier Marine Services Vince DiOrio is an Information Systems major at a local college. To help pay for tuition, he works part-time three days a week at a nearby marina, Krier Marine Services. Vince works in the business office, and his responsibilities range from making coffee to keeping the company's books.

Recently, Jim Krier, the owner of the marina, asked Vince if he could help computerize the payroll for their part-time employees. He explained that the employees work a different number of hours each week for different rates of pay. Jim does the payroll manually now and finds it time-consuming. Moreover, whenever he makes an error, he is embarrassed and annoyed at having to take the additional time to correct it. Jim was hoping Vince could help him.

Vince immediately agrees to help. He tells Jim that he knows how to use Excel and that he can build a spreadsheet that will save him time and reduce errors. Jim and Vince meet. They review the present payroll process and discuss the desired outcomes of the payroll spreadsheet. Figure 1-30 is a sketch of the output Jim wants to get.

Figure 1-30 ◀
Sketch of
worksheet

Krier Marine Services Weekly Payroll
Week Ending 10/15

Employee	Hours	Pay Rate	Gross Pay
Bramble	15	7	formula
Juarez	28	5	"
Smith	30	7	"
DiOrio	22	6	"
Total			formula

1. Open the workbook Payroll in the Cases folder for Tutorial 1 on your Student Disk.
2. Use the Save As command to save the workbook as Payroll 2.
3. Complete the worksheet by performing the following tasks:
   a. Enter the employee hours in column B.
   b. Enter the employee pay rate in column C.
   c. In column D, enter the formulas to compute gross pay for each employee. (*Hint*: Use Hours times Pay Rate.)
   d. In cell D9, enter the SUM function to calculate total gross pay.
4. Save the workbook.
5. Print the worksheet.
6. Remove the hours for the four employees.
7. Enter the following hours: 18 for Bramble, 25 for Juarez, 35 for Smith, and 20 for DiOrio.
8. Print the new worksheet.

Lab Assignments

Spreadsheets

These Lab Assignments are designed to accompany the interactive Course Lab called Spreadsheets. To start the Spreadsheets Lab, click the Start button on the Windows 95 taskbar, point to Programs, point to Course Labs, point to New Perspectives Applications, and click Spreadsheets. If you do not see Course Labs on your Programs menu, see your instructor or technical support person.

Spreadsheets Spreadsheet software is used extensively in business, education, science, and the humanities to simplify tasks that involve calculations. In this Lab you will learn how spreadsheet software works. You will use spreadsheet software to examine and modify worksheets, as well as to create your own worksheets.

1. Click the Steps button to learn how spreadsheet software works. As you proceed through the Steps, answer all of the Quick Check questions that appear. After you complete the Steps, you will see a Quick Check Summary report. Follow the instructions on the screen to print this report.
2. Click the Explore button. Click OK to display a new worksheet. Click File, and then click Open to display the Open dialog box. Click the file Income, then press the Enter key to open the Income and Expense Summary worksheet. Notice that the worksheet contains labels and values for income from consulting and training. It also contains labels and values for expenses such as rent

and salaries. The worksheet does not, however, contain formulas to calculate Total Income, Total Expenses, or Profit. Do the following:

a. Calculate the Total Income by entering the formula =SUM(C4:C5) in cell C6.

b. Calculate the Total Expenses by entering the formula =SUM(C9:C12) in cell C13.

c. Calculate Profit by entering the formula =C6-C13 in cell C15.

d. Manually check the results to make sure you entered the formulas correctly.

e. Print your completed worksheet that shows your results.

3. You can use a spreadsheet to keep track of your grade in a class. Click the Explore button to display a blank worksheet. Click File and then click Open to display the Open dialog box. Click the file Grades to open the Grades worksheet. This worksheet contains all the labels and formulas necessary to calculate your grade based on four test scores.

Suppose you receive a score of 88 out of 100 on the first test. On the second test, you score 42 out of 48. On the third test, you score 92 out of 100. You have not taken the fourth test yet. Enter the appropriate data on the Grade worksheet to determine your grade after taking three tests. Print out your worksheet.

4. Worksheets are handy for answering "what if" questions. For example, suppose you decide to open a lemonade stand. You're interested in how much profit you can make each day. What if you sell 20 cups of lemonade? What if you sell 100? What if the cost of lemons increases?

In Explore, open the file Lemons and use the worksheet to answer questions a through d, then print the worksheet for item e:

a. What is your profit if you sell 20 cups a day?

b. What is your profit if you sell 100 cups a day?

c. What is your profit if the price of lemons increases to $.07 and you sell 100 cups?

d. What is your profit if you raise the price of a cup of lemonade to $.30? (Lemons still cost $.07 and you assume you will sell 100 cups.)

e. Suppose your competitor boasts that she sold 50 cups of lemonade in one day and made exactly $12.00. On your worksheet, adjust the cost of cups, water, lemons, and sugar, and the price per cup to show a profit of exactly $12.00 for 50 cups sold. Print this worksheet.

5. It is important to make sure the formulas in your worksheet are accurate. An easy way to test this is to enter 1s for all the values on your worksheet, and then check the calculations manually. In Explore, open the worksheet Receipt, which calculates sales receipts. Enter 1 as the value for Item 1, Item 2, and Item 3. Enter .01 for the Sales Tax rate. Now, manually calculate what you would pay for three items that cost $1.00 each in a state where sales tax is 1% (.01). Do your manual calculations match those of the worksheet? If not, correct the formulas in the worksheet and print out a formula report of your revised worksheet.

6. In Explore, create your own worksheet showing your household budget for one month. Make sure you put a title on the worksheet. Use formulas to calculate your total income and your total expenses for the month. Add another formula to calculate how much money you were able to save. Print a formula report of your worksheet. Also, print your worksheet, showing realistic values for one month.

Creating a Worksheet

Producing a Sales Comparison Report for MSI

In this tutorial you will:

- Plan, build, test, document, preview, and print a worksheet

- Enter labels, values, and formulas

- Calculate a total using the AutoSum button

- Copy formulas using the fill handle and Clipboard

- Learn about relative, absolute, and mixed references

- Use the AVERAGE, MAX, and MIN functions to calculate values in the worksheet

- Spell check the worksheet

- Insert a row

- Reverse an action using the Undo button

- Move a range of cells

- Format the worksheet using AutoFormat

- Center printouts on a page

- Customize worksheet headers

CASE

Motorcycle Specialties Incorporated

Motorcycle Specialties Incorporated (MSI), a motorcycle helmet and accessories company, provides a wide range of specialty items to motorcycle enthusiasts throughout the world. MSI has its headquarters in Atlanta, Georgia, but it markets its products in North America, South America, Australia, and Europe.

The company's Marketing and Sales Director, Sally Caneval, meets regularly with the regional sales managers who oversee global sales in each of the four regions in which MSI does business. This month, Sally intends to review overall sales in each region for the last two fiscal years and present her findings at her next meeting with the regional sales managers. She has asked you to help her put together a report that summarizes this sales information.

Specifically, Sally wants the report to show total sales for each region of the world for the two most recent fiscal years. Additionally, she wants to see the percentage change between the two years. She also wants the report to include the percentage each region contributed to the total sales of the company in 1999. Finally, she wants to include summary statistics on the average, maximum, and minimum sales for 1999.

In this session you will learn how to plan and build a worksheet; enter labels, numbers, and formulas; and copy formulas to other cells.

Developing Worksheets

Effective worksheets are well planned and carefully designed. A well-designed worksheet should clearly identify its overall goal. It should present information in a clear, well-organized format, and include all the data necessary to produce the results that address the goal of the application.

Further, the process of developing a good worksheet includes the following planning and execution steps:

- Determine the worksheet's purpose, what it will include, and how it will be organized

- Enter the data and formulas into the worksheet

- Test the worksheet

- Edit the worksheet to correct any errors or make modifications

- Document the worksheet

- Improve the appearance of the worksheet

- Save and print the completed worksheet

Planning the Worksheet

Sally begins developing a worksheet that compares global sales by region over two years by first creating a planning analysis sheet. Her **planning analysis sheet** helps her answer the following questions:

1. What is the goal of the worksheet? This helps to define the problem to solve.

2. What are the desired results? This information describes the **output**—the information required to help solve the problem.

3. What data is needed to calculate the results you want to see? This information is the **input**—data that must be entered.

4. What calculations are needed to produce the desired output? These calculations specify the formulas used in the worksheet.

Sally's completed planning analysis sheet is shown in Figure 2-1.

Figure 2-1 ◀
Planning
analysis sheet

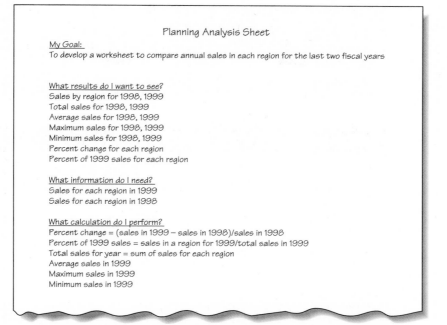

Planning Analysis Sheet

My Goal:
To develop a worksheet to compare annual sales in each region for the last two fiscal years

What results do I want to see?
Sales by region for 1998, 1999
Total sales for 1998, 1999
Average sales for 1998, 1999
Maximum sales for 1998, 1999
Minimum sales for 1998, 1999
Percent change for each region
Percent of 1999 sales for each region

What information do I need?
Sales for each region in 1999
Sales for each region in 1998

What calculation do I perform?
Percent change = (sales in 1999 − sales in 1998)/sales in 1998
Percent of 1999 sales = sales in a region for 1999/total sales in 1999
Total sales for year = sum of sales for each region
Average sales in 1999
Maximum sales in 1999
Minimum sales in 1999

Next, Sally makes a rough sketch of her design, including titles, column headings, row labels, and where data values and totals should be placed. Figure 2-2 shows Sally's sketch. With these two planning tools, Sally is now ready to enter the data into Excel and build the worksheet.

Figure 2-2 ◀
Sketch of
worksheet

Motorcycle Specialties Incorporated
Sales Comparison 1999 with 1998

Region	Year 1999	Year 1998	% Change	% of 1999 Sales
North America	365000	314330	0.16	0.28
South America	354250	292120	0.21	0.28
Australia	251140	262000	-0.04	0.19
Europe	310440	279996	0.11	0.24
Total	1280830	1148446	0.12	

Average	320207.5
Maximum	365000
Minimum	251140

Building the Worksheet

You will use Sally's planning analysis sheet, Figure 2-1, and the rough sketch shown in Figure 2-2 to guide you in preparing the sales comparison worksheet. You will begin by establishing the layout of the worksheet by entering titles and column headings. Next you will work on inputting the data and formulas that will calculate the results Sally needs.

To start Excel and organize your desktop:

1. Start Excel as usual.

2. Make sure your Student Disk is in the appropriate disk drive.

3. Make sure the Microsoft Excel and Book1 windows are maximized.

Entering Labels

When you build a worksheet, it's a good practice to enter the labels before entering any other data. These labels will help you identify the cells where you will enter data and formulas in your worksheet. As you type a label in a cell, Excel aligns the label at the left side of the cell. Labels that are too long to fit in a cell spill over into the cell or cells to the right, if those cells are empty. If the cells to the right are not empty, Excel displays only as much of the label as fits in the cell. Begin creating the sales comparison worksheet for Sally by entering the two-line title.

To enter the worksheet title:

1. If necessary, click cell **A1** to make it the active cell.

2. Type **Motorcycle Specialties Incorporated** and press the **Enter** key. Since cell A1 is empty, the title appears in cell A1 and spills over into cells B1, C1, and D1. Cell A2 is now the active cell.

TROUBLE? If you make a mistake while typing, remember that you can correct errors with the Backspace key. If you notice the error only after you have pressed the Enter key, then double-click the cell to activate Edit mode, and use the edit keys on your keyboard to correct the error.

3. In cell A2 type **Sales Comparison 1999 with 1998** and press the **Enter** key.

Next, you will enter the column headings defined on the worksheet sketch in Figure 2-2.

To enter labels for the column headings:

1. If necessary, click cell **A3** to make it the active cell.

2. Type **Region** and press the → key to complete the entry. Cell B3 is the active cell.

3. In cell **B3** type **Year 1999** and press the → key.

Sally's sketch shows that three more column heads are needed for the worksheet. Enter those next.

4. Enter the remaining column heads as follows:
Cell C3: **Year 1998**
Cell D3: **% Change**
Cell E3: **% of 1999 Sales**
See Figure 2-3.

TROUBLE? If any cell does not contain the correct label, either edit the cell or retype the entry.

Figure 2-3 ◀
Worksheet
after titles and
column
headings
entered

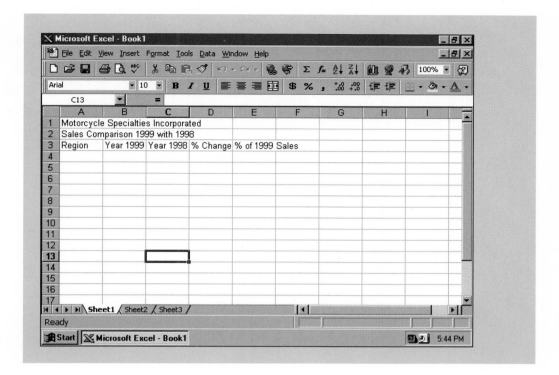

Recall that MSI conducts business in four different regions of the world, and the spreadsheet needs to track the sales information for each region. So Sally wants labels reflecting the regions entered into the worksheet. Enter these labels next.

To enter the regions:

1. Click cell **A4**, type **North America,** and press the **Enter** key.

2. In cell A5 type **South America,** and press the **Enter** key.

3. Type **Australia** in cell A6, and **Europe** in cell A7.

The last set of labels to be entered identify the summary information that will be included in the report.

To enter the summary labels:

1. In cell A8 type **Total** and press the **Enter** key.

2. Type the following labels into the specified cells:
   Cell A9: **Average**
   Cell A10: **Maximum**
   Cell A11: **Minimum**
   See Figure 2-4.

Figure 2-4
Worksheet
after all labels
have been
entered

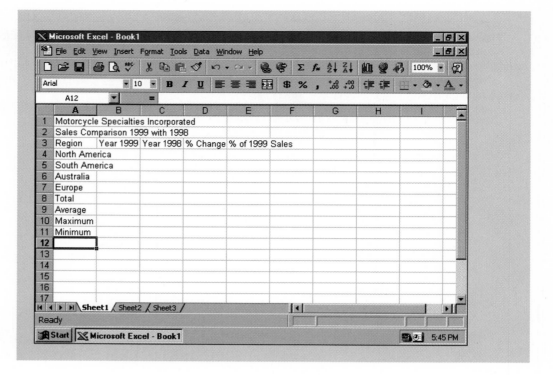

The labels that you just entered into the worksheet will help to identify where the data and formulas need to be placed.

Entering Data

Recall that values can be numbers, formulas, or functions. The next step in building the worksheet is to enter the data, which in this case is the numbers representing sales in each region during 1998 and 1999.

To enter the sales values for 1998 and 1999:

1. Click cell **B4** to make it the active cell. Type **365000** and press the **Enter** key. See Figure 2-5. Notice that the region name, North America, is no longer completely displayed in cell A4 because cell B4 is no longer empty. Later in the tutorial you will learn how to increase the width of a column in order to display the complete contents of cells.

Excel

Figure 2-5 ◀
Worksheet with
label truncated
in cell

label truncated

label spills over
to cell B5

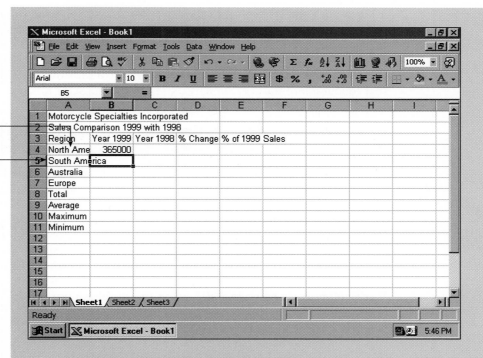

2. In cell B5 type **354250** and press the **Enter** key.

3. Enter the values for cells B6, **251140**, and B7, **310440**.

Next, type the values for sales during 1998.

4. Click cell **C4**, type **314330**, and press the **Enter** key.

5. Enter the remaining values in the specified cells as follows:
Cell C5: **292120**
Cell C6: **262000**
Cell C7: **279996**
Your screen should now look like Figure 2-6.

Figure 2-6 ◀
Worksheet
after sales for
1998 and 1999
entered

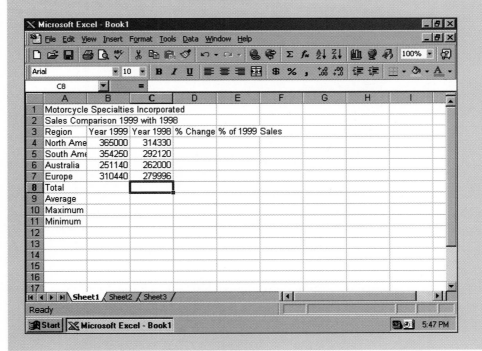

Now that you have entered the labels and data, you need to enter the formulas that will calculate the data to produce the output, or the results. The first calculation Sally wants to see is the total sales for each year. To determine total sales for 1999, you would simply sum the sales from each region for that year. In the previous tutorial you used the SUM function to calculate the weighted total score for the Scottsdale golf site by typing that function into the cell. Similarly, you can use the SUM function to calculate total sales for each year for MSI's comparison report.

Using the AutoSum Button

Since the SUM function is used more often than any other function, Excel includes the AutoSum button on the Standard toolbar. This button automatically creates a formula that contains the SUM function. To do this, Excel looks at the cells adjacent to the active cell, makes an assumption as to which cells you want to sum, and displays a formula based on its best determination about the range you want to sum. You can press the Enter key to accept the formula, or you can select a different range of cells to change the range in the formula. You will use the AutoSum button to calculate the total sales for each year.

To calculate total sales in 1999 using the AutoSum button:

1. Click cell **B8** because this is where you want to display the total sales for 1999.

2. Click the **AutoSum** button Σ on the Standard toolbar. Excel enters a SUM function in the selected cell and determines that the range of cells to sum is B4:B7, the range directly above the selected cell. See Figure 2-7. In this case, that's exactly what you want to do.

Figure 2-7 ◀
Using the
AutoSum tool

outline of cells
to be summed

range of cells
to be summed

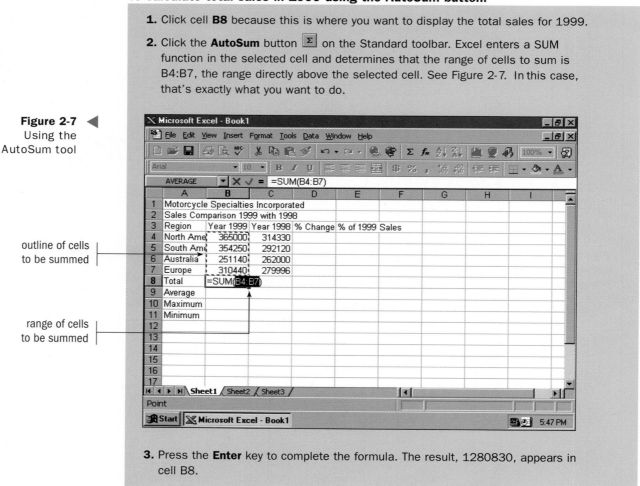

3. Press the **Enter** key to complete the formula. The result, 1280830, appears in cell B8.

Now use the same approach to calculate the total sales for 1998.

To calculate total sales in 1998 using the AutoSum button:

1. Click cell **C8** to make it the active cell.

2. Click the **AutoSum** button Σ on the Standard toolbar.

3. Press the **Enter** key to complete the formula. The result, 1148446, appears in cell C8.

Next, you need to enter the formula to calculate the percent change in sales for North America between 1999 and 1998.

Entering Formulas

Recall that a formula is an equation that performs calculations in a cell. By entering an equal sign (=) as the first entry in the cell, you are telling Excel that the numbers or symbols that follow constitute a formula, not just data. Reviewing Sally's worksheet plan, you note that you need to calculate the percent change in sales in North America. The formula is:

percent change in sales for North America =
(1999 sales in North America - 1998 sales in North America)/1998 sales in North America

So, in looking at the worksheet, the formula in Excel would be:

(B4-C4)/C4

If a formula contains more than one arithmetic operator, Excel performs the calculations in the standard order of precedence of operators shown in Figure 2-8. The **order of precedence** is a set of predefined rules that Excel uses to calculate a formula unambiguously by determining which part of the formula to calculate first, which part second, and so on.

Figure 2-8 ◀
Order of precedence operations

Order	Operator	Description
1	^	Exponentiation
2	* or /	Multiplication or division
3	+ or −	Addition or subtraction

Exponentiation has the highest rank, followed by multiplication and division, and finally addition and subtraction. For example, because multiplication has precedence over addition, in the formula =3+4*5 the result of the formula is 23.

When a formula contains more than one operator with the same order of precedence, Excel performs the operation from left to right. Thus, in the formula =4*10/8, Excel multiplies 4 by 10 before dividing the product by 8. The result of the calculation is 5. You can enter parentheses in a formula to make it easier to understand or to change the order of operations. Excel always performs any calculations contained in parentheses first. In the formula =3+4*5, the multiplication is performed before the addition. If instead you wanted the formula to add 3+4 and then multiply the sum by 5, you would enter the formula =(3+4)*5. The result of the calculation is 35.

Now enter the percent change formula as specified in Sally's planning sheet.

To enter the formula for the percent change in sales for North America:

1. Click cell **D4** to make it the active cell.

2. Type **=(B4-C4)/C4** and press the **Enter** key. Excel performs the calculations and displays the value 0.1612 in cell D4. The formula is no longer visible in the cell. If you select the cell, the result of the formula appears in the cell, and the formula you entered appears in the formula bar.

Next, you need to enter the percent change formulas for the other regions, as well as the percent change for the total company sales. You could type the formula =(B5-C5)/C5 in cell D5, the formula =(B6-C6)/C6 in cell D6, the formula =(B7-C7)/C7 in cell D7, and the formula =(B8-C8)/C8 in cell D8. However, this approach is time-consuming and error prone. Instead, you can copy the formula you entered in cell C4 (percent change in North American sales) into cells D5, D6, D7, and D8. **Copying** duplicates the underlying formula in a cell into other cells, automatically adjusting cell references to reflect the new cell address. Copying formulas from one cell to another saves time and reduces the chances of entering incorrect formulas when building worksheets.

Copying a Formula Using the Fill Handle

You can copy formulas using menu commands, toolbar buttons, or the fill handle. The **fill handle** is a small black square located in the lower-right corner of the selected cell, as shown in Figure 2-9. In this section you will use the fill handle to copy the formulas. In other situations you can also use the fill handle for copying values and labels from one cell or a group of cells.

Figure 2-9 ◄
Fill handle

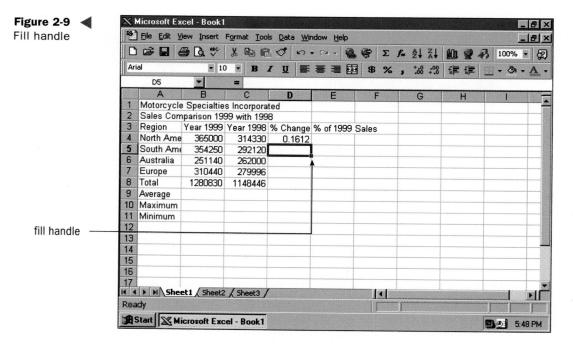

fill handle ———

COPYING CELL CONTENTS WITH THE FILL HANDLE

- Click the cell that contains the label, value, or formula you want to copy. If you want to copy the contents of more than one cell, select the range of cells you want to copy.
- To copy to adjacent cells, click and drag the fill handle to outline the cells where you want the copy or copies to appear, and then release the mouse button.

You want to copy the formula from cell D4 to cells D5, D6, D7, and D8.

To copy the formula from cell D4 to cells D5, D6, D7, and D8:

1. Click cell **D4** to make it the active cell.

2. Position the pointer over the fill handle (in the lower-right corner of cell D4) until the pointer changes to $+$.

3. Click and drag the pointer down the worksheet to outline cells D5 through D8. See Figure 2-10.

Figure 2-10 ◀
Copying a
formula

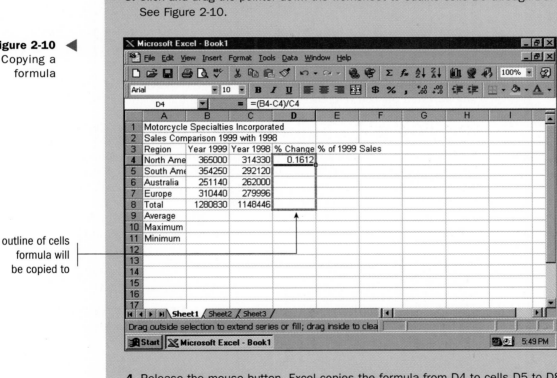

outline of cells
formula will
be copied to

4. Release the mouse button. Excel copies the formula from D4 to cells D5 to D8. Values now appear in cells D5 through D8.

5. Click any cell to deselect the range. See Figure 2-11.

Figure 2-11 ◀
Worksheet
after formula
copied

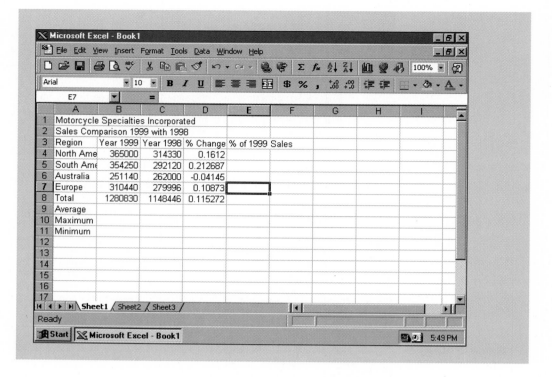

Notice that Excel didn't copy the formula =(B4-C4)/C4 exactly. Rather, it automatically adjusted the cell references for each new formula location. Why did that happen?

Copying a Formula Using Relative References

When you copy a formula that contains cell references, Excel automatically adjusts the cell references for the new locations. For example, when Excel copied the formula from cell D4, =(B4-C4)/C4, it automatically changed the cell references in the formula to reflect the formula's new position in the worksheet. So in cell D5 the cell references adjust to =(B5-C5)/C5. Cell references that change when copied are called **relative cell references**.

Take a moment to look at the formulas in cells D5, D6, D7, and D8.

To examine the formulas in cells D5, D6, D7, and D8:

1. Click cell **D5**. The formula =(B5-C5)/C5 appears in the formula bar.

When Excel copied the formula from cell D4 to cell D5, the cell references changed. The formula =(B4-C4)/C4 became =(B5-C5)/C5 when Excel copied the formula down one row to row 5.

2. Examine the formulas in cells D6, D7, and D8. Notice that the cell references were adjusted for the new locations.

Copying a Formula Using an Absolute Reference

According to Sally's plan, in the worksheet you need to display the percent that each region contributed to the total sales in 1999. For example, if the company's total sales were $100,000 and sales in North America were $25,000, then sales in North America would be 25% of total sales. To complete this calculation for each region you need to divide each region's sales by the total company sales, as shown in the following formulas:

Contribution by North America	=B4/B8
Contribution by South America	=B5/B8
Contribution by Australia	=B6/B8
Contribution by Europe	=B7/B8

First, enter the formula to calculate the percent North America contributed to total sales.

To calculate North America's percent of total 1999 sales:

1. Click cell **E4** to make it the active cell.

2. Type **=B4/B8** and press the **Enter** key to display the value .284971 in cell E4.

Cell E4 displays the correct result. Sales in North America for 1999 were 365,000, which is approximately .28 of the 1,280,830 in total sales in 1999. Next, you decide to copy the formula in cell E4 to cells E5, E6, and E7.

To copy the percent formula in cell E4 to cells E5 through E7:

1. Click cell **E4**, and then move the pointer over the fill handle in cell E4 until it changes to $+$.

2. Click and drag the pointer to cell E7 and release the mouse button.

3. Click any blank cell to deselect the range. The message "#DIV/0!" appears in cells E5 through E7. See Figure 2-12.

Figure 2-12 ◀
Error message
displayed in
worksheet after
copying formula

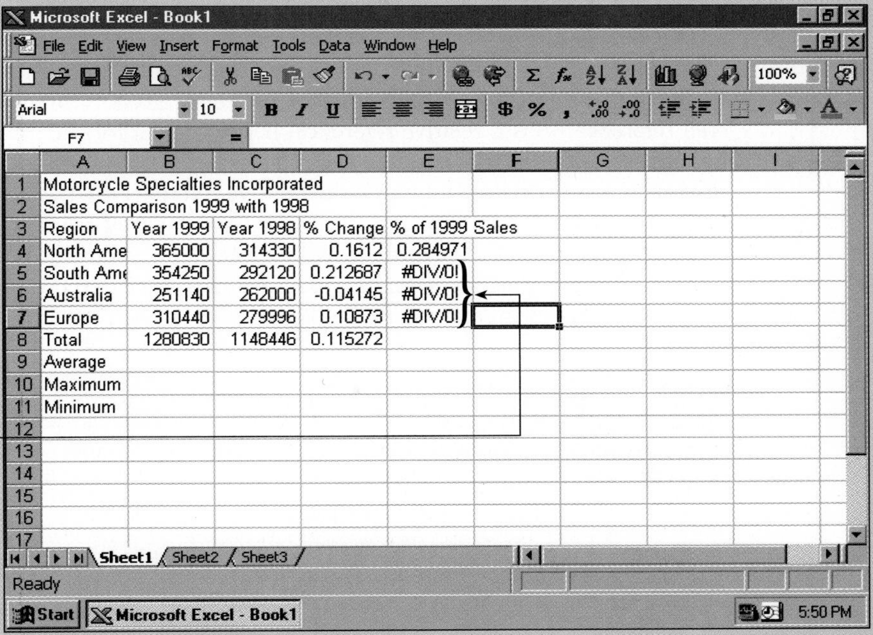

error message

Something is wrong. Cells E5 through E7 display "#DIV/0!," a message that means that Excel was instructed to divide by zero. Take a moment to look at the formulas you copied into cells E5, E6, and E7.

To examine the formulas in cells E5 through E7:

1. Click cell **E5** and look at the formula displayed in the formula bar, =B5/B9. The first cell reference changed from B4 in the original formula to B5 in the copied formula. That's correct because the sales data for South America is entered in cell B5. The second cell reference changed from B8, in the original formula to B9, which is not correct. The correct formula should be =B5/B8 because the total sales are in cell B8, not cell B9.

2. Look at the formulas in cells E6 and E7 and see how the cell references changed in each formula.

As you observed, the cell reference to total company sales (B8) in the original formula was changed to B9, B10, and B11 in the copied formulas. The problem with the copied formulas is that Excel adjusted *all* the cell references relative to their new location.

Absolute Versus Relative References

Sometimes when you copy a formula, you don't want Excel to change all cell references automatically to reflect their new positions in the worksheet. If you want a cell reference to point to the same location in the worksheet when you copy it, you must use an absolute reference. An **absolute reference** is a cell reference in a formula that does not change when copied to another cell.

To create an absolute reference, you insert a dollar sign ($) before the column and row of the cell reference. For example, the cell reference $B$8 is an absolute reference, whereas the cell reference B8 is a relative reference. If you copy a formula that contains the absolute reference $B$8 to another cell, the cell reference to $B$8 does not change. On the other hand, if you copy a formula containing the relative reference B8 to another cell, the reference to B8 changes. In some situations, a cell might have a **mixed reference**, such as $B8; in this case, when the formula is copied, the row number changes but the column letter does not.

To include an absolute reference in a formula, you can type a dollar sign when you type the cell reference, or you can use the F4 key to change the cell reference type while in Edit mode.

REFERENCE window

EDITING CELL REFERENCE TYPES

- Double-click the cell that contains the formula you want to edit.
- Use the arrow keys to move the insertion point to the part of the cell reference you want to change.
- Press the F4 key until the reference is correct.
- Press the Enter key to complete the edit.

To correct the problem in your worksheet, you need to use an absolute reference, instead of a relative reference, to indicate the location of total sales in 1999. That is, you need to change the formula from =B4/B8 to =B4/$B$8. The easiest way to make this change is in Edit mode.

To change a cell reference to an absolute reference:

1. Click cell **E4** to move to the cell that contains the formula you want to edit.

2. Double-click the mouse button to edit the formula in the cell. Notice that each cell reference in the formula in cell E4 appears in a different color and the corresponding cells referred to in the formula are outlined in the same color. This feature is called Range Finder and is designed to make it easier for you to check the accuracy of your formula.

3. Make sure the insertion point is to the right of the division (/) operator, anywhere in the cell reference B8.

4. Press the **F4** key to change the reference to $B$8.

   TROUBLE? If your reference shows the **mixed reference** B$8 or $B8, continue to press the F4 key until you see $B$8.

5. Press the **Enter** key to update the formula in cell E4.

Cell E4 still displays .284971, which is the formula's correct result. But remember, the problem in your original formula did not surface until you copied it to cells E5 through E7. To correct the error, you need to copy the revised formula and then check the results. Although you can again use the fill handle to copy the formula, you can also copy the formula using the Clipboard and the Copy and Paste buttons on the Standard toolbar.

Copying Cell Contents Using the Copy and Paste Method

You can duplicate the contents of a cell or range by making a copy of the cell or range and then pasting the copy into one or more locations in the same worksheet, another worksheet, or another workbook.

When you copy a cell or range of cells, the copied material is placed on the Clipboard. You can copy labels, numbers, dates, or formulas.

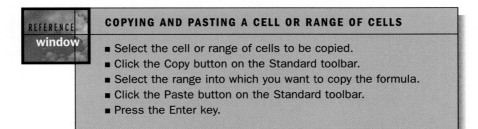

REFERENCE window	COPYING AND PASTING A CELL OR RANGE OF CELLS
	■ Select the cell or range of cells to be copied.
	■ Click the Copy button on the Standard toolbar.
	■ Select the range into which you want to copy the formula.
	■ Click the Paste button on the Standard toolbar.
	■ Press the Enter key.

You need to copy the formula in cell E4 to the Clipboard and then paste that formula into cells E5 through E7.

To copy the revised formula from cell E4 to cells E5 through E7:

1. Click cell **E4** because it contains the revised formula that you want to copy.

2. Click the **Copy** button 🖿 on the Standard toolbar. A moving dashed line surrounds cell E4, indicating that the formula has been copied and is available to be pasted into other cells.

3. Click and drag to select cells **E5** through **E7**.

4. Click the **Paste** button 🖿 on the Standard toolbar. Excel adjusts the formula and pastes it into cells E5 through E7.

5. Click any cell to deselect the range and view the formulas' results. Press the **Escape** key to clear the Clipboard and remove the dashed line surrounding cell E4. See Figure 2-13.

Figure 2-13 ◀
Results of
copying the
formula with
an absolute
reference

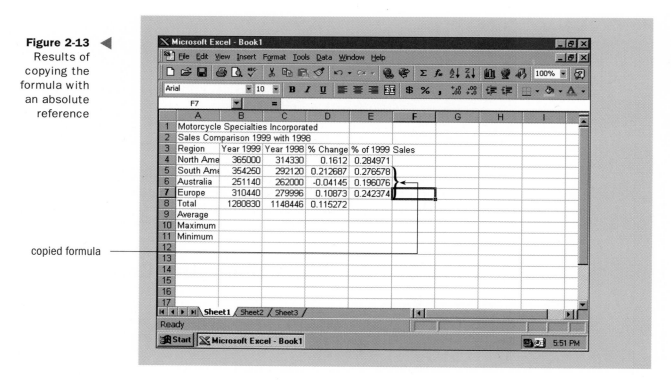

copied formula ───

Copying this formula worked. When you pasted the formula from cell E4 into the range E5:E7, Excel automatically adjusted the relative reference (B4), while using the cell reference ($B$8) for all absolute references. You have now implemented most of the design as specified in the planning analysis sheet. Now rename the worksheet to accurately describe its contents, then save the workbook to your Student Disk before entering the formulas to compute the summary statistics.

Renaming the Worksheet

Before saving the workbook, look at the sheet tab in the lower-left corner of the worksheet window: the sheet is currently named Sheet1—the name Excel automatically uses when it opens a new workbook. Now that your worksheet is taking shape, you want to give it a more descriptive name that better indicates its contents. Change the worksheet name to Sales Comparison.

To change a worksheet name:

1. Double-click the **Sheet1** sheet tab to select it.

2. Type the new name, **Sales Comparison**, over the current name, Sheet1. Click any cell in the worksheet. The sheet tab displays the name "Sales Comparison."

Saving the New Workbook

Now you want to save the workbook. Because this is the first time you have saved this workbook, you will use the Save As command and name the file MSI Sales Report.

To save the workbook as MSI Sales Report:

1. Click **File** on the menu bar, and then click **Save As** to display the Save As dialog box.

2. In the File name text box, type **MSI Sales Report** but don't press the Enter key yet. You still need to check some other settings.

3. Click the **Save in** list arrow, and then click the drive containing your Student Disk.

4. In the folder list, double-click the **Tutorial.02** folder to select the folder into which you want to save the workbook. Your Save As dialog box should look like the dialog box in Figure 2-14.

Figure 2-14 ◀
Saving the worksheet as MSI Sales Report

enter name of worksheet here

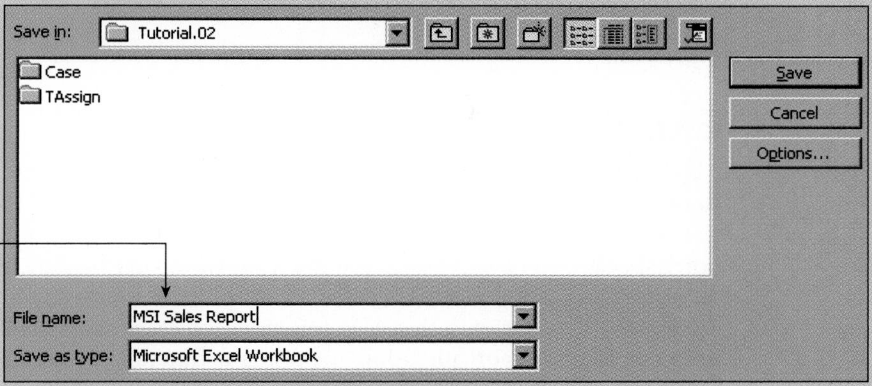

Save in:	📁 Tutorial.02								

📁 Case
📁 TAssign

Save
Cancel
Options...

File name: MSI Sales Report

Save as type: Microsoft Excel Workbook

5. Click the **Save** button to save the workbook.

TROUBLE? If you see the message "Replace Existing MSI Sales Report?" click the Yes button to replace the old version with the current version.

Quick Check

1 | Describe how AutoSum works.

2 | In cell C5 you have the formula =A5+B5. After you copy this formula to cell C6, the formula in cell C6 would appear in the formula bar as _____.

3 | In the formula =A5+B5, A5 and B5 are examples of _____ references.

4 | In the formula =A8+(1+$C$1), $C$1 is an example of a(n) _____.

5 | When you copy a formula using the Copy 📋 and Paste 📋 buttons on the Standard toolbar, Excel uses the _____ to temporarily store the formula.

6 | The _____ is a small black square located in the lower-right corner of a selected cell.

7 | Describe the steps you take to change the name of the sheet tab.

8 | List the steps to follow to create a worksheet.

Now that you have planned and built the Sales Comparison worksheet by entering labels, values, and formulas, you need to complete the worksheet by entering some functions and format the worksheet. You will do this in Session 2.2.

SESSION 2.2

In this session you will finish the worksheet as you learn how to enter several statistical functions, increase the column width, insert a row between the titles and column headings, move the contents of a range to another location, and apply one of the Excel predefined formats to the report. You will also spell check the worksheet, and preview and print it.

Excel Functions

According to Sally's planning analysis sheet, you still need to enter the formulas for the summary statistics. To enter these statistics you'll use three Excel functions, AVERAGE, MAX, and MIN. The many Excel functions help you enter formulas for calculations and other specialized tasks, even if you don't know the mathematical details of the calculations. As you recall, a function is a calculation tool that performs a predefined operation. You are already familiar with the SUM function, which adds the values in a range of cells. Excel provides hundreds of functions, including a function to calculate the average of a list of numbers, a function to find a number's square root, a function to calculate loan payments, and a function to calculate the number of days between two dates. Figure 2-15 shows how Excel organizes these functions into categories.

Figure 2-15 ◄
Excel function categories

Function Category	Examples of Functions in This Category
Financial	Calculate loan payments, depreciation, interest rate, internal rate of return
Date & Time	Display today's date and/or time; calculate the number of days between two dates
Math & Trig	Round off numbers; calculate sums, logs, and least common multiple; generate random numbers
Statistical	Calculate average, standard deviation, and frequencies; find minimum, maximum; count how many numbers are in a list
Lookup & Reference	Look for a value in a range of cells; find the row or column location of a reference
Database	Perform crosstabs, averages, counts, and standard deviation for an Excel database
Text	Convert numbers to text; compare two text entries; find the length of a text entry
Logical	Perform conditional calculations
Information	Return information about the formatting, location, or contents of a range

Each function has a **syntax**, which specifies the order in which you must type the parts of the function and where to put commas, parentheses, and other punctuation. The general syntax of an Excel function is:

$$NAME(argument1,argument2,...)$$

The syntax of most functions requires you to type the function name followed by one or more arguments in parentheses. Function **arguments** specify the values that Excel must use in the calculation, or the cell references that Excel must include in the calculation. For example, in the function SUM(A1:A20) the function name is SUM and the argument is A1:A20, which is the range of cells you want to total.

You can use a function in a simple formula such as =SUM(A1:A20), or a more complex formula such as =SUM(A1:A20)*52. As with all formulas, you enter the formula that contains a function in the cell where you want to display the results. The easiest way to enter a function in a cell is to use the Paste Function button on the Standard toolbar, which leads you step-by-step through the process of entering a formula containing a function.

If you prefer, you can type the function directly into the cell. Although the function name is always shown in uppercase, you can type it in either uppercase or lowercase. Also, even though parentheses enclose the arguments, you need not type the closing parenthesis if the function ends the formula. Excel automatically adds the closing parenthesis when you press the Enter key to complete the formula.

According to Sally's planning analysis sheet, the next step is to calculate the average regional sales for 1999.

AVERAGE Function

AVERAGE is a statistical function that calculates the average, or the arithmetic mean. The syntax for the AVERAGE function is:

$$\text{AVERAGE(\textit{number1,number2,...})}$$

Generally, when you use the AVERAGE function, *number* is a range of cells. To calculate the average of a range of cells, Excel sums the values in the range, then divides by the number of non-blank cells in the range.

REFERENCE
window

USING THE PASTE FUNCTION BUTTON

- Click the cell where you want to display the results of the function. Then click the Paste Function button on the Standard toolbar to open the Paste Function dialog box.
- Click the type of function you want in the Function category list box.
- Click the function you want in the Function name list box.
- Click the OK button to open a second dialog box.
- Accept the default information or enter the information you want the function to use in its calculations.
- Click the OK button to close the dialog box and display the results of the function in the cell.

Sally wants you to calculate the average sales in 1999. You'll use the Paste Function button to enter the AVERAGE function, which is one of the statistical functions.

To enter the AVERAGE function using the Paste Function button:

1. Click cell **B9** to select the cell where you want to enter the AVERAGE function.

2. Click the **Paste Function** button on the Standard toolbar to display the Paste Function dialog box.

   TROUBLE? If the Office Assistant opens and offers help on this feature, click the No option button.

3. Click **Statistical** in the Function category list box.

4. Click **AVERAGE** in the Function name list box. See Figure 2-16. The syntax for the AVERAGE function, AVERAGE(*number1,number2,...*), is displayed beneath the Function category box.

Figure 2-16 ◄
Paste Function
dialog box

syntax for
AVERAGE Function

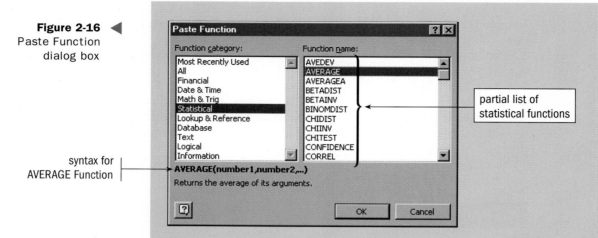

partial list of
statistical functions

5. Click the **OK** button to open the AVERAGE dialog box. Notice that the range B4:B8 appears in the Number1 text box, and =AVERAGE(B4:B8) appears in the formula bar. See Figure 2-17.

Figure 2-17 ◄
AVERAGE
dialog box

range includes
cell B8

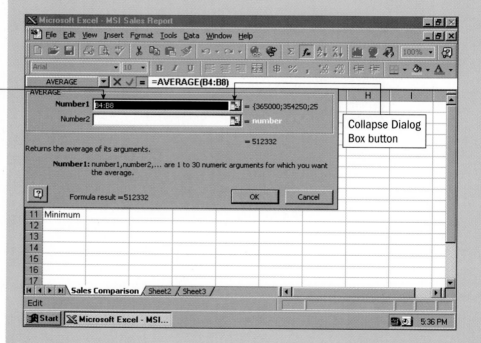

Collapse Dialog
Box button

Excel has incorrectly included the total sales for 1999 (cell B8) in the range to calculate the average. The correct range is B4:B7.

6. Click the **Collapse Dialog Box** button to the right of the Number1 text box to collapse the dialog box to the size of one row. This makes it easier for you to identify and select the correct range.

7. Position the cell pointer over cell **B4**, click and drag to select the range **B4:B7**, and then click the **Collapse Dialog Box** button. The collapsed dialog box is restored and the correct range, B4:B7, is displayed in the Number1 text box. The formula =AVERAGE(B4:B7) is displayed in the formula bar.

8. Click the **OK** button to close the dialog box and return to the worksheet. The average, 320207.5, now appears in cell B9.

According to your plan, you need to enter a formula to find the largest regional sales amount in 1999. To do this, you'll use the MAX function.

MAX Function

MAX is a statistical function that finds the largest number. The syntax of the MAX function is:

$$MAX(number1, number2,...)$$

In the MAX function, *number* can be a constant number such as 345, a cell reference such as B6, or a range of cells such as B5:B16. You can use the MAX function to simply display the largest number or to use the largest number in a calculation. Although you can use the Paste Function to enter the MAX function, this time you'll type the MAX function directly into cell B10.

To enter the MAX function by typing directly into a cell:

1. If necessary, click cell **B10** to select it as the cell into which you want to type the formula that uses the MAX function.

2. Type **=MAX(B4:B7)** and press the **Enter** key. Cell B10 displays 365000, the largest regional sales amount in 1999.

Next, you need to find the smallest regional sales amount in 1999. For that, you'll use the MIN function.

MIN Function

MIN is a statistical function that finds the smallest number. The syntax of the MIN function is:

$$MIN(number1, number2,...)$$

You can use the MIN function to display the smallest number or to use the smallest number in a calculation.

You'll enter the MIN function directly into cell B11, using the pointing method.

Building Formulas by Pointing

Excel provides several ways to enter cell references into a formula. One is to type the cell references directly, as you have done so far in all the formulas you've entered. Another way to put a cell reference in a formula is to **point** to the cell reference you want to include while creating the formula. To use the pointing method to enter the formula, you click the cell or range of cells whose cell references you want to include in the formula. You may prefer to use this method to enter formulas, because it minimizes typing errors.

Now enter the formula to calculate the minimum sales by using the pointing method.

To enter the MIN function using the pointing method:

1. If necessary, click cell **B11** to move to the cell where you want to enter the formula that uses the MIN function.

2. Type **=MIN(** to begin the formula.

3. Position the cell pointer in cell **B4**, and then click and drag to select cells **B4** through **B7**. As you drag the mouse over the range, notice that the message "4Rx1C" appears in a ScreenTip, informing you that four rows and one column have been selected. Release the mouse button, and then press the **Enter** key. Cell B11 displays 251140, the smallest regional sales amount for 1999. See Figure 2-18.

Figure 2-18 ◀
Worksheet after labels, numbers, formulas, and functions entered

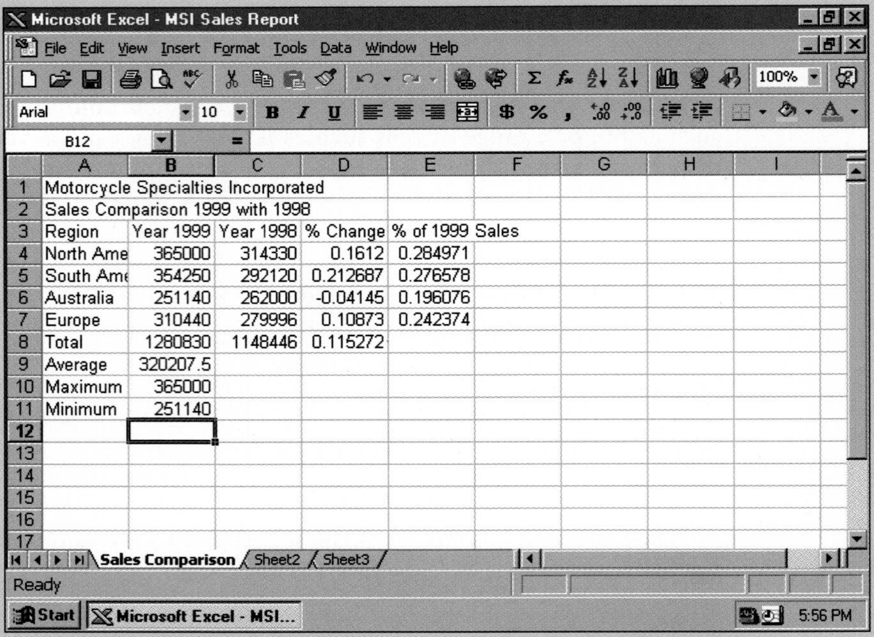

Now that the worksheet labels, values, formulas, and functions have been entered, Sally reviews the worksheet.

Testing the Worksheet

Before trusting a worksheet and its results, you should test it to make sure you entered the correct formulas. You want the worksheet to produce accurate results.

Beginners often expect their Excel worksheets to work correctly the first time. Sometimes they do work correctly the first time, but even well-planned and well-designed worksheets can contain errors. It's best to assume that a worksheet has errors and test it to make sure it is correct. While there are no rules for testing a worksheet, here are some approaches:

- Entering **test values**, numbers that generate a known result, to determine whether your worksheet formulas are accurate. For example, try entering a 1 into each cell. After you enter the test values, you compare the results in your worksheet with the known results. If the results on your worksheet don't match the known results, you probably made an error.

- Entering **extreme values**, such as very large or very small numbers, and observing their effect on cells with formulas.

- Working out the numbers ahead of time with pencil, paper, and calculator, and comparing these results with the output from the computer.

Sally used the third approach to test her worksheet. She had calculated her results using a calculator (Figure 2-2) and then compared them with the results on the screen (Figure 2-18). The numbers agree, so she feels confident that the worksheet she created contains accurate results.

Spell Checking the Worksheet

You can use the Excel spell check feature to help identify and correct spelling and typing errors. Excel compares the words in your worksheet to the words in its dictionary. If Excel finds a word in your worksheet not in its dictionary, it shows you the word and some suggested corrections, and you decide whether to correct it or leave it as is.

REFERENCE window	**CHECKING THE SPELLING IN A WORKSHEET**
	■ Click cell A1 to begin the spell check from the top of the worksheet. ■ Click the Spelling button on the Standard toolbar. ■ Change the spelling or ignore the spell check's suggestion for each identified word. ■ Click the OK button when the spell check is complete.

You have tested your numbers and formulas for accuracy. Now you can check the spelling of all text entries in the worksheet.

To check the spelling in a worksheet:

1. Click cell **A1** to begin spell checking in the first cell of the worksheet.

2. Click the **Spelling** button on the Standard toolbar to check the spelling of the text in the worksheet. A message box indicates that Excel has finished spell checking the entire worksheet. No errors were found.

   TROUBLE? If the spell check does find a spelling error in your worksheet, use the Spelling dialog box options to correct the spelling mistake and continue checking the worksheet.

Improving the Worksheet Layout

Although the numbers are correct, Sally does not want to present a worksheet without a more polished appearance. She feels that there are a number of simple changes you can make to the worksheet that will improve its layout and make the data more readable. Specifically, she asks you to increase the width of column A so that the entire region names are displayed, insert a blank row between the titles and column headings, move the summary statistics down three rows from their current location, and apply one of the pre-defined Excel formats to the worksheet.

Changing Column Width

Changing the column width is one way to improve the appearance of the worksheet, making it easier to read and interpret data. In Sally's worksheet, you need to increase the width of column A so that the entire labels for North America and South America appear in their cells.

Excel provides several methods for changing column width. For example, you can click a column heading or click and drag the pointer to select a series of column headings and then use the Format menu. You can also use the dividing line between column headings in the column header row. When you move the pointer over the dividing line between two column headings, the pointer changes to ↔. You can then use the pointer to drag the dividing line to a new location. You can also double-click the dividing line to make the column as wide as the longest text label or number in the column.

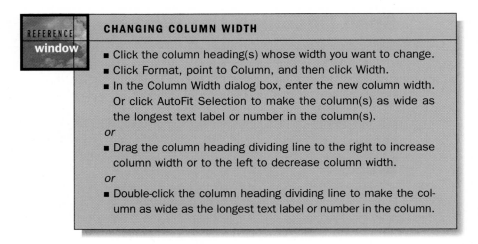

REFERENCE window

CHANGING COLUMN WIDTH

- Click the column heading(s) whose width you want to change.
- Click Format, point to Column, and then click Width.
- In the Column Width dialog box, enter the new column width. Or click AutoFit Selection to make the column(s) as wide as the longest text label or number in the column(s).

or

- Drag the column heading dividing line to the right to increase column width or to the left to decrease column width.

or

- Double-click the column heading dividing line to make the column as wide as the longest text label or number in the column.

Sally has asked you to change column A's width so that the complete region name is displayed.

To change the width of column A:

1. Position the pointer ⊕ on the A in the column heading area.

2. Move the pointer to the right edge of the column heading dividing columns A and B. Notice that the pointer changes to the resize arrow ✛.

3. Click and drag the resize arrow to the right, increasing the column width 12 characters or more, as indicated in the ScreenTip that pops up on the screen.

4. Release the mouse button. See Figure 2-19.

Figure 2-19 ◄
Worksheet
after width of
column A
increased

now entire contents
of cell displayed

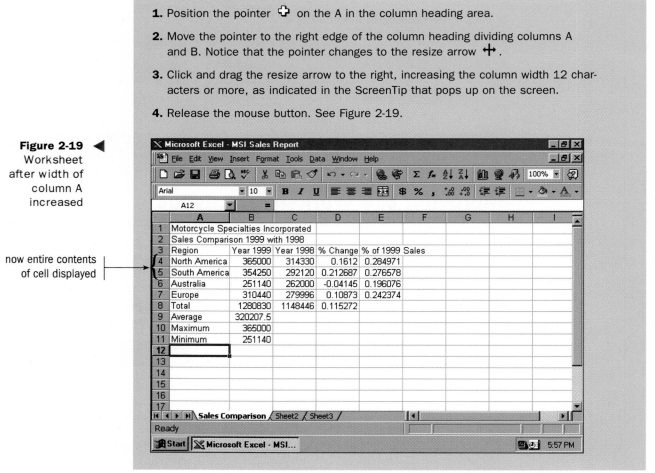

Next, you need to insert a row between the title and the column heading.

Inserting a Row into a Worksheet

At times, you may need to add one or more rows or columns to a worksheet to make room for new data or to make the worksheet easier to read. The process of inserting columns and rows is similar; you select the number of columns or rows you want to insert and then use the Insert command to insert the columns or rows. When you insert rows or columns, Excel repositions other rows and columns in the worksheet and automatically adjusts cell references in formulas to reflect the new location of values used in calculations.

REFERENCE
window

INSERTING A ROW OR COLUMN

- Click any cell in the row/column above which you want to insert the new row/column (or select a range of rows/columns above which you want to insert new rows/columns).
- Click Insert and then click Rows/Columns. Above the selected range, Excel inserts one row/column for every row/column in the selected range.

Sally wants one blank row between the titles and column headings in her worksheet.

To insert a row into a worksheet:

1. Click cell **A2**.

2. Click **Insert** on the menu bar, and then click **Rows**. Excel inserts a blank row above the original row 2. All other rows shift down one row. See Figure 2-20.

Figure 2-20 ◀
Worksheet after one row inserted above original row 2

row inserted in wrong position

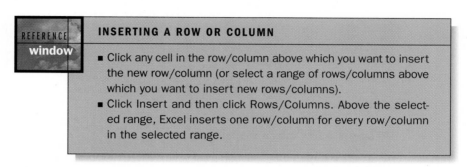

The blank row isn't really where you wanted it. You inserted a row between the two lines of the title instead of between the title and the column heading. To correct this error you can either delete the row or use the Undo button. If you need to delete a row or column, select the row(s) or column(s) you want to delete, then click Delete on the Edit menu, or press the Delete key on your keyboard. You use the Undo button because it is a feature you find valuable in many situations.

Using the Undo Button

The Excel Undo button lets you cancel recent actions one at a time. Click the Undo button to reverse the last command or delete the last entry you typed. To reverse more than one action, click the arrow next to the Undo button and click the action you want to undo on the drop-down list.

Now use the Undo button to reverse the row insertion.

To reverse the row insertion:

1. Click the **Undo** button 🔙 on the Standard toolbar to restore the worksheet to its status before the row was inserted.

Now you can insert the blank row in the correct place—between the second line of the worksheet title and the column heads.

To insert a row into a worksheet:

1. Click cell **A3** because you want to insert one row above row 3. If you wanted to insert several rows, you would select as many rows as you wanted to insert before using the Insert command.

2. Click **Insert** on the menu bar, and then click **Rows**. Excel inserts a blank row above the original row 3. All other rows shift down one row. See Figure 2-21.

Figure 2-21 ◀
Worksheet
after one row
inserted

row inserted in
desired location ⟶

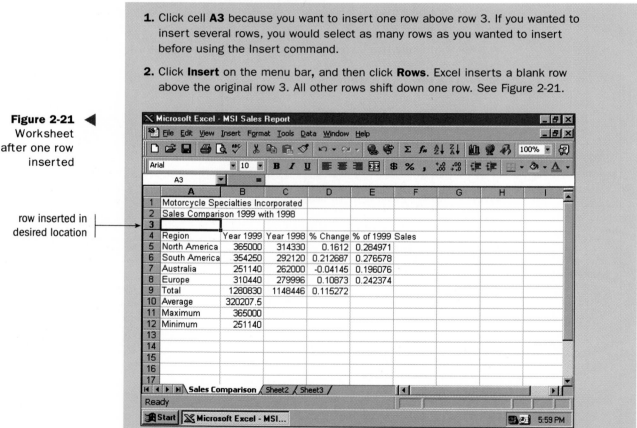

Adding a row changed the location of the data in the worksheet. For example, the percent change in North American sales, originally in cell D4, is now in cell D5. Did Excel adjust the formulas to compensate for the new row? Check cell D5 and any other cells you want to view to verify that the cell references were adjusted.

To examine the formula in cell D5 and other cells:

1. Click cell **D5**. The formula =(B5-C5)/C5 appears in the formula bar. You originally entered the formula =(B4-C4)/C4 in cell D4 to calculate percent change in North America. Excel automatically adjusted the cell reference to reflect the new location of the data.

2. Inspect other cells below row 3 to verify that their cell references were automatically adjusted when the new row was inserted.

Sally has also suggested moving the summary statistics down three rows from the present location to make the report easier to read. So, you will need to move the range of cells containing the average, minimum, and maximum sales to a different location in the worksheet.

Moving a Range Using the Mouse

To place the summary statistics three rows below the other data in the report, you could use the Insert command to insert three blank rows between the total and average sales. Alternatively, you could use the mouse to move the summary statistics to a new location. Since you already know how to insert a row, try using the mouse to move the summary statistics to a new location. This technique is called **drag-and-drop**. You simply select the cell range you want to move and use the pointer to drag the cells' contents to the desired location.

REFERENCE window	**MOVING A RANGE USING THE MOUSE**
	■ Select the cell or range of cells you want to move.
	■ Place the mouse pointer over any edge of the selected range until the pointer changes to an arrow.
	■ Click and drag the outline of the range to the new worksheet location.
	■ Release the mouse button.

Sally has asked you to move the range A10 through B12 to the new destination area A13 through B15.

To move a range of cells using the drag-and-drop technique:

1. Select the range of cells **A10:B12**, which contains the sales summary statistics you want to move.

2. Place the mouse pointer over any edge of the selected range until the pointer changes to an arrow ⇖ . See Figure 2-22.

Figure 2-22 ◀
Range to
be moved

pointer shape
indicates you can
move selected range

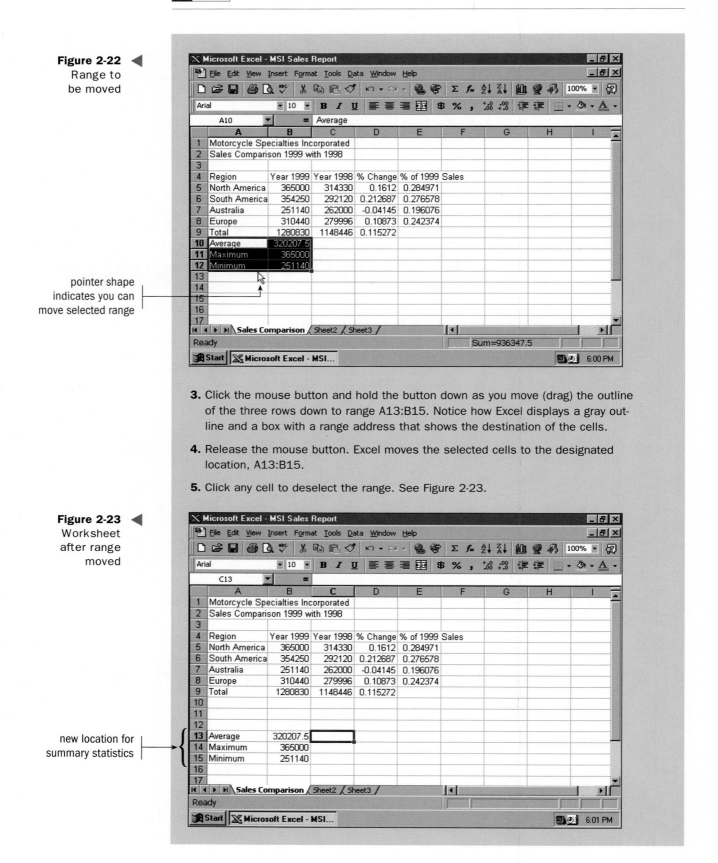

3. Click the mouse button and hold the button down as you move (drag) the outline of the three rows down to range A13:B15. Notice how Excel displays a gray outline and a box with a range address that shows the destination of the cells.

4. Release the mouse button. Excel moves the selected cells to the designated location, A13:B15.

5. Click any cell to deselect the range. See Figure 2-23.

Figure 2-23 ◀
Worksheet
after range
moved

new location for
summary statistics

Next, Sally wants you to use the Excel AutoFormat feature to improve the worksheet's appearance by emphasizing the titles and aligning numbers in cells.

Using AutoFormat

The **AutoFormat** feature lets you change your worksheet's appearance by selecting from a collection of predesigned worksheet formats. Each worksheet format in the AutoFormat collection gives your worksheet a more professional appearance by applying attractive fonts, borders, colors, and shading to a range of data. AutoFormat also adjusts column widths, row heights, and the alignment of text in cells to improve the worksheet's appearance.

REFERENCE window	**USING AUTOFORMAT**
	■ Select the cells you want to format. ■ Click Format, and then click AutoFormat. ■ Select a format style from the Table Format list. ■ Click the OK button to apply the format.

Now you'll use AutoFormat's Simple format to improve the worksheet's appearance.

To apply AutoFormat's Simple format:

1. Select cells **A1:E9** as the range you want to format using AutoFormat.

2. Click **Format** on the menu bar, and then click **AutoFormat**. The AutoFormat dialog box opens. See Figure 2-24.

Figure 2-24 ◀
AutoFormat
dialog box

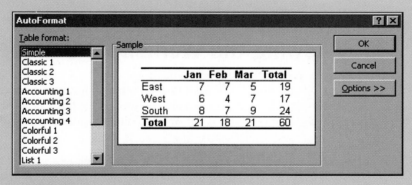

3. The Table format box lists the available formats. The format called "Simple" is selected and the Sample box shows how the Simple format looks when applied to a worksheet.

4. Click each of the formats from Simple down to Accounting 1. Notice the different font styles and colors of each format shown in the Sample box.

5. Click the **Simple** format, and then click the **OK** button to apply this format.

6. Click any cell to deselect the range. Figure 2-25 shows the newly formatted worksheet.

Figure 2-25 ◄
Worksheet
after using the
Simple
AutoFormat

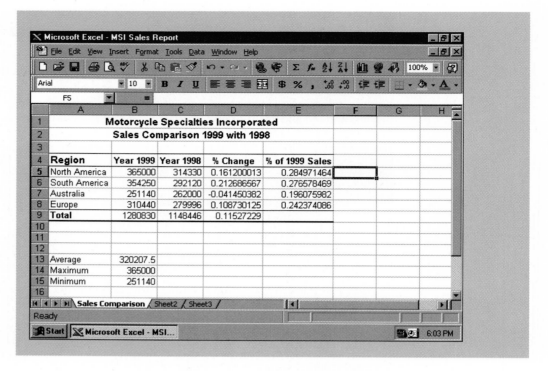

You show the worksheet to Sally. She's impressed with the improved appearance and decides to hand it out to the regional sales managers at their next meeting. She asks you to print it so she can make copies.

Previewing the Worksheet Using Print Preview

Before you print a worksheet, you can use the Excel Print Preview window to see how it will look when printed. The **Print Preview window** shows you margins, page breaks, headers, and footers that are not always visible on the screen. If the preview isn't what you want, you can close the Print Preview window and change the worksheet before printing it.

To preview the worksheet before you print it:

1. Click the **Print Preview** button ⟨⟩ on the Standard toolbar. After a moment Excel displays the worksheet in the Print Preview window. See Figure 2-26.

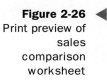

Figure 2-26 ◀
Print preview of
sales
comparison
worksheet

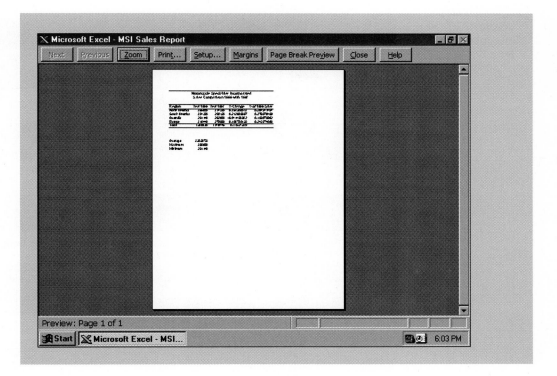

When Excel displays a full page in the Print Preview window, you might have difficulty seeing the text of the worksheet because it is so small. Don't worry if the preview isn't completely readable. One purpose of the Print Preview window is to see the overall layout of the worksheet and how it will fit on the printed page. If you want a better view of the text, you can use the Zoom button.

To display an enlarged section of the Print Preview window:

1. Click the **Zoom** button to display an enlarged section of the Print Preview.

2. Click the **Zoom** button again to return to the full-page view.

Notice that the Print Preview window contains several other buttons. Figure 2-27 describes each of these buttons.

Figure 2-27 ◄
Description of
Print Preview
buttons

Clicking this Button	Results in
Next	Moving forward one page
Previous	Moving backward one page
Zoom	Magnifying the Print Preview screen to zoom in on any portion of the page; click again to return to full-page preview
Print	Printing the document
Setup	Displaying the Page Setup dialog box
Margins	Changing the width of margins, columns in the worksheet and the position of headers and footers
Page Break Preview	Showing where page breaks occur in the worksheet and which area of the worksheet will be printed; you can adjust where data will print by inserting or moving page breaks
Close	Closing the Print Preview window
Help	Activating Help

Looking at the worksheet in Print Preview, you observe that it is not centered on the page. By default, Excel prints a worksheet at the upper left of the page's print area. You can specify that the worksheet be centered vertically, horizontally, or both.

Centering the Printout

Worksheet printouts generally look more professional centered on the printed page. You decide that Sally would want you to center the sales comparison worksheet both horizontally and vertically on the printed page.

To center the printout:

1. Click the **Setup** button to display the Page Setup dialog box.

2. Click the **Margins** tab. See Figure 2-28. Notice that the preview box displays a worksheet positioned at the upper-left edge of the page.

Figure 2-28
Margins tab of
Page Setup
dialog box

indicates that
worksheet will be
displayed in upper-
left corner of page

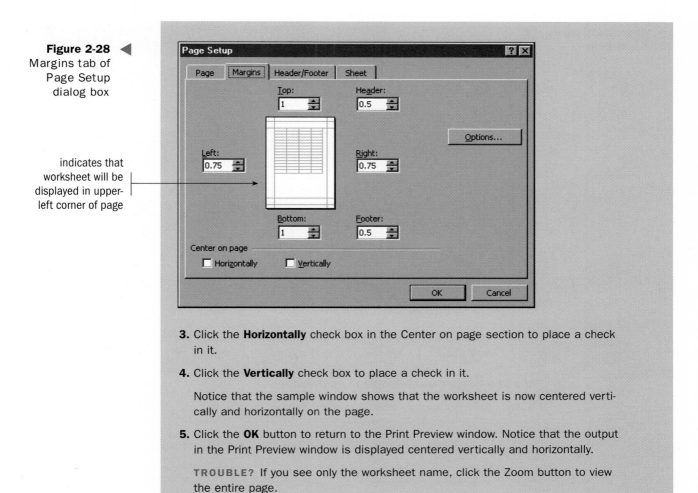

3. Click the **Horizontally** check box in the Center on page section to place a check in it.

4. Click the **Vertically** check box to place a check in it.

Notice that the sample window shows that the worksheet is now centered vertically and horizontally on the page.

5. Click the **OK** button to return to the Print Preview window. Notice that the output in the Print Preview window is displayed centered vertically and horizontally.

TROUBLE? If you see only the worksheet name, click the Zoom button to view the entire page.

Adding Headers and Footers

Headers and footers can provide you with useful documentation on your printed worksheet, such as the name of the person who created the worksheet, the date it was printed, and its filename. The **header** is text printed in the top margin of every worksheet page. A **footer** is text printed in the bottom margin of every page. Headers and footers are not displayed in the worksheet window. To see them, you must preview or print the worksheet.

Excel uses formatting codes in headers and footers to represent the items you want to print. Formatting codes produce dates, times, and filenames that you might want a header or footer to include. You can type these codes, or you can click a formatting code button to insert the code. Figure 2-29 shows the formatting codes and the buttons for inserting them.

Figure 2-29 ◀
Header
and footer
formatting
buttons

Button	Button Name	Formatting Code	Action
A	Font	none	Sets font, text style, and font size
	Page Number	&[Page]	Inserts page number
	Total Pages	&[Pages]	Inserts total number of pages
	Date	&[Date]	Inserts current date
	Time	&[Time]	Inserts current time
	Filename	&[File]	Inserts filename
	Sheet name	&[Tab]	Inserts name of active worksheet

Sally asks you to add a header that includes the filename and today's date. She also wants you to add a footer that displays the page number.

To add a header and a footer to your worksheet:

1. In the Print Preview window, click the **Setup** button to open the Page Setup dialog box, and then click the **Header/Footer** tab.

2. Click the **Custom Header** button to display the Header dialog box.

3. With the insertion point in the Left section box, click the **Filename** button [icon]. The code &[File] appears in the Left section box.

   TROUBLE? If you clicked the wrong code, double-click the code, press the Delete key, then repeat Steps 2 and 3.

4. Click the **Right section** box to move the insertion point to the Right section box.

5. Click the **Date** button [icon]. The code &[Date] appears in the Right section box. See Figure 2-30.

Figure 2-30 ◀
Inserting
formatting
codes into
the Header
dialog box

formatting code to
display workbook
filename

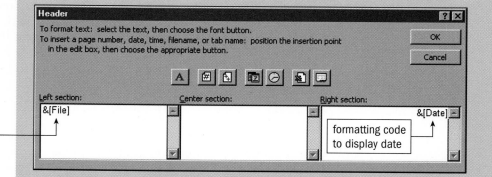

TROUBLE? If you clicked the wrong code, double-click the code, press the Delete key, then repeat Step 5.

6. Click the **OK** button to complete the header and return to the Page Setup dialog box. Notice that the header shows the filename on the left and the date on the right.

7. Click the **Custom Footer** button to display the Footer dialog box.

8. Click the **Center section** box to move the insertion point to the Center Section box.

9. Click the **Page Number** button 🔲. The code &[Page] appears in the Center section box.

10. Click the **OK** button to complete the footer and return to the Page Setup dialog box. Notice that the footer shows the page number in the bottom center of the page.

11. Click the **OK** button to return to the Print Preview window. The changed header appears in the Print Preview window.

12. Click the **Close** button to exit the Print Preview window and return to the worksheet.

You'll use the Print button on the Standard toolbar to print one copy of the worksheet with the current settings. First, save the worksheet before printing it.

To save your page setup settings:

1. Click the **Save** button 🔲 on the Standard toolbar.

2. Click the **Print** button 🖨 on the Standard toolbar. See Figure 2-31.

   TROUBLE? If you see a message that indicates that you have a printer problem, click the Cancel button to cancel printing. Check your printer to make sure it is turned on and is online; also make sure it has paper. Then go back and try Step 2 again. If you have no printer available, click the Cancel button.

Figure 2-31 ◀
Printed
worksheet

Motorcycle Specialties Incorporated
Sales Comparison 1999 with 1998

Region	Year 1999	Year 1998	% Change	% of 1999 Sales
North America	365000	314330	0.161200013	0.284971464
South America	354250	292120	0.212686567	0.276578469
Australia	251140	262000	-0.041450382	0.196075982
Europe	310440	279996	0.108730125	0.242374086
Total	1280830	1148446	0.11527229	

Average	320207.5			
Maximum	365000			
Minimum	251140			

Sally reviews the printed worksheet and is satisfied with its appearance. She will make four copies to be distributed to the regional managers at the next meeting.

Documenting the Workbook

Documenting the workbook provides valuable information to those using the workbook. Documentation includes external documentation as well as notes and instructions within the workbook. This information could be as basic as who created the worksheet and the date it was created, or it could be more detailed, summarizing formulas and layout.

Depending on the use of the workbook, the required amount of documentation varies. Sally's planning analysis sheet and sketch for the sales comparison worksheet are one form of external documentation. This information can be useful to someone who would need to modify the worksheet in any way because it states the goals, required input, output, and the calculations used.

One source of internal documentation would be a worksheet that is placed as the first worksheet in the workbook, such as the Title Sheet worksheet in the workbook you worked with in Tutorial 1 to determine the best location for the new Inwood golf course. In more complex workbooks, this sheet may also include an index of all worksheets in the workbook, instructions on how to use the worksheets, where to enter data, how to save the workbook, and how to print reports. This documentation method is useful because the information is contained directly in the workbook and can easily be viewed upon opening the workbook, or printed if necessary. Another source of internal documentation is the **Property dialog box**. This dialog box enables you to electronically capture information such as the name of the workbook's creator, the creation date, the number of revisions, and other information related to the workbook.

If you prefer, you can include documentation in each sheet of the workbook. One way is to attach notes to cells by using the Comments command to explain complex formulas and assumptions.

The worksheet itself can be used as documentation. Once a worksheet is completed, it is a good practice to print and file a "hard" copy of your work as documentation. This hard copy file should include a printout of each worksheet with the values displayed and another printout of the worksheet displaying the cell formulas.

Displaying and Printing Worksheet Formulas

You can document the formulas you entered in a worksheet by displaying and printing them. When you display formulas, Excel shows the formulas you entered in each cell instead of showing the results of the calculations. You want a printout of the formulas in your worksheet for documentation.

To display worksheet formulas:

1. Click **Tools** on the menu bar, and then click **Options** to open the Options dialog box.

2. Click the **View** tab, and then click the **Formulas** check box in the Window options section to place a check in it.

3. Click the **OK** button to return to the worksheet. The width of each column nearly doubles to accommodate the underlying formulas. See Figure 2-32.

Figure 2-32 ◀
Displaying
formulas in a
worksheet

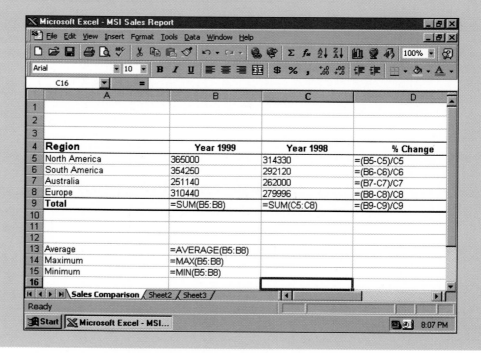

Now print the worksheet with the formulas displayed. Before printing the formulas you need to change the appropriate settings in the Page Setup dialog box to show the gridlines and the row/column headings, center the worksheet on the page, and fit the printout on a single page.

To adjust the print setups to display formulas:

1. Click **File** on the menu bar, and then click **Page Setup** to display the Page Setup dialog box.

2. Click the **Sheet** tab to view the sheet options. Click the **Row and Column Headings** check box to print the row numbers and column letters along with the worksheet results.

3. Click the **Gridlines** check box to place a check in it and select that option.

4. Click the **Page** tab, and then click the **Landscape** option button. This option prints the worksheet with the paper position so it is wider than it is tall.

5. Click the **Fit to** option button in the Scaling section of the Page tab. This option reduces the worksheet when you print it, so it fits on the specific number of pages in the Fit to check box. The default is 1.

6. Click the **Print Preview** button to open the Print Preview window.

7. Click the **Print** button. See Figure 2-33.

Figure 2-33 ◀
Printout of
worksheet
formulas

	A	B	C	D	E
1					
2					
3					
4	Region	Year 1999	Year 1998	% Change	% of 1999 Sales
5	North America	365000	314330	=(B5-C5)/C5	=B5/$B$9
6	South America	354250	292120	=(B6-C6)/C6	=B6/$B$9
7	Australia	251140	262000	=(B7-C7)/C7	=B7/$B$9
8	Europe	310440	279996	=(B8-C8)/C8	=B8/$B$9
9	Total	=SUM(B5:B8)	=SUM(C5:C8)	=(B9-C9)/C9	
10					
11					
12					
13	Average	=AVERAGE(B5:B8)			
14	Maximum	=MAX(B5:B8)			
15	Minimum	=MIN(B5:B8)			

After printing the formulas, return the worksheet so it displays the worksheet values.

To turn off the formulas display:

1. Click **Tools** on the menu bar, and then click **Options** to open the Options dialog box.

2. Click the **View** tab if necessary, and then click **Formulas** to remove the check mark next to that option to deselect it.

3. Click the **OK** button to return to the worksheet. The formulas are no longer displayed.

4. Close the workbook and exit Excel.

Quick Check

1. To move a range of cells, you must _____ the range first.

2. A _____ is text that is printed in the top margin of every worksheet page.

3. _____ is a command that lets you change your worksheet's appearance by selecting a collection of predesigned worksheet formats.

4. Describe how to insert a row or a column.

5. To reverse your most recent action, which button should you click?
   a. [icon]
   b. [icon]
   c. [icon]

6. Describe how you use the pointing method to create a formula.

7. To display formulas instead of values in your worksheet, you choose what command?

8. If your worksheet has too many columns to fit on one printed page, you should try _____ orientation.

You have planned, built, formatted, and documented Sally's sales comparison worksheet. It is ready for her to present to the regional sales managers at their next meeting.

Tutorial Assignments

After Sally meets with the regional sales managers for MSI, she decides it would be a good idea to provide the managers with their own copy of the sales comparison worksheet, so they can update the report with next year's sales data, and also modify it to use for their own sales tracking purposes. Before passing it on to them, she wants to provide more documentation, and add some additional information that the managers thought would be useful to them. Complete the following for Sally:

1. Start Windows and Excel, if necessary. Insert your Student Disk into the appropriate disk drive. Make sure the Excel and Book1 windows are maximized.

2. Open the workbook MSI1 in the TAssign folder for Tutorial 2 on your Student Disk.

3. Save your workbook as MSI Sales Report 2 in the TAssign folder for Tutorial 2 on your Student Disk.

4. Make Sheet2 the active sheet. Use Sheet2 to include information about the workbook. Insert the information in Figure 2-34 into Sheet2. Increase the width of column A as necessary.

Figure 2-34 ◀

Cell	Text Entry
A1	Motorcycle Specialties Incorporated
A3	Created By:
A4	Date created:
A6	Purpose:
B3	enter your name
B4	enter today's date
B6	Sales report comparing sales by region for 1999 with 1998

5. Change the name of the worksheet from Sheet2 to Title Sheet.

6. Print the Title Sheet sheet.

7. Make Sales Comparison the active sheet.

8. Open the Office Assistant and enter the search phrase "Insert a column" to obtain instruction on inserting a new column into a worksheet. Insert a new column between columns C and D.

9. In cell D4 enter the heading "Change."

10. In cell D5 enter the formula to calculate the change in sales for North America from 1998 to 1999. (*Hint*: Check that the figure in cell D5 is 50670.)

11. Copy the formula in D5 to the other regions and total (D6 through D9) using the fill handle.

12. Calculate summary statistics for 1998. In cell C13 display the average sales, in cell C14 display the maximum, and in cell C15 display the minimum.

13. Save the workbook.

14. Print the sales comparison worksheet.

15. a. Use the Office Assistant to learn how to attach comments to a cell. List the steps.
    b. Insert the following comment into cell F4: "Divide 1999 sales in each region by total sales in 1999."

16. Open the MSI3 workbook and save it as MSI Report 4.
    a. Use the AutoSum button to compute the totals for 1998 and 1999. Print the worksheet. Are the results correct?
    b. Replace the values in the range B5:C8 with "1". Print the worksheet. Are the results correct? Why do you think this problem occurred?
    c. Use the pointing method to correct the formula. Print the worksheet.

17. a. Use the Office Assistant to learn how to use row and column headers in your formulas to create formulas (enter the search phrase "labels as formulas").
    b. Open the MSI5 workbook and save it as MSI Report 6.
    c. In cell D5, calculate the change in sales in North America from 1998 to 1999 using the labels in columns B and C.
    d. Copy the formula in D5 to the other regions and total (D6 through D9) using the fill handle.
    e. Print the worksheet.
    f. Print the formulas.
    g. Save the worksheet.

18. Open the MSI7 workbook and save it as MSI Report 8.
    a. Activate the Sales Comparison sheet and select the range A1:E9. Copy the selected range to the Clipboard. Activate Sheet2 and paste the selected range to the corresponding cells in Sheet2. Apply the Classic 1 AutoFormat to this range. Print Sheet2.
    b. Insert a new sheet using the Worksheet command from the Insert menu. Return to the Sales Comparison sheet and copy the range A1:E9 to the corresponding cells in the new sheet. Apply the 3D Effects 2 AutoFormat to this range. Print this sheet.
    c. Use the Delete Sheet command from the Edit menu to delete the Title Sheet sheet.
    d. Move the Sales Comparison sheet so it is the third sheet in the workbook.
    e. Save the workbook.

Case Problems

1. Magazine Circulation Report You are a research analyst in the marketing department of a large magazine publisher. You have been assigned the task of compiling circulation data on the company's competition. Circulation statistics for the top six magazines appear in Figure 2-35.

Figure 2-35 ◀

Magazine	Prior Year	Current Year
Better Homes & Gardens	8000	8002
Family Circle	5138	5108
Good Housekeeping	4975	5101
National Geographic	9925	9787
Reader's Digest	16300	16256
TV Guide	15337	14920

1. Open a new workbook and enter the data from Figure 2-35 in a worksheet.

2. Use the AutoSum button to compute total circulation for all six magazines listed for both the current year and the prior year.

3. Use the Paste Function dialog box to compute the average circulation for all six magazines for both the current and the prior year.

4. For each magazine, create and enter a formula to compute the increase/decrease in circulation compared to the prior year.

5. Use AutoFormat to improve the appearance of the worksheet. Use Classic 1 as the format.

6. Rename the sheet Total Circulation.

7. Use a sheet in the workbook to enter your name, the date created, and the purpose of this sheet. Rename the sheet Title Sheet.

8. Save the worksheet as Magazine in the Case folder for Tutorial 2.

9. Print both the worksheets.

2. Compiling Data on the U.S. Airline Industry The editor of *Aviation Week and Space Technology* has asked you to research the current status of the U.S. airline industry. You collect information on the revenue-miles and passenger-miles for each major U.S. airline (Figure 2-36).

Figure 2-36 ◄

Revenue-Miles and Passenger-Miles for Major U.S. Airlines

Airline	Revenue-Miles (in 1000s of miles)	Passenger-Miles (in 1000s of miles)
American	26851	2210871
Continental	9316	622543
Delta	21515	1862276
Northwest	20803	1924288
US Air	9855	1542800
Trans World	16228	1188124
United	35175	3673152

You want to calculate the following summary information to use in the article:

- total revenue-miles for the U.S. airline industry
- total passenger-miles for the U.S. airline industry
- each airline's share of the total revenue-miles
- each airline's share of the total passenger-miles
- average revenue-miles for U.S. airlines
- average passenger-miles for U.S. airlines

Complete these steps:

1. Open a new workbook and enter the labels and data from Figure 2-36.

2. In cell A2, insert a second line to the title that reads:

    Compiled by: *XXXX*

   where *XXXX* is your name.

3. Enter the formulas to compute the total and average revenue-miles and passenger-miles. Use the SUM and AVERAGE functions where appropriate. Remember to include row labels to describe each statistic.

4. Add a column to display each airline's share of the total revenue-miles. Remember to include a column heading. You decide the appropriate location for this data.

5. Add a column to display each airline's share of the total passenger-miles. Remember to include a column heading. You decide the appropriate location for this data.

6. Name the worksheet Mileage Data.

7. Save the worksheet as Airline in the Case folder for Tutorial 2.

8. Print the worksheet. Center the report, no gridlines, and place the date in the upper-right corner of the header.

9. Select an AutoFormat to improve the appearance of your output.

10. Save your workbook.

11. Print the worksheet, centered on the page, no gridlines or row and column headings.

12. Print the formulas for the worksheet. Include row and column headings in the output.

3. Fresh Air Sales Incentive Program Carl Stambaugh is assistant sales manager at Fresh Air Inc., a manufacturer of outdoor and expedition clothing. Fresh Air sales representatives contact retail chains and individual retail outlets to sell the Fresh Air line.

This year, to spur sales, Carl has decided to run a sales incentive program for sales representatives. Each sales representative has been assigned a sales goal 15% higher than his or her total sales last year. All sales representatives who reach this new goal will be awarded an all-expenses-paid trip for two to Cozumel, Mexico.

Carl wants to track the results of the sales incentive program with an Excel worksheet. He has asked you to complete the worksheet by adding the formulas to compute:

■ actual sales in 1999 for each sales representative

■ sales goal in 1999 for each sales representative

■ percent of goal reached for each sales representative

He also wants a printout before he presents the worksheet at the next sales meeting. Complete these steps:

1. Open the workbook Fresh (in the Case folder for Tutorial 2 on your Student Disk). Maximize the worksheet window and save the workbook as Fresh Air Sales Incentives in the Case folder for Tutorial 2.

2. Complete the worksheet by adding the following formulas:
   a. 1999 Actual for each employee = Sum of Actual Sales for each quarter
   b. Goal 1999 for each employee = 1998 Sales X (1 + Goal % increase)
   c. % Goal reached for each employee = 1999 Actual / 1999 Goal

   (*Hint:* Use the Copy command. Review relative versus absolute references.)

3. Make the formatting changes using an AutoFormat to improve the appearance of the worksheet.

4. Print the worksheet, centered horizontally and vertically, and add an appropriate header. Add your name and date in the footer.

5. At the bottom of the worksheet (three rows after the last sales rep) add the average, maximum, and minimum statistics for columns C through I.

6. Save the workbook.

7. Print the worksheet.

8. As you scroll down the worksheet, the column headings no longer appear on the screen, making it difficult to know what each column represents. Use the Help system to look up "Freezing Panes." Implement this feature in your worksheet. Save the workbook. Explain the steps you take to freeze the panes.

4. Stock Portfolio for Juan Cortez Your close friend, Juan Cortez, works as an accountant at a local manufacturing company. While in college, with a double major in accounting and finance, Juan dabbled in the stock market and expressed an interest in becoming a financial planner and running his own firm. To that end, he has continued his professional studies in the evenings with the aim of becoming a certified financial planner. He has already begun to provide financial planning services to a few clients. Because of his hectic schedule as a full-time accountant, part-time student taking evening classes, and part-time financial planner with client visits on the weekends, Juan finds it difficult to keep up with the data processing needs for his clients. You have offered to assist him until he completes his studies for the certified financial planner exams.

Juan asks you to set up a worksheet to keep track of a stock portfolio for one of his clients.

Open a new workbook and do the following:

1. Figure 2-37 shows the data you will enter into the workbook. For each stock, you will enter the name, number of shares purchased, and purchase price. Periodically, you will also enter the current price of each stock so Juan can review the changes with his clients.

2. In addition to entering the data, you need to make the following calculations:
   a. Cost = No of shares * Purchase price
   b. Current Value = No of shares * Current price
   c. Gains/Losses = Current value minus Cost
   d. Totals for Cost, Current value, and Gains/Losses

   Enter the formulas to calculate the Cost, Current Value, Gains/Losses, and Totals.

3. Save the workbook as Portfolio in the Case folder for Tutorial 2.

Figure 2-37 ◀

Stock	No. Of Shares	Purchase Price	Cost	Current Price	Current Value	Gains/ Losses
PepsiC	100	50.25		52.50		
FordM	250	31		30		
AT&T	50	60		61.25		
IBM	100	90.25		95.75		
Xerox	50	138		134		
Total						

4. Print the worksheet. Center the worksheet horizontally and vertically. Add an appropriate header.

5. Apply an AutoFormat that improves the appearance of the worksheet. Save the worksheet as Portfolio 2. Print the worksheet.

6. Print the formulas for the worksheet. Include row and column headings in the printed output.

7. Clear the prices in the Current price column of the worksheet.

8. Enter the following prices:

   PepsiC   55
   FordM   29.5
   AT&T   64
   IBM   91.25
   Xerox   125

   Print the worksheet.

9. From the financial section of your newspaper, look up the current price of each stock (all these stocks are listed on the New York Stock Exchange). Enter these prices in the worksheet. Print the worksheet.

Developing a Professional-Looking Worksheet

Producing a Projected Sales Report for the Pronto Salsa Company

Excel

CASE

Pronto Salsa Company

Anne Castelar owns the Pronto Salsa Company, a successful business located in the heart of Tex-Mex country. She is working on a plan to add a new product, de Chili Guero Medium, to Pronto's gourmet salsa line.

Anne wants to take out a bank loan to purchase additional food-processing equipment to handle the production increase the new salsa requires. She has an appointment with her bank loan officer at 2:00 this afternoon. To prepare for the meeting, Anne creates a worksheet to show the projected sales of the new salsa and the expected effect on profits. Although the numbers and formulas are in place on the worksheet, Anne has no time to format the worksheet for the best impact. She planned to do that now, but an unexpected problem with today's produce shipment requires her to leave the office for a few hours. Anne asks you to complete the worksheet. She shows you a printout of the unformatted worksheet and explains that she wants the finished worksheet to look very professional—like those you see in business magazines. She also asks you to make sure that the worksheet emphasizes the profits expected from sales of the new salsa.

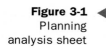

SESSION

3.1

In this session you will learn how to make your worksheets easier to understand through various formatting techniques. You will format values using Currency formats, Number formats, and Percentage formats. You will also change font styles and font sizes, and change the alignment of data within cells and across columns. As you perform all these tasks, you'll find the Format Painter button an extremely useful tool.

Opening the Workbook

After Anne leaves, you develop the worksheet plan in Figure 3-1 and the worksheet format plan in Figure 3-2.

Figure 3-1 ◀
Planning
analysis sheet

Planning Analysis For Projected Sales Report

My Goal
To format the worksheet so it produces a professional-looking printout

What results do I want to see?
The profits that are expected from sales of the new salsa product

What information do I need?
The unformatted worksheet

What calculations will I perform?
None; formulas have already been entered

Figure 3-2 ◀
Format plan

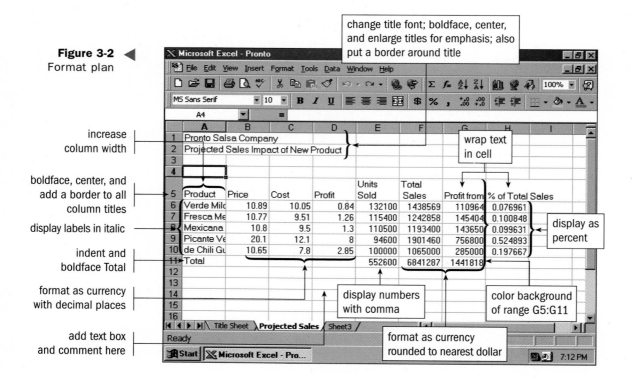

Anne has already entered all the formulas, numbers, and labels. Your main task is to format this information so it is easy to read and understand, and appears professional. This can be accomplished on two levels—by formatting the detailed data in the worksheet and by enhancing the appearance of the worksheet as a whole.

On the data level, you decide that the numbers should be formatted according to their use. For example, the product prices need to appear as dollar values. Secondly, the column and row labels need to fit within their cells. Also, the labels need to stand out more. To enhance the worksheet as a whole, you need to structure it so that related information is visually grouped together using lines and borders. Anne also wants certain areas of the worksheet that contain key information to stand out, and color may be a useful tool for this.

With all that needs to be done before Anne's 2:00 meeting, you decide that the best place to begin is with formatting the data within the worksheet. Once that is done, you will work to improve the worksheet's overall organization and appearance.

Now that the planning is done, you are ready to start Excel and open the workbook of unformatted data that Anne created.

To start Excel and organize your desktop:

1. Start Excel as usual.

2. Make sure your Student Disk is in the appropriate disk drive.

3. Make sure the Microsoft Excel and Book1 windows are maximized.

Now you need to open Anne's file and begin formatting the worksheet. Anne stored the workbook as Pronto, but before you begin to change the workbook, save it using the filename Pronto Salsa Company. This way, the original workbook, Pronto, remains unchanged in case you want to work through this tutorial again.

To open the Pronto workbook and save the workbook as Pronto Salsa Company:

1. Click the **Open** button 📧 on the Standard toolbar to display the Open dialog box.

2. Open the **Pronto** workbook in the Tutorial.03 folder on your Student Disk.

3. Click **File** on the menu bar, and then click **Save As** to display the Save As dialog box.

4. In the File name text box, change the filename to **Pronto Salsa Company**.

5. Click the **Save** button to save the workbook under the new filename. The new filename, Pronto Salsa Company, appears in the title bar.

   TROUBLE? If you see the message "Replace existing file?" click the Yes button to replace the old version of Pronto Salsa Company with your new version.

6. Click the **Projected Sales** sheet tab. See Figure 3-3.

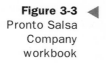

Figure 3-3 ◀
Pronto Salsa
Company
workbook

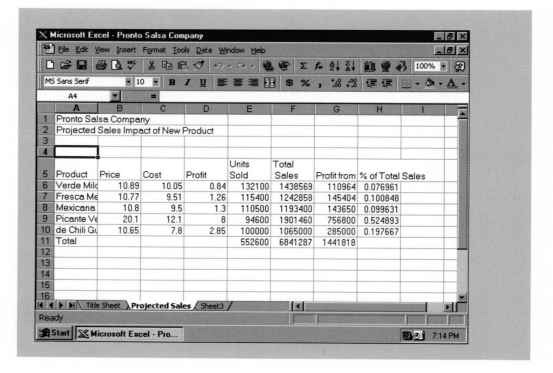

Studying the worksheet, you notice that the salsa names do not fit in column A. It is easy to widen column A, but if you do, some of the worksheet will scroll off the screen. Other formatting tasks are easier if you can see the entire worksheet, so you decide to do these tasks first.

Formatting Worksheet Data

Formatting is the process of changing the appearance of the data in worksheet cells. Formatting can make your worksheets easier to understand, and draw attention to important points.

In the previous tutorial you used AutoFormat to improve the appearance of your worksheet. AutoFormat applies a predefined format to your entire workbook. AutoFormat is easy to use, but its predefined format might not suit every worksheet. If you decide to customize a workbook's format, you can use the extensive Excel formatting options. When you select your own formats, you can format an individual cell or a range of cells.

Formatting changes only the appearance of the worksheet; it does not change the text or numbers stored in the cells. For example, if you format the number .123653 using a Percentage format that displays only one decimal place, the number appears in the worksheet as 12.4%; however, the original number, .123653, remains stored in the cell. When you enter data into cells, Excel applies an automatic format, referred to as the General format. The **General format** aligns numbers at the right side of the cell, uses a minus sign for negative values, and displays numbers without trailing zeros to the right of the decimal point. You can change the General format by using AutoFormat, the Format menu, the Shortcut menu, or toolbar buttons.

There are many ways to access the Excel formatting options. The Format menu provides access to all formatting commands. See Figure 3-4.

Figure 3-4 ◄
Format menu

The Shortcut menu provides quick access to the Format dialog box. See Figure 3-5. To display the Shortcut menu, make sure the pointer is positioned within the range you have selected to format, and then click the right mouse button.

Figure 3-5 ◄
Shortcut menu

The Formatting toolbar contains formatting buttons, including the style and alignment buttons, and the Font Style and Font Size boxes. See Figure 3-6.

Figure 3-6 ◄
Formatting
toolbar buttons

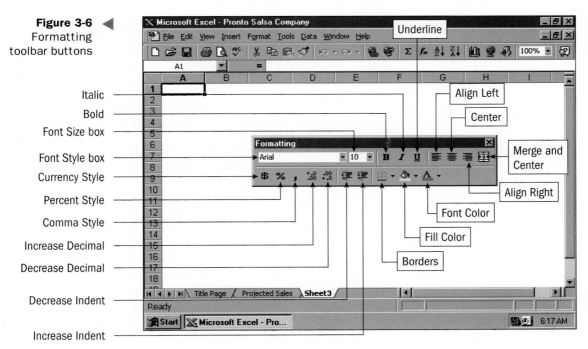

Most experienced Excel users develop a preference for which menu or buttons they use to access the Excel formatting options; however, most beginners find it easy to remember that all formatting options are available from the Format menu.

Looking at Anne's worksheet, you decide to change the appearance of the data first.

Changing the Appearance of Numbers

When the data in the worksheet appears as numbers, you want each number to appear in a style appropriate for what it is representing. The Excel default General format is often not the most appropriate style. For example, dollar values may require the dollar symbol ($) and thousand markers, and these can be applied to numerical data simply by changing the data's format. You can also standardize the number of decimal places displayed in a cell through formatting. Excel has a variety of predefined number formats. Figure 3-7 describes some of the most commonly used formats.

Figure 3-7 ◀
Commonly used
number formats

Category	Display Option
General	Excel default Number format; displays numbers without dollar signs, commas, or trailing decimal places
Number	Sets decimal places, negative number display, and comma separator
Currency	Sets decimal places and negative number display, and inserts dollar signs and comma separators
Accounting	Specialized monetary value format used to align dollar signs, decimal places, and comma separators
Date	Sets date or date and time display
Percentage	Inserts percent sign to the right of a number with a set number of decimal places

To change the number formatting, you select the cell or range of cells to be reformatted, and then use the Format Cells command or the Formatting toolbar button to apply a different format.

Currency Formats

In reviewing Anne's unformatted worksheet, you recognize that there are several columns of data that reflect currency. You decide to apply the Currency format to the Cost, Price, and Profit columns.

You have several options when formatting values as currency. You need to decide the number of decimal places you want displayed; whether or not you want to see the dollar sign; and how you want negative numbers to look. Keep in mind that if you want the currency symbols and decimal places to line up within a column, you should choose the Accounting format, rather than the Currency format.

In the Pronto Salsa Company worksheet, you want to apply the Currency format to the values in columns B, C, and D. The numbers will be formatted to include a dollar sign with two decimal places. You also decide to display negative numbers in the worksheet in parentheses.

To format columns B, C, and D using the Currency format:

1. Select the range **B6:D10**.

2. Click **Format** on the menu bar, and then click **Cells** to display the Format Cells dialog box.

3. If necessary, click the **Number** tab. See Figure 3-8.

Figure 3-8 ◀
Number tab of
Format Cells
dialog box

4. Click **Currency** in the Category list box. The Number tab changes to display the Currency formatting options, as shown in Figure 3-9. Notice that a sample of the selected format appears near the top of the dialog box. As you make further selections, the sample automatically changes to reflect your choices.

Figure 3-9 ◀
Selecting a
Currency
format

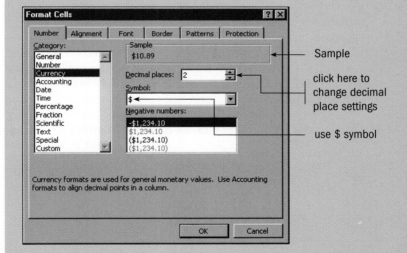

Notice that 2 decimal places is the default setting. A dollar sign ($) appears in the Symbol list box, indicating that the dollar sign will be displayed. If you are using a different currency, click the down arrow in the Symbol list box to select the currency symbol you want to display. Given the current options selected, you only need to select a format for negative numbers.

5. Click the third option **($1,234.10)** in the Negative numbers list box.

6. Click the **OK** button to format the selected range.

7. Click any cell to deselect the range and view the new formatting. See Figure 3-10.

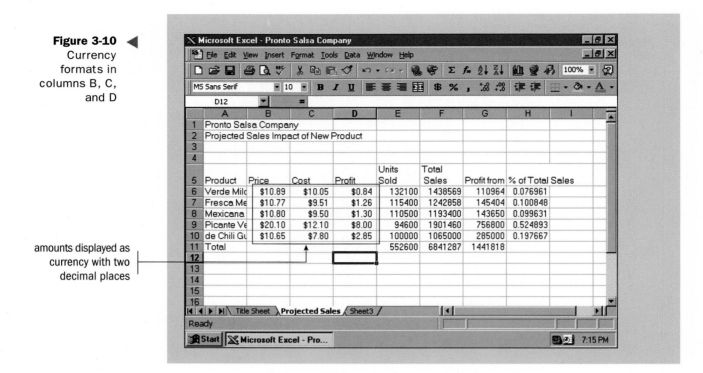

Figure 3-10 ◄
Currency
formats in
columns B, C,
and D

amounts displayed as
currency with two
decimal places

When your worksheet has large dollar amounts, you might want to use a Currency format that does not display any decimal places. To do this you use the Decrease Decimal button on the Formatting toolbar, or change the decimal places setting in the Format Cells dialog box. Currency values displayed with no decimal places are rounded to the nearest dollar: $15,612.56 becomes $15,613; $16,507.49 becomes $16,507; and so on.

You decide to format the Total Sales column as currency rounded to the nearest dollar.

To format cells F6 through F11 as currency rounded to the nearest dollar:

1. Select the range **F6:F11**.

2. Click **Format** on the menu bar, and then click **Cells** to display the Format Cells dialog box.

3. If necessary, click the **Number** tab.

4. Click **Currency** in the Category list box.

5. Click the **Decimal places** spin box down arrow twice to change the setting to 0 decimal places. Notice that the sample format changes to reflect the new settings.

6. Click the **OK** button to apply the format. Notice that Excel automatically increased the column width to display the formatted numbers.

7. Click any cell to deselect the range.

After formatting the Total Sales figures in column F, you realize you should have used the same format for the numbers in column G. To save time, you simply copy the formatting from column F to column G.

The Format Painter Button

The Format Painter button on the Standard toolbar lets you copy formats quickly from one cell or range to another. You simply click a cell containing the formats you want to copy, click the Format Painter button, and then use the click-drag technique to select the range to which you want to apply the copied formats.

Excel

To copy the format from cell F6:

1. Click cell **F6** because it contains the format you want to copy.

2. Click the **Format Painter** button ⬚ on the Standard toolbar. As you move the pointer over the worksheet cells, notice that the pointer turns to ⬚.

3. Position ⬚ over cell G6, and then click and drag to select cells **G6:G11**. When you release the mouse button, the cells appear in the Currency format, rounded to the nearest dollar—the same format used in cells F6 through F11.

4. Click any cell to deselect the range and view the formatted Profit from Sales column. See Figure 3-11.

Figure 3-11 ◀
Worksheet
after Format
Painter used to
copy formats

number symbols
indicate column width
needs to increase

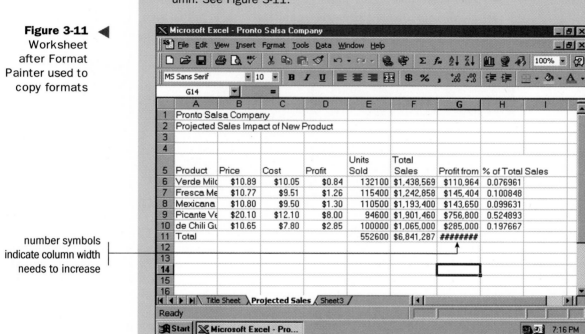

As you review the changes on the screen, you notice that cell G11 contains number symbols (######) instead of values. This is because the formatting change has caused the data to exceed the width of the cell.

Number Symbol (###) Replacement

If a number is too long to fit within a cell's boundaries, Excel displays a series of number symbols (###) in the cell. The number symbols indicate that the number of digits in the value exceeds the cell's width. The number or formula is still stored in the cell, but the current cell width is not large enough to display the value. To display the value, you just need to increase the column width. One way you can do this is to use the Shortcut menu.

To replace the number symbols by increasing the column width:

1. Position the pointer on the column heading for column G.

2. Right-click the mouse button to display the Shortcut menu.

3. Click **Column Width** to display the Column Width dialog box.

4. Type **9** in the Column Width box.

5. Click the **OK** button to view the total sales, $1,441,818.

6. Click any cell to view the formatted data.

Now the cells containing price, cost, profit, total sales, and profit from sales are formatted as currency. Next, you want to apply formats to the numbers in columns E and H so that they are easier to read.

Number Formats

Like Currency formats, the Excel Number formats offer many options. You can select Number formats to specify

- the number of decimal places displayed
- whether to display a comma to delimit thousands, millions, and billions
- whether to display negative numbers with a minus sign, parentheses, or red numerals

---

REFERENCE window	**FORMATTING NUMBERS**
	■ Select the cells you want the new format applied to.
	■ Click Format, click Cells, and then click the Numbers tab in the Format Cells dialog box.
	■ Select a format category from the Category list box.
	■ Select the desired options for the selected format.
	■ Click the OK button.

To access all Excel Number formats, you can use the Number tab in the Format Cells dialog box. You can also use the Comma Style button, the Increase Decimal button, and the Decrease Decimal button on the Formatting toolbar to select some Number formats.

Looking at your planning sheet and sketch, you can see that the numbers in column E need to be made easier to read by changing the format to include commas.

To format the contents in column E with a comma and no decimal places:

1. Select the range **E6:E11**.

2. Click the **Comma Style** button on the Formatting toolbar to apply the Comma Style. The default for the Comma Style is to display numbers with two places to the right of the decimal. Use the Decrease Decimal button on the Formatting toolbar to decrease the number of decimal places displayed in cells formatted with the Comma Style to zero.

3. Click the **Decrease Decimal** button on the Formatting toolbar twice to display the number with no decimal places.

4. Click any cell to deselect the range and view the formatted Units Sold column. See Figure 3-12.

Figure 3-12 ◀
Cells formatted
with Number
format

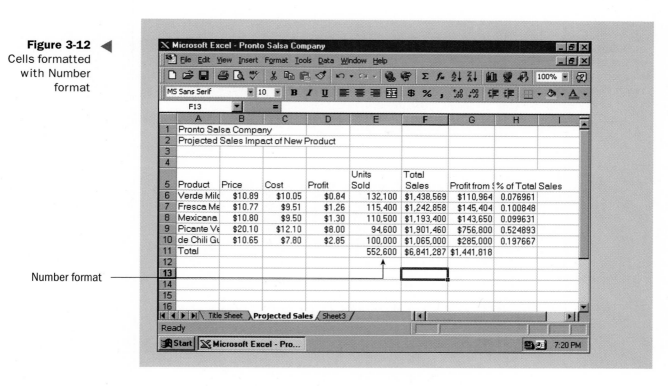

Number format ──────────

Looking at the numbers in column H, you realize that they are difficult to interpret and decide that you do not need to display so many decimal places. What are your options for displaying percentages?

Percentage Format

When formatting values as percentages, you need to select how many decimal places you want displayed. The Percentage format with no decimal places displays the number 0.18037 as 18%. The Percentage format with two decimal places displays the same number as 18.04%. If you want to use the Percentage format with two decimal places, you select this option using the Number tab in the Format Cells dialog box. You can also use the Percent Style button on the Formatting toolbar, and then click the Increase Decimal button twice to add two decimal places.

Your format sketch specifies a Percentage format with no decimal places for the values in column H. You could use the Number tab to choose this format. But it's faster to use the Percent Style button on the Formatting toolbar.

To format the values in column H as a percentage with no decimal places:

1. Select the range **H6:H10.**

2. Click the **Percent Style** button on the Formatting toolbar.

3. Click any cell to deselect the range and view the Percent Style. See Figure 3-13.

Figure 3-13 ◀
Percent of total
sales formatted
with Percent
Style

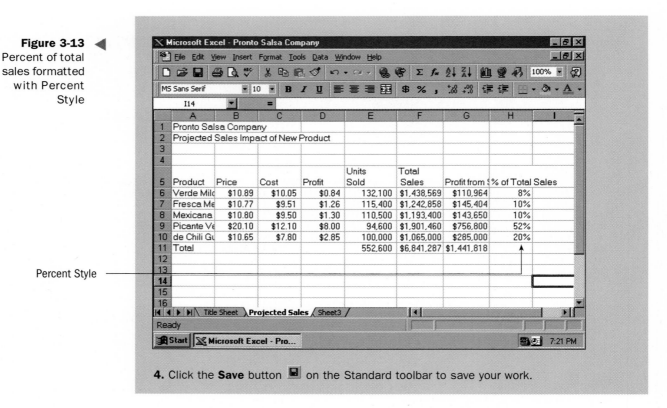

Percent Style

4. Click the **Save** button 🖫 on the Standard toolbar to save your work.

You review the worksheet. You have now formatted all the numbers in the worksheet appropriately. The next step in formatting Anne's worksheet is to improve the alignment of the data in the cells.

Aligning Cell Contents

The **alignment** of data in a cell is the position of the data relative to the right and left edges of the cell. Cell contents can be aligned on the left or right side of the cell, or centered in the cell. When you enter numbers and formulas, Excel automatically aligns them on the cell's right side. Excel automatically aligns text entries on the cell's left side. The default Excel alignment does not always create the most readable worksheet. Figure 3-14 shows a worksheet with the column titles left-aligned and the numbers in the columns right-aligned.

Figure 3-14 ◀
Poorly
formatted
worksheet

column titles
left-aligned

numbers
right-aligned

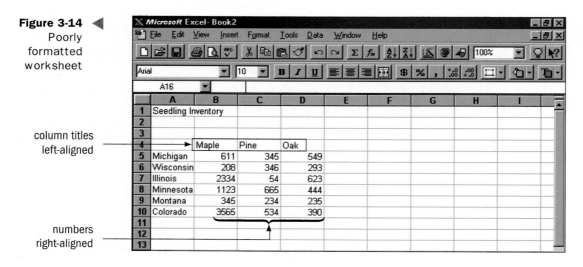

Notice how difficult it is to figure out which numbers go with each column title. Centering or right-aligning column titles would improve the readability of the worksheet in Figure 3-14. As a general rule, you should center column titles, format columns of numbers so that the decimal places are in line, and leave columns of text aligned on the left. You can change the alignment of cell data using the four alignment tools on the Formatting toolbar, or you can access additional alignment options by selecting the Alignment tab in the Format Cells dialog box.

To center the column titles:

1. Select the range **A5:H5**.

2. Click the **Center** button ≣ on the Formatting toolbar to center the cell contents.

3. Click any cell to deselect the range and view the centered titles. See Figure 3-15.

Figure 3-15 ◄
Worksheet with
centered
column titles

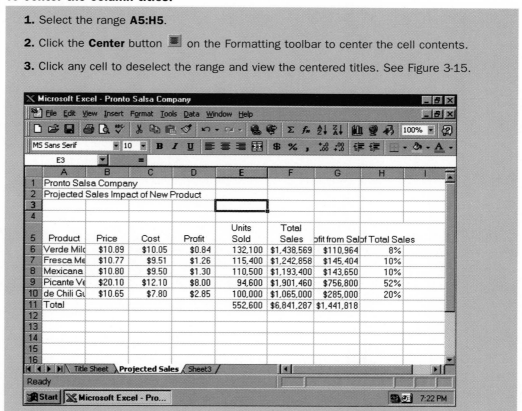

Notice that the column titles in columns G and H are not fully displayed. Although you could widen the column widths of these two columns to display the entire text, the Excel Wrap Text option enables you to display a label within a cell.

Wrapping Text in a Cell

As you know, if you enter a label that's too wide for the active cell, Excel extends the label past the cell border and into the adjacent cells—provided those cells are empty. If you select the Wrap Text option, Excel will display your label entirely within the active cell. To accommodate the label, the height of the row in which the cell is located is increased, and the text is "wrapped" onto the additional lines.

Now wrap the column titles in columns G and H.

To wrap text within a cell:

1. Select the range **G5:H5**.

2. Click **Format** on the menu bar, and then click **Cells** to display the Format Cells dialog box.

3. Click the **Alignment** tab. See Figure 3-16.

Figure 3-16 ◄
Alignment tab
of Format Cells
dialog box

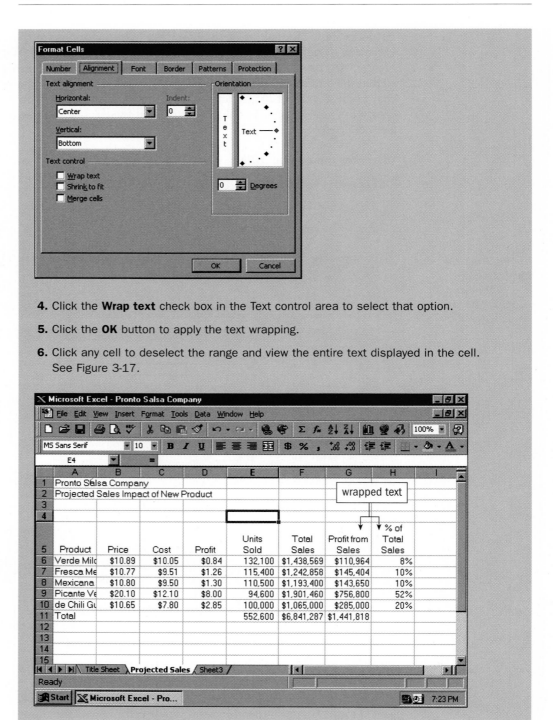

4. Click the **Wrap text** check box in the Text control area to select that option.

5. Click the **OK** button to apply the text wrapping.

6. Click any cell to deselect the range and view the entire text displayed in the cell. See Figure 3-17.

Figure 3-17 ◄
Wrapping text
in a cell

Now you will center the main worksheet titles.

Centering Text Across Columns

Sometimes you might want to center a cell's contents across more than one column. This is particularly useful for centering titles at the top of a worksheet. Now you will use the Center Across Selections option from the Format Cells dialog box to center the worksheet titles in cells A1 and A2 across columns A through H.

To center the worksheet titles across columns A through H:

1. Select the range **A1:H2**.

2. Click **Format**, click **Cells**, and if necessary click the **Alignment** tab in the Format Cells dialog box.

3. Click the arrow next to the Horizontal text alignment list box to display the horizontal text alignment options.

4. Click the **Center Across Selection** option to center the title lines across columns A through H.

5. Click the **OK** button.

6. Click any cell to deselect the range. See Figure 3-18.

Figure 3-18 ◀
Worksheet with titles centered across several columns

cell contents centered across columns A through H

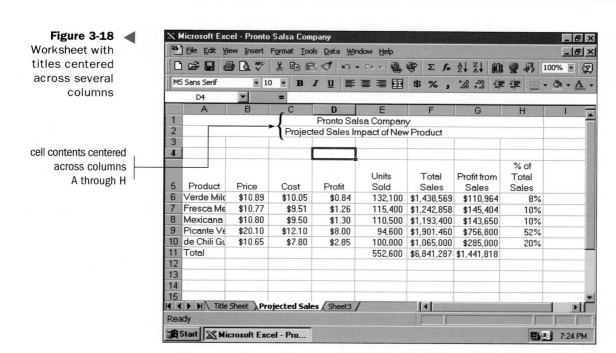

Indenting Text Within a Cell

When you type text in a cell it is left-aligned. You can indent text from the left edge by using the Increase Indent button on the Formatting toolbar or the Index spinner button in the Alignment tab of the Format Cells dialog box. You decide to indent the word "Total" to provide a visual cue of the change from detail to summary information.

To indent text within a cell:

1. Click cell **A11** to make it the active cell.

2. Click the **Increase Indent** button 🔲 on the Formatting toolbar to indent the word "Total" within the cell.

3. Click the **Save** button 🔲 on the Standard toolbar to save the worksheet.

You check your plan and confirm that you selected formats for all worksheet cells containing data, and that the data within the cells is aligned properly. The formatting of the worksheet contents is almost complete. Your next task is to improve the appearance of the labels by changing the font style of the title and the column headings.

You decide to use the Bold button on the Formatting toolbar to change some titles in the worksheet to boldface.

Changing the Font, Font Style, and Font Size

A **font** is a set of letters, numbers, punctuation marks, and symbols with a specific size and design. Figure 3-19 shows some examples. A font can have one or more of the following **font styles**: regular, italic, bold, and bold italic.

Figure 3-19 ◀
Selected fonts

Font	Regular Style	Italic Style	Bold Style	Bold Italic Style
Times	AaBbCc	*AaBbCc*	**AaBbCc**	***AaBbCc***
Courier	AaBbCc	*AaBbCc*	**AaBbCc**	***AaBbCc***
Garamond	AaBbCc	*AaBbCc*	**AaBbCc**	***AaBbCc***
Helvetica Condensed	AaBbCc	*AaBbCc*	**AaBbCc**	***AaBbCc***

Most fonts are available in many sizes, and you can also select font effects, such as strikeout, underline, and color. The Formatting toolbar provides tools for changing font style by applying boldface, italics, underline, and increasing or decreasing font size. To access other font effects, you can open the Format Cells dialog box from the Format menu.

REFERENCE window

CHANGING FONT, FONT STYLE, AND FONT SIZE

- Select the cells you want the new format to apply to.
- Click Format, click Cells, and then click the Font tab in the Format Cells dialog box.
- Select a typeface from the Font list box.
- Select a font style from the Font style list box.
- Select a type size from the Size list box.
- the OK button.
  or
- Select the cells you want the new format to apply to.
- Select the font, font size, and font style using the buttons on the Formatting toolbar.

You begin by formatting the word "Total" in cell A11 in boldface letters.

To apply the boldface font style:

1. If necessary, click cell **A11**.

2. Click the **Bold** button **B** on the Formatting toolbar to set the font style to boldface. Notice that when a style like bold is applied to a cell's content, the toolbar button appears depressed to indicate that the style is applied to the active cell.

You also want to display the column titles in boldface. To do this, first select the range you want to format, and then click the Bold button to apply the format.

To display the column titles in boldface:

1. Select the range **A5:H5**.

2. Click the **Bold** button 𝐁 on the Formatting toolbar to apply the boldface font style.

3. Click any cell to deselect the range.

Next, you decide to display the salsa products' names in italics.

To italicize the row labels:

1. Select the range **A6:A10**.

2. Click the **Italic** button 𝐼 on the Formatting toolbar to apply the italic font style.

3. Click any cell to deselect the range and view the formatting you have done so far. See Figure 3-20.

Figure 3-20 ◀
Bold and Italic
formats applied

bold

italic

text indented

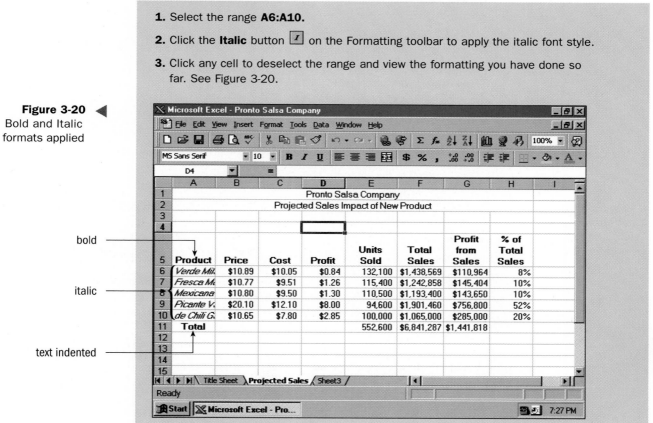

Next, you want to change the font and size of the worksheet titles for emphasis. You use the Font dialog box (instead of the toolbar) so you can preview your changes. Remember, although the worksheet titles appear to be in columns A through F, they are just spilling over from column A. To format the titles, you need to select only cells A1 and A2—the cells where the titles were originally entered.

To change the font and font size of the worksheet titles:

1. Select the range **A1:A2**.

2. Click **Format** on the menu bar, and then click **Cells** to display the Format Cells dialog box.

3. Click the **Font** tab. See Figure 3-21.

Figure 3-21
Font tab in
Format Cells
dialog box

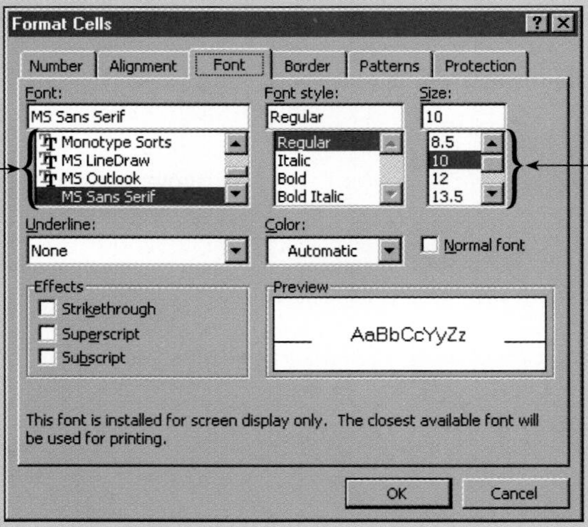

select new
font here

change font
size here

4. Use the Font box scroll bar to find the Times New Roman font. Click the **Times New Roman** font to select it.

5. Click **Bold** in the Font style list box.

6. Click **14** in the Size list box. A sample of the font appears in the Preview box.

7. Click the **OK** button to apply the new font and font size to the worksheet titles.

8. Click any cell to deselect the titles. See Figure 3-22.

Figure 3-22
Titles after new
font and font
size applied

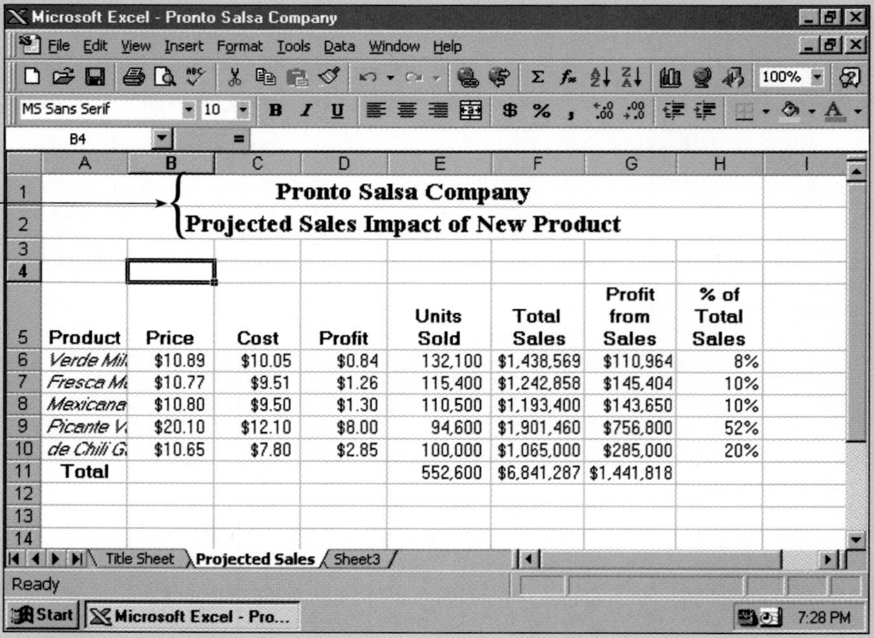

reformatted title

9. Click the **Save** button 🖫 on the Standard toolbar to save the worksheet.

You hope Anne will approve of the Times New Roman font—it looks like the font on the Pronto salsa jar labels.

Quick Check

1. If the number .128912 is in a cell, what will Excel display if you:
   a. Format the number using the Percentage format with no decimal places
   b. Format the number using the Currency format with 2 decimal places and the dollar sign

2. List three ways you can access formatting commands, options, and tools.

3. Explain why Excel might display 3,045.39 in a cell, but 3045.38672 in the formula bar.

4. List the options available on the Formatting toolbar for aligning data.

5. What are the general rules you should follow for aligning column headings, numbers, and text labels?

6. Explain two ways to completely display a label that currently is not entirely displayed.

7. The _____ copies formats quickly from one cell or range to another.

8. A series of ####### in a cell indicates _____.

Now that you have finished formatting the data in the worksheet, you need to enhance the worksheet's appearance and readability as a whole. You will do this in Session 3.2 by applying borders, colors, and a text box.

SESSION 3.2

In this session you learn how to enhance a worksheet's overall appearance by adding borders and color. You will use the Drawing toolbar to add a text box and graphic to the worksheet, and use landscape orientation to print the worksheet.

Adding and Removing Borders

A well-constructed worksheet is clearly divided into zones that visually group related information. Figure 3-23 shows the zones on your worksheet. Lines, called **borders**, can help to distinguish different zones of the worksheet and add visual interest.

Figure 3-23
Information zones

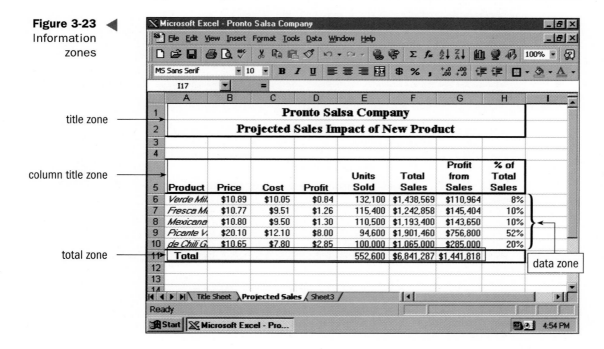

title zone
column title zone
total zone
data zone

You can create lines and borders using either the Borders button on the Formatting toolbar, or the Border tab in the Format Cells dialog box. You can place a border around a single cell or a group of cells using the Outline option. To create a horizontal line, you place a border at the top or bottom of a cell. To create a vertical line, you place a border on the right or left side of a cell.

The Border tab lets you choose from numerous border styles, including different line thicknesses, double lines, dashed lines, and colored lines. With the Borders button, your choice of border styles is more limited.

To remove a border from a cell or group of cells, you can use the Border tab in the Format Cells dialog box. To remove all borders from a selected range of cells, select the None button in the Presets area.

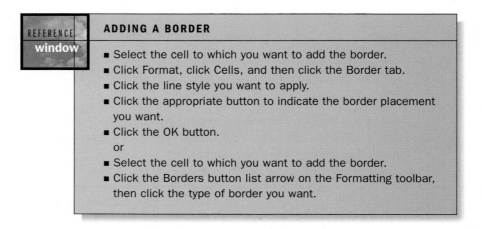

REFERENCE window

ADDING A BORDER

- Select the cell to which you want to add the border.
- Click Format, click Cells, and then click the Border tab.
- Click the line style you want to apply.
- Click the appropriate button to indicate the border placement you want.
- Click the OK button.
  or
- Select the cell to which you want to add the border.
- Click the Borders button list arrow on the Formatting toolbar, then click the type of border you want.

You decide that a thick line under all column titles will separate them from the data in the columns. To do this, you use the Borders button on the Formatting toolbar.

To underline column titles:

1. If you took a break after the last session, make sure Excel is running and the Projected Sales worksheet of the Pronto Salsa Company workbook is open.

2. Select the range **A5:H5**.

3. Click the **Borders** button list arrow ▣ on the Formatting toolbar. The Borders palette appears. See Figure 3-24.

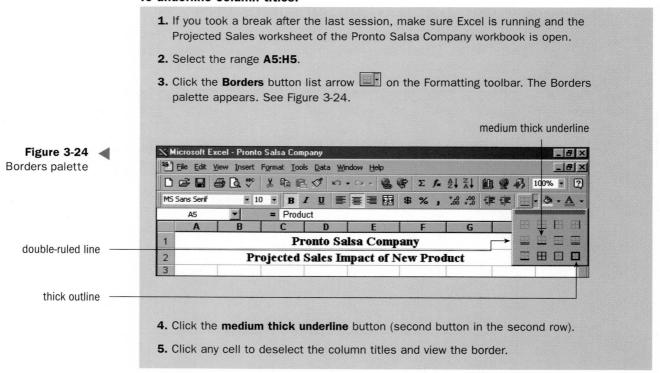

Figure 3-24 ◀
Borders palette

medium thick underline

double-ruled line

thick outline

4. Click the **medium thick underline** button (second button in the second row).

5. Click any cell to deselect the column titles and view the border.

You also want a line to separate the data from the totals in row 11, and a double-ruled line below the totals. This time you use the Border tab in the Format Cells dialog box to apply borders to cells.

To add a line separating the data and the totals and a double-ruled line below the totals:

1. Select the range **A11:H11**.

2. Click **Format** on the menu bar, click **Cells**, and then click the **Border** tab in the Format Cells dialog box. See Figure 3-25.

Figure 3-25 ◀
Border tab from
Format Cells
dialog box

applies selected line
style to top border

applies selected line
style to bottom border

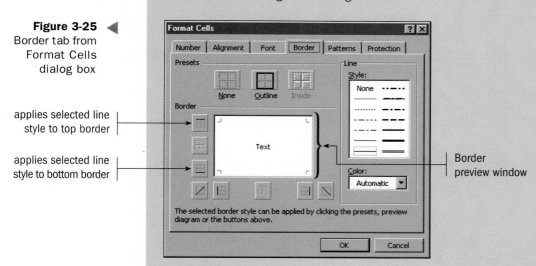

Border
preview window

3. Click the **medium thick line** in the Line Style box (third from the bottom in the second column).

4. Click the **top border** button. A thick line appears at the top of the Border preview window.

5. Click the **double-ruled line** in the Line Style box.

6. Click the **bottom border** button. A double-ruled line appears at the bottom of the Border preview window.

7. Click the **OK** button to apply the borders.

8. Click any cell to deselect the range and view the borders. See Figure 3-26.

Figure 3-26 ◀
Borders applied
to worksheet

medium thick line ———

double-ruled line ———

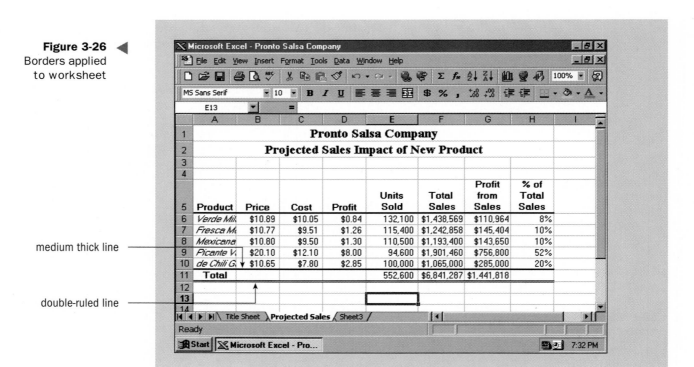

You consult your format sketch and see that you planned a border around the title zone to add a professional touch. You decide to add this border next.

To place an outline border around the title zone:

1. Select the range **A1:H2**.

2. Click the **Borders** button list arrow [icon] on the Formatting toolbar to display the Borders palette.

3. Click the **thick outline** button in the last row.

4. Click any cell to deselect the titles and view the border.

5. Click the **Save** button [icon] on the Standard toolbar to save the worksheet.

In addition to a border around the title zone, you want to add color to emphasize the Profit from Sales column.

Using Color for Emphasis

Patterns and colors provide visual interest, emphasize worksheet zones, or indicate data-entry areas. You should base the use of patterns or colors on the way you intend to use the worksheet. If you print the worksheet in color and distribute a hard copy of it, or if you plan to use a color projection device to display your worksheet on screen, you can take advantage of the Excel color formatting options. If you do not have a color printer, you can use patterns. It is difficult to predict how colors you see on your screen will be translated into gray shades on your printout.

REFERENCE window	APPLYING PATTERNS AND COLOR
	■ Select the cells you want to fill with a pattern or color. ■ Click Format, click Cells, and then click the Patterns tab in the Format Cells dialog box. ■ Select a pattern from the Pattern drop-down list. If you want the pattern to appear in a color, select a color from the Pattern palette, too. ■ If you want a colored background, select it from the Cell shading color palette. You can also select colors by clicking the Color button on the Formatting toolbar and then clicking the color you want.

You want your worksheet to look good when you print it in black and white on the office laser printer, but you also want it to look good on the screen when you show it to Anne. You decide that a yellow background will enable the Profit from Sales column to stand out and looks fairly good on the screen and the printout. You apply this format using the Patterns tab in the Format Cells dialog box.

To apply a color to the Profit from Sales column:

1. Select the range **G5:G11**.

2. Click **Format** on the menu bar, click **Cells**, and then click the **Patterns** tab in the Format Cells dialog box. See Figure 3-27.

Figure 3-27 ◀
Color palette in the Patterns tab of the Format Cells dialog box

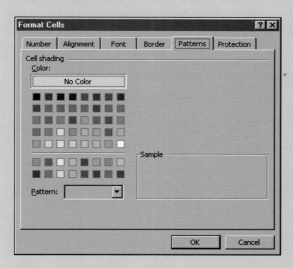

3. Click the **yellow square** in the fourth row (third square from the left) of the Cell shading Color palette.

4. Click the **OK** button to apply the color.

5. Click any cell to deselect the range and view the color in the Profit from Sales column. See Figure 3-28.

Figure 3-28 ◄
Worksheet
after applying
color to
a column

yellow background —

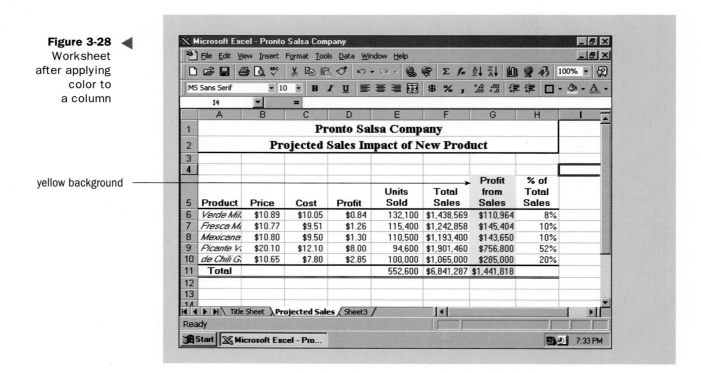

You delayed changing the width of column A because you knew that doing so would cause some columns to scroll off the screen, forcing you to scroll around the worksheet to format all the labels and values. Now that you have finished formatting labels and values, you can change the width of column A to best display the information in that column. To do this, you can use the Shortcut menu to change the column width.

To change the column width using the Shortcut menu:

1. Position the pointer on the column heading for column A.

2. Right-click the mouse button to display the Shortcut menu.

3. Click **Column Width** to display the Column Width dialog box.

4. Type **25** in the Column Width text box.

5. Click the **OK** button.

6. Click any cell to deselect the column and view the results of the column width change. See Figure 3-29.

Figure 3-29 ◀
Results of
changing
column width

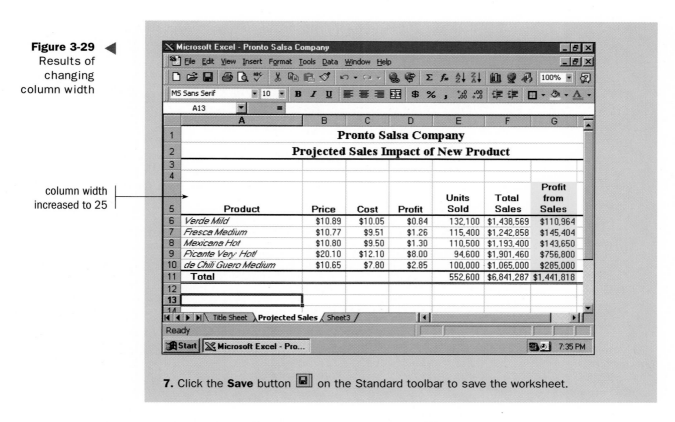

column width
increased to 25

7. Click the **Save** button 🖫 on the Standard toolbar to save the worksheet.

Adding Comments to the Worksheet

The Excel Text Box feature lets you display a comment in a worksheet. A comment is like an electronic Post-It note that you paste inside a rectangular text box in the worksheet.

To add a comment to your worksheet, you first create a text box, then you simply type the text in the box. You create a text box using the Text Box button, which is located on the Drawing toolbar.

Activating a Toolbar

Excel provides many toolbars. You have been using two: the Standard toolbar and the Formatting toolbar. Some of the other toolbars include the Chart toolbar, the Drawing toolbar, and the Visual Basic toolbar. To activate a toolbar, it's usually easiest to use the toolbar Shortcut menu, but to activate the Drawing toolbar you can simply click the Drawing button on the Standard toolbar. When you finish using a toolbar, you can easily remove it from the worksheet.

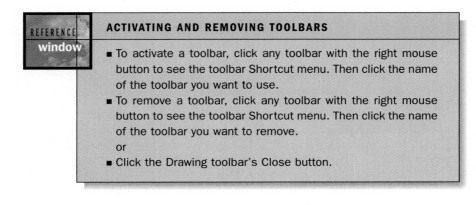

REFERENCE
window

ACTIVATING AND REMOVING TOOLBARS

- To activate a toolbar, click any toolbar with the right mouse button to see the toolbar Shortcut menu. Then click the name of the toolbar you want to use.
- To remove a toolbar, click any toolbar with the right mouse button to see the toolbar Shortcut menu. Then click the name of the toolbar you want to remove.
  or
- Click the Drawing toolbar's Close button.

You need the Drawing toolbar to accomplish your next formatting task. (If your Drawing toolbar is already displayed, skip the following step.)

To display the Drawing toolbar:

1. Click the **Drawing** button 🖾 on the Standard toolbar.

The toolbar might appear in any location in the worksheet window; this is called a **floating toolbar**. You don't want the toolbar obstructing your view of the worksheet, so drag it to the bottom of the worksheet window, to **anchor** it there. (If your toolbar is already anchored at the bottom of the worksheet window, or at the top, skip the next set of steps.)

To anchor the Drawing toolbar to the bottom of the worksheet window:

1. Position the pointer on the title bar of the Drawing toolbar.

2. Click and drag the toolbar to the bottom of the screen.

3. Release the mouse button to attach the Drawing toolbar to the bottom of the worksheet window. See Figure 3-30.

Figure 3-30 ◀
Drawing toolbar
attached
to bottom
of window

Drawing toolbar ————

Text Box tool ————

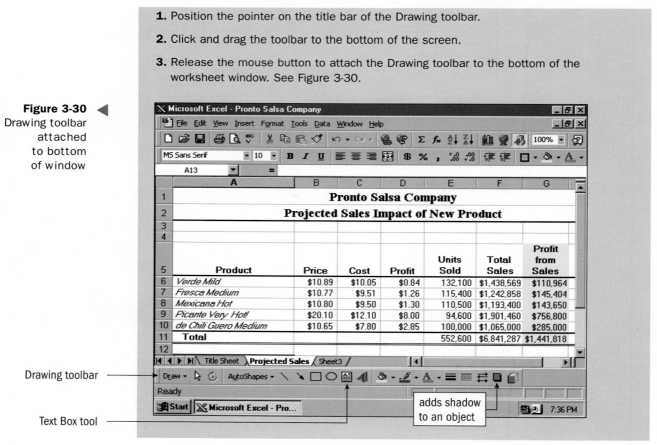

Now that the Drawing toolbar is where you want it, you proceed with your plan to add a comment to the worksheet.

Adding a Text Box

A **text box** is a block of text that sits in the worksheet. It is useful for adding comments to worksheets and charts. The text box is one example of a graphic object. With Excel you can create a variety of graphic objects, such as boxes, lines, circles, arrows, and text boxes. To move, modify, or delete an object, you first select it by moving the pointer over the object until the pointer changes to ⬚ , then clicking. Small square handles indicate that the object is selected. Use these handles to adjust the object's size, change its location, or delete it.

Excel

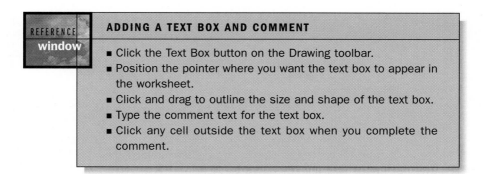

REFERENCE window

ADDING A TEXT BOX AND COMMENT

- Click the Text Box button on the Drawing toolbar.
- Position the pointer where you want the text box to appear in the worksheet.
- Click and drag to outline the size and shape of the text box.
- Type the comment text for the text box.
- Click any cell outside the text box when you complete the comment.

You want to draw attention to the new salsa product's low price and high profit margin. To do this, you plan to add a text box to the bottom of the worksheet that contains a comment about expected profits.

To add a comment in a text box:

1. Scroll the worksheet so you can see rows 7 through 21.

2. Click the **Text Box** button 📧 on the Drawing toolbar. As you move the pointer inside the worksheet area, the pointer changes to ↓. Position the crosshair of the pointer at the top of cell **A13** to mark the upper-left corner of the text box.

3. Click and drag + to cell **C18**, and then release the mouse button to mark the lower-right corner of the text box. See Figure 3-31.

You are ready to type the text into the text box.

Figure 3-31 ◀
Creating a text box

text box ⟶

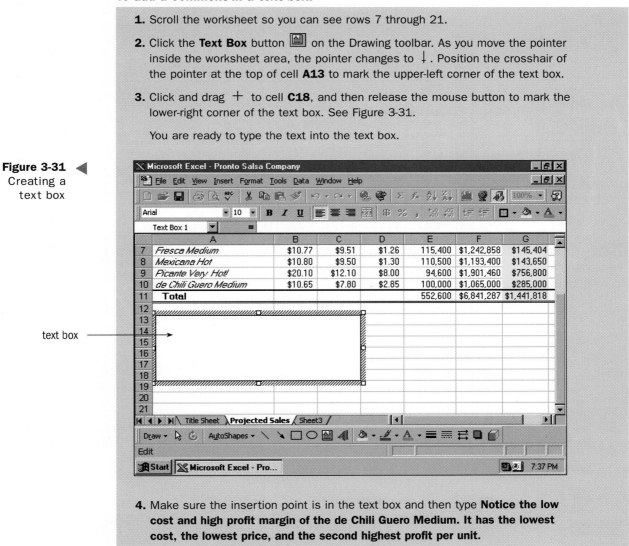

4. Make sure the insertion point is in the text box and then type **Notice the low cost and high profit margin of the de Chili Guero Medium. It has the lowest cost, the lowest price, and the second highest profit per unit.**

You want to use a different font style to emphasize the name of the new salsa product in the text box.

To italicize the name of the new salsa product:

1. Position I in the text box just before the word "de Chili."

2. Click and drag I to the end of the word "Medium", and then release the mouse button.

   TROUBLE? Don't worry if the text in your text box is not arranged exactly like the text in the figure. If the size of your text box differs slightly from the one in the figure, the lines of text might break differently.

3. Click the **Italic** button 🇮 on the Formatting toolbar.

4. Click any cell to deselect the product name, which now appears italicized. See Figure 3-32.

Figure 3-32 ◀
Italicizing text
in the text box

italicized text ——

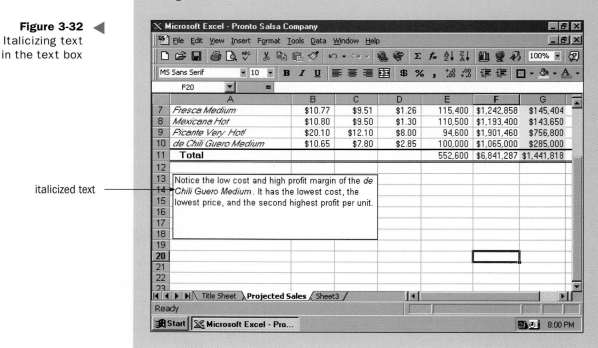

You decide to change the text box size so that there is no empty space at the bottom.

To change the text box size:

1. Click the **text box** to select it and display the patterned border with handles.

2. Position the pointer on the center handle at the bottom of the text box. The pointer changes to ↕.

3. Click and drag ↕ up to shorten the box, and then release the mouse button.

You want to change the text box a bit more by adding a drop shadow to it.

To add a shadow to the text box:

1. Make sure the text box is still selected. (Look for the patterned border and handles.)

2. Click the **Shadow** button 🔲 on the Drawing toolbar to display the gallery of Shadow options. See Figure 3-33.

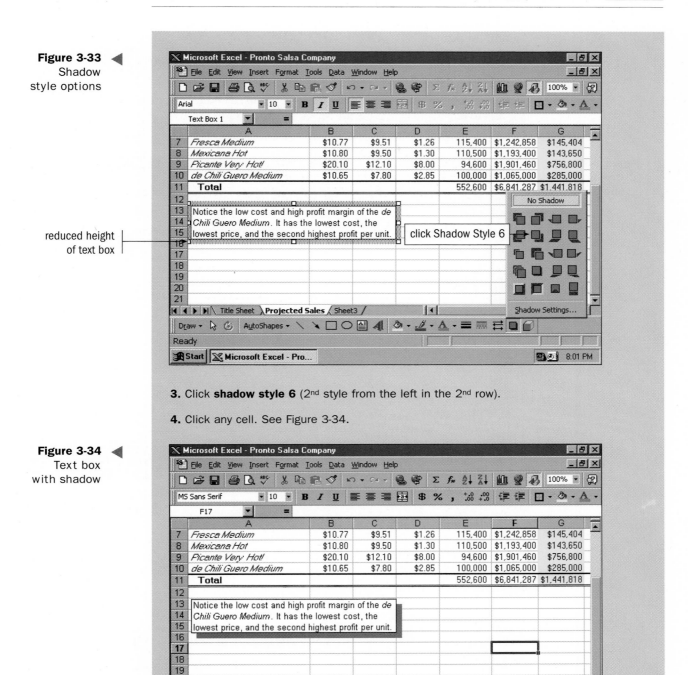

Figure 3-33
Shadow
style options

reduced height
of text box

3. Click **shadow style 6** (2nd style from the left in the 2nd row).

4. Click any cell. See Figure 3-34.

Figure 3-34
Text box
with shadow

Adding an Arrow

You decide to add an arrow pointing from the text box to the row with information on the new salsa.

To add an arrow:

1. Click the **Arrow** button ⬉ on the Drawing toolbar. As you move the mouse pointer inside the worksheet, the pointer changes to +.

2. Position + on the top edge of the text box in cell **B12**. To ensure a straight line, press and hold the **Shift** key as you drag + to cell **B10**, and then release the mouse button. See Figure 3-35.

Figure 3-35 ◀
Creating
an arrow

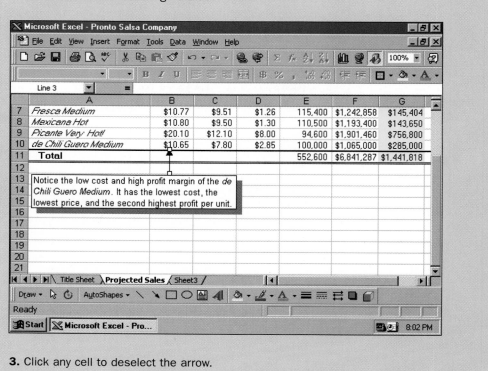

3. Click any cell to deselect the arrow.

You want the arrow to point to cell D10 instead of B10, so you need to reposition it. Like a text box, an arrow is an Excel object. To modify the arrow object, you must select it. When you do so, two small square handles appear on it. You can reposition either end of the arrow by dragging one of the handles.

To reposition the arrow:

1. Scroll the worksheet until row 5 appears as the first visible row in the window.

2. Move the pointer over the arrow object until the pointer changes to ✥.

3. Click the **arrow**. Handles appear at each end of the arrow.

4. Move the pointer to the top handle on the arrowhead until the pointer changes to ↘.

5. Click and drag + to cell **D10**, and then release the mouse button.

6. Click any cell to deselect the arrow object. See Figure 3-36.

Figure 3-36
Moving
the arrow

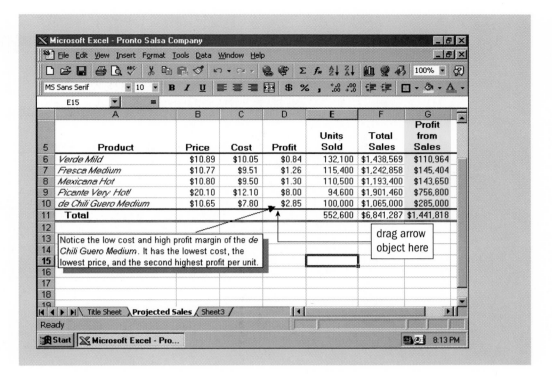

Now that the text box is finished, you can remove the Drawing toolbar from the worksheet.

To remove the Drawing toolbar:

1. Click the **Drawing** button ![] on the Standard toolbar. The Drawing toolbar is removed from the window, and the Drawing button ![] no longer appears depressed (selected).

2. Press **Ctrl + Home** to make cell A1 the active cell.

3. Click the **Save** button ![] on the Standard toolbar to save your work.

You have now made all the formatting changes and enhancements to Anne's worksheet. She has just returned to the office, and you show her the completed worksheet. She is very pleased with how professional the worksheet looks, but she thinks of one more way to improve the appearance of the worksheet. She asks you to remove the gridlines from the worksheet display.

Controlling the Display of Gridlines

Although normally the boundaries of each cell are outlined in black, Anne has decided that the appearance of your worksheet will be more effective if you remove the display of gridlines. To remove the gridline display, you deselect the Gridlines option in the View tab of the Options dialog box.

To remove the display of gridlines in the worksheet:

1. Click **Tools** on the menu bar, click **Options**, and if necessary, click the **View** tab in the Options dialog box.

2. Click the **Gridlines** check box in the Window option to remove the check and deselect the option.

3. Click the **OK** button to display the worksheet without gridlines. See Figure 3-37.

Figure 3-37 ◀
Worksheet
without
gridlines

no gridlines →

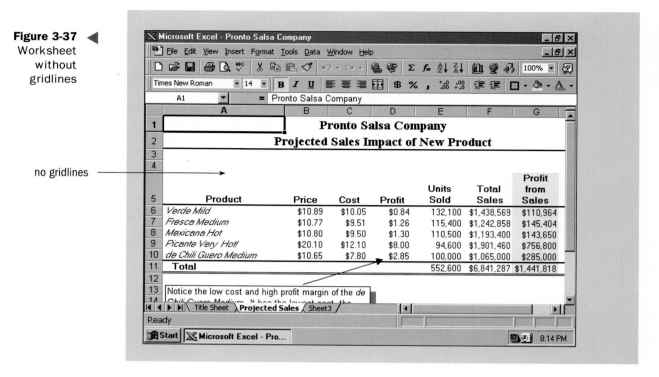

Now you are ready to print the worksheet.

Printing the Worksheet

Before you print a worksheet, you can use the Excel Print Preview window to see how it will look when printed. Recall that the Print Preview window shows you margins, page breaks, headers, and footers that are not always visible on the screen.

To preview the worksheet before you print it:

1. Click the **Print Preview** button 🔍 on the Standard toolbar to display the first worksheet page in the Print Preview window. See Figure 3-38.

Figure 3-38 ◀
Print Preview

active Next button
indicates more pages

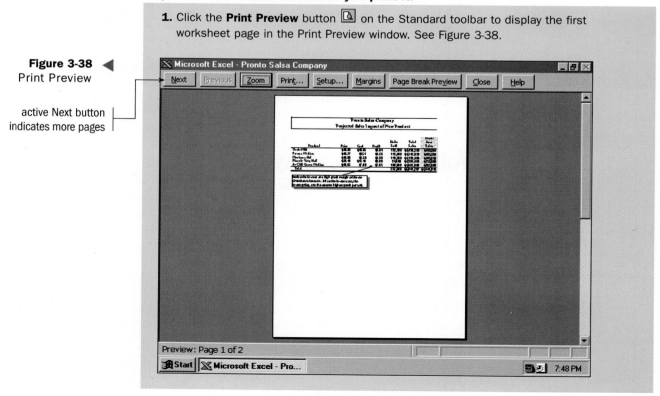

2. Click the **Next** button to preview the second worksheet page. Only one column appears on this page.

3. Click the **Previous** button to preview the first page again.

Looking at the Print Preview, you see that the worksheet is too wide to fit on a single page. You realize that if you print the worksheet lengthwise, however, it will fit on a single sheet of paper.

Portrait and Landscape Orientations

Excel provides two print orientations, portrait and landscape. **Portrait orientation** prints the worksheet with the paper positioned so it is taller than it is wide. **Landscape orientation** prints the worksheet with the paper positioned so it is wider than it is tall. Because some worksheets are wider than they are tall, landscape orientation is very useful.

You can specify print orientation using the Page Setup command on the File menu or using the Setup button in the Print Preview window. Use the landscape orientation for the Projected Sales worksheet.

To change the print orientation to landscape:

1. In the Print Preview window, click the **Setup** button to display the Page Setup dialog box. If necessary, click the **Page** tab.

2. Click the **Landscape** option button in the Orientation section to select this option.

3. Click the **OK** button to return to the Print Preview window. See Figure 3-39. Notice the Landscape orientation; that is, the page is wider than it is tall.

Figure 3-39 ◀
Landscape
orientation

Next button no
longer active

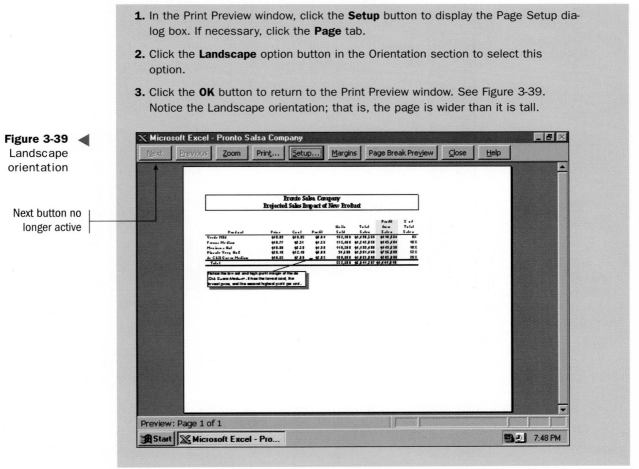

Before printing the worksheet, center the output on the page, and use the header/footer tab to document the printed worksheet.

To center the printed output:

1. Click the **Setup** button to display the Page Setup dialog box. Click the **Margins** tab.

2. Click the **Center on page Horizontally** check box to place a check in it and select that option.

Next, modify the printed footer by adding the date in the left section, and Anne's name in the right section.

To change the worksheet footer:

1. Click the **Header/Footer** tab, and then click the **Custom footer** to display the Footer dialog box.

2. In the Left section box, click the **Date** button 🖼 to display &Date in the Left section box.

3. Click the **Right section** box, then type **Prepared by Anne Castelar.**

4. Click the **OK** button to complete the footer and return to the Page Setup dialog box. See Figure 3-40.

Figure 3-40 ◀
Page Setup
after changing
the footer

from right section
of Custom Footer
dialog box

from left section
of Custom Footer
dialog box

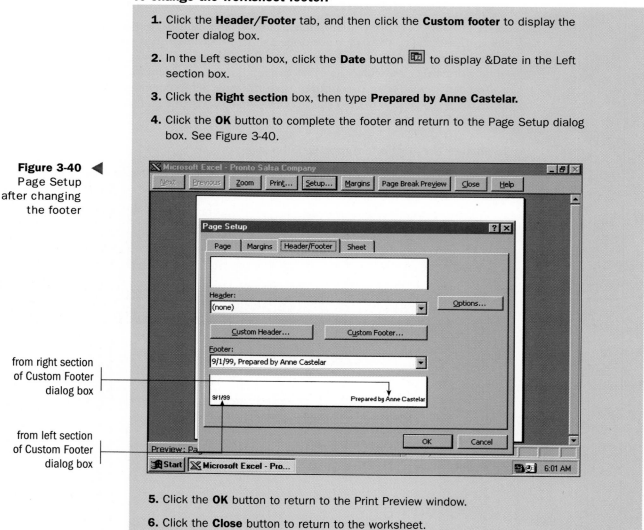

5. Click the **OK** button to return to the Print Preview window.

6. Click the **Close** button to return to the worksheet.

The worksheet is ready to print, but you always save your work before printing.

To save your page setup settings and print the worksheet:

1. Click the **Save** button 🖫 on the Standard toolbar.

2. Click the **Print** button 🖨 on the Standard toolbar. The worksheet prints. See Figure 3-41.

TROUBLE? If you see a message that indicates that you have a printer problem, click the Cancel button to cancel the printout. Check your printer to make sure it is turned on and is online; also make sure it has paper. Then go back and try Step 2 again. If you have no printer available, click the Cancel button.

Figure 3-41 ◄
Printed
worksheet

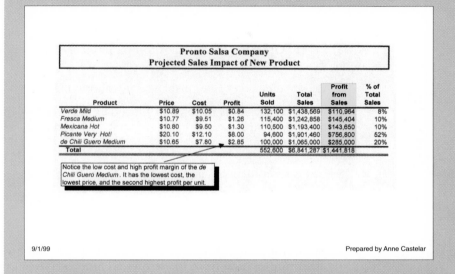

TROUBLE? If the title for the last two columns didn't print completely, you need to increase the row height for row 5. Select row 5. Drag the border below row 5 until the row height is 42.75 or greater (check the reference area of the formula bar). Click the Print button.

Now that you are done formatting the worksheet, close the workbook and exit Excel.

3. Close the workbook and exit Excel.

Quick Check

1. List two ways you can place a double-ruled line at the bottom of a range of cells.

2. Describe how to activate the Drawing toolbar.

3. To move, modify, or delete an object, you must _____ it first.

4. A _____ is a block of text that is placed in the worksheet.

5. _____ orientation prints the worksheet with the paper positioned so it is taller than it is wide.

6. If you are asked to remove the gridlines from the worksheet display, you will do what to the worksheet?

7. An arrow is an example of a _____.

You have completed formatting the Projected Sales worksheet and are ready to give it to Anne to check over before she presents it at her meeting with the bank loan officer.

Tutorial Assignments

After you show Anne the Projected Sales worksheet, the two of you discuss alternative ways to improve the worksheet's appearance. You decide to make some of these changes and give Anne the choice between two formatted worksheets. Do the following:

1. Start Windows and Excel, if necessary. Insert your Student Disk into the appropriate disk drive. Make sure the Excel and Book1 windows are maximized. Open the workbook Pronto2 in the TAssign folder for Tutorial 3 and save as Pronto3.

2. Center the percentages displayed in column H.

3. Make the contents of cells A10 through H10 bold to emphasize the new product. Make any necessary column-width adjustments.

4. Apply the color yellow to cells A1 through H2.

5. Right-align the label in cell A11.

6. Draw a vertical line to separate the product names from the rest of the data (the line begins in row 6 and continues to row 10).

7. Enter your name in the footer so that it appears on the printout of the worksheet. Make sure the footer also prints the date and filename. Remove any other information from the header and footer.

8. Make sure the Page Setup menu settings are set for centered horizontally and vertically, no row/column headings, and no cell gridlines.

9. Preview the printout to make sure it fits on one page. Save and print the worksheet.

10. Fill the text box with the color yellow so that it appears as a "yellow sticky note."

11. Change the color of the two-line title to red (the text, not the background color).

12. In step 4 you applied the color yellow to the cells A1 through H2. Remove the yellow color so that the background is the same as the rest of your worksheet.

13. If you answered steps 10, 11, or 12, save the worksheet as Pronto4.

14. a. Study the worksheet shown in Figure 3-42. Then open the Office Assistant and inquire about rotating and merging text in a cell.

Figure 3-42 ◀

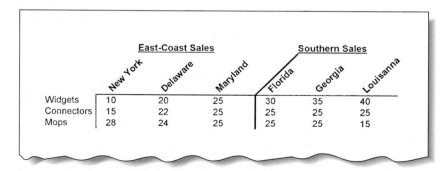

b. Open the workbook Explore3 and save it as Explore3 Solution.

c. Use the Rotate Text formatting feature to change the worksheet so it is similar to Figure 3-42. Make any other changes to make the worksheet as similar as possible to the one shown in Figure 3-42.

d. Save and print the worksheet.

Case Problems

1. Jenson Sports Wear Quarterly Sales Carl is the national sales manager for Jenson Sports Wear, a company that sells sports wear to major department stores. He has been using an Excel worksheet to track the results of a sales incentive program in which his sales staff has been participating. He has asked you to format the worksheet so it looks professional. He also wants a printout before he presents the worksheet at the next sales meeting. Complete these steps to format and print the worksheet:

1. Start Windows and Excel, if necessary. Insert your Student Disk into the appropriate disk drive. Make sure the Excel and Book1 windows are maximized. Open the workbook Running in the Case folder for Tutorial 3 on your Student Disk. Maximize the worksheet window and save the workbook as Running2 in the Case folder for Tutorial 3.

2. Complete the worksheet by doing the following:

   a. Calculating totals for each product
   b. Calculating quarterly subtotals for the Shoes and Shirts departments
   c. Calculating totals for each quarter and an overall total

3. Modify the worksheet so it is formatted as shown in Figure 3-43.

4. Use the Page Setup dialog box to center the output both horizontally and vertically.

5. Add the filename, your name, and the date in the footer section and delete the formatting code &[File] from the Center section of the header.

6. Save the worksheet.

7. Preview the worksheet and adjust the page setup as necessary for the printed results you want.

8. Print the worksheet.

 9. Place the comment "Leading product" in a text box. Remove the border from the text box. (*Hint*: Use the Format Object dialog box.) Draw an oval object around the comment. (*Hint*: Use the Oval tool on the Drawing toolbar.) Draw an arrow from the edge of the oval to the number in the worksheet representing the leading product. Save and print the worksheet. Your printout should fit on one page.

Figure 3-43 ◀

Jenson Sports Wear
Quarterly Sales by Product

Shoes	Qtr 1	Qtr 2	Qtr 3	Qtr 4	Total
Running	1,750	2,050	2,125	2,200	8,125
Tennis	2,450	2,000	2,200	2,400	9,050
Basketball	1,150	1,300	1,450	1,500	5,400
Subtotal	5,350	5,350	5,775	6,100	22,575

Shirts	Qtr 1	Qtr 2	Qtr 3	Qtr 4	Total
Tee	900	1,100	1,000	1,050	4,050
Polo	2,000	2,100	2,200	2,300	8,600
Sweat	250	250	275	300	1,075
Subtotal	3,150	3,450	3,475	3,650	13,725
Total	8,500	8,800	9,250	9,750	36,300

2. Age Group Changes in the U.S. Population Rick Stephanopolous works for the U.S. Census Bureau and has been asked by his manager to prepare a report on changes in the U.S. population. Part of his report focuses on age group changes in the population from 1970 through 1980. Rick has created a worksheet that contains information from the U.S. Census reports from these years, and he is ready to format it. Complete these steps to format the worksheet:

1. Start Windows and Excel, if necessary. Insert your Student Disk into the appropriate disk drive. Make sure the Excel and Book1 windows are maximized. Open the workbook Census in the Case folder for Tutorial 3, and then save the workbook as US Population in the Case folder for Tutorial 3.

2. Make the formatting changes shown in Figure 3-44, adjusting column widths as necessary.

3. Use the Page Setup dialog box to modify the header so that the Right section consists of your name, a space, the current date, and the filename. Delete the contents of the Center section of the header.

4. Save the workbook.

5. Preview and print the worksheet. Your printout should fit on one page.

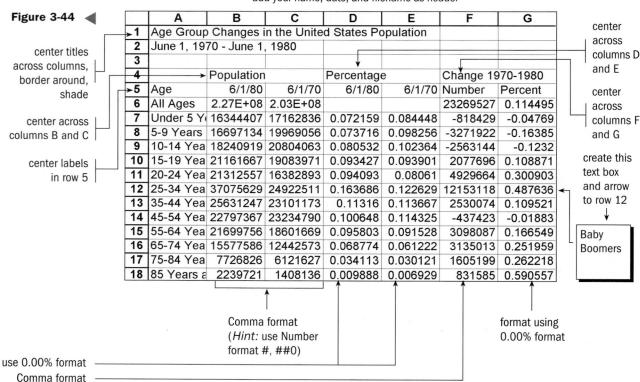

Figure 3-44

add your name, date, and filename as header

center titles across columns, border around, shade

center across columns B and C

center labels in row 5

center across columns D and E

center across columns F and G

create this text box and arrow to row 12

Baby Boomers

Comma format (*Hint:* use Number format #, ##0)

format using 0.00% format

use 0.00% format

Comma format

6. Change the border color of the text box from black to red. Change the color of the arrow to red. Save the workbook as US Population2. If you have access to a color printer, print the worksheet.

3. State Recycling Campaign Fred Birnbaum is working as an intern in the state's Waste Disposal Department. They have a pilot project on recycling for three counties (Seacoast, Metro, and Pioneer Valley). You have been asked to complete the worksheet and format it for presentation to their board of directors.

1. Start Windows and Excel, if necessary. Insert your Student Disk into the appropriate disk drive. Make sure the Excel and Book1 windows are maximized. Open the workbook Recycle in the Case folder on your Student Disk and save it as Recycle2.

2. Add two columns to calculate yearly totals for tons and a dollar value for each material in each county.

3. Insert three rows at the top of the worksheet to include:

   State Recycling Project
   Material Reclamation 1999
   <blank row>

4. Format the worksheet until you feel confident that the board of directors will be impressed with the appearance of the report.

5. Rename the worksheet Recycle Data.

6. Save the worksheet.

7. Print the worksheet centered horizontally and vertically on the page, using landscape orientation.

8. Remove the gridlines from the display. Use the Border tab of the Format Cells dialog box to place the recycle data, cells A6 to K20, in a grid. Save the workbook as Recycle3.

9. Change the magnification of the sheet so you can view the recycle data on the screen without having to scroll. (*Hint*: Use the Zoom control on the Standard toolbar.)

4. Cash Budgeting at Halpern's Appliances Fran Valence, the business manager for Halpern's Appliances, a small retail appliance store, is in the process of preparing a cash budget for January. The store has a loan that must be paid the first week in February. Fran wants to determine whether the business will have enough cash to make the loan payment to the bank.

Fran sketches the projected budget so that it will have the format shown in Figure 3-45.

Figure 3-45 ◄

Halpern's Appliances Cash Budget
Projected Cash Receipts and Disbursements
January 1, 1999
Cash balance, January 1, 1999   xxxx
Projected receipts during January:
       Cash sales during month   xxxx
       Collections from credit sales   xxxx
              Total cash receipts   xxxx
Projected disbursements during January:
       Payments for goods purchased   xxxx
       Salaries   xxxx
       Rent   xxxx
       Utilities   xxxx
              Total cash disbursements   xxxx
Cash balance, January 31, 1999   xxxx

Do the following:

1. Start Windows and Excel, if necessary. Insert your Student Disk into the appropriate disk drive. Make sure the Excel and Book1 windows are maximized.

2. Use only columns A, B, and C to create the worksheet sketched in Figure 3-45.

3. Use the following formulas in your worksheet:

   a. Total cash receipts = Cash sales during month + Collections from credit sales
   b. Total cash disbursements = Payments for goods purchased + Salaries + Rent + Utilities
   c. Cash Balance, January 31, 1999 = Cash Balance, January 1, 1999 + Total cash receipts - Total cash disbursements

Figure 3-46 ◀

Budget Item	Amount
Cash balance at beginning of month	32000
Cash sales during month	9000
Collections from credit sales	17500
Payments for goods purchased	15000
Salaries	4800
Rent	1500
Utilities	800

4. Enter the data in Figure 3-46 into the worksheet.

5. Use the formatting techniques you learned in this tutorial to create a professional-looking worksheet.

6. Save the worksheet as Budget in the Case folder for Tutorial 3 on your Student Disk.

7. Print the projected cash budget.

8. After printing the budget Fran remembers that starting in January the monthly rent increases by $150. Modify the projected cash budget accordingly. Print the revised cash budget.

9. Add a footnote to the title Halpern's Appliances Cash Budget title line so it appears as

Halpern's Appliances Cash Budget[1]
Add the line
[1]Prepared by <insert your name>

two rows after the last row. (*Hint*: Check out Superscript in the Font tab of the Format Cells dialog box.) Save the workbook as Budget1. Print the revised budget.

Creating Charts

Charting Sales Information for Cast Iron Concepts

OBJECTIVES

In this tutorial you will:

■ Identify the elements of an Excel chart

■ Learn which type of chart will represent your data most effectively

■ Create an embedded chart

■ Move and resize a chart

■ Edit a chart

■ Change the appearance of a chart

■ Place a chart in a chart sheet

■ Select nonadjacent ranges

■ Work with 3-D chart types

■ Add a picture to a chart

CASE

Cast Iron Concepts

The regional sales manager of Cast Iron Concepts (CIC), a distributor of cast iron stoves, Andrea Puest, is required to present information on how well the company's products are selling within her territory. Andrea sells in the New England region, which currently includes Massachusetts, Maine, and Vermont. She sells four major models—Star Windsor, Box Windsor, West Windsor, and Circle Windsor. The Circle Windsor is CIC's latest entry in the cast iron stove market. Due to production problems it was only available for sale the last four months of the year.

Andrea will make a presentation before the Director of Sales for CIC and the other regional managers next week when the entire group meets at corporate headquarters. Andrea gives you the basic data on sales in her territory for the past year. She must report on how well each model is moving in total for the region as well as within each state she covers. She knows that this kind of information is often understood best when it is presented in graphical form. So, she thinks she would like to show this information in a column chart as well as in a pie chart. You will help her prepare for her presentation by creating the charts she needs.

SESSION

4.1

In this session you will learn about the variety of Excel chart types and learn to iden-tify the elements of a chart. You will learn how to create a column chart and learn a number of techniques for improving your chart, including moving and resizing it, adding and editing chart text, enhancing a chart title by adding a border, and using color for emphasis.

Excel Charts

Andrea's sales data is saved in a workbook named Concepts. You will generate the charts from the data in this workbook.

To start Excel, open the Concepts workbook, and rename it:

1. Start Excel as usual.

2. Open the **Concepts** workbook in the Tutorial.04 folder on your Student Disk.

    The Title Sheet sheet appears as the first sheet in the workbook. You can type your name and the current date and then save the workbook under a new name.

3. Type your name and the current date in the appropriate cells in the Title Sheet sheet.

4. Save the workbook as **Cast Iron Concepts**. After you do so, the new filename appears in the title bar.

5. Click the **Sales Data** tab to move to that sheet. See Figure 4-1.

Figure 4-1 ◀
Sales Data
worksheet in
Cast Iron
Concepts
workbook

	A	B	C	D	E	F	G	H	
1		Windsor Stove Sales							
2		Massachusetts	Vermont	Maine	Totals				
3	Star	418,679	272,522	175,000	$ 866,201				
4	Box	337,102	227,150	130,808	$ 695,060				
5	West	239,312	143,400	191,500	$ 574,212				
6	Circle	46,325	10,390	24,615	$ 81,330				
7	Totals	$ 1,041,418	$653,462	$521,923	$2,216,803				
8									
9									

The worksheet shows the annual sales in dollars for each Windsor stove model by state. The total sales during the year for each model are in column E, and the total sales for each state appear in row 7.

It is easy to visually represent this kind of worksheet data. You might think of these graph-ical representations as "graphs"; however, in Excel they are referred to as **charts**. Figure 4-2 shows the 14 chart types within Excel that you can use to represent worksheet data.

Each chart type has two or more subtypes that provide various alternative charts for the selected chart type. For example, the Column chart type has seven subtypes, as shown in Figure 4-3. You can find more information on chart types and formats in the *Microsoft Excel User's Guide*, in the Excel Help facility, and in the Excel Chart Wizard.

Figure 4-2 ◄
Excel chart
types

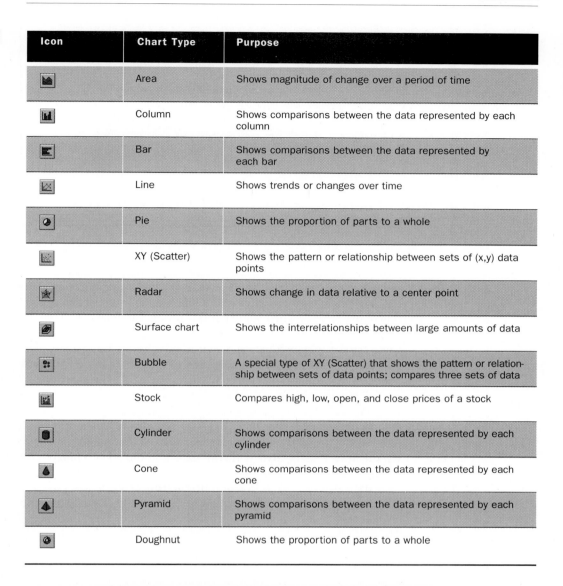

Icon	Chart Type	Purpose
	Area	Shows magnitude of change over a period of time
	Column	Shows comparisons between the data represented by each column
	Bar	Shows comparisons between the data represented by each bar
	Line	Shows trends or changes over time
	Pie	Shows the proportion of parts to a whole
	XY (Scatter)	Shows the pattern or relationship between sets of (x,y) data points
	Radar	Shows change in data relative to a center point
	Surface chart	Shows the interrelationships between large amounts of data
	Bubble	A special type of XY (Scatter) that shows the pattern or relationship between sets of data points; compares three sets of data
	Stock	Compares high, low, open, and close prices of a stock
	Cylinder	Shows comparisons between the data represented by each cylinder
	Cone	Shows comparisons between the data represented by each cone
	Pyramid	Shows comparisons between the data represented by each pyramid
	Doughnut	Shows the proportion of parts to a whole

Figure 4-3 ◄
Chart subtypes
for Column
chart type

Chart Subtype Icon	Description
	Clustered column
	Stacked column
	100% Stacked column
	Clustered column with 3-D visual effect
	Stacked column with 3-D visual effect
	100% Stacked column with 3-D visual effect
	3-D column

Figure 4-4 shows the elements of a typical Excel chart. Understanding the Excel chart terminology is particularly important so you can successfully construct and edit charts.

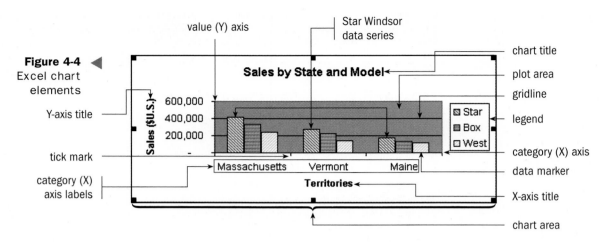

Figure 4-4 ◀
Excel chart
elements

The entire chart and all its elements are contained in the **chart area**. The **plot area** is the rectangular area defined by the axis, with the Y-axis forming the left side and the X-axis forming the base; in Figure 4-4 the plot area is in gray. The **axis** is a line that borders one side of the plot area, providing a frame for measurement or comparison in a chart. Data values are plotted along the **value** or **Y-axis**, which is typically vertical. Categories are plotted along the **category** or **X-axis**, which is usually horizontal. Each axis in a chart can have a title that identifies the scale or categories of the chart data; in Figure 4-4 the **X-axis title** is "Territories" and the **Y-axis title** is "Sales ($U.S.)." The **chart title** identifies the chart.

A **tick mark label** identifies the categories, values, or series in the chart. **Tick marks** are small lines that intersect an axis like divisions on a ruler, and represent the scale used for measuring values in the chart. Excel automatically generates this scale based on the values selected for the chart. **Gridlines** extend the tick marks on a chart axis to make it easier to see the values associated with the data markers. The **category names** or **category labels**, usually displayed on the X-axis, correspond to the labels you use for the worksheet data.

A **data point** is a single value originating from a worksheet cell. A **data marker** is a graphic representing a data point in a chart; depending on the type of chart, a data marker can be a bar, column, area, slice, or other symbol. For example, sales of the Star Windsor stove in Massachusetts (value 418,679 in cell B3 of the worksheet on your screen) is a data point. Each column in the chart in Figure 4-4 that shows the sales of Windsor stoves is a data marker. A **data series** is a group of related data points, such as the Star Windsor sales shown as red column markers in the chart.

When you have more than one data series, your chart will contain more than one set of data markers. For example, Figure 4-4 has three data series, one for each Windsor stove. When you show more than one data series in a chart, it is a good idea to use a **legend** to identify which data markers represent each data series.

Charts can be placed in the same worksheet as the data; this type of chart is called an **embedded chart**, and enables you to place the chart next to the data so it can easily be reviewed and printed on one page. You can also place a chart in a separate sheet, called a **chart sheet**, which contains only one chart and doesn't have rows and columns. In this tutorial you will create both an embedded chart and a chart that resides in a separate chart sheet.

Planning a Chart

Before you begin creating a chart you should plan it. Planning a chart includes the following steps:

- identifying the data points to be plotted, as well as the labels representing each data series and categories for the X-axis

- choosing an appropriate chart type

- sketching the chart, including data markers, axes, titles, labels, and legend

- deciding on the location of the chart within the workbook

Remember, Andrea wants to compare sales for each model in each state in which she sells. She thinks that a column chart is the best way to provide her audience with an accurate comparison of sales of Windsor stoves in her New England territory. She also needs to show how total sales in her territory are broken down by stove model. When showing parts of a whole, a pie chart is most effective, so she will create a pie chart to use in her presentation as well.

Andrea sketched the column chart and pie chart shown in Figure 4-5.

Figure 4-5
Sketch of
column and
pie charts

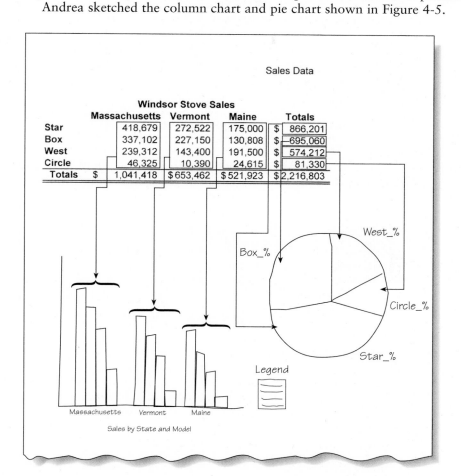

The sketches show roughly how Andrea wants the charts to look. It is difficult to envision exactly how a chart will look until you know how the data series looks when plotted; therefore, you don't need to incorporate every detail in the chart sketch. As you construct the charts, you can take advantage of Excel previewing capabilities to try different formatting options until your charts look just the way you want.

Create the column chart first. In looking at the sketch for this chart, note that Andrea wants to group the data by states; that is, the four models are shown for each of the three states. The names of the states in cells B2:D2 of the worksheet will be used as category labels. The names of each stove model, in cells A3:A6, will represent the legend text. The data series for the chart are in rows B3:D3, B4:D4, B5:D5, and B6:D6.

Creating a Column Chart

After studying Andrea's sketch for the column chart, you are ready to create it, using the Sales Data worksheet. When you create a chart, you first select the cells that contain the data you want to appear in the chart and then you click the Chart Wizard button on the Standard toolbar. The Chart Wizard consists of four dialog boxes that guide you through the steps required to create a chart. Figure 4-6 identifies the tasks you perform in each of the Chart Wizard dialog boxes.

Figure 4-6 ◄
Tasks
performed in
each step of
the Chart
Wizard

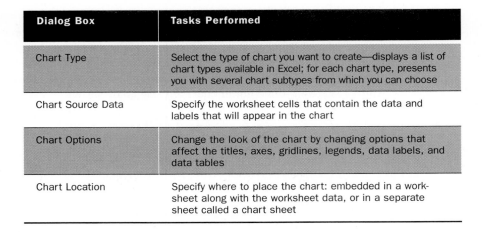

Dialog Box	Tasks Performed
Chart Type	Select the type of chart you want to create—displays a list of chart types available in Excel; for each chart type, presents you with several chart subtypes from which you can choose
Chart Source Data	Specify the worksheet cells that contain the data and labels that will appear in the chart
Chart Options	Change the look of the chart by changing options that affect the titles, axes, gridlines, legends, data labels, and data tables
Chart Location	Specify where to place the chart: embedded in a worksheet along with the worksheet data, or in a separate sheet called a chart sheet

You know that Andrea intends to create a handout of the worksheet and chart, so you want to embed the column chart in the same worksheet as the sales data, making it easier for her to create a one-page handout.

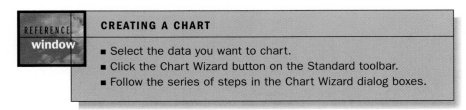

REFERENCE
window

CREATING A CHART

- Select the data you want to chart.
- Click the Chart Wizard button on the Standard toolbar.
- Follow the series of steps in the Chart Wizard dialog boxes.

Before activating the Chart Wizard you will need to select the cells containing the data the chart will display. If you want the column and row labels to appear in the chart, include the cells that contain them in your selection as well. For this chart, select the range A2 through D6, which includes the sales of each Windsor stove model in the three states as well as names of the stove models and states.

To create the column chart using the Chart Wizard:

1. Select cells **A2:D6**, making sure no cells are highlighted in column E or row 7.

   Now that you have selected the chart range, you use the Chart Wizard to create the column chart.

2. Click the **Chart Wizard** button 📊 on the Standard toolbar to display the Chart Wizard - Step 1 of 4 - Chart Type dialog box. See Figure 4-7.

   TROUBLE? If the Office Assistant appears on your screen, click the button next to the message "No, don't provide help now" to close the Office Assistant.

   This first dialog box asks you to select the type of chart you want to create. The Chart type list box displays each of the 14 chart types available in Excel. The default chart type is the Column chart type. To the right of the Chart type list box is a gallery of chart subtypes for the selected chart. Select the chart type you want to create.

Excel

Figure 4-7 ◄
Chart Wizard -
Step 1 of 4 -
Chart Type
dialog box

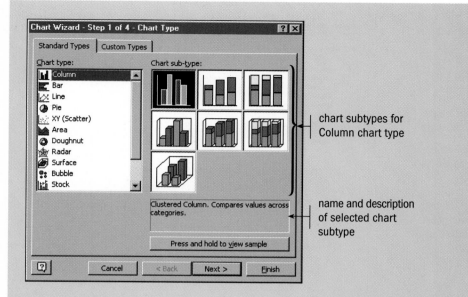

chart subtypes for
Column chart type

name and description
of selected chart
subtype

You want to create a column chart.

3. If necessary, click the **Column** chart type (the default) to select it. Seven Column chart subtypes are displayed. The Clustered Column chart subtype is the default subtype for the Column chart type. Click and hold the **Press and hold to view sample** button to display a preview of the Clustered Column chart subtype. See Figure 4-8. Release the mouse button.

To view any other Column chart subtype, select another subtype option and click the Press and hold to view sample button.

Figure 4-8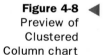
Preview of
Clustered
Column chart
type

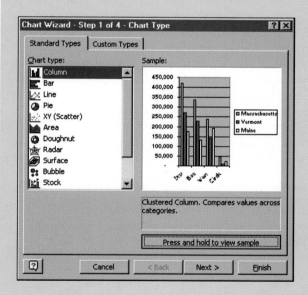

You decide to use the Clustered Column chart type, the default selection.

4. Click the **Next** button to display the Chart Wizard - Step 2 of 4 - Chart Source Data dialog box. See Figure 4-9. In this step you confirm or specify the worksheet cells that contain the data and labels to appear in the chart.

Figure 4-9 ◀
Chart Wizard -
Step 2 of 4 -
Chart Source
Data dialog box

current appearance
of chart

Andrea wants states
as category labels

Excel treating
columns in worksheet
as the data series

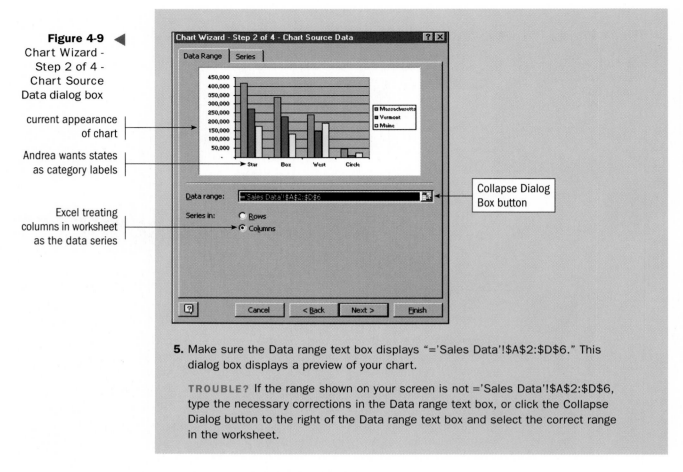

Collapse Dialog
Box button

5. Make sure the Data range text box displays "='Sales Data'!$A$2:$D$6." This
dialog box displays a preview of your chart.

TROUBLE? If the range shown on your screen is not ='Sales Data'!$A$2:$D$6,
type the necessary corrections in the Data range text box, or click the Collapse
Dialog button to the right of the Data range text box and select the correct range
in the worksheet.

In Step 2, you can also modify how the data series is organized—by rows or by
columns—using the **Series in** option. In Figure 4-9, the chart uses the columns in the
worksheet as the data series. To see how the chart would look if the rows in the worksheet were used as the data series, you can modify the settings in this dialog box.

Does the sample chart shown on your screen and in Figure 4-9 look like the sketch
Andrea prepared (Figure 4-5)? Not exactly. The problem is that the Chart Wizard
assumes that if the range to plot has more rows than columns (which is true in this case),
then the data in the columns (states) becomes the data series. Andrea wants the stove
models (rows) as the data series, so you need to make this change in the dialog box.

To change the data series and continue the steps in the Chart Wizard:

1. Click the **Rows** option button in the Series in area of the dialog box. The sample
chart now shows the stove models as the data series and the states as category
labels. See Figure 4-10.

Figure 4-10
Rows as data
series

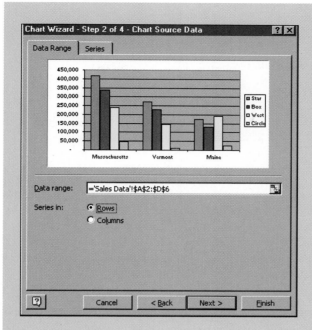

2. Click the **Next** button to display the Chart Wizard - Step 3 of 4 - Chart Options dialog box. See Figure 4-11. A preview area displays the current appearance of the chart. This tabbed dialog box enables you to change various chart options, such as titles, axes, gridlines, legends, data labels, and data tables. As you change these settings, check the preview chart in this dialog box to make sure you get the look you want.

Now add a title for the chart.

Figure 4-11
Chart Wizard -
Step 3 of 4 -
Chart Options
dialog box

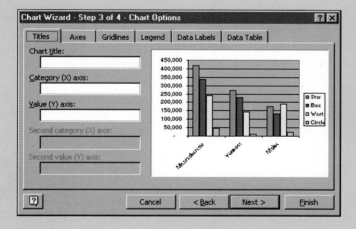

3. If necessary click the **Titles** tab, click the **Chart title** text box, and then type **Sales by State** for the chart title. Notice that the title appears in the preview area.

4. Click the **Next** button to display the Chart Wizard - Step 4 of 4 - Chart Location dialog box. See Figure 4-12. In this fourth dialog box you decide where to place the chart. You can place a chart in a worksheet, an embedded chart, or place it in its own chart sheet. You want to embed this chart in the Sales Data worksheet, which is the default option.

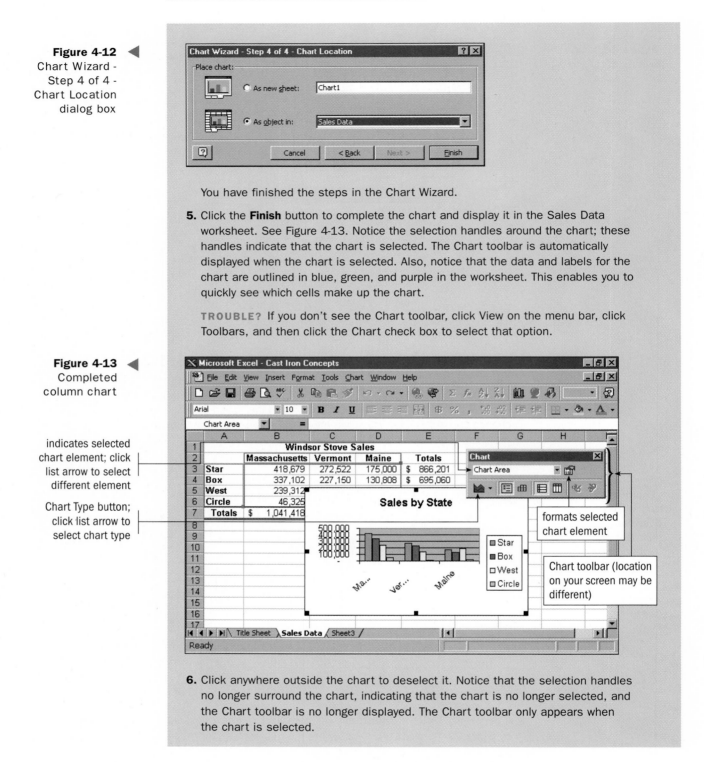

Figure 4-12 ◄
Chart Wizard -
Step 4 of 4 -
Chart Location
dialog box

You have finished the steps in the Chart Wizard.

5. Click the **Finish** button to complete the chart and display it in the Sales Data worksheet. See Figure 4-13. Notice the selection handles around the chart; these handles indicate that the chart is selected. The Chart toolbar is automatically displayed when the chart is selected. Also, notice that the data and labels for the chart are outlined in blue, green, and purple in the worksheet. This enables you to quickly see which cells make up the chart.

TROUBLE? If you don't see the Chart toolbar, click View on the menu bar, click Toolbars, and then click the Chart check box to select that option.

Figure 4-13 ◄
Completed
column chart

indicates selected
chart element; click
list arrow to select
different element

Chart Type button;
click list arrow to
select chart type

6. Click anywhere outside the chart to deselect it. Notice that the selection handles no longer surround the chart, indicating that the chart is no longer selected, and the Chart toolbar is no longer displayed. The Chart toolbar only appears when the chart is selected.

After reviewing the column chart, you think that the area outlined for the chart is too small to highlight the comparison between models. You also note that you need to move the chart so that it does not cover the worksheet data.

Excel

Moving and Resizing a Chart

When you use the Chart Wizard to create an embedded chart, Excel displays the chart in the worksheet. The size of the chart may not be large enough to accentuate relationships between data points or display the labels correctly. Since a chart is an object, you can move, resize, or copy it like any object in the Windows environment. However, before you can move, resize, or copy a chart, you must select, or **activate** it. You select a chart by clicking anywhere within the chart area. Small black squares, called **selection handles** or **sizing handles**, appear on the boundaries of the chart, indicating that it is selected. You will also notice that some of the items on the menu bar change to enable you to modify the chart instead of the worksheet.

You decide to move and resize the chart before showing it to Andrea.

To change the size and position of the chart:

1. Scroll the worksheet until row 8 appears as the first row in the window.

2. Click anywhere within the white area of the chart border to select the chart. Selection handles appear on the chart border. See Figure 4-14.

Figure 4-14 ◀
Selected chart

menu bar has changed because chart is activated

Name box indicates selected object

selection handles

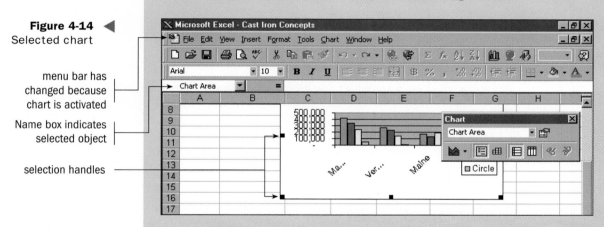

> **TROUBLE?** If the Name box does not display the name "Chart Area," click the Chart Objects list box arrow on the Chart toolbar to display the list of chart objects. Select Chart Area.

> **TROUBLE?** If the Chart toolbar is in the way, click and drag it to the bottom of the window to anchor it there.

3. Position the pointer anywhere on the chart border. The pointer changes to ↖. Click and hold down the mouse button as you drag the chart down and to the left until you see the upper-left corner of the dashed outline in column A of row 8. Release the mouse button to view the chart in its new position.

Now increase the width of the chart.

4. Position the pointer on the right center selection handle. When the pointer changes to ↔, hold down the mouse button and drag the selection handle to the right until the chart outline reaches the right edge of column G. Release the mouse button to view the resized chart. See Figure 4-15.

Figure 4-15
Chart after
being moved
and resized

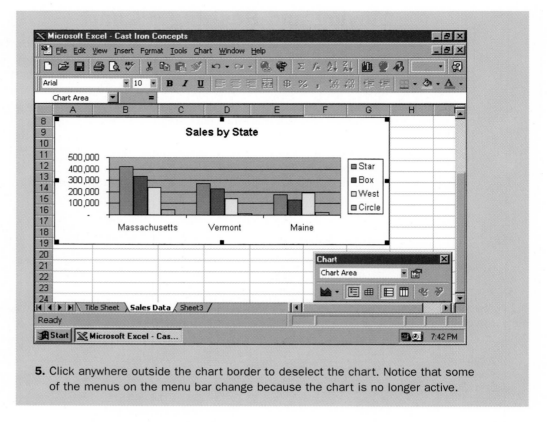

5. Click anywhere outside the chart border to deselect the chart. Notice that some of the menus on the menu bar change because the chart is no longer active.

The chart is repositioned and resized. You show Andrea the chart embedded in her Sales Data worksheet. As she reviews the chart, Andrea notices an error in the value entered for West Windsor stoves sold in Maine.

Updating a Chart

Every chart you create is linked to the worksheet data. As a result, if you change the data in a worksheet, Excel automatically updates the chart to reflect the new values. Andrea noticed that sales of West Windsor in Maine were entered incorrectly. She accidentally entered sales as 191,500, when the correct entry should have been 119,500. Correct this data entry error and observe how it changes the column chart.

To change the worksheet data and observe changes to the column chart:

1. Observe the height of the data marker for the West model in Maine (yellow data marker) in the column chart.

2. Scroll the worksheet until row 2 appears as the first row of the worksheet window.

3. Click cell **D5**, and then type **119500** and press the **Enter** key. See Figure 4-16. The total West sales (cell E5) and total sales for Maine (cell D7) automatically change. In addition, Excel automatically updates the chart to reflect the new source value. Now the data marker for the West Windsor sales in Maine is shorter.

Figure 4-16
Modified
column chart
after chart's
source data
changed

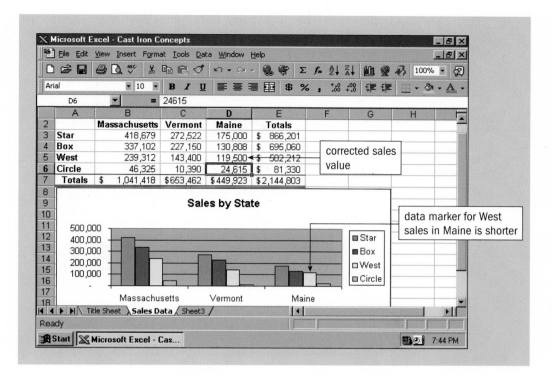

Now that the data for the West stove sales in Maine is corrected, you review the chart with Andrea for ways you can improve the presentation of the chart data.

Modifying an Excel Chart

You can make many modifications to a chart, including changing the type of chart, the text, the labels, the gridlines, and the titles. To make these modifications, you need to activate the chart. Selecting, or activating, a chart, as mentioned earlier, allows you to move and resize it. It also gives you access to the Chart commands on the menu bar and displays the Chart toolbar to use as you alter the chart.

After reviewing the column chart, Andrea believes that the Circle Windsor will distract the audience from the three products that were actually available during the entire period. Recall that the Circle Windsor was only on the market for four months and even then there were production problems. She wants to compare sales only for the three models sold during the entire year.

Revising the Chart Data Series

After you create a chart, you might discover that you specified the wrong data range, or you might decide that your chart should display different data series. Whatever your reason, you do not need to start over in order to revise the chart's data series.

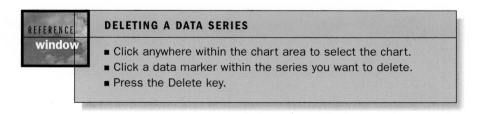

REFERENCE window

DELETING A DATA SERIES

- Click anywhere within the chart area to select the chart.
- Click a data marker within the series you want to delete.
- Press the Delete key.

Andrea asks you to remove the data series representing the Circle Windsor model from the column chart.

To delete the Circle Windsor data series from the column chart:

1. Click anywhere within the chart border to select the chart.

2. Click any data marker representing the Circle data series (any light blue data marker). Selection handles appear on each column of the Circle Windsor data series and a ScreenTip is displayed identifying the selected chart item. See Figure 4-17.

Figure 4-17 ◀
Chart with
Circle data
series selected

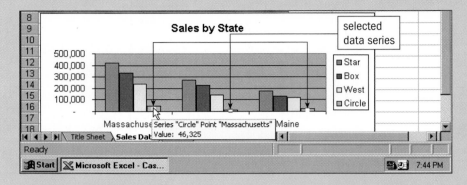

3. Press the **Delete** key. See Figure 4-18. Notice that the Circle Windsor data series is removed from the chart.

Figure 4-18 ◀
Column chart
after data
series removed

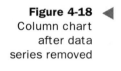

TROUBLE? If you deleted the wrong data series, click the Undo button and repeat Steps 2 and 3.

Andrea reviews her sketch and notices that the chart title is incomplete; the intended title was "Sales by State and Model." She asks you to make this change to the chart.

Editing Chart Text

Excel classifies the text in your charts in three categories: label text, attached text, and unattached text. **Label text** includes the category names, the tick mark labels, the X-axis labels, and the legend. Label text often derives from the cells in the worksheet; you usually specify it using the Chart Wizard.

Attached text includes the chart title, X-axis title, and Y-axis title. Although attached text appears in a predefined position, you can edit it, and move it using the click-drag technique.

Unattached text includes text boxes or comments that you type in the chart after it is created. You can position unattached text anywhere in the chart. To add unattached text to a chart, you use the Text Box tool on the Drawing toolbar.

As noted earlier, you need to change the chart title to "Sales by State and Model." To do this you must select the chart, select the chart title, and then add "and Model" to the title.

To revise the chart title:

1. If the chart is not selected, click the **chart** to select it.

2. Click the **chart title** object to select it. Notice that the object name Chart Title appears in the Name box and as a ScreenTip; also, selection handles surround the Chart Title object.

3. Position the pointer in the chart title text box at the end of the title and click to remove the selection handles from the Chart Title object. The pointer changes to an insertion point I.

   TROUBLE? If the insertion point is not at the end of the title, press the End key to move it to the end.

4. Press the **spacebar** and type **and Model**, and then click anywhere within the chart border to complete the change in the title and deselect it.

Checking Andrea's sketch, you notice that the Y-axis title was not included. To help clarify what the data values in the chart represent, you decide to add "Sales ($U.S.)" as a Y-axis title. You use the Chart Option command on the Chart menu to add this title.

To add the Y-axis title:

1. Make sure that the chart is still selected.

2. Click **Chart** on the menu bar, and then click **Chart Options** to display the Chart Options dialog box. If necessary, click the **Titles** tab.

3. Click the **Value (Y) axis** text box, and then type **Sales ($U.S.)**.

4. Click the **OK** button to close the Chart Options dialog box.

5. If necessary, scroll the worksheet so that the entire chart is displayed.

6. Click anywhere within the chart border to deselect the Y-axis title. See Figure 4-19.

Figure 4-19 ◀
Chart after title modified and value axis label inserted

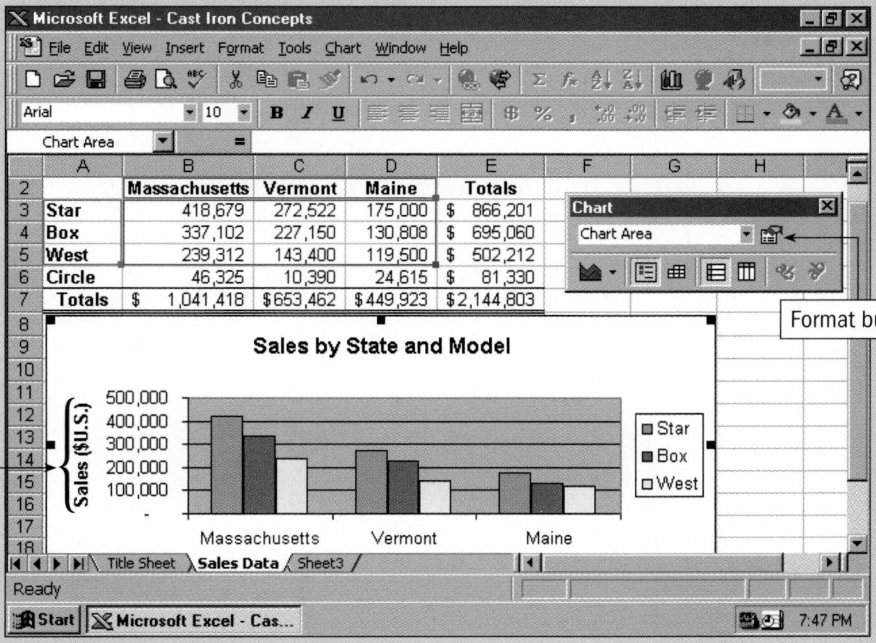

Now that the titles accurately describe the chart data, Andrea asks you to add data labels to show the exact values of the Star Windsor data series—CIC's leading model.

Adding Data Labels

A **data label** provides additional information about a data marker. Depending on the type of chart, data labels can show values, names of data series (or categories), or percentages. You can apply a label to a single data point, an entire data series, or all data markers in a chart.

REFERENCE window	**ADDING A DATA LABEL**
	■ Select the chart. ■ Select a single data marker, entire data series, or all data markers in the chart. ■ Click Chart, click Chart Options, and then click Data Labels. ■ Click the option for the type of label you want to add. ■ Click OK.

In this case, Andrea wants to add data labels to the Star model data series.

To apply data labels to a data series:

1. If the column chart is not selected, click anywhere within the chart border to select it.

2. Click any **Star Windsor data marker** (blue data marker) within the chart. Selection handles appear on all columns in the Star Windsor data series.

   To format any chart element, you can use the Format button on the Chart toolbar. The Format button's ToolTip name and function change depending on what chart element is selected for formatting. The list box that appears to the left of the Format button on the toolbar also displays the name of the currently selected chart element. In this case, the Star Windsor data series marker is selected, so the Format button on the Chart toolbar appears as the Format Data Series button, and when selected, opens the Format Data Series dialog box.

3. Click the **Format Data Series** button 🖻 on the Chart toolbar to display the Format Data Series dialog box. Click the **Data Labels** tab if necessary. See Figure 4-20.

Figure 4-20 ◄
Active Data
Labels tab in
Format Data
Series dialog
box

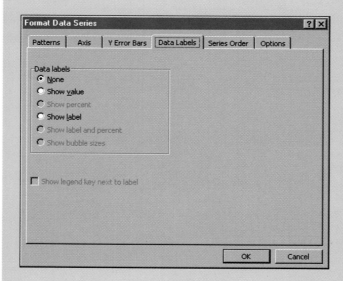

4. Click the **Show value** option button.

5. Click the **OK** button to display the column chart with data labels. See Figure 4-21.

Figure 4-21 ◀
Chart with data
labels

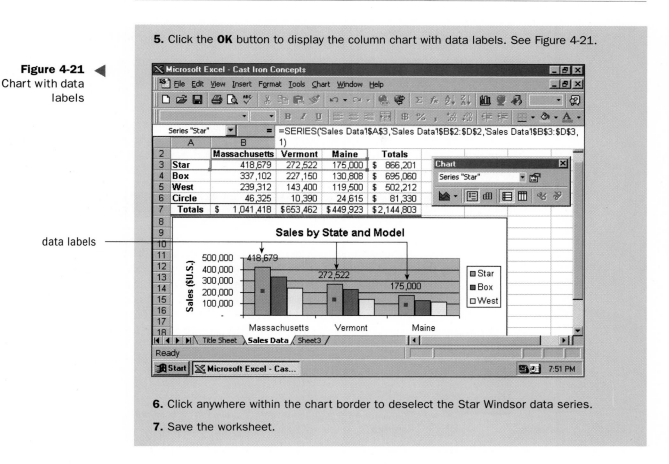

6. Click anywhere within the chart border to deselect the Star Windsor data series.

7. Save the worksheet.

Andrea is pleased with the changes in the chart's appearance. Now, she wants to add visual interest to the chart, making it look more polished.

Enhancing the Chart's Appearance

There are many ways to give charts a more professional look. The use of different font styles, types, and sizes can make chart labels and titles stand out. Also, using colors, borders, and patterns can make a chart more interesting to view.

Andrea thinks that a border and some color could accentuate the title of the chart.

Emphasizing the Title with Border and Color

The chart title is an object that you can select and format using the menu options or the toolbar buttons. Now make the changes to the chart title.

To display the title with border and color:

1. Click the **chart title** to select it and display selection handles. Now that the chart title is selected, notice that the Format button 🖻 on the Chart toolbar becomes the Format Chart Title button, and the Format button list box displays "Chart Title."

2. Click the **Format Chart Title** button 🖻 on the Chart toolbar to display the Format Chart Title dialog box, and then, if necessary, click the **Patterns** tab.

3. Click the **Weight** list arrow in the Border section to display a list of border weights.

4. Click the **second line** in the list.

5. Click the **gray** square in the Color palette (fourth row, last column) in the Area section.

6. Click the **OK** button to apply the format changes to the chart title, and then click anywhere within the chart area to deselect the title.

Andrea thinks that the chart looks better with its title emphasized. Now she wants you to work on making the data markers more distinctive. They certainly stand out on her computer's color monitor, but she is concerned that this will not be the case when she prints the chart on the office's black and white printer.

Changing Colors and Patterns

Patterns add visual interest to a chart and they can be useful when your printer has no color capability. Although your charts appear in color on a color monitor, if your printer does not have color capability, Excel translates colors to gray shades when printing. It's difficult to distinguish some colors, particularly darker ones, from one another when Excel translates them to gray shades and then prints them. To solve this potential problem, you can make your charts more readable by selecting a different pattern for each data marker.

To apply a different pattern to each data series you use the Patterns dialog box.

REFERENCE window	**SELECTING A PATTERN FOR A DATA MARKER**
	■ Make sure the chart is selected.
	■ Select the data marker or markers to which you want to apply a pattern.
	■ Click the Format Data Series button on the Chart toolbar to display the Format Data Series dialog box.
	■ Click the Patterns tab, click the Fill Effects button, and then click the Pattern tab to display a list of patterns.
	■ Click the pattern you want to apply, and then click the OK button twice to close the dialog boxes.

You want to apply a different pattern to each data series.

To apply a pattern to a data series:

1. Make sure the chart is selected.

2. Click any data marker for the Star data series (blue data marker) to display selection handles for all three data markers for that data series.

3. Click the **Format Data Series** button on the Chart toolbar to display the Format Data Series dialog box.

4. If necessary, click the **Patterns** tab, and then click the **Fill Effects** button to display the Fill Effects dialog box. Click the **Pattern** tab to display the Pattern palette. See Figure 4-22.

Figure 4-22 ◀
Pattern options
in Fill Effects
dialog box

dark downward
diagonal pattern

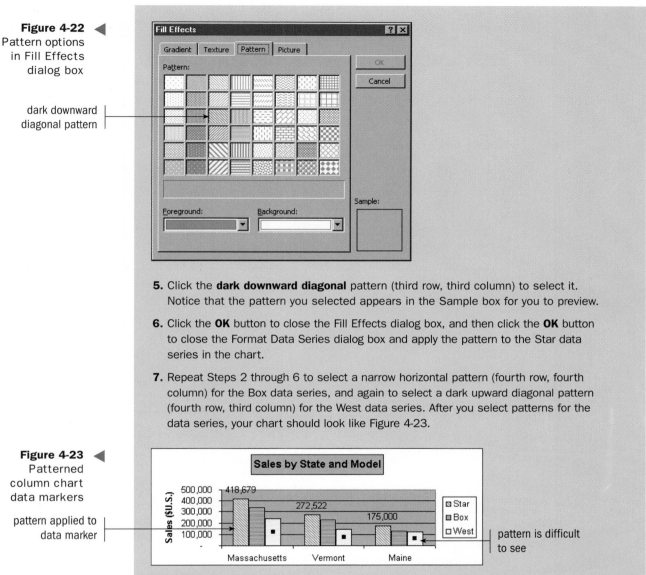

5. Click the **dark downward diagonal** pattern (third row, third column) to select it. Notice that the pattern you selected appears in the Sample box for you to preview.

6. Click the **OK** button to close the Fill Effects dialog box, and then click the **OK** button to close the Format Data Series dialog box and apply the pattern to the Star data series in the chart.

7. Repeat Steps 2 through 6 to select a narrow horizontal pattern (fourth row, fourth column) for the Box data series, and again to select a dark upward diagonal pattern (fourth row, third column) for the West data series. After you select patterns for the data series, your chart should look like Figure 4-23.

Figure 4-23 ◀
Patterned
column chart
data markers

pattern applied to
data marker

pattern is difficult
to see

You notice that the West markers appear to have no pattern applied because the pattern is very difficult to see when applied against the yellow color. You decide to change the color of the West markers to a darker color—green, so the pattern will be more visible.

To change the color of data markers:

1. If the West data markers are not selected, click any one of them to select the data markers for that data series.

2. Click the **Format Data Series** button on the Chart toolbar to display the Format Data Series dialog box.

3. If necessary, click the **Patterns** tab, click the **Fill Effects** button, and then click the **Pattern** tab in the Fill Effects dialog box to display the patterns palette.

4. In the Pattern tab, click the **Background** list arrow to display a color palette. Click the **green** square in the third row, third column, and click the **OK** button to close the Fill Effects dialog box and return to the Format Data Series dialog box.

5. Click the **OK** button to close the Format Data Series dialog box, and then click anywhere outside the chart border to deselect the chart.

You show the chart to Andrea, and she decides that it is ready to be printed and duplicated for distribution at the meeting.

Previewing and Printing the Chart

Before you print you should preview the worksheet to see how it will appear on the printed page. Remember, Andrea wants the embedded chart and the worksheet data to print on one page that she can use as a handout at the meeting.

To save and print an embedded chart:

1. Click the **Save** button 🖫 on the Standard toolbar to save the workbook.

2. Click the **Print Preview** button 🔍 on the Standard toolbar to display the Print Preview window.

3. Click the **Print** button to display the Print dialog box, and then click the **OK** button. See Figure 4-24.

Figure 4-24 ◀
Printout of worksheet with embedded column chart

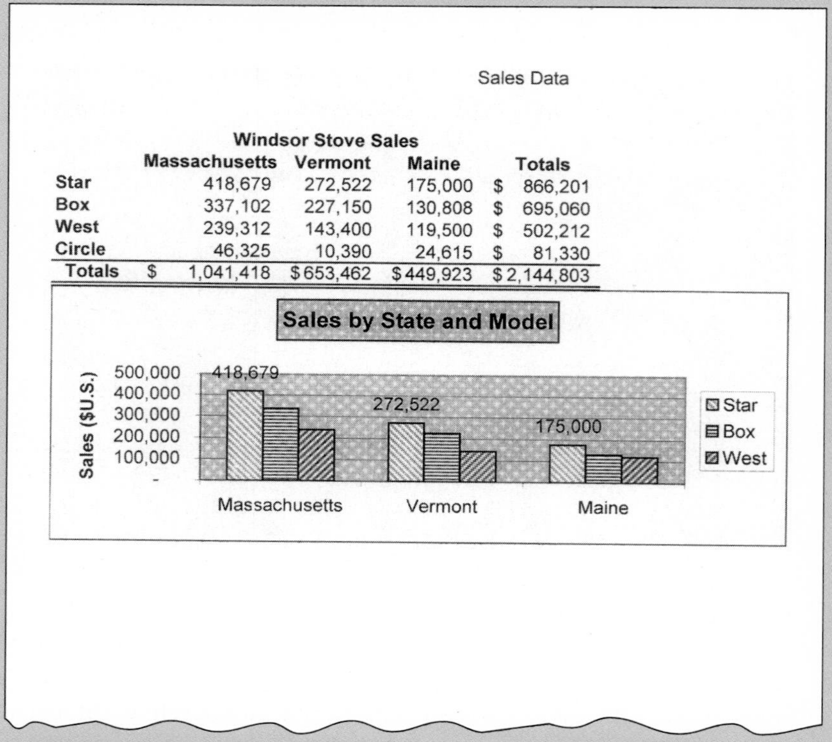

Sales Data

Windsor Stove Sales

	Massachusetts	Vermont	Maine	Totals
Star	418,679	272,522	175,000	$ 866,201
Box	337,102	227,150	130,808	$ 695,060
West	239,312	143,400	119,500	$ 502,212
Circle	46,325	10,390	24,615	$ 81,330
Totals	$ 1,041,418	$ 653,462	$ 449,923	$ 2,144,803

Sales by State and Model

Quick Check

1 A column chart is used to show _____.

2 When you click an embedded chart, it is _____

3 Explain how to revise a chart's data series.

4 How do you move an embedded chart to a new location using the mouse?

5 Describe the action you're likely to take before beginning Step 1 of the Chart Wizard.

6 What happens when you change a value in a worksheet that is the source of data for a chart?

7 What is the purpose of a legend?

8 Explain the difference between a data point and a data marker.

You have finished creating the column chart showing stove sales by state and model for Andrea. Next, you need to create the pie chart showing total stove sales by model. You will do this in Session 4.2.

SESSION

4.2

In this session you will create a pie chart. You will also learn how to select nonadjacent ranges, how to change a 2-D pie chart to a 3-D pie chart, and how to "explode" a slice from a pie chart. You will also learn how to use chart sheets and how to add a border to a chart.

Creating a Chart in a Chart Sheet

Now Andrea wants to show the contribution of each Windsor model to the total stove sales. Recall from the planning sketch she did (Figure 4-5) that she wants to use a pie chart to show this relationship.

A pie chart shows the relationship, or proportions, of parts to a whole. The size of each slice is determined by the value of that data point in relation to the total of all values. A pie chart contains only one data series. When you create a pie chart, you generally specify two ranges. Excel uses the first range for the category labels and the second range for the data series. Excel automatically calculates the percentage for each slice, draws the slice to reflect the percentage of the whole, and gives you the option of displaying the percentage as a label in the completed chart.

Andrea's sketch (see Figure 4-5) shows estimates of each stove's contribution and how she wants the pie chart to look. The pie chart will have four slices, one for each stove model. She wants each slice labeled with the stove model's name and its percentage of total sales. Because she doesn't know the exact percentages until Excel calculates and displays them in the chart, she put "__%" on her sketch to show where she wants the percentages to appear.

Creating a Pie Chart

You begin creating a pie chart by selecting the data to be represented from the worksheet. You refer to your worksheet and note in the sketch that the data labels for the pie slices are in cells A3 through A6 and the data points representing the pie slices are in cells E3 through E6. You must select these two ranges to tell the Chart Wizard the data that you want to chart, but you realize that these ranges are not located next to each other in the worksheet. You know how to select a series of adjacent cells; now you need to learn how to select two separate ranges at once.

Selecting Nonadjacent Ranges

A **nonadjacent range** is a group of individual cells or ranges that are not next to each other. Selecting nonadjacent ranges is particularly useful when you construct charts because the cells that contain the data series and these that contain the data labels are often not side by side in the worksheet. When you select nonadjacent ranges, the selected cells in each range are highlighted. You can then format the cells, clear them, or use them to construct a chart.

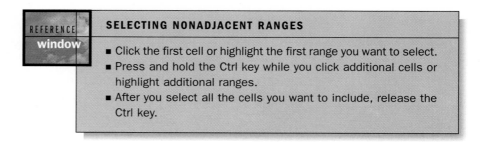

SELECTING NONADJACENT RANGES

- Click the first cell or highlight the first range you want to select.
- Press and hold the Ctrl key while you click additional cells or highlight additional ranges.
- After you select all the cells you want to include, release the Ctrl key.

Now select the nonadjacent ranges to be used to create the pie chart.

To select range A3:A6 and range E3:E6 in the Sales Data sheet:

1. If you took a break after the last session, make sure that Excel is running, the Cast Iron Concepts workbook is open, and the Sales Data worksheet is displayed.

2. Click anywhere outside the chart border to make sure the chart is not activated. Press **Ctrl + Home** to make cell A1 the active cell.

3. Select cells **A3** through **A6**, and then release the mouse button.

4. Press and hold the **Ctrl** key while you select cells **E3** through **E6**, and then release the mouse and the Ctrl key. The two nonadjacent ranges are now selected: A3:A6 and E3:E6. See Figure 4-25.

   TROUBLE? If you don't select the cells you want on your first try, click any cell to remove the highlighting, then go back to Step 2 and try again.

Figure 4-25
Selecting nonadjacent cell ranges

nonadjacent ranges selected

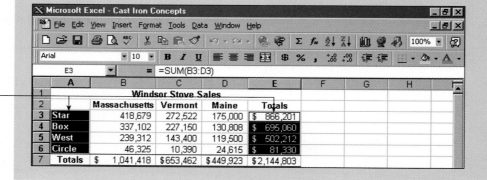

This time you'll place your new chart in a **chart sheet**, a special sheet that contains only one chart. It does not have the rows and columns of a regular worksheet. If you have many charts to create, you may want to place each chart in a separate chart sheet to avoid cluttering the worksheet. This approach also makes it easier to locate a particular chart because you can change the name on the chart sheet tab.

To create a pie chart in a chart sheet:

1. Click the **Chart Wizard** button [icon] on the Standard toolbar to display the Chart Wizard - Step 1 of 4 - Chart Type dialog box.

   TROUBLE? If the Office Assistant appears on your screen, click the button next to the message "No, don't provide help now" to close the Office Assistant.

   You want to create a pie chart.

2. Click the **Pie** chart type to select it. Six Pie chart subtypes are displayed. The Two-dimensional Pie chart subtype is the default subtype for the Pie chart type. Click the **Press and hold to view sample** button to display a preview of the Pie chart type.

You decide to use the default chart subtype.

3. Click the **Next** button to display the Chart Wizard - Step 2 of 4 - Chart Source Data dialog box. Make sure the Data range text box displays "='Sales Data'!$A$3:$A$6,'Sales Data'!$E$3:$E$6." This dialog box also displays a preview of your chart.

   TROUBLE? If the range shown on your screen is not "='Sales Data'!$A$3:$A$6, 'Sales Data'!$E$3:$E$6," type the necessary corrections in the Data range text box, or click the Collapse Dialog button located to the right of the Data range text box and select the correct range in the worksheet.

4. Click the **Next** button to display the Chart Wizard - Step 3 of 4 - Chart Options dialog box.

   Add a title for the chart.

5. If necessary, click the **Titles** tab, click the **Chart title** text box, and then type **Sales by Model** for the chart title. Notice that the title appears in the preview area.

6. Click the **Data Labels** tab, and then click the **Show label and percent** option button to place the label and percent next to each slice.

   Now remove the legend because it is no longer needed.

7. Click the **Legend** tab, and then click the **Show legend** check box to remove the check and deselect that option.

8. Click the **Next** button to display the Chart Wizard - Step 4 of 4 - Chart Location dialog box. Recall that in the fourth dialog box you decide where to place the chart. You can place a chart in a worksheet, or place it in its own chart sheet. You want to place this chart in a chart sheet.

9. Click the **As new sheet** option button to place the chart in the Chart1 chart sheet.

   You have finished the steps in the Chart Wizard.

10. Click the **Finish** button to complete the chart. The new chart, along with the Chart toolbar, appears in the chart sheet named Chart1. The chart sheet is inserted into the workbook before the worksheet on which it is based. If necessary, click the white portion of chart area to select the chart. See Figure 4-26.

Figure 4-26 ◀
Pie chart in a
chart sheet

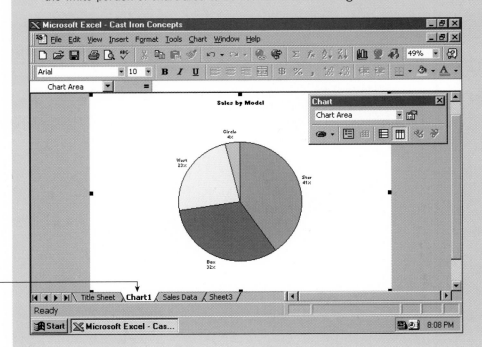

default name for
first chart sheet

After reviewing the pie chart, Andrea asks you to change the current pie chart to a three-dimensional design to give the chart a more professional look.

Changing the Chart Type from 2-D to 3-D

As you recall, Excel provides 14 different chart types that you can choose from as you create a chart. You can also access these chart types after the chart is created and change from one type to another. To change the chart type, you can use the Chart Type command on the Chart menu or the Chart Type button on the Chart toolbar to make this change. You'll use the Chart toolbar to change this 2-D pie chart to a 3-D pie chart.

To change the pie chart to a 3-D pie chart:

1. Make sure the chart area is selected, and then click the **Chart Type** arrow on the Chart toolbar to display a palette of chart types. See Figure 4-27.

TROUBLE? If the Chart toolbar is not displayed on the screen, click View on the menu bar, point to Toolbars, and click the Chart check box to display the Chart toolbar.

Figure 4-27 ◀
Palette of chart types

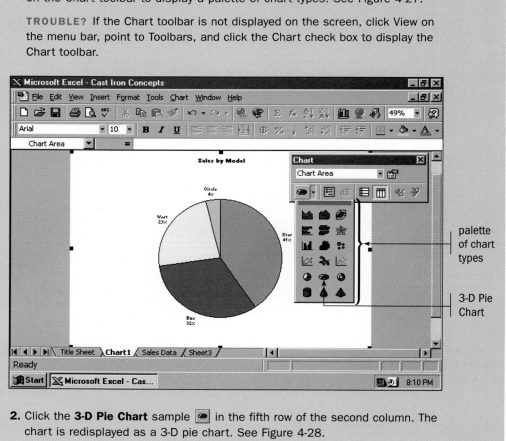

palette of chart types

3-D Pie Chart

2. Click the **3-D Pie Chart** sample in the fifth row of the second column. The chart is redisplayed as a 3-D pie chart. See Figure 4-28.

Figure 4-28 ◀
3-D pie chart

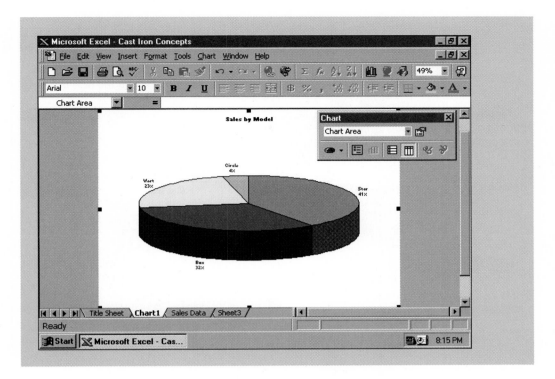

In her presentation, Andrea plans to emphasize the importance of the Star model because it is her best-selling model in the New England territory. She decides to "explode" the Star slice.

Exploding a Slice of a Pie Chart

When you create a pie chart, you may want to focus attention on a particular slice in the chart. You can present the data so a viewer can easily see which slice is larger or smaller—for example, which product sold the most. One method of emphasizing a particular slice over others is by separating the slice from the rest of the pie. The *cut* slice is more distinct because it is not connected to the other slices. A pie chart with one or more slices separated from the whole is referred to as an **exploded pie chart**.

REFERENCE
window

EXPLODING A SLICE OF A PIE CHART

- Click the pie chart, and then click the slice you want to explode.
- Drag the selected slice away from the center of the chart.

Andrea asks you to explode the slice that represents sales for the Star model.

To explode the slice that represents the Star model sales:

1. Click anywhere in the pie chart to select it. One selection handle appears on each pie slice and the Name box indicates that Series 1 is the selected chart object.

2. Now that you have selected the entire pie, you can select one part of it, the Star slice. Position the pointer over the slice that represents Star model sales. As you move the pointer over this slice, the ScreenTip "Series 1 Point: "Star" Value: $866,201 (41%)" is displayed. Click to select the slice. Selection handles now appear on only this slice.

3. With the pointer on the selected slice, click and hold down the mouse button while dragging the slice to the right, away from the center of the pie chart. As you drag the slice, an outline of the slice marks your progress.

4. Release the mouse button to leave the slice in the new position. See Figure 4-29.

Figure 4-29 ◀
Pie chart with
exploded slice

exploded slice

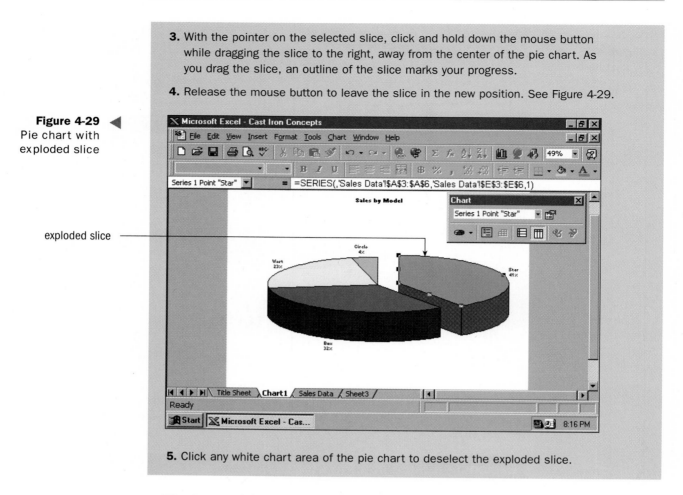

5. Click any white chart area of the pie chart to deselect the exploded slice.

The Star model now is exploded in the pie chart, but Andrea still isn't satisfied. You suggest moving the slice to the front of the pie.

Rotating a 3-D Chart

When working with a 3-D chart, you can modify the view of your chart to change its perspective, elevation, or rotation. You can change the elevation to look down on the chart or up from the bottom. You can also rotate the chart to adjust the placement of objects on the chart. Now rotate the chart so that the Star slice appears at the front of the chart.

To change the 3-D view of the chart:

1. Click **Chart** on the menu bar, and then click **3-D View** to display the 3-D View dialog box. See Figure 4-30.

Figure 4-30 ◀
3-D View dialog
box

clockwise rotation
arrow button

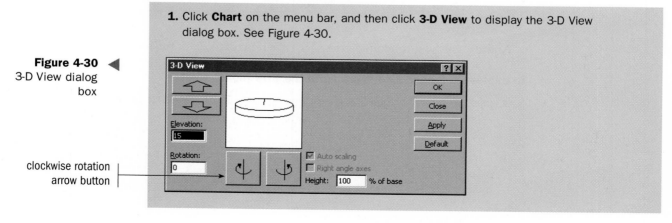

2. Click the **clockwise rotation arrow** button until the Rotation box shows 90; as you do this, notice that the pie chart sketch rotates to show the new position.

3. Click the **OK** button to apply the changes. See Figure 4-31.

Figure 4-31 ◄
3-D pie chart
after view
rotated to
display cut
slice in front

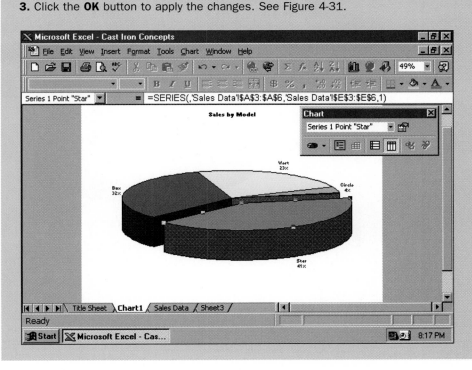

After looking over the chart, you decide to increase the size of the chart labels so that they are easier to read.

Formatting Chart Labels

You can change the font type, size, style, and the color of text in a chart using the Formatting toolbar buttons.

You look at the chart and decide that it will look better if you increase the size of the data labels from 10 to 14 points.

To change the font size of the chart labels:

1. Click any one of the four data labels to select all the data labels. Selection handles appear around all four labels, and the Name box displays "Series 1 Data Labels."

2. Click the **Font Size** list arrow on the Formatting toolbar, and then click **14**.

Now increase the font size of the title to 20 points.

To change the font size of the chart title:

1. Click the **chart title** to select it. Selection handles appear around the title.

2. Click the **Font Size** list arrow on the Formatting toolbar, and then click **20**.

3. Click any white area of the pie chart to deselect the title. See Figure 4-32.

Figure 4-32 ◀
3-D pie chart
after font size
of data labels
and title
increased

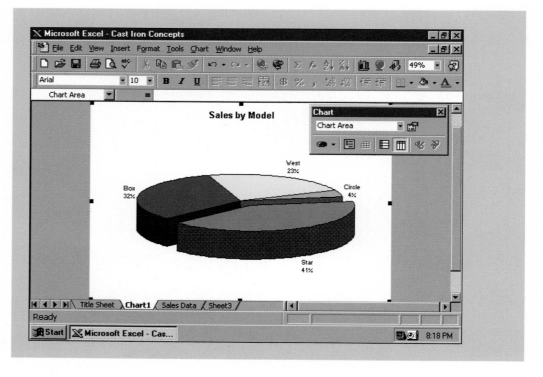

The pie chart looks good but Andrea has one last request. She asks you to apply a blue texture to the chart background.

Applying a Texture Fill Effect to the Chart Background

You can apply texture or gradient fill effects to chart walls, floors, bars, columns, and chart and plot background areas. These fill effects provide a professional look. You want to change the white chart area of the pie chart to a blue texture.

To apply a texture fill effect to the chart background:

1. Make sure the chart area is selected. If it is not, click the white area around the pie chart.

2. Click the **Format Chart Area** button 📷 on the Chart toolbar to display the Format Chart Area dialog box.

3. If necessary, click the **Patterns** tab, click the **Fill Effects** button to display the Fill Effects dialog box, and then click the **Texture** tab. See Figure 4-33.

Figure 4-33 ◀
Texture options
in Fill Effects
dialog box

blue tissue
paper texture

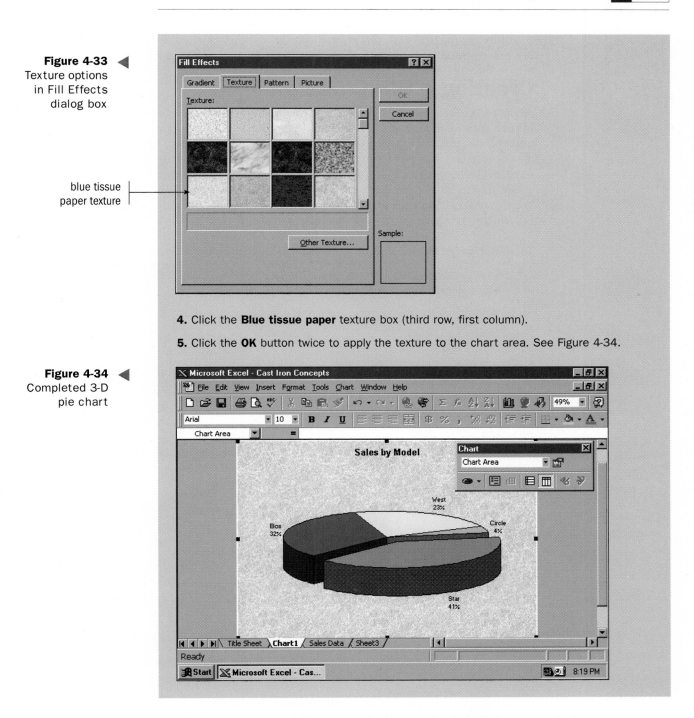

Figure 4-34 ◀
Completed 3-D
pie chart

4. Click the **Blue tissue paper** texture box (third row, first column).

5. Click the **OK** button twice to apply the texture to the chart area. See Figure 4-34.

The chart is now complete. You decide to print it and show it to Andrea.

Printing the Chart from the Chart Sheet

When you create a chart in a separate sheet, you can print that sheet separately. If necessary, you can make page setup decisions for the chart sheet alone. In this case, the chart in the chart sheet is ready for printing. You don't need to change any setup options. Now that the 3-D pie chart is complete, save the workbook and print a copy of the chart.

To save the workbook and print the chart:

1. Click the **Save** button 🖫 on the Standard toolbar to save the workbook.

2. Click the **Print** button 🖨 on the Standard toolbar to print the chart.

Andrea is pleased with the printed chart and believes it will help her when she makes her presentation next week.

Creating a Bar Chart

Andrea decides to spend some time during her presentation reviewing sales of all stoves in each state in her territory. She recalls from one of her college classes that both the bar and column chart are useful for comparing data by categories. The bar chart may have an advantage if you have long labels, because the category labels in bar charts are easier to read. Andrea asks you to prepare a bar chart comparing sales of all stoves by state.

To prepare this chart, you will first select the cells containing the chart you will display. For this chart, select the range B2 through D2 for the category axis (states) and B7 through D7 for the data series (total sales in each state).

To select range B2:D2 and range B7:D7 in the Sales Data sheet:

1. Click the **Sales Data** tab to activate the Sales Data worksheet, and then press **Ctrl + Home** to make cell A1 the active cell.

2. Select cells **B2:D2**, and then release the mouse button.

3. Press and hold the **Ctrl** key while you select cells **B7:D7**, and then release the mouse and the Ctrl key. The two nonadjacent ranges are now selected: B2:D2 and B7:D7.

   TROUBLE? If you don't select the cells you want on your first try, click any cell to remove the highlighting, and then go back to Step 2 and try again.

Place the bar chart in a separate chart sheet so that Andrea can easily locate it.

To create a bar chart in a chart sheet:

1. Click the **Chart Wizard** button 📊 on the Standard toolbar to display the Chart Wizard - Step 1 of 4 - Chart Type dialog box.

   You want to create a bar chart.

2. Click the **Bar** chart type to select it. Six Bar chart subtypes are displayed. The Clustered Bar chart is the default subtype for the Bar chart. Click the **Press and hold to view sample** button to display a preview of the Clustered Bar chart subtype.

   You decide to use the Clustered Bar chart type.

3. Click the **Next** button to display the Chart Wizard - Step 2 of 4 - Chart Source Data dialog box. Make sure the Data range box displays "='Sales data'!$B$2:$D$2,'Sales Data'!$B$7:$D$7." This dialog box also displays a preview of your chart.

   TROUBLE? If the range shown on your screen is not "='Sales data'!$B$2:$D$2, 'Sales Data'!$B$7:$D$7," type the necessary corrections in the Data range text box, or click the Collapse Dialog button and select the correct range in the worksheet.

4. Click the **Next** button to display the Chart Wizard - Step 3 of 4 - Chart Options dialog box.

   Add a title for the chart.

5. If necessary, click the **Titles** tab, and then click the **Chart title** text box. Type **Sales by State** for the chart title. Notice that the title appears in the preview area. Click the **Category (X) axis** title box, and then type **Territories**. Click the **Value (Y) axis** title box, and then type **Sales ($U.S.)**.

   Since there is only one data series, remove the legend.

6. Click the **Legend** tab and then click the **Show legend** check box to remove the check and deselect that option.

7. Click the **Next** button to display the Chart Wizard - Step 4 of 4 - Chart Location dialog box. You want this chart to be placed in a chart sheet.

8. Click the **As new sheet** option button to place this chart in a chart sheet, and then type **Bar Chart** in the As new sheet text box to rename the chart sheet.

You have finished the steps in the Chart Wizard.

9. Click the **Finish** button to complete the chart. The new chart, along with the Chart toolbar, appears in the chart sheet named Bar Chart. The chart sheet is inserted into the workbook before the worksheet on which it is based. See Figure 4-35.

Figure 4-35 ◀
Bar chart in a
chart sheet

categories are
organized vertically

values are displayed
horizontally

Andrea reviews the bar chart and believes it will focus the audience's attention on sales in each state.

Using Pictures in a Bar Chart

When making a presentation, an interesting way to enhance a bar or column chart is to replace the data markers with graphic images, thereby creating a picture chart. Any graphic image that can be copied to the Clipboard can serve as the basis for a picture chart. Andrea wants you to use a picture of the Windsor stove from CIC's latest catalog as the data marker in your bar chart.

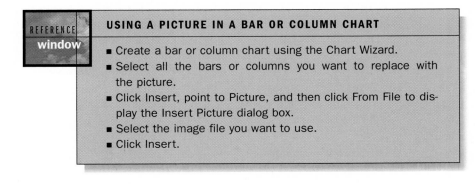

REFERENCE window

USING A PICTURE IN A BAR OR COLUMN CHART

■ Create a bar or column chart using the Chart Wizard.
■ Select all the bars or columns you want to replace with the picture.
■ Click Insert, point to Picture, and then click From File to display the Insert Picture dialog box.
■ Select the image file you want to use.
■ Click Insert.

The graphic image of the Windsor stove is located in the Tutorial.04 folder on your Student Disk. The file is named Stove. To replace the plain bars with the graphic image, you need to select one bar or column of the chart and use the Picture command on the Insert menu.

To insert the picture into the bar chart:

1. Click any column in the chart so that all three data markers are selected.

2. Click **Insert** on the menu bar, point to **Picture,** and then click **From File** to display the Insert Picture dialog box.

3. Make sure Tutorial.04 is the folder shown in the Look In list box, and then click **Stove**.

4. Click the **Insert** button to insert the picture into the chart. The three bars are each filled by the picture of the stove. See Figure 4-36. Notice that each picture is "stretched" to fit the bar it fills.

Figure 4-36 ◀
Picture chart with stretched graphic

Stove graphic

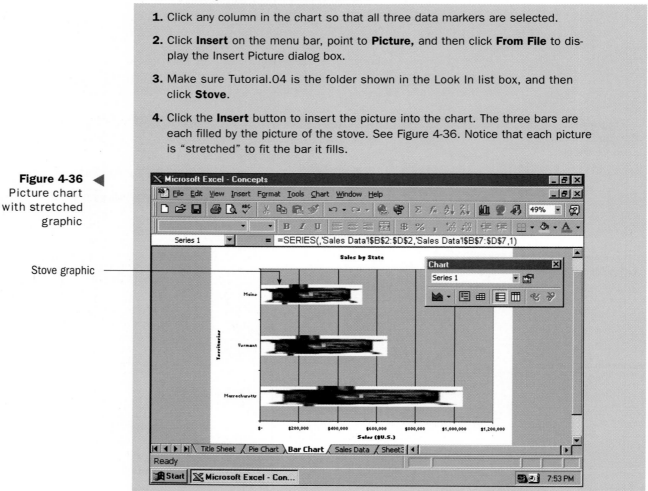

When you insert a picture into a bar or column chart, Excel automatically stretches the picture to fill the space formerly occupied by the marker. Some pictures stretch well, but others become distorted, and detract from, rather than add to, the chart's impact.

Stretching and Stacking Pictures

As an alternative to stretching a picture, you can stack the picture so that it appears repeatedly in the bar, reaching the height of the original bar in the chart. You'll stack the Windsor stove picture in your chart to improve its appearance.

The value axis has tick mark labels at 200000, 400000, 600000, and so on. To match the axis labels, you'll stack one stove each 200000 units.

To stack the picture:

1. If the handles have disappeared from the bars, click any bar in the chart to select all the bars.

2. Click the **Format Data Series** button on the Chart toolbar to display the Format Data Series dialog box, and if necessary, click the **Patterns** tab.

3. Click the **Fill Effects** button to display the Fill Effects dialog box, and then click the **Picture** tab.

4. Click the **Stack and scale to** option button. Accept the Units/Picture value.

5. Click the **OK** button to close the Fill Effects dialog box, and then click the **OK** button to close the Format Data Series dialog box and return to the chart sheet and display the data markers as stacked stoves.

6. Click the white area of the chart to deselect the data markers. See Figure 4-37.

Figure 4-37 ◄
Picture chart with stacked graphic

stacked graphic image

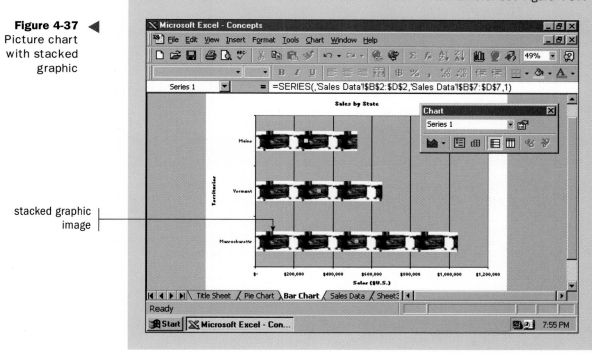

Andrea likes the picture chart, but is not sure how her audience will react to this type of chart. She wants to think about it. She asks you to save the workbook with the picture chart included and will let you know in the morning whether to print the picture chart or return to the bar chart. If Andrea asks you to remove the pictures and return to the original bars for the data markers, you will select the data series, click Edit, click Clear, and then click Formats.

Now save the workbook.

To save the workbook:

1. Click the **Title Sheet** tab to make it the active worksheet.

2. Click the **Save** button on the Standard toolbar.

3. Close the workbook and exit Excel.

Quick **Check**

1 Define the following terms in relation to a pie chart:
a. data point
b. data marker
c. data series

2 Explain how to select cells A1, C5, and D10 at the same time.

3 What type of chart shows the proportion of parts to a whole?

4 When creating charts, why is it important to know how to select nonadjacent ranges?

5 Explain the difference between an embedded chart and a chart placed in a chart sheet.

6 Explain how to rotate a 3-D pie chart.

7 Explain how to explode a slice from a pie chart.

8 When you change a two-dimensional pie chart to a 3-D pie chart, you change the _____.

You have finished creating the column chart, pie chart, and bar chart that Andrea needs for her presentation.

Tutorial Assignments

After having the night to think about it, Andrea comes to work the next morning and asks you to create one more chart for her presentation. Do the following:

1. Start Windows and Excel, if necessary. Insert your Student Disk into the disk drive. Make sure that the Excel and Book1 windows are maximized. Open the file Concept2 in the TAssign folder for Tutorial 4.

2. Save the file under the new name Cast Iron Concepts 2 in the TAssign folder.

3. Type your name and the current date in the Title Sheet sheet.

4. In the Sales Data sheet select the nonadjacent ranges that contain the models (A3:A6) and the total sales for each model (E3:E6).

5. Use the Chart Wizard to create a clustered column chart with 3-D visual effect. Place the completed chart in a chart sheet.

6. As you are creating the chart, remove the legend and add "Total Stove Sales by State" as the chart title.

7. Rename the chart sheet "3D Column."

8. After the chart is completed, increase the font size of the title and axis labels so that they are easier to read.

 9. Put a box around the chart's title, using a thick line for a border. Add a drop shadow to the border.

10. Save the workbook. Print the chart. Include your name, the filename, and the date in the footer for the printed chart.

 11. Select the walls chart element and apply a 1-color gradient fill effect. You select an appropriate color.

 12. Select the value axis and change its scale so that the major unit is 150000.

13. Open the Office Assistant and learn how you can show the worksheet data in a data table, which is a grid at the bottom of the chart. (*Hint*: Search on "add data table to a chart.") Add a data table to your chart. Increase the font size associated with the data table.

14. Save the workbook, and then print the chart.

15. Switch to the Sales Data worksheet and do the following:

   a. Change the color of the West Windsor pattern to brown.

   b. Move the legend to the bottom of the chart. Increase the height of the chart, so it has a more professional look.

   c. Annotate the column chart with the note "Star model—best seller in Massachusetts!" by adding a text box and arrow using the tools on the Drawing toolbar.

   d. Save the workbook, and then print the Sales Data sheet with the embedded chart.

Case Problems

1. Illustrating Production Data at TekStar Electronics You are executive assistant to the President of TekStar Electronics, a manufacturer of consumer electronics. You are compiling the yearly manufacturing reports and have collected production totals for each of TekStar's four U.S. manufacturing plants. The workbook TekStar contains these totals. Now you need to create a 3-D pie chart showing the relative percentage of CD players each plant produced.

   1. Open the workbook Tekstar in the Case folder for Tutorial 4 and add the necessary information to the Title Sheet sheet to create a summary of the workbook. Save the workbook as TekStar Electronics in the Case folder for Tutorial 4.

   2. Activate the Units Sold sheet. Use the Chart Wizard to create a 3-D pie chart in a chart sheet that shows the percentage of CD players produced at each plant location. Use the Pie with 3-D Visual Effect subtype.

   3. Enter "Production of CD Players" as the chart title. Show "Label" and "Percent" as the data labels. Remove the legend.

   4. Pull out the slice representing the Chicago plant's CD player production.

   5. Increase the font size of the title and data labels so that they are easier to read.

   6. Name the chart sheet 3D Pie Chart.

   7. Preview and print the chart sheet. Save your work.

   8. Create an embedded chart comparing sales of all the products by city. Select the appropriate range and then use the Chart Wizard to create a clustered bar chart. Use the products as the data series and the cities as the X-axis (category) labels. Enter "Production by Product and Plant Location" as the title.

   9. Move the bar chart under the table, and then enhance the chart in any way you think appropriate.

   10. Preview and print the embedded bar chart. Save your work.

11. Create a clustered column chart with 3-D visual effect comparing the production of VCRs by city. Remove the legend. Place the chart in a chart sheet named "VCRs."

   a. Add a data table (a grid in a chart that contains the numeric data used to create the chart) to the chart. (*Hint*: Use the Office Assistant to find out how to add a data table to a chart.)

   b. Save the workbook, and then print the chart.

2. Dow Jones Charting You are working for a stock analyst who is planning to publish a weekly newsletter. One regular component of the newsletter will be a 15-week chart tracking the Dow Jones average. Create the chart that can be used for the newsletter.

1. Open the workbook DowJones in the Case folder for Tutorial 4. Save the workbook as Dow Jones 8-2-96 in the Case folder for Tutorial 4.

2. Use the Chart Wizard to create an embedded line chart (Line subtype) in the Data worksheet. Specify "Dow Jones Average" as the chart title and "Index" as the title for the Y-axis. Do not add a legend or X-axis title.

3. Place the chart to the right of the present worksheet data and resize it until you are satisfied with its appearance.

4. Edit the chart as follows:

   a. Change the line marker to a thick line.
   b. Apply a texture fill effect to the chart area. You decide the texture.
   c. Change the color of the plot area to a shade of yellow.
   d. Angle the text upward for the dates on the category axis.

5. Save your workbook. Preview and print the embedded chart.

6. Add the text box "Inflation Worries Wall Street" pointing to 7-26-96.

7. Save your workbook. Print the chart.

8. The Dow Jones average for the week ending 8-9-96 was 5500.

   a. Add this data to the last row of the worksheet.
   b. Modify the chart by plotting the 15-week period beginning 5-3-96 and ending 8-9-96.
   c. Save the workbook as Dow Jones 8-9-96. Preview your work and print only the chart. Center the chart vertically and horizontally on the page.

3. New York Chronicle You are working as an intern for Jeff Sindle, business economist, of the *New York Chronicle*—a New York newspaper with circulation in New York City and Long Island. The paper is planning to publish an economic profile of the region and you are assisting in this project.

1. Open the workbook NewYork in the Case folder for Tutorial 4. Save the workbook as New York Economic Data. Create three charts, each in its own chart sheet.

2. First, create a 3-D pie chart that compares the population of the six geographic areas in the study. Title the chart and enhance it as you think appropriate. Rename the chart sheet to reflect the chart it contains.

3. Create a clustered column chart that compares the number of establishments in retail and services by the six geographic areas. (*Hint*: Categorize by type of establishment; each geographic area is a data series.) Title the chart and enhance it as you think appropriate. Rename the chart sheet to reflect the chart it contains.

4. Create a clustered bar chart comparing sales/receipts by geographic area (categorize by geographic area; the data series is sales/receipts). Title the chart and enhance it as you think appropriate. Rename the chart sheet to reflect the chart it contains.

5. Add a title sheet that includes your name, date created, purpose, and a brief description of each sheet in the workbook.

6. Save the workbook.

7. Print the entire workbook (title and data worksheet and the three chart sheets).

4. Duplicating a Printed Chart Look through books, business magazines, or textbooks for your other courses to find an attractive chart. Select one, photocopy it, and create a worksheet that contains the data displayed in the chart. You can estimate the data values plotted in the chart. Do your best to duplicate the chart you found. You might not be able to duplicate the chart fonts or colors exactly, but choose the closest available substitutes. When your work is complete, save it as Duplicate Chart in the Case folder for Tutorial 4, preview it, and print it. Submit the photocopy of the original as well as the printout of the chart you created.

Answers to Quick Check Questions

SESSION 1.1

1 cell

2 open

3 D2

4 b

5 click the "Sheet2" sheet tab

6 press Ctrl + Home

SESSION 1.2

1 8; D1 + E1 + F1 + G1+ H1 + I1 + J1 + K1

2 B4, B5, B6, C4, C5, C6, D4, D5, D6

3 a. text
   b. value
   c. value
   d. formula
   e. text
   f. formula
   g. text

4 Active sheet(s), Print

5 Print, File

6 c

7 When you exit Excel, the workbook is erased from RAM. So if you want to use the workbook again you need to save it to disk. Click File, then click Save As.

8 press the Delete key

9 revising the contents of one or more cells in a worksheet and observing the effect this change has on all other cells in the worksheet

SESSION 2.1

1 Select the cell where you want the sum to appear. Click the AutoSum button. Excel suggests a formula which includes the SUM function. To accept the formula press the Enter key.

2 =A6+B6

3 cell references. If you were to copy the formula to other cells, these cells are relative references

4 absolute reference

5 Windows clipboard

6 fill-handle

7 double-click the sheet tab, then type the new name, then press the Enter key or click any cell in the work-sheet to accept the entry

8 determine the purpose of the worksheet, enter the data and formulas, test the worksheet; correct errors, improve the appearance, document the worksheet, save and print

SESSION 2.2

1 select

2 header

3 Autoformat

4 Click any cell in the row above which you want to insert a row. Click Insert, then click Row

5 c

6 Assuming you are entering a formula with a function, first select the cell where you want to place a formula, type =, the function name and a left parenthesis, then click and drag over the range of cells to be used in the formula. Press the Enter key.

7 click Tools, click Options, then in the View tab, click the Formula check box

8 Landscape

SESSION 3.1

1 a. 13%; b. $0.13

2 Click Format, click Cells; right-click mouse in cell you want to format; use buttons on the Formatting toolbar

3 the data in the cell is formatted with the Comma style using two decimal places

4 Left Align button, Center button, Right Align button, and Merge and Center button

5 Center column headings, right-align numbers, and left-align text

6 Position the mouse pointer over the column header, right-click the mouse and click Column Width. Enter the new column width in the Column Width dialog box. Position the mouse pointer over the right edge of the column you want to modify, then click and drag to increase the column width.

7 Format Painter button

8 The column width of a cell is not wide enough to display the numbers, and you need to increase the column width

SESSION 3.2

1 use the Borders Tab on the Format Cells dialog box, or the Borders button on the Formatting toolbar

2 Click the Drawing button on the Standard toolbar

3 select

4 text box

5 Portrait

6 Click Tools, click View tab, then click the Gridlines check box to remove the check from the check box

7 Excel (graphic) object

SESSION 4.1

1   comparisons among items or changes in data over a period of time

2   selected; also referred to as activated

3   Select the appropriate chart, click Chart Menu, then click Source Data. Click the Collapse dialog box button, then select values to be included in the chart, press the Enter key, then click the OK button

4   Select the chart, move the pointer over the chart area until the pointer changes to an arrow then click and drag to another location on the worksheet

5   select the range of cells to be used as the source of data for the chart

6   the data marker that represents that data point will change to reflect the new value

7   identifies the pattern or colors assigned to the data series in a chart

8   A data point is a value in the worksheet, while the data marker is the symbol (pie slice, column, bar, and so on) that represents the data point in the chart

SESSION 4.2

1   a. a value that originates from a worksheet cell
    b. a slice in a pie chart that represents a single point
    c. a group of related data points plotted in a pie chart that originate from rows or columns in a worksheet

2   Select the A1, then press and hold down the CTRL key and select cells C5 and D10

3   pie chart

4   often, the data you want to plot is not in adjacent cells

5   an embedded chart is a chart object placed in a worksheet and saved with the worksheet when the workbook is saved; a chart sheet is a sheet in a workbook that contains only a chart

6   Select the pie chart you want to rotate, click Chart on the menu bar then click 3-D View to display the 3-D View dialog box. Click either rotate button to rotate the chart.

7   Select the slice you want to "explode," then click and drag the slice away from the center.

8   chart type

Microsoft®
Excel 97

LEVEL II

TUTORIALS

Read This **Before You Begin**

STUDENT DISKS

To complete Excel 97 Tutorials 5–7 you need 2 Student Disks. Your instructor will either provide you with Student Disks or ask you to make your own.

If you are supposed to make your own Student Disks, you will need 2 blank, formatted high-density disks. You will need to copy a set of folders from a file server or standalone computer onto your disks. Your instructor will tell you which computer, drive letter, and folders contain the files you need. The following table shows you which folders go on each of your disks, so that you will have enough disk space to complete all the tutorials, Tutorial Assignments, and Case Problems:

Student Disk	Write this on the disk label	Put these folders on the disk
1	Student Disk 1: Tutorials 5 and 7	Tutorial.05 and Tutorial.07
2	Student Disk 2: Tutorial 6	Tutorial.06

Please note, the Tutorial.05 and Tutorial.07 folders must go on Student Disk 1.

When you begin each tutorial, be sure you are using the correct Student Disk. See the inside front or inside back cover of this book for more information on Student Disk files, or ask your instructor or technical support person for assistance.

COURSE LAB

Tutorial 1 features an interactive Course Lab to help you understand spreadsheet concepts. There are Lab Assignments at the end of the tutorial that relate to this Lab. To start the Lab, click the Start button on the Windows 95 Taskbar, point to Programs, point to Course Labs, point to New Perspectives Applications, and click Spreadsheets.

USING YOUR OWN COMPUTER

If you are going to work through this book using your own computer, you need:

■ **Computer System** Microsoft Windows 95 or Microsoft Windows NT Workstation 4.0 (or a later version) and Microsoft Excel 97 must be installed on your computer. This book assumes a typical installation of Microsoft Excel 97.

■ **Student Disks** Ask your instructor or lab manager for details on how to get the Student Disks. You will not be able to complete the tutorials or end-of-tutorial assignments in this book using your own computer until you have Student Disks. The Student Files may also be obtained electronically over the Internet. See the inside front or inside back cover of this book for more details.

■ **Course Lab** See your instructor or technical support person to obtain the Course Lab software for use on your own computer.

To complete Excel 97 Tutorials 5–7 your students must use a set of files on 2 Student Disks. These files are included in the Instructor's Resource Kit, and they may also be obtained electronically over the Internet. See the inside front or inside back cover of this book for more details. Follow the instructions in the Readme file to copy the files to your server or standalone computer. You can view the Readme file using WordPad. Once the files are copied, you can make Student Disks for the students yourself, or you can tell students where to find the files so they can make their own Student Disks.

COURSE LAB SOFTWARE

The Course Lab software is distributed on a CD-ROM included in the Instructor's Resource Kit. Refer to the Readme file for essential technical notes related to running the Lab in a multi-user environment. Once you have installed the Course Lab software, your students can start the Lab from the Windows 95 desktop by following the instructions in the Course Lab section above.

COURSE TECHNOLOGY STUDENT FILES AND LAB SOFTWARE

You are granted a license to copy the Student Files and Course Lab software to any computer or computer network used by students who have purchased this book.

Working with Excel Lists

Managing Faculty Data at North State University

OBJECTIVES

In this tutorial you will:

- Identify the elements of an Excel list

- Freeze rows and columns

- Sort data in a list

- Use a data form to enter, search for, edit, and delete records

- Filter data in a list using AutoFilters

- Apply conditional formatting to a range

- Create natural language formulas

- Insert subtotals into a list

- Use the subtotals outline view

- Insert page breaks using Page Break Preview

- Summarize a list using pivot tables

CASE

North State University

Janice Long is the dean of the College of Business Administration at North State University. The College of Business Administration has three academic departments: management, marketing, and accounting. Each faculty member holds an academic rank, such as professor or associate professor. Most faculty members are hired as instructors or assistant professors. After a period of time, he or she might be promoted to associate professor and then to full professor. Faculty salaries usually reflect the faculty member's rank and length of service in the department.

The dean frequently asks you to locate and summarize information about the College of Business Administration faculty. This week, she has several important budget and staffing meetings to attend for which she will need to produce detailed and specific information on her faculty. She asks for your help to compile the necessary data. She has provided an Excel worksheet that contains the name, academic rank, department, hire date, salary, and sex of each faculty member in the College of Business Administration. She asks you to use the worksheet to create several reports that will organize the information to produce the specific output she requires for each meeting.

SESSION 5.1

You already know how to use Excel to perform calculations using numeric data or values you enter into worksheet cells. In this lesson you will learn how to use Excel to manage lists of data. You will discover how easy it is to sort the information in a worksheet, to add and delete data, and to search for specific information. You will also learn how to filter the information to display only data meeting certain criteria.

Introduction to Lists

One of the more common uses of a worksheet is to manage lists of data, such as client lists, phone lists, and transaction lists. Excel provides you with the tools to manage such tasks. Using Excel, you can store and update data, sort data, search for and retrieve data, summarize and compare data, and create reports.

In Excel a **list** is a collection of similar data stored in a structured manner, in rows and columns. Figure 5-1 shows a portion of the College of Business Administration faculty list. Within an Excel list, each column represents a **field** that describes some attribute or characteristic of an object, person, place, or thing. In this situation, a faculty member's last name, the department in which the faculty member works, and the faculty member's annual salary are examples of fields. When related fields are grouped together in a row, they form a **record**, a collection of fields that describes a person, place, or thing. For example, the data for each faculty member—first name, last name, department, rank, year hired, sex, and salary—represents a record. A collection of related records makes up an Excel list.

Figure 5-1 ◀
Portion of faculty list

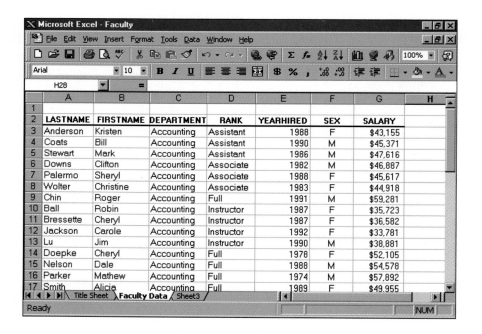

If you have worked with spreadsheets before, you may associate the term "database" with what Excel now calls a list. Since the introduction of Excel Version 5, Microsoft refers to database tables in Excel worksheets as lists. The term **database** refers to files created using database management software, such as dBASE, Access, and Paradox. In this tutorial we focus on Excel lists.

Planning and Creating a List

Before you create a list you will want to do some planning. As you spend time thinking about how you will use the list, consider the types of reports, queries, and searches you may need. This process should help you determine the kind of information to include for each record and the contents of each field. As with most projects, the planning you do will help you avoid redesigning the list later.

To create the faculty list she has given you to work with, the dean first determined her information requirements. As a way of documenting the information requirements of the faculty list, she developed a **data definition table** that describes the fields she plans to maintain for each faculty member at the College of Business Administration. Figure 5-2 shows the data definition table the dean developed to define her data requirements. She used this as a guide in creating the faculty list.

Figure 5-2 ◀
Data definition
table for
faculty list

Field Name	Description
LASTNAME	Faculty member's last name
FIRSTNAME	Faculty member's first name
DEPARTMENT	Name of department (accounting, finance, and management)
RANK	Faculty rank (instructor, assistant, associate, and full)
YEARHIRED	Year in which faculty member was hired
SEX	Female (F) or male (M)
SALARY	Annual salary

Once you determine the design of your list, you can create the list in a worksheet. You can use a blank worksheet, or one that already contains data.

When creating a list in Excel, use the following guidelines:

- The top row of the list should contain a **field name**, a unique label describing the contents of the data in the rows below it. This row of field names is sometimes referred to as the **field header row**.

- Field names can contain up to 255 characters. Usually a short name is easier to understand and remember. Short field names also enable you to display more fields on the screen at one time.

- You should boldface the field names, change the font, or use a different color to make it easier for Excel to distinguish between the data in the list and the field names.

- Each column should contain the same kind of information for each row in the list.

The list should be separated from any other information in the same worksheet by at least one blank row and one blank column because Excel automatically determines the range of the list by identifying blank rows and columns. For the same reason, you should avoid blank rows and columns within the list.

Now open the workbook the dean created to help you maintain the data on faculty at North State University's College of Business Administration.

To open the Faculty workbook:

1. Start Excel. Make sure your Student Disk is in the appropriate drive, and then open the workbook **Faculty** in the Tutorial.05 folder on your Student Disk, and immediately save it as **CBA Faculty**.

2. Switch to the **Faculty Data** sheet to display the faculty list. See Figure 5-3. The dean's worksheet contains the list of faculty at the College of Business Administration. Currently there are 41 faculty. Each faculty record is stored as a separate row (rows 3 through 43). There are seven fields for each faculty record (columns A through G). Notice that the field names have been boldfaced to make it easier for Excel to distinguish the field names from the data in the list.

   To become familiar with the data, you decide to scroll the faculty list.

Figure 5-3 ◄
Faculty list

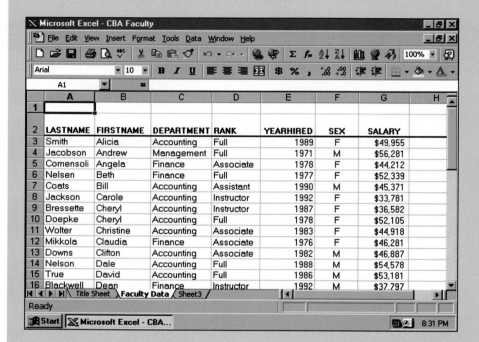

3. Click the **vertical scroll bar down arrow** to scroll to the bottom of the list (row 43). As you scroll, notice that the column headings are no longer visible.

4. After viewing the last record in the faculty list, press **Ctrl + Home** to return to cell A1.

You want to keep the column headings on the screen as you scroll the faculty list because not being able to see the column headings makes it difficult to know what the data in each column represents.

Freezing Rows and Columns

You can freeze rows and columns so they will not scroll off the screen as you move around the worksheet. This lets you keep headings on the screen as you work with the data in a large worksheet.

REFERENCE window	**FREEZING ROWS AND COLUMNS**
	■ Select the cell below and to the right of row(s) or column(s) you want to freeze.
	■ Click Window, and then click Freeze Panes.

You decide to freeze the row with the column headings and the LASTNAME column so that they remain on the screen as you scroll the list.

To freeze rows and columns:

1. Click cell **B3** to make it the active cell.

2. Click **Window** on the menu bar, and then click **Freeze Panes** to freeze the rows above row 3 and the columns to the left of column B. Excel displays dark horizontal and vertical lines to indicate which rows and columns are frozen.

    Now scroll the list.

3. Click the **vertical scroll bar down arrow** to scroll down to the bottom of the list (row 43). As you scroll, notice that the column headings remain visible. See Figure 5-4.

dark horizontal and vertical
lines indicate which columns
and rows are frozen

Figure 5-4 ◄
Faculty list
with column
labels visible as
you scroll

column labels
remain on screen

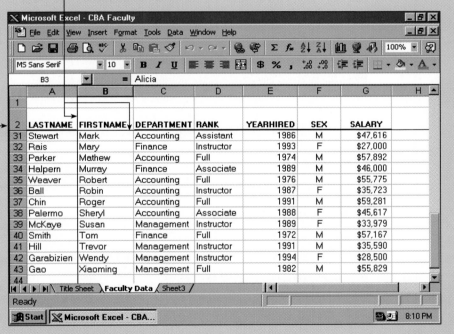

4. Click the **horizontal scroll bar right arrow**. As you scroll to the right, notice that column A, LASTNAME, remains visible.

5. Press **Ctrl + Home** to return to cell B3. Notice that Ctrl + Home no longer returns you to cell A1—instead it returns you to the cell directly below and to the right of the frozen row and column.

To unfreeze the rows and columns, you would select Unfreeze Panes from the Window menu.

Sorting Data

In preparation for her meetings this week, the dean wants a list of faculty members sorted by last name, so she can have quick access to faculty data when not near a computer. She asks you to prepare a list of all faculty, alphabetized by last name.

When you initially enter records into a list, each new record is placed at the bottom of the list. To rearrange records in a list, you sort based on the data in one or more of the fields (columns). The fields you use to order your data are called **sort fields** or **sort keys**.

For example, to sort the faculty list alphabetically by last name, you order the data using the values in the LASTNAME field. LASTNAME becomes the sort field. Because LASTNAME is the first sort field, and in this case the only sort field, it is the **primary** sort field.

Before you complete the sort, you will need to decide whether you want to put the list in ascending or descending order. **Ascending order** arranges labels alphabetically from A to Z, and numbers from smallest to largest. **Descending order** arranges labels in reverse alphabetical order from Z to A, and numbers from largest to smallest. In both ascending and descending order, any blank fields are placed at the bottom of the list. For the quick reference list of faculty, the dean wants to sort the list by last name in ascending order.

Sorting a List Using One Sort Field

To sort data in an Excel worksheet, you can use the Sort Ascending and Sort Descending buttons on the Standard toolbar, or you can use the Sort command on the Data menu. The easiest way to sort data when there is only one sort key is to use the Sort Ascending or Sort Descending buttons on the Standard toolbar. If you are sorting using more than one sort key, you should use the Sort command on the Data menu to specify the columns on which you want to sort.

REFERENCE window	**SORTING USING A SINGLE SORT FIELD** ■ Click any cell in the column you want to sort by. ■ Click the Sort Ascending or Sort Descending button on the Standard toolbar to sort the data.

Produce the dean's alphabetized list by sorting the faculty list using LASTNAME as the sort field.

To sort a list using a single sort field:

1. Click any cell in the LASTNAME column.

2. Click the **Sort Ascending** button [⬇] on the Standard toolbar. The data is sorted in ascending order by last name. See Figure 5-5.

   TROUBLE? If you selected the wrong column before sorting the list, and your data is sorted in the wrong order, you can undo it. To undo a sort, click the Undo button [↶ ▾] on the Standard toolbar.

Figure 5-5
Faculty list
sorted by
last name

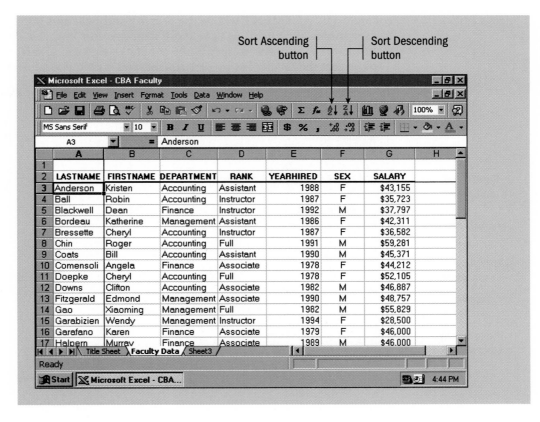

The dean also requests a list of faculty sorted alphabetically by department, and within each department, sorted alphabetically by last name.

Sorting a List Using More than One Sort Field

Sometimes sorting by one sort field results in ties. A **tie** occurs when more than one record has the same value for a field. For example, if you sort the faculty list on the DEPARTMENT field, all employees with the same department name would be grouped together. To break a tie you can sort the list on multiple fields. For example, you can sort the faculty list by department, and then by last name within each department. In this case, you specify the DEPARTMENT field as the **primary sort field** and the LASTNAME field as the **secondary sort field**.

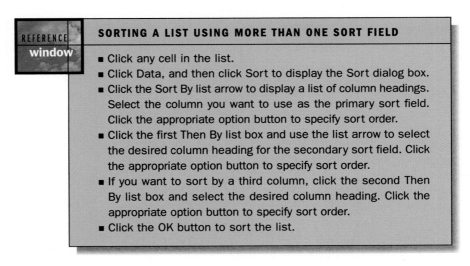

REFERENCE
window

SORTING A LIST USING MORE THAN ONE SORT FIELD

- Click any cell in the list.
- Click Data, and then click Sort to display the Sort dialog box.
- Click the Sort By list arrow to display a list of column headings. Select the column you want to use as the primary sort field. Click the appropriate option button to specify sort order.
- Click the first Then By list box and use the list arrow to select the desired column heading for the secondary sort field. Click the appropriate option button to specify sort order.
- If you want to sort by a third column, click the second Then By list box and select the desired column heading. Click the appropriate option button to specify sort order.
- Click the OK button to sort the list.

The dean asked you to sort by department and then alphabetically by last name within each department. To prepare this second list, you will need to sort the data using two columns: DEPARTMENT will be the primary sort field and LASTNAME will be the secondary sort field. When you have more than one sort key, you should use the Sort command on the Data menu to specify the columns you want to sort.

Now sort the faculty list by department, and within department by last name.

To sort the records by department and within department by last name:

1. Click any cell in the list.

2. Click **Data** on the menu bar, and then click **Sort** to display the Sort dialog box. See Figure 5-6.

Figure 5-6 ◀
Sort dialog box

primary sort key

specify secondary
sort key here

specify third
sort key here

use to specify a
custom sort order

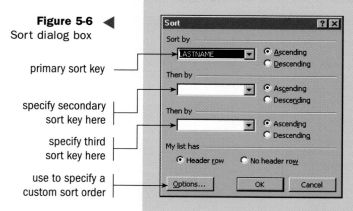

3. Click the **Sort By** list arrow to display the list of column headings, and then click **DEPARTMENT**.

4. If necessary, click the **Ascending** option button to specify that you want to sort the DEPARTMENT field in ascending order.

   Now specify the secondary sort field.

5. Click the first **Then By** list arrow to display the list of column headings, and then click **LASTNAME**.

6. Make sure the Ascending option button is selected.

7. Click the **OK** button to sort the records by department and within department by last name. See Figure 5-7.

Figure 5-7 ◀
Faculty list
sorted by
department
and within
department by
last name

sorted by last name
within accounting
department

sorted in ascending
order by department

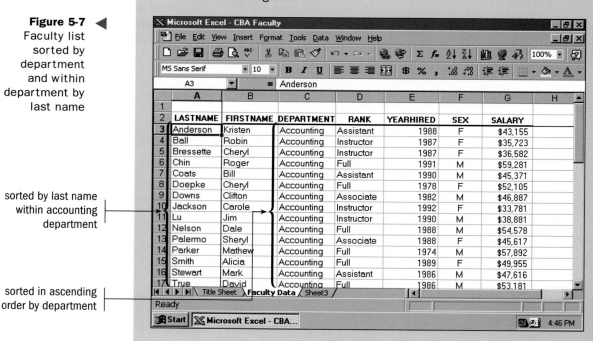

8. Scroll the list to view the data sorted by department and within department by last name.

9. Save the workbook.

Now the dean has a list of faculty members sorted by department and within department by last name. This will make finding information about faculty members much easier.

Maintaining a List Using a Data Form

The dean has several changes regarding the faculty status that need to be reflected in the faculty list. First, the accounting department has hired an instructor, Mary Hutch, to teach the introductory accounting courses. Her record needs to be added to the faculty list. Second, Kevin Mack just received official confirmation on his promotion to associate professor. Kevin's record must be updated to reflect his change in rank and new salary of $45,000. Finally, Wendy Garabizien retired at the end of the term; her record needs to be deleted from the faculty list. The dean asks you to update the faculty list to reflect these changes.

One of the easiest ways to maintain a list in Excel is to use a data form. A **data form** is a dialog box in which you can add, find, edit, and delete records in a list. A data form displays one record at a time, as opposed to the table of rows and columns you see in the worksheet. Although you can use the worksheet to make changes directly to the list, using the data form can help prevent mistakes that can occur if you accidentally enter data in the wrong column or in a row above or below the correct one.

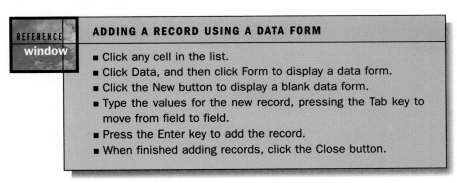

REFERENCE
window

ADDING A RECORD USING A DATA FORM

- Click any cell in the list.
- Click Data, and then click Form to display a data form.
- Click the New button to display a blank data form.
- Type the values for the new record, pressing the Tab key to move from field to field.
- Press the Enter key to add the record.
- When finished adding records, click the Close button.

Begin updating the faculty list by adding Mary Hutch's data, using the data form.

To add a new record using the data form:

1. Click any cell in the list.

2. Click **Data**, and then click **Form** to display the Faculty Data data form. The first record in the list appears. See Figure 5-8. Notice that Excel uses the worksheet name, Faculty Date, as the title of the data form.

Figure 5-8
Faculty Data
data form

labels from
column headings
of faculty list

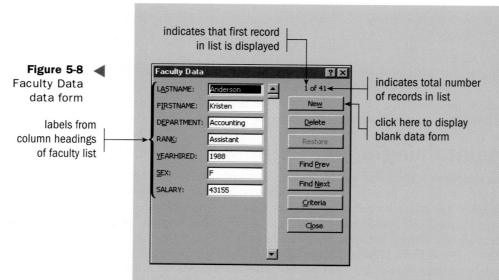

indicates that first record
in list is displayed

indicates total number
of records in list

click here to display
blank data form

The names that appear on the left side of the data form are taken from the header row of the faculty list.

In the upper-right corner of the form, there is information on how many records are in the list and which row is currently selected.

Now add the new record.

3. Click the **New** button to display a blank data form. Notice that the label "New Record" appears in the upper-right corner of the data form. Enter the values for the record in the text boxes next to each field name.

4. Type **Hutch** in the LASTNAME text box, and then press the **Tab** key to move to the FIRSTNAME text box.

   TROUBLE? If you pressed the Enter key instead of the Tab key, a blank data form appears. Click the Find Prev button to return to the previous record, the record you were entering, and continue entering the data.

5. Type **Mary** in the FIRSTNAME text box, and then press the **Tab** key to move to the DEPARTMENT text box.

6. Type **Accounting** in the DEPARTMENT text box, and then press the **Tab** key to move to the RANK text box. Continue entering the remaining data. Remember to press the Tab key after you complete each entry.

   RANK: **Instructor**

   YEARHIRED: **1999**

   SEX: **F**

   SALARY: **28000**

7. Press the **Enter** key to add the record to the bottom of the list.

   The data form is blank again, ready for you to add a new record. But since you don't have any new records to add now, return to the worksheet.

8. Click the **Close** button to close the data form and return to the worksheet.

   Confirm that the new record has been added to the faculty list. It should appear at the bottom of the list.

9. Click cell **A3** to make it the active cell.

10. Press **End +** ↓ to move to the last record in the list, in cell A44. Verify that the last record contains the data for Mary Hutch.

11. Press **Ctrl + Home** to return to cell B3.

Now you can make the other updates to the faculty list. You still need to complete two tasks: change Kevin Mack's rank and salary, and delete Wendy Garabizien's record. Although you can manually scroll through the list to find a specific record, with larger lists of data this method is slow and prone to error. The quicker and more accurate way to find a record is to use the data form's search capabilities. You will use this method to make Kevin Mack's changes and delete Wendy Garabizien's record.

Using the Data Form to Search for Records

You can use the data form to search for a specific record or group of records. When you initiate a search, you specify the search criteria, or instructions for the search. Excel starts from the current record and moves through the list, searching for any records that match the search criteria. If Excel finds more than one record that matches the search criteria, it displays the first record that matches the criteria. You can use the Find Next button in the data form to display the next record that matches the search criteria.

You need to find Kevin Mack's record to change his salary. Use the data form to find this record.

To search for a record in a list using the data form:

1. Make sure the active cell is inside the faculty list.

2. Click **Data**, and then click **Form** to display the Faculty Data data form.

3. Click the **Criteria** button to display a blank data form. The label "Criteria" in the upper-right corner of the data form indicates that the form is ready to accept search criteria.

Enter the search criteria in the appropriate field.

4. Click the **LASTNAME** text box, and then type **Mack**.

If necessary, you can enter multiple criteria. If you enter multiple criteria, all criteria must be met for Excel to find a match.

5. Click the **Find Next** button to display the next record in the list that meets the specified criteria—LASTNAME equal to Mack. See Figure 5-9.

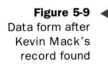

Figure 5-9 ◀
Data form after
Kevin Mack's
record found

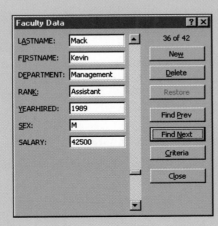

Kevin Mack is the record you're looking for. However, if more than one employee were named Mack and this was not the record you were interested in, you could click the Find Next button again and the next record meeting the search criteria would be displayed.

If no records meet the search criteria, no message is displayed. Instead, the data form simply displays the current record.

Now update his record.

6. Double-click the **RANK** text box, and then type **Associate**.

7. Double-click the **SALARY** text box, and then type **45000**.

8. Click the **Close** button to return to the faculty list. The rank and salary for Kevin Mack have been updated.

9. Scroll the list to verify that Kevin Mack's salary is now $45,000, and then press **Ctrl + Home** to return to cell B3.

Now complete the final update to the list, deleting Wendy Garabizien's record.

Using the Data Form to Delete a Record

To delete Wendy Garabizien's record, you will again use the search criteria to find the record. If you enter the full name as the search criteria, the spelling must be absolutely correct; otherwise there will be no match and Wendy Garabizien's record won't be found. As an alternative, the data form allows you to use wildcard characters when you enter search criteria. A **wildcard character** is a symbol that stands for one or more characters. Excel recognizes two wildcards: the question mark (?) and the asterisk (*).

REFERENCE window	**DELETING A RECORD USING A DATA FORM**
	■ Click any cell in the list.
	■ Click Data, and then click Form to display a data form.
	■ Locate and display the record you want to delete.
	■ Click the Delete button, and then click the OK button to confirm the deletion.

You use the asterisk (*) wildcard to represent any group of characters. For example, if you use "Gar*" as the search criteria for LASTNAME, Excel will find all the records with a last name that begins with Gar, no matter what letters follow. You use the question mark (?) to substitute for a single character. For example, enter "Richm?n" as the search criteria and you might find Richman, Richmen, or Richmon.

Since there is a chance of entering Wendy Garabizien's name incorrectly, use the asterisk wildcard character to help find her record.

To search for a record using a wildcard character:

1. Click any cell in the list, click **Data**, and then click **Form** to display the Faculty Data data form.

2. Click the **Criteria** button to begin entering the search criteria.

Specify the new search criteria.

3. Click the **LASTNAME** text box, and then type **Gar***. See Figure 5-10.

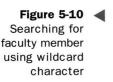
Figure 5-10 ◀
Searching for
faculty member
using wildcard
character

wildcard character

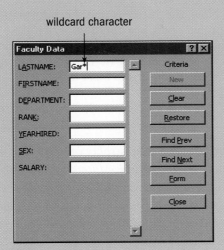

4. Click the **Find Next** button to display the first record in the list that contains the letters Gar as the first three letters of the last name. Karen Garafano is not the record you want to delete.

   TROUBLE? If you did not retrieve Karen Garafano's record, click the Close button, click Data on the menu bar, and then click Form before repeating Steps 1 through 4.

5. Click the **Find Next** button to display the next record that contains the letters Gar at the beginning of the name. Wendy Garabizien is the record you're looking for.

6. Click the **Delete** button. A message box appears, warning you that the displayed record will be permanently deleted from the list.

7. Click the **OK** button to confirm the record deletion. Wendy Garabizien's record has been deleted from the list, and the next record in the list is displayed in the data form.

8. Click the **Close** button to close the data form and return to the worksheet.

9. Print the list so the dean has a printout of the most current faculty information.

Quick Check

1. A row within a data list is often called a _____.

2. A column within a data list is often called a _____.

3. In Excel, a _____ is a collection of similar data stored in a structured manner.

4. Explain how to order a student list so that all students in the same major appear together in alphabetical order by the student's last name.

5. The _____ button in the Data Form is used to add a record to a list.

6. You have a list of 250 employees. Explain how to find Jin Shinu's record using the data form.

7. A _____ sort key is a field used to arrange records in a list.

8. If you sort the faculty list from the most recent start date to the earliest start date, you have sorted the faculty in _____ order.

You have now provided the dean with a current list of all faculty members, sorted alphabetically by department. Now she requires specific information on only some of the faculty at different levels on her staff. She could work with the complete list to find this information, but a customized list limited to just the information she requires would be more useful to her. You can help the dean by filtering the faculty list to show just the information she requires. You will do this in Session 5.2.

SESSION 5.2

In this session you will learn to filter a list to display only specific information using AutoFilters, and you will learn how to customize filters to meet more complex criteria. You will use conditional formatting to highlight data in the list. You will also expand the list to include a new field using natural language formulas, and insert subtotals to display summary information in the list. Finally, you will use Page Break Preview to insert custom page breaks for printing the list.

Filtering a List Using AutoFilters

Now that the dean has the full list of faculty organized for easy reference, she is ready to use the list to prepare the reports she needs for her upcoming meetings. The first scheduled meeting is with the other deans at NSU—their task is to form a university-wide accreditation committee comprising faculty representatives from each of the individual colleges and departments at the university. The dean needs to select a faculty member from the College of Business Administration to serve on the committee. She wants to select a senior faculty member and asks you for a list of full professors.

To get a list of faculty members who are full professors you could scan the entire faculty list. However, with large lists locating the data you need can be difficult and time-consuming. Sorting can help because you group the data; however, you're still working with the entire list. You could use a data form, but if you use a data form to find records that meet specified criteria, you will only display one record at a time. A better solution is to have Excel find the specific records you want, displaying only these records in the worksheet. This process of "hiding" certain records and viewing the ones you want is called **filtering** your data. All records that do not meet your criteria are temporarily hidden from view.

REFERENCE window

FILTERING A LIST WITH AUTOFILTER

- Click any cell in the list.
- Click Data, point to Filter, and then click AutoFilter to insert list arrows next to each column label in your list.
- Click the list arrow in the column that contains the data you want to filter.
- Click the criteria you want to filter.

The Excel AutoFilter feature allows you to filter your data so you view only the records you want. You will use this feature to create a list of full professors in the College of Business Administration.

To filter a list using the AutoFilter command:

1. If you took a break after the last session, make sure Excel is running, the CBA Faculty workbook is open, and the Faculty Data worksheet is displayed. Make sure the active cell is within the faculty list.

2. Click **Data**, point to **Filter**, and then click **AutoFilter**. See Figure 5-11. List arrows appear next to each column label in the list. To see a list of filtering criteria for a specific column, click the list arrow next to the column heading.

Figure 5-11 ◀
Faculty list after AutoFilter feature activated

filtering arrow next to each column heading

3. Click the **RANK column** list arrow in cell D2 to display a list of criteria you can use to filter the data. See Figure 5-12. Besides the unique values—Assistant, Associate, Full, and Instructor—in the RANK column, three other choices appear that apply to every column. Figure 5-13 describes these three options.

Figure 5-12 ◀
Filtering options for the RANK field

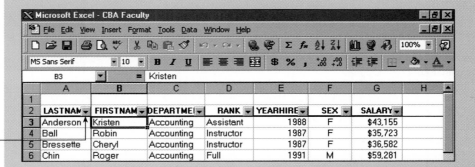

these options appear in all columns

list of filtering options

Figure 5-13 ◀
Default filtering options

Option	Description
All	Displays all items in the column and removes filtering for the column
Top 10	Displays the top or bottom *n* items in the list
Custom	Specifies more complex criteria

Now select your criteria for filtering the data.

4. Click **Full** to display only full professors. See Figure 5-14. In the status bar, Excel displays the number of records found out of the total records in the list. Review the list to verify that only records with a value equal to Full in the RANK column are visible. Excel hides all rows (records) that do not have the value Full in this column.

Figure 5-14 ◄
Faculty list displaying only full professors

blue arrow indicates column used to filter list

gaps in row numbers

indicates number of records found out of all records in list

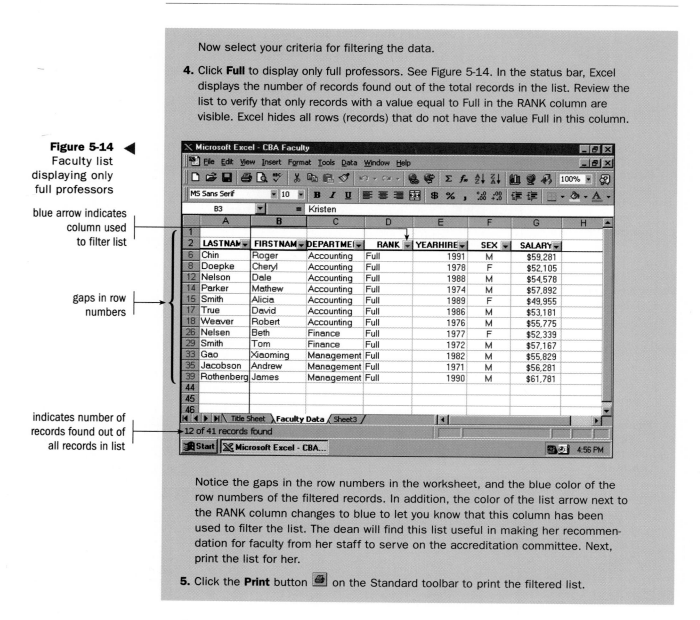

Notice the gaps in the row numbers in the worksheet, and the blue color of the row numbers of the filtered records. In addition, the color of the list arrow next to the RANK column changes to blue to let you know that this column has been used to filter the list. The dean will find this list useful in making her recommendation for faculty from her staff to serve on the accreditation committee. Next, print the list for her.

5. Click the **Print** button 🖨 on the Standard toolbar to print the filtered list.

If you need to, you can further restrict the records that appear in the filtered list by selecting entries from another drop-down list. For instance, if the dean wanted to select from a pool of female faculty with a rank of full professor, you could simply click the SEX column and then click F.

To filter by more than one criterion:

1. Click the **SEX column** list arrow, in cell F2, and then click **F** to display the female full professors. See Figure 5-15.

Figure 5-15 ◄
Faculty list
showing female
full professors

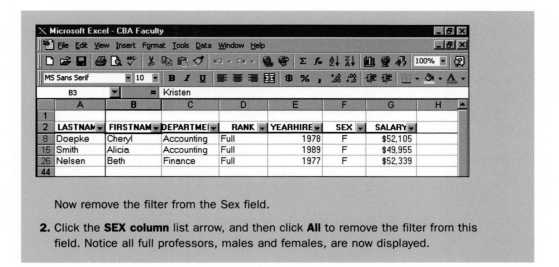

Now remove the filter from the Sex field.

2. Click the **SEX column** list arrow, and then click **All** to remove the filter from this field. Notice all full professors, males and females, are now displayed.

Now that you have provided the dean with the list of full professors, restore the list so all the records can be viewed again.

To restore all the data to the list:

1. Click **Data**, point to **Filter**, and then click **Show All**. All the records appear in the worksheet, but all the list arrows remain next to the column headings. Therefore, you can continue to customize the list by filtering it to show certain data.

Now that the list again shows all the faculty records, the dean has a more complex task, which requires you to provide specific information based on customized criteria.

Using Custom AutoFilters to Specify More Complex Criteria

Although you can often find the information you need by selecting a single item from a list of values in the filter list, there are times when you need to specify a custom set of criteria to find certain records. **Custom AutoFilters** allow you to specify relationships other than "equal to" to filter records. For instance, the dean will be meeting with the university's budget director, Bin Chi, later this week to review the College of Business Administration's budget needs for the next fiscal cycle. She received a memo today from the budget office asking for a list of faculty earning over $50,000 a year hired during the 1980s. The dean asks you to print this information. You can develop a custom set of criteria using the Custom option in the AutoFilter list to retrieve these records for the dean.

To use a custom AutoFilter to filter a list:

1. Click the **YEARHIRED** list arrow, and then click **Custom** to display the Custom AutoFilter dialog box. See Figure 5-16.

click here for a list of
comparison operators

criteria boxes

Figure 5-16
Custom
AutoFilter
dialog box

operator boxes

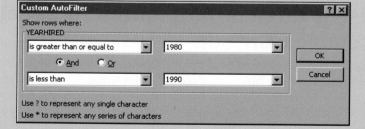

The operator list box, the first list box in the Show rows where section of the dialog box, lets you specify a comparison operator by selecting an item from a list.

The criteria list box, the list box to the right of the operator list box, lets you specify the field value by typing a value or selecting an item from a list.

The And and Or option buttons are used if you want to display rows that meet two conditions for the field. You select And to display rows that meet both criteria. You select Or to display rows that meet either criterion.

2. Click the **first operator** list arrow, and then click **is greater than or equal to**.

3. Click the **first criteria** list box, and then type **1980** in the list box.

4. If necessary, click the **And** option button.

5. Click the **second operator** list arrow, and then click **is less than**.

6. Click the **second criteria** list box, and then type **1990**. See Figure 5-17.

Figure 5-17
Custom
AutoFilter
dialog box
showing
custom criteria

Custom AutoFilter			? X
Show rows where:			
┌YEARHIRED─			
is greater than or equal to ▼	1980 ▼		OK
⦿ And ○ Or			Cancel
is less than ▼	1990 ▼		
Use ? to represent any single character			
Use * to represent any series of characters			

7. Click the **OK** button to display the filtered list consisting of all faculty hired between 1980 and 1989.

You have only some of the information the dean requires, however, because she also needs to know all the faculty hired during the 1980s who earn more than $50,000. So, further restrict the filtered list to those faculty earning more than $50,000.

8. Click the **SALARY** list arrow, and then click **Custom** to display the Custom AutoFilter dialog box.

9. Click the **first operator** list arrow, click **is greater than** from the list of operators, click the **first criteria** list box, and then type **50000**.

10. Click the **OK** button to view the filtered list showing faculty hired between 1980 and 1989 earning more than $50,000. See Figure 5-18.

Figure 5-18 ◄
Filtered list
showing faculty
hired between
1980 and 1989
earning more
than $50,000

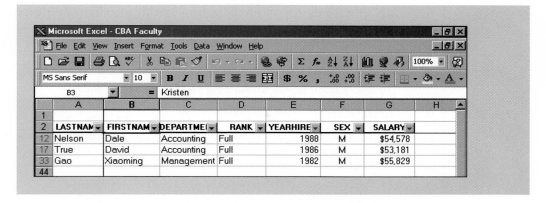

You show the list to the dean. She asks you to sort the list in descending order by salary.

To sort the filtered list, and then restore all the records to the list:

1. Click any field in the SALARY column.

2. Click the **Sort Descending** button ![ZA] on the Standard toolbar to sort the filtered list in descending order by salary.

3. Click the **Print** button ![printer] on the Standard toolbar to print the list.

   After printing the list you give it to the dean. You can now remove all the filters to return to the original complete faculty list.

4. Click **Data**, point to **Filter**, and then click **AutoFilter** to remove all the filters. All the records are displayed and the list arrows no longer appear in the column headings.

The dean wants to be able to quickly identify faculty earning more than $50,000 and asks you to apply the new Excel conditional formatting feature to the SALARY field.

Using Conditional Formatting

Excel lets you apply **conditional formatting**—formatting that appears only when data in the cell meets conditions that you specify. Using this feature you can specify up to three conditions that apply to the value of a cell or the formula that produces the value. For each condition, you specify the formatting (font, font style, font color, border, etc.) that will be applied to the cell if the condition is true.

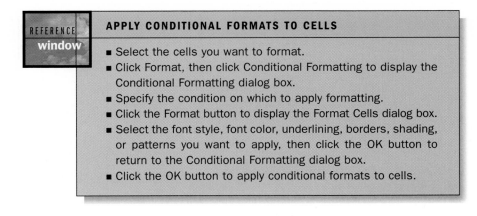

REFERENCE
window

APPLY CONDITIONAL FORMATS TO CELLS

■ Select the cells you want to format.
■ Click Format, then click Conditional Formatting to display the Conditional Formatting dialog box.
■ Specify the condition on which to apply formatting.
■ Click the Format button to display the Format Cells dialog box.
■ Select the font style, font color, underlining, borders, shading, or patterns you want to apply, then click the OK button to return to the Conditional Formatting dialog box.
■ Click the OK button to apply conditional formats to cells.

Since the dean wants to be able to quickly identify faculty earning more than $50,000, you decide to apply conditional formatting to any cell in the SALARY field containing a value exceeding $50,000, so that the background color of these cells is green.

Now apply the conditional formatting to the SALARY field.

To apply conditional formatting to the SALARY field:

1. Select the range **G3:G43**.

2. Click **Format** on the menu bar, and then click **Conditional Formatting** to display the Conditional Formatting dialog box. See Figure 5-19. First, specify the condition that will be applied to the salary range.

click here to see list of comparison operators

Figure 5-19 ◄
Conditional
Formatting
dialog box

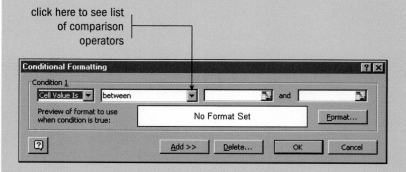

3. Since the contents of the cells in the SALARY field are values, as opposed to formulas or text, make sure Cell Value Is appears in the Condition 1 list box.

Next, choose the comparison operator to compare with the cell value.

4. Click the **list arrow** in the second list box to display a list of comparison operators, and then click **greater than**. Notice the number of boxes changes to reflect the comparison operator you should use.

Now enter the value.

5. Click the **third** list box for Condition 1, and type **50000**. The condition has been defined. If you needed to, you could specify two additional conditions.

Now define the formatting to be applied to the cell or range if the condition is true.

6. Click the **Format** button in the Conditional Formatting dialog box to display the Format Cells dialog box.

7. Click the **Patterns** tab, and then click the color **green** from the Cell Shading palette (fourth row, fourth column).

8. Click the **OK** button to return to the Conditional Formatting dialog box. Notice that green shading appears in the Preview box.

9. Click the **OK** button to apply the conditional formatting to the selected cells.

10. Click any cell to deselect the range. See Figure 5-20. Notice that the background color of several cells in the range is now green.

Figure 5-20
Faculty
list after
conditional
formatting
applied

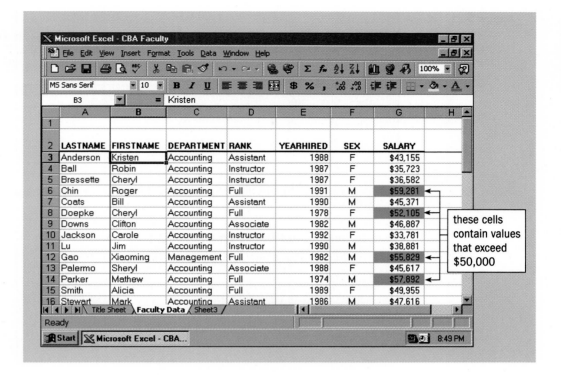

Note that if the value of the cell changes and no longer meets the specified condition(s), Excel temporarily suppresses the formats associated with that cell. However, the conditional formats remain applied to the cells until you remove them, even when none of the conditions are met and the specified cell formats are not displayed.

The dean has a request for information she needs for her meeting with the budget director, and she meets with you to discuss how the faculty list can be used in this task.

Creating Natural Language Formulas

Bin, the budget director, is getting ready to start the next budget cycle. He asks each college dean to provide him with a list of faculty and the proposed salary for each faculty member for next year. Currently, the plan is to increase each faculty member's salary by three percent to keep pace with inflation. The report requested by Bin should list each faculty member by department, and should include a departmental subtotal for the PROPOSED SALARY field.

You will need to add a new field to the faculty list—PROPOSED SALARY—a calculated field equal to each faculty member's current salary times 1.03.

Although you can use cell references to build this formula, Excel 97 has a feature, natural language formulas, which can be used to create such formulas. **Natural language formulas** allow you to use column headers and row labels in building formulas. For example, in Figure 5-21 you have two labels, Sales and Expenses, which identify the values in cells B1 and B2. These labels can be used to build the formula to compute net income. Instead of entering the formula =B1-B2, the natural language formula =Sales - Expenses was used to calculate net income.

Figure 5-21 ◀
Example of
natural
language
formula

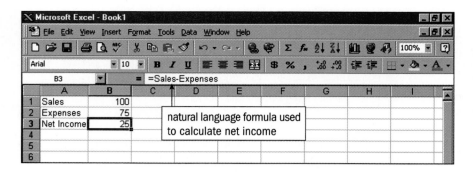

Now, add the PROPOSED SALARY field to the faculty list using a natural language formula.

To enter and format the column heading for proposed salary:

1. Click cell **H2**, and then type **PROPOSED SALARY**.

2. Click cell **G2**, click the **Format Painter** button, on the Standard toolbar, and then click cell **H2** to copy the format in cell G2 to cell H2.

3. Click **Format** on the menu bar, and then click **Cells** to display the Format Cells dialog box.

4. Click the **Alignment** tab, click the **Wrap Text** check box, and then click the **OK** button to apply text wrapping to cell H2.

Now enter the formula to calculate the proposed salary.

To create a natural language formula:

1. In cell H3, type **=salary*1.03**, and then press the **Enter** key. "Salary" in the formula is the column heading. Excel uses the corresponding cell in the SALARY column (G3) to multiply times 1.03.

   Apply the format used in the SALARY field to the PROPOSED SALARY field.

2. Format cell H3 using Currency style with zero decimal places.

3. Copy the formula in cell H3 to the range H4:H43. Scroll to the top of the list.

4. Click any cell to deselect the range. See Figure 5-22. Notice on Figure 5-22, column B is not visible, unless you scroll to the left. Depending on the size of your monitor, column B may or may not be visible.

Figure 5-22 ◀
Faculty list
with new field

natural language
formula

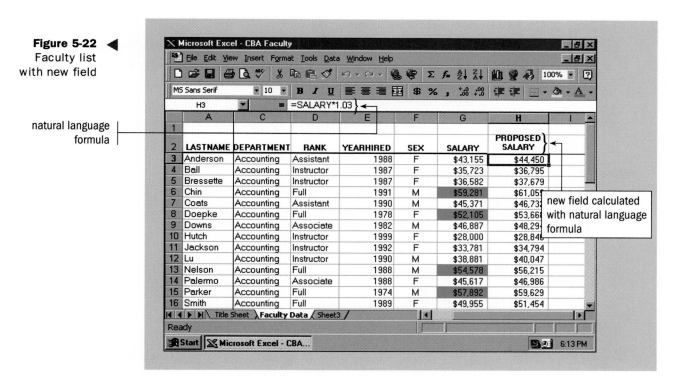

Now that the PROPOSED SALARY field has been added to the list, you can prepare the information for the dean. Remember, this report will list the faculty by department, followed by totals for each department.

Inserting Subtotals into a List

Excel can summarize data in a list by inserting subtotals. The Subtotals command offers many kinds of summary information, including counts, sums, averages, minimums, and maximums. The Subtotals command automatically inserts a subtotal line into the list for each group of data in the list. A grand total line is also added to the bottom of the list. Since Excel inserts subtotals whenever the value in a specified field changes, you need to sort the list so records with the same value in a specified field are grouped together before you can use the subtotals command.

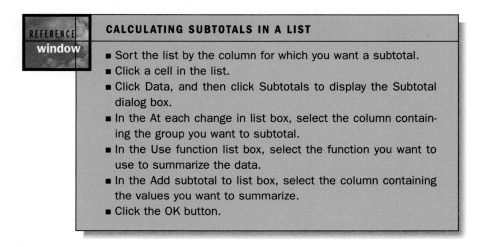

REFERENCE
window

CALCULATING SUBTOTALS IN A LIST

- Sort the list by the column for which you want a subtotal.
- Click a cell in the list.
- Click Data, and then click Subtotals to display the Subtotal dialog box.
- In the At each change in list box, select the column containing the group you want to subtotal.
- In the Use function list box, select the function you want to use to summarize the data.
- In the Add subtotal to list box, select the column containing the values you want to summarize.
- Click the OK button.

To supply Bin with the information he requested, you will develop a list of faculty, sorted by department, with subtotals calculated for the PROPOSED SALARY field. Each subtotal will be inserted after each departmental grouping.

To calculate subtotals by department:

1. If the list is not sorted by department, click any cell in the DEPARTMENT column, and then click the **Sort Ascending** button 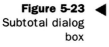 on the Standard toolbar. The list is sorted by department.

   Now calculate the subtotals in the list.

2. Click **Data** on the menu bar, and then click **Subtotals** to display the Subtotal dialog box. See Figure 5-23.

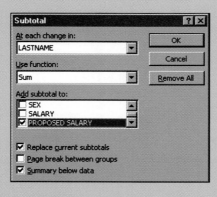

Figure 5-23 ◄
Subtotal dialog
box

3. Click the **At each change in** list arrow, and then click **DEPARTMENT** to select the column containing the field for which you want subtotals.

4. If necessary, click the **Use function** list arrow, and then click **Sum** to select the function you want to use to summarize the data.

   You want departmental subtotals for the PROPOSED SALARY field.

5. In the Add subtotal to list box, scroll the list and, if necessary, remove any check marks in the category check boxes, and then click the **PROPOSED SALARY** check box, the column containing the field you want to summarize.

6. Make sure the Replace current subtotals and the Summary below data check boxes are checked so that the subtotals appear below the related data.

7. Click the **OK** button to insert subtotals into the list. Subtotals are added to the PROPOSED SALARY column, showing the total salaries for each department.

8. Scroll through the list to be sure you can see all the subtotals and the grand total at the bottom. If necessary, increase the column width so you can view the subtotal values. See Figure 5-24. Notice the Outline buttons to the left of the worksheet, which show the levels of detail possible while the Subtotals command is active.

Figure 5-24 ◀
Faculty list
with subtotals

Level 3
Outline button

Outline buttons that
control the level of
detail you see

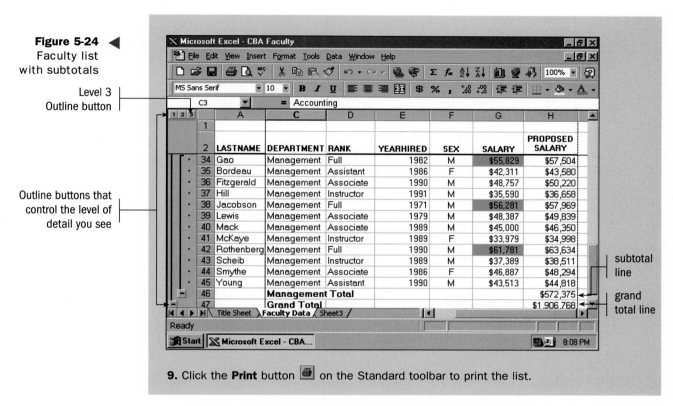

9. Click the **Print** button on the Standard toolbar to print the list.

The subtotals are useful for the dean to see, but she asks if there is a way to isolate the different subtotal sections so that she can focus on them individually.

Using the Subtotals Outline View

In addition to displaying subtotals, the Subtotals command "outlines" your worksheet so you can control the level of detail that is displayed. The three Outline buttons displayed at the top of the outline area in Figure 5-24 allow you to show or hide different levels of detail in your worksheet. By default, Level 3 is active. Level 3 displays the most detail—the individual faculty records, the subtotals, and the grand total. If you click the Level 2 Outline button, Excel displays the subtotals and the grand total but not the individual records. If you click the Level 1 Outline button, Excel displays only the grand total.

Now, use the Outline buttons to prepare a report that includes only subtotals and the grand total.

To use the Outline buttons to hide the details:

1. Click the **Level 2** Outline button. Scroll the worksheet until all subtotals are visible. See Figure 5-25. Notice that the worksheet hides the individual faculty records and shows only the subtotals for each department and the grand total.

Figure 5-25 ◀
Subtotals after
Level 2 Outline
button selected

Level 2 Outline button

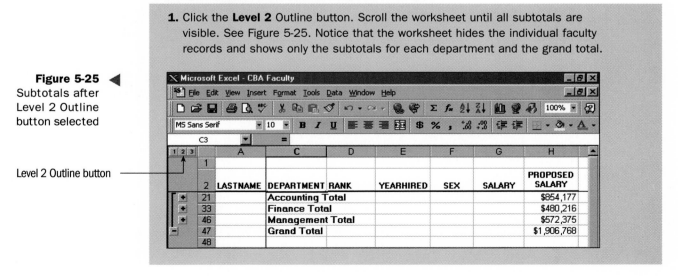

2. Print the worksheet.

3. Click the **Level 3 Outline** button to show all the records again.

The dean is very pleased with the way you have manipulated the faculty list to provide her with the data she needs. She now needs printouts she can hand out to the various department heads.

Printing the List Using Page Breaks

When you printed the faculty list, it printed on one page. The dean has asked that the data for each department be printed on a separate page so copies can be shared with each department head as well as the budget director. You can use the Page Break Preview button from the Print Preview window to view where Excel breaks pages in your worksheet and to change either a horizontal or a vertical page break.

To insert a page break to start a new page:

1. Click the **Print Preview** button 🔍 on the Standard toolbar to display the faculty list. Notice that only one page is needed to print the list.

2. Click the **Page Break Preview** button to view a version of the worksheet that shows the entire print area with page breaks and page numbers superimposed on it. Excel is now in Page Break Preview view. See Figure 5-26.

> TROUBLE? If the message, "Welcome to Page Break View. You can adjust where the page breaks are by clicking and dragging with your mouse" is displayed, click the check box, and then click the OK button, so the message is not displayed again.

Figure 5-26 ◄
Page Break
Preview view

Select All button ——

click here to indicate
row where page break
will occur

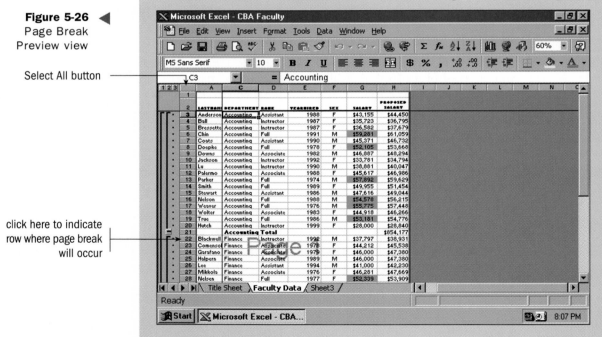

Page Break Preview is different from Print Preview in that you can make some modifications to the worksheet in this mode.

3. Click the **row selector** button to the left of column A at row 22, the row where you want to start a new page.

4. Click **Insert** on the menu bar, and then click **Page Break**.

5. Repeat Steps 3 and 4 to insert a page break at row 34. Notice that after you insert the page break, a thick blue line appears to indicate where the break is located.

6. Repeat Steps 3 and 4 to insert a page break at row 47 so that the grand total is *not* printed on the same page as the management department data.

7. If necessary, increase the column width of column H so that you can view the grand total.

8. Click the **Print** button 🖨 on the Standard toolbar to print the faculty list on separate pages for each department.

   Because you will not need these page breaks for future printouts of the faculty list, remove them now.

9. To remove all the page breaks, click the **Select All** button located at the intersection of the row and column headings of your worksheet (if necessary, refer to Figure 5-26), click **Insert** on the menu bar, and then click **Reset All Page Breaks**.

   Now return to normal view.

10. Click **View** on the menu bar, and then click **Normal**. The worksheet returns to normal view.

Now that you have prepared and printed the list with subtotals, you can remove the subtotals from the list.

To remove the subtotals from the list:

1. Click any cell in the list, click **Data**, and then click **Subtotals** to display the Subtotal dialog box.

2. Click the **Remove All** button to remove the subtotals from the list.

3. Click **Ctrl + Home** to return to the top of the list.

4. Save the worksheet.

Quick Check

1. Explain the relationship between the Sort and Subtotals commands.

2. If you have a list of students sorted by major and you wanted to print the students in each major on a separate page, you would use the _____.

3. If you had a worksheet with the column headings Shares and Cost Per Share, and entered the formula =*Shares * Cost Per Share* to compute Total Cost, you were using a _____ formula.

4. If you have a list of 300 students in the College of Business Administration and wanted to print only finance majors, you would use the _____ command from the _____ menu.

5. Explain how you can display a list of marketing majors with a GPA of 3.0 or greater from a list of 300 students.

6. Once subtotals are displayed, you can use the _____ button to control the level of detail displayed.

7. _____ enables formatting to appear only when the data in a cell meets a condition you specify.

You have supplied the dean with the information she needs for her meeting with the budget director to review financial plans for the next fiscal cycle. Now the dean needs to generate some information for a meeting with the affirmative action task force. You will work with the CBA faculty list in the next session to gather the information she needs for that meeting.

SESSION

5.3

In this session you will learn to summarize data from an Excel list in different formats using the PivotTable Wizard.

Creating and Using Pivot Tables to Summarize a List

An Excel list can contain a wealth of information, but because of the large amounts of detailed data, it is often difficult to form a clear overall view of the information. You can use a pivot table to help organize the information. A **pivot table** is a special type of table that enables you to group and summarize an Excel list into a concise, tabular format for easier reporting and analysis. A pivot table summarizes data in different categories using functions such as COUNT, SUM, AVERAGE, MAX, and MIN.

All pivot tables have similar elements. These include **column fields**, **row fields**, and **page fields**. Typically, the values in descriptive fields, such as department, rank, year hired, and sex, appear in pivot tables as rows, columns, or pages. In creating a pivot table, you also specify which fields you want to summarize. Salaries, sales, and costs are examples of fields that you usually summarize. In pivot table terminology these are known as **data fields**.

One advantage of pivot tables is that you can easily rearrange, hide, and display different categories in the pivot table to provide alternative views of the data. This ability to "pivot" your table—for example, change column headings to row positions and vice versa—gives the pivot table its name and makes it a powerful analytical tool.

The dean now wants some tabulated information for an affirmative action report. She first reviewed the data within the faculty list to try to get a feel for whether men and women in comparable positions are making comparable salaries. She became overwhelmed and asked you to set up a pivot table.

You consider the information that the dean wants and create a pivot table plan (Figure 5-27) and a pivot table sketch (Figure 5-28). Your plan and sketch will help you work with the PivotTable Wizard to produce the pivot table you want.

Figure 5-27 ◀
Pivot table plan
for calculating
average
salaries

Pivot Table Plan

My Goal:
Create a table that compares female and male average salary for each academic rank

What results do I want to see?
Average female salary for each rank
Average male salary for each rank
Overall average female salary
Overall average male salary
The average at each rank for males and females combined

What information do I need?
The table rows will show the data for each rank
The table columns will show the data for each sex
The table will summarize salary data

What calculation method will I use?
The salary data will be averaged for each rank and sex

Figure 5-28 ◀
Sketch of table
to compare
average
salaries

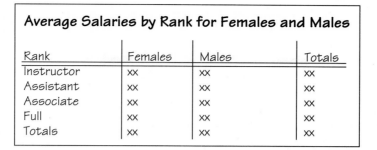

Rank	Females	Males	Totals
Instructor	xx	xx	xx
Assistant	xx	xx	xx
Associate	xx	xx	xx
Full	xx	xx	xx
Totals	xx	xx	xx

Average Salaries by Rank for Females and Males

Now you are ready to create a pivot table summarizing average faculty salaries of men and women by rank.

Creating a Pivot Table

To create the pivot table for the dean, you can use the Excel PivotTable Wizard to guide you through a four-step process. Although the PivotTable Wizard will prompt you for the information necessary to create the table, the preliminary plan and sketch you created will be helpful in achieving the layout the dean wants.

Defining the Layout of the Pivot Table

In the third step of the PivotTable Wizard you specify which fields contain the data you want to summarize, and specify how the data will be summarized by selecting from functions such as COUNT, SUM, AVERAGE, MAX, and MIN. In addition to identifying the data to be summarized, you also specify how the data is to be arranged; that is, what fields will appear as column, row, and page headings in the pivot table.

In this step the fields are represented by a set of field buttons. You create the layout by dragging the field buttons into any of the four areas of the sample pivot table: ROW, COLUMN, PAGE, or DATA.

In the pivot table you are creating, you will compute average salaries for each rank and sex. The values in the RANK field will appear as row labels, the values in the SEX field will appear as column headings, and the SALARY field will be the data that is summarized.

Now that you have done some planning, you are ready to create the pivot table for the dean.

REFERENCE
window

CREATING A PIVOT TABLE

- Identify the source of data for the pivot table.
- Identify the location of the data.
- Identify the layout of the pivot table—define the row, column, page, and data fields for the table.
- Specify the location, name, and other options for the pivot table.

Most often when creating a pivot table, you begin with a list stored in a worksheet. In this case, you will use the faculty list in the Faculty Data worksheet to create the pivot table.

To create a pivot table:

1. Click any cell in the list, click **Data**, and then click **PivotTable Report** to display the PivotTable Wizard - Step 1 of 4 dialog box. See Figure 5-29. In this dialog box, you specify the source of the data that is to be used to create the pivot table. You can select from an Excel list; an external data source, such as a dBASE file; multiple consolidation ranges; or another pivot table. To develop the average salaries pivot table, you use the Excel list in the Faculty Data worksheet.

TROUBLE? If the Office Assistant appears, select the option "No, don't provide help now."

Figure 5-29
PivotTable
Wizard -
Step 1 of 4
dialog box

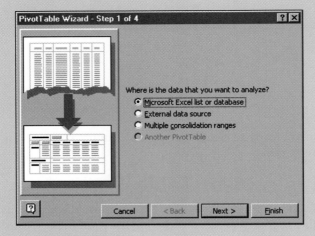

2. Make sure the Microsoft Excel list or database option is selected, and then click the **Next** button to display the PivotTable Wizard - Step 2 of 4 dialog box. See Figure 5-30.

Figure 5-30
PivotTable
Wizard - Step
2 of 4 dialog
box

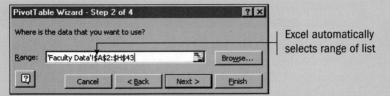

Excel automatically
selects range of list

At this point, you need to identify the location of the data you are going to summarize in the pivot table.

Since the active cell is located within the range of the Excel list (Step 1), the Wizard automatically selects the range of the faculty list, 'Faculty Data'!$A$2:$H$43, as the source of data for the pivot table.

TROUBLE? If the Range box in the PivotTable Wizard - Step 2 of 4 displays "Database" instead of 'Faculty Data'!$A$2:$H$43 as the source of the data, click the Next button to go to Step 3 of the PivotTable Wizard. If an error message displays when you click the Next button, click the Collapse Dialog box button and select the range A2:H43, and then continue to Step 3.

3. Click the **Next** button to display the PivotTable Wizard - Step 3 of 4 dialog box. See Figure 5-31. In this dialog box you specify the layout of the pivot table. Notice the field buttons on the right side of the dialog box and the diagram to the left of the field buttons. They are used to specify the layout of the pivot table.

Figure 5-31
PivotTable
Wizard - Step
3 of 4 dialog
box

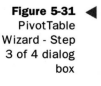

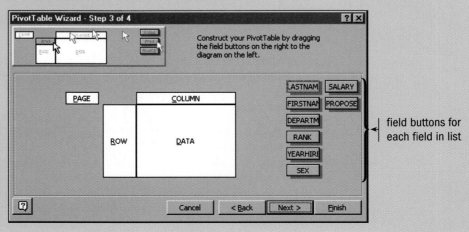

field buttons for
each field in list

4. Click the **RANK** field button and drag it to the ROW area of the sample pivot table. When you release the mouse button, the RANK button appears in the ROW area. See Figure 5-32. When the Wizard is finished, the pivot table will contain a row label for each unique value in the RANK field.

Figure 5-32 ◄
Sample pivot
table area

RANK button dragged
to ROW area

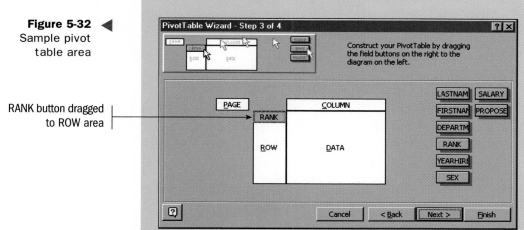

TROUBLE? If you moved the wrong field into the sample pivot table area, you can remove it by dragging it anywhere outside the diagram.

5. Click and drag the **SEX** field button to the COLUMN area of the sample pivot table. When you release the mouse button, the SEX button appears in the COLUMN area. When the Wizard is finished, the pivot table will contain a column label for each unique value in the SEX field.

6. Click and drag the **SALARY** field button to the DATA area of the sample pivot table. When you release the mouse button, a Sum of SALARY button appears in the DATA area. See Figure 5-33. When the Wizard is finished, the pivot table will contain the sum of the SALARY field entries for each combination of the SEX and RANK field entries.

Figure 5-33 ◄
Sample pivot
table area with
entries in ROW,
COLUMN, and
DATA areas

SEX field is
column label

SALARY field to
be summarized

RANK field is
row label

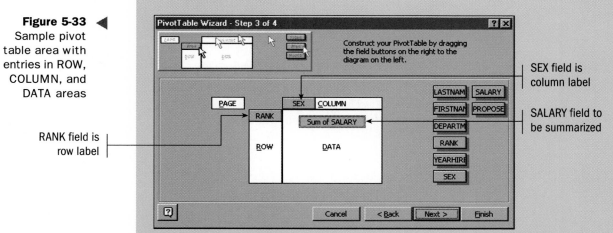

By default, the PivotTable Wizard uses the SUM function for calculations involving numeric values in the DATA area, and the COUNT function for nonnumeric values. If you want to use a different summary function, such as AVERAGE, MAX, or MIN, you can double-click the field button in the DATA area and select the summary function from a list of available functions in the PivotTable Field dialog box.

Now compute average salaries.

7. Double-click the **Sum of SALARY** button in the DATA area to display the PivotTable Field dialog box. See Figure 5-34.

Figure 5-34 ◀
PivotTable Field
dialog box

select this summary
function

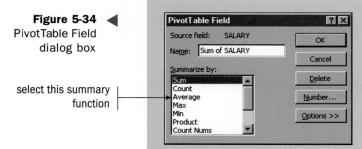

8. Click **Average** in the Summarize by list box, and then click the **OK** button to return to the PivotTable Wizard - Step 3 of 4 dialog box. Notice that the summary button in the DATA area indicates Average of SALARY. The third step is complete.

9. Click the **Next** button to display the PivotTable Wizard - Step 4 of 4 dialog box. See Figure 5-35.

Figure 5-35 ◀
PivotTable
Wizard - Step
4 of 4 dialog
box

In this final dialog box of the PivotTable Wizard you decide where to place the pivot table—either in a new worksheet or in an existing worksheet. Place the pivot table in a new worksheet.

10. Make sure the New worksheet option button is selected, and then click the **Finish** button to create the pivot table. A new worksheet, Sheet1, containing the pivot table, appears to the left of the Faculty Data sheet. See Figure 5-36. Notice that the field buttons RANK and SEX appear as part of the pivot table. Additionally, the PivotTable toolbar is displayed. Figure 5-37 describes the tools available on this toolbar.

TROUBLE? If the PivotTable toolbar does not appear on your screen, click View on the menu bar, click Toolbars, and then click PivotTable.

Figure 5-36 ◀
Pivot table
showing
average
salaries for
males and
females by rank

SEX field button ——

RANK field button ——

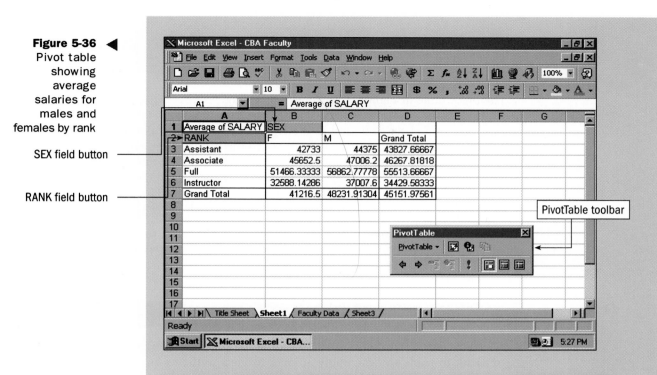

Figure 5-37 ◀
PivotTable
toolbar

Button	Name	Function
PivotTable	PivotTable	Shortcut menu of all pivot table commands
	PivotTable Wizard	Accesses the PivotTable Wizard so you can create or modify a pivot table
	PivotTable Field	Displays the PivotTable Field dialog box so you can modify the options for the selected field
	Show Pages	Displays each page of a pivot table page field in a new worksheet in the same workbook
	Ungroup	Ungroups the values in a selected field
	Group	Groups selected items; lets you group numeric items, dates, or times into ranges
	Hide Detail	Hides detail lines for a selected field in a pivot table
	Show Detail	Shows detail lines for a selected field in a pivot table
	Refresh Data	Updates the contents of the pivot table based on changes made to the source data
	Select Label	Selects just the labels in the table for formatting
	Select Data	Selects just the data in the table for formatting
	Select Label and Data	Selects the data and the labels in the table for formatting

11. Rename the worksheet **AvgSalary**.

12. Save the workbook.

The pivot table in Figure 5-36 shows the average salaries paid to faculty members in each rank, by males and females. Although the data in a pivot table may look like data in any other worksheet, you cannot directly enter or change data in the DATA area of the pivot table, because the pivot table is linked to the source data. Any changes that affect the pivot table must first be made to the Excel list. Later in the tutorial you will update a faculty member's salary and learn how to reflect that change in the pivot table.

Changing the Layout of a Pivot Table

Although you cannot change the values inside the pivot table, there are many ways you can change the layout, formatting, and computational options of a pivot table. For example, once the pivot table is created, you have numerous ways of rearranging, adding, and removing fields.

Formatting Numbers in the Pivot Table

As the dean runs off to a meeting, she mentions to you that the numbers in the pivot table are difficult to read. You can apply number formats to the cells in the pivot table just as you would format any cell in a worksheet. You will format the average salary using the Currency style.

To specify the number format for pivot table values:

1. Select the range **B3:D7**.

2. Click the **Currency Style** button 🔘 on the Formatting toolbar. Click the **Decrease Decimal** button 🔘 on the Formatting toolbar twice to reduce the number of decimal places to zero. The pivot table is displayed with the Currency format applied to the cells in the DATA area of the table.

3. Click any cell to deselect the range and view the newly formatted pivot table. See Figure 5-38.

Figure 5-38 ◀
Pivot table after formatting

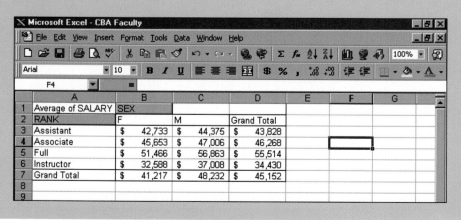

With the numbers formatted, the data in the pivot table is much easier to interpret.

Repositioning a Field in the Pivot Table

Recall that the benefit of a pivot table is that it summarizes large amounts of data into a readable format. Once you have created the table, you can also choose to view the same data from different angles. At the top of the pivot table's ROW and COLUMN areas are field buttons that enable you to change, or pivot, the view of the data by dragging these buttons to different locations in the pivot table.

The dean reviews the tabular format of the pivot table you have created, and decides it might be more useful if it displayed males and females as row classifications under rank. Reposition the column headings for the SEX field (females and males) as row labels.

To move a column field to a row field in the pivot table:

1. Click and drag the **SEX** field button below the RANK field button. See Figure 5-39. Notice that when you click and drag in the COLUMN area, your mouse pointer changes to ⬚. After you drag into the ROW area, the mouse pointer changes to ⬚.

Figure 5-39 ◀
Repositioning
SEX field
button in pivot
table

indicates pivot table
is being rearranged

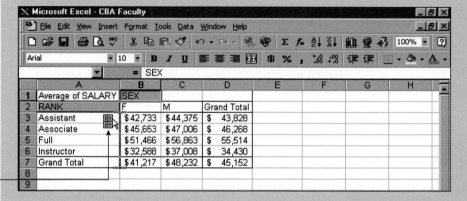

2. Release the mouse button. See Figure 5-40. The pivot table is reordered so that the SEX field is treated as a row field instead of a column field.

    TROUBLE? If the SEX field appears to the left of the RANK field, click the Undo button ⟳ ▾ on the Standard toolbar to undo the last step and then repeat Step 1. When you drag the SEX field button, just drag the button into the blank area under the RANK button. If you drag the button much further to the left, you will change the order of the fields.

Figure 5-40 ◀
Rearranged
pivot table

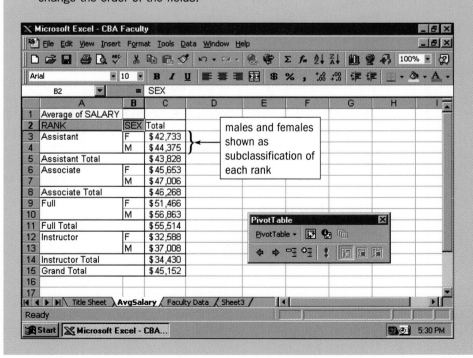

After viewing the pivot table in the new arrangement, the dean decides she prefers the original layout.

3. Click the **SEX** field button and drag it above the RANK field button. The pivot table again looks like Figure 5-38.

Sorting Items Within the Pivot Table

After reviewing the pivot table the dean asks you to rearrange it so that it displays the rank with the highest average salary first. To complete this task, you can sort the data in the pivot table.

To sort a pivot table:

1. Click cell **D3** to place the cell pointer in the cell that contains the field you want to sort.

2. Click the **Sort Descending** button [Z↓] on the Standard toolbar. See Figure 5-41. The full professor rank is now the first rank in the pivot table.

Figure 5-41 ◀
Pivot table
after values
sorted

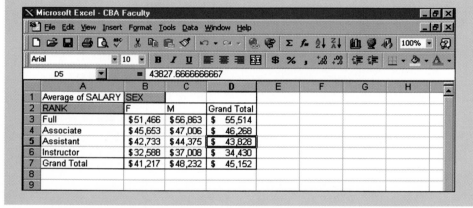

Adding a Field to a Pivot Table

You can expand a pivot table by adding columns, rows, page fields, and data fields; this creates a more informative table. For example, the dean believes that a more accurate comparison of average salaries would include the DEPARTMENT field. Adding this field to the pivot table enables you to calculate average salaries based on an additional breakdown—one that categorizes faculty in each rank into departmental classifications as well as by sex. The dean thinks the additional information will be useful in her discussion with the affirmative action task force, and she asks you to add it to the pivot table.

To add a field to the pivot table:

1. Click any cell in the pivot table.

2. Click the **PivotTable Wizard** button [⊞] on the PivotTable toolbar to display the PivotTable Wizard - Step 3 of 4 dialog box.

   TROUBLE? If the PivotTable toolbar is in the way, drag it to a different location on your screen.

3. Click and drag the **DEPARTMENT** field button into the ROW area, immediately below the RANK field button, and release the mouse button. See Figure 5-42.

Figure 5-42 ◀
PivotTable
Wizard – Step 3
of 4 after
adding
DEPARTMENT
field button

DEPARTMENT field
added |

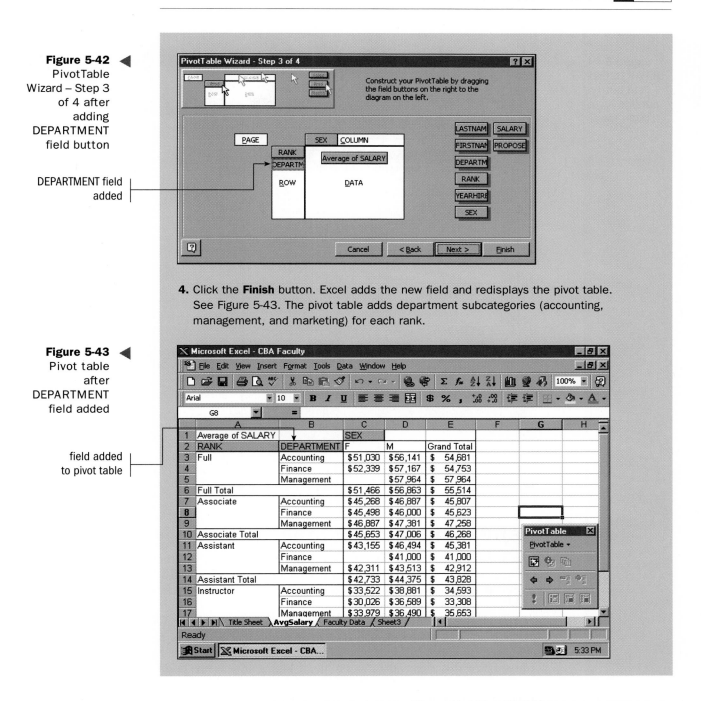

4. Click the **Finish** button. Excel adds the new field and redisplays the pivot table. See Figure 5-43. The pivot table adds department subcategories (accounting, management, and marketing) for each rank.

Figure 5-43 ◀
Pivot table
after
DEPARTMENT
field added

field added |
to pivot table |

Removing a Field from the Pivot Table

If you decide you want to remove a field from the pivot table, just drag the field button outside the pivot table. The dean reviews the pivot table showing the data arranged by rank, department, and sex. While she thinks this is important information, she feels the additional breakdown is not needed to show the difference in average salaries between men and women. She asks you to remove the DEPARTMENT field from the pivot table.

To remove a field from the pivot table:

1. Click and drag the **DEPARTMENT** field button outside the pivot table range. When the field button is outside the pivot table, it changes to ✖. See Figure 5-44.

Figure 5-44 ◄
DEPARTMENT
field button
outside pivot
table range

remove this field
button

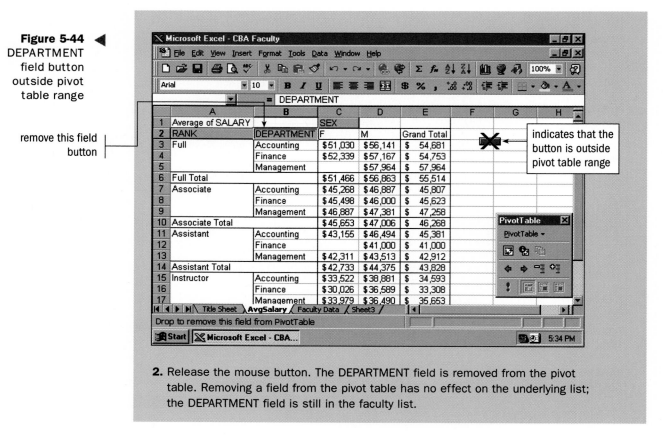

2. Release the mouse button. The DEPARTMENT field is removed from the pivot table. Removing a field from the pivot table has no effect on the underlying list; the DEPARTMENT field is still in the faculty list.

Recall that you cannot change the data in the pivot table; you can simply rearrange it, or format it. So if you were to receive updated information, how would you update the values in the pivot table?

Refreshing a Pivot Table

Recall that in order to change the data in the pivot table, you must make the changes to the original list first; then you need to update the pivot table. To update a pivot table so it reflects the current state of the faculty list, you need to update, or "refresh," the pivot table using the Refresh command.

You receive a memo from the dean informing you that Jodie Weeks, a faculty member in the finance department, will receive an additional $3,000 in salary because her merit increase was approved. Her new salary is $36,052. Update her record in the faculty list and see how this affects the pivot table. (Make a note at this point that the average salary for female instructors is $32,588.) Observe whether there is any change in the pivot table after you update Jodie Weeks' salary.

To update Jodie Weeks' salary:

1. Activate the **Faculty Data** worksheet, and then click any cell in the list.

2. Click **Data** on the menu bar, and then click **Form** to display the Faculty Data data form dialog box.

3. Click the **Criteria** button to display a blank data form.

Enter the search criteria in the appropriate field.

4. Click the **LASTNAME** text box, and then type **Weeks**.

5. Click the **Find Next** button to display the next record in the list that meets the specified criteria—LASTNAME equal to Weeks.

6. Change Jodie Weeks' salary to **$36,052**.

7. Click the **Close** button. The salary for Jodie Weeks has been updated.

   Now return to the pivot table to observe whether there is any change in the average salary for female instructors.

8. Switch to the **AvgSalary** worksheet. Notice that the average salary for female instructors remains at $32,588.

Because the pivot table is not automatically updated when data in the source list is updated, the pivot table must be "refreshed."

To refresh a pivot table:

1. Select any cell inside the pivot table.

2. Click the **Refresh Data** button 🔲 on the PivotTable toolbar to update the pivot table. See Figure 5-45. The new average salary for female instructors is $33,017.

Figure 5-45 ◄
Pivot table
after being
refreshed

this average changed ────

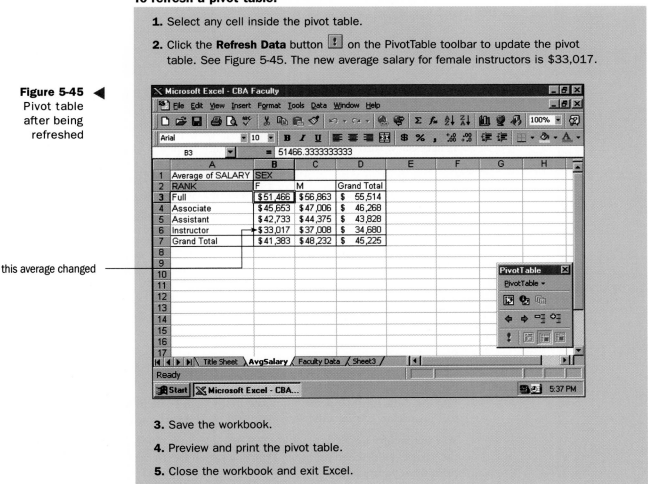

3. Save the workbook.

4. Preview and print the pivot table.

5. Close the workbook and exit Excel.

The dean is pleased with the appearance of the pivot table. The table shows that the average salary paid to females is lower in every rank than the average salary paid to males.

Quick Check

1. What is the default calculation method for numeric data in a pivot table?

2. After the data in a list has been updated, you would have to _____ the pivot table in order to see an updated version of it.

3 Fields such as region, state, country, and zip code are most likely to appear as _____ in a pivot table.

4 Assume that you have a list of students, and included in the list is a code for males and females and a field identifying the student major. Which tool, AutoFilter or pivot table, would you use in each of the following situations:
a. You want a list of all females majoring in history.
b. You want a count of the number of males and females in each major at your institution.

You have modified and added data to an Excel list. You have also filtered the data in the list in numerous ways to highlight certain budget information that the dean of the College of Business Administration needs for her meeting with the university's budget director. Finally, you have created pivot tables from the list to further organize the information into specialized reports that the dean can use in her upcoming meetings with the affirmative action task force.

Tutorial Assignments

The dean has asked for more information about the College of Business Administration faculty.

To provide the answers she asks you to complete the following:

1. If necessary, start Excel and make sure your Student Disk is in the appropriate disk drive. Open the workbook Faculty2 in the TAssign folder for Tutorial.05 on your Student Disk, and save it as CBA Faculty 2. Type your name and date in the title sheet, then move to the Faculty Data sheet.

2. Add the following information for a new faculty member.

   Last name = Gerety

   First name = Estelle

   Department = Management

   Rank = Assistant

   Year hired = 1999

   Sex = F

   Salary = 42500

3. Use the data form to determine how many faculty members hold the rank of full professor. Explain the steps you followed to get your answer.

4. Sort the faculty list by sex, within sex by rank, and within rank by salary. Arrange the salaries in descending order. Print the sorted list so that males and females print on separate pages.

5. Use the Subtotals command to count how many males and how many females are on the faculty. Print the faculty list with the subtotals.

6. Use the AutoFilter command to display all females in the accounting department. Sort by last name. Print the filtered list.

7. Further refine the list from question 6 so you display all female accounting faculty hired after 1990. Print the list.

8. Use the AVERAGE function to determine the average faculty salary. Based on this information, print a list of all faculty earning above the average salary.

9. Use conditional formatting to boldface the YEARHIRED field for faculty hired before 1980. Print the faculty list.

10. Use the Subtotals command to compute the average salary paid by department.

11. Based on question 10, use the appropriate Outline button to display only the subtotals and the grand total. Print the result.

12. Create a pivot table to show the maximum salary by rank and sex. Place your pivot table in a blank worksheet, leaving room for a title. Format your pivot table to produce an attractive printout. Add an appropriate title. Rename the pivot table sheet using an appropriate name. Print the pivot table.

13. Modify the pivot table in question 12 to also display the minimum salary by rank and sex. Print the modified pivot table. (*Hint:* Check out the top 10 option in the list of available AutoFilters.)

14. Use AutoFilters to produce and then print the faculty with the top five salaries in descending order.

15. Print a list of faculty sorted by department and within department by last name. Include only the last name, department, year hired, and gender in the output. (*Hint:* Use the Office Assistant to learn about hiding columns.) After printing the report, unhide the columns.)

16. When you used the Page Break command in the tutorial to print each department's faculty on a separate page, you may have noticed that the column headings appeared only on the first page. Use the Print Area and Print Title sections of the Page Setup dialog box (Sheet tab), along with the Page Break command, to print the column headings on each page.

17. In column I, create a new calculated field using a natural language formula reflecting an alternative Proposed Salary of a 4 1/2% increase.

18. Save and close the workbook.

Case Problems

1. Inventory at OfficeMart Business Supplies You are an assistant buyer at OfficeMart Business Supplies, a retail business supply store. Your boss, Ellen Kerrigan, created an Excel workbook containing product and pricing information for inventory items purchased from each primary vendor. Ellen is preparing her monthly order for EB Wholesale Office Supplies, one of OfficeMart's suppliers. She has asked you to print a list of all back-ordered EB Wholesale products so you can include them in the order. She would also like a list of all discontinued items so you can remove those items from the catalog. Do the following:

1. If necessary, start Excel and make sure your Student Disk is in the appropriate disk drive. Open the workbook Office in the Case folder for Tutorial.05 on your Student Disk and save it as Office Supplies.

2. Freeze the panes so the column headings and the Part number row labels remain on the screen as you scroll the office supplies list.

3. Print the items in each status category on a separate page.

4. Display only the records for back-ordered items (Status = B). Sort the back-ordered items by part description. Print the records for back-ordered items.

5. Apply conditional formatting to all discontinued products (Status = D) so that for each discontinued product the status code appears in red.

6. Add a new field to the list. Name the field Retail Value and format appropriately. For each inventory item, calculate the value at retail (quantity on hand multiplied by retail) using a natural language formula. Format the numbers in the new field. Print the list so it prints on one page.

7. Use the Subtotals command to compute the total retail value of the inventory by status category (B, D, and S). Print the list with subtotals.

8. Prepare the same list with subtotals as in question 7, but exclude all records whose retail value is zero.

9. Prepare a pivot table to summarize the retail value of inventory by status category. For each status category, include a count of the number of different items (this is not the sum of the quantity on hand), the total retail value, and the average retail value. Place the pivot table in a new sheet. Assign a descriptive name to the sheet. Print the pivot table.

10. Display only the discontinued items (Status = D). Copy these records to a blank worksheet. Rename the worksheet Discontinued. Print the list of discontinued items.

11. Save and close the workbook.

2. Creating a Current Membership List for Shih Tzu Fanciers of America Jennifer Santarelli is the membership coordinator for the Shih Tzu Fanciers of America, a nonprofit organization for owners, fanciers, and breeders of Shih Tzu dogs. The organization maintains a membership list. The list includes the first name, last name, address, city, state, and zip code for approximately 100 current members.

The board of the Shih Tzu Fanciers of America (STFA) has asked Jennifer to prepare a report on the current membership, showing the number of members in each state and the total current membership.

It has been some time since Jennifer used the list features in Excel. She has tried to create the report but has run into trouble, so she asks you to help her use the PivotTable Wizard to create a pivot table.

Do the following:

1. If necessary, start Excel and make sure your Student Disk is in the appropriate drive. Open the Members workbook in the Case folder for Tutorial.05 on your Student Disk and save it as Current Members.

2. Freeze the column headings and last name row labels.

3. Add the following record. After you add this record, how many records are in the list? How did you determine this?

   Last name = CLEMENTE

   First name = HELEN

   Address = 111 ANGEL WAY

   City = PHOENIX

   State = AZ

   Zip code = 85628 (format as appropriate)

4. Explain how you can quickly find the last record in the list.

5. Explain how you can quickly find Nelson Cruz's record.

6. Sort the list by state, and within state by last name. Print the list so all the fields appear on one page. (*Hint:* You will still have more than one page of output.)

7. Prepare a pivot table to summarize the number of members in each state. Print the pivot table. Name the worksheet StateCount.

8. Use the Subtotals command to count the number of members in each state. Print the list with subtotals for each state, with each state on a separate page.

9. Print a list of all members in Florida and Colorado, sorted by state and within state by last name. Again, all fields should appear on one page.

10. Print the same data as question 8, but include only last name, city, and state in the output. (*Hint*: Use the Office Assistant, if necessary, to learn how to hide columns.)

11. Modify the output from question 10 so the column headings appear on each page. Use the Print Area and Print Title sections of the Page Setup dialog box (Sheet tab) along with the Page Break command, to print Column headings on each page.

12. Save and close the workbook.

3. Sales Analysis at Medical Technology, Inc. Medical Technology, Inc. distributes supplies to hospitals, medical laboratories, and pharmacies. Records of all customer and accounts receivable data are available to department managers on the company's mainframe computer. Tom Benson, the manager of credit and collections, was reviewing this data and noticed that the outstanding balances of several customers in Rhode Island and Massachusetts appeared to be higher than the average customer balances. He believes the average customer balance to be approximately $4,000. He wants to study these accounts in more detail with the goal of creating a plan to bring these accounts closer to the average balance.

Tom was able to download the necessary data from the company's mainframe, and he set up an Excel list.

Do the following:

1. If necessary, start Excel and make sure your Student Disk is in the appropriate disk drive. Open the workbook Medical in the Case folder for Tutorial.05, and then save it as Med Tech.

2. Sort the list by sales rep (ascending) and within sales rep by year-to-date (YTD) sales (descending). Print the sorted list.

3. Insert subtotals (SUM) on YTD sales by type of customer. Print the list with only subtotals and grand total included. After printing, remove the subtotals.

4. Use conditional formatting to display all customers with YTD sales above 50000 in blue text, and apply boldface.

5. Display all customers with a balance owed above $25000 who are from Rhode Island. Sort the list in descending order by balance owed. How many customers are in this list? Which customer owes the most? Print the list.

6. Print a list of customers that have the word "lab" anywhere in the customer name. Explain how you got your results.

7. Prepare a pivot table summarizing total YTD sales by sales rep. Format the pivot table, and then print it. Name the pivot table sheet Sales Rep.

8. Using the pivot table you prepared in question 7, sort total YTD sales in descending order. Print the modified pivot table.

9. There appears to be a problem in the collection of money (balance) owed for one state and one type of customer. Identify the state and customer type that has the highest average outstanding balance. Print a report that supports your observation.

10. Save and close the workbook.

4. Revenue at the Tea House Arnold Tealover, sales manager for Tea House Distributors, is getting ready for a semi-annual meeting at the company headquarters. At this meeting, Arnold plans to present summary data on his product line. The data he has accumulated consists of revenues by product, by month, and by region for the last six months. Help him summarize and analyze the data. Do the following:

1. If necessary, start Excel and make sure your Student Disk is in the appropriate drive. Open the workbook TeaHouse in the Case folder for Tutorial.05 on your Student Disk, and save it as TeaHouse Revenue.

2. Improve the formatting of the revenue field.

3. Freeze the column headings so they remain on the screen as you scroll the worksheet.

4. Revenue for Duke Gray Tea for June in the West region was $51,100. Use the data form to enter Duke Gray Tea, June, West, 51100.

5. Sort the tea list by product and within product by month. Insert subtotals by product and also by month for each product. Print the information for each product on a separate page.

6. Use conditional formatting to display revenue below $25000 hired.

7. Use the Subtotals command to display total sales by product. Print the list with subtotals.

8. Use the Outline buttons to display only the subtotals and grand total. Print this information.

9. Sort the data by month and within month by region. The months should appear in January through December sequence. (*Hint*: Click the Options button in the sort dialog box to customize your sort options.) Print the list.

10. Determine which product was the company's best seller during May or June in the West region. Print the list that supports your answer.

11. You want to determine which month had the highest sales and which region had the lowest sales. Prepare one pivot table that provides you with the information you can use to determine the answer to both questions. Use a text box to place the answer in the sheet with the pivot table. Name the sheet with the pivot table MaxMin. Print the pivot table.

12. Summarize each product's revenue using a pivot table. Use the data in the pivot table to create a pie chart of total revenue by product. Print the pivot table and pie chart on one page. Name the sheet Product Summary.

13. Sort the list by region. Print the data for each region on a separate page. Use Page Break Preview to drag the automatic page breaks to the appropriate locations. (*Hint*: You may also need to insert additional page breaks manually.)

14. Sort the data by region. The region should appear in the following sequence: North, South, East, West. Print the list. (*Hint*: Use online Help to search on customizing, sort order.)

15. Save and close the workbook.

Integrating Excel with Other Windows Programs and the World Wide Web

Creating Integrated Documents for Country Gardens

OBJECTIVES

In this tutorial you will:

- Learn about Object Linking and Embedding (OLE)

- Paste a graphic object into an Excel worksheet

- Embed a WordArt object in Excel

- Link an Excel worksheet to a Word document

- Update linked documents

- Embed an Excel chart in a Word document

- Complete a mail merge using an Excel list and a Word document

- View documents from a mail merge

- Preview and print a mail-merged document

- Create hyperlinks to connect files

- Convert worksheet data to HTML format

Country Gardens

CASE

Nearly fifteen years ago, Sue Dickinson began growing and selling plants and herbs from her 15-acre farm in Bristol, New Hampshire. At the urging of her customers, she opened a small shop in her barn and originally called the shop The Country Gardener. Today, Sue's business, renamed Country Gardens, has grown to include three shops, located in Derry, New Hampshire; Dunstable, Massachusetts; and the newest one in Burlington, Vermont.

The customer base has grown from townspeople and neighbors to include garden centers, nurseries, and landscaping companies throughout the Northeast who purchase products in bulk to stock their own greenhouses. This year, Country Gardens has received the much-prized recognition as the largest grower and greens supplier in New England, a title established by the New England Growers and Horticultural Association (NEGHA).

Sue has decided to offer her products through a mail-order catalog. The catalog will give Sue's customers an opportunity to better plan their own stock and gardening needs by previewing the available products, prices, and quantities a few months before the products are needed. This approach will also allow her to better monitor market trends and customer needs as she tracks orders—products, dollar volume, and purchase dates.

Sue wants to display a flyer at the checkout counter announcing the year's new products to the customers who visit the three stores. In addition to inserting the company logo, she can use WordArt, a shared program that comes with all Microsoft Office 97 programs, to dress up the new products table.

Sue also has drafted the body of a letter to her customers, highlighting the company's recent award from NEGHA, introducing the mail-order catalog, and previewing ten new products that will be available this year. To show this information in an easy-to-understand format, she plans to include a table outlining the ten new products to be offered in the catalog. In addition, she wants the letter to include a chart that NEGHA has supplied depicting the company's status as the top area grower. She will then merge an Excel list containing her customer addresses to the list.

Lastly, Sue wants her customers who use the Internet and the World Wide Web to have access to the new products information online. She will create a Web page showing the new products information.

You'll complete the flyer, the letter, and the Web page for Sue using the integration features of Excel, which allow you to easily incorporate information from documents created in other programs.

SESSION

6.1

In this session you will learn about the different methods of integrating information between Windows programs to create compound documents. You will paste a logo into an Excel worksheet, create WordArt, link an Excel workbook to a Word document, and embed an Excel chart into a Word document.

Methods of Integration

Like Sue, you may occasionally need to copy data between two or more programs to produce the type of document you require. This type of document is referred to as a **compound document**—a document made up of parts created in more than one program. For example, you may want to incorporate data from a worksheet, a graphic design, or a chart, and insert it into a word-processed report.

Excel is part of a suite of programs called Microsoft Office 97. In addition to Excel, the Office programs consist of Word, a word processing program; Access, a database program; PowerPoint, a program used for creating presentations; and Outlook, a personal information manager. Microsoft Office also contains some auxiliary programs, such as WordArt, that allow you to customize your documents even further. All of these programs can share information, which saves time and ensures consistency.

There are essentially three ways to copy data between Windows programs; you can use pasting, linking, or embedding. Regardless of the method used, a copy of the data appears in the compound document. Figure 6-1 provides a description of each of these methods, and examples of when each method would be appropriate.

Figure 6-1 ◀
Comparison of methods of integrating information

Method of Sharing	Description	Use When
Copying and pasting	Places a copy of the information in a document	You will be exchanging the data between the two documents only once, and it doesn't matter if the data changes.
Linking	Displays an object in the destination document but doesn't store it there—only the location of the source document is stored in the destination document	You want to use the same data in more than one document, and you need to ensure that the data will be current and identical in each document. Any changes you make to the source document will be reflected in the destination document(s).
Embedding	Displays and stores an object in the destination document	You want the source data to become a permanent part of the destination document, or the source data will no longer be available to the destination document. Any changes you make to either the destination document or the source document will not affect the other.

Pasting Data

You can **paste** an object, such as a range of cells or a chart, from one program to another using copy-and-paste operations. This creates a static copy of the data. For example, you can paste a range of cells from an Excel worksheet into a Word document, and use it as part of your Word document.

Once you paste an object from one program into another, that data is now part of the new document, and can only be altered in that document's program. The pasted data has no connection to the source document. For example, if you paste a range of cells from Excel into a Word document, you can only edit or change that data using the Word commands and features. The pasted data becomes a table of text and numbers, just as if you had entered it directly from the keyboard. There is no connection to the Excel worksheet. Once you have pasted the range of cells, any changes in the Excel worksheet are not reflected in the Word document. In order for changes in the worksheet to appear in the Word document, you need to repeat the copy-and-paste operation. Pasting is used when you need to perform a one-time exchange of information between programs.

Object Linking and Embedding

There are situations when copying and pasting information into a document is not the best solution. Excel supports a technology called **Object Linking and Embedding** (OLE). This technology enables you to copy and paste objects—a graphic file, a worksheet range, a chart, or a sound file—in such a way that the data is associated with its source. For example, using OLE (pronounced oh-lay) you can insert a worksheet or chart into a Word document as either a linked object or an embedded object.

OLE involves the exchange of information between two programs, called the **source** or **server program** and the **destination** or **client program**. The source is the program in which the data was created. The destination is the program that receives the data. For example, if you insert an Excel pivot table into a Word document, Excel is the source program and Word is the destination program.

Using OLE, you can share data between programs by creating a **link** between files. Linking files lets information created in one file be displayed in another file. When an object is linked, the data is stored in the original source file. For example, you can link a chart from a worksheet to a Word document. Although the chart appears in the Word document, it actually exists as a separate file. The destination document simply displays the object. In effect, the destination document stores a **reference** (location and name of the source file) to the object in the source file. Thus, only one copy of the original, or source, object exists. If you make changes to the original object, changes also appear in the destination document. With only one version of the object, every document containing a link to the source object uses the same copy of the object.

Embedding lets you store data from multiple programs—for example, a worksheet or chart—directly in the destination document. The information is totally contained in one file. The copied object, which is embedded, exists as a separate object within the destination document. To make changes to the embedded object, you edit the embedded object directly from within the destination document. The embedded object has no link to the original source document, which means that changes to the embedded object do not alter the original object. This also means that the changes you make to the original source data do not appear in the embedded document.

The main differences between objects that are linked and objects that are embedded are where the data is stored and how it is updated after you place it in the destination document. Figure 6-2 illustrates the differences between linking and embedding.

Figure 6-2 ◄
Embedding
contrasted
with linking

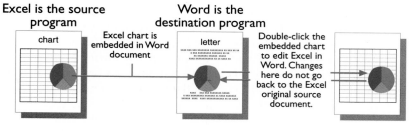

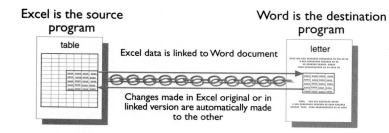

Planning the Integration

Recall that Sue has two documents she wants to create. First, she wants to create a flyer to be placed next to each cash register in the three stores. The flyer will describe the ten new products being offered. The table of the products and their prices is contained in an Excel file, Products. To create the flyer, Sue needs to paste the company logo at the top, which she can do using Excel's Insert command, as this will be a one-time exchange of data. Then, she will use WordArt to insert a visually pleasing title above the product table.

In the case of the customer letter, Sue has already created the body of the letter in Word. However, the Excel new products table must be linked to the Word document because the prices of some of the products might change, and both customer letter and product work-sheet will need to show the latest prices. The NEGHA pie chart depicting Country Gardens as the leading area grower needs to be integrated into the customer letter as well. Sue knows the data in the chart will not change, but she might need to modify the chart's size and appearance once it is integrated into the letter. To do this, Sue will want to use the Excel commands for modifying a chart; therefore she decides to embed the chart. Figure 6-3 shows Sue's plan for integrating these pieces to create the flyer and the customer letter.

Figure 6-3 ◄
Sue's
Integration
plans for the
flyer and
customer letter

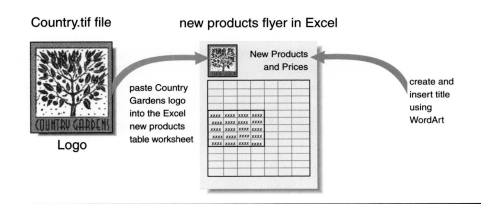

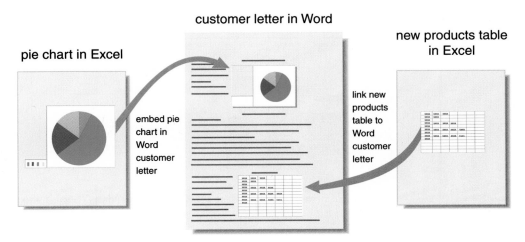

Creating the New Products Flyer

Sue wants to complete the flyer first. To create this document, she needs to insert the Country Gardens logo, a graphic file, into the Excel worksheet, Products, that contains the table of new products. She also needs to create and then insert a WordArt image in the Excel worksheet.

To open the products table:

1. Start Excel as usual. Make sure your Student Disk is in the appropriate disk drive.

2. Open the Excel workbook named **Products** in the Tutorial.06 folder on your Student Disk. Use the Save As command to save the file as **New Products**.

3. Activate the **New Products** sheet. See Figure 6-4.

Figure 6-4 ◀
New Products
worksheet

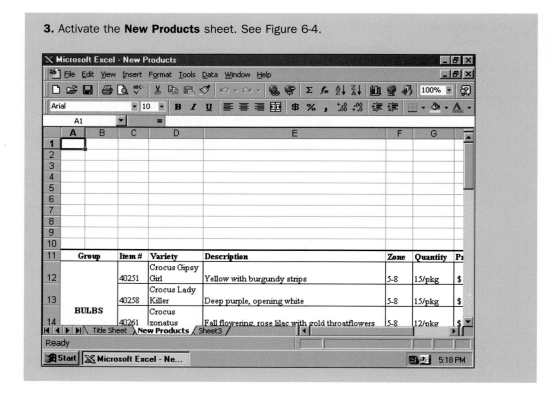

You are now ready to insert the Country Gardens logo at the top of the new products table.

To insert the company logo into the worksheet:

1. Make sure cell A1 is selected.

2. Click **Insert** on the menu bar, point to **Picture**, and then click **From File** to display the Insert Picture dialog box.

3. Make sure the Look in list box displays the Tutorial.06 folder, click **Country** in the list of available fonts, and then click the **Insert** button to paste the company logo into the worksheet. See Figure 6-5. Notice that the Picture toolbar appears on the screen while the graphic object is selected. The Picture toolbar contains tools you can use to change the characteristics of a graphic image. For example, you can crop the image, or adjust its brightness.

Figure 6-5 ◄
Worksheet
after company
logo inserted

company logo ──→

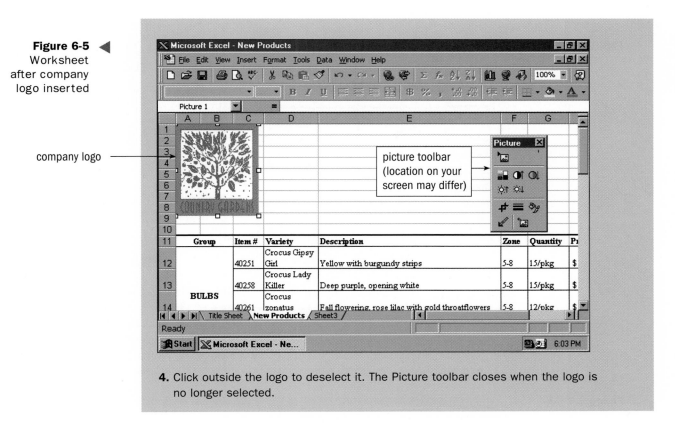

4. Click outside the logo to deselect it. The Picture toolbar closes when the logo is no longer selected.

Sue still needs to add a title to the new products table.

Inserting WordArt into an Excel Worksheet

When Sue reviews her work so far, she knows that her table shows the basic data but it does nothing to attract her customers' attention. To add some pizzazz, she would like you to use WordArt, a shared application available to all Office programs. WordArt enables you to add special graphic effects to your documents. You can bend, rotate, and stretch the text, and insert the graphic object in other documents, such as an Excel worksheet.

To prepare Sue's flyer, you will start WordArt while in Excel, create the graphic object, and then return to Excel to insert the object into the Excel worksheet.

To create a WordArt graphic object:

1. If necessary, click the **Drawing** button ![icon] on the Standard toolbar to display the Drawing toolbar. You can access the WordArt program from the Drawing toolbar.

2. Click the **Insert WordArt** button ![icon] on the Drawing toolbar to display a gallery of WordArt special effects styles. See Figure 6-6.

Figure 6-6 ◀
WordArt styles

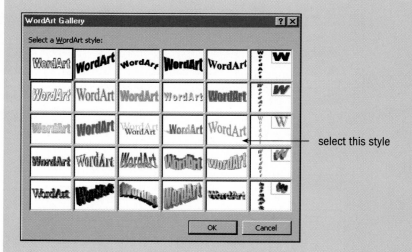

select this style ⟵

3. Click the WordArt style in the third row, fifth column, and then click the **OK** button to open the Edit WordArt Text dialog box. See Figure 6-7. In this dialog box, you specify the text you want to appear in the WordArt style you selected. If you want, you can also change the font, font size, and font style in the dialog box. For now, just type the text you want as the title of the worksheet. You will adjust the font size and style as necessary after you see how it appears in the worksheet.

Figure 6-7 ◀
Edit WordArt
Text dialog box

4. Type **New Products & Prices** and then click the **OK** button to place the WordArt graphic on your worksheet. See Figure 6-8. Notice that the WordArt toolbar is displayed while the WordArt object is selected. Figure 6-9 describes each button on the WordArt toolbar.

TROUBLE? If the WordArt toolbar is not displayed on your screen, click View on the menu bar, point to Toolbars, and then click WordArt to place a check next to this option and display the WordArt toolbar on your screen.

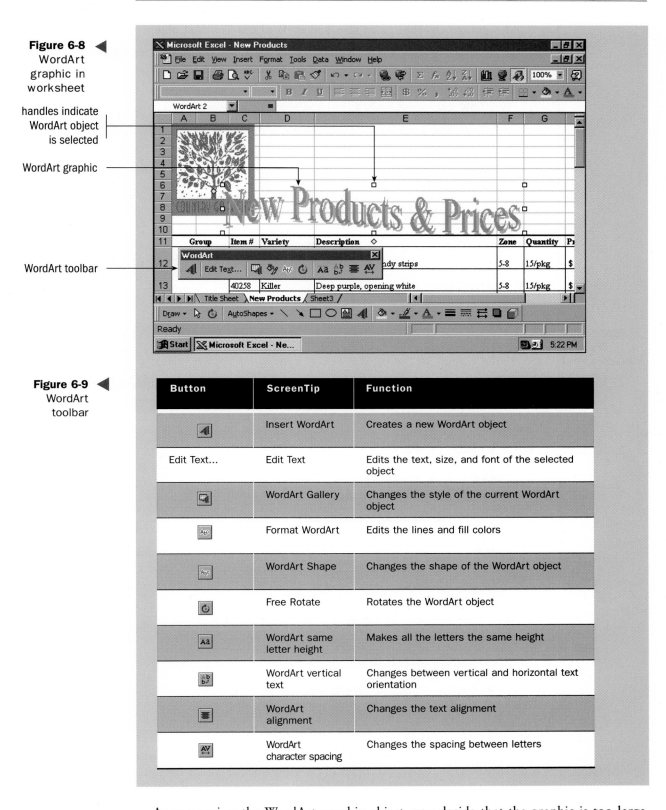

Figure 6-8
WordArt
graphic in
worksheet

handles indicate
WordArt object
is selected

WordArt graphic

WordArt toolbar

Figure 6-9
WordArt
toolbar

Button	ScreenTip	Function
	Insert WordArt	Creates a new WordArt object
Edit Text...	Edit Text	Edits the text, size, and font of the selected object
	WordArt Gallery	Changes the style of the current WordArt object
	Format WordArt	Edits the lines and fill colors
	WordArt Shape	Changes the shape of the WordArt object
	Free Rotate	Rotates the WordArt object
	WordArt same letter height	Makes all the letters the same height
	WordArt vertical text	Changes between vertical and horizontal text orientation
	WordArt alignment	Changes the text alignment
	WordArt character spacing	Changes the spacing between letters

As you review the WordArt graphic object, you decide that the graphic is too large. You decide to change the point size from 36 to 24 points and apply a bold style to make the graphic stand out. To make these changes, you need to return to the WordArt program because when you insert WordArt into an Excel worksheet, the object is embedded. This means that in order to modify the object, you need access to its source program's commands and features.

To change the font point size and style of the WordArt object:

1. Make sure the graphic object is selected, and then click the **Edit Text** button on the WordArt toolbar to return to the Edit WordArt Text dialog box.

2. Click the **Size** list arrow and click **24**. Click the **Bold** button, and then click the **OK** button. You return to the New Products worksheet.

   Now move the graphic object above the new products table, and to the right of the logo.

3. Make sure the graphic object is selected, and then position the pointer over the graphic until the pointer changes to a four-headed arrow ✛ .

4. Click and drag the WordArt object to the top of row 4 in column E. As you drag the object, an outline of the object indicates its placement on the worksheet. Release the mouse button.

   TROUBLE? If the Country Gardens logo moves instead of the WordArt object, click Undo, select the WordArt object, and repeat Steps 3 and 4.

5. Click anywhere outside the graphic so it is no longer selected. See Figure 6-10.

Figure 6-10 ◄
WordArt
graphic after
being moved
and edited

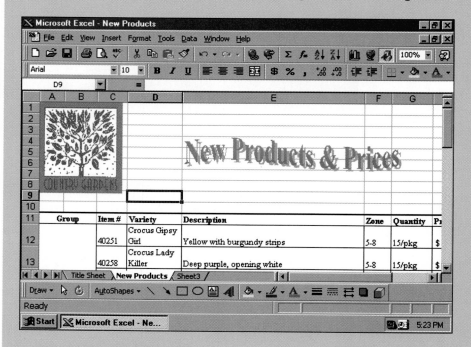

6. Save the worksheet.

7. Preview and print the worksheet for Sue.

8. Click the **Drawing** button 🖉 on the Standard toolbar to remove the Drawing toolbar.

Sue is pleased with how professional the worksheet looks with the company logo and WordArt. She can print copies of the table now, and distribute them as flyers at each store.

Excel

Linking an Excel Worksheet to a Word Document

Now Sue needs to link the new products table created in Excel and the customer letter created in Word. As you know, Sue maintains her new product and pricing information in an Excel workbook. She wants to include the new products table in a letter to her customers. Since the product and pricing information is always subject to change, the copy-and-paste method is not the appropriate method to integrate these documents. Recall that pasting only allows you to change or modify the pasted object from the destination program. Sue wants the most current pricing information to appear both in the original source file—the new products worksheet—and the destination document—the customer letter. Therefore, a better solution is to create a link between data copied from Excel to Word. When she creates a link between the documents, if the data changes in the source document, these changes automatically appear in the destination document. For example, Sue believes that the price of bulbs will most likely change when she receives a signed quote from her supplier. It's possible that she won't receive this quote until right before she plans to send out the letter. Therefore, you'll link the table from the New Products workbook to the Customer Letter document so that you can make changes to the Excel new products table and have these changes automatically reflected in the Word document.

REFERENCE window	LINKING AN OBJECT
	■ Start the source program, open the file containing the object to be linked, select the object or information you want to link to the destination program, and then click the Copy button on the Standard toolbar.
	■ Start the destination program, open the file that will contain the link to the copied object, position the insertion point where you want the linked object to appear, click Edit, and then click Paste Special.
	■ Click the Paste link option button, select the option you want in the As list box, and then click the OK button.

Sue has given you the Word file containing her letter. You need to link the new products table to the customer letter. First you need to select the new products table, which is the Excel object to be linked.

To link the new products table to the customer letter:

1. Make sure the New Products sheet is the active sheet. Select the range of cells **A11:H21** to select the new products table.

2. Click the **Copy** button ▣ on the Standard toolbar to copy the data to the Clipboard.

Now, you need to start Word, and then open the customer letter document.

To start Word and open the customer letter document:

1. Make sure your Student Disk is in the appropriate disk drive. Click the **Start** button on the taskbar, point to **Programs**, and then click **Microsoft Word** to start this program.

2. Open the **Letter** document, which is located in the Tutorial.06 folder on your Student Disk. Sue's letter to the Country Gardens customers is displayed in the document window in page layout view. See Figure 6-11.

> TROUBLE? If your document does not show the nonprinting characters, click the Show/Hide button ¶ on the Standard toolbar.

Next you'll save the file with a new name. That way, the original letter remains intact on your Student Disk, in case you want to restart the tutorial.

Figure 6-11 ◄
Beginning of
customer letter

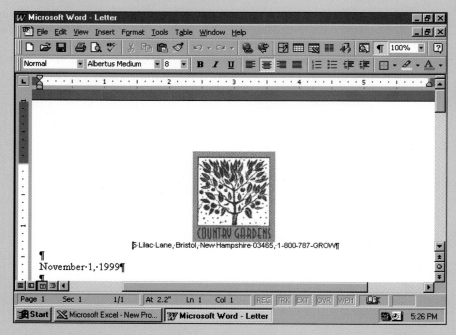

3. Use the Save As command to save the file as **Customer Letter** in the Tutorial.06 folder on your Student Disk.

Now link the Excel new products table to the customer letter.

4. Scroll the document and position the insertion point to the left of the paragraph mark above the paragraph that begins, "You will receive...." This is where you want the product and pricing data to appear. See Figure 6-12.

Figure 6-12 ◄
Placement of
product table in
customer letter

position insert point

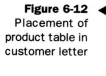

Excel

5. Click **Edit** on the menu bar, and then click **Paste Special**. The Paste Special dialog box opens. See Figure 6-13.

Figure 6-13 ◀
Paste Special
dialog box

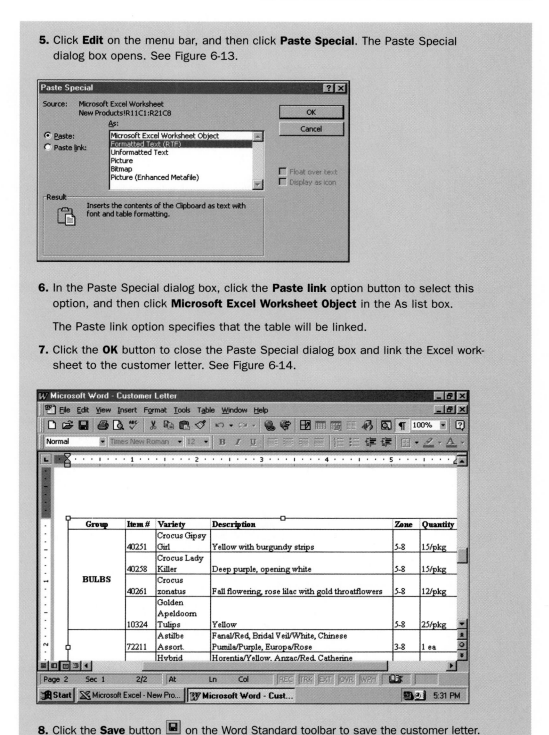

6. In the Paste Special dialog box, click the **Paste link** option button to select this option, and then click **Microsoft Excel Worksheet Object** in the As list box.

The Paste link option specifies that the table will be linked.

7. Click the **OK** button to close the Paste Special dialog box and link the Excel worksheet to the customer letter. See Figure 6-14.

Figure 6-14 ◀
New products
table in Word
document

Group	Item #	Variety	Description	Zone	Quantity
	40251	Crocus Gipsy Girl	Yellow with burgundy strips	5-8	15/pkg
	40258	Crocus Lady Killer	Deep purple, opening white	5-8	15/pkg
BULBS	40261	Crocus zonatus	Fall flowering, rose lilac with gold throatflowers	5-8	12/pkg
	10324	Golden Apeldoom Tulips	Yellow	5-8	25/pkg
	72211	Astilbe Assort.	Fanal/Red, Bridal Veil/White, Chinese Pumila/Purple, Europa/Rose	3-8	1 ea
		Hybrid	Horentia/Yellow, Anzac/Red, Catherine		

8. Click the **Save** button 🖫 on the Word Standard toolbar to save the customer letter.

Sue has just received the signed quote from her bulb supplier. As she expected, some of the prices have changed. She would now like you to update the new products table.

Updating Linked Objects

Now that you have linked the new products table from Excel to the customer letter, you can make changes to the source document, the Excel new products table, and the changes will automatically be reflected in the destination file. When making changes, you can have one or both files open.

To update the new products table in Excel:

1. Click the **Microsoft Excel** button on the taskbar to switch to the New Products workbook. Make sure the New Products sheet is the active sheet.

2. Click any cell to deselect the table and press the **Esc** key to remove the data from the Clipboard.

   The price of Crocus Gipsy Girl bulbs has changed from $2.95 to $3.95 each.

3. Enter **3.95** in cell H12.

   Now check to see if this change is reflected in the customer letter.

4. Click the **Microsoft Word** button on the taskbar to switch to the customer letter, and then scroll to view the price of Crocus Gipsy Girl bulbs. Because you linked the table from Excel to Word, the change you just made to the price of product 40251, Crocus Gipsy Girl bulbs, also appears in the destination document. See Figure 6-15.

Figure 6-15 ◀
Customer letter
with updated
price

updated price ——

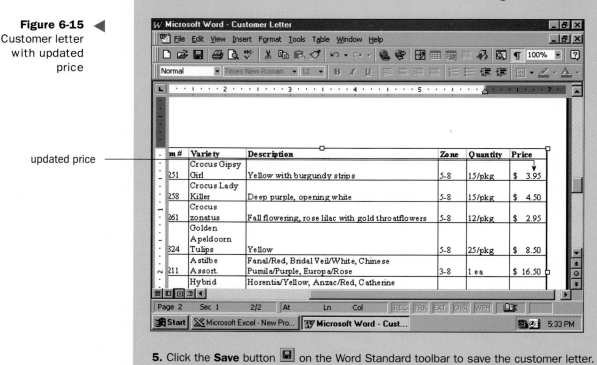

5. Click the **Save** button 🖫 on the Word Standard toolbar to save the customer letter.

What would happen if you were working on the new products table in Excel without the Word document open? Would the information still be updated in the customer letter? To find out, make the remaining changes to the prices for bulbs with the customer letter closed. You can then reopen the customer letter to ensure that the changes appear there as well.

To change the linked object with the Word document closed:

1. Click **File** on the Word menu bar, and then click **Close** to close the Customer Letter document.

2. Click the **Microsoft Excel** button on the taskbar to switch to the New Products workbook.

3. Enter **4.95** in cell H13, and then enter **3.25** in cell H14.

4. Click the **Save** button 🔲 on the Excel Standard toolbar.

5. Close the Excel workbook.

   Now reopen the customer letter to confirm that the prices have been updated in the linked new products table.

6. Click the **Microsoft Word** button on the taskbar. Click **File** on the menu bar, and then click **1 Customer Letter**.

7. Scroll the document to view the linked table. Notice that the new bulb prices appear in the linked table in Word. See Figure 6-16.

Figure 6-16 ◀
Linked table
after all prices
updated

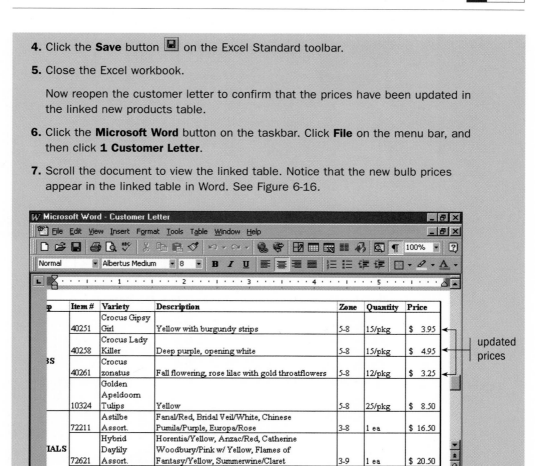

8. Save the letter.

The customer letter is almost complete. Now Sue just needs you to add the NEGHA pie chart.

Embedding an Excel Chart in a Word Document

Sue wants her letter to include the pie chart from NEGHA showing Country Gardens as the top grower in the area for 1999. Sue knows the data for the chart will not change, so there is no need for her to link the pie chart in her Word letter to the source file. Therefore, she decides to embed it. That way, if the pie chart needs to be resized or moved once it is in the customer letter, she can make these changes using Excel chart commands. (Recall that when you embed an object, you automatically have access to the object's source program's commands and features to manipulate it in the destination program.)

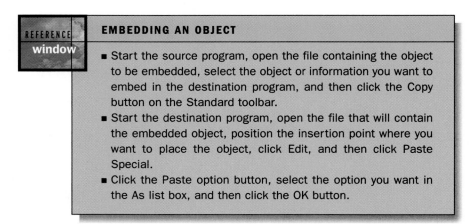

Now you can embed the pie chart in the customer letter.

To embed the Excel chart in the Word document:

1. Click the **Microsoft Excel** button on the taskbar to switch to Excel. Open the **NEGHA** workbook, which is located in the Tutorial.06 folder on your Student Disk. The workbook is displayed in the worksheet window. See Figure 6-17.

Figure 6-17 ◀
NEGHA pie
chart

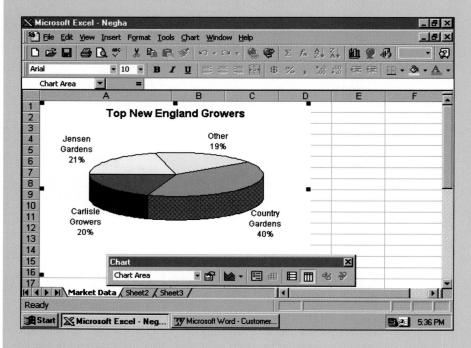

2. If necessary, click the **chart area** (the white area around the pie) to select the chart. When the chart is selected, handles appear on the chart area.

3. Click the **Copy** button on the Excel Standard toolbar to copy the chart to the Clipboard. The chart now appears with a rotating dashed line around its frame, indicating that it has been copied.

4. Click the **Microsoft Word** button on the taskbar to return to the Customer Letter document.

5. Scroll to page 1 of the Customer Letter document, and then click to the left of the paragraph mark immediately above the paragraph that begins "Since 1985 Country Gardens...." to position the insertion point where you need to embed the pie chart. See Figure 6-18.

Figure 6-18 ◀
Placement of
pie chart in
customer letter

position insertion
point here

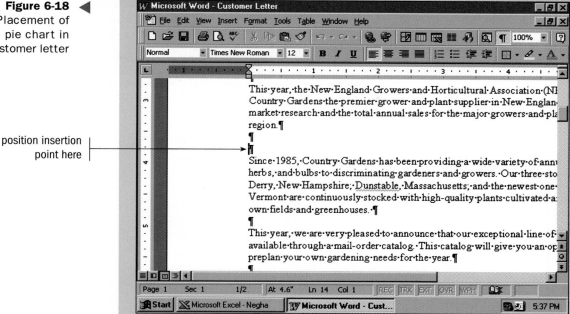

6. Click **Edit** on the menu bar, and then click **Paste Special**. The Paste Special dialog box opens. See Figure 6-19.

Figure 6-19 ◀
Paste Special
dialog box with
settings for
paste

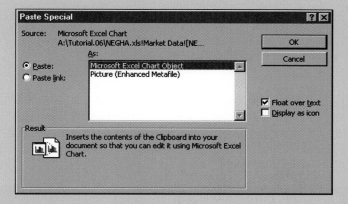

7. Make sure the Paste option button is selected. This option will embed the chart.

8. In the As list box, make sure Microsoft Excel Chart Object is selected as the object to be embedded.

   TROUBLE? If the Microsoft Excel Chart Object option does not appear in the As list box, you might not have selected and copied the chart correctly. Click the Cancel button, and then repeat Steps 1 through 8, making sure that when you select the chart, handles appear around the chart area, and that when you copy the chart, a rotating dashed line appears around the chart area.

9. Click the **OK** button. The Paste Special dialog box closes, and after a few moments, the Excel pie chart appears embedded in the letter. See Figure 6-20.

Figure 6-20 ◀
Customer letter
with embedded
pie chart

embedded pie chart —

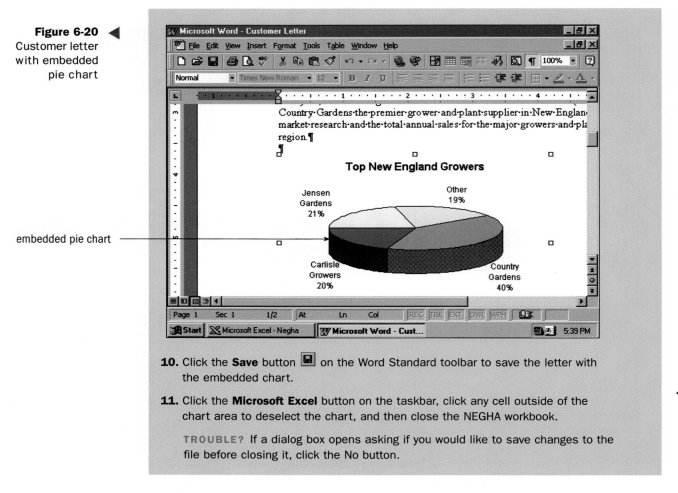

10. Click the **Save** button 🖫 on the Word Standard toolbar to save the letter with the embedded chart.

11. Click the **Microsoft Excel** button on the taskbar, click any cell outside of the chart area to deselect the chart, and then close the NEGHA workbook.

   TROUBLE? If a dialog box opens asking if you would like to save changes to the file before closing it, click the No button.

After reviewing the letter with the embedded pie chart, Sue decides that the Country Gardens slice should be "exploded" so the reader's attention is drawn to the fact that Country Gardens' percentage of the market is greatest. Because you embedded the chart (as opposed to just copying and pasting it), you can use Excel chart commands from within the Word document to modify the chart.

Modifying an Embedded Object

When you make changes to an embedded object within the destination program, the changes are made to the embedded object only; the original object in the source program is not affected. When you select an embedded object, the menu commands on the destination program's menu bar change to include the menu commands of the embedded object's source program. You can then use these commands to modify the embedded object.

   Now that you have embedded the pie chart in Word, you can modify it by exploding the Country Gardens pie slice.

Excel

To edit the pie chart from within Word:

1. Click the **Microsoft Word** button on the taskbar.

2. Double-click the **chart** to select it. After a moment, a thick border appears around the chart, and the Excel Chart menu is displayed at the top of the Word window. See Figure 6-21. Notice that the embedded object appears within the Excel row and column borders. You can now edit this object in place using Excel commands. Thus, you have access to all of the Excel features while you are in Word.

Figure 6-21
Embedded object selected for editing

still in Word

Excel menus and toolbars

embedded object (pie chart) appears in Excel

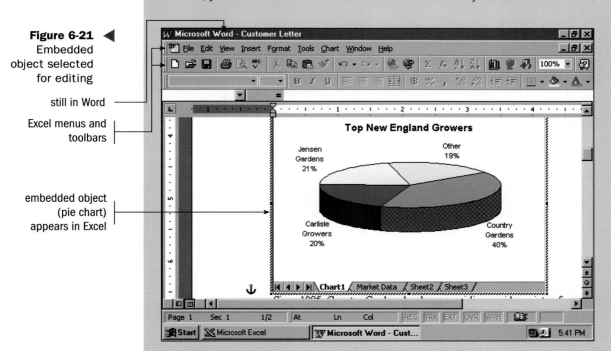

TROUBLE? If the floating Chart toolbar appears, click its Close button to close it.

Now you can modify the chart.

3. Click anywhere within the **chart** to select it, and then click the **Country Gardens slice** to select it. Selection handles now appear on only this slice.

4. With the pointer on the selected slice, click and drag the Country Gardens slice down and to the right, and then release the mouse button. The Country Gardens slice is exploded.

5. Click outside of the chart area to deselect the chart and return the window to the display of Word commands and features only. See Figure 6-22.

Figure 6-22 ◄
Pie chart in
Word document
after slice
exploded

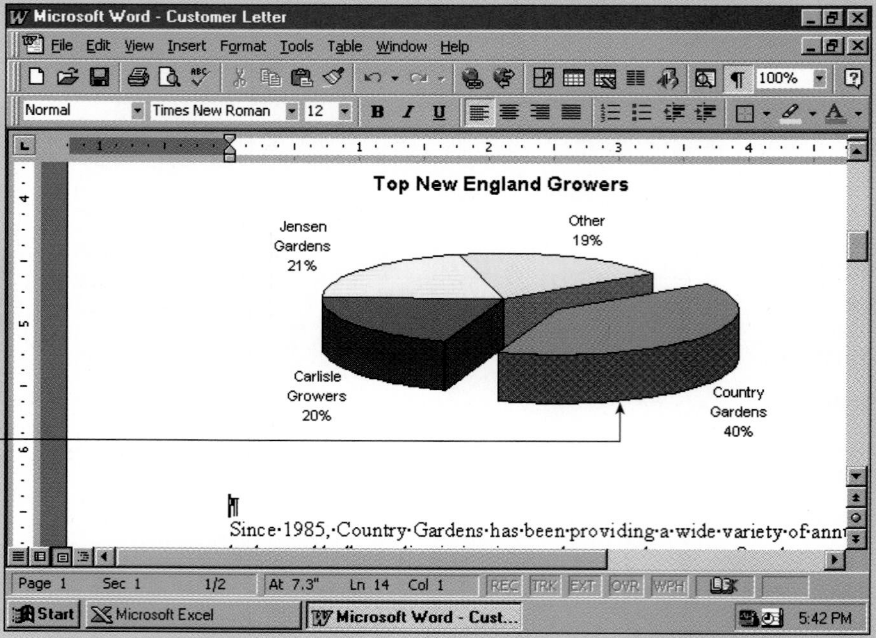

exploded slice ────────

6. Click the **Save** button 💾 on the Word Standard toolbar to save the Customer Letter document.

Quick Check

1. When linking objects, you use the _____ command on the Edit menu.

2. OLE stands for _____.

3. If two documents are _____ using OLE, changing the source document will automatically change the destination document.

4. You can create special text effects using _____.

5. Updating an embedded object (has, has no) effect on the original source object.

6. You have embedded a range of cells in a Word document. Describe what happens when you double-click the embedded object.

7. When you _____ an object, that object is now part of the new document, and can only be altered from within that document's program.

8. You should _____ an object if you plan to use the same data in several documents and need to ensure that the data will be identical in each document.

Now that you have completed the body of the customer letter, Sue is ready for you to send it to the Country Gardens Vermont customers. You can do this through a mail merge. You will do this in Session 6.2.

SESSION

6.2

In this session, you will plan and complete a mail merge by inserting merge fields into a form letter that links to data in an Excel list.

Customizing a Form Letter Using an Excel List

Sue is ready to send out the completed promotional letter announcing the new mail-order catalog and introducing the new products. She has decided to customize the customer letter by inserting the customer's name and address into each letter. Using her customer list, which is maintained in Excel, she plans separate mailings to coincide with promotional events at each of her company's three stores. For instance, the store in Burlington, Vermont has an open house planned next month and Sue wants to send the letter to only those customers in Vermont so that they receive the letter in advance of the open house. Later, she will do a separate mailing for New Hampshire customers to coincide with a fall festival, and then a separate mailing to Massachusetts customers to coincide with the Dunstable store's participation in a town fair.

In this section, you'll complete the customer letter for Sue by merging it with the names and addresses of Country Gardens' Vermont customers. This data is stored as an Excel list. Therefore, you will again be integrating Excel data with a Word document.

Planning the Form Letter

Sue plans to use the Mail Merge feature of Word to send the customer letter you completed in the previous session to each Country Gardens customer in Vermont. She will be sending the same letter, a form letter, to each customer; only the name and address will change. A **form letter** is a Word document that contains standard paragraphs of text and a minimum of variable text, usually just the names and addresses of the letter recipients. The **main document** of a form letter contains the text that stays the same in each letter, as well as the **merge fields** that tell Word where to insert the variable information into each letter. The variable information, the information that changes from letter to letter, is contained in a **data source**, which can be another Word document, an Excel list, an Access database, or some other source. The main document and the data source work together—when you merge the main document with the data source, Word replaces the merge fields with the corresponding field values from the data source. The process of merging the main document with the data source is called a **mail merge**.

In this case, Sue's customer letter will be the main document and a customer list maintained in Excel containing the names and addresses of Country Gardens customers will be the data source. Figure 6-23 shows Sue's plan for the form letter.

Figure 6-23 ◀
Sue's plan for
the form letter

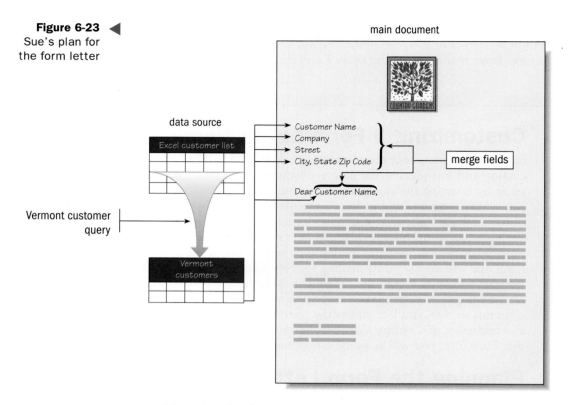

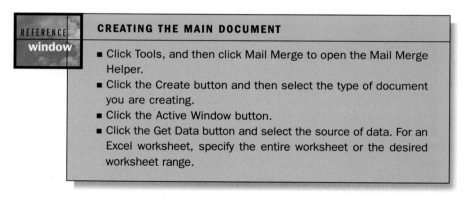

Note that the data source contains all Country Gardens customers. Sue first wants to send the letter to only the Vermont customers.

REFERENCE
window

CREATING THE MAIN DOCUMENT

- Click Tools, and then click Mail Merge to open the Mail Merge Helper.
- Click the Create button and then select the type of document you are creating.
- Click the Active Window button.
- Click the Get Data button and select the source of data. For an Excel worksheet, specify the entire worksheet or the desired worksheet range.

To help simplify the mail merge process, you will use the Word Mail Merge Helper, which guides you through the steps of the mail merge.

Specifying a Main Document and a Data Source

A mail-merged main document can be a new or existing Word document. In this case, the main document is Sue's customer letter.

Now you need to specify the customer letter as the main document and the Excel customer list as the data source.

To specify the main document and the data source:

1. If you took a break after the last session, make sure that Excel and Word are running, and the Customer Letter document is open and displayed on your screen.

2. Scroll to the top of the letter, click **Tools** on the menu bar, and then click **Mail Merge**. The Mail Merge Helper dialog box opens. See Figure 6-24. The dialog box displays the three tasks you need to perform: creating the main document, creating or getting a data source, and merging the main document with the data source.

Figure 6-24 ◄
Mail Merge
Helper dialog
box

click to choose the
type of merge
document

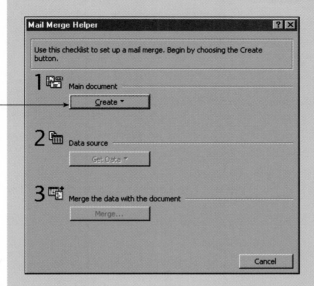

The type of merge document you need to create is a form letter.

3. Click the **Create** button in the Main document section to display the list of main document types. Click **Form Letters**. Word displays a message box asking whether you want to use the active window as the main document or create a new main document. In this case, you want to use the open document, Customer Letter, as the main document.

4. Click the **Active Window** button. The area below the Create button now indicates the type of mail merge (Form Letters) and the file path and name of the main document (Customer Letter).

   You have now established Customer Letter as the main document. Next you need to specify the data source, the source of the variable information that will be inserted into the main document during the merge process. The data source is an Excel workbook named Customers.

5. Click the **Get Data** button in the Data source section of the Mail Merge Helper dialog box, and then click **Open Data Source**. The Open Data Source dialog box opens.

   The Customers workbook is located in the Tutorial.06 folder on your Student Disk.

6. Make sure that the Tutorial.06 folder is displayed in the Look in list box.

   Because the dialog box currently shows only the Word documents in the selected folder, you need to change the entry in the Files of type list box to show the Excel files.

7. Click the **Files of type** list arrow, and then click **MS Excel Worksheets**. The dialog box now shows a list of all the Excel files in the Tutorial.06 folder on your Student Disk.

8. Click **Customer** and then click the **Open** button. A Microsoft Excel dialog box opens, in which you can choose the data source—either the entire spreadsheet or the range containing the customer list. In this case, you need to specify the range Customers. See Figure 6-25.

Figure 6-25 ◀
Choose data
source

click this data source ──────

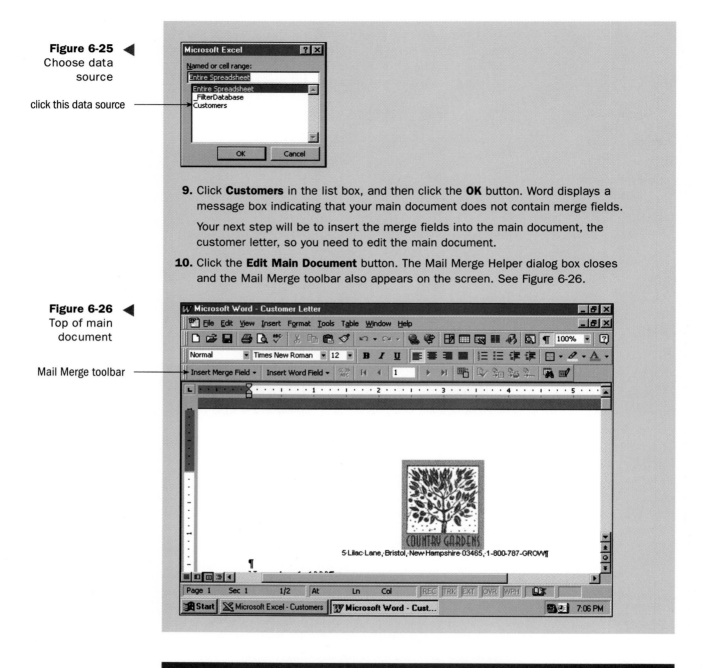

9. Click **Customers** in the list box, and then click the **OK** button. Word displays a message box indicating that your main document does not contain merge fields.

   Your next step will be to insert the merge fields into the main document, the customer letter, so you need to edit the main document.

10. Click the **Edit Main Document** button. The Mail Merge Helper dialog box closes and the Mail Merge toolbar also appears on the screen. See Figure 6-26.

Figure 6-26 ◀
Top of main
document

Mail Merge toolbar ──────

Inserting the Merge Fields

Because you now have a data source to use with the main document, you can go back to the main document and identify which fields to pull into the document and where to place each. This process is called **inserting merge fields**. As noted earlier, a merge field is a special instruction that tells Word where to insert the variable information from the data source into a form letter.

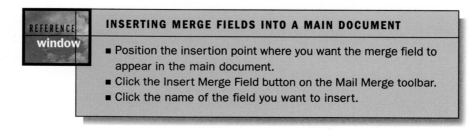

REFERENCE
window

INSERTING MERGE FIELDS INTO A MAIN DOCUMENT

- Position the insertion point where you want the merge field to appear in the main document.
- Click the Insert Merge Field button on the Mail Merge toolbar.
- Click the name of the field you want to insert.

Excel

To complete Sue's form letter, you need to insert seven merge fields, one for each of the following pieces of information: customer name, company name (if any), street, city, state, and zip code—all for the inside address—and customer name again in the salutation of the letter.

To insert the merge fields into the customer letter document:

1. Scroll the document window and position the insertion point in the blank paragraph directly above the salutation ("Dear,"). This is where the customer's name and address will appear.

2. Press the **Enter** key to insert a blank line, and then click the **Insert Merge Field** button on the Mail Merge toolbar. A list of the available merge fields is displayed. See Figure 6-27.

Figure 6-27 ◄
Inserting merge fields into main document

available fields from customer list

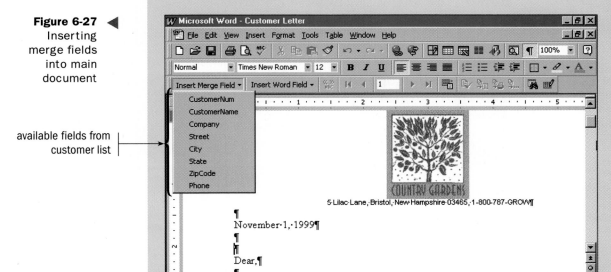

3. Click **CustomerName** to select this field. See Figure 6-28. Word inserts the field name into the document, enclosed in chevron symbols (<< >>). The chevrons distinguish the merge fields from the rest of the text in the main document.

Figure 6-28 ◄
Main document after one merge field inserted

merge field

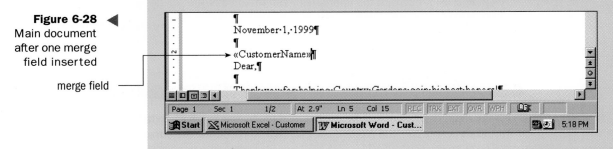

The company name (if any) should appear on the line below the customer name.

4. Press the **Enter** key to move the insertion point to the next line, click the **Insert Merge Field** button on the Mail Merge toolbar, and then click **Company**. Word inserts the Company merge field into the document.

5. Repeat Step 4 to insert the **Street** field on the third line of the inside address.

6. Repeat Step 4 to insert the **City** field on the fourth line of the inside address. The State and ZipCode fields must appear on the same line as the City field, with a comma and a space separating the city and state, and a space separating the state and zip code.

7. Type **,** (a comma), press the **Spacebar**, click the **Insert Merge Field** button on the Mail Merge toolbar, and then click **State**.

8. Press the **Spacebar**, click the **Insert Merge Field** button on the Mail Merge toolbar, and then click **ZipCode**.

9. Press the **Enter** key to insert a blank line between the inside address and the salutation. The final merge field you need to insert is the CustomerName field again, after the word "Dear" in the salutation of the letter.

10. Position the insertion point between the "r" in the word "Dear" and the comma following it, press the **Spacebar**, click the **Insert Merge Field** button on the Mail Merge toolbar, and then click **CustomerName**. The merge fields are now complete. See Figure 6-29.

Figure 6-29 ◀
All merge fields inserted into main document

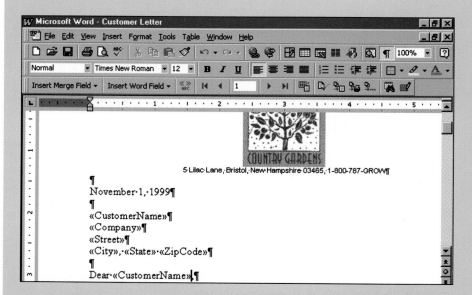

TROUBLE? Compare your screen with Figure 6-29 and make sure there are no extra spaces or punctuation around the merge fields. If you need to delete a merge field, highlight the entire field, and then press the Delete key.

11. Click the **Save** button on the Word Standard toolbar to save the letter.

Performing the Mail Merge

With the main document and merge fields in place, you're ready to merge the main document with the data source—the Excel customer list—to produce the customized letter.

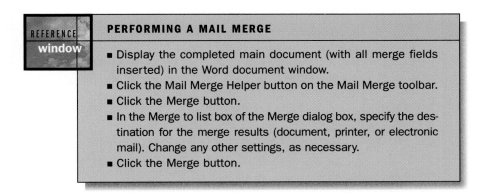

REFERENCE
window

PERFORMING A MAIL MERGE

■ Display the completed main document (with all merge fields inserted) in the Word document window.
■ Click the Mail Merge Helper button on the Mail Merge toolbar.
■ Click the Merge button.
■ In the Merge to list box of the Merge dialog box, specify the destination for the merge results (document, printer, or electronic mail). Change any other settings, as necessary.
■ Click the Merge button.

In this case, Sue wants the merge results placed in a new document, so that she can check the merged form letters before printing them. First she needs to specify the records that are to be included in the mail merge—customers in Vermont.

To specify selection criteria for records to retrieve from the data source:

1. Click the **Mail Merge Helper** button 🖳 on the Mail Merge toolbar. The Mail Merge Helper dialog box opens.

2. Click the **Merge** button to display the Merge dialog box. See Figure 6-30.

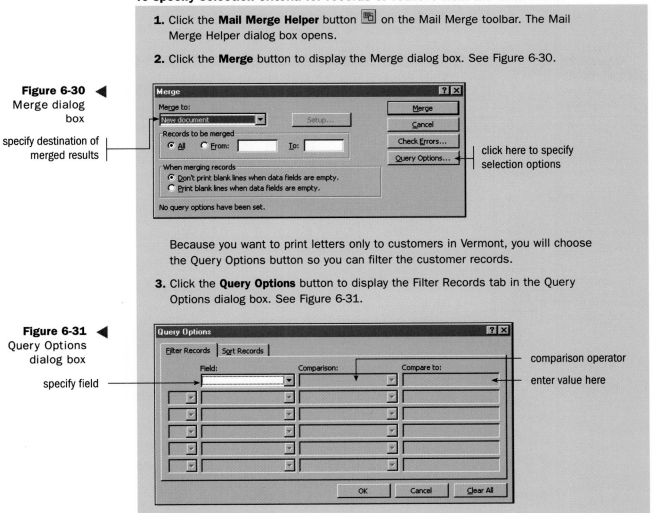

Figure 6-30 ◀
Merge dialog box

specify destination of merged results

click here to specify selection options

Because you want to print letters only to customers in Vermont, you will choose the Query Options button so you can filter the customer records.

3. Click the **Query Options** button to display the Filter Records tab in the Query Options dialog box. See Figure 6-31.

Figure 6-31 ◀
Query Options dialog box

specify field

comparison operator

enter value here

4. Click the **Field** list arrow to display the list of fields from the customer list. Scroll the list until the State field appears. Click **State** to select the field you want to base your selection on. Notice that the Comparison operator box now displays the default operator—Equal to. Accept the default comparison operator and enter a value to compare the State field to.

5. Make sure the insertion point is in the Compare to text box and then type **VT**.

6. Click the **OK** button to return to the Merge dialog box.

You are now ready to merge the data with the letter. You can merge the data to a new document, or merge directly to the printer, electronic mail, or fax. Sue wants to check the merged document before printing, so you will merge to a new document.

7. Click the **Merge** button. The Excel data is merged with the Word form letter and placed in a new document named Form Letters1 (the default name supplied by Word). The form letter for each of the five Vermont customers is contained in the merged document, each separated by a section break.

8. Scroll the document until you can see the first merged address. Word replaced each merge field with the appropriate Excel data. See Figure 6-32.

Figure 6-32 ◀
Merged results in new document

first Vermont customer in Excel customer list

document contains 5 two-page letters

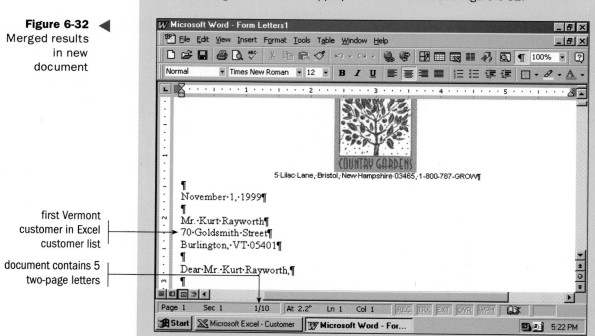

Notice that the merged document contains 10 pages. Each letter is two pages long, and there are five letters in all.

9. Use the buttons in the vertical scroll bar to page through the merged document. Notice that in addresses that do not include a company name, the blank line is suppressed. Also, notice that each two-page form letter is separated from the others by a section break.

Now you'll save the merged document and then close it.

10. Save the document as **Merged Customer Letters** in the Tutorial.06 folder on your Student Disk.

11. Close the Merged Customer Letters document. You return to the main document, the customer letter.

Excel

Viewing Merged Documents

When you're working with mail-merge documents, you don't have to open the document containing the merge results in order to view them. You can view the merged documents right from the main document.

The View Merged Data button on the Mail Merge toolbar lets you check the merge results quickly. When you click this button, Word displays information from the first data record in place of the merge fields. You can then use the navigation buttons on the Mail Merge toolbar to view the results for other data records. You'll practice using the navigation buttons to view the merge results.

To view the merge results from the main document:

1. Click the **View Merged Data** button on the Mail Merge toolbar. Word displays the information from the first merged letter in place of the merge fields. See Figure 6-33.

Figure 6-33 ◀
Viewing merged results from main document

View Merged Data button

first record

previous record

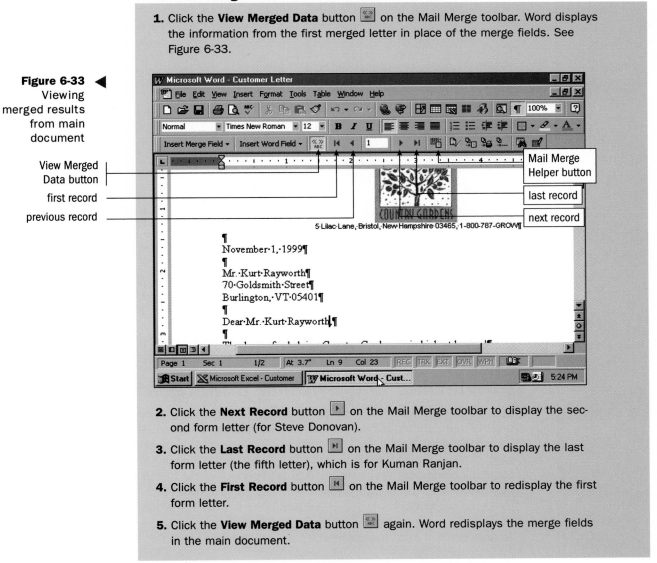

Mail Merge Helper button

last record

next record

2. Click the **Next Record** button on the Mail Merge toolbar to display the second form letter (for Steve Donovan).

3. Click the **Last Record** button on the Mail Merge toolbar to display the last form letter (the fifth letter), which is for Kuman Ranjan.

4. Click the **First Record** button on the Mail Merge toolbar to redisplay the first form letter.

5. Click the **View Merged Data** button again. Word redisplays the merge fields in the main document.

Sue has just learned that one of her customers, Williston Lawn Services, has moved to a different location. She asks you to enter the new address for this customer in Excel and then re-merge the Word document with the data.

To change the address and then re-merge the document:

1. Click the **Microsoft Excel** button on the taskbar to switch to Excel.

2. Use the data form to locate Williston Lawn Services (customer number 192) and change the Street entry to **10 Main Street**.

3. Click the **Microsoft Word** button on the taskbar to switch back to Word.

4. Click the **View Merged Data** button 🔲 on the Mail Merge toolbar. Word displays the information from the first merged letter.

The record for Williston Lawn Services is the second record (in the mail merge).

5. Click the **Next Record** button ▶ on the Mail Merge toolbar to select the next record. Word displays the record for Williston Lawn Services. Note that the data has been updated to show the new street address (10 Main Street).

Although the main document now shows the updated record data, the document containing the merge results—Merged Customer Letters—still contains the old address, because it contains only the results of the previous merge. In order to update the Merged Customer Letters document, you need to re-merge the main document with the data source and then save the updated merge results.

6. Click the **Mail Merge Helper** button 🔲 on the Mail Merge toolbar. The Mail Merge Helper dialog box opens.

7. Click the **Merge** button to open the Merge dialog box, and then click the **Merge** button. The mail merge results are displayed in a new document window.

8. Scroll through the results until you find the address for Williston Lawn Services. Note that it now includes the updated street data.

Now you need to save the merge results as Merged Customer Letters to overwrite the existing document.

9. Use the Save As command to save the document containing the merge results as **Merged Customer Letters**, answer **Yes** to the prompt for overwriting the existing file, and then close the Merged Customer Letters document. You return to the main document, which still displays the data for Williston Lawn Services.

After viewing the merged documents, Sue decides to print just one of the letters to check its appearance and layout before printing all the letters.

Previewing and Printing a Merged Document

You can preview and print a merged document in the same way that you do any Word document—using the Print Preview and Print buttons on the Standard toolbar. For the sample letter Sue wants to print, she decides that it would be best to print one that includes a company name in the address. This will allow her to make sure that the additional line for the company name does not cause a bad page break across the two pages of the letter. Because the main document already displays the data for Williston Lawn Services, which includes the company name, you can preview and print this merged letter.

To preview and print the merged letter for Williston Lawn Services:

1. Click the **Print Preview** button 🔲 on the Standard toolbar. Both pages of the letter are displayed in Print Preview. See Figure 6-34.

Figure 6-34 ◀
Merged letter
for Williston
Lawn Services
in Print Preview

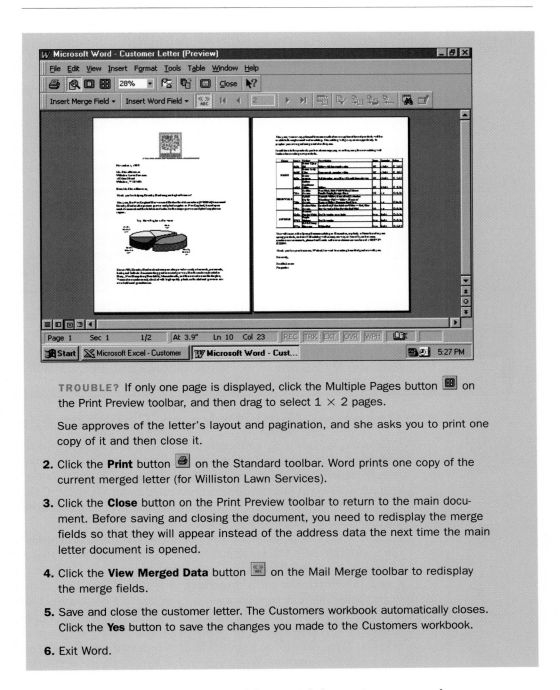

TROUBLE? If only one page is displayed, click the Multiple Pages button ⊞ on the Print Preview toolbar, and then drag to select 1 × 2 pages.

Sue approves of the letter's layout and pagination, and she asks you to print one copy of it and then close it.

2. Click the **Print** button 🖨 on the Standard toolbar. Word prints one copy of the current merged letter (for Williston Lawn Services).

3. Click the **Close** button on the Print Preview toolbar to return to the main document. Before saving and closing the document, you need to redisplay the merge fields so that they will appear instead of the address data the next time the main letter document is opened.

4. Click the **View Merged Data** button 《》/ABC on the Mail Merge toolbar to redisplay the merge fields.

5. Save and close the customer letter. The Customers workbook automatically closes. Click the **Yes** button to save the changes you made to the Customers workbook.

6. Exit Word.

Sue plans on reviewing the printed letter with her assistants to make sure everyone approves of it before she prints and mails all the form letters.

Quick Check

1. The _____ document of a form letter contains the text that stays the same, as well as the _____ .

2. A _____ contains the variable information in a form letter.

3. During the mail merge process you updated the customer list in Excel and then observed the updated address in the merged customer letter. That process illustrates _____ .

4. How do you insert merge fields into a main document?

5. How do you view merged documents directly from the main document?

Sue is pleased with her finished letter, which integrates her Excel data. She is confident that it will contribute to the successful promotion of Country Gardens.

SESSION 6.3

In this session, you will create hyperlinks between documents so that you can easily access other information from a single document. You will learn how to navigate a series of hyperlinks using the Web toolbar. You will also learn how to convert an Excel worksheet to HTML format so you can display Excel data as a Web document.

Creating Hyperlinks to Connect Files

In Sessions 6.1 and 6.2, you worked with several files from two different programs, Excel and Word, that contained related information. To do this, you opened each program, and then navigated between the two using their program buttons on the taskbar. With Excel 97, you can now insert links to documents created using Microsoft Office programs. These links allow you to easily navigate to different documents created in different programs, without having to launch each program first.

To link various documents, you can use a hyperlink. A **hyperlink** is an object (computer file pathname or address, text, or graphic) in a document that you can click to access information in other locations in that document or in other documents. This system of linked information is called **hypertext**. A hyperlink can be a filename, a word, a phrase, or a graphic that has been assigned an address to a file located elsewhere. If the hyperlink is a filename or text, the hyperlink will be displayed in color and as underlined text. If the hyperlink is a graphic, there is no visual cue until you position your mouse over the graphic. Then the mouse pointer changes to a pointing hand 👆 and displays the location of the link's destination. When you click a hyperlink, the destination document is brought into memory and displayed on the screen. This hyperlink may reference

- a document created in Word, Excel, PowerPoint, or Access
- a section farther down in the same document
- a document on the World Wide Web

Hyperlinks offer a new way of making information available. Files containing hyperlinks are called **hyperlink documents**. Using the hyperlinks available to you in a hyperlink document, you are able to jump from one topic to the next in whatever order you want, regardless of where they reside.

As more hyperlinks are added between and within various documents, a structure emerges that you can navigate, traveling from hyperlink to hyperlink, following a path of information and ideas. You have already worked with such a structure when you accessed the Excel online Help system. By clicking a keyword or phrase, you were able to access additional information on the topic you were interested in. The Excel online Help system is an example of a series of hyperlink documents.

Inserting a Hyperlink

Sue asks you to place a hyperlink in the New Products workbook to the Merged Customer Letters (Word file) and to the Customers workbook (Excel file). With the files connected she can easily jump to the other files if she wants to recall specific information. For instance, by including links to the customer list and the merged customer letter she can check a customer's name, or make sure she sent a letter to an important new client—while working in the New Products workbook.

REFERENCE window

INSERTING A HYPERLINK

- Select the text, graphic, or cell where you want to insert the hyperlink, and then click the Insert Hyperlink button on the Standard toolbar to display the Insert Hyperlink dialog box.
- Type the address of the Web page or file you want to jump to. If you are not sure of the filename, click the Browse button to display the Link to File dialog box. Find and select the file you want to link to.
- If you want to jump to a particular location within the file, enter the location in the Named location in file text box.
- Click the Use relative path for hyperlink check box if you want the Excel destination's relative file address.

To insert a hyperlink into an Excel worksheet:

1. If you took a break after the last session, make sure Excel is running and your Student Disk is in the appropriate disk drive.

2. Open the **New Products** workbook located in the Tutorial.06 folder on your Student Disk.

3. Make sure the Title Sheet sheet is active, and then click cell **A10**. The Title Sheet is where you want to insert the hyperlinks to the other files Sue works with when using this workbook.

4. Type **Cross Reference to Related Documents**, and then press the **Enter** key.

5. Click cell **A10**, and then click the **Bold** button [B] on the Standard toolbar.

   Enter the text you want to use as a reference.

6. Click cell **A11**, type **Merged Customer Letters**, and press the **Enter** key.

7. In cell A12 type **Customer List**, and then press the **Enter** key.

   Now you need to specify the location of the destination file for each hyperlink. You do this using the Insert Hyperlink button on the Standard toolbar.

8. Click cell **A11** and then click the **Insert Hyperlink** button [icon] on the Standard toolbar to display the Insert Hyperlink dialog box. See Figure 6-35.

   TROUBLE? If the message "You should save this document before creating a hyperlink...." appears, click the Yes button and save the document before inserting the link.

Figure 6-35 ◀
Insert
Hyperlink
dialog box

enter destination
file for the link

click here to view contents
of selected drive

Enter the address of the merged customer letter, which is its filename.

9. Click the **Browse** button in the Link to file or URL section to open the Link to File dialog box. Make sure your Student Disk is in the appropriate disk drive, and the Tutorial.06 folder is specified in the Look in list box.

10. Click **Merged Customer Letters** and then click the **OK** button.

11. Make sure the Use relative path for hyperlink check box is checked so that the Path section of the dialog box will show only the name of the file and not the drive letters. Therefore, in the event that you decide at a later time to move the file to another folder, you will not have to insert a new address for the hyperlink to that file.

12. Click the **OK** button to close the dialog box. Notice that the hyperlink text is colored and underlined, which indicates the text is a hyperlink.

13. Click cell **A12** and repeat Steps 8-12 to create a hyperlink to the Customer workbook. See Figure 6-36.

Figure 6-36 ◀
Hyperlinks
inserted into
Title Sheet

hyperlinks

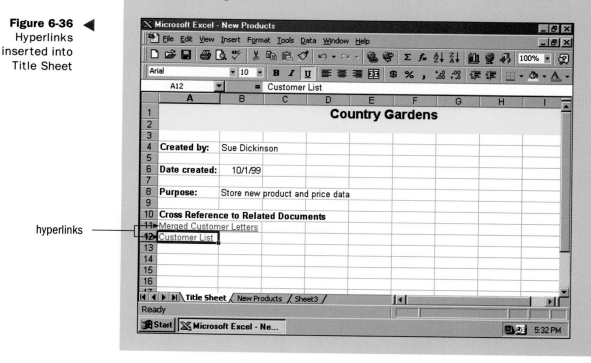

Now that you have created the hyperlinks, you should test them.

Testing Hyperlinks

Now that you have created the hyperlinks, you decide to test them to make sure each one links to the correct location. Recall that by clicking a hyperlink you jump to the referenced location. First, test the hyperlink to the merged customer letters.

To test the Merged Customer Letters hyperlink:

1. Position the pointer over the text **Merged Customer Letters** in cell A11. The pointer changes to a pointing hand 🖑, and a ScreenTip showing the address of the linked document appears.

2. Click the **Merged Customer Letters** hyperlink. Word launches and the Merged Customer Letters document opens on your screen. See Figure 6-37. Notice that the Web toolbar also appears on your screen. Figure 6-38 describes the function of each button on the Web toolbar in navigating between documents that contain hyperlinks.

Figure 6-37 ◀
Merged
Customer
Letters
document
opened from
hyperlink

Web toolbar (location
on your screen
may differ)

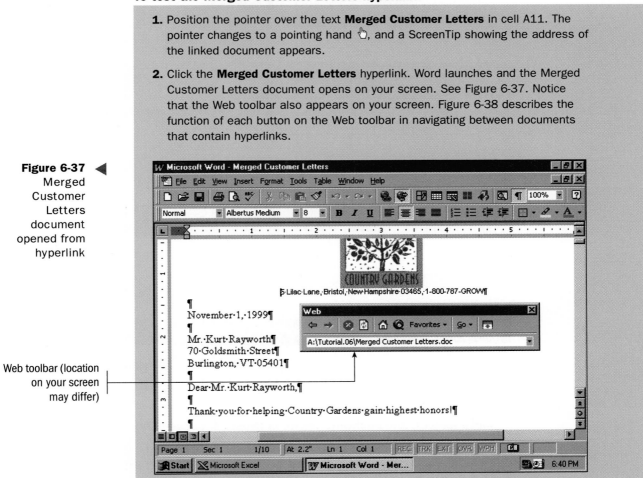

Figure 6-38 ◀
Function of
buttons on
Web toolbar

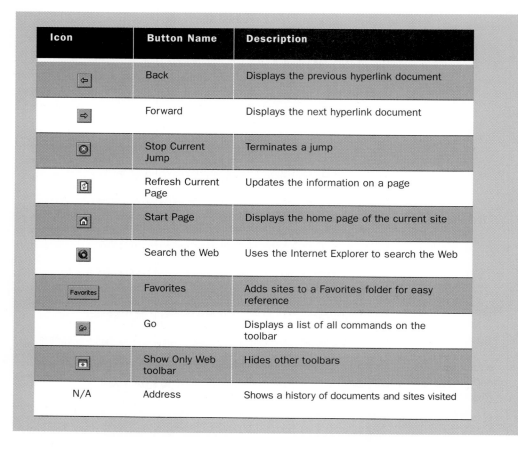

Icon	Button Name	Description
⇐	Back	Displays the previous hyperlink document
⇒	Forward	Displays the next hyperlink document
⊗	Stop Current Jump	Terminates a jump
▢	Refresh Current Page	Updates the information on a page
⌂	Start Page	Displays the home page of the current site
◎	Search the Web	Uses the Internet Explorer to search the Web
Favorites	Favorites	Adds sites to a Favorites folder for easy reference
Go	Go	Displays a list of all commands on the toolbar
▣	Show Only Web toolbar	Hides other toolbars
N/A	Address	Shows a history of documents and sites visited

Navigating Between the Hyperlink Documents

After reviewing the letter, you are ready to return to Excel. Instead of using the program button on the taskbar, use the navigational buttons on the Web toolbar to move forward and backward between the hyperlink documents.

To move forward and backward between hyperlink documents:

1. Click the **Back** button ⇐ on the Web toolbar to return to the title sheet for the New Products workbook. Notice that the hyperlink reference has changed color, indicating that you have used the hyperlink at least once to jump to the linked document.

2. Click the **Customer List** hyperlink. The Customers workbook opens.

3. Click the **Back** button ⇐ on the Web toolbar to return to the New Products workbook.

   TROUBLE? If the Web toolbar does not appear, click View on the menu bar, click Toolbars, and then click Web. Repeat Step 3.

4. Click the **Forward** button ⇒ on the Web toolbar to jump to the Customers workbook again.

5. Click the **Back** button ⇐ on the Web toolbar to return to the New Products workbook.

6. Save and then close the New Products workbook. Notice that the Customer workbook automatically closed. Remove the Web toolbar.

7. Switch to Word, close the Word document, and then exit Word.

Sue is pleased to have the hyperlinks in place for navigating between these related Country Gardens documents.

Publishing Excel Data on a Web Page

The **World Wide Web** (WWW), commonly called the Web, is a structure of documents connected electronically over **the Internet**, which is a large computer network made up of smaller networks and computers all connected electronically. Each document on the Web is called a **Web document** or **Web page**. These documents store different types of information, including text, graphics, sound, animation, and video. A Web page often includes hypertext links to other Web documents. These hypertext links point to other Web pages and allow you to follow related information by jumping from computer to computer to retrieve the desired information. Each Web page or document has a specific address, called its Uniform Resource Locator, or more commonly, **URL**. The URL indicates where the Web document is stored on the Web.

As a progressive businessperson, Sue recognized early the potential marketing power of the Internet. Understanding this potential, she hired a small firm to develop her company's documents to be placed on the Web. This provides Sue with another means to inform her customers of new Country Gardens products and events, in addition to the customer letter and the in-store flyers.

Now, she plans to develop an additional Web page showing her new products list. Fortunately, Sue can use her existing New Products worksheet to create this Web page. However, she will need to make some modifications first. In order for a document to be usable as a Web document, it needs to be formatted in a particular way.

Converting an Excel Worksheet to HTML Format

When people access the World Wide Web, they use a software program, called a **Web browser**, that enables them to access, view, and navigate all the Web documents on the Web. Web browsers recognize files that are in the HTML format. Therefore, any document that is to be available on the Web needs to be in this HTML format. **HTML**, short for HyperText Markup Language, is the language in which your data needs to be formatted in order to be accessible on the Web. In order to display your Excel data on the Web you need to convert it to HTML Format. Excel workbook data can easily be converted to HTML format. Only then can the workbook be used as a Web document.

Sue has asked you to convert the new products table in the New Products worksheet to HTML format. Excel provides a Wizard that walks you through the process of converting an Excel range or chart to HTML format.

To open the New Products workbook and start the Internet Assistant Wizard:

1. Open the New Products workbook and make sure the New Products sheet is activated. Press **Ctrl + Home** to return to the top of the worksheet.

2. Select the range **A11:H21**. This is the range containing the new products table that you want to convert to HTML format.

3. Click **File** on the menu bar, and then click **Save as HTML** to open the Internet Assistant Wizard - Step 1 of 4 dialog box. See Figure 6-39.

TROUBLE? If the Office Assistant opens, click "No, don't provide help now" to close it.

TROUBLE? If the Save as HTML command does not appear on the File menu, click Tools on the menu bar, then click Add-Ins to display the Add-Ins dialog box. Click the Internet Assistant Wizard check box, and then click OK to install the Internet Assistant. Repeat Step 3. (If you don't see the Internet Assistant Wizard in the Add-Ins dialog box, check with your instructor or technical support person.)

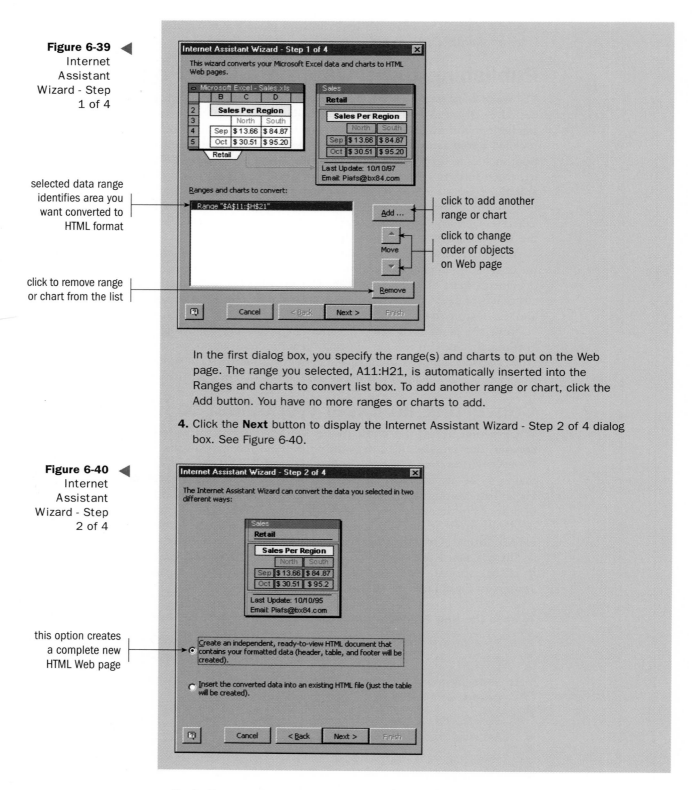

Figure 6-39 ◀
Internet
Assistant
Wizard - Step
1 of 4

selected data range
identifies area you
want converted to
HTML format

click to add another
range or chart

click to change
order of objects
on Web page

click to remove range
or chart from the list

In the first dialog box, you specify the range(s) and charts to put on the Web
page. The range you selected, A11:H21, is automatically inserted into the
Ranges and charts to convert list box. To add another range or chart, click the
Add button. You have no more ranges or charts to add.

4. Click the **Next** button to display the Internet Assistant Wizard - Step 2 of 4 dialog
box. See Figure 6-40.

Figure 6-40 ◀
Internet
Assistant
Wizard - Step
2 of 4

this option creates
a complete new
HTML Web page

In the Internet Assistant Wizard – Step 2 of 4 dialog box, you specify whether you want
to create a complete new Web page or insert the range into an existing Web page. Sue
wants to insert the new products table as a separate Web page, which is the default option.

To create a complete Web page:

1. Make sure the Create an independent, ready-to-view HTML document option button is selected, and then click the **Next** button to display the Internet Assistant Wizard - Step 3 of 4 dialog box. See Figure 6-41.

Figure 6-41 ◀
Internet
Assistant
Wizard - Step
3 of 4

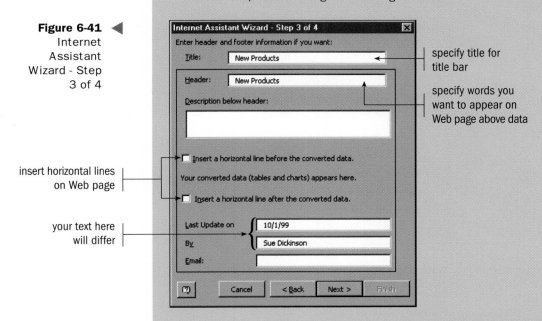

In Step 3 of the Internet Assistant Wizard, you lay out your Web page. You specify the title you want displayed in the title bar of the Web browser. You also enter any information you want to appear above or below your worksheet data. In the Header section, you type the text you want to appear above the data in the worksheet at the top of the Web document. You can also enter text in the Description below header box. These lines of text appear below the header. You can also insert horizontal lines, the date the file was last updated, and your Internet e-mail address. Now enter the information for Sue's Web page.

2. Highlight the default Web page title in the Title textbox, and then type **Country Gardens Web Page**.

   TROUBLE? If you pressed the Enter key and accidentally advanced to the Internet Assistant Wizard – Step 4 of 4 dialog box, click the Back button to return to Internet Assistant – Step 3 of 4.

3. Press the **Tab** key to move to the **Header** text box, and then type **New Product List** to place this text above the new products table on your Web page.

4. Click the **Insert a horizontal line after the converted data** check box to place a line below the new products table to serve as a separator from the other information on your Web page.

   Now enter the date the page was updated, the name of the person creating the Web page, and an e-mail address to contact.

5. Type **10/1/99** in the Last Update on text box.

6. Type **Sue Dickinson** in the By text box.

7. Type **sd@cg.com** in the Email text box. The completed dialog box appears in Figure 6-42.

Figure 6-42 ◀
Internet
Assistant
Wizard - Step 3
of 4 completed

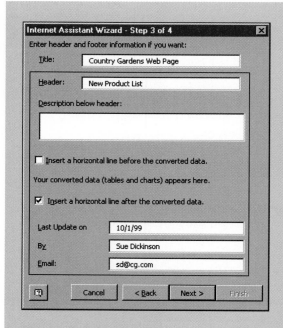

8. Click the **Next** button to display the Internet Assistant Wizard - Step 4 of 4 dialog box. See Figure 6-43.

Figure 6-43 ◀
Internet
Assistant
Wizard - Step 4
of 4 completed

accept default ──────

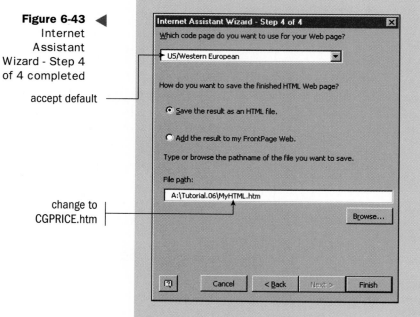

change to
CGPRICE.htm

In the final step of the Internet Assistant Wizard, you specify the location and name of the HTML file you are creating.

9. Make sure that the Save the result as an HTML file option button is selected so your work is saved as an HTML file.

Change the default filename MyHTML.htm to CGPRICE.htm.

10. In the File path text box, select just the filename, **MyHTML.htm**, and replace it with **CGPRICE.htm**. See Figure 6-44.

Figure 6-44 ◀
Internet
Assistant
Wizard - Step 4
of 4 after
filename
change

new filename

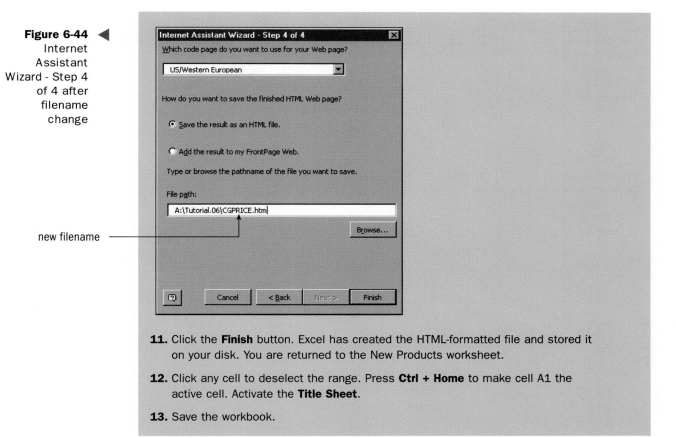

11. Click the **Finish** button. Excel has created the HTML-formatted file and stored it on your disk. You are returned to the New Products worksheet.

12. Click any cell to deselect the range. Press **Ctrl + Home** to make cell A1 the active cell. Activate the **Title Sheet**.

13. Save the workbook.

Viewing an HTML File Using a Web Browser

You have completed your Web page and it is now saved on your Student Disk as CGPRICE.htm. The file extension .htm indicates that it is in HTML format, and therefore readable using a Web browser. Before the document is made accessible on the World Wide Web, Sue wants to view her Web page to confirm that her layout appears as she wants it to. To see how it will appear to people viewing it from the Web using a Web browser, you can open the HTML file on your Student Disk using your own Web browser.

To view the CGPrice HTML file:

1. Click **View** on the menu bar, point to **Toolbars**, and then click **Web**. Excel displays the Web toolbar.

2. Click the **Go** button [Go] on the Web toolbar, and then click **Open**. Excel displays the Open Internet Address dialog box, in which you can specify the URL of the Internet site or the name of the HTML file you want to view.

3. Click the **Browse** button. Excel displays the Browse dialog box. If necessary, use the Look In text box to display the contents of the Tutorial.06 folder on your Student Disk, click **CGPRICE**, and then click the **Open** button. Excel returns to the Open Internet Address dialog box and displays the address for the HTML file.

4. Click the **OK** button. Excel opens the Internet Explorer (or the Web browser installed on your computer) and displays the CGPrice HTML file. See Figure 6-45.

Figure 6-45 ◀
Viewing New
Product List
Web page from
a Web browser

the appearance of
your Web page may
differ depending on
the Web browser
you are using

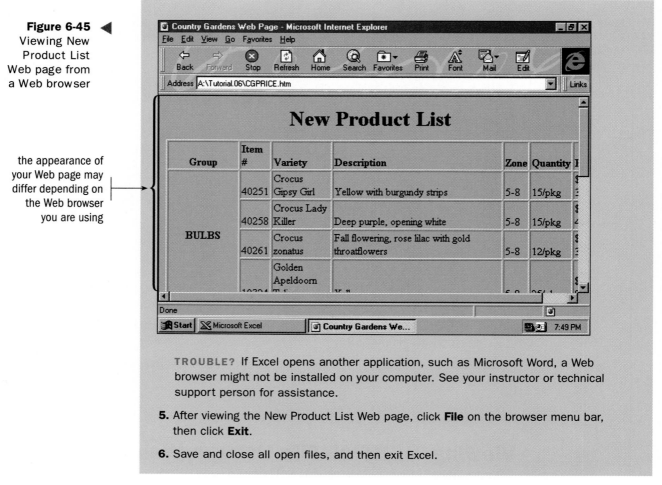

TROUBLE? If Excel opens another application, such as Microsoft Word, a Web browser might not be installed on your computer. See your instructor or technical support person for assistance.

5. After viewing the New Product List Web page, click **File** on the browser menu bar, then click **Exit**.

6. Save and close all open files, and then exit Excel.

Sue is very pleased with the New Product List Web page. It is ready to be added to the series of Web documents Country Gardens currently has available on the World Wide Web.

Quick Check

1. _____ is the language used to present documents on the World Wide Web.

2. You can jump to a document by clicking a _____.

3. A hyperlink can be a _____, _____, or _____.

4. The _____ button on the Standard toolbar is used to insert a hyperlink.

5. You use the _____ and the _____ buttons on the _____ toolbar to move forward and backward between hyperlink documents.

6. A software program called a _____ _____ enables you to access Web documents.

7. To convert Excel data to HTML format, you issue the _____ command.

8. The file extension _____ indicates that the file is in HTML format.

Sue is very pleased to have informed her customers of the new products using a variety of methods—distributing flyers, mailing customized letters, and creating a Web document to be viewed on the World Wide Web.

Tutorial Assignments

Sue is ready to send the merged customer letter to the Massachusetts Country Gardens customers. She also wants to add the NEGHA pie chart to a Web page to be viewable online. Finally, she needs to inform her advisory board, a group of local business professionals, about the company's new products and the NEGHA recognition. Help Sue with these tasks.

Do the following:

1. Start Word and open the document CustLtr2 in the TAssign folder for Tutorial.06 and save it as Customer Letter 2.
2. Use the Merge Mail Helper to modify the selection criteria so only the Massachusetts customers in the city of Andover are selected. Rearrange the letter with the modified criteria. Close the Form Letters 1 document without saving it. (Note: The document Customer Letter 2 is still open.)
3. Print the letter for Ronald Kooienga.
4. Return to the customer list in Excel and change the street address of Ron Kooienga (Customer Number 133) to 20 Freedom Trail. Print the revised letter. Save Customer Letter 2 and exit Word.
5. Open the workbook NEGHA in the TAssign folder for Tutorial.06. This workbook contains a pie chart comparing sales of the top growers in New England. Sue wants to add this chart as a new page on her Web site. Use the Internet Assistant Wizard to create a Web page named NEGHA.htm. The title bar should have the title "Country Gardens," and the Header should be "Top Growers in New England." Add any other information you think is appropriate to Step 3 of the Internet Assistant Wizard. Open your Web browser and view the Web document. Print the Web page from your browser.
6. Open the workbook NewProd2 and save it as New Products 2. Use this workbook to answer questions 7 through 11.
7. Activate the New Products worksheet. Use WordArt to create your own graphic. The text of the graphic is "New Products & Prices." Place the graphic above the new products list. Experiment with some of the features on the WordArt and Drawing toolbar. Save the workbook. Print the worksheet with the graphic.
8. Activate the Title sheet and add a hyperlink to the NEGHA workbook in cell A14. Instead of using a word or phrase as the hyperlink, use the file address of the NEGHA workbook in the TAssign folder for Tutorial.06 as the hyperlink.

9. In cell A15, create a hyperlink to the GardenNet home page on the WWW. Its URL is http://trine.com/GardenNet/. The hyperlink text should be "GardenNet."
10. In cells A17:A18, create a WordArt object with the text "Store Sales." Use the WordArt graphic as a hyperlink to the MonSales worksheet.
11. Save the New Products 2 workbook. Print the Title Sheet worksheet. Close the workbook.
12. Sue has written a letter to her advisory board telling them of the Country Gardens new products and their sales. Open the letter AdvLetr in the TAssign folder for Tutorial.06 and save it as Advisory Board Letter. Open the workbook MonSales in the TAssign folder for Tutorial.06 and save it as MonSales2. Link the MonSales2 worksheet to the Word document Advisory Board Letter. Print the letter.
13. Add the sales for Massachusetts (Figure 6-46) to the worksheet and print the advisory board letter again. Save and close both the letter and the workbook.

Figure 6-46 ◀

Item #	Variety	MA
40251	Crocus Gipsy Girl	600
40258	Crocus Lady Killer	550
40261	Crocus Zonatus	400
10324	Golden Apeldoorn Tulips	200
72211	Astilbe Assort.	300
72621	Hybrid Daylily Assort.	100
74311	Garden Phlox Assort.	650
82480	Exactum Persian Violet	1000
87345	Purple Verbena	500
87730	Salvia Cherry Blossom	450

14. Open the letter AdvLetr in the TAssign folder for Tutorial.06 and save it as Advisory Board Letter2. Open the workbook MonSales in the TAssign folder for Tutorial.06 and embed it in the Advisory Board Letter2. Add the sales for Massachusetts (Figure 6-46) to the worksheet in the Word document. Save and print the letter. Close Word.

15. Use Windows Explorer to compare the file size of the two Word documents: Advisory Board Letter and Advisory Board Letter2 in the TAssign folder for Tutorial.06. What is the file size in bytes of each file? Explain the difference in file sizes.

16. Sue is beginning to prepare a PowerPoint presentation for the Growers Association meeting. Create a new PowerPoint presentation. Create a first slide that has the title "Country Gardens" and a subtitle "The Past 15 Years." Include a second slide that shows Country Gardens as the top grower in New England. Embed the Pie Chart from the NEGHA workbook in the TAssign folder for Tutorial.06 into slide 2. Resize the chart as necessary. In the presentation, explode the Country Gardens slice. Print the two slides on one page. Save the presentation as "Growers" in the TAssign folder for Tutorial.06 and exit PowerPoint.

17. Close all open files.

Case Problems

1. Reporting Sales for Toy World Store manager Fred Galt must report to the regional manager each week. He faxes a memo each week to the regional sales office indicating his recommendations regarding any special sales or promotions he feels will be needed, based on the summary sales information he includes in the report. Fred maintains a worksheet that summarizes sales in units and dollars for each day of the week. This sales summary is included in his weekly report, and on the company's Web page.

Do the following:

1. If necessary, start Excel and make sure your Student Disk is in the appropriate drive. Open ToyStore.xls in the Case folder for Tutorial.06. This is Fred's partially completed worksheet. Save it as Toystore Sales.

2. Complete the worksheet by computing total sales in dollars for each day (including the formula for Saturday) by multiplying the number of units sold of each product by the price per unit (the price table is in the upper-right corner of the worksheet). Also, compute total sales for each product and the total sales for the store. (*Hint*: Check number for Monday through Friday: Total store sales = $86,993.90.)

3. Save the worksheet.

4. Start Word and open the document ToyLtr and save it as Toy Memo.

5. Link the worksheet range A1:F15 to the memo. Print the memo.

6. Saturday evening, Fred faxes the memo to the regional manager, indicating that sales are on target for the week, and no special promotions are necessary at this time. Update store sales for Saturday using the following data: 22,6,18,14. Save the workbook.

7. Print the memo.

8. Save the memo and exit Word.

9. Create a Web page named ToySales.htm which includes the range A7:F15. You decide what information should be entered on Step 3 of the Internet Assistant Wizard. Open your Web browser and view the Web document. Print the page from your Web browser.

10. Use WordArt to replace the title "Store Analysis" with the title "Toy World Sales." Print the worksheet excluding the Product Price Table.

11. Save and close the workbook.

2. Quarterly Sales at Happy Morning Farms Casandra Owens is product manager for a line of breakfast cereals at Happy Morning Farms. Casandra is waiting for one figure so that she can complete her Sales Report—Summarized by State for next week's Operations Management Team (OMT) meeting. As she is working on the report, she receives an urgent call from one of her sales representatives indicating that he needs Casandra in Denver immediately to deal with a customer problem that requires management attention. Casandra realizes that she will not be able to make the next OMT meeting, so she plans to complete her report on the road. She will get the last figure she needs, finish the report, and then fax it to John Styles, who will represent her at the meeting. Before she leaves the office, Casandra decides to embed her data in a memo.

1. If necessary, start Excel and make sure your Student Disk is in the appropriate drive. Open the workbook StSales in the Case folder for Tutorial.06.

2. Open the Word document StMemo in the Case folder for Tutorial.06 and save it as State Sales Memo.

3. Embed the StSales worksheet in the Word document, State Sales Memo, which can be found in the Case folder for Tutorial.06.

4. Save the Word document with the embedded worksheet.

5. Print the memo with the embedded worksheet.

6. After arriving in Denver Casandra gets a call with the missing sales figure—sales in Idaho this quarter were $21. Update the Word document by entering the Idaho sales number in the embedded worksheet.

7. Save the Word document and print the memo again. Close the Word document.

8. Print the source worksheet, StSales. Comment on the sales data in the source worksheet versus the sales data in the Word document.

9. Now repeat the process using a different approach. Open the workbook StSales in the Case folder for Tutorial.06 and save it as State Sales.

10. Open the Word document StMemo1 in the Case folder for Tutorial.06 and save the document as State Sales Memo1.

11. Link cell D49 in the State Sales workbook to the end of the first sentence in the State Sales Memo1 Word document. (Hint: For the best placement of the linked object, use the Unformatted text option instead of Microsoft Excel Worksheet object when you link the object.) Save the document. Print the letter.

12. Update the State Sales workbook by entering the Idaho sales number ($21).

13. Save the Word document. Print the State Sales Memo1.

14. At the bottom of the State Sales Memo1 document, add the line "Details for Sales are in the State Sales workbook." Create a hyperlink in the Word document to the State Sales workbook. The hyperlink text should be "State Sales workbook." Save the Word document. Test the hyperlink.

15. Save and close any open documents.

3. Horizons State Alumni Office Charlene Goodwin, director of alumni affairs, has been planning a marketing "blitz" in which she will use three methods to reach Horizons' alumni. For campus visitors she will develop a flyer inviting friends of HSU to visit the campus store to view its new line of Horizons affinity products. For World Wide Web users, she plans to create a Web page highlighting these products. For alumni, she plans a letter announcing the affinity products that alums can order using a mail-order form. Help her get these jobs completed.

Do the following:

1. If necessary, start Excel and make sure your Student Disk is in the appropriate drive. Open the workbook AlumProd in the Case folder for Tutorial.06, and save it as Alumni Products. This is the product list.
2. Open the Word document Alumltr in the Case folder for Tutorial.06 and save it as Alumni Letter. Link the product list from the Alumni Products workbook beginning at the line [insert price list here]. Remember to remove the note [insert price list here]. Print the letter with the linked object.
3. You notice an error in the product list—the price of item 3 should be $75. Return to Excel and correct the error in the worksheet. Print the letter. Save and close the Word document.
4. Create a logo for Horizons State using WordArt. Insert it at the top of the product list in the Alumni Products workbook. Save the workbook and print the price list with your graphic.
5. Create a Web page for the product list in the Alumni Products workbook (do not include the WordArt graphic in the range) using the Internet Assistant Wizard. You decide the titles, headers, ruled lines, and so on you want to include on the page. Name the page HorzPrc.htm. View the page using your Web browser. Print the Web page using your Web browser.
6. Create a title sheet with appropriate information to describe the workbook. Print the title sheet.
7. In the title sheet, insert a hyperlink to the Word document Alumni Letter.

8. In the title sheet, insert a hyperlink to your institution's Web page.
9. Save and close any open files.

4. Inwood Design Group of Japan Spurred by the Japanese passion for the sport, golf enjoys unprecedented popularity in Japan. Inwood Design Group plans to build a world-class golf course, and one of the four sites under consideration is Chiba Prefecture, Japan. Other possible sites are Kauai, Hawaii; Edmonton, Canada; and Scottsdale, Arizona. You and Mike Nagochi are members of the site selection team for Inwood Design Group. The team is responsible for collecting information on the sites, evaluating that information, and recommending the best site for the new golf course.

Your team identified five factors likely to determine the success of a golf course: climate, competition, market size, topography, and transportation. The team has collected information on these factors for all the four potential golf course sites.

Mike created a worksheet that the team can use to evaluate the four sites. He brought the completed worksheet to the group's meeting so that the team could analyze the information and recommend a site to management.

Prepare a memo to the site selection committee with your team's findings. Do the following:

1. If necessary, start Excel and make sure your Student Disk is in the appropriate drive. Open the workbook Inwood in the Case folder for Tutorial.06. Save the workbook as Inwood 1. Review the worksheet.
2. Open Word and write a brief memo to the site selection committee. State your recommendation for a site selection and reason(s). Support your narrative by referencing the Weighted Score section of the Inwood worksheet. Paste the Weighted Score section of the worksheet into your memo.
3. Save the Word document as Inwood Memo in the Case folder for Tutorial.06.
4. Print the memo. Close Word.
5. Explain why pasting rather than linking or embedding is appropriate in this situation.
6. In the Inwood 1 workbook, activate the Title Sheet and insert a hyperlink to the Inwood Memo. Test the hyperlink.

7. Use your Web browser to access one of the following sites: www.yahoo.com, or www.altavista.com. Use the information at these Web sites to locate an interesting golf-related Web site. In the Inwood 1 workbook, below the hyperlink to the Inwood Memo, insert a hyperlink to this site.
8. Replace the Inwood Design Group title in the Title Sheet with a WordArt image with the same text.
9. Save the Inwood 1 workbook, print the title sheet, then close and exit the workbook.

Developing an Excel Application

Employee 401(k) Planning at CableScan

OBJECTIVES

In this tutorial you will:

■ Arrange worksheet in sections

■ Assign data validation rules to a cell

■ Assign and use range names

■ Use IF and FV functions in formulas

■ Create a series using AutoFill

■ Protect worksheets

■ Delete unnecessary sheets from a workbook

■ Plan and record Excel macros

■ Run a macro using menu commands

■ Run a macro using a shortcut key

■ View Visual Basic for Applications code

■ Run a macro using a button object

CASE

CableScan

CableScan intends to implement a 401(k) plan this year, and Mary Kincaid, benefits administrator, will travel to the company's three sites to present the plan and its features to all of the employees. A 401(k) plan is a retirement savings program that allows employees to deduct funds from their monthly pay, before taxes, provided that they invest them directly into various options within the 401(k) plan.

To introduce the 401(k) plan, Mary will hold formal meetings at each company location. At the meetings, she will give employees an audio-visual presentation that includes an overview of the plan, the administrative procedures, and the investment options. Because there are currently no other retirement plans available to the employees, other than personal savings, the company wants to be sure that there is high participation in the 401(k) plan. Management has set a goal of 80 percent of all eligible employees to participate in the plan. To help ensure this high rate of participation, the company will match, dollar for dollar, whatever the employee contributes, up to four percent of the employee's salary. Additionally, employees can contribute up to a total of 20 percent of their salaries.

Mary has asked you to work with individual employees after each of the formal presentations by answering any questions they may have. She also wants to provide an Excel workbook that can be used by employees to determine the appropriate amount they can contribute to the plan, and see the effects different amounts will have on their retirement savings over the next five to 30 years. Employees can use this workbook to conduct their own what-if analyses on their retirement plans.

In this tutorial you will develop a more complex workbook than you have in any previous tutorial. You'll build it in three sessions. In this session you will start the process by dividing your worksheet into separate sections for input and calculations. You'll use the Excel data validation feature to specify the type of data that a cell can store. You'll assign names to cells and use these names instead of cell addresses to build the formulas in your worksheet. Finally, you'll use the IF function to build formulas where the value you store in a cell depends on the result of a condition.

Planning the 401(k) Workbook Application

You have been asked to develop a simple investment model that will allow each CableScan employee to see the effect (dollar accumulation) of investing a percent of his or her current salary each year at an annual return on investment over a 30-year period. You can use Excel to create a workbook that the employees can use to make these calculations and plan their retirement funding.

You realize that many of the employees at CableScan are familiar with Excel, and will have no trouble using a 401(k) planning workbook. However, there are others who will require assistance in using the workbook, and you will be working with those employees one-on-one after Mary presents the plan. Because the CableScan employees using the workbook will be of varying skill levels with Excel and computers in general, you want the workbook to be as easy to use as possible. It needs to produce valuable information clearly, while being nearly foolproof to use.

Figures 7-1 and 7-2 show the planning analysis sheet and the sketch that Mary has created to assist you in completing the workbook. You can see from the planning analysis sheet that the formulas to be used in the workbook are somewhat complex. Fortunately, Excel provides a few means of simplifying complex formulas. Mary also wants you to build the worksheet so that employees enter only valid data in the correct cells in the worksheet. Note in the sketch in Figure 7-2 that the worksheet will be divided into manageable sections—sections where the employee provides (inputs) information, and sections containing information produced from calculating the input to produce output. Also note that the workbook allows the employee to view and analyze the information numerically and graphically, by including a line chart.

Figure 7-1 ◀
Planning
analysis sheet

Planning Analysis Sheet

<u>My Goal</u>
To develop a simple investment planning worksheet

<u>What information do I need?</u>
Name of employee
Current salary
Percent of salary invested—enter a percent of salary. NOTE: The maximum percent an employee can contribute is 20 percent.
Annual rate of return—enter as a percent

<u>What calculations do I need to perform?</u>
Employee contribution—monthly = current salary * percent of salary invested/12
Employer contribution—monthly = monthly employee contribution
NOTE: Remember that for every dollar employee contributes, employer invests a dollar, up to 4% of employee's salary; employer invests nothing above 4% of employee's salary
Total monthly contribution = monthly employee contribution + monthly employer contribution
Value of investment at 5, 10, 15, 20, 25, and 30 years. NOTE: use
=FV(monthly rate of return, number of periods, total monthly contribution) to compute future value of investment

<u>What output do I want to see?</u>
Table showing future value of investment at 5, 10, 15, 20, 25, and 30 years
Line chart displaying future value of investment

Figure 7-2 ◄
Sketch of
worksheet plan

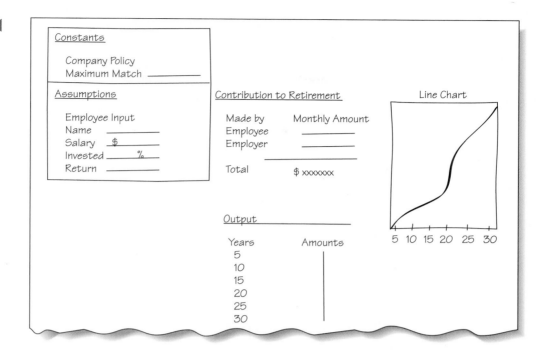

Use these planning documents to build the worksheet for Mary. She has already started to create the workbook.

Open the 401k file and examine the work Mary has done so far.

To open the 401k workbook and save the workbook as 401kPlan:

1. Start Excel. Make sure your Student Disk is in the appropriate disk drive, open the workbook **401k** in the Tutorial.07 folder on your Student Disk, and immediately save it as **401kPlan**.

2. Click the **401kPlan** sheet tab. In the 401kPlan worksheet, the labels and column headings have already been entered. See Figure 7-3.

Figure 7-3 ◄
Initial
401kPlan
worksheet

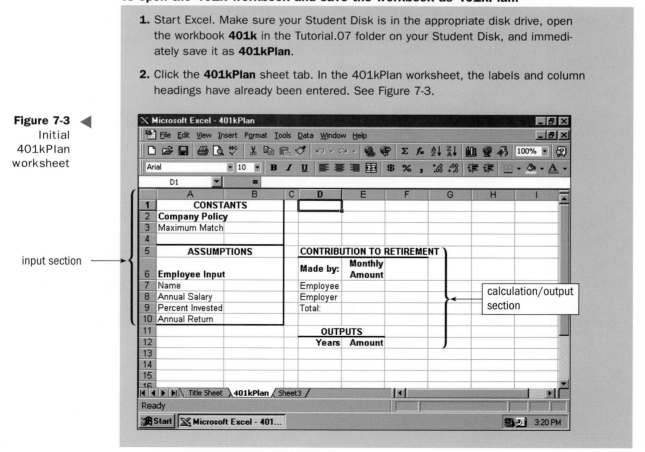

Arranging a Worksheet in Sections

Since many people will be using the worksheet, and will want to change assumptions such as current salary, percent of salary invested, and annual return on investment, Mary has divided her worksheet into two sections: input and calculation/output. The **input section** contains the data values used in formulas. Sometimes the input section is said to contain the worksheet's **initial conditions and assumptions** because the results of the worksheet are based on the values in the input section. A second section, the **calculation/output section**, performs the calculations and displays the results of the model. The formulas in this section do not contain constants; instead they reference cells in the input section. For example, the formula to calculate the monthly employee contribution to the 401(k) plan (cell E7) will reference cells B8 and B9 in the input section, which contain values for the employee's salary and the percent of salary the employee invests in the 401(k) plan, rather than constants, such as 30000 and .05.

Dividing the worksheet into sections has the following benefits:

- The user knows exactly where to enter and change values—in the input area. Changes to the worksheet are made only to values in the input area.

- The user clearly sees what factors affect the results of the worksheet.

- The user doesn't have to change specific values in formulas to reflect new assumptions.

Entering Initial Values

Now that you have examined the current status of the workbook, it's time for you to continue creating the 401(k) application. Since the labels and headings have already been entered, you'll begin by entering and formatting the values shown in Figure 7-4.

Figure 7-4 ◄
Initial
assumptions

Cell	Value	Formatting
B3	.04	Percent style
B7	Mike Tobey	
B8	30000	Currency style, no decimal place
B9	.05	Percent style
B10	.08	Percent style

To enter and format the input values:

1. Click cell **B3**, type **.04**, and press the **Enter** key. Return to cell B3 and click the **Percent style** button [%] on the Formatting toolbar.

2. Click cell **B7** and enter the remaining values and formatting shown in Figure 7-4. When you're finished entering the data, your input section of the worksheet should look like Figure 7-5.

Figure 7-5 ◄
Input section
after values
entered

input section ─→

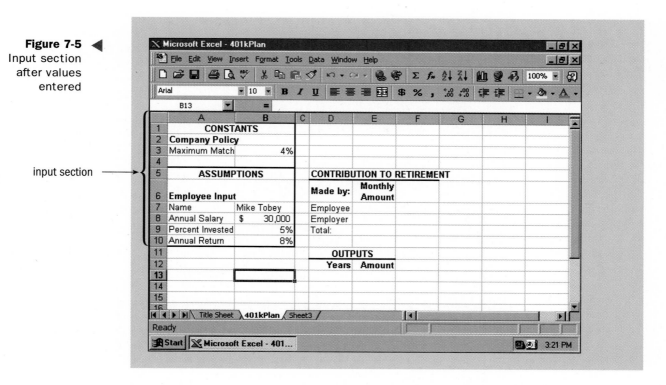

Mary is concerned that an employee may accidentally enter invalid data into the work-sheet, which will result in output that is not correct. For example, employees are not allowed to invest more than 20 percent of their salary in the 401(k) plan. If an employee entered a value greater than 20 percent of his or her salary, the value of future investments would be inaccurate, because the plan does not allow for this level of investment.

You can use the Excel data validation feature to prevent a user from entering an invalid value. This will allow you to minimize errors introduced by the workbook user.

Validating Data Entry

One way to make sure the correct data is entered in a cell or range is to use the Excel data validation feature to restrict the information being entered in the worksheet. For instance, you can specify the type of data (whole numbers, dates, time, or text) allowed in a cell, as well as the range of acceptable values (for example, numbers between 1 and 100). If you wish, you can display an input message that appears when a user enters data in a given cell, reminding the user of valid entries for this cell. You can also display an error message when the user enters an invalid entry. Since the maximum percentage of salary an employee can invest is 20, Mary asks you to establish a validation rule so that a user cannot exceed this limit.

Specifying Data Type and Acceptable Values

The first step in using the data validation feature is to specify the type of data as well as the acceptable values allowed in a cell or range of cells. You need to specify that in cell B9 only decimal values less than or equal to .2 (or 20 percent) are permitted.

To specify a data type and acceptable values:

1. Click cell **B9**, the cell where you want to apply data validation.

2. Click **Data** on the menu bar, and then click **Validation** to display the Data Validation dialog box. See Figure 7-6. This dialog box allows you to specify the parameters for the validation, the message that appears as the user inputs a value, and an error alert message that appears if the user enters an invalid value.

Figure 7-6 ◀
Settings tab of
Data Validation
dialog box

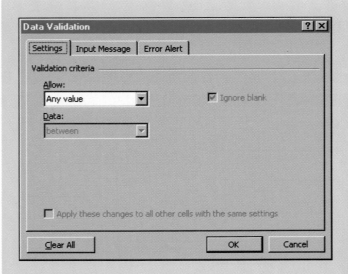

3. Make sure the Settings tab is selected, click the **Allow** list arrow, and then click **Decimal** from the list of allowable data types. Notice the number of text boxes in the dialog box changed to reflect the selection you made in the Allow list box.

Next, specify the range of values you will allow.

4. Click the **Data** list arrow, and then click **less than or equal to**. Notice that when you select this data operator, additional text boxes appear in the dialog box, allowing you to further specify the criteria for validation.

5. In the Maximum text box, type **.2**. The data validation rule of a value of less than or equal to 20 percent is now specified.

   TROUBLE? If you accidentally pressed the Enter key or clicked the OK button and the Data Validation dialog box closed, you can reopen the dialog box by clicking Data on the menu bar, and then clicking Validation.

Next, establish a prompt that will appear when users select that cell, indicating the type of data they can enter into the cell.

Specifying an Input Message

Now create an input prompt that informs the user what kind of data is allowed in the selected cell. The message will appear as a ScreenTip beside the cell when the user selects it. Although the input message is optional, Mary asks you to include the input message "Percent of salary invested by employee cannot exceed 20%," as an aid to the user during data entry.

To enter a data validation input message:

1. In the Data Validation dialog box, click the **Input Message** tab. See Figure 7-7.

Figure 7-7 ◀
Input Message
tab of Data
Validation
dialog box

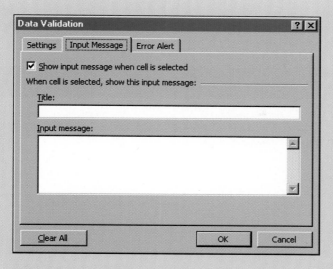

2. Make sure the Show input message when cell is selected check box is checked. This will ensure that the message will appear when the user selects the cell.

3. Click the **Title** text box, and then type **Valid Data**. This title will be at the top of the input message when it appears.

4. Click the **Input message** text box, and then type **Percent of salary invested by employee cannot exceed 20%**. This message will be displayed as a ScreenTip beside the cell being validated whenever the user selects that cell.

The input message that you have entered will help minimize the chances for employees to enter an invalid percent of salary value. However, if users still enter a value above 20 percent, then you want them to be prompted to reenter a correct percentage.

Specifying an Error Alert Style and Message

You can also use the Data Validation dialog box to establish an error alert message, which is a message that appears if an invalid entry is typed in the cell. This message should inform the user of the error, and identify a means to correct the error and enter a valid value.

Now create an appropriate error alert message for this cell.

To enter the error alert message:

1. In the Data Validation dialog box, click the **Error Alert** tab. See Figure 7-8.

Figure 7-8 ◀
Error Alert
tab of Data
Validation
dialog box

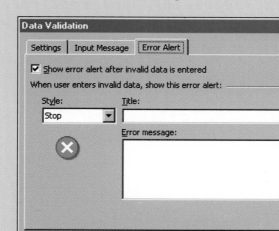

2. Make sure the Show error alert after invalid data is entered check box is checked. Now select the message style: Stop, Warning, or Information. Figure 7-9 describes the function of each style.

Figure 7-9 ◀
Error
message
alert styles

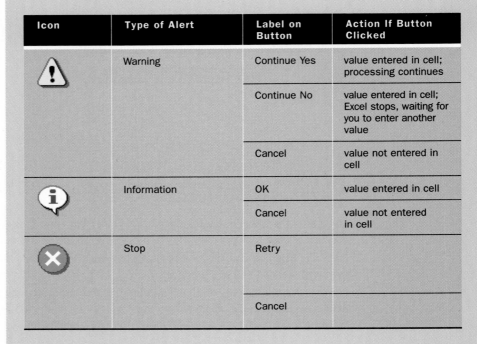

Icon	Type of Alert	Label on Button	Action If Button Clicked
⚠	Warning	Continue Yes	value entered in cell; processing continues
		Continue No	value entered in cell; Excel stops, waiting for you to enter another value
		Cancel	value not entered in cell
ⓘ	Information	OK	value entered in cell
		Cancel	value not entered in cell
✕	Stop	Retry	
		Cancel	

You decide to use the Stop style, since you don't want to continue data entry until the percent invested is 20 percent or less.

3. If necessary, click the **Style** list arrow, and then click **Stop**.

Now specify the error alert message.

4. In the Title text box, type **Invalid Data**.

5. In the Error message text box, type **You entered a value above 20%. A valid percent is 20% or less**.

6. Click the **OK** button to close the Data Validation dialog box.

The data validation rule is completely specified. Now test the validation rule to make sure it is working correctly when invalid data is entered in the cell.

To test data validation:

1. If necessary, click cell **B9**. The input message for Valid Data is displayed. See Figure 7-10.

Figure 7-10 ◀
Display of input
message

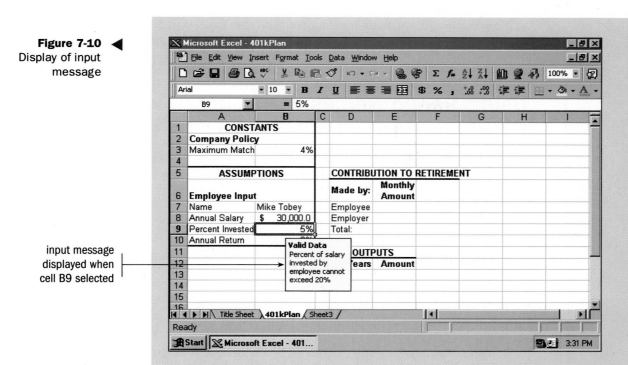

input message
displayed when
cell B9 selected

Now attempt to enter an invalid value.

2. Type **.25** and press the **Enter** key. The error alert message for Invalid Data is displayed. See Figure 7-11. Your choices are to click Retry to correct the value, or click Cancel to start all over. You decide to correct the value.

Figure 7-11 ◀
Display of error
alert message

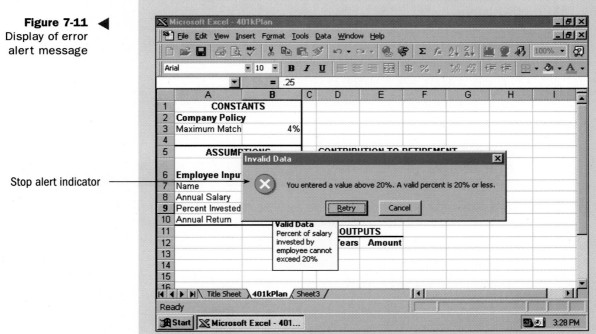

Stop alert indicator

3. Click the **Retry** button. Cell B9 is highlighted and Excel waits for you to enter a corrected value.

4. Type **.05** and press the **Enter** key. Excel recognizes this entry as valid and moves the cell pointer to the next cell, cell B10.

Now that you have made the data entry process easier and less error-prone for users, enter the formulas needed to perform the calculations in the workbook. Some of the formulas are complex. To avoid overwhelming users, you want to simplify the formulas a bit. This will also allow users to clearly see how the inputs are calculated to produce the output.

Using Range Names

So far in Excel you have always referred to cells by their addresses. Excel provides a valuable feature that allows you to assign a name to a cell or a range of cells so you don't have to remember the cell address. A **range name** is a descriptive name you assign to a cell or range of cells that can then be used to reference the cell or range of cells in formulas, print ranges, etc.

The ability to name a cell or range allows

- easier formula construction and entry

- improved documentation and clarification of the meaning of formulas

- navigation of large worksheets simply by using the Go To command to move the pointer to a named range

- specification of a print range

Range names must begin with a letter or the underscore character (_). After the first letter, any character, letter, number, or special symbol—except hyphens and spaces—is acceptable. You can assign names of up to 255 characters, although short, meaningful names of 5-15 characters are more practical.

REFERENCE window	**DEFINING A CELL OR RANGE NAME**
	▪ Select the cell or range of cells you want to name.
	▪ Click Insert, point to Name, and then click Define to display the Define Name dialog box.
	▪ Type the range name in the Names in workbook text box.
	▪ Click Add to add the name to the Names in workbook list.
	▪ Click the OK button to return to the worksheet.

Defining a Range Name

You decide to assign range names to several cells in the input area. This will make it easier for you when you create the formulas to be used to calculate the output. Use the range name MaxMatch in cell B3, Salary in cell B8, Invested in cell B9, and Return in cell B10.

To define a range name:

1. Click cell **B8**, the cell you want to assign a range name.

2. Click **Insert** on the menu bar, point to **Name**, and then click **Define** to display the Define Name dialog box. See Figure 7-12 Notice that Excel has already placed the name Annual_Salary in the Names in workbook text box using the text label in the cell to the left of the selected cell. You can keep that name or change it by typing a new name in the text box. In this case, shorten the name to Salary.

Figure 7-12 ◀
Define Name
dialog box

name suggested
by Excel

address name
is assigned to

click here to remove
a selected
range name

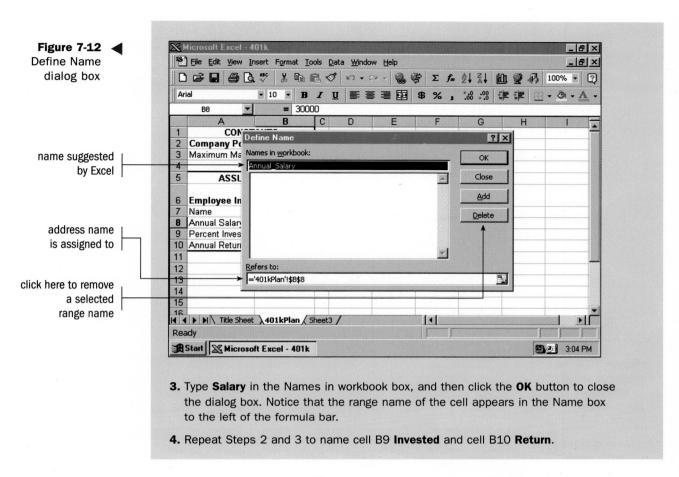

3. Type **Salary** in the Names in workbook box, and then click the **OK** button to close the dialog box. Notice that the range name of the cell appears in the Name box to the left of the formula bar.

4. Repeat Steps 2 and 3 to name cell B9 **Invested** and cell B10 **Return**.

As you have noticed, the range name of the selected cell appears in the Name box to the left of the formula bar. This Name box allows you to work with named ranges more easily.

Using the Name Box to Define a Range Name

You can also use the Name box as another means of assigning names to cells. You can use this Name box to define a range, or to select and move to an already defined range. Assign the name MaxMatch to cell B3 using the Name box.

To assign a range name using the Name box:

1. Click cell **B3**, the cell you want to name.

2. Click the **Name** box to the left of the formula bar. See Figure 7-13.

Figure 7-13 ◀
Using the Name
box to assign a
range name

Name box

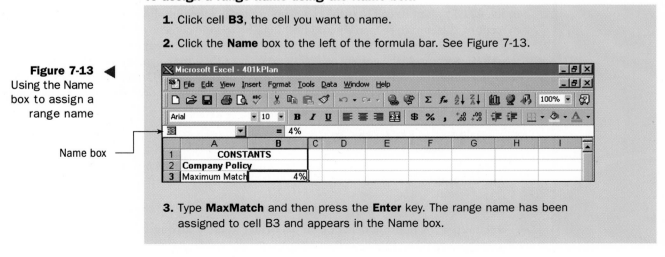

3. Type **MaxMatch** and then press the **Enter** key. The range name has been assigned to cell B3 and appears in the Name box.

Now that you have assigned names to the input cells, you can use them as you create the formulas for the 401(k) investment model. First, calculate the amount the employee plans to invest each month.

Using a Range Name in a Formula

You can use the name of a cell or range in a formula instead of cell addresses as you enter your formulas into the worksheet. Rather than using the formula =B8*B9/12 to compute the amount the employee plans to invest each month, you can enter the formula using the range names =*Salary*Invested/12*. Now enter the formula to compute the monthly employee contribution.

To enter a formula using a range name:

1. Click cell **E7**, the cell where you calculate the monthly amount the employee contributes to the retirement plan.

2. Type **= Salary*Invested/12** and press the **Enter** key. Excel performs the calculations and displays the value 125.

3. Click cell **E7** and examine the formula in the formula bar. Notice that the range names appear in the formula instead of the cell addresses. See Figure 7-14.

Figure 7-14 ◀
Range names
appear in
formula bar

formula bar displays
range names

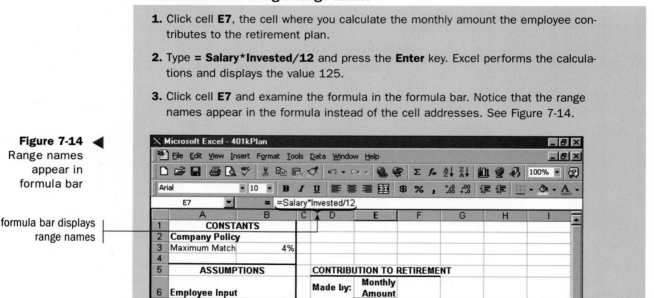

Next you need to enter a formula to calculate the amount of money the employer will contribute to the employee's 401(k) investment. The formula to calculate the employer's contribution is not as straightforward as the one for the employee's contribution. The amount the employer contributes depends on the percent of salary the employee invests in the 401(k) plan. Recall that the company policy is to match dollar for dollar up to four percent of the employee's salary and nothing above four percent of the employee's salary. This calculation requires that you determine whether the employee is contributing more than four percent. If the employee is investing more than four percent of his or her salary, then the employer will only match four percent of the salary. On the other hand, if the employee is investing four percent or less, the employer will contribute an amount equal to the employee contribution.

Inserting the IF Function

There are many situations where the value you store in a cell depends on certain conditions. For example:

- An employee's gross pay may depend on whether that employee worked overtime.
- A taxpayer's tax rate depends on his or her taxable income.
- A customer's charge depends on whether the size of the order entitles that customer to a discount.

In Excel, the IF function allows you to evaluate a specified condition, performing one action if the condition is true and another action if the condition is false. The IF function has the following format:

IF(*logical_test*, *value_if_true*, *value_if_false*)

where

- A *logical_test* evaluates a logical expression (condition) as either True or False.

- A *value_if_true* is the value returned if the *logical_test* is True.

- A *value_if_false* is the value returned if the *logical_test* is False.

An example may help illustrate how the IF function works. Suppose you need to determine whether an employee earns overtime pay, that is, whether he or she worked more than 40 hours in a week. Figure 7-15 illustrates the logic of this function.

Figure 7-15 ◀
Flow chart of
the IF function

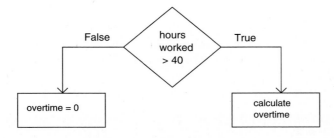

Using the IF function syntax

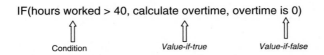

In this example, the condition is the comparison between the hours an employee works and 40 hours. The *value_if_true* is returned if an employee works more than 40 hours; then the condition is true and overtime pay is calculated. The *value_if_false* is returned if an employee works 40 hours or less; then the condition is false and overtime pay is 0.

The most common condition, a simple condition, is a comparison between two expressions. An **expression** may be a cell or range, a number, a label, a formula, or another function that represents a single value. For example, B5, B6*B7, and "West" are expressions. In addition to expressions, a condition contains a comparison operator. A **comparison operator** indicates a mathematical comparison, such as less than or greater than. Figure 7-16 shows the comparison operators allowed in Excel.

Figure 7-16 ◄
Comparison
operators

Type of Comparison	Comparison Operator Symbol
Less than	<
Greater than	>
Less than or equal to	<=
Greater than or equal to	>=
Equal to	=
Not equal to	<>

A comparison operator is combined with an expression to form a condition. For example, say the hours worked value is stored in D10; then the condition "the number of hours worked is greater than 40" would be expressed in Excel as IF(D10>40...). Figure 7-17 illustrates several examples of conditional situations and how they can be expressed in Excel.

Figure 7-17 ◄
Examples of
conditional
situations

Conditional Situation	Excel Formula
If salesperson's sales are > 5000 THEN return the value 0.1 (10% bonus) ELSE return the value 0.05 (5% bonus)	=IF(B24>5000,0.1,0.05) Note: cell B24 stores salesperson's sales
IF company's region code equals 3 THEN return the label East ELSE return the label Other	=IF(N7=3,"East","Other") Note: cell N7 stores code for region
IF person's age is less than 65 THEN amount x under 65 rate ELSE amount x 65 or over rate	=IF(A21<65,B21*C21,B21*D21) Note: cell A21 stores person's age; cell B21 stores amount; cell C21 stores under 65 rate; and cell D21 stores 65 or over rate

Mary developed a flowchart to establish the logic behind the formula needed to calculate the employer's matching contribution to the 401(k) plan. See Figure 7-18.

Figure 7-18 ◄
Flow chart of
employer's
monthly
matching
contribution

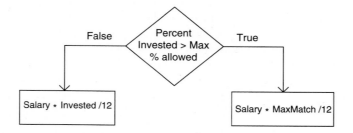

Now enter the IF function needed to calculate the employer's monthly matching contribution to the 401(k) plan.

To enter the IF function:

1. Click cell **E8** to select the cell where you want to enter the IF function.

2. Click the **Paste Function** button [*fx*] on the Standard toolbar to display the Paste Function dialog box. Click **Logical** in the Function category list box, click **IF** in the Function name list box, and then click the **OK** button to open the IF function dialog box.

   TROUBLE? If the Office Assistant opens and offers help on this feature, click the No button.

   Now enter the condition.

3. In the Logical_test text box, type **Invested>MaxMatch**.

4. Click the **Value_if_true** text box, and then type **Salary*MaxMatch/12**, the value to be returned if the condition is true.

5. Click the **Value_if_false** text box, and then type **Salary*Invested/12**, the value to be returned if the condition is false. See Figure 7-19.

Figure 7-19 ◀
IF function dialog box after arguments entered

formula developed by Excel based on your entries in the IF function dialog box

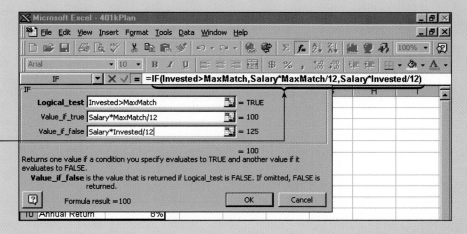

6. Click the **OK** button. Excel places the IF function in the worksheet. Since the condition, in this case, is True, the value 100 appears in cell E8. Notice that the formula =IF(Invested>MaxMatch,Salary*MaxMatch/12,Salary*Invested/12) appears in the formula bar.

Now compute the total amount invested each month, which is the sum of the employee and employer contributions.

To calculate the total contribution:

1. Click cell **E9**, click the **AutoSum** button [Σ], and press the **Enter** key. The total amount invested is 225.

   Now name cell E9 TotContribution.

2. Return to cell **E9**, click the **Name** box, type **TotContribution**, and press the **Enter** key.

   TROUBLE? If the label TotContribution appears in cell E9, click the Undo button [↶] on the Standard toolbar, and then click the Name box, type TotContribution, and press the Enter key.

3. Format the range **E7:E9** using the Currency style and zero decimal places.

4. Click any cell to deselect the range.

5. Save the workbook.

Quick Check

1. When you select a named cell or range, the name appears in the _____.

2. Which of the following are invalid range names?
   a. Annual_Total
   b. 3rdQtr
   c. Qtr3
   d. Annual total

3. During data validation, the error alert message is displayed _____.

4. Rather than enter constants in formulas, you should reference values from a separate section of your worksheet referred to as the _____.

5. When you restrict the information being placed in a particular cell, you are applying _____.

6. During data validation, the input message is displayed when you _____.

7. When the value you store in a cell depends on certain conditions, you should consider using a(n) _____ in your formula.

8. The symbol <= is an example of a _____.

You have completed the input section of the 401kPlan worksheet. By applying data validation rules, defining range names, and using range names and IF functions to create formulas, you have made the worksheet easier for you to develop and the numerous CableScan employees to use. In Session 7.2 you will complete the worksheet's calculation/output section.

SESSION

7.2

In this session you will finish the 401(k) planning workbook by entering the remaining formulas using the Excel AutoFill feature and FV function, creating a line chart, and protecting worksheet cells.

Computing the Retirement Fund

The last set of calculations will determine the dollars accumulated over time, or the total retirement fund, often called the "retirement nest egg." In the first column, range D13:D18, the values 5, 10, 15, 20, 25, 30—representing the years left until retirement—need to be entered. Although you can type these numbers, there is an easier approach you can use when the values represent a series.

Creating a Series Using AutoFill

When working in Excel you sometimes need to enter a series of data. You enter one or two initial values in a series of numbers, dates, or text, and using the **AutoFill** feature, Excel completes the series for you. Figure 7-20 shows several series that AutoFill recognizes and automatically completes. You can quickly enter the series of data with the assistance of the fill handle. Enter the series 5, 10, 15, 20, 25, and 30 to represent the number of years left until retirement.

Figure 7-20 ◀
Examples
of series
completed
using AutoFill

Initial Value	Remaining Series
Sunday	Monday, Tuesday, Wednesday, ...
1/10/99	1/11/99, 1/12/99, 1/13/99
Qtr1	Qtr2, Qtr3, Qtr4
January	February, March, April, May, ...

To generate a series using AutoFill:

1. If you took a break after the last session, make sure Excel is running, the 401kPlan workbook is open, and the 401kPlan sheet is active.

2. Scroll the worksheet so row 5 is the first visible row in the worksheet window.

3. In cell D13, enter **5**. In cell D14, enter **10**.

4. Select the range **D13:D14**.

5. Click and drag the fill handle in cell D14 through cells D15:D18. Notice that a ScreenTip displays each number in the series as you drag the mouse pointer. Release the mouse button. Excel has created the series, using the interval between the two selected values.

6. Click any cell to deselect the range. See Figure 7-21.

Figure 7-21 ◀
Series created
using AutoFill

series →

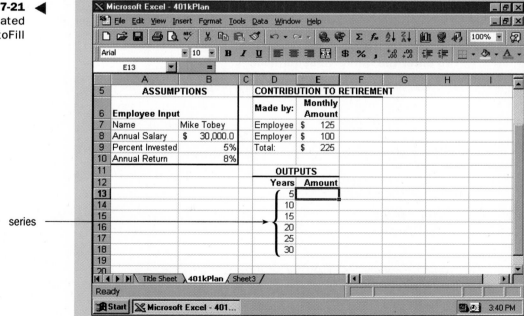

Inserting the FV Function

Now enter the formula to calculate the future value of the investment, the retirement nest egg. The future value of an investment is its value at some future date based on a series of cash flows of equal amounts made over a number of periods earning a constant interest rate. You will use the financial function FV to compute the future value of the investment. The FV function has the following format:

$$FV(\textit{rate, nper, pmt})$$

where

- *rate* is the interest rate per period.
- *nper* is the number of periods in which payments will be made.
- *pmt* is the payments made each period. It cannot change over the life of the investment.

This is one of several financial functions available in Excel. Figure 7-22 lists some of the other Excel financial functions.

Figure 7-22 ◄
Selected
financial
functions

Function Name	Description
PV	Computes the present value of a series of equal payments
PMT	Computes the periodic payment required to amortize a loan over a specified number of periods
RATE	Computes the rate of return of an investment that generates a series of equal periodic payments
DDB	Computes an asset's depreciation using the double-declining balance method
IRR	Computes an internal rate of return for a series of periodic cash flows

Now enter the future value formula, using the Paste Function button on the Standard toolbar.

To enter the future value formula:

1. Click cell **E13** to select the cell where you want to enter the FV function.

2. Click the **Paste Function** button 🔣 on the Standard toolbar to display the Paste Function dialog box. Click **Financial** in the Function category list box, click **FV** in the Function name list box, and then click the **OK** button to open the FV function dialog box. See Figure 7-23.

   TROUBLE? If the Office Assistant opens offering help on this feature, click the No button.

Figure 7-23 ◄
FV function
dialog box

name of function

arguments

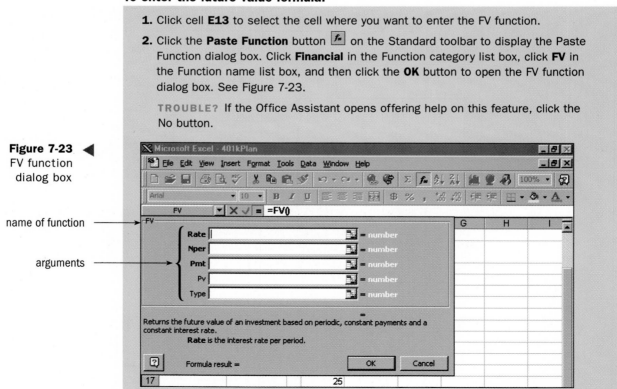

Now enter the arguments for this function. First, calculate the monthly return on the investment by dividing the annual return by 12.

3. In the Rate text box, type **Return/12**. Notice that the monthly return of .006666667 appears to the right of the Rate text box.

Next, calculate the number of monthly payments during the life of the investment.

4. In the Nper (number of periods) text box, type **D13*12**. Notice that 60, the number of months in five years, appears to the right of the Nper text box.

Now, enter the total amount invested each month.

5. In the Pmt text box, type **TotContribution** and press the **Enter** key. The value ($16,532.29) appears as a red negative value. See Figure 7-24. This value, ($16,532.29), means that if an investment of $225 is made each month for 60 months and earns interest at a rate of 0.67% per month, you will have accumulated $16,532.29 in 5 years. By default, Excel shows this value as a negative number. You think the employees will be confused if they see the value of their investment as a negative number, so edit the formula and place a minus sign in front of the function name in order to display the future value as a positive number.

TROUBLE? If the width of column E is too narrow, increase the column width to display the value.

Figure 7-24 ◀
Future value computation for five years

future value appears
as negative number

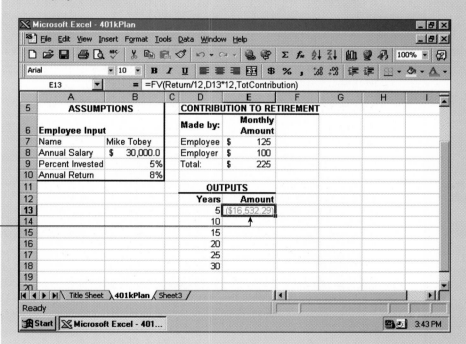

6. Double-click cell **E13**. Position the insertion point to the right of the equal sign (=) and type -, and then press the **Enter** key. The value appears as a positive number.

7. Copy the formula in cell E13 to cells **E14:E18**.

8. Format the range using the Currency style with zero decimal places.

9. Click any cell to deselect the range. See Figure 7-25.

Figure 7-25 ◄
Future value
computations
over 30-year
period in
five-year
increments

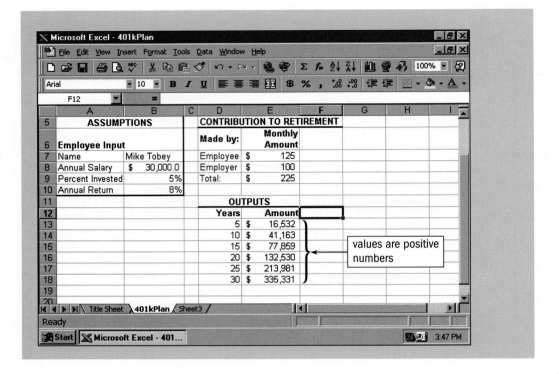

The output table showing the dollars accumulated over 30 years is complete. Now display this information as a line chart showing the accumulation of dollars over the 30-year period.

To create the line chart:

1. Select the range **D13:E18**.

2. Click the **Chart Wizard** button on the Standard toolbar to display the Chart Wizard - Step 1 of 4 - Chart Type dialog box.

3. Click the **Line** chart type. Seven line chart subtypes are displayed. Click the **Line** chart subtype (the first subtype).

4. Click the **Next** button to display the Chart Wizard - Step 2 of 4 - Chart Source Data dialog box. On the Data tab, make sure the Data range box displays ='401kPlan'!$D$13:$D$18. Click the **Series** tab. With Series1 selected in the Series section, click the **Remove** button. Click the **Category (X) axis labels** box, click the **Collapse dialog box** button, and select the range **D13:D18**. Click the **Collapse (Expand) dialog box** button to return to the Chart Wizard. See Figure 7-26.

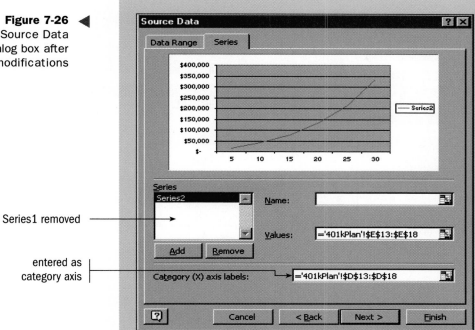

Figure 7-26
Source Data
dialog box after
modifications

Series1 removed

entered as
category axis

5. Click the **Next** button to display the Chart Wizard - Step 3 of 4 - Chart Options dialog box.

   Next, add a title to the chart.

6. If necessary, click the **Titles** tab, click the **Chart title** text box, and type **Retirement Nest Egg** for the chart title. Click the **Category (X) axis** title box, and then type **Years in future**. Click the **Value (Y) axis** title box, and then type **Dollars**.

   Since there is only one data series, remove the legend, as it is not needed.

7. Click the **Legend** tab and then click the **Show Legend** check box to remove the check and deselect that option.

8. Click the **Next** button to display the Chart Wizard - Step 4 of 4 - Chart Location dialog box. Embed the chart in the 401kPlan worksheet (the default option).

9. Click the **Finish** button to complete the chart and display it in the 401kPlan worksheet. See Figure 7-27.

Figure 7-27 ◀
Completed
line chart

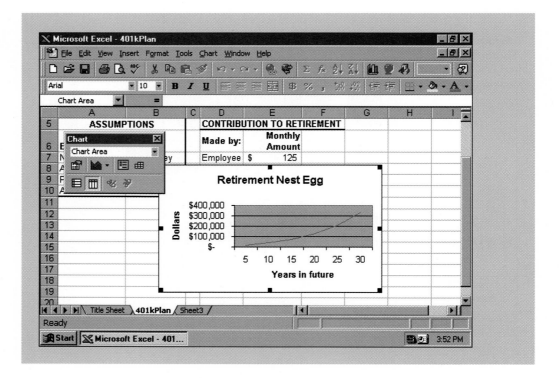

You need to move and resize the chart to improve its appearance.

To change the size and position of the chart:

1. Scroll the worksheet until row 5 appears as the first visible row and column D as the first visible column in the worksheet window.

2. Move and resize the chart object so it appears in the range F6:L18. See Figure 7-28.

Figure 7-28 ◀
Line chart after
being moved
and resized

floating Chart toolbar
may appear in a
different location
on your screen

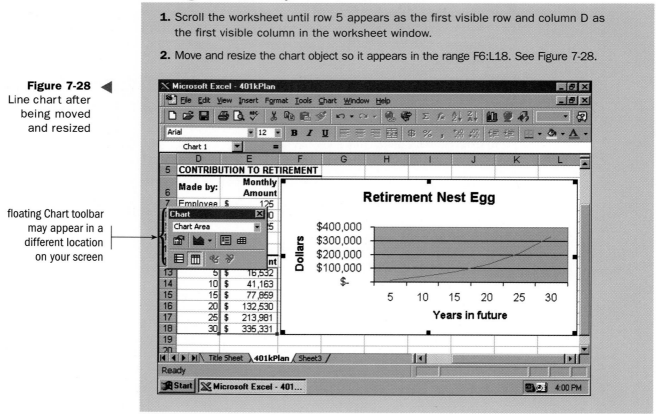

Now enhance the chart's appearance.

To improve the appearance of the chart:

1. Double-click the **Series 2** (Line object) to display the Format Data Series dialog box. On the Patterns tab, click the **Weight** list arrow, select the thickest line weight, and then click the **OK** button.

2. Click the **Value-Axis** object, and then click the **Format Axis** button on the Chart toolbar to display the Format Axis dialog box. Click the **Font** tab, click **8** in the Size list box, and then click the **OK** button.

3. Click the **Category-Axis** object, and then click the **Format Axis** button on the Chart toolbar to display the Format Axis dialog box. If necessary, click the **Font** tab, click **8** in the Size list box, then click the **OK** button. See Figure 7-29.

Figure 7-29 ◄
Final version
of line chart

thicker line

8-point font size

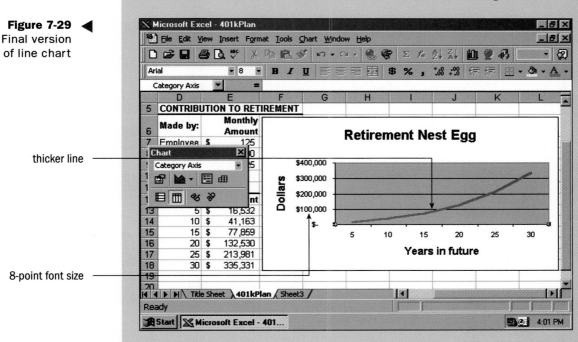

4. Click anywhere outside the chart area to deselect the chart.

5. Save the workbook.

Now that all the components of the worksheet are complete, you still need to make a few enhancements to make the worksheet less susceptible to user error. Mary realizes that others will use the worksheet to explore what-if alternatives, and she worries about a user accidentally deleting the formatting or formulas in the calculation/output section of the worksheet. To preserve your work, Mary asks you to protect all the cells in the worksheet except the cells in the input section.

Protecting Cells in a Worksheet

When you **protect** a worksheet, data in protected cells cannot be changed. Once you have protected worksheet cells, the data in these cells can be viewed, but not edited or modified. Once you protect a worksheet, you cannot enter data, insert or delete rows, or change cell formats or column widths. Only the values in unprotected cells can be changed.

Unlocking Individual Cells

Most of the time you will not want to lock every cell in a worksheet. For example, in a worksheet that you share with others, you might want to protect the formulas and formatting, but leave particular cells unprotected so that necessary data may be entered. When you want to protect some but not all worksheet cells, you implement protection by following a two-step process. By default all cells in a worksheet have the locked property turned on, which means the cell is capable of being protected. First you need to identify the cells you want unprotected and turn off the "lock" associated with each of these cells. Once you have "unlocked" the selected cells, you activate the protection command to "turn on" protection for the remaining cells. Figure 7-30 illustrates this process.

Figure 7-30 ◄
Process of protecting worksheet cells

Default Status

By default, every cell in the worksheet has a locked property turned on, which means each cell has the capability of being protected, but at this step no cell is protected. You can enter data in any cell.

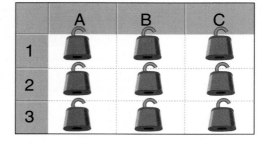

Step I

The worksheet after some cells have their locks removed (locked property turned off). At this step no cell is protected. You can enter data in any cell.

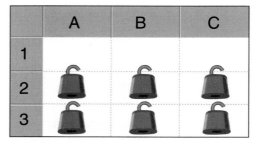

Step II

The worksheet after the Protect Sheet command has been activated. The cells in the bottom two rows are protected—no data may be entered in these cells. You can still enter data in the first row.

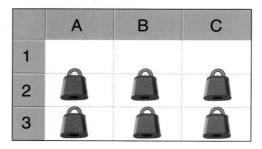

REFERENCE window

PROTECTING CELLS

- Select the cells you want to remain unprotected.
- Click Format, and then click Cells to display the Format Cells dialog box.
- In the Format Cells dialog box, click the Protection tab.
- Remove the check from the Locked check box, and then click the OK button.
- Click Tools, point to Protection, and then click Protect Sheet to display the Protect Sheet dialog box.
- If desired, enter a password in the Protect Sheet dialog box, and then reenter the password in the Confirm Password dialog box.

You start by unlocking the range of cells where the user can enter data, which in this case would be the input area of the 401kPlan worksheet. Then activate the protection for the rest of the worksheet, which will protect the data and formulas you do not want the employees to change.

To unlock the cells for data entry:

1. Click cell **A5** to make it the active cell, so you can view the input section.

2. Select the range **B7:B10**, the cells the user can change and therefore do not require protection.

3. Click **Format** on the menu bar, and then click **Cells** to display the Format Cells dialog box.

4. Click the **Protection** tab. By default, the Locked check box contains a check. See Figure 7-31.

Figure 7-31 ◀
Protection tab
of Format Cells
dialog box

check means cell
is capable
of being locked

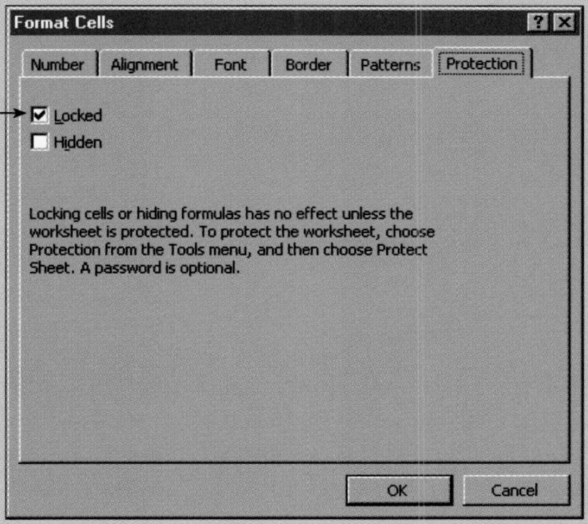

5. Click the **Locked** check box to remove the check.

6. Click the **OK** button. Nothing visible happens to the worksheet to show that cells are unlocked.

Since Excel does not provide any on-screen indication of the protection status of individual cells, you decide to change the background color of the unlocked cells to distinguish them from the protected cells. This will be a nice visual cue for the employees using the worksheet, indicating which cells they should use to input their investment information.

To change the fill color of unprotected cells:

1. If necessary, select cells **B7:10**.

2. Click the **Fill color** button list arrow [icon] on the Formatting toolbar to display the Color palette.

3. Click **Yellow** in the fourth row, third column of the Color palette.

4. Click any cell to view the yellow color applied to the unprotected cells.

Protecting the Worksheet

Now that you have unlocked the cells for data entry, you will turn on protection for the entire worksheet to protect every cell that you didn't unlock.

When you protect the worksheet, Excel lets you enter a password that must be used to unprotect the worksheet. If you specify a password, you must make sure to remember it so you can unprotect the worksheet in the future. Unless you are working on confidential material, it's probably easier not to use a password at all.

To turn protection on:

1. Click **Tools** on the menu bar, point to **Protection**, and then click **Protect Sheet** to display the Protect Sheet dialog box. See Figure 7-32. The Password text box lets you enter a password of your choice. The Contents check box locks the cells in the sheet. The Objects check box prevents changes to charts or graphical objects, and the Scenarios check box locks any scenario you've created.

Figure 7-32 ◀
Options for protecting a worksheet

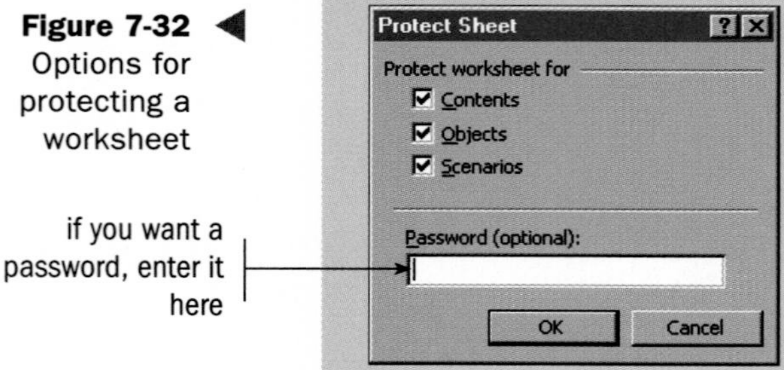

if you want a password, enter it here

2. Click the **OK** button. If you had entered a password, a Confirm Password dialog box would appear and you would be asked to retype the same password to make sure you remember it and that you entered it correctly the first time.

Testing Cell Protection

After protection is enabled, you cannot change a locked cell. Before you distribute the workbook to the employees to use, you decide to test the worksheet to assure yourself that protection has been implemented successfully.

To test worksheet protection:

1. Click cell **E13**, and then try typing **40000**. A message indicating that this cell is locked and cannot be changed is displayed. See Figure 7-33.

Figure 7-33 ◀
Message displayed when you attempt to change a protected cell

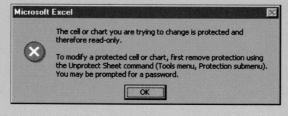

2. Click the **OK** button to continue.

   Now enter a value in a cell that is unlocked.

3. Click cell **B8**, type **40000**, and press the **Enter** key. Notice that the calculation and outputs changed.

Now that you are done creating the workbook, and have customized it so it is user-friendly and appropriate for use by all CableScan employees, you give it to Mary to review. She is very pleased with the finished workbook. Her only suggestion is to further simplify the workbook by removing any unnecessary sheets. She thinks this will eliminate any possibility of people trying to enter data in the wrong area of the workbook.

Deleting Unnecessary Worksheets

If you want to remove an empty worksheet or a worksheet you no longer need, you can delete it. You decide to delete Sheet3 since it is not used in the 401(k) application.

To delete a worksheet:

1. Click the **Sheet3** tab to activate the Sheet3 worksheet.

2. Click **Edit**, and then click **Delete Sheet**. Excel displays a message letting you know that the selected sheet will be permanently deleted.

3. Click the **OK** button. Notice that Excel has deleted Sheet3 from the workbook.

4. Save the workbook.

Quick Check

1. You can use the Excel _____ feature to complete a series of numbers, dates, or text values.

2. Why were the unprotected cells filled with color?

3. Protecting a worksheet is a two-step process. You _____ and then you _____.

4. How does cell protection differ from data validation?

5. What happens when you try to enter a value in a protected cell?

6. The FV function stands for _____. This function is found in the _____ category.

You have now completed the worksheet. In this next section you will create two macros that will simplify some of the tasks a user performs when using this workbook.

SESSION

7.3

In this session you will learn what macros are, and how they can be used to automate tasks in a workbook for the user. You will also plan and create two macros using the Excel macro recorder.

Automating Tasks Using Macros

Typically macros are used to automate repetitive tasks. A **macro** is a series of commands and functions that you can initiate whenever you want to perform a particular task. That is, you create them to automatically perform a series of Excel operations, such as menu selections, dialog box selections, range selections, or keystrokes. They carry out repetitive tasks more quickly than you can yourself, making your work more productive while helping you make fewer errors. For example, you can create macros to automate the following tasks:

■ Move through a large worksheet quickly.

- Add a date and time stamp to a cell in the current worksheet.

- Extract data from an Excel list and create a chart.

- Print several reports from a worksheet, each with different print specifications.

- Apply a common set of formats to any sheet in a workbook.

Macros simplify the use of workbooks for both experienced and novice users. In reviewing the 401kPlan workbook with Mary, you realize that macros would be useful to include in this workbook. You know that all users will need to clear the input section to enter data as it changes. You also know that people will most likely want to have a hard copy of some or all of the worksheet. Therefore, printing is another task that would be good to simplify.

Creating Macros

You can create a macro in two ways: you can use the macro recorder to record your keystrokes and mouse actions as you perform them (recording the selection of ranges, menu commands, dialog box options, etc.), or you can write your own macros by entering a series of commands in the **Visual Basic for Applications (VBA)** programming language, which tells Excel how to do a particular task.

The easiest way to create a macro in Excel is to use the macro recorder. When you record a macro, Excel automatically translates your keystrokes and mouse actions into Visual Basic instructions (code) that you can play back, or run, whenever you want to repeat those particular keystrokes and tasks. Excel records your actions, and then translates them into a series of instructions in the Visual Basic for Applications (VBA) programming language. When you run the macro, the instructions are read and executed in sequence, thereby duplicating the actions you performed when you recorded the macro.

In this section, you will create two macros using the macro recorder. The first will be a ClearInputs macro that will automate the task of clearing values from the input section of the workbook, so the user can enter new data. The second macro you will create will be a Print macro, which will simplify the printing process.

Planning Macros

As with most complex projects, you need to plan your macro. Decide what you want to accomplish and the best way to go about doing it. Once you know the purpose of the macro, you should carry out the keystrokes or mouse actions before you actually record them. Going through each step before recording a macro might seem like extra work, but it reduces the chances of error when you actually create the macro.

Mary realizes that many different employees will use the worksheet and will enter different sets of input assumptions. She wants you to create a macro that will automatically clear the values in the input section and place the cell pointer in cell B7—ready for the user to enter a new set of data.

She sits down at her computer and goes through the steps to include in the macro before you actually record them. This way you will be familiar with the steps to include in the macro, and the chances for errors in the macro are fewer. Figure 7-34 lists the steps Mary plans to include in the macro.

Figure 7-34 ◀
Planning the
ClearInputs
macro

Action	Result
Select the range B7:B10	Highlights the range you want to clear of data
Press the Delete key	Clears the contents of the selected range
Click cell B7	Makes cell B7 the active cell

Recording the ClearInputs Macro

After planning the macro, you are ready to record it. There are several actions you need to take before actually recording the macro. First, you want to decide on an appropriate name for the macro. For example, the first macro Mary asked you to create is for clearing the input section of any values, so a good name for this macro would be ClearInputs. A macro name can be up to 255 characters long; it must begin with a letter, and it can contain only letters, numbers, and the underscore character. No spaces or other punctuation marks are permitted. For multiple-word macros such as Clear Inputs you can use initial caps (ClearInputs) or the underscore (Clear_Inputs).

When you record a macro, every keystroke and mouse click is stored by Excel. Therefore, your second task before you can record the macro is to specify where you want the macro stored. The macro is stored in the form of a Visual Basic for Applications program, and its storage location plays a part in how you will be able to access and use the macro once it is created. There are three possible locations you can choose to store the macro. By default, Excel assumes you want to store the recorded macro as part of the current workbook. In this case, Excel stores the recorded macro in a hidden module that is part of the workbook. Macros stored in a workbook are available only when the workbook is open. If a workbook is closed, the macros stored within the workbook can't be used. Use this storage option to store macros that you plan to use only when using this workbook. If you use some macros on a regular basis, you may want to make them available at all times. In that case, you would choose to store the macros in the Personal Macro workbook. With this option, Excel stores the macro in a special workbook file named Personal Macro. When you start Excel, this workbook is opened and hidden automatically, making the macros in it available to any open workbook.

You can also store the macro in a new workbook file. In this case, Excel opens another workbook to store the recorded macro. To use macros stored in another workbook, you need to open the workbook with the macros as well as the workbook containing the application.

In addition to considering where you want to store your macro, before you record a macro you also need to make sure your worksheet is set up exactly as you want it to exist at the time you play back the recorded macro. This may involve opening a specific workbook, activating a specific sheet in which you want the macro to run, and moving to the location where you want to start recording. Otherwise the macro may not work as planned, and you may have to record it again.

REFERENCE window

RECORDING A MACRO

- Click Tools, point to Macro, and then click Record New Macro to display the Record Macro dialog box.
- In the Macro name text box, type a name for the macro.
- If you want to run the macro by pressing a keyboard shortcut key, enter a letter in the Shortcut key text box.
- In the Store macro in list box, click the location where you want to store the macro.
- In the Description text box, type a description of the macro.
- Click the OK button. The macro recorder starts recording.
- Perform the tasks you want the macro to automate.
- Click the Stop Recording button on the Stop Recording toolbar, or click Tools, point to Macro, and then click Stop Recording to stop the recording process.

When you record a macro, you name and describe it. You can also set up a shortcut key to run the macro, and specify the workbook in which to store the macro.

To record a macro to delete a range of cells:

1. If you took a break after the last session, make sure Excel is running, the 401kPlan workbook is open, and the 401kPlan sheet is active. If necessary, press **Ctrl + Home** to make cell A1 the active cell.

   Now start the macro recorder.

2. Click **Tools** on the menu bar, point to **Macro**, and then click **Record New Macro** to display the Record Macro dialog box. See Figure 7-35.

Figure 7-35 ◀
Record Macro
dialog box

enter new name here —

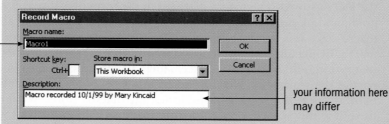

your information here
may differ

Excel proposes a default name for the macro. This default macro name consists of the word "Macro" and a number corresponding to the number of macros you have recorded in the workbook in the current work session. You should change the macro name to a name more descriptive of what the macro will do. Name the macro ClearInputs.

3. Type **ClearInputs** in the Macro name text box.

   Now specify the location of your macro. You want the macro to be accessible only to this workbook, and when this workbook is open. Therefore, you want to store the macro as part of this workbook.

4. Make sure the option This Workbook is selected in the Store macro in list box.

   Notice that Excel provides a brief description indicating the date the macro is being recorded and by whom. You can add additional comments to explain the purpose of the macro.

5. Click anywhere within the **Description** text box. If the insertion point is not at the end of the default description, move it there. Press the **Enter** key to start a new line. Type **Clear the values from the input section**. See Figure 7-36.

Figure 7-36 ◀
Completed
Record Macro
dialog box

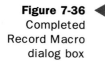
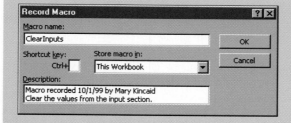

6. Click the **OK** button to start recording the macro. See Figure 7-37. Excel returns to the worksheet and the message "Recording" appears in the status bar at the bottom of the screen. You are now in Record mode and all keystrokes and mouse clicks will be recorded until you stop the macro recorder.

Figure 7-37 ◀
Stop Recording
toolbar

click here to stop
recording of macro

Relative Reference
button

status bar indicates
macro is being
recorded

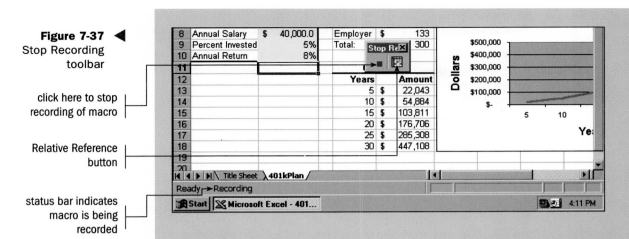

Notice that the Stop Recording toolbar is also displayed. This toolbar contains two buttons, the Stop Recording button and the Relative Reference button. By default Excel uses absolute references while recording macros. If you wanted a macro to select cells regardless of the position of the cell pointer in the worksheet when you run the macro, then you would click the Relative Reference button to record macros using relative references. When you have finished entering all tasks, you can use the Stop Recording button to stop the macro recorder.

TROUBLE? If a warning message appears indicating that the macro name already exists, click the Yes button and proceed to record the tasks in your macro. Excel replaces the existing macro with whatever you now record.

Now perform the tasks you want recorded.

To perform the steps to be recorded:

1. Select the range **B7:B10**.

2. Press the **Delete** key. The input section is now cleared.

3. Click cell **B7** to make it the active cell.

   You have completed the actions that you want recorded. Next, you will stop the macro recorder.

4. Click the **Stop Recording** button ▪ on the Stop Recording toolbar. Notice that the message "Recording" is no longer displayed in the status bar.

   TROUBLE? If you forget to turn off the macro recorder, it continues to record all of your actions. If this happens to you, you may need to delete the macro and record it again. To delete the macro, click Tools on the menu bar, point to Macro, and then click Macros in the Macros dialog box, select ClearInputs in the Macro Name list, and then click the Delete button. Click the Yes button to verify you want to delete the macro.

You have completed recording your first macro. Now test the macro by running it.

Running the ClearInputs Macro from the Tools Menu

After recording a macro, you can play it back, or run it, at any time. When you run a macro, you are telling Excel to execute the previously recorded instructions contained within the macro. It is a good idea to run the macro directly after you create it, as a test to ensure that it works correctly. If it doesn't work correctly, you can:

- re-record the macro using the same macro name as before
- delete the recorded macro and then record the macro again
- edit the incorrect macro by opening the Visual Basic Editor

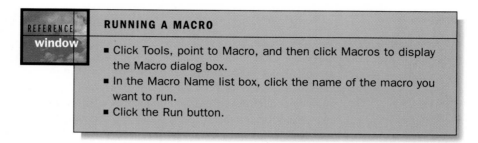

REFERENCE window

RUNNING A MACRO

- Click Tools, point to Macro, and then click Macros to display the Macro dialog box.
- In the Macro Name list box, click the name of the macro you want to run.
- Click the Run button.

The first time you run the macro, you are testing it to determine whether it works as expected. Run the macro you just created to see if it automatically clears the values from the input section. To do this, you need to first enter values in the section to be cleared.

To run a macro using the Macro command on the Tools menu:

1. Enter a new set of input values in cells B7:B10. Enter **Mary Higgins**, **45000**, **.02**, **.06**.

2. Scroll to the calculation/output section to see the results of the new set of input assumptions.

3. Press **Ctrl + Home** to move to cell A1.

   Now save the workbook before running the macro for the first time in case anything goes wrong while running it.

4. Click the **Save** button 🖫 on the Standard toolbar to save the workbook.
   Use the ClearInputs macro to erase the input values.

5. Click **Tools** on the menu bar, point to **Macro**, and then click **Macros** to display the Macro dialog box. See Figure 7-38. A list of all macros found in all open workbooks appears in the Macro Name list box.

Figure 7-38 ◀
Macro dialog
box

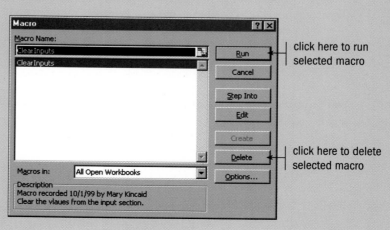

click here to run selected macro

click here to delete selected macro

Select the name of the macro you want to run.

6. If necessary, click **ClearInputs** to display ClearInputs in the Macro Name text box, and then click the **Run** button. Excel executes the ClearInputs macro and clears the values in cells B7:B10. See Figure 7-39.

Figure 7-39
Worksheet after
macro run

input values cleared ⟶

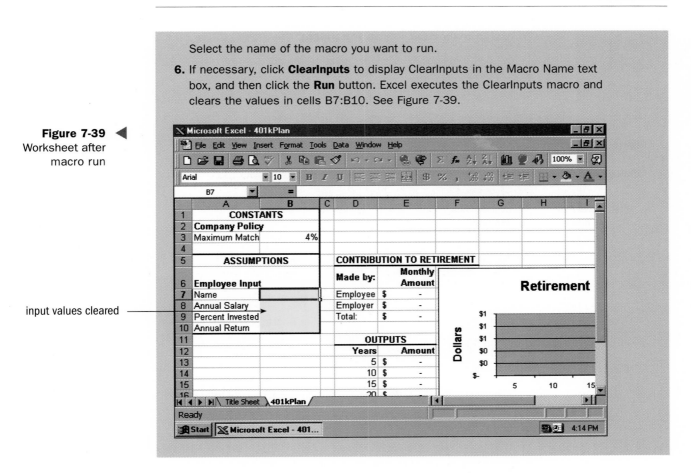

The macro ran successfully. Now that you know the macro works, you want to make it easy for users to run. There are several ways to do this.

Creating a Macro Shortcut Key

You can use the Macro command on the Tools menu to run macros that you execute infrequently, but this approach is inconvenient if you need to run the macro often. There are several ways to make it easier to run a macro. You can:

- assign the macro to a shortcut key that enables you to run the macro by using a combination of the Ctrl key and a letter key

- assign the macro to a command that appears on one of the Excel menus

- assign the macro to a button on a toolbar

- assign the macro to a drawing object

A quick way to run a macro is to assign it to a shortcut key, a key you press along with the Ctrl key to run the macro. The shortcut key is a single uppercase or lowercase letter. If you use this option, you can run the macro by holding down the Ctrl key and pressing the shortcut key. Normally you assign a shortcut key when you first record a macro; however, if you didn't create a shortcut key at the time you recorded the macro you can still assign one to the macro.

Mary asks you to create a shortcut key to execute the ClearInputs macro. She wants users to type Ctrl + c to execute the macro.

To assign a shortcut key to the macro:

1. Click **Tools** on the menu bar, point to **Macro**, and then click **Macros** to display the Macro dialog box.

2. If necessary, click **ClearInputs**, and then click the **Options** button to open the Macro Options dialog box. See Figure 7-40.

Figure 7-40 ◀
Macro Options
dialog box

enter shortcut
key here

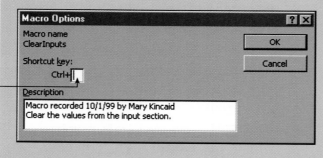

Assign a keyboard shortcut to the macro.

3. Make sure the insertion point is in the Shortcut key text box, type **c**, and then click the **OK** button to return to the Macro dialog box. Click the **Cancel** button to return to the worksheet. The shortcut key is now assigned to the ClearInputs macro.

Now test the shortcut key to see if the macro runs when Ctrl + c is pressed.

To test the shortcut key:

1. Enter a new set of input values. In cells B7:B10, enter **FJ Miles, 50000, .06, .10**.

2. Press **Ctrl + c** to run the macro. The input values are erased and B7 is the active cell.

   Note that shortcut keys are case-sensitive, so if a user types Ctrl + Shift C, the shortcut will not run the ClearInputs macro.

The shortcut key successfully ran the macro. Now let's take a look at the code behind the ClearInputs macro.

Viewing the ClearInputs Macro Code

As you may have realized, you can successfully record and run a macro without looking at or understanding the instructions underlying it. For simple macros this approach is fine. There will be times, however, when you may welcome the greater flexibility that comes from understanding the commands underlying the recorded macro.

As Excel records your actions, it translates them into a series of instructions in the Visual Basic for Applications programming language. Figure 7-41 represents the Visual Basic code generated while your ClearInputs macro was recorded.

Figure 7-41
VBA code for
ClearInputs
macro

start of macro

comments

body macro

end of macro

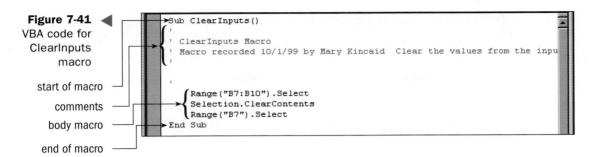

```
Sub ClearInputs()
'
' ClearInputs Macro
' Macro recorded 10/1/99 by Mary Kincaid  Clear the values from the inpu
'

    Range("B7:B10").Select
    Selection.ClearContents
    Range("B7").Select
End Sub
```

Visual Basic for Applications Code

The Visual Basic for Applications code shown in Figure 7-41 has the following components: **Sub/End Sub** are keywords that mark the beginning and end of a macro. The keyword Sub in the statement

    Sub ClearInputs()

signals the start of the macro. It is followed by the macro name ClearInputs and then by left and right parentheses. The keywords End Sub signal the end of the macro. **Comments** are statements that explain or document what is happening in the macro. Any line of the code that is preceded by an apostrophe is a comment and is ignored by Excel when the macro is run. In Figure 7-41, Excel includes as comments the macro name, the date recorded, and the description you entered in the Record Macro dialog box.

The **body of the macro** is the series of statements between Sub and End Sub representing the VBA translation of the actions you performed while recording the macro. In Figure 7-41 the statement

    Range("B7:B10").Select

is the VBA equivalent of selecting the range B7:B10.

The next statement

    Selection.ClearContents

is the VBA equivalent of pressing the Delete key to clear the contents of the selected range.

The last statement

    Range("B7").Select

is the VBA equivalent of clicking B7 to make it the active cell.

Now that you have viewed the code behind the macro, you're ready to create your next macro, a macro to print a portion of the 401kPlan worksheet.

Recording the Print401k Macro

Because your worksheets may be large, containing input sections, data, tables, reports, charts, etc., you may want to use a macro to help you simplify the steps for printing different parts of a worksheet. Also, the addition of one or more print macros will make the printing process much easier for other users.

After an employee has made changes to certain input values and viewed the revised table and chart, Mary wants the employee to be able to print a hard copy of the worksheet for his or her records. Some employees may only want to print the table and chart from the 401k worksheet. Instead of the user having to establish print settings to get the output of just the table and chart, for example, you could create a macro to print just these sections of the worksheet. Because you would be printing only part of the worksheet, you would need to specify the print area for the portion of the worksheet you are printing. Mary also wants the user's output to automatically have informative headers and footers. Before printing, the user should also be able to view the output in the Print Preview window. Figure 7-42 shows the planning for this macro. Using this planning sheet, record the macro for Mary. Mary suggests that you name the macro Print401k and that it be stored just in this workbook. Now, set up the worksheet just the way you want it before you begin the macro recorder.

Figure 7-42 ◄
Planning the
Print401k
macro

Action	Result
Click File, click Page Setup	Opens the Page Setup dialog box
Click the Sheet tab, click Print area, type D5:L18	Defines print area
Click Margins, click Horizontally check box	Horizontally centers output
Click Header/Footer tab, click Custom Header, click the Tab Name button, click OK	Defines custom header
Click Custom Footer, click Date, click OK	Defines custom footer
Click Print Preview	Displays output in Print Preview window
Click Close	Closes Print Preview window
Click cell A5	Makes cell A5 the active cell

To record the Print401k macro:

1. Enter a new set of input values. Enter **Tammy Beach**, **25000**, **.1**, **.12** in the appropriate cells in range B7:B10. Click cell **A1**.

   Now start the macro recorder.

2. Click **Tools** on the menu bar, point to **Macro**, and then click **Record New Macro** to display the Record Macro dialog box.

   Excel proposes Macro2 as the name for the macro, because this is the second macro you have recorded during this work session. Change the name of the macro to Print401k.

3. Type **Print401k** in the Macro name text box.

   Now add a shortcut key.

4. Click the **Shortcut key** text box, and then type **p**.

   Add an additional comment to explain the purpose of the macro.

5. Place the insertion point at the end of the default description. Press the **Enter** key and type **Print preview output table and chart**.

6. Click the **OK** button to start the macro recorder.

7. Click **File** on the menu bar, and then click **Page Setup** to display the Page Setup dialog box.

   By default, Excel prints the entire worksheet. To print only a part of the worksheet, you must specify the part you want.

8. Click the **Sheet** tab of the Page Setup dialog box, click the **Print area** text box, and then type **D5:L18**.

   Now specify the print settings so the output is centered horizontally.

9. Click the **Margins** tab, and then check the **Horizontally** check box to select it.

Excel

10. Click the **Header/Footer** tab, and then click the **Custom Header** button. In the center section, click the **Tab Name** button, and then click the **OK** button.

11. Click the **Custom Footer** button, click the **Date** button 🖻 in the Right section, and then click the **OK** button.

Review the output in the Print Preview window.

12. Click the **Print Preview** button on the right side of the dialog box to preview the output. See Figure 7-43.

Figure 7-43 ◄
Print Preview
as result of
running macro

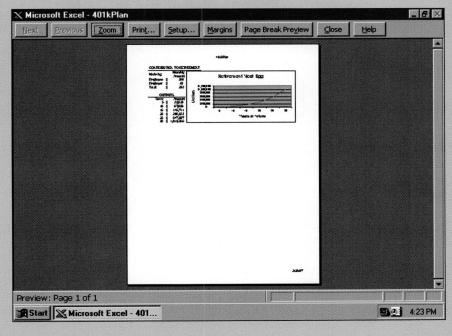

13. Click the **Close** button to close the Print Preview window and return to the 401kPlan sheet. Note that you cannot stop the macro until you leave the Print Preview window.

14. Click cell **A5** to make it the active cell.

You have completed the tasks for the macro; now turn off the macro recorder.

15. Click the **Stop Recording** button ■ on the Stop Recording toolbar to stop recording the macro.

Now test the Print401k macro using the shortcut key.

To test the macro using the shortcut key:

1. Save the workbook.

2. Press **Ctrl + p** to run the macro. Excel displays the output table and chart in the Print Preview window.

3. If you want a hard copy, click the **Print** button on the Print Preview toolbar, and then click the **OK** button in the Print dialog box; otherwise click the **Close** button.

The shortcut key successfully ran the print macro. However, Mary thinks it may be easier for a user to run the print macro by clicking a button placed on the worksheet. Mary asks you to create this button.

Assigning the Print401k Macro to a Button on the Worksheet

Another way to run a macro is to assign it to a command button object. You place the command button object on a worksheet, assign the macro to the button, and then run the macro by clicking the button. This approach makes the macro easier to use. It will speed up your own work, as well as make the macro easier for others to run.

 REFERENCE window | **ASSIGNING A MACRO TO A BUTTON OBJECT ON A WORKSHEET**

- Click the Button button on the Forms toolbar.
- Position the mouse pointer where you want the button, and then click and drag the mouse pointer until the button is the size and shape you want.
- Release the mouse button. The button appears on the worksheet with a label and the Assign Macro dialog box opens.
- Select the name of the macro that you want to assign to the button from the Macro Name list box.
- Click the OK button.

Since the workbook is still protected, you need to turn protection off in order to make any changes to the worksheet (except in unlocked cells), such as placing a button on the worksheet.

To turn protection off:

1. Click **Tools** on the menu bar, point to **Protection**, and then click **Unprotect Sheet**. The worksheet is unprotected. If you had password-protected the worksheet, the Unprotect Sheet dialog box would open so that you could enter the password.

Now place a command button object on the worksheet.

To place a button object on the worksheet and assign a macro to the button:

1. Click cell **D2**.

   Next, display the Forms toolbar, which contains the tools you need to place the button object.

2. Click **View** on the menu bar, point to **Toolbars**, and then click **Forms** to display the Forms toolbar. If necessary, drag the Forms toolbar out of the way. See Figure 7-44.

Figure 7-44 ◀
Forms toolbar
displayed in
worksheet
window

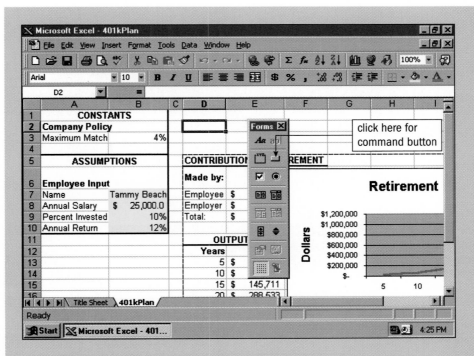

Now place a command button on the worksheet.

3. Click the **Button** button 🔲 on the Forms toolbar. Now position the mouse pointer in the worksheet where you want the button to appear.

4. Position the mouse pointer in the upper-left corner of cell D2. Click and drag the mouse pointer until the box covers the range D2:E3. When you release the mouse button, the Assign Macro dialog box opens. See Figure 7-45. Here you select the macro that will be run when this button is clicked by the user. This is referred to as assigning a macro to a button object.

Figure 7-45 ◀
Assign Macro
dialog box

select this macro →

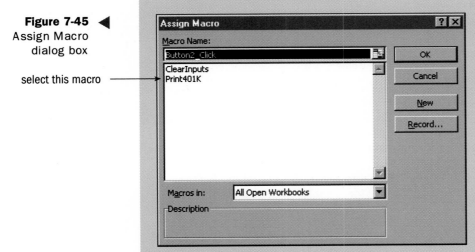

5. Click **Print401k** in the Macro Name list box, and then click the **OK** button. The macro is assigned to the command button object. The button object appears on the worksheet. It is selected (sizing handles appear around the button), and the default name Button 2 appears as a label on the button.

TROUBLE? If the button is too small, too large, or in the wrong location, you can resize or move it just as you move or resize any object. If the button is not selected, press the Ctrl key while moving the mouse pointer on top of the button, and then click the mouse. Selection handles appear around the button, indicating that you can move or resize it.

TROUBLE? If the Forms toolbar is in the way, click and drag it to move it out of the way, or click the Forms toolbar Close button to remove it from the screen.

Now change the name on the button to one that indicates the function of the macro assigned to it.

6. Highlight the label on the command button and type **Print 401k Report**. See Figure 7-46.

Figure 7-46 ◄
Command button to run Print401k macro

command button with new label

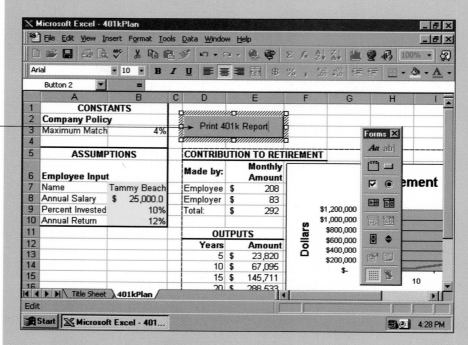

7. Click anywhere in the worksheet to deselect the button.

8. If you haven't already removed the Forms toolbar, click its **Close** button to remove it now.

Now test the command button to make sure it runs the macro.

To test the Print401k macro using the command button:

1. Type **.08** in cell B10 and press the **Enter** key.

2. Click the **Print 401k Report** button. Excel displays the output and chart in the Print Preview window.

3. If you want a hard copy, click the **Print** button on the Standard toolbar and then click the **OK** button in the Print dialog box; otherwise click the **Close** button.

Your Print401k macro worked successfully using the button object.

4. Save the workbook, and then close it and exit Excel.

Quick Check

1. A _____ automates repetitive tasks.

2. You can create a macro by _____ or _____.

3. A recorded macro stores instructions in the _____ programming language.

4. Name three ways to run a macro.

5. Macros are stored in a _____, _____, or _____.

6. To stop recording a macro, you _____.

7. What is the purpose of a shortcut key?

8. "Print Chart" is a valid macro name. (True/False)

You have created a workbook for the CableScan employees that will allow them to easily and efficiently plan and establish 401(k) plans.

Tutorial Assignments

After the formal presentation at the first of CableScan's three sites, you have received feedback from the employees on how to improve the usability of the 401kPlan workbook. Do the following:

1. If necessary, start Excel and make sure your Student Disk is in the appropriate disk drive. Open the workbook 401kPln2 in the TAssign folder for Tutorial.07 and save it as 401kPlan3. Since this workbook contains macros, Excel displays a message informing you of this. Click the Enable Macros button to continue.

2. Remove cell protection from the worksheet.

3. Specify a data validation rule for the Salary value, cell B8. You want to allow integer values between 5000 and 150000.

4. Test the data validation. Enter a salary of 200000. What happens?

5. Modify the data validation you just assigned in cell B8 to include an input message. The message should state "Valid salary values are between 5000 and 150000" and have the title Valid Data.

6. Modify the data validation you assigned in cell B8 to include an error alert message. The error message should have the title Invalid Data, and the message should state "You entered a value less than $5000 or greater than $150,000." Use the Warning style in defining the error alert.

7. Test the data validation again. Enter a value of 200,000. What happens?

8. Change the error alert style to Information. Enter 200000 as the current salary. What happens?

9. Assign the name Contributions to the range E7:E8. Replace the formula in cell E9 with the formula =Sum(Contributions). What value is displayed in E9?

10. The FV function in cell E13 assumes that payments are made at the end of the month. A more realistic assumption is that payments are made at the beginning of the month. Use the Paste Function button on the Standard toolbar to modify the FV function in cell E13 by placing a 1 in the Type argument. Copy the modified formula to the other cells in the output table. Use the Print 401k Report button to print the worksheet.

11. Modify the IF function in cell E8 so the condition is expressed Invested <=MaxMatch instead of MaxMatch > Invested. Modify the other arguments of the IF function so you get the same results as in the tutorial. What formula did you enter in cell B9?

12. Plan and create a macro to print preview the entire worksheet except the range A1:B4. Include the label "CableScan 401k Plan" as a custom header in the center setting and change the page orientation to Landscape. Name the macro PrintWorksheet. Assign a shortcut key to the macro. Place a button on the worksheet next to the Print 401k Report button. Label the button Print Worksheet. Test your macro twice, using the Print Worksheet button and the shortcut key. (*Note:* By default, the macro button does not print.)

13. Delete Sheet3 from the workbook, and then save and close the workbook.

14. a. Open a new workbook and use AutoFill to create the series Q197,Q297,Q397,Q497,Q198,Q298,...,Q199,...,Q499. Print the series.
    b. What values must be entered in the worksheet in order for Excel to recognize the pattern and create this series?
    c. What value does Excel display after Q499?
    d. Save the workbook as AutoFill Exercise in the TAssign folder for Tutorial.07 on your Student Disk.

15. Open a new workbook and create two macros that are identical, except that in the first case you'll record the macro using absolute references and in the second, you'll record the macro using relative references. Both macros enter a company's name and address into three worksheet cells. Figure 7-47 describes the steps required for each macro.

Figure 7-47 ◄

Name of Macro: NameAddress1 Shortcut key: x Description: using absolute references
Click cell A1
Type Adobe Development Corporation
In cell A2, type 101 Terra Way
In cell A3, type Tucson, AZ

Name of Macro: NameAddress2 Shortcut key: y Description: using relative references
Click Relative Reference button
Click cell A1
Type Adobe Development Corporation
In cell A2, type 101 Terra Way
In cell A3, type Tucson, AZ
Click Relative Reference button

Do the following:
   a. Record the NameAddress1 macro as described in Figure 7-47.
   b. Before you record the second macro, clear the contents of cells A1:A3, and then make A3 the active cell.
   c. Record the Name Address2 macro described in Figure 7-47.
   d. Activate Sheet2.
   e. Click cell D5 and run the NameAddress1 macro using the shortcut key.
   f. Click cell D12 and run the NameAddress2 macro using the shortcut key.
   g. Activate Sheet3.
   h. Click cell D5 and run the NameAddress1 macro.
   i. Click cell D12 and run the NameAddress2 macro.
   j. Save the workbook as Relative vs. Absolute in the TAssign folder for Tutorial.07. Close the workbook.

Comment on the differences between the two macros.

Case Problems

1. Travel Expense Worksheet for Tax Purposes Jack Conners, an accountant for a manufacturing company, has been preparing tax returns on weekends and evenings for several years to earn extra income. Although Jack uses a commercial tax package to prepare tax returns for his friends and clients, he has discovered that the package doesn't provide any assistance in determining the portion of a business trip that is tax deductible. Jack has asked you to develop a worksheet to determine deductible travel expenses that he can use with a client who travels on business.

The IRS rules state that a taxpayer can deduct travel expenses incurred while pursuing a business purpose. Those travel expenses include transportation, lodging, incidentals, and 50% of meals. Incidentals are items such as local transportation, telephone calls, laundry, and similar small items that are necessary while traveling. Sometimes a trip may involve both business and personal activities. If fewer than 50% of the travel days are devoted to business, the IRS rule states that none of the transportation expenses are deductible; otherwise the transportation expenses are fully deductible. The costs for lodging, meals, and incidentals are deductible to the extent that they are related specifically to business activities. Only 50% of meals associated with business travel, such as taking a client to lunch, are deductible.

Figure 7-48 incorporates the information you need to complete the travel expense worksheet.

Figure 7-48 ◀

```
Inputs
  Name of taxpayer
  Dates of travel
  Destination
  Purpose
  Number of travel days: business
  Number of travel days: personal
  Transportation (total cost)
  Lodging (cost per day)
  Meals (cost per day)
  Incidentals (cost per day)


Calculations
  Transportation = IF Number of travel days: business is greater than Number of travel days: personal THEN
              Transportation = Transportation (total cost)
          ELSE
              Transportation = 0
          END IF
  Lodging = Number of travel days (business) x  Lodging (cost per day)
  Meals = Number of travel days  (business) x Meals (cost per day) x 50%
  Incidentals = Number of travel days (business) x Incidentals (cost per day)
  Total deductible travel expense = Transportation + Lodging + Meals + Incidentals
```

Do the following:

1. If necessary, start Excel and make sure your Student Disk is in the appropriate disk drive.

2. Prepare a travel expense worksheet based on the information in Figure 7-48. Name the sheet Travel.

3. Divide the worksheet into two sections: input and calculation/output. As you develop the input section, assign range names to each cell.

4. The IRS guideline limits the deduction for meals to $75 per day, unless the taxpayer has receipts to justify a higher expense. Set up a data validation rule in the input section to comply with this guideline. You should include an input message and determine appropriate text for the message. Also, include an error alert message using the Warning style. You determine the text of the error alert message. Test the data validation.

5. Use the range names to build the formulas in the calculation section of your worksheet.

6. Improve the appearance of the worksheet, so you have a professional-looking report you can output.

7. Print the worksheet using Taxpayer 1 data from Figure 7-49.

Figure 7-49 ◀

Input Field	Taxpayer 1	Taxpayer 2
Name of taxpayer	Ken Turner	Ellen Wymer
Dates of travel	Jan 5 - Jan 12	April 21 - April 28
Destination	Austin, TX	San Antonio, TX
Purpose	Sales call	Consulting
Number of travel days (business)	5	3
Number of travel days (personal)	3	5
Transportation (total cost)	350	375
Lodging (cost per day)	125	110
Meals (cost per day)	50	60
Incidentals (cost per day)	20	15

8. Save the worksheet as Travel Expense in the Case folder for Tutorial.07 on your Student Disk.

9. Print the formulas for the worksheet. Include row and column headers. Output the formulas on one page.

10. Create macros to clear the input section and print the worksheet. Assign each macro to a button. Use Taxpayer 2 data from Figure 7-49 to test your macros.

11. Apply cell protection to all cells in the worksheet except cells in the input section. Test the cell protection. Assign a color to identify the range that is unprotected.

12. Delete any unused worksheets in the workbook, then save and close the workbook.

2. Sales Agreement Application for Desert Dreams Desert Dreams, a self-contained community, is being developed in New Mexico by Adobe Sun Corporation as an environment that appeals to people of all ages. Desert Dreams offers lifestyle features such as an 18-hole golf course, clubhouse, state-of-the-art fitness center, swimming and tennis center, hiking and bike paths, and open space with beautiful desert views. In addition, the floorplans for the houses in the development are said to be the best in the area as well as winners of numerous architectural awards.

Interest in the community has been abundant. To assist the sales associates, you have been asked to develop a Sales Agreement worksheet to use with potential home buyers as they finalize the sale of a home.

The worksheet should summarize the total purchase price, which consists of the cost of the lot, the base price of the home, and the cost of extras (options). In addition, the worksheet should lay out the payment schedule for two alternative financing schedules: a cash plan and a mortgage payment plan. Figure 7-50 shows the information you need to include in your worksheet.

Figure 7-50 ◀

Input
  Name of buyer
  Lot cost
  Base price of home
  Options

Calculations
  Purchase price = lot cost + base price of home + options

  Financing Plan - Mortgage

Deposit at signing sales agreement	$5000
Down payment at start of construction	(15% x total purchase price) less deposit
Final payment at closing	total purchase price less (down payment and deposit)
Total cash paid out	sum of 3 payments

  Financing Plan - Cash

Deposit at signing sales agreement	$10000
Down Payment at start of construction	(30% x total purchase price) less deposit
Payment at start of framing	(35% x total purchase price) less deposit
Final payment at closing	total purchase price less (sum of 3 payments) less cash Discount
Cash discount	2.5% of base price
Total cash paid out	sum of 4 payments
Total purchase price	total cash paid out plus cash discount

Do the following:

1. If necessary, start Excel and make sure your Student Disk is in the appropriate disk drive.

2. Design the worksheet with the two users in mind. Make it useful to sales associates as they enter data but also attractive and easy to follow for home buyers, who will receive a copy of the sales agreement. Consider dividing the worksheet into input and calculation/output sections. In your calculation/output section include a payment schedule for both the mortgage and cash financing plans. Use the information in Figure 7-50 as you build your worksheet. Name the sheet Sales Agreement.

3. Apply the following data validation rules:

   ■ base price of home does not exceed $300,000

   ■ lot prices are between $20,000 and $100,000

   For each rule you should include an appropriate input and error alert message.

4. Create and use range names as you build formulas and in any other way you see fit. (*Hint*: Values in the input section and selected calculations are the most useful choices for range names.)

5. Format an attractive sales agreement worksheet, using features you have learned throughout the tutorials.

6. Save your workbook as Sales Agreement in the Case folder for Tutorial.07 on your Student Disk.

7. Enter the data in Figure 7-51, and then print the worksheet.

Figure 7-51 ◀

Name of buyer	Helen Chomas
Lot cost	25,000
Base price	150,000
Options	12500

8. Develop macros to:
    a. Clear input values from your input section. Name this macro ClearInputs and assign it to a button.
    b. Print the portion of the worksheet that includes inputs and costs of both financing plans. Name this macro PrintData, and assign it to a button.

9. Helen Chomas has just selected some additional options which increased the options cost to $15000. Make this change to the input section of your worksheet and use your PrintData macro to print a new output of the financing plans.

10. Create a title sheet. Print the title sheet.

11. Use the Index tab in the Help dialog box to learn how to "paste" range names and their associated addresses into your worksheet. Create a section in your title sheet to include all range name information in your worksheet. Print the modified title sheet.

12. Protect all cells in your worksheet except the cells where a user enters input values.

13. Save your worksheet, and then print the worksheet formulas. Remember to include row and column headers in your output.

14. Modify the Financing Plan - Mortgage to include a line for the monthly mortgage payment. Assume 8% annual interest, 25 years, and amount borrowed (use final payment at closing). Use the Office Assistant to learn about the PMT function. Use your print macro to output the Sales Agreement worksheet.

15. Save and close the workbook.

3. Customer Billing for Apex Auto Rental Apex Auto Rental is the only car rental company in a midwest city. The company has been in business for two years. John Prescott, president and founder of Apex, has asked you to help him computerize the bills he gives to his customers.

Apex rents two types of cars: compact and luxury. The current rental rates are shown in Figure 7-52.

Figure 7-52 ◀

Type	Charge/Day	Charge/Mile
Compact	$38	$0.22
Luxury	$50	$0.32

1. If necessary, start Excel and make sure your Student Disk is in the appropriate disk drive.

2. Develop a worksheet that calculates and prints customer bills. Divide your workbook into the following sheets:

   ■ A title sheet that includes a title, your name, date developed, filename, and purpose.

   ■ A worksheet for the customer bill. Name the worksheet Customer Bill. The customer bill should include the information shown in Figure 7-53. Divide your worksheet into input, calculation, and output sections. Use the layout in Figure 7-54 to design your output section. As you create your input and calculation sections, assign range names to these cells.

Figure 7-53 ◀

Assumptions
  Rental rate information (Figure 7-52)

Rental Inputs
  Customer name
  Type of car (compact or luxury)
  Number of days rented
  Number of miles driven

Calculations
  Charge per day (depends on type of car rented, which is entered in input section. Get charge from rental rate information)
  Charge per mile (depends on type of car rented, which is entered in input section. Get charge from rental rate information)
  Amount due = (days driven x charge/day) + (miles driven x charge/mile)

Figure 7-54 ◀

Apex Car Rental
Customer Bill

Customer Name: xxxxxxxxxxxxxxx

Type of Car: xxxxxxxxxx

Days Driven: x   **Charge/Day:** xx

Miles Driven: xxxx   **Charge/Mile:** xx

Amount Due: $ x,xxx.xx

---

3. Apply the data validation rules from Figure 7-55 to the input section. You decide on appropriate input and error alert messages.

Figure 7-55 ◀

Field	Rule
Number of days	< 30
Number of miles	< 5000
Type of car	List (use values from rental rate information)

4. Use the range names as you build the formulas for the customer bill.

5. Improve the appearance of your worksheet.

6. Save your worksheet as Apex Rental.

7. Enter the Customer 1 data from Figure 7-56 into the input section of your worksheet. Print the entire worksheet.

Figure 7-56 ◀

Input Field	Customer 1	Customer 2
Customer name	Masirsa Elders	Henry Fuller
Type of car	Compact	Luxury
Days driven	2	7
Miles driven	150	1200

8. Create macros to

   ■ clear the rental input section. Name this macro ClearInputs. Assign the macro to a button.

   ■ print only the customer bill. Name this macro PrintBill and assign it to a button.

   Use the Customer 2 data from Figure 7-56 to test your macros.

9. Print the formulas (include row and column headers).

10. Apply cell protection to the worksheet cells, while permitting the user to enter data in the input section. Use color or shading to identify the unprotected area.

4. Managing Tours for Executive Travel Services Executive Travel Services (ETS) of San Diego is a travel agency that specializes in selling packaged tours to business executives from Fortune 500 companies. ETS was started in 1982 by Tom Williams, a retired executive from a Fortune 500 company. As an executive, Tom often wished he could socialize with other top executives in an informal setting for several days so he founded ETS. ETS books tours that last from one to three weeks. The tours are designed to let executives enjoy a variety of activities while becoming acquainted with other executives.

In the last several months, the number of tour requests has nearly doubled. ETS accidentally overbooked several of its more popular tours. Tom decided to develop an Excel list that could be used to provide information necessary to avoid future overbooking problems. One of his first steps was to develop the data definition shown in Figure 7-57.

Figure 7-57 ◀

Field Name	Description
Tour	Tour name
Month	Month tour is scheduled to start
Type	Type of tour: Golf, Photo, or Relax
Sold	Number of seats sold for tour
Open	Number of seats still open for sale
Price	Price of tour

The Excel list was created to track the Tours information. Tom would like you to make several changes to improve the operation of the tour management. Do the following:

1. If necessary, start Excel and make sure your Student Disk is in the appropriate disk drive. Open the ETS1.XLS workbook in the Case folder for Tutorial.07 and save it as Executive Tours. Review the Tours list. What is missing from the list?

2. Complete the information in the Title Sheet worksheet. Activate the Tours Data sheet and add the appropriate field names in the order in which they are listed in the data definition. Center and bold each field name.

3. Replace the report title and subtitle with a WordArt graphic.

4. Tom wants to know how much revenue the tours are producing. Add a Revenue field to the Excel list and place it immediately to the right of the Price field (column G). Revenue for a tour is calculated as the number of seats sold for a tour multiplied by the price charged for the tour. Add the column heading Revenue in cell G7. Use the Format Painter button to copy the formats in cell F7 to G7. Use a natural language formula to build a formula to compute revenue for each tour.

5. Insert a formula in cell G5 to sum the revenue for all tours. Assign the range name TotalRevenue to this cell (G5). Use color, shading, or some other enhancement to draw attention to the total revenue cell. In cell F5 enter the label Revenue.

6. Use the Pivot Table feature to produce a report that summarizes tour revenues by month and type of tour. Enhance the appearance of the report. Place the pivot table on a separate page. Name the sheet RevenueSummary. Print it.

7. Use the Zoom box on the Standard toolbar to change the magnification so you can see all the columns in the list without scrolling.

8. Insert a new sheet into the workbook and in it, prepare a professional-looking income statement for ETS based on the model in Figure 7-58. Name the sheet IncomeStmt. As you enter the input assumption section in this sheet, assign range names to each cell in this section.

Figure 7-58 ◄

Revenue:

Total revenue = sum of revenue from all tours (use the formula =*TotalRevenue* to link to total revenue in the Tours Data sheet)

Expenses:

Commissions = Commission rate × Total revenue

Administration = Administrative rate × Total revenue

Reservation System = Reservation system rate × Total revenue

Supplies = 6000 + Supplies rate × Total revenue

Rent = 12000

Miscellaneous = 5000

Total expenses = sum of all expenses

Net Income = Total revenue - Total expenses

Input Assumptions:

Commission rate   25%

Reservation system rate 35%

Administrative rate   5%

Supplies rate   3.6%

9. Use the ranges as you enter the formulas to build the income statement.

10. Save the worksheet. Print the formulas for the income statement (include row and column headings in the output).

Questions 11-13 involve the creation of macros.

11. Create three macros to sort the Tours list. The macros should sort by:

    - Tour

    - Type field as the first sort key and Tour field as the second sort key

    - Revenue (descending order)

    Assign each macro to a button that when clicked performs the desired sort. Place the buttons in a convenient location on the Tours Data sheet. Test the macro.

12. Create a macro that will print the Tours list. Assign the macro to a button. Label the button. Place the button in a convenient location on the Tours Data sheet. Test the macro.

13. Create a macro to print the income statement and input assumptions. Assign the macro to a button. Label the button. Place the button in a convenient location on the IncomeStmt sheet. Test the macro.

14. Based on the income statement and the Goal Seek feature, determine how high the commission rate must be raised for ETS to break even (net income zero). Print the input assumptions and income statement on a single sheet.

15. Apply cell protection to all cells in the IncomeStmt sheet except the cells in the input section and save the workbook.

Answers to Quick Check Questions

SESSION 5.1

1. Record
2. Field
3. List
4. Sort by major and within major by last name
5. New button
6. Assuming you have the fields FirstName and LastName as part of the employee list, you would click the Criteria button in the Data Form dialog box. In the FirstName field text box type "Jin"; in the LastName field text box type "Shinu". Click the Find Next button to display the record in the data form.
7. Primary; alternative answer might be sort field or sort key
8. Descending

SESSION 5.2

1. In order to have Excel calculate subtotals correctly, you must first sort the data because the subtotals are inserted whenever the value in the specified field changes.
2. Page Break Preview view
3. Natural language
4. AutoFilter, Data
5. Use the AutoFilter feature. Click the Major field filter arrow and then click Marketing. For the GPA field, click Custom from the list of filtering options. Enter the comparison operator > and the constant 3.0 to form the condition GPA greater than 3.0.
6. Outline
7. Conditional formatting

SESSION 5.3

1. Sums the field
2. Refresh
3. Rows, columns, or pages
4. a. AutoFilter
   b. Pivot table

SESSION 6.1

1. Paste Special
2. Object linking and embedding
3. Linked
4. WordArt
5. Has no effect
6. The Excel menus and toolbar replace the menus and toolbar in the Word window. The embedded object now has column and row headings and the sheet tabs appear. Excel becomes the active program.
7. Embed
8. Link

SESSION 6.2

1 Main, merge fields
2 Merge field
3 Linking
4 Position the insertion point where you want the merge field; click the Insert Merge Field button, and then click the name of field you want to insert.
5 Click the View Merged Data button on the Mail Merge toolbar

SESSION 6.3

1 HyperText Markup language, Web
2 Hyperlink
3 file address, text, graphic image
4 Insert Hyperlink
5 Forward, Back, Web
6 Web browser
7 Save As HTML
8 .htm

SESSION 7.1

1 Name box
2 b and d
3 If you enter a value that violates the validation rule
4 Input section
5 Data validation
6 When you enter a cell
7 IF function
8 Comparison operator

SESSION 7.2

1 AutoFill
2 To help users identify them
3 Remove the Locked property from cells you want to be able to enter data into, activate the Protect Sheet command
4 Cell protection prevents you from entering any data in a protected cell. Assuming a cell is unprotected, data validation allows you to specify what values users are allowed to enter in the cell.
5 A message box appears informing you that the cell is protected
6 Future Value; Financial

SESSION 7.3

1 Macro
2 recording, or entering Visual Basic code
3 Visual Basic for Applications or VBA
4 Shortcut key (Ctrl + letter), command button object, Run button from Macro dialog box
5 Current workbook, another workbook, Personal Macro workbook
6 Click the Stop Recording Macro button
7 To quickly execute the macro
8 False. Macro names cannot contain embedded blanks. Use an underscore.

Microsoft®
Excel 97

LEVEL III

TUTORIALS

Read This **Before You Begin**

TUTORIAL 8

Working with Multiple Worksheets and Workbooks

Creating Grading Sheets at MidWest University

OBJECTIVES

In this tutorial you will:

- Insert, name, and move worksheets

- Create worksheet groups

- Edit multiple worksheets at the same time

- Consolidate information from multiple worksheets and workbooks

- Create a workbook template

- Learn how to store templates

- Create a lookup table and use Excel's lookup function

 CASE

MidWest University

Professor Karen White teaches Calculus in the Mathematics Department at MidWest University, a liberal arts school that draws students from the midwest and from across the United States. Her Calculus 223 course is one of the most popular courses in the department. Because her Calculus course is required for Computer Science, as well as several other majors, at the university, Professor White's lecture is filled with over 200 students each semester. Students attend Professor White's weekly lecture, as well as smaller biweekly discussion sections with a teaching assistant, or TA, to receive extra instruction, discuss special topics, and work on problems. In addition to leading discussion sections, the four TAs assigned to Professor White's lecture are responsible for grading all the homework assignments, mid-term exams, and final exams of the students in their sections. Professor White's TAs teach three discussion sections, each with about twenty students per section.

In the past, Professor White and her TAs have used hand-written grading sheets to keep track of homework and exam scores, and to calculate final grades. Professor White feels that the accuracy and efficiency of record-keeping for her Calculus course could be greatly improved if the TAs used Microsoft Excel for these tasks instead. She also thinks automating the record-keeping process would save time for her TAs, who carry full course loads in addition to their assistantships.

Professor White has asked you to use Excel to create a grading workbook that her TAs can use to both record the progress of their students and to give her an overall picture of how well all the classes, and each of her assistants, is doing. For each TA's sections, the workbook must be able to calculate the average of the homework and exam results, weight each one according to the values Professor White determines, and automatically assign a final letter grade. Professor White would also like to be able to combine the results from each TA's workbook into a single summary workbook, so she can combine and compare the information to evaluate TA performance. In addition, she would like to use Excel to automatically assign grades based on students' numeric scores.

As you plan a spreadsheet solution that meets Professor White's needs, you review her requirements. You know that you will need a worksheet that can display both the detail and summary information clearly, that can be readily distributed to the TAs, and that will have a consistent format so you can easily combine the results. To meet these goals, you explore the possibility of using multiple worksheets with Excel.

E | **8.3**

SESSION

8.1

In this session you'll learn how to work with multiple worksheets, including inserting and moving worksheets. You'll learn how to work with groups of worksheets at the same time. Finally, you'll be introduced to 3-D cell references that allow you to summarize data from several worksheets.

Why Use Multiple Worksheets?

One of the most useful ways to organize information in your workbooks is to use multiple worksheets. Using multiple worksheets makes it easier for you to group your information. For example, a company with branches located in different regions could place sales information for each region on a separate worksheet. The workbook's users could then view regional sales information by clicking a sheet in the workbook, rather than scrolling through a large and complicated worksheet.

By using multiple worksheets, you can also more easily hide information that might not be of interest to all users. For example, if your director is only interested in the bottom line, the first worksheet could contain your conclusions and summary data, with more detailed information available on separate worksheets.

You can also use separate worksheets to organize your reports, since it is easier to print a single worksheet than it is to select and define a print area within a worksheet and then print it.

Finally, if individual worksheets in a single workbook contain the same type of data and formatting (which is often true of documents like regional sales reports), Excel allows you to edit several worksheets simultaneously and to easily combine the results of several worksheets, saving you time.

Whenever you use multiple worksheets, it's important to plan the content and organization carefully.

Planning a Multiple-Sheet Workbook

Before creating a workbook with multiple worksheets, you should consider how you will organize the sheets to create a coherent and easy-to-use document. Organization is particularly important if other people will be using your workbook. One way of organizing your workbook is to create a title sheet, data sheets, and a summary sheet.

As you know, a **title sheet** describes the workbook's content, structure, and purpose. Sometimes called a **documentation sheet**, it is usually the first worksheet in a workbook. The title sheet should include any information that you think would help other people who might use your workbook. It should list the source of the data, the assumptions you used in creating the workbook, and any conclusions you've derived from analyzing the workbook data. The title sheet should enable anyone who opens your workbook to use it without additional assistance from you. While the Excel File Properties dialog box and cell notes are useful tools for documenting worksheets, every well-designed workbook also should contain a title sheet.

After the title sheet, place a worksheet for each area or group you use to collect and present your information. These **data sheets** could contain data on different sales regions, departments, or areas of production. Data sheets can contain both data and charts.

Finally, if the information from each of the data sheets can be summarized, you should place this information in a **summary worksheet**. In the sales example, the summary worksheet could contain total sales figures for all the individual regions. You can place the summary sheet either at the start of the workbook after the title sheet, or at the end. If you, or the people who will use the workbook, are more interested in the overall picture than in the details, place the summary worksheet at the beginning of the workbook. On the other hand, if you want your workbook to tell a "story" to the user, where the details area is just as important as the final product, place the summary worksheet at the end of the workbook.

Professor White has sketched out the workbook structure she envisions, shown in Figure 8-1. The workbook will have a title sheet that will include the TA's name, contact information, office hours, and class times for each of his or her sections. You'll place grades for each section on a separate worksheet. Since you know Professor White is as interested in the details as in the summary information, you'll place a summary of the discussion section grades on a summary sheet at the end of the workbook. Later on, you'll summarize the information on these summary sheets from each TA's workbook into a single workbook for Professor White to use.

Figure 8-1 ◄
Proposed structure of the grading workbook each TA will use

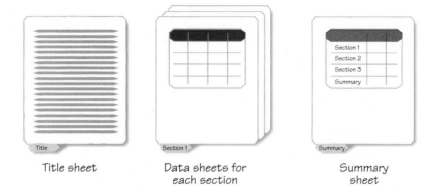

Title sheet   Data sheets for   Summary
                          each section   sheet

Inserting a Worksheet

To create Professor White's grading workbook, you begin by starting Excel, saving the new workbook, and creating a separate sheet for the title sheet and for each of the sections he or she teaches. Since you are the author of this workbook and the person who will be responsible for maintaining it, you will also add your name and the date that the workbook was created.

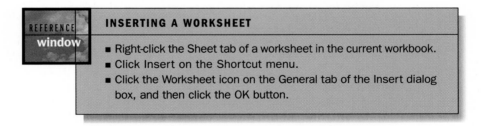

REFERENCE
window

INSERTING A WORKSHEET

- Right-click the Sheet tab of a worksheet in the current workbook.
- Click Insert on the Shortcut menu.
- Click the Worksheet icon on the General tab of the Insert dialog box, and then click the OK button.

First you'll create a new workbook and a new sheet.

To create the new workbook and insert a new worksheet:

1. Start Excel as usual, and make sure your Student Disk is in the appropriate drive.

2. Save the blank workbook that appears as **Grades** in the Tutorial.08 folder on your Student Disk.

3. Right-click the **Sheet1** sheet tab, and then click **Insert** on the Shortcut menu.

4. Click the **Worksheet** icon, as shown in Figure 8-2, and then click the **OK** button.

Figure 8-2 ◀
Insert
dialog box

click to insert a
worksheet into the
workbook

your contents
might differ

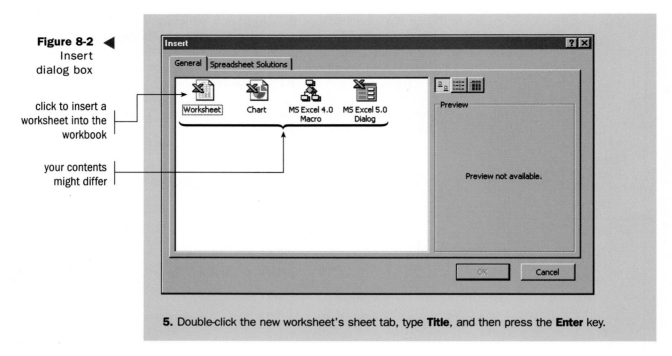

5. Double-click the new worksheet's sheet tab, type **Title**, and then press the **Enter** key.

Next, you'll enter title sheet information.

To set up the title sheet:

1. Enter the following titles in the Title worksheet:

Cell A1: **TA Name**

Cell A2: **Office**

Cell A3: **Phone #**

Cell A4: **Office Hours**

Cell A6: **Section 1**

Cell A7: **Section 2**

Cell A8: **Section 3**

Cell A10: **Purpose:**

Cell A13: **Workbook:**

Cell A14: **Created by:**

Cell A15: **Date Created:**

Cell B5: **Section Times**

Cell C5: **Location**

Now enter the purpose of the worksheet.

2. Click cell **B10**, type **To record the grades for the Section 1 - Section 3** and then press the **Enter** key.

3. In cell B11, enter the following text: **discussion groups of Prof. White's Calculus 223 lecture.**

4. Type **Grades** in cell B13.

5. Enter your name and the date in cells B14 and B15.

6. Apply the boldface style to the ranges **A1:A10** and **B5:C5**. Adjust the width of column **A** to make the column fit its content, resize columns **B** and **C** to **25.00**, and then press **Ctrl + Home** to return to cell A1. See Figure 8-3.

Figure 8-3
Completed
Title sheet

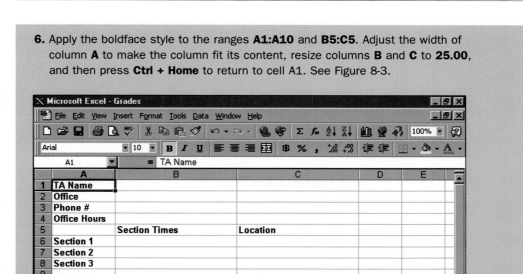

You'll leave the rest of the title sheet to be completed by the TAs when they start using your workbook. Next you'll set up the individual grading sheets.

Moving Worksheets

Now that you have created a title sheet, you'll create the grading sheet for each discussion section. Each of Professor White's four TAs teaches three discussion sections, so you'll be inserting three grading sheets into the workbook.

As you saw when you created the Title sheet, Excel places new worksheets directly to the left of the currently selected sheet. Since you want the Title sheet to be the first sheet in the workbook, you'll have to move the new grading sheet directly to the right of the Title sheet. You can do this using drag and drop.

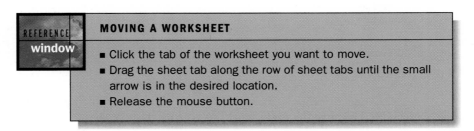

REFERENCE
window

MOVING A WORKSHEET

- Click the tab of the worksheet you want to move.
- Drag the sheet tab along the row of sheet tabs until the small arrow is in the desired location.
- Release the mouse button.

Try moving the first grading sheet now.

To insert and move the first grading sheet:

1. Right-click the **Title** sheet tab, and then click **Insert** on the shortcut menu.

2. Make sure the Worksheet icon is selected, and then click the **OK** button.

3. Double-click the tab of the new worksheet, type **Section 1**, and then press the **Enter** key.

4. Click **Section 1** tab, and then hold down the mouse button so that your pointer changes to ⬚, and drag it to the right until the ▼ is directly to the right of the Title sheet.

5. Release the mouse button.

The new sheet moves to its new location to the right of the Title sheet. You'll follow the same steps to add two new grading sheets for the other two sections.

To insert additional grading sheets into the workbook:

1. Right-click the **Section 1** sheet tab, and then click **Insert** on the Shortcut menu.

2. Make sure the Worksheet icon is selected and click the **OK** button.

3. Double-click the new worksheet's tab, type **Section 2**, and then press the **Enter** key.

4. Drag the Section 2 sheet tab and drop it directly to the right of the Section 1 sheet tab.

5. Repeat Steps 1 through 4 to create a grading sheet for Section 3. Drag the Section 3 sheet directly to the right of the Section 2 sheet. Your workbook should look like Figure 8-4.

Figure 8-4 ◄
Grades workbook with three grading sheets

new worksheets inserted into the workbook

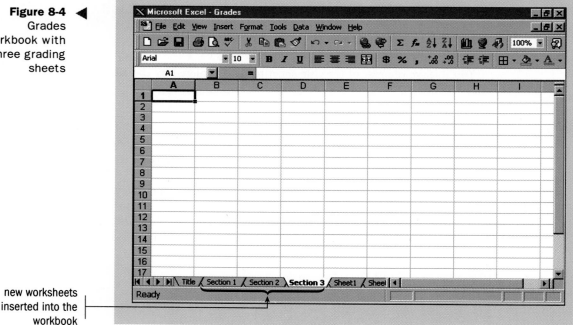

Your workbook now contains the title sheet and the grading sheets you need. Next you'll remove the extra worksheets from the workbook, which you can do in one step by creating a worksheet group.

Working with Worksheet Groups

When you start the Excel program, it opens a new workbook with three blank worksheets (although your version of Excel might be set up to display a different number of worksheets). You don't need these additional sheets in Professor White's workbook, so you can delete them. You could delete the sheets one at a time, but it's more efficient to select the entire group of worksheets and delete them all at once.

To group and delete the worksheets:

1. Click the **Sheet1** sheet tab.

2. Press and hold down the **Shift** key and click the rightmost worksheet in the work-book (you might have to click the Last Worksheet button 🔲 to see it.) All three sheet tabs become white, indicating that they are selected.

3. Right-click any one of the selected sheets, and then click **Delete** on the Shortcut menu.

4. Click the **OK** button to confirm the deletion. The blank worksheets are deleted from your workbook.

Your workbook is now set up according to Professor White's sketch. Next you'll add column titles to the Section 1 worksheet grading sheets, which you can then copy to the other worksheets.

Copying Information Across Worksheets

The process you used to select multiple worksheets for deletion is called **grouping**. Grouping the blank worksheets in the Grading workbook made it easy to delete them, but grouping has other uses as well. You can enter formulas, format and copy values into a worksheet group, or create range names for each sheet in the group. If you have several worksheets that will share a common format, you can format them all at once by using a worksheet group.

Professor White hands you a handwritten grading sheet from a previous semester, shown in Figure 8-5. She would like the grading sheets in your workbook to have the same structure as this sheet.

Figure 8-5 ◀
Professor White's grading sheet

Student ID	Homework 1	Homework 2	Homework 3	Homework 4	Exam 1	Exam 2	Final	Overall	Grade
1001	90	95	92	88	96	89	91	90	A
1002	81	88	85	70	88	72	80	81	B
1003	85	85	90	95	86	92	95	93	A
1004	81	78	65	75	80	72	76	75	BC
1005	99	65	100	99	100	100	95	95	A
1006	81	90	92	85	88	85	86	86	AB
1007	70	100	72	75	75	70	71	74	BC
1008	95	95	95	90	91	92	88	88	AB
1009	94	100	100	81	100	91	93	96	A
1010	100	95	81	96	96	84	89	88	AB
1011	100	100	100	100	100	100	98	98	A
1012	95	94	92	96	95	93	97	97	A
1013	100	100	92	96	100	91	94	98	A
1014	70	75	70	72	76	69	78	77	BC
1015	85	92	81	88	91	84	87	86	B
1016	81	68	75	60	81	65	71	70	C
1017	88	92	84	87	90	65	85	87	AB
1018	75	72	71	75	73	81	71	70	C
1019	92	81	84	85	87	65	87	86	B
1020	94	96	93	90	95	84	91	90	AB

Professor White scores homework and exams on a 100-point scale. She then calculates an overall average of each student's scores and assigns a letter grade based on the average. Since she gives the same assignments and tests for every section, you can create column titles for the Section 1 grading sheet, and then copy them to the Section 2 and Section 3 worksheets.

To add column titles to the Section 1 worksheet:

1. Click the **Section 1** sheet tab.

2. Type **ID** in cell A1, and then press the **Tab** key.

3. Type **Home1** in cell B1, and then press the **Tab** key.

4. Continue entering the following column titles in the first row of the worksheet: **Home2**, **Home3**, **Home4**, **Exam1**, **Exam2**, and **Final**. See Figure 8-6.

Figure 8-6
Column titles for the Section 1 grading worksheet sheet

grading worksheet titles

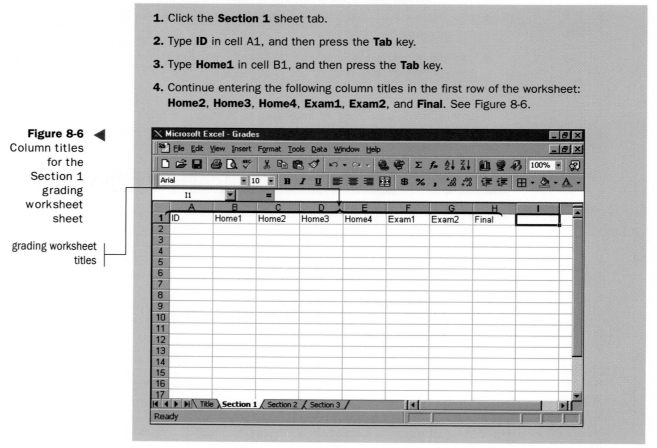

With the titles in place, you'll group the worksheets and use the Excel Fill Across Worksheets command to copy the titles to the other two grading sheets.

To copy the Section 1 column titles:

1. Select the range **A1:H1**.

2. Press and hold down the **Shift** key and click the **Section 3** tab, and then release the Shift key.

3. Click **Edit** on the menu bar, point to **Fill**, and then click **Across Worksheets**.

4. Click the **All** option button, and then click the **OK** button.

The Fill Across Worksheets command only copies the cells that you've selected. When you use the Fill Across Worksheets command, you can copy the contents of the selected cells only, the formats, or both. In the preceding steps, you copied both the cell contents and formats.

Excel

GROUPING AND UNGROUPING WORKSHEETS

- Click the sheet tab of the first worksheet in the group, press and hold down the Shift key, and then click the sheet tab of the last sheet in the group.
- To select non-consecutive worksheets, press and hold down the Ctrl key, and then click the sheet tab of each worksheet you want to include.
- To ungroup worksheets, either click the sheet tab of a work-sheet not in the group, or right-click the tab of one of the sheets in the group, and select Ungroup Sheets on the Shortcut menu.

To begin working with the individual grading sheets again, you must first ungroup them. You can ungroup worksheets in one of two ways: You can click a sheet in the work-book that is not part of the worksheet group, or you can use the Ungroup Sheets com-mand on the worksheet's Shortcut menu, which you'll do in the following steps.

To ungroup the worksheets and view your changes:

1. Right-click the sheet tab of any of the selected sheets.

2. Click **Ungroup Sheets** on the Shortcut menu.

3. Click the **Section 2** tab, and then click the **Section 3** tab. You can see that the titles you entered on the Section 1 worksheet are copied into both the Section 2 and Section 3 worksheets.

With the basic structure of the grading sheets in place, your next task will be to enter formulas that summarize the students' test scores. This information is available in another workbook. For now, close and save the Grades workbook.

To close and save the Grades workbook:

1. Click the **Title** sheet tab, and then press **Ctrl + Home** to return to cell A1.

2. Save and close the Grades workbook, leaving Excel running.

You're now ready to work with some sample data.

Entering Text and Formulas into a Worksheet Group

Professor White has given you the scores of former students in her class from a previous semester. This data has been placed in the Grades2 workbook. Open this workbook now.

To open the Grades2 workbook and save it as Grades3:

1. Open the **Grades2** workbook in the Tutorial.08 folder on your Student Disk and save the workbook as **Grades3**.

The workbook has the same structure as the one you just created. Take a moment to look at the sample data on the worksheet for each section.

To view the sample data in Section 1:

1. Click the **Section 1** sheet tab. The Section 1 worksheet displays scores for all the homework assignments, exams, and the final exam for each of 20 students. See Figure 8-7.

Figure 8-7 ◀
Sample student scores in the Section 1 worksheet

sample student scores

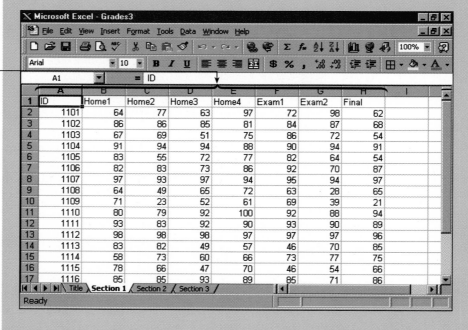

2. Look at the Section 2 and Section 3 worksheets, and verify that they also contain sample scores, and then return to the Section 1 worksheet.

As you look over the grading sheets, you realize that you still have to create a column for each student's overall score. In Professor White's grading system, homework is 20 percent of the grade, the two mid-term exams are 40 percent, and the final exam is 40 percent. To create this column for all three grading sheets, you could add a column to the Section 1 grading sheet that calculates this weighted average and then use the Fill Across Worksheets command to transfer the formula to the remaining sheets. Another option, which will save you a step, is to group the three grading sheets together and enter the formula simultaneously in all three sheets. You'll try this method now.

To add the weighted average to all grading sheets:

1. With the Section 1 tab still selected, press and hold down the **Shift** key and click the **Section 3** tab to group the worksheets. Notice that the word "[Group]" appears in the title bar, indicating that a group is selected.

2. Click cell **I1**, type **Overall**, and then press the **Enter** key. Now you'll enter the formula for the weighted averages.

3. In cell I2, type **=0.2*AVERAGE(B2:E2)+0.4*AVERAGE(F2:G2)+0.4*H2** and then press the **Enter** key. The first student's average score of 73.85 appears in cell I2. Now you'll copy the formula to calculate the averages for the rest of the students.

   TROUBLE? If pressing the Enter key does not select cell I2, your installation of Excel might have been set up to use the Enter key in a different way. Use the mouse to select cell I2 instead.

4. Select the range **I2:I21**.

5. Click **Edit** on the menu bar, point to **Fill**, and then click **Down**.

The weighted average scores for the Section 1 worksheet are displayed in Figure 8-8.

Figure 8-8
Weighted
averages for
sample student
scores

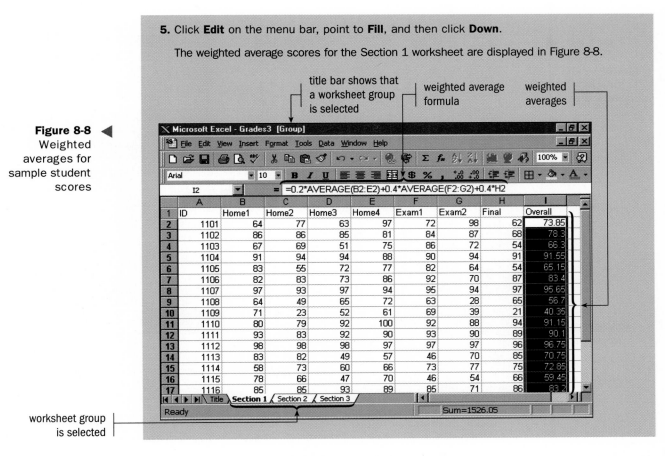

title bar shows that
a worksheet group
is selected

weighted average
formula

weighted
averages

worksheet group
is selected

Since you have grouped the worksheets, the formulas you entered in the Section 1 worksheet should also have been entered in the corresponding cells on the other worksheets in the group. To check that this actually occurred, view the Section 2 worksheet. You can view different sheets in the group without ungrouping the worksheets.

To view the Section 2 worksheet:

1. Click the **Section 2** sheet tab.

The worksheet displays the new column of weighted averages shown in Figure 8-9.

Figure 8-9
Weighted averages for Section 2 sample scores

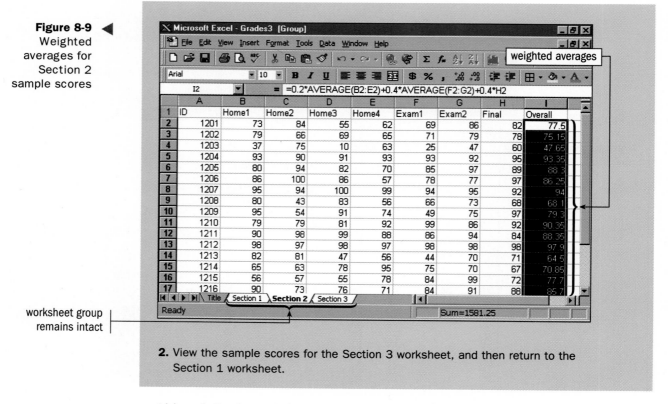

2. View the sample scores for the Section 3 worksheet, and then return to the Section 1 worksheet.

Although Professor White's grading sheet from last semester included only the individual scores for each test and the weighted average for each student, it would probably be helpful for her and her TAs to see the section average for each homework or exam. Then they could quickly see how the whole section scored on an exam or homework assignment. To create section averages, you will add an additional row to each grading sheet that averages the scores entered into the columns.

To insert a formula calculating homework and exam averages:

1. Click cell **A22**, type **Average**, and then press the **Tab** key.

2. In cell B22, type **=AVERAGE(B2:B21)** and then press the **Tab** key. The value 79 appears in cell B22.

3. Select the range **B22:I22**.

4. Click **Edit** on the menu bar, point to **Fill**, and then click **Right**.

Figure 8-10 displays the Section 1 averages for homework assignments and exams.

Figure 8-10
Section 1
averages for
homework
assignments
and exams

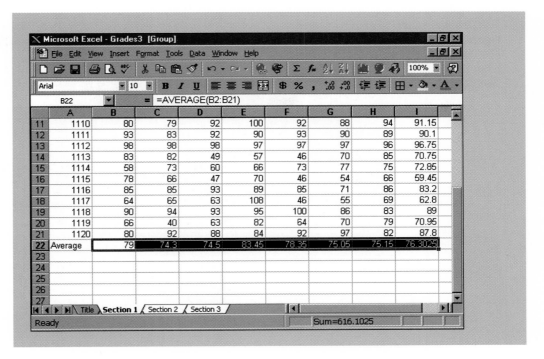

	A	B	C	D	E	F	G	H	I
11	1110	80	79	92	100	92	88	94	91.15
12	1111	93	83	92	90	93	90	89	90.1
13	1112	98	98	98	97	97	97	96	96.75
14	1113	83	82	49	57	46	70	85	70.75
15	1114	58	73	60	66	73	77	75	72.85
16	1115	78	66	47	70	46	54	66	59.45
17	1116	85	85	93	89	85	71	86	83.2
18	1117	64	65	63	108	46	55	69	62.8
19	1118	90	94	93	95	100	86	83	89
20	1119	66	40	63	82	64	70	79	70.95
21	1120	80	92	88	84	92	97	82	87.8
22	Average	79	74.3	74.5	83.45	78.35	75.05	75.15	76.3025
23									
24									
25									
26									
27									

Title / **Section 1** / Section 2 / Section 3

Ready   Sum=616.1025

Since the three grading sheets are still grouped together, the formulas in the Section 1 worksheet are also entered into the Section 2 and Section 3 worksheets.

Now that you have entered the formulas that will calculate the section averages Professor White and her TAs need, you'll now format the worksheet to make it attractive and readable.

Formatting a Worksheet Group

You have used worksheet groups to insert formulas and text into more than one worksheet at once. You can also use groups to simultaneously format the appearance of multiple worksheets. You decide to add decimals to the test scores, and use one of the Excel built-in worksheet designs to format the column titles and the test scores on your grading sheets.

To format the column averages, totals, and scores:

1. Make sure the Section 1 worksheet is selected, and that the three section worksheets are still grouped.

2. Select the range **I2:I21**, and then click the **Increase Decimal** button on the Excel toolbar.

3. Select the range **B22:I22**, and then click the **Increase Decimal** button on the Excel toolbar three times.

4. Select the range **A1:I22**, click **Format** on the menu bar, and then click **AutoFormat**.

5. Click **Classic 3** from the Table format list, and then click the **OK** button.

6. Press **Ctrl + Home** to return to cell A1.

   The worksheet is now formatted with the Classic 3 AutoFormat. See Figure 8-11.

Figure 8-11 ◄
Formatted
Section 1
worksheet

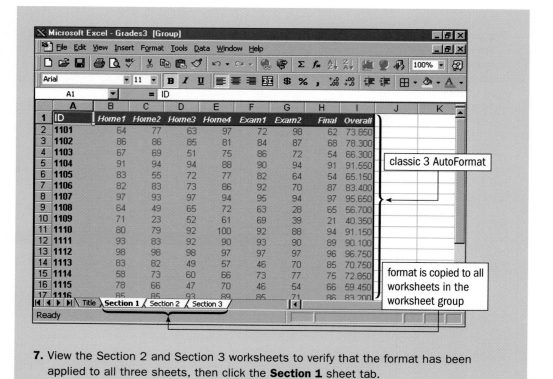

7. View the Section 2 and Section 3 worksheets to verify that the format has been applied to all three sheets, then click the **Section 1** sheet tab.

Creating a Summary Worksheet

Now that you have used sample scores in your workbook to calculate student and section averages, and formatted the worksheets, you'll now summarize the data from the three sections into a single worksheet. Using the summary worksheet, the TAs can get a quick overview of how the sections are performing.

First, you'll create the summary worksheet. You can save time by using the techniques you've learned so far to copy the format of the grading sheets into the new summary worksheet. First insert a blank sheet at the end of the workbook.

To insert the summary sheet at the end of the workbook:

1. Right-click the **Section 1** tab, and then click **Ungroup Sheets** on the Shortcut menu.

2. Right-click the **Section 1** tab again, click **Insert** on the shortcut menu and then double-click the **Worksheet** icon.

3. Drag the new worksheet to the end of the workbook, and then rename it **Summary**.

Next, you will use the Fill Across Worksheets command to copy only the formats from the Section 3 worksheet into the Summary worksheet. After copying the formats, you'll copy the column titles.

To copy the formats and column titles into the Summary worksheet:

1. Click the **Section 3** tab, and then press and hold down the **Shift** key, and click the **Summary** tab.

2. Select the cell range **A1:I22**.

3. Click **Edit** on the menu bar, point to **Fill**, and then click **Across Worksheets**. The Fill Across Worksheets dialog box opens, asking if you want to fill the contents, formats, or both.

4. Click the **Formats** option button, and then click the **OK** button. Now, you'll copy the column titles to the Summary worksheet.

5. Select the cell range **A1:I1**, click **Edit** on the menu bar, point to **Fill**, and then click **Across Worksheets**.

6. Click the **Contents** option button, and then click the **OK** button.

The grading sheet that you used to create the Summary sheet contains information for 20 students, while the Summary sheet will summarize the results from only three sections, so you'll have to remove the unnecessary rows from the table.

To complete the Summary sheet:

1. Ungroup the worksheets and then select the **Summary** sheet.

2. Select the cell range **A5:I21**, click **Edit** on the menu bar, and then click **Delete**.

3. Click the **Shift cells up** option button, and then click the **OK** button.

4. Click cell **A1**, type **Section**, and then press the **Enter** key.

5. Enter the following in column A:

   Cell A2: **1**

   Cell A3: **2**

   Cell A4: **3**

   Cell A5: **All**

6. Press **Ctrl + Home** to return to cell A1.

   Figure 8-12 shows the final layout of the Summary sheet.

Figure 8-12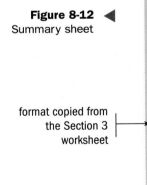
Summary sheet

format copied from
the Section 3
worksheet

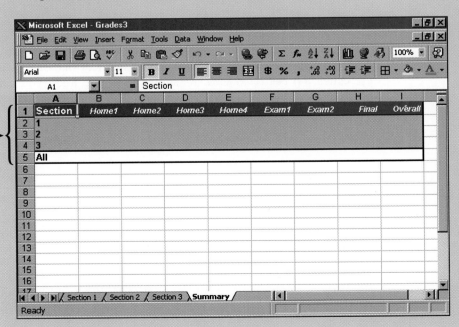

Having set up the Summary sheet, you are ready to start consolidating the information from the individual sections.

Consolidating Data with 3-D References

When you **consolidate** worksheet data, you summarize the results contained in several worksheets (or workbooks) into a single worksheet by using formulas. Consolidation formulas can sum sales figures from several regional sales worksheets, or simply report the values from several different worksheets, in one easy-to-read table. In your grading workbook, you want to add a summary worksheet that consolidates grading information from the individual sections, showing the section averages for each homework assignment and exam. You'll then use this information to calculate an overall average, pooling information from all the sections that the TA is teaching. Figure 8-13 shows a diagram of the consolidation you'll be creating.

Figure 8-13 ◄
Consolidating
the Section
worksheets

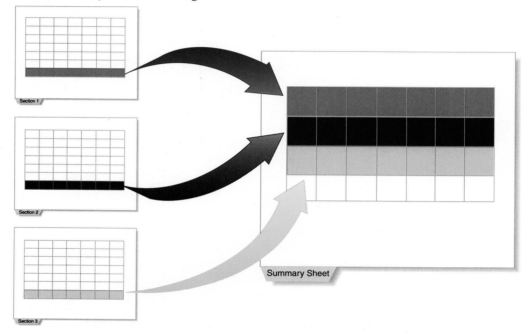

To consolidate data in a workbook, you need to know some of the basic rules for referencing cells in other worksheets. Cell references that specify cells in other worksheets are called **3-D cell references**. As shown in Figure 8-14, you can consider the rows and columns as representing two dimensions. The worksheets themselves comprise the third dimension.

Figure 8-14 ◀
The three
dimensions of
a workbook

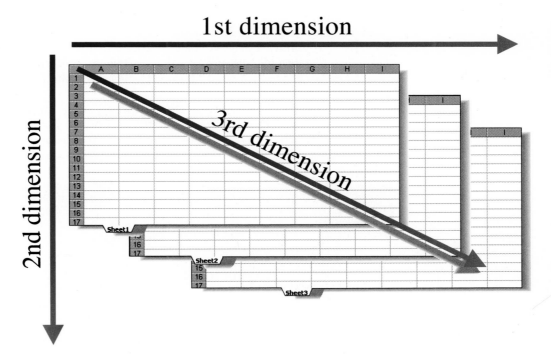

A 3-D cell reference must include not only the rows and columns that contain the data you want to reference, but also the sheet location. The general form of a 3-D cell reference is:

Sheet Range!Cell Range

The **sheet range** is the range of worksheets that you're referencing. It can be a single sheet or a group of worksheets (if the group is contiguous). The **cell range** portion of the 3-D cell reference is the range of cells on the worksheet or worksheets. For example, if you want to reference the cell range B2:B21 on the Section 1 worksheet, the 3-D cell reference is 'Section 1'!B2:B21. An exclamation point always separates the sheet range from the cell range.

If the names of the worksheets contain spaces, you must enclose the sheet range within single quotation marks. For example, if a 3-D cell reference refers to cell B21 on the Section 1 worksheet, you would enter the sheet reference as 'Section 1'!B21. On the other hand, cell B21 on the Summary worksheet would have a 3-D cell reference of Summary!B21, with no quotation marks.

A sheet range that covers a group of worksheets must include the first and last sheet names in the range, separated by a colon. For example, the 3-D cell reference 'Section 1:Section 3'!A1, refers to the A1 cells in the Section 1, Section 2, and Section 3 worksheets. When you are including several worksheets in the sheet range, you do not enclose each worksheet name in quotation marks, even if the sheet name contains spaces—just the sheet range. In other words, the sheet range 'Section 1:Section 3' is correct, but 'Section 1':'Section 3' will cause Excel to display an error message.

You can use functions to cover the same cell range on several different worksheets with a 3-D cell reference. For example, if you wanted to calculate the average of the I22 cells in the three grading sheets from the Grades workbook, you would use the following function:

=AVERAGE('Section 1:Section 3'!I22)

You enter 3-D cell references either by typing the reference or by selecting the appropriate cells with the mouse as you're entering the formula. If you are using the mouse, you must first select the sheet range, followed by the cell range.

You should use caution when working with 3-D cell references. Calculations or charts based on data on a worksheet might become inaccurate if you move the worksheet. Similarly, if you move a new worksheet into the middle of a sheet range referred to elsewhere by a 3-D formula reference, the data on the new worksheet might be included in the calculation. It's generally a good idea not to move worksheets around in your workbook if they contain 3-D cell references.

In the range B2:I5 of the Summary worksheet, you'll create consolidation formulas that will display the average scores from each of the three sections taught by the TA. Your formulas will contain 3-D cell references that refer to the appropriate cells on the individual grading sheets. You'll start by entering the averages from the Section 1 worksheet.

REFERENCE window	**INSERTING A FORMULA USING A 3-D CELL REFERENCE**
	■ Select the cell where you want the formula to appear. ■ Type = and the function name, if any. ■ Click the sheet tab for the sheet containing the cell (or cells) that you want to reference. ■ To reference a range of worksheets, press and hold down the Shift key, and then click the tab of the last sheet in the range. ■ Click the cell range you want to reference. ■ Finish the formula and then press the Enter key.

You'll begin by consolidating the averages from Section 1 into the Summary worksheet.

To insert the Section 1 averages into the Summary worksheet:

1. Click cell **B2** on the Summary worksheet.

2. Type **=** (an equal sign)

3. Click the **Section 1** sheet tab (you might have to scroll through the sheet tabs to see it.)

4. Click cell **B22** and then press the **Enter** key.

   The value 79 appears in the Summary sheet cell B2. Now go back and view the formula.

5. Click cell **B2** and see that the formula ='Section 1'!B22 appears in the formula bar. Now that you know the formula is correct, you'll copy it to the other summary cells for Section 1.

6. Select the range **B2:I2** on the Summary sheet.

7. Click **Edit** on the menu bar, point to **Fill**, and then click **Right**.

   The 3-D cell references for the Section 1 worksheet averages now display on the Summary worksheet. See Figure 8-15.

Figure 8-15 ◀
Summary
scores for the
Section 1
grading
worksheet

3-D cell reference ─

Section 1 grade
averages ─

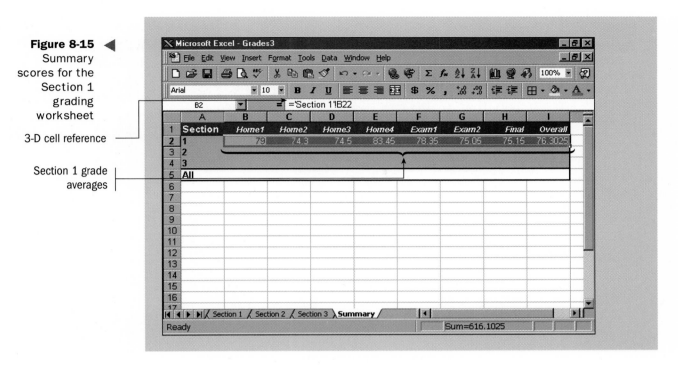

Now you'll fill in the rest of the table for the Section 2 and Section 3 sample grades.

To insert the Section 2 and Section 3 averages:

1. Click cell **B3**.

2. Type **=** and then click the **Section 2** sheet tab.

3. Click cell **B22** and then press the **Enter** key. The value 79.2 appears in the Summary sheet cell B3.

4. Select the range **B3:I3** on the Summary sheet, click **Edit** on the menu bar, point to **Fill**, and then click **Right**. The Section 2 averages are copied to the Summary sheet.

5. Click cell **B4**.

6. Type **=** and then click the **Section 3** tab.

7. Click cell **B22** and then press the **Enter** key. The value 74.3 appears in the Summary sheet cell B4.

8. Select the range **B4:I4** on the Summary sheet.

9. Click **Edit** on the menu bar, point to **Fill**, and then click **Right**. The Section 3 averages appear.

10. Press **Ctrl + Home** to return to cell A1.

   Figure 8-16 shows the Summary sheet with the average scores from each section.

Figure 8-16 ◄
Summary
scores for all
grading
worksheets

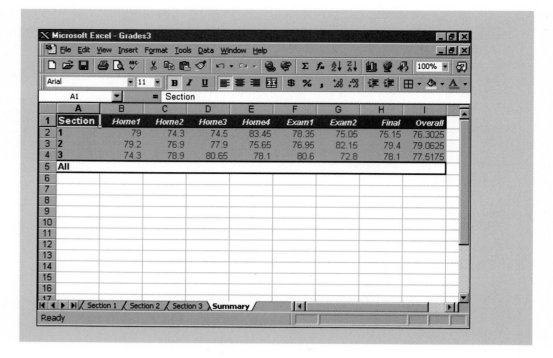

Now you'll complete the final part of the summary table, the average across all sections for homework assignments and exams.

To insert overall averages:

1. With the Summary sheet still selected, click cell **B5**.

2. Type **=AVERAGE(** to begin the function.

3. Click the **Section 1** sheet tab, press and hold down the **Shift** key and click the **Section 3** tab. The formula bar shows that the worksheet range for the three sections has been entered into the function.

4. Click cell **B22**, type **)** (a closing parenthesis), and then press the **Enter** key.

   Excel inserts the formula, "=AVERAGE('Section 1:Section 3'!B22)" into cell B5, displaying the value 77.5.

5. On the Summary sheet, select the range **B5:I5**, and then click **Edit** on the menu bar, point to **Fill**, and click **Right**. The overall averages for all tests for all sections appear in the All row. Now you'll format the numbers to match those on the grading sheets.

6. Select the cell range **B2:I5**, and then click the **Increase Decimal** button ⬚ on the Formatting toolbar three times. All the numbers should now have three decimal places.

7. Press **Ctrl + Home** to return to cell A1.

   Figure 8-17 shows the completed Summary sheet.

Excel

Figure 8-17 ◀
Completed
Summary
worksheet

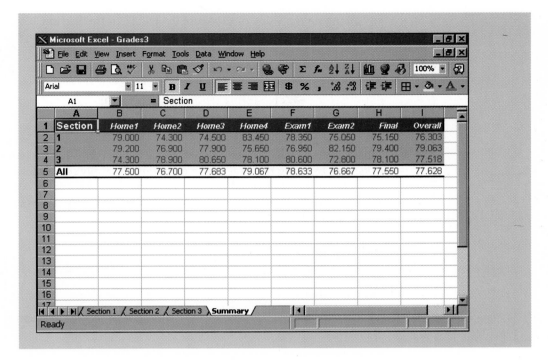

The summary table you've just created will be automatically updated whenever sample scores in the grading sheets are added or changed. To test this feature, you decide to change one of the sample scores in the Section 1 worksheet. First, notice that the current overall average for Section 1 is 76.303 and the average across all three sections is 77.628.

To change one of the values in the Section 1 worksheet:

1. Click the **Section 1** sheet tab.

2. Click cell **H2**, type **92**, and then press the **Enter** key.

3. Click the **Summary** sheet tab.

Figure 8-18 shows the revised values in the Summary worksheet.

Figure 8-18 ◀
Revised
Summary
worksheet

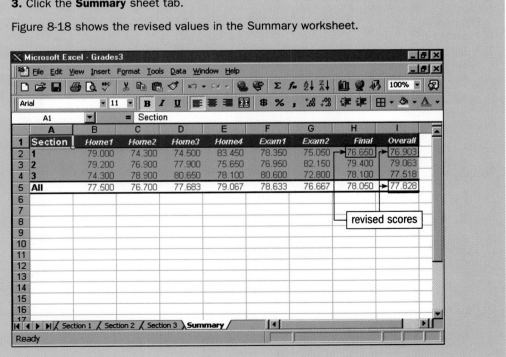

By changing the value of the score in cell H2 of the Section 1 worksheet from 62 to 92, the overall average for Section 1 is increased from 76.303 to 76.903 and the overall average for all sections is automatically increased from 77.628 to 77.828.

Now that you've completed your grading worksheets, you can print them using worksheet groups.

Printing Worksheet Groups

Now that you've completed the grading workbook, you decide to print it, but first you'll set up the pages. You can set up your pages individually, or you can quickly format all the worksheets by using the Page Setup command to apply to all the worksheets in the group. You decide to print the grading sheets and the Summary sheet centered on the page both vertically and horizontally, with the worksheet name in the page header and the workbook name in the page footer.

To print the grading sheets and the Summary sheet:

1. Select the range of worksheets from the **Section 1** to **Summary**.

2. Click **File** on the menu bar, and then click **Page Setup**.

3. Click the **Margins** tab and then click the **Center of page Horizontally** and **Vertically** check boxes.

4. Click the **Header/Footer** tab, click **Section 1** in the Header list box, and then click **Grades3** in the Footer list box to place the worksheet name in the header and the workbook name in the footer for all the worksheets in the group.

   TROUBLE? If Section 1 does not appear in your list box, but Summary does, this just means you clicked the Summary tab first when you selected the range. Click Cancel, reselect the group, then reopen the dialog box and continue.

5. Click the **Print Preview** button and verify that the same page setup has been used for all sheets in the worksheet group, using the Next and Previous buttons at the top of the Preview window to view each sheet. Figure 8-19 displays the Section 1 worksheet in Print Preview.

Figure 8-19 ◀
Print Preview of the Section 1 worksheet

title bar indicates that a worksheet group is selected

grading table centered on page

workbook name

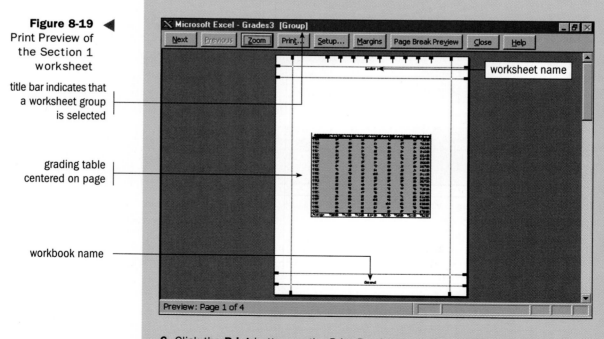

6. Click the **Print** button on the Print Preview toolbar, and then click the **OK** button to print the selected worksheets.

7. Click the **Title** tab so that the next time this worksheet is opened, the user sees the Title sheet.

8. Save and close the Grades 3 workbook.

Using a worksheet group has made it possible to format and print all the grading worksheets at the same time.

Quick Check

1. Explain how to insert a new worksheet directly to the right of the active sheet.

2. What is a worksheet group?

3. How do you select and deselect a worksheet group?

4. How do you copy text and formulas from one worksheet into a range of worksheets?

5. What are the two parts of a 3-D cell reference?

6. What is the 3-D cell reference in the Section 1 worksheet?

7. What is the 3-D cell reference in the Sheet1 through Sheet10 worksheets?

In this session, you have created a workbook with multiple worksheets, inserted and moved worksheets, created worksheet groups, and combined data from separate worksheets into a consolidation worksheet that TAs can use to compare the performance of their discussion sections. In the next session you'll see how templates can help Professor White and the TAs share the workbook you have created.

SESSION
8.2

In this session you will create and use Excel templates. You'll learn how Excel organizes templates on your computer and how to use some of the built-in templates Excel provides.

Using Templates

In the last session you created a workbook that the TAs in Professor White's Calculus lecture will use to maintain grading records for their discussion sections. But how should you make the new workbook available to them? One possibility is to simply give a copy of the workbook to each user. However, there is a potential problem with this approach: Once the file leaves your hands, you have no way of controlling the changes the TAs will make to it. You would like to have a single workbook file that will be available to them, but that will always retain the format you created. One way of doing this is to create a template.

A **template** is a workbook that contains specific content and formatting that you can use as a model for other similar workbooks. A template can include standardized text such as page headers and row and column labels, as well as formulas, macros, and customized menus and toolbars. When you open a template, Excel opens a blank workbook with content and formatting identical to the template. You then add data to the blank workbook and save it as an Excel file with any name you choose. The original template will retain its original design and formats for the next time you or another user need to create another workbook based on it. This is very useful if you want several users to maintain a workbook containing the same types of information. The original workbook design will always be available to them because they will only save files based on the template. The template itself will remain unchanged.

Excel has several templates that are automatically installed on your hard disk when you install the program. In fact, whenever you start Excel and see the blank workbook called Book1, you are actually using a workbook that's based on a template known as the **default template**. Excel also includes several specialized templates that you can use for specific tasks, such as creating an accounting ledger or sales worksheet.

Opening a Workbook Based on a Template

To see how templates work, you'll create a new workbook based on one of the built-in Excel templates.

> **REFERENCE window**
>
> **OPENING A WORKBOOK BASED ON A TEMPLATE**
>
> ■ Click File and then click New.
> ■ Click the icon representing that template you want to use.
> ■ Click the OK button.

You'll open an Excel Invoice template, so you can get an idea of how the grading template you'll create for Professor White will look when the TAs open it.

To open a built-in template:

1. If you took a break at the end of the last session, make sure Excel is running.

2. Click **File** on the menu bar, and then click **New**. The New dialog box opens.

   TROUBLE? If a new, blank workbook opened instead of the New dialog box, you probably clicked the New button on the Standard toolbar. In order to open a template, you must use the New command from the File menu, not the New button on the toolbar.

3. Click the **Spreadsheet Solutions** tab.

   The tab displays icons representing templates, shown in Figure 8-20.

Figure 8-20 ◀
Built-in templates provided by Excel

built-in templates ─────

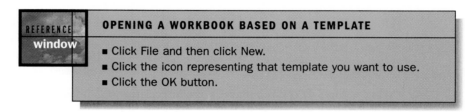

TROUBLE? Depending upon how Office 97 or Excel was installed on your system, you might see different workbook templates. If you don't see the invoice template, open any other template.

Next, you'll open a blank workbook based on the Invoice template.

4. Click the **INVOICE** icon and then click the **OK** button.

5. Click the **Enable Macros** option button to enable the macros that are included with the INVOICE template.

Excel opens the workbook shown in Figure 8-21.

Figure 8-21 ◀
INVOICE template

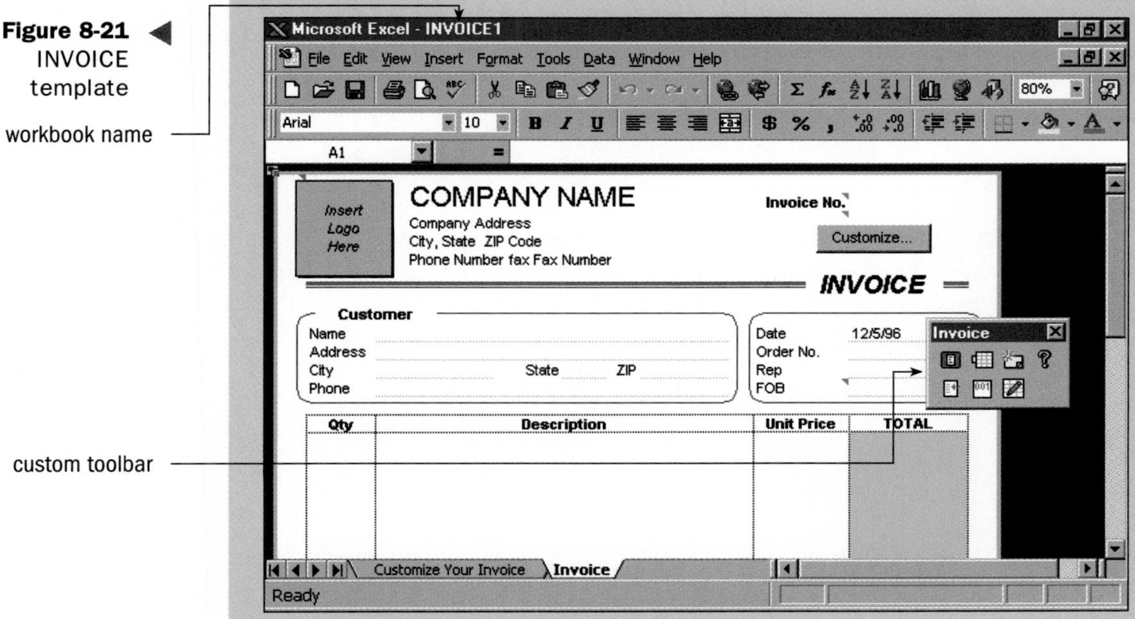

workbook name

custom toolbar

Figure 8-21 displays a workbook based on the INVOICE template. Notice that the name in the title bar is not INVOICE but INVOICE1. Just as the blank workbooks you see when you first open Excel have the sequential names Book1, Book2 and so forth, a workbook based on a template always displays the name of the template, followed by a sequential number, in the title bar. Any additions you make to this workbook will only affect the new document you are creating, and will not affect the INVOICE template itself. However if you want to save your changes, you would save the Invoice1 workbook in the same way you save the Book1 workbook that you see when you first start Excel. The next time you create a new workbook based on this template, you'll be presented with the same workbook and workbook features.

Having seen how to create a workbook based on a template, you can close the Invoice1 workbook. You do not need to save your changes.

To close the INVOICE1 workbook:

1. Click **File** on the menu bar, and then click **Close**.

2. Click the **No** button when prompted to save your changes.

Now that you've seen how to access a template, you can see how useful a template would be for Professor White's TAs. You can make your grading sheet into a template, make it available to the TAs, and they can create grading sheet documents based on your template. At regular intervals, they can submit their sheets to you or Professor White, who can easily consolidate the information because it will have the same structure and format on all the worksheets.

Next you'll learn how to make your workbook into a template, and learn about storing templates in the correct location, so it is available to those who need it.

Creating and Storing a Workbook Template

To create a template, you simply save an Excel workbook as a template file using the Save As command. Excel will then automatically convert the workbook to a template file. You decide to try this with the grading workbook you created in the last session.

REFERENCE window	SAVING A WORKBOOK AS A TEMPLATE
	■ Click File and then click Save As.
	■ Click the Save as type list arrow, and then select Template.
	■ Click the Save button.

A workbook named Grades4 has been placed on your Student Disk. The Grades4 workbook contains the same formulas and formats that you created in the last session, except that the sample data has been removed. You'll open the Grades4 workbook and save it as a template file now.

To save the Grades4 workbook as a template file:

1. Open the **Grades4** workbook in the Tutorial 8 folder on your Student Disk. Notice that it has the same structure as the previous workbook. Now you'll save it as a template.

2. Click **File** on the menu bar, and then click **Save As** to open the Save As dialog box.

3. Type **Grading Sheet** in the File name text box, and then press the **Tab** key.

4. Click the **Save as type** list arrow, and click **Template** in the list.

5. In the Save in list box, locate the Tutorial.08 folder on your Student Disk.

   TROUBLE? When you select the Template file type, Excel might automatically open a folder named "Template." As you'll see, Excel is preset to put all template files in this folder. But since you might not have access to your computer network's Template folder, you should save the template file to your Student Disk.

6. Click the **Save** button. Excel saves the Grades4 workbook as a template named Grading Sheet on your Student Disk.

7. Close the Grading Sheet template.

Once you've converted a workbook to a template, you have to make the template accessible to other users. To do this, you have to understand how Excel stores templates.

Using the Templates Folder

To use a template file like the one you just created, the template must be placed in the Templates folder that is in the Microsoft Office folder on your computer or network. You cannot create a workbook based on your template unless it's in the Templates folder.

Depending upon your computer environment, you might not be able to modify the contents of your Templates folder. If Excel and Microsoft Office are installed on a computer network, only the network administrator may have permission to modify it. For that reason, the material that follows is provided for you to review, but you might not be able to perform the steps on your system. If you would like to work with the Templates

Excel

folder yourself, but are not sure if you have access to it, ask your instructor or the technical support person in your computer lab.

The exact location of the Templates folder depends on how Microsoft Office was installed on your computer. For example, if the Microsoft Office folder is located on drive C of your computer, then the Templates folder is located in the C:\Program Files\Microsoft Office\Templates directory. Figure 8-22 shows the location of the Templates folder as in Windows Explorer.

Figure 8-22 ◀
Contents of a
Templates
folder

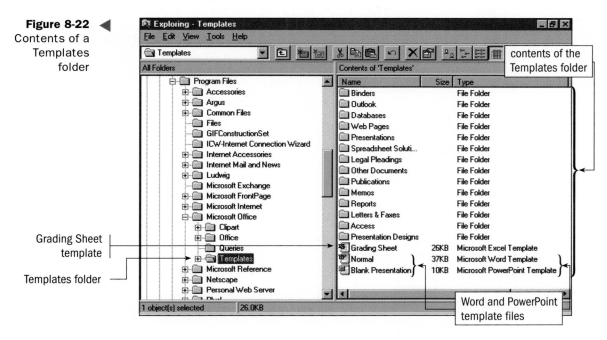

If you did have access to the Templates directory, your Grading worksheet would appear as in Figure 8-22. Template files are displayed with a different icon than workbooks. Windows 95 displays Excel workbooks with a 🗒 icon and Excel templates with a 🗒 icon. Template files you use in other Office 97 applications (in this case, Word and PowerPoint) appear in this folder as well.

When a template is placed in the Templates folder, its icon will appear on the General tab in the New dialog box. Figure 8-23 shows the Excel New dialog box that corresponds to the Templates folder from Figure 8-22. It displays your Grading Sheet template but not the Word or PowerPoint template files, because you are viewing it from within Excel.

Figure 8-23 ◀
New dialog box
containing the
Grading Sheet
template

icon for the Grading
sheet template

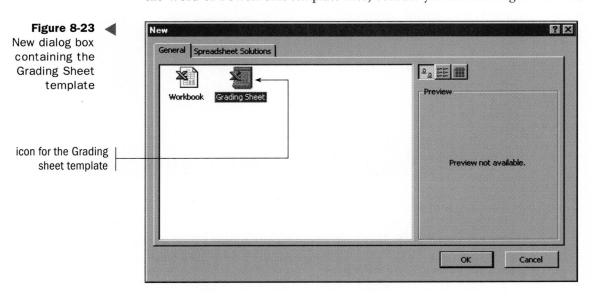

The Templates folder can include subfolders. These subfolders are used to organize and group the different Office 97 template files. The Templates folder shown in Figure 8-22 contains several subfolders. Subfolders are displayed in the New dialog box as separate dialog sheets. Not all subfolders are displayed as tabs, however; only those subfolders that contain Excel template files will appear in the Excel New dialog box.

You could move your template file to a folder called "Classroom" to distinguish it from other templates that the TAs might be using. Figure 8-24 shows the contents of a Classroom subfolder with the Grading Sheet template file you created earlier.

Figure 8-24 ◄
Classroom
subfolder of the
Templates
folder

Grading Sheet
template

Classroom subfolder
of the Templates
folder

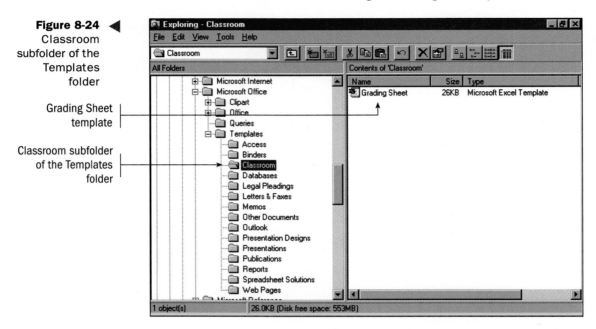

When TAs want to access this template, they can use the Excel File New command and then click the Classroom tab to display the template, as shown in Figure 8-25.

Figure 8-25 ◄
Classroom tab
in the New
dialog box

Grading sheet
template icon

Classroom tab

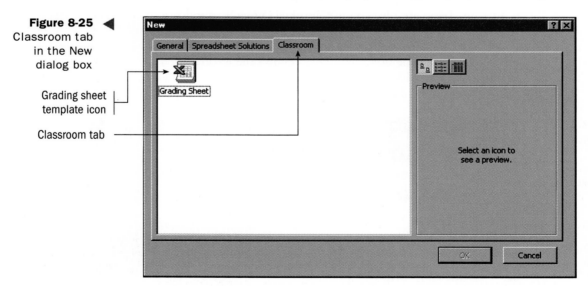

Because MidWest University has installed Office 97 on the campus network, your Grading Sheet template would be readily available to Professor White's four TAs, as shown in Figure 8-26. If you decide to make changes to the template, you can place the updated template file on the network. The TAs could then easily create new workbooks based on your revised template.

Excel

Figure 8-26 ◀
Accessing the
Grading Sheet
template

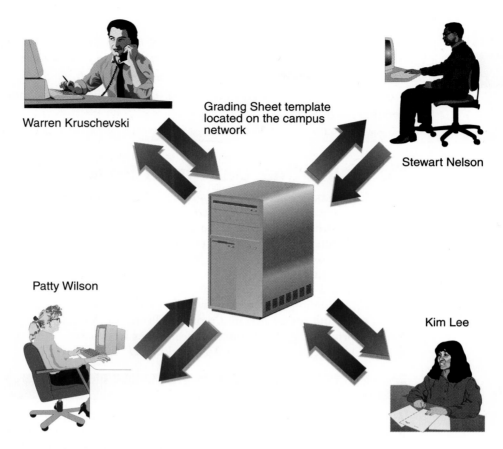

Warren Kruschevski

Grading Sheet template
located on the campus
network

Stewart Nelson

Patty Wilson

Kim Lee

If your template was indeed placed on the university network, TAs would then use it to create their grading workbooks, which they would then turn in to you or Professor White. You'll use their workbooks created from your template to help you design the next version of the Grading Sheet workbook.

Quick Check

1. What is a template?

2. How do you save a file as a template?

3. Where must you store your templates?

4. What is the default workbook template?

5. How would you place a template into its own tab in the File New dialog box?

6. What are two advantages of using a template instead of simply distributing a workbook file?

You have created the grading workbook template and learned about the importance of placing them in the correct location. In the next session you'll learn how to consolidate information from the TAs' completed workbooks into a single workbook that Professor White will use to evaluate all the sections of her Calculus 223 course.

SESSION 8.3

In this session you will learn how to consolidate information from several workbooks. You'll learn how Excel retrieves and updates information from those workbooks and how you can manually update that information yourself. Finally, you'll learn how to create a lookup table and how to use the Excel lookup functions to retrieve information from the table.

Consolidating Data from Several Workbooks

In the last session you saved your grading sheet as a template. Since then, the template has been made available to Professor White's four TAs. They have used the template to create a workbook containing the grades they assigned to students in their sections. Professor White would like you to create a workbook that consolidates the data from the TAs' workbooks into a single file. She'll use the consolidated file to monitor the performance of the students and the TAs as the semester progresses.

A workbook has been created for you, with the name "White." It has a title worksheet and a consolidation worksheet in which you'll place the summary grades from each TA. You'll open and resave this in a moment. Professor White wants you to place summary grade information on the Summary sheet of her workbook. To do this, you'll have to create a 3-D cell reference to each TA's workbook.

3-D Cell References to Other Workbooks

A 3-D cell reference to a workbook is similar to the 3-D cell references you created earlier in Session 1. The difference is that you'll add the name of the workbook to the reference, instead of the name of a worksheet. The general form of a 3-D cell reference that includes the workbook is:

Location[*Workbook name*]*Sheet Range*!*Cell Range*

The **location** is the drive and folder that contains the workbook to which you are creating the reference. For example, assume you want to create a reference to the cell range B5:E5 on the "Summary Info" worksheet of the Sales.xls workbook, and the workbook is located in the Business folder on drive E of your computer. In this case, the 3-D cell reference is:

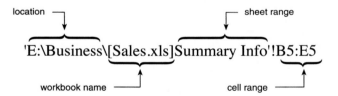

As you did earlier when you used sheet references with the sample data, you enclose the Location[Workbook name]Sheet Range portion of the 3-D cell reference in single quotation marks if there are any blank spaces in the location, workbook, or worksheet names. For example, 'E:\Business\[Sales.xls]Summary Info' needs quotation marks, while E:\Business\[Sales.xls]Summary does not.

If you are referring to workbooks located in the same folder as the active workbook, you do not need to include the location information in your cell reference. Excel will assume that, if you do not specify a location, you want to use workbooks located in the active workbook's folder, and it will add the location information for you automatically.

The four TAs assigned to Professor White's lecture have stored their grading sheets in the following files: TA1, TA2, TA3, and TA4. Since each TA has created his or her workbook from the template you created earlier, you know where the relevant information has been stored. For example, you know that the name of each TA should be entered on the Title sheet of each workbook in cell B1 (recall Figure 8-3). With that in mind, you can create a reference to that cell in Professor White's Summary Grades workbook.

To open the workbook and add a reference to each TA's name:

1. If you took a break after the last session, make sure Excel is running.

2. Open the **White** workbook in the Tutorial.08 folder on your Student Disk, and save it as **Summary Grades**.

3. Click the **Summary** tab.

4. Click cell **A2**.

   Now you'll enter the 3-D cell reference that will enter the name of the first TA in this cell.

5. Type **=[TA1]Title!B1** and then press the **Enter** key. The name "Stewart Nelson" appears in cell A2.

6. Click the **A2** cell again and notice that Excel has automatically inserted the path indicating the location of the TA1 workbook file into the cell reference.

Next, you'll continue entering the references to the remaining TA names. You'll use a reference to the TA2 workbook to enter Patty Wilson's name in cell A3, TA3 to enter Kim Lee's name in A4, and TA4 to enter Warren Kruschevski's in A5.

To complete the column of TA names:

1. Click cell **A3**.

2. Type **=[TA2]Title!B1** and then press the **Enter** key. Patty Wilson's name appears in cell A3.

3. In cell A4, enter **=[TA3]Title!B1**. Kim Lee's name appears.

4. In cell A5 enter **=[TA4]Title!B1**. Warren Kruschevski's name appears.

Figure 8-27 displays the completed column of TA names.

Figure 8-27 ◀
TA names pulled from the grading sheet workbook

TA names from the TA1, TA2, TA3, and TA4 workbooks

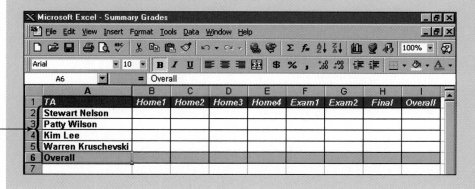

Next, you'll need to reference the average scores that are recorded on the Summary sheet of each TA's workbook in cells B5:I5 (see Figure 8-17). As with the column of TA names, you can create columns of homework and exam averages, but here you can use the Fill Right command, since the structure of the Summary sheet from Figure 8-17 is identical to the Summary sheet in the Summary Grades workbook. Start with the grades for Stewart Nelson's discussion sections in row 2.

To create a reference to Stewart Nelson's grading averages:

1. Click cell **B2**.

2. Type **=[TA1]Summary!B5** and then press the **Enter** key. The value 77.50 appears in cell B2.

3. Select the range **B2:I2**.

4. Click **Edit** on the menu bar, point to **Fill**, and then click **Right**.

Excel fills in the average scores for homework and exams for Stewart Nelson's discussion sections. See Figure 8-28. Excel has automatically inserted the location of Stewart's workbook in the formula for cell B2.

Figure 8-28 ◀
Summary scores from the TA1 workbook

homework and exam scores from the TA1 workbook

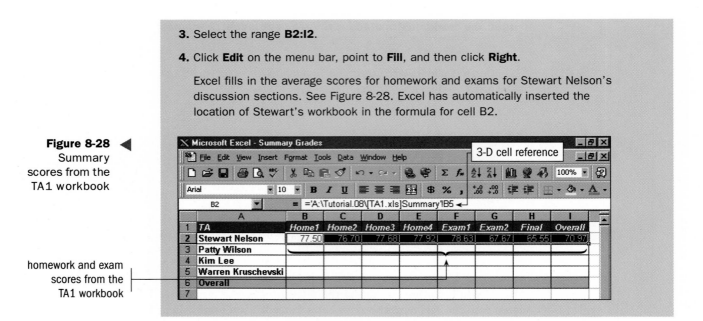

Next you'll fill in the scores for the other TAs. Patty Wilson's scores are in the TA2 workbook, Kim Lee's are in TA3, and Warren Kruschevski's are in TA4.

To add references to the rest of the exam scores:

1. Click cell **B3**.

2. Type **=[TA2]Summary!B5**, and then press the **Enter** key. The value 79.07 appears in cell B3.

3. Select the range **B3:I3** and fill to the right using the keyboard shortcut **Ctrl + R**.

   Note that you can use the keyboard shortcut Ctrl + R in place of the Edit, Fill, and Right commands.

4. Click cell **B4**, type **=[TA3]Summary!B5**, and then press the **Enter** key. The value 83.60 appears.

5. Select the range **B4:I4**, and then press **Ctrl + R** to fill to the right.

6. Click cell **B5**, type **=[TA4]Summary!B5**, and then press the **Enter** key. The value 84.63 appears.

7. Select the range **B5:I5**, and then press **Ctrl + R** to fill to the right.

   Your screen should display all the average scores for each TA, as shown in Figure 8-29.

Figure 8-29 ◀
Summary scores from the TA1–TA4 workbooks

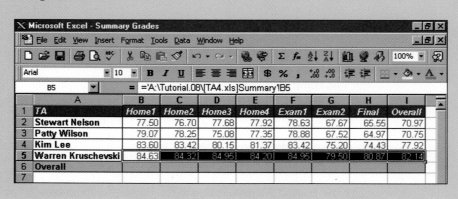

Excel

Finally, Professor White would like you to calculate the overall average scores for the four TAs. You can place these values in row 6.

To calculate the average of the TA grades:

1. Click cell **B6**.

2. Enter the formula **=AVERAGE(B2:B5)**. The value 81.20 appears in cell B6.

3. Select the range **B6:I6**, and then press **Ctrl + R** to fill to the right.

4. Press **Ctrl + Home** to return to cell A1.

    The average scores for each TA appear in row 6 of the summary worksheet. See Figure 8-30.

Figure 8-30 ◀
Completed summary worksheet

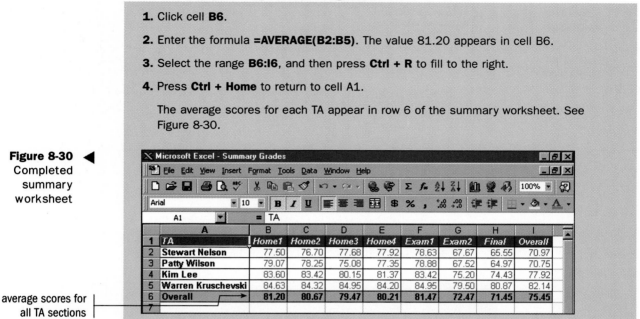

average scores for all TA sections

From your Summary sheet, Professor White will be able to see that two of the TAs, Stewart Nelson and Patty Wilson, have section averages well below the other two. She will most likely want to look into the reasons for this.

When you created the 3-D references in Professor White's Summary Grades workbook, you actually created a link between the Summary workbook and the TA's workbooks You'll learn how to examine these links in the next section.

Working with Linked Workbooks

When you create a 3-D cell reference to another workbook, you are also creating a **link**, or a "live" connection, between one workbook and another. Because the workbooks are linked, a change in one TA's workbook will cause a change in the Summary workbook. You've already seen this principle in action within workbooks when you changed a value in one of the section grading sheets and saw the Summary sheet values update automatically.

Professor White has talked to a student who feels that a test item was incorrectly marked wrong on her final exam. After reviewing the problem, Professor White decides that the student is right, which will increase her final exam score from 85 to 95. The student's ID number is 1107, and she is in Stewart Nelson's first discussion section. If Professor White wants to update the grading sheet, how will she know which workbook to access? She can view the list of linked workbooks.

To view the list of links:

1. Click **Edit** on the menu bar, and then click **Links**.

    Figure 8-31 shows the list of workbooks linked to the Summary Grades workbook.

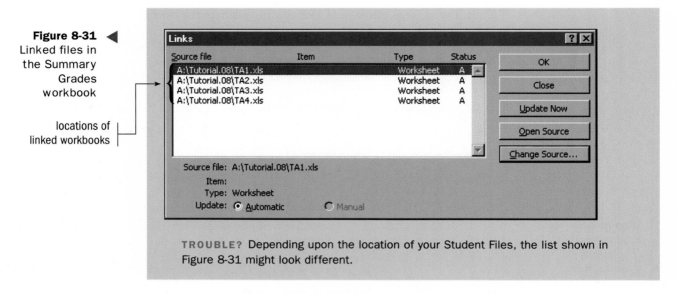

Figure 8-31
Linked files in
the Summary
Grades
workbook

locations of
linked workbooks

TROUBLE? Depending upon the location of your Student Files, the list shown in
Figure 8-31 might look different.

Professor White knows that because Stewart Nelson covers the first set of discussion
sections, his grades will be in the TA1 workbook.

REFERENCE
window

OPENING A LINKED WORKBOOK

- Click Edit and then click Links.
- Click the name of the workbook you want to open from the list
  of linked workbooks.
- Click the Open Source button.

Professor White can open Stewart Nelson's workbook through the Links dialog box,
which you'll do next.

To open the TA1 workbook:

1. Click **TA1.xls** in the Source file list box.

2. Click the **Open Source** button.

   Excel opens the TA1 workbook.

3. Click the **Section 1** tab, type **95** in cell H8, and then press the **Enter** key.
   Figure 8-32 shows the new values.

Figure 8-32 ◀
Section 1
worksheet
revised grade

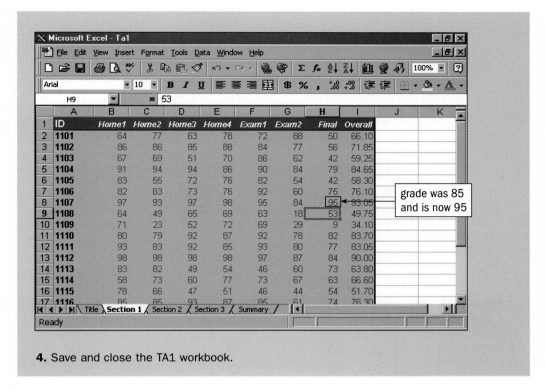

4. Save and close the TA1 workbook.

After changing the student's final exam grade, the average final exam grade in Stewart Nelson's discussion sections, in cell H2 of the Summary worksheet, has increased from 65.55 to 65.72 and the average of his overall scores in cell I2 has increased from 70.97 to 71.04.

Opening and changing a source file in this way will automatically update the formulas to which it is linked in the workbook. If the Summary workbook is closed when you change the source, when you reopen it Excel will ask you if you want to update links to other files. If you click the Yes button, Excel retrieves any new or updated data. This guarantees that the workbook contains accurate and timely information.

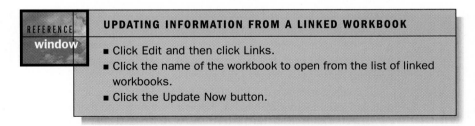

REFERENCE window

UPDATING INFORMATION FROM A LINKED WORKBOOK

■ Click Edit and then click Links.
■ Click the name of the workbook to open from the list of linked workbooks.
■ Click the Update Now button.

Professor White would like to know what would happen if one of her TAs makes changes to the linked file while she is working on the Summary Grades workbook. You explain that when this happens, she can manually update the link to that workbook. For example, what if, while she was changing the grade of the student in Stewart Nelson's discussion section, Kim Lee was making changes in her grading sheet workbook? In that case, Professor White could retrieve the new information from Kim's source file by manually updating the link. You show her how to update the link to Kim Lee's grading sheet, located in the TA3 workbook.

To update information from the TA3 workbook:

1. Click **Edit** on the menu bar, and then click **Links**.

2. Click **TA3.xls** in the Source file list box.

3. Click the **Update Now** button.

4. Click the **OK** button.

Any changes that Kim may have saved to her TA3.xls workbook will now be incorporated into the Summary Grades workbook. Since the end of the semester is approaching, Professor White turns her attention to assigning final letter grades to each of her students, which she will do by using lookup tables.

Using Lookup Tables

Professor White has reviewed each of the grades her TAs recorded. She has noted the overall average scores and has opened the workbooks containing the individual scores. Based on what she has seen, she has decided on a grading scale that determines the letter grades she wants to assign to each score category. Figure 8-33 shows the grading scale and the letter grades she has created.

Figure 8-33 ◄
Professor White's grading scale

compare values ⟶

OVERALL SCORE	GRADE	GRADE POINT
0 - < 30	F	0.0
30 - < 50	D	1.0
50 - < 60	C	2.0
60 - < 70	BC	2.5
70 - < 77	B	3.0
77 - < 84	AB	3.5
84 - 100	A	4.0

Professor White could just give this table to her TAs and have them manually enter each student's letter grade. But it would be much more efficient to have the letter grades automatically entered into the grading sheet workbooks using a lookup table. A **lookup table** consists of rows and columns of information organized into separate categories. For example, the table in Figure 8-33 displays seven different categories in the overall score column. If you knew what a student's score was, you could determine the student's letter grade or grade point average from the table by finding the appropriate row in the table and then looking in the letter grade or grade point column. You'll enter Professor White's grading scale as an Excel lookup table.

The categories for the lookup table are usually located in the table's first row or column and are called **compare values**, because an individual student's score is compared to each category to determine the grade. The value that is sent to the table is called the **lookup value**. In Figure 8-33, the first column contains compare values and each student's score is the lookup value.

A lookup table can have many different columns or rows to incorporate more pieces of information. Professor White's grading table displays both the letter grade and the corresponding grade point average. To use this lookup table, you have to specify both the lookup value (the student's test score) and whether you're interested in retrieving the student's grade or grade point average. See Figure 8-34.

Figure 8-34
Using a lookup
table

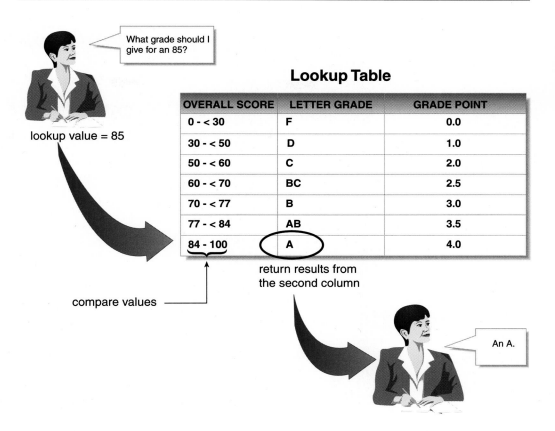

Professor White wants you to enter the values from Figure 8-33 into the Summary Grades workbook. Because of the way Excel works with lookup tables, you'll only insert the lowest value that a student needs to receive a particular letter grade in the compare values column of the table. In other words, placing an '84' in the row for a letter grade of A means that students who score 84 or above will receive an A. A value of 77 in the row for the AB grade means that students who score above 77 but less than 84 will receive an AB. You'll see how Excel uses these categories to retrieve the correct grades in a moment.

To create the lookup table:

1. Insert a worksheet to the right of the Summary sheet.

2. Rename the new sheet **Grades**

3. Enter the following values on the **Grades** sheet:

   Cell A1: **Score**

   Cell B1: **Grade**

   Cell C1: **Grade Point**

   Cell A2: **0**

   Cell A3: **30**

   Cell A4: **50**

   Cell A5: **60**

   Cell A6: **70**

   Cell A7: **77**

   Cell A8: **84**

4. Enter the remaining grades and grade point averages from the table in Figure 8-33 to columns B and C in the Grades worksheet.

5. Press **Ctrl + Home** to return to cell A1. See Figure 8-35.

Figure 8-35 ◀
Grades lookup
table

compare values

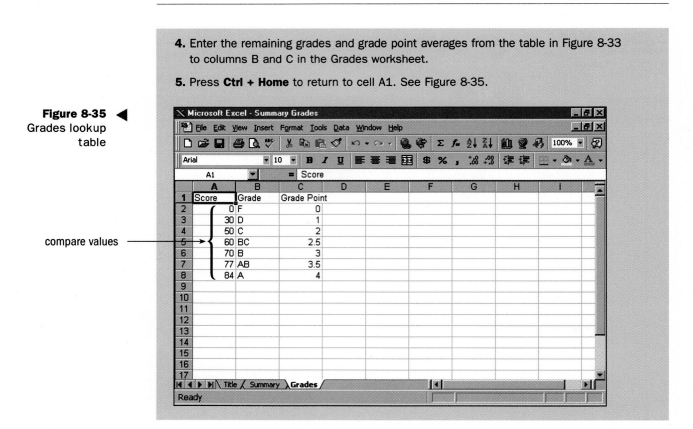

Finally, you should give a range name to your lookup table. While this is not necessary to use the lookup table, a range name will make it easier for others to refer to values in the table, since they would only have to learn the range name and not the cell reference.

To name the lookup table:

1. Select the range **A1:C8**.

2. Click **Insert** on the menu bar, point to **Name**, and then click **Define**.

3. Type **Grade_Scale** in the Names in workbook text box, and click the **OK** button.

4. Save your changes and close the workbook.

Now that you've created the lookup table, you'll see how Professor White's TAs can use it to enter letter grades.

Using Lookup Functions

To retrieve a value, in this case a letter grade, from a lookup table, you can use an Excel lookup function. In a **lookup function**, you specify the location of the lookup table, the lookup value, and the column or row that contains the values you want retrieved from the table. Excel has two lookup functions: the VLOOKUP function and the HLOOKUP function. The **VLOOKUP** (or vertical lookup) function is used for lookup tables in which the compare values are placed into the first column of the table, while the HLOOKUP

Excel

(or horizontal lookup) function places the compare values in the table's first row. With the lookup table you created in Professor White's workbook, you'll use the VLOOKUP function, since the compare values were placed in the table's first column. The form of the VLOOKUP function is:

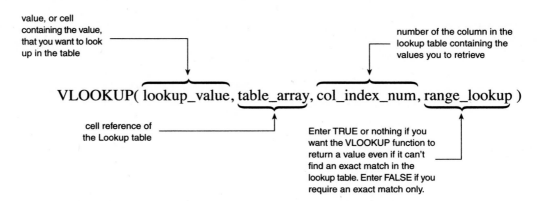

value, or cell containing the value, that you want to look up in the table

number of the column in the lookup table containing the values you to retrieve

VLOOKUP(lookup_value, table_array, col_index_num, range_lookup)

cell reference of the Lookup table

Enter TRUE or nothing if you want the VLOOKUP function to return a value even if it can't find an exact match in the lookup table. Enter FALSE if you require an exact match only.

The VLOOKUP formula can look imposing, but once you look at each piece of the function, you'll find it easier to understand. The first part of the function you'll enter is the lookup value. The **lookup value** is, as you saw above, the value that you want to enter into the table. It can either be a value or a reference to a cell that contains a value or a text string. In this case, the lookup values are the students' final numeric scores in the TA1 through TA4 workbooks. The **table_array** is the cell reference that specifies the location of the lookup table. In the lookup table you just created, the table array would be Summary!A1:C8, or if you use the range name you created, Summary!Grade_Scale. The **col_index_num** is the column number of the lookup table containing the information that you want retrieved. For example, a col_index_num of 1 returns the value in the first column of the lookup table, a col_index_num of 2 returns the value from the second column and so forth. You'll want the VLOOKUP function to look at column 2, the letter grade column, and retrieve the appropriate grade.

The **range_lookup** is a logical value that can be either TRUE or FALSE. It tells VLOOKUP how to match the compare values in the first column of the table with your lookup value. If the range_lookup value is TRUE or omitted, VLOOKUP retrieves values even if there is not an exact match between the lookup value and the compare values. In this case, Excel uses the largest compare value that is less than lookup value. If the range_lookup value is FALSE, the VLOOKUP function will search for only exact matches. If it fails to find an exact match, the function will return the #N/A error value. In the case of Professor White's grades lookup table, you would use a range_lookup value of TRUE (or nothing), because you do not have a letter grade assigned for every possible score.

Recall that when you created the lookup table, you entered the lower end of the range for each letter grade in the compare values column. The VLOOKUP function compares each lookup value with the compare values in the lookup table. Because the range lookup value is TRUE, the function looks for the largest compare value that is less than the lookup value score. Therefore the lookup table values must be sorted in ascending order, from the lowest compare value to the highest. If a score of 65 is sent to the lookup table shown in Figure 8-36, the VLOOKUP function moves down the Score column until it reaches the value of 70, the lowest score at which one can get a B. This is the first compare value that is greater than 65, which means that the largest compare value that is less than the lookup value is 60. The VLOOKUP function will then return a letter grade of BC for a score of 65, which, according to Professor White's original grading table in Figure 8-33, is the correct letter grade.

Figure 8-36
Using the
VLookup
function with
an inexact
match

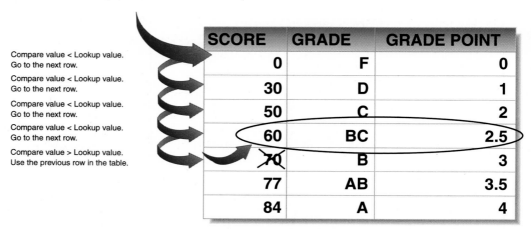

Lookup Value = 65

Compare value < Lookup value.
Go to the next row.

Compare value < Lookup value.
Go to the next row.

Compare value < Lookup value.
Go to the next row.

Compare value < Lookup value.
Go to the next row.

Compare value > Lookup value.
Use the previous row in the table.

SCORE	GRADE	GRADE POINT
0	F	0
30	D	1
50	C	2
60	BC	2.5
70	B	3
77	AB	3.5
84	A	4

Since the VLOOKUP function seems to be just what you need to assign letter grades automatically, you'll add the function to Stewart Nelson's grading sheet in the TA1 workbook. In this tutorial, you'll only add the function to TA1; you can add it to TA2, TA3, and TA4 at another time.

On the Section 1 worksheet of the Grading workbook, you'll add a column that will contain the final letter grade for each student. By entering the VLOOKUP function in that column, you'll have Excel enter the appropriate grade automatically.

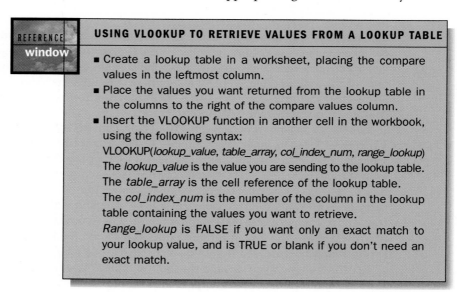

REFERENCE window

USING VLOOKUP TO RETRIEVE VALUES FROM A LOOKUP TABLE

- Create a lookup table in a worksheet, placing the compare values in the leftmost column.
- Place the values you want returned from the lookup table in the columns to the right of the compare values column.
- Insert the VLOOKUP function in another cell in the workbook, using the following syntax:
  VLOOKUP(*lookup_value, table_array, col_index_num, range_lookup*)
  The *lookup_value* is the value you are sending to the lookup table.
  The *table_array* is the cell reference of the lookup table.
  The *col_index_num* is the number of the column in the lookup table containing the values you want to retrieve.
  Range_lookup is FALSE if you want only an exact match to your lookup value, and is TRUE or blank if you don't need an exact match.

You have all the information you need to set up the VLOOKUP function. The lookup values are each student's overall score in column I. The lookup table is located in the Summary Grades workbook under the range name Grade_Scale. The grades that will be assigned to each student are located in the second column of that table. Finally you'll omit the range_lookup logical value because you are not trying to find an exact match. See Figure 8-37.

Figure 8-37 ◀
Applying the
VLOOKUP
function to the
grading
workbook

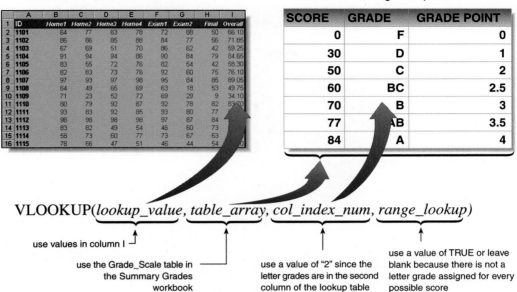

Student homework and exam scores

Grading lookup table

VLOOKUP(*lookup_value, table_array, col_index_num, range_lookup*)

use values in column I

use the Grade_Scale table in
the Summary Grades
workbook

use a value of "2" since the
letter grades are in the second
column of the lookup table

use a value of TRUE or leave
blank because there is not a
letter grade assigned for every
possible score

You'll begin by opening the TA1 workbook and entering the lookup function in a new Grades column that you'll add to the worksheet.

To add a column of final grades to the worksheet:

1. Open the **TA1** workbook from the Tutorial.08 folder on your Student Disk,

2. Group the worksheets for **Section 1** through **Section 3**.

3. Click cell **J1**, enter **Grade**. Now you'll connect the first Grade cell with the lookup table that will determine each grade.

4. In cell J2, type **=VLOOKUP(I2,'Summary Grades'!Grade_Scale,2)** and then press the **Enter** key.

   You have instructed Excel to look in cell I2 of the Grade Scale worksheet, and to retrieve the letter grade for that score based on the lookup table in the Summary Grades workbook. The grade BC appears in cell J2. Now you'll copy the formula in J2 to the grade cells below it.

   TROUBLE? If you receive an error message stating that Excel cannot find the Summary Grades workbook, verify that you've typed the name of the file correctly. The Summary Grades workbook should be in the same folder as the current workbook you're editing.

5. Select the range **J2:J21** and fill down using the keyboard shortcut **Ctrl + D**.

   The rest of the grades appear in column J. Now you'll format the values in the column.

6. Select the range **I1:I22**, and then click the **Format Painter** button 🖑 on the Standard toolbar.

7. Select the range **J1:J22** to format the Grades column.

8. Select the range **J1:J21**, click the **Center** button 🔳 on the Formatting toolbar, and then press **Ctrl + Home** to return to cell A1.

   Figure 8-38 shows the final version of the table. Because you've grouped the three grading sheets, the VLOOKUP formula and cell formats have been added to all three worksheets. A quick glance at the grades assigned to the students indicates a fairly even mix of letter grades.

Figure 8-38
Grades for
Stewart
Nelson's
students

VLOOKUP formula
is copied to all
worksheets in
the group

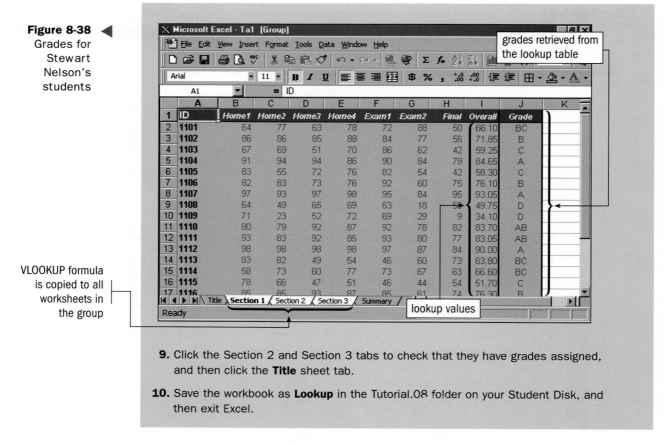

9. Click the Section 2 and Section 3 tabs to check that they have grades assigned, and then click the **Title** sheet tab.

10. Save the workbook as **Lookup** in the Tutorial.08 folder on your Student Disk, and then exit Excel.

With the lookup table in place, if Stewart makes a change in one of his student's homework or exam scores, or if Professor White revises her grading scale, the grades in column J can be automatically updated. This is much more accurate and efficient than simply entering the grades by hand.

You've completed your work with the grading workbooks for Professor White's calculus classes. You can use the Lookup workbook as an example of how to use the lookup function for the other grading workbooks.

Quick Check

1. What is the 3-D cell reference for the A1:A10 cell range on the Sales Info worksheet in the Product Report workbook located in the Reports folder on drive D?

2. How does a 3-D cell reference to a workbook differ from a 3-D reference to a worksheet?

3. How would you view a list a links to other workbooks in your current workbook?

4. Define lookup table, lookup value, and compare value.

5. What are two of the functions that Excel uses to retrieve values from a lookup table?

6. What is the range_lookup value? What does a value of TRUE mean for the range-lookup value?

In this tutorial, you have worked with multiple worksheets and workbooks, learned about templates, and used the Excel VLOOKUP function. Professor White is pleased with the grading sheets you've created. She'll look over your work and let you know if she has any changes she wants you to make.

Tutorial Assignments

Professor White has looked over the grading workbooks you've created. Based on her suggestions, you've made some formatting changes to the documents. She has a couple of items that she wants you to add to her new Summary Grades workbook and to each of her TA's grading sheet workbooks. In her Summary Grades workbook, she would like you to add a worksheet containing contact information for each TA retrieved from the TA1-TA4 workbooks, and she would like you to add to a column with the student's grade point to each TA's grading sheet. To make Professor White's modifications, do the following:

1. If necessary, start Excel, and make sure your Student Disk is in the appropriate drive. Open the Calc223 workbook in the TAssign folder for Tutorial 8, and save it as Calc223 Grades. When you are asked if you want to update links, click the Yes button.

2. Insert a new worksheet between the Title sheet and the Summary worksheet, and name it TA Info.

3. Enter the following column titles:

   Cell A1: "Sections 1-3"

   Cell B1: "Sections 4-6"

   Cell C1: "Sections 7-9"

   Cell D1: "Sections 10-12"

4. Increase the size of columns A through D to 20.00.

5. Enter a 3-D cell reference in cell A2 referring to cell B1 in the Title sheet of the TA1 workbook (*Hint*: Enter the 3-D cell reference yourself; do not use the mouse to select the cell in the TA1 workbook.)

6. Select the range A2:A5 and use the Edit, Fill, Down command to fill in information about the TA's office, phone number, and office hours.

7. Repeat the last two steps on columns B through D, referencing the TA information for Patty Wilson, Kim Lee, and Warren Kruschevski located in the TA2, TA3, and TA4 workbooks.

8. Center the column headings, format the TA Info worksheet with the Classic 3 AutoFormat.

9. Print the TA Info worksheet.

10. Close the Calc223 Grades workbook, saving your changes.

11. Open the TA1 workbook from the TAssign folder for Tutorial 8, and then save it as SNelson.

12. Group the three section grading sheets, select all the cells with information in them, and copy the format from the Section 1 worksheet into the Section 2 and Section 3 worksheets using the Fill Across Worksheets command.

13. In column J, use the VLOOKUP function to add the grade point average for each student to each of the three grading sheets using the grading table found in the Calc223 Grades workbook. (*Hint*: The lookup table in the Calc223 Grades workbook has the range name, Grade_Scale.)

14. Calculate the grade point average for the three sections in the TA1 workbook. What are the three grade point averages?

15. Format the Grade column on all three sheets to match the formatting of the Overall column.

16. Print the three grouped grading sheets with a common page setup format: Center the table of scores and grades on the page, place your name in the page header and the date in the page footer.

17. Ungroup the worksheets and save your changes.

Case Problems

1. Consolidating Copier Sales at DOC-Centric DOC-Centric makes six brands of copiers. They track sales information from four sales regions—north, south, east and west—in a sales workbook. You've been asked by your supervisor, Peter Mitchell, to format the workbook and to create a summary worksheet that will sum up the sales information from all four regions. To do this, you'll use the Excel worksheet grouping feature and 3-D cell references.

Do the following:

1. If necessary, start Excel, and make sure your Student Disk is in the appropriate drive. Open the Copiers workbook in the Cases folder for Tutorial 8 on your Student Disk, and save it as Copier Sales.

2. Enter the workbook name, your name, and the date in cells B5, B6 and B7 of the Title Sheet worksheet.

3. Insert a new sheet in the workbook titled Total Sales at the end of the workbook.

4. Using the Edit, Fill Across Sheets command, copy the row titles and column titles from the East worksheet into the Total Sales worksheet.

5. In cell B3, insert the SUM function, summing values in the B3 cells from all four worksheets from the North worksheet to the East worksheet.

6. Copy the formula in cell B3 into the range B3:F9.

7. Group the worksheets from North to Total Sales.

8. Format the sales numbers with the Comma style, but reduce the number of decimal places shown to 0.

9. Select the range A1:F9 and format the entire table(s) using the Classic 2 Autoformat table style.

10. Ungroup the worksheets and print the Total Sales worksheet.

11. Save your changes.

12. Remove the data in the range B3:E8, but not any formulas, from the 4 region sales worksheets and the Summary sheet, and remove the workbook name, your name and the date from the Title sheet.

13. Save the empty workbook as a template with the name Copier Sales Form in the Cases folder for Tutorial.08 on your Student Disk.

14. Print the template and close the workbook.

2. Examining Sales Information at Kitchen WareHouse Jaya Torres tracks the sales of kitchen appliances at Kitchen WareHouse. Kitchen WareHouse has stores in five regions. Jaya has recorded the monthly sales of refrigerators, microwaves, ovens, and dishwashers for each region in a workbook titled Kitchen located in the Cases folder for Tutorial 8 on your Student Disk. Jaya would like to include a worksheet that consolidates the sales information from the five regions. She would also like to take advantage of the Excel lookup feature to allow users to quickly retrieve the total sales of a particular product in a specific month.

Jaya has already placed an empty worksheet in her workbook that will be the summary sheet. The worksheet's title is All Regions. She wants you to add formulas to the table that sum the sales for each product in each month across the five sales regions.

She has also included a worksheet entitled Sales Results, in which she wants you to use the VLOOKUP function to allow a user to enter the month number and the product ID code, and have the total sales appear in a cell labeled "Units Sold."

Do the following:

1. If necessary, start Excel, and make sure your Student Disk is in the appropriate drive. Open the Kitchen workbook in the Cases folder for Tutorial 8 on your Student Disk, and then save it as Kitchen Warehouse.

2. Enter the new workbook name, your name, and the date in cells B3, B4, and B5 of the Title sheet.

3. In cell B4 of the Summary worksheet, enter a formula that sums the values in cell B4 from the Region 1 to Region 5 worksheets.

4. Copy the formula you created in cell B4 into the range B4:N8 in the Summary worksheet

5. Save the workbook and print the Summary worksheet.

6. Assign the range name Total_Sales to cellsA3:N8 in the Summary worksheet. This will be the lookup table used in the following step.

7. In cell B5 of the Sales Results worksheet, create a lookup formula using the VLOOKUP function with the following parameters:

   ■ The lookup value is the product number entered into cell B4.

   ■ The lookup table is the table referenced by the range name, Total_Sales.

   ■ The col_index_num is equal to the month number entered into cell B3 plus 1.

   ■ The value of the range_lookup parameter is FALSE.

8. Test the lookup function by using it to answer the following questions:

   a. How many refrigerators were sold in all regions in January?

   b. How many dishwashers were sold in all regions over the entire year?

   c. How many appliances were sold in all regions in March?

d. How many ovens were sold in all regions in June?

9. Print and save the final version of the Kitchen Warehouse workbook.

3. Using the VLOOKUP and MATCH Functions to Create a Stock Index Reporter Kelly Watkins is an investment counselor at Davis and Burns. Some of the many kinds of information that she refers to in her job are the daily stock indices on the New York Stock Exchange (NYSE). The indices are measures of changes in the market value of NYSE common stocks, adjusted to elimin1ate the effects of new stock listings, and deleted stock listings. There are four subgroup indices—Industrial, Transportation, Utility, and Finance, and a Composite index combining the values of the other four. Kelly would like to be able to find the closing value of any of these subgroups on any particular day. She has some raw data for the 1990 NYSE. She would like you to help her create a simple workbook in which she would only need to enter the date and the name of the subgroup and have Excel tell her the closing value.

She wants this "index reporter" to be friendly and easy to use, since she plans on sharing it with other people who might not be experienced computer users. So she wants you to remove such things as code numbers from the function of the index reporter.

You'll use the MATCH function to solve this problem. The MATCH function operates like the lookup functions, except that it indicates the location of matching values in a list of values. For example, in matching the word "Composite" to the list {Date, Composite, Industrial, Transport, Utility, Finance}, the MATCH function would return the value "2" since Composite is the second item in the list. You can use the MATCH function to replace the col_index_num parameter in the VLOOKUP function. Instead of having the user indicate the column number from a lookup table, the user can enter one column title and have the MATCH function return the column number. The syntax of the MATCH function is

MATCH(lookup_value,lookup_array,match_type)

where *lookup_value* is the value you want to find, *lookup_array* is the column or row containing the values, and *match_type* is a variable that determines the type of match you want. Set match_type to 0 for exact matches. For more information, see the Excel Office Assistant Help file on the MATCH function.

With these new functions, you are ready to create the index reporter for Kelly. Do the following:

1. If necessary, start Excel, and make sure your Student Disk is in the appropriate drive. Open the Index workbook in the Cases folder for Tutorial 8 on your Student Disk, and save it as NYSE Index.

2. Enter your name, the date, and the workbook name in the Title sheet.

3. In the Index Data worksheet, name the range A1:F1561 as Closing_Values.

4. In the Index Data worksheet, name the range A1:F1 as Index_Groups.

5. In the Reporter worksheet, enter a VLOOKUP formula in cell C6, using the following parameters:

   ▪ The lookup value is the date entered in cell C4.

   ▪ The lookup table is the range name, Closing_Values.

   ▪ The col_index_num is the number entered in cell C5.

   ▪ The range_lookup value is FALSE to ensure that only exact matches will be returned.

6. Test the VLOOKUP function by entering a date from the period covered in the Index Data sheet and an index number representing one of the indices. Verify that the function gives the correct values for the date and column number you entered (*Hint*: The values you would enter into C5 are 2 for Composite, 3 for Industrial and so forth.)

7. Replace the cell reference, C5, in the VLOOKUP formula that you just created with the following formula: MATCH(C5,Index_Groups,0).

8. Test your new function by writing the date in cell C4 and the name of the index in cell C5. Verify that this function will display the correct closing value for the index, or in the event of faulty data, will display a #N/A.

9. Use the new function to answer the following questions:

   What was the Composite index's closing value on 10/4/90?

   What was the Industrial index's value on that date?

   What was the Transport index on 3/14/90?

10. Print the Reporter sheet with the results of the last lookup, and then save and close the NYSE Index workbook.

4. Projected Income Statement for The Bread Bakery Your supervisor, David Keyes, has asked you to prepare the annual projected income statement for The Bread Bakery—a company specializing in fine baked breads. You've been given workbooks from three regions in the country. Each workbook has quarterly projected income statements for three of the company's products: French baguettes, sourdough wheat bread, and sourdough white bread. David wants you to summarize each workbook for him, reporting the following annual totals in a new worksheet:

Net sales

Total cost of goods

Gross profit

Total operating expenses

Earnings before tax

Return on sales

The last figure, return on sales, is calculated by dividing the earnings before taxes by the net sales. Once you have added this information to each workbook, he wants you to consolidate the information from the three regional workbooks, reporting in a single workbook, the same information for the entire company.

Do the following:

1. If necessary, start Excel, and make sure your Student Disk is in the appropriate drive. Open each regional sales workbook in the Cases folder for Tutorial 8 on your Student Disk. Open the R1 workbook and save it as North, save the R2 workbook as South, the R3 workbook as Southwest.

2. In each regional sales workbook, enter your name, the name of the workbook, and the date on the Title sheet.

3. Place a worksheet named Summary near the beginning of each regional sales workbook, right after the Title sheet. The Summary sheet should total all the Projected Income Statement figures in row 19 for the four quarters.

4. Format the Summary sheet using any format you choose.

5. Create the company's total projected income report from scratch, save it as Bread Bakery Report in the Cases folder for Tutorial 8 on your Student Disk.

6. Create a title sheet in the Bread Bakery Report workbook containing your name and the date.

7. Create a summary worksheet in the Bread Bakery Report workbook consolidating the information from the Summary worksheets in the North, South, and Southwest workbooks you've created.

8. The format and design of the Bread Bakery Report workbook is up to you.

9. Print the Summary sheets from the four workbooks you've created.

Data Tables and Scenario Management

Performing Cost-Volume-Profit Analysis Under Different Scenarios for Davis Blades

Excel

OBJECTIVES

In this tutorial you will:

- Examine cost-volume-profit relationships

- Learn the principles of multiple what-if analyses

- Use one-variable data tables to perform a what-if analysis

- Use two-variable data tables to perform a what-if analysis

- Create scenarios to perform what-if analyses

- Create a scenario summary report to save your conclusions

CASE

Davis Blades

Davis Blades is a manufacturer of in-line skates in Madison, Wisconsin and has retail outlets across the central and midwestern regions of the country. Davis Blades has been in business for four years, and sales have increased each year due to the increasing popularity of rollerblading as a sport and as a form of exercise across all age groups. The company carries six models of in-line skates at various prices. One of its most popular products is the Professional model, a high-quality in-line skate that is popular with men and women who participate in roller hockey leagues.

While the company sales figures have increased each year, the sales manager of the North Central region, Anne Costello, regularly monitors manufacturing costs, overhead expenses, and pricing policies to make sure Davis Blades remains profitable in the rapidly changing business environment. She asks you to create a report describing the profitability of the Professional model for her region. She gives you information detailing the expenses involved in creating the Professional model, as well as its retail price per unit. She wants you to use this information to calculate monthly operating income generated by the Professional model, using several assumptions regarding sales price and sales volume. With this information, she will be able to make sound business decisions to keep the product profitable.

In this session you'll examine the basic principles of cost-volume-profit analysis. You'll learn about data tables and how they can help you describe the relationship between cost, volume, and profits under different sets of circumstances. You'll learn about one- and two-variable data tables and how to create and display them.

Principles of Cost-Volume-Profit Relationships

One of Anne Costello's major tasks at Davis Blades is to quantify the different factors that affect the company's profitability. For example, if the company sells an additional 10,000 pairs of in-line skates a month, how much additional income will that generate? How much additional expense would be incurred? How many pairs does the company need to sell each month in order to break even?

You can find answers to questions like these by using cost-volume-profit analysis. **Cost-volume-profit (CVP) analysis** expresses the relationship between a product's expenses (cost), its volume (units sold), and the resulting profit. CVP analysis is an important business decision-making tool because it helps managers quickly and easily predict the effects of cutting overhead or raising prices on profit. While volume and profit are straightforward terms, you should understand the types of expenses that are part of CVP calculations.

Types of Expenses

The first component of CVP analysis is cost, or expense. A business like Davis Blades has three types of expenses. **Variable expenses** change in direct proportion to the number of units produced. For example, Davis Blades must purchase raw materials to create its in-line skates, such as leather and bearings. As it increases the number of units it produces, it must spend more money on raw materials. So raw material is a variable expense for Davis Blades, because the expense increases with higher quantities. To give you an idea how much expenses increase, Anne tells you that one pair of Professionals costs the company $25 in raw materials and $15 in manufacturing expenses. The graph in Figure 9-1 displays the company's variable expenses. As the number of units increases (shown on the horizontal x-axis), so does the cost of material (shown on the vertical y-axis). If Davis Blades produces 500 units, its variable expenses are $20,000. If it produces no in-line skates, its variable expense is zero.

Figure 9-1 ◀
Graph of
variable
expenses

500 units cost
$20,000 in
variable expenses

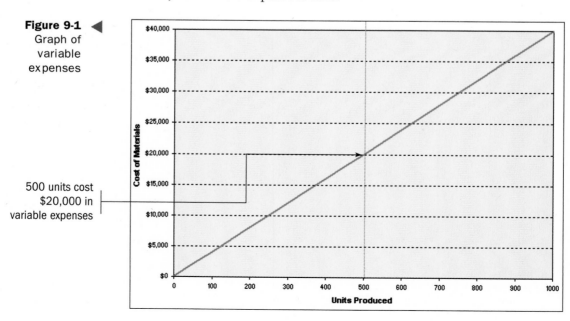

Anne tells you that Davis Blades sells the Professional for a unit price of $99 a pair. If you deduct the variable expenses ($40) from the unit price, it might seem like the company earns a profit of about $60 from each unit. It doesn't, however, because it also has to pay for a second type of expense, fixed expense. A **fixed expense** is an expense that Davis Blades must pay regardless of the number of units it sells. For example, machinery leasing or office rental does not change with an increase or decrease in production. Davis Blades spends about $60,000 a month on fixed expenses, even if it doesn't sell any units of the Professional.

Mixed expenses are part variable and part fixed. Salaries are sometimes a mixed expense. For example, Davis Blades has some employment expenses regardless of how many units it produces, such as the salaries of the office manager and the marketing staff. But salary costs will increase if the company decides to hire new manufacturing employees to accommodate an increase in production.

By adding its variable, fixed, and mixed expenses, Davis Blades can predict how much it costs to produce a specific number of Professionals. Figure 9-2 displays the North Central region's monthly expenses—variable, fixed, and mixed—as they relate to the number of in-line skates produced.

Figure 9-2
Graph of total monthly expenses

y-axis shows combined cost of variable, fixed, and mixed expenses

500 units cost $80,000 in total expenses

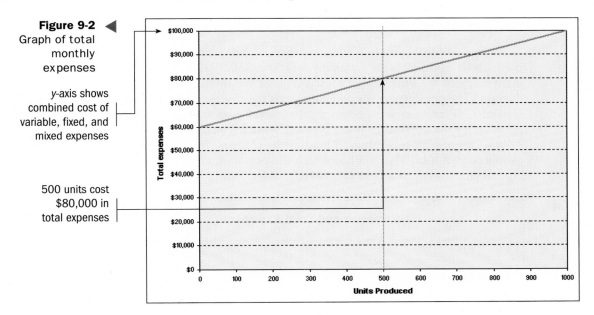

This chart more accurately represents Davis Blades' expenses. If Davis Blades produces no in-line skates, it would still have $60,000 in total expenses. If it produces 500 units, its total expenses would be $80,000. With a better picture of Davis Blades' expenses, you can calculate another important component of CVP analysis: the break-even point.

The Break-Even Point

As Davis Blades increases the volume of in-line skates it sells, it increases its revenue, as shown in Figure 9-3. Since a pair of Professional in-line skates sells for $99, its revenue for 500 pairs would be about $50,000.

Figure 9-3 ◄
Graph of
revenue per
number of
units sold

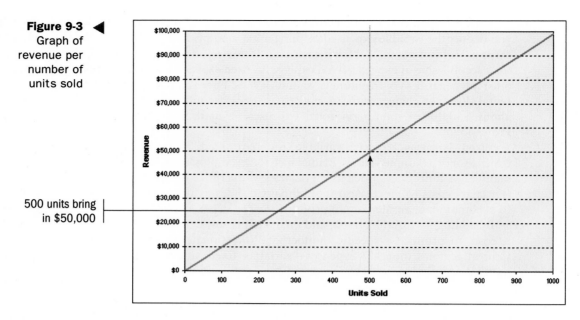

500 units bring
in $50,000

As you saw in Figure 9-2, total expenses at 500 units would be $80,000. So if Davis Blades sells 500 units, the company will lose $30,000 ($80,000 minus $50,000). How many units of the Professional must it sell for the revenue to equal the total cost of production? The point where the revenue equals the cost is called the **break-even point**. For this reason, CVP analysis is sometimes called **break-even analysis**. Any money the company earns above the break-even point is called **operating income**, or profit.

You can present a break-even analysis by charting revenue and expenses versus units produced and sold. The point at which the two lines cross is the break-even point. This type of chart is called a **Cost-Volume-Profit chart**. Figure 9-4 shows a typical CVP chart.

Figure 9-4 ◄
Revenue and
total expenses

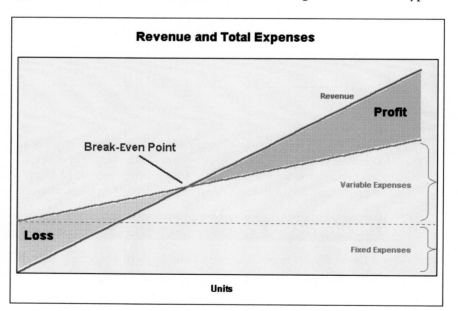

Using a chart like this, you can quickly determine what unit sales volume is necessary for a company to show a profit from a particular product.

Planning Income and Expenses at Davis Blades

Anne wants to determine the number of units Davis Blades has to sell to break even and then produce operating income. She also wants to see the cost-volume-profit picture at

Excel

Davis Blades, so she can make sure its prices reflect the cost of doing business. To help you obtain this information, she has given you a worksheet containing income and expense figures for the Professional in-line skates for a typical month. You will use these figures as the basis for a CVP analysis using Excel. The workbook is stored as Davis on your Student Disk. You'll open it and save it as Break-even Analysis.

To open the Davis workbook and view the datasheet:

1. Start Excel as usual, insert your Student Disk in the appropriate drive, open the file **Davis** from the Tutorial.09 folder on your Student Disk and save the file as **Break-even Analysis**.

2. Type **Break-even Analysis** in cell B3, type your name in cell B4, and type the date in cell B5.

3. Click the **CVP Data** sheet tab. Figure 9-5 shows Anne's sales and expense figures.

   TROUBLE? Don't worry that you can't see the entire worksheet shown in Figure 9-5. Your screen hides the lower portion; it is shown here so you can see the entire contents of the worksheet.

Figure 9-5 ◄
Professional
CVP data for
the North
Central region

	A	B	C	D
1		**Davis Blades** The *Professional* Model Monthly Income Statement: North Central Region		
2	**Revenue**			
3		Units Sold	1,200	
4		Price per Unit	$99	
5		Total Revenue	$118,800 ◄— total revenue	
6	**Variable Expenses**			
7		Units Produced	1,200	
8		Material Cost per Unit	$25	
9		Total Material Cost	$30,000	
10		Manufacturing Cost per Unit	$15	
11		Manufacturing Expenses	$18,000	
12		Total Variable Expense	$48,000	
13	**Fixed Expenses**			
14		Leasing	$5,000	
15		Salary and benefits	$45,000	
16		Advertisement	$5,000	
17		Administrative	$5,000	
18		Total Fixed Expense	$60,000	
19	**Summary**			
20		Total Expenses	$108,000	
21		Operating Income	$10,800	
22				

subtract total
expenses from total
revenue to arrive at
operating income

add variable and fixed
expenses to arrive
at total expenses

The CVP Data sheet contains an Income Statement, showing the Professional's price per unit and anticipated sales volume for a one-month period. It also shows the variable and fixed expenses Davis Blades incurs by producing that quantity of the Professional model in-line skates. No mixed expenses are reported. As you can see in Figure 9-5, each pair of Professionals sells for $99. The total material cost per unit ($25) and manufacturing cost per unit ($15) is $40. If David Blades sells 1,200 units of the Professional, variable costs for manufacturing and materials will total $48,000. The total fixed expenses for each month are $60,000. The formula in cell C21 calculates the operating income by subtracting total expenses from total revenue. If the North Central region of Davis Blades can produce and sell 1200 units, they can cover their variable and fixed expenses and show a profit of $10,800.

Anne would like to know what would happen to monthly operating income if the region's monthly sales of the Professional increased to 1,300 units.

To calculate income for sales of 1,300 units:

1. Click cell **C3**.

2. Type **1300** and press the **Enter** key. Scroll down to see that the monthly operating income for Davis Blades for sales of the Professional model increases to $16,700 as shown in cell C21.

3. Scroll back up and enter **1200** in cell C3 to return the Break-even Analysis workbook back to its original state.

You call Anne and give her the new income figure. Anne decides that she would like to have income calculations for sales levels ranging from 800 to 1500 units per month. To do this, you could enter each sales figure individually in cell C3 and record the results as you go, but it would be much easier to have Excel do the work for you. You can use Excel to create a data table that will calculate the operating income for any sales level you specify.

One-Variable Data Tables

One of the advantages of spreadsheets is that they allow you to quickly see how changing variables (items that can change), such as sales price or sales volume, can affect the value of a calculated figure like operating income. The ability to investigate different possibilities is called **what-if analysis**. You just performed a what-if analysis for Anne by determining the effect that increasing sales by 100 units per month had on operating income. You changed the Units Sold value to produce the Operating Income value. Sometimes you'll want to create what-if analyses for a number of values for a particular variable. In the Davis Blades case, you might want to look at sales of 1,000, 1,200, and 1,300 units. Organizing and presenting these different possibilities in a table makes the information easier to view and use. Excel provides this feature with data tables. **Data tables** are a way of organizing and displaying the results of multiple what-if analyses. Excel supports two kinds of data tables: one-variable data tables and two-variable data tables. You'll examine the one-variable data table first.

Start by identifying two cells on your worksheet: the input cell and the result cell. The **input cell** is a cell in the worksheet containing a value that you want to change. The **result cell** is the cell containing the outcome you want to examine. For example, you might know that your home mortgage has a monthly payment of $840.85 at an interest rate of 9.50%. Figure 9-6 illustrates these conditions.

Figure 9-6 ◄
Input and
result cells

	A	B	C	D
1				
2		**Mortgage Loan Analysis**		
3				
4		**Current Conditions**		
5		**Down Payment**	$0	
6		**Interest Rate**	9.50%	← input cell
7		**Term (months)**	360	
8		**Loan Amount**	$100,000	
9		**Payment**	$840.85	← result cell
10				

You're wondering what will happen to the monthly payment if you refinance the loan at a different interest rate. The value you want to change is the interest rate—cell C6 in this example. So cell C6 is the input cell. The outcome you want to examine is the monthly payment—cell C9. Therefore, cell C9 is the result cell.

You'd like to calculate monthly payments for a whole set of possible interest rates. Those possible interest rates are called **input values**; they are variations of the number in the input cell. The input cell C6 currently has the value 9.50%. You'd like to try input values of 8.75%, 9.00%, 9.25%, and so on. Based on those input values, you want to produce **result values** that are the outcome of each input value you use. For example, if you use an input value of 8.75%, your result value is a monthly payment of $786.70. Figure 9-7 displays the relationship between input values and result values.

Figure 9-7 ◀
Substituting
input values for
the input cell
to arrive at
result values

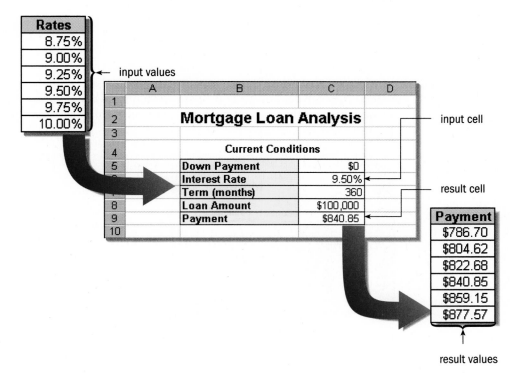

A **one-variable data table** is a table containing input values that are substituted, one at a time, for the value in the input cell of the worksheet, to calculate the result values, which are then displayed next to the input values. Figure 9-8 shows a one-variable data table for the Mortgage Loan Analysis worksheet, with current conditions for the loan on the left and the data table on the right. The data table lists the input values (the possible interest rates) in the left column and the result values (the corresponding monthly payment for each interest rate) in the right column.

Figure 9-8 ◄
One-variable
data table

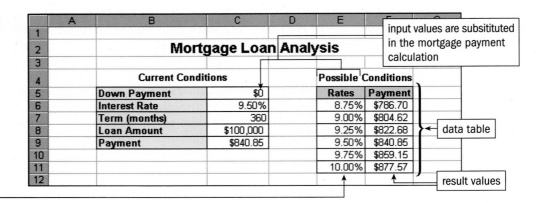

input values

Input values and result values can be placed in either rows or columns, but the input values must be placed in the *first* row or column.

Although one-variable input tables are limited to a single row or column of input values, they can contain several rows or columns of result values. Figure 9-9, for example, shows the monthly loan data table with two columns of result values: the monthly payment and the total payments for the mortgage.

Figure 9-9 ◄
One-variable
data table with
two columns
of result values

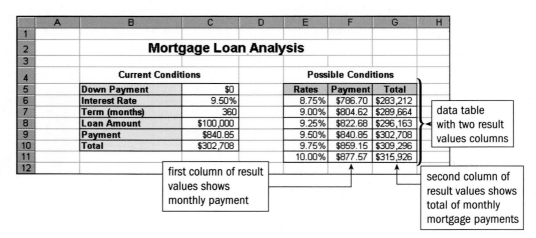

Now that you have seen what a one-variable data table looks like, you are ready to create your own in the Break-even Analysis workbook.

Creating a One-Variable Data Table

To supply the information Anne needs, you'll create a one-variable data table that allows you to evaluate the financial situation when varying quantities of Professional in-line skates are sold. You'll specify input values from 800 to 1500 units sold per month in increments of 100. The input cell is cell C3, the number of units sold. The result cells are the total revenue (cell C5), total expenses (cell C20) and income (cell C21). You'll need to designate three columns that will display the result values for each of the result cells. Figure 9-10 shows the areas of the worksheet you'll work with.

Figure 9-10 ◄
Planning a
one-variable
data table

input cell ———

total revenue
result cell

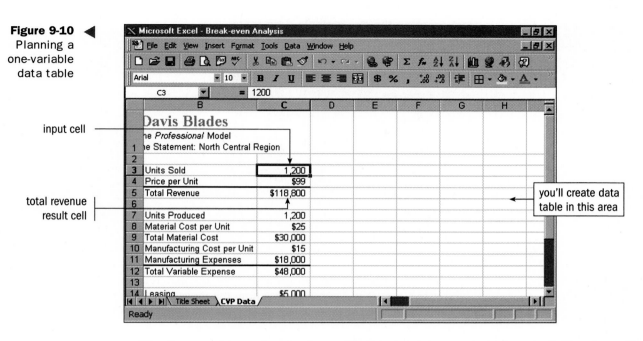

The first step in creating the data table is to create a row (or column) of titles that will identify the parts of the table. After these headings, you'll insert formulas that reference the input and result cells. These formulas will then substitute each of your input values— 800 units, 900 units, and so on—and generate corresponding result values.

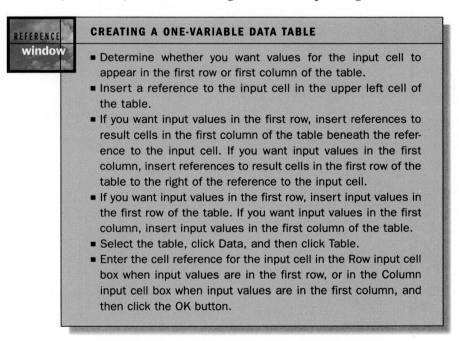

REFERENCE
window

CREATING A ONE-VARIABLE DATA TABLE

- Determine whether you want values for the input cell to appear in the first row or first column of the table.
- Insert a reference to the input cell in the upper left cell of the table.
- If you want input values in the first row, insert references to result cells in the first column of the table beneath the reference to the input cell. If you want input values in the first column, insert references to result cells in the first row of the table to the right of the reference to the input cell.
- If you want input values in the first row, insert input values in the first row of the table. If you want input values in the first column, insert input values in the first column of the table.
- Select the table, click Data, and then click Table.
- Enter the cell reference for the input cell in the Row input cell box when input values are in the first row, or in the Column input cell box when input values are in the first column, and then click the OK button.

You're ready to create the data table to address Anne's sales concerns.

To start creating the one-variable data table:

1. Enter **Units** in cell E2. Enter the remaining labels as follows:

Cell F2: **Revenue**

Cell G2: **Expenses**

Cell H2: **Income**

2. Now enter references to the Units Sold, Revenue, Expenses, and Income cells.

Cell E3: **=C3**

Cell F3: **=C5**

Cell G3: **=C20**

Cell H3: **=C21**

Now that you've entered headings and formulas that reference the input and result cells, you insert a column (or row) containing the input values. In this case you'll insert a column containing the range of values from 800 units sold to 1500.

To enter the input values:

1. Enter **800** in cell E4.

2. Enter **900** in cell E5.

3. Select the range **E4:E5**, and then drag the fill handle to extend the range to cell **E11**. After you release the mouse button, Excel fills the range with the units sold values ranging from 800 to 1500 in increments of 100. See Figure 9-11.

Figure 9-11 ◀
Entering
input values

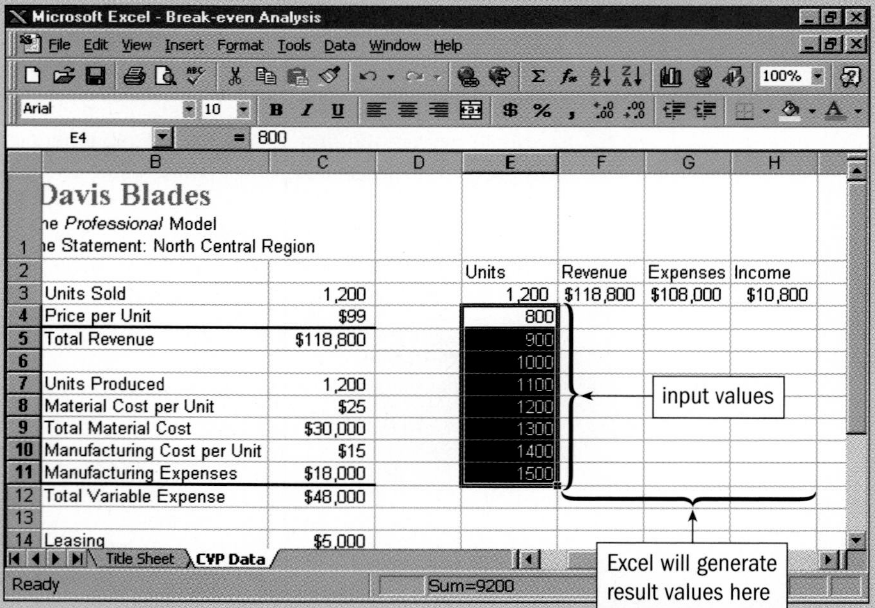

The final step in creating the one-variable data table is to instruct Excel to fill the table with the result values. To do this, you select the range of the data table (excluding any headings you've created) and run Excel's Data Table command. You will then need to designate the input cell and indicate whether the input values are in column or row format. Since your input values are in a column, you will use the Column input cell option. If you had oriented the table so that the input values were in a single row, you would use the Row input cell option.

To complete the one-variable data table:

1. Select the range **E3:H11**, click **Data** on the menu bar, and then click **Table**. The Table dialog box opens. Now you'll specify that the input cell is cell C3 and that it is in column format.

2. Type **C3** in the Column input cell box to reference the cell containing the units sold. See Figure 9-12.

Figure 9-12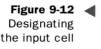
Designating the input cell

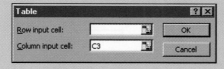

3. Click the **OK** button. Excel places values into the data table as shown in Figure 9-13.

Figure 9-13
Generating data table result values

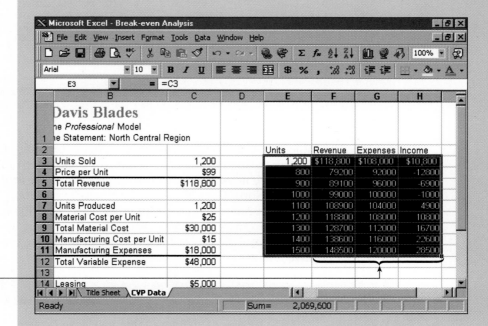

three columns of result values

Before trying to interpret the table, you'll make it easier to read by reformatting the values. You can do this quickly using the Format Painter tool on the toolbar.

To format the values in the table:

1. Select the range **E3:H3** and click the **Format Painter** button ⟨icon⟩ on the Standard toolbar. Now you'll apply the format of the range you selected to the values in the table.

2. Select the range **E4:H11** to apply the currency formats.

3. Click cell **E2** to deselect the range. Figure 9-14 displays the final one-variable data table, with the values in currency format.

Figure 9-14 ◀
Formatted
data table

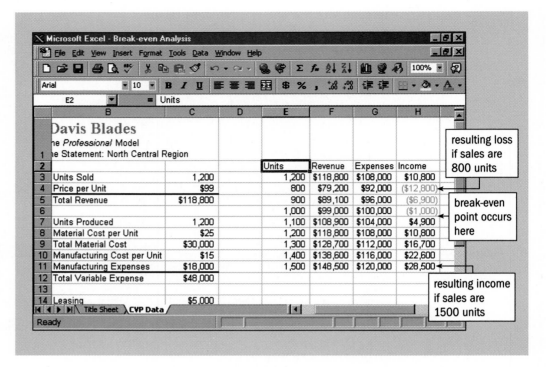

The data table uses the formulas in cells C5 (Total Revenue), C20 (Total Expenses), and C21 (Operating Income) to calculate results for each input value (Number of units). You can use the table to answer Anne's question. If sales of the Professional model fall to 800 units a month in North Central region, Anne will be reporting a loss of $12,800. On the other hand, if the region can increase monthly sales to 1,500 units, she will be able to report an operating income of $28,500. The break-even point lies somewhere between 1000 and 1100 units, because it is at these levels that operating income goes from a negative to a positive number.

Charting a One-Variable Data Table

You could give Anne a copy of the data table you have created, but the results will be much clearer if you include a CVP chart along with the table. The chart will give her a better picture of the relationship between the three variables. To create the chart, you'll need figures for the number of units sold, revenue, and expenses, which are all in the one-variable data table you've created.

To create the CVP chart:

1. Select the range **E2:G11**, click **Insert** on the menu bar, and then click **Chart**.

   TROUBLE? If the Office Assistant appears, click the No, don't provide help now button.

2. Click **XY (Scatter)** in the Chart type list box, click the **Scatter with data points connected by lines without markers** chart type as shown in Figure 9-15, and then click the **Next** button twice.

Figure 9-15 ◀
Creating a CVP
scatter chart

scatter charts
plot one variable
against another →

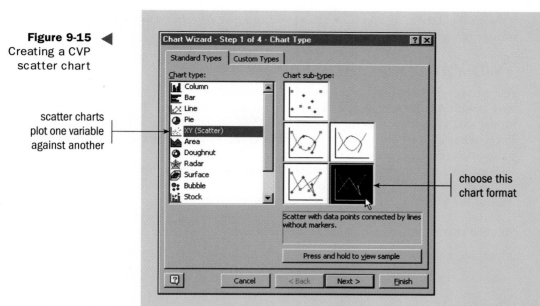

choose this
chart format

Now you'll label the chart and the horizontal axis so that others will know how to interpret the chart.

3. Type **Cost-Volume-Profit** in the Chart title box, and press the **Tab** key.

4. Type **Units Sold** in the Value (X) Axis box, and click the **Next** button. Now you'll specify that you want the chart placed on a separate sheet.

5. Click the **As new sheet** option button, and type **CVP Chart** in the As new sheet text box.

6. Click the **Finish** button. Figure 9-16 displays the completed chart.

Figure 9-16 ◀
CVP chart

break-even point ──

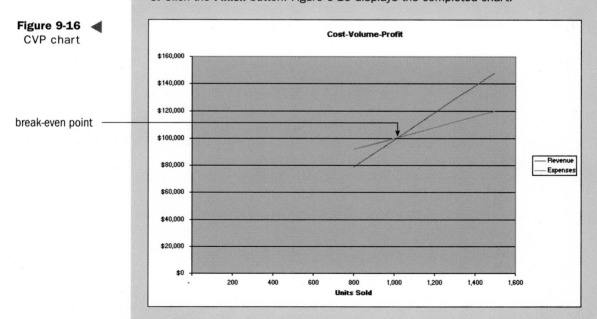

Excel plots each of the points in your data table and connects them with a line. The black line represents revenue and the pink line represents expenses. If you locate the 800 units sold mark on the x-axis and look straight up to the lines, you'll see that expenses exceed revenue—in other words, a loss of about $12,000. If you locate 1,400 units on the x-axis, you can see that revenue exceeds expenses by about $22,000. These loss and profit figures agree with the ones in the data table for the same levels of units sold.

With the data table and CVP chart, you can give Anne a comprehensive picture of the impact of varying sales levels upon both expenses and revenue.

Two-Variable Data Tables

Anne has reviewed your figures and incorporated them into her plans. But now competitive conditions have changed. A rival company, Street-Wise, is selling an in-line skate model that competes with the Professional. The model sells for $10 less. Anne wants to know what kind of cost-volume-profit results she would see if Davis Blades reduced the price of the Professional by $10.

Because data tables are dynamic, changes in the worksheet are automatically reflected in the data table. To see the effect of changing the unit price in the data table, you'll change the value in cell C4 from $99 to $89.

To view the effect of changing the sales price:

1. Click the **CVP Data** sheet tab to return to the sales worksheet.
2. Enter **89** in cell C4. Figure 9-17 shows the updated worksheet and data table. Note that the monthly operating income (assuming 1,200 units sold) is now an operating loss of $1,200 as shown in cell C21.

Figure 9-17 Effect of changing Professional sale price

	A	B	C	D	E	F	G	H	I
1	Davis Blades The *Professional* Model Monthly Income Statement: North Central Region								
2	**Revenue**				Units	Revenue	Expenses	Income	
3		Units Sold	1,200		1,200	$106,800	$108,000	($1,200)	
4		Price per Unit	$89		800	$71,200	$92,000	($20,800)	
5		Total Revenue	$106,800		900	$80,100	$96,000	($15,900)	
6	**Variable Expenses**				1,000	$89,000	$100,000	($11,000)	
7		Units Produced	1,200		1,100	$97,900	$104,000	($6,100)	
8		Material Cost per Unit	$25		1,200	$106,800	$108,000	($1,200)	
9		Total Material Cost	$30,000		1,300	$115,700	$112,000	$3,700	
10		Manufacturing Cost per Unit	$15		1,400	$124,600	$116,000	$8,600	
11		Manufacturing Expenses	$18,000		1,500	$133,500	$120,000	$13,500	
12		Total Variable Expense	$48,000						
13	**Fixed Expenses**								
14		Leasing	$5,000						
15		Salary and benefits	$45,000						
16		Advertisement	$5,000						
17		Administrative	$5,000						
18		Total Fixed Expense	$60,000						
19	**Summary**								
20		Total Expenses	$108,000						
21		Operating Income	($1,200)						
22									

data table result values update automatically

operating income now shows a loss

3. Click the **CVP Chart** tab to view the chart. The break-even point, where the Revenue and Expenses lines intersect, has moved to the right, indicating that David Blades would have to sell more units at this lower price to break even. Now return the price to its original level.
4. Click the **CVP Data** tab, and enter **99** in cell C4. The one-variable data table and the rest of the worksheet now display their prior values.

Based on the information from Figure 9-17, the region would have to sell between 1200 and 1300 units of its Professional model per month to break even at a unit price of $89. Moreover, the region would have to sell between 1,400 and 1,500 units per month to generate the same operating income as selling 1,200 units of the Professional for $99.

When she learns these results, Anne decides that she would like to see how other prices for this model affect her region's monthly operating income, in conjunction with the varying levels of units sold. She asks you to give her the operating income for unit prices of $88, $90, $92, $94, $96 and $98, and for monthly sales volumes of 800 to 1500 units, in increments of 100 units. This means you now have to analyze the effects of two variables: price and sales in units.

You can analyze the effect of these two variables with a two-variable data table. As the name implies, a **two-variable data table** uses two input cells to create its result values. Figure 9-18 shows an example of a two-variable data table that calculates mortgage costs.

Figure 9-18 ◀
Two-variable
data table

input cells

nput values for
input cell C6

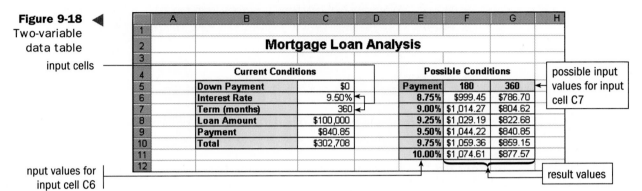

There are two input cells: cell C6, the interest rate, and cell C7, the number of months before the loan is repaid (180 or 360 months). Notice that the first row of the data table displays different values for the Term input cell (180 and 360 months). The first column of the data table displays different values of the Interest Rate input cell (8.75% to 10%, in increments of .25%). At the intersection of each interest rate and term length, the table displays the monthly payment that would result from the conditions. For example, a 180-month term at a 9.50% interest rate yields a monthly payment of $1,044.22 (cell F9).

Unlike one-variable data tables, two-variable data tables allow you to display only one set of result values in the workbook. For Anne's workbook, you'll have to choose whether you want to display revenue, expenses, or income, because you can display only one.

Next, you'll create a two-variable table in Excel to obtain the information Anne needs.

Creating a Two-Variable Table

Anne wants to see how income levels will vary with varying unit prices and sales volumes, so your result cell is C21, Operating Income. As with the one-variable data table, your first task in creating a two-variable data table will be to create the row and column input values. The row input values will be the unit prices and the column input values will be the sales volumes. You can copy these from your one-variable data table because they are the same.

REFERENCE
window

CREATING A TWO-VARIABLE DATA TABLE

- Insert a reference to the input cell in the upper-left cell of the table.
- Beneath the upper-left cell, enter a column of input values for your table.
- To the right of the upper-left cell, fill in the row with the second set of input values.
- Select the table, click Data, and then click Table.
- In the Row input cell box, enter the input cell corresponding to the row of input values.
- In the Column input cell box, enter the input cell corresponding to the column of input values.
- Click the OK button.

Now you'll create the two-variable data table that reflects both changing unit prices and changing sales volume. You'll place it below the one-variable table.

To enter the row and column headings for the two-variable data table:

1. On the **CVP Data** tab, enter **$88** in cell F14 to begin the row of unit prices.

2. Enter **$90** in cell G14. Now you'll fill in the row in price increments of $2.

3. Select the range **F14:G14**, and then drag the fill handle to extend the range to **K14**. After you release the mouse button, Excel fills the range with unit prices ranging from $88 to $98, in increments of $2. See Figure 9-19.

Figure 9-19 ◀
Entering input values for unit price input cell

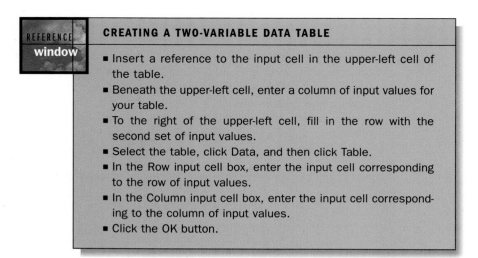

Now you'll copy the column input values from the one-input table.

4. Select the range **E4:E11**, and click the **Copy** button on the Standard toolbar.

5. Click cell **E15** and click the **Paste** button on the Standard toolbar. The row and column input values are now complete.

Excel

In two-variable tables, you must always place a reference to the result cell in the upper left corner of the table. Now that the input values are entered, you'll insert a reference to the Operating Income result cell, cell C21. Since placing a value in this location might confuse someone viewing your table, you'll format the cell to hide the actual value. Instead of displaying the reference, you'll display a title describing the contents on the input column.

To insert a reference to the result cell in the two-variable table:

1. Click cell **E14**, type **=C21**, and press the **Enter** key. The current operating income appears. Now you'll format the cell to hide the actual value and instead display a title for the Units Sold column.

2. Right-click cell **E14** and click **Format Cells** on the shortcut menu. The Format Cells dialog box opens. Normally, you use this dialog box to assign standard formats to cell values. In this case, however, you'll use the Custom format to display a label in cell E14.

3. Click the **Number** tab and click **Custom** in the Category list box. Now you'll replace the default format code with a label that will display in the cell.

4. Drag to select the entire format code displayed in the Type box. Now enter the label that will replace it.

5. Type **"Units Sold"** (include the quotation marks). See Figure 9-20.

Figure 9-20 ◀
Formatting the
result cell
reference

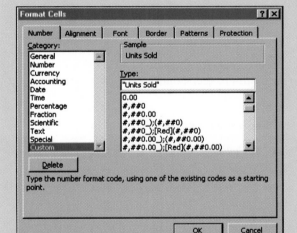

6. Click the **OK** button.

   The label "Units Sold" appears in cell E14. The underlying formula entered in that cell, however, remains intact.

   TROUBLE? If the Units Sold text that appears in your cell E14 appears incorrect, you may have forgotten to include the quotation marks. Go back and insert them now and then press the Enter key.

   Now you'll enter a heading row above the prices, and center it across the columns.

7. Enter **Price per Unit** in cell F13.

8. Select the range **F13:K13** and click the **Merge and Center** button 🔳 on the Formatting toolbar. The heading row is now centered above the range of prices.

9. Click cell **E14**. Your two-variable table should now look like Figure 9-21.

Figure 9-21 ◀
Data table
ready to
receive result
values

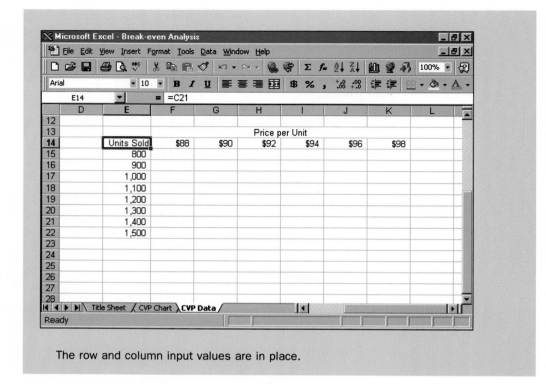

The row and column input values are in place.

Now that you've set up the table, Excel can fill in the operating income result values based on the varying levels of the two input cells: the units sold cell, C3, and the price per unit cell, C4. You do this with the same Data Table command you used earlier to create a one-variable data table, except that with a two-variable input table, you enter values in both the row and column input cells.

To complete the two-variable table:

1. Select the range **E14:K22**, click **Data** on the menu bar, and then click **Table**. The Table dialog box opens.

2. Type **C4** in the Row input cell box to refer to the cell containing the unit price, and press the **Tab** key.

3. Type **C3** in the Column input cell box to refer to the cell containing the number of units sold. See Figure 9-22.

Figure 9-22 ◀
Designating
input cells for a
two-variable
data table

units sold input cell ———

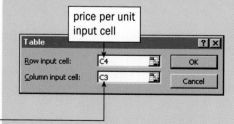

4. Click the **OK** button. Excel places the result values into the data table. Next you'll format the values in the table using the same currency format as the operating income cell.

5. Click cell **C21** and click the **Format Painter** button on the Standard toolbar.

6. Select **F15:K22** to format the income values in currency format.

7. Click **E14** to deselect the range F15:K22. Figure 9-23 shows the completed two-variable data table. You might have to scroll to display the complete table.

Figure 9-23
Completed two-variable data table

break-even point at $90 per unit

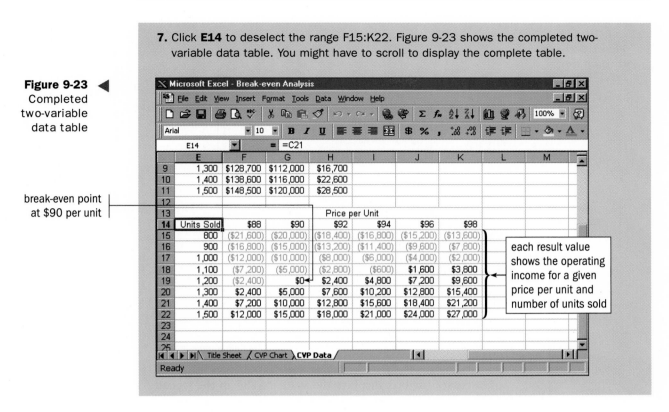

Based on the results shown in Figure 9-23, you tell Anne that if Davis Blades reduces the price of the Professional to $90 to match the price offered by Street-Wise, the region will break even at the current sales volume of 1200 units per month. However if sales drop by 100 units, the region will show a loss of $5000 per month. On the other hand, the region could still show a positive operating income at that sales volume if the unit price is $92 or more.

Charting a Two-Variable Data Table

To illustrate the effects of different combinations of unit price and sales volume on operating income, you'll chart the data in the table.

To begin creating the CVP chart:

1. Select the range **E15:K22**, click **Insert** on the menu bar, and then click **Chart**.

2. Click **XY (Scatter)** in the Chart type list box, click the **Scatter with data points connected by lines without markers** box, and then click the **Next** button.

3. Click the **Series** tab and click the **Name** text box.

   Because of the structure of the two-variable table, you must manually insert the unit prices into the chart's legend. You can do this by entering the names for each series.

4. Click the **Collapse dialog box** button, click cell **F14** on the CVP Data worksheet, and then press the **Enter** key. The address for cell F14 appears in the Name box. See Figure 9-24.

Figure 9-24 ◄
Setting up the
CVP chart

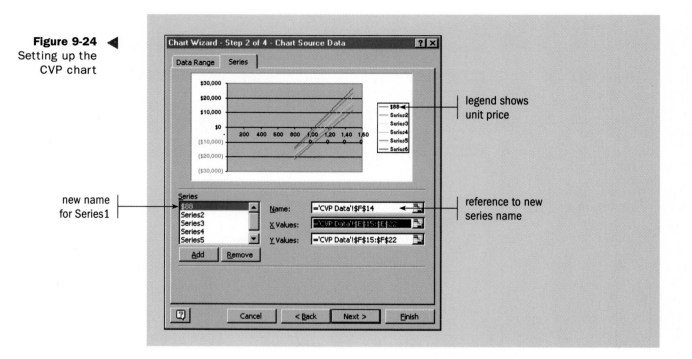

The Series list box displays the value "$88" in the legend for Series1 and the Name box shows the reference "="CVP Data"!$F$14". You could have typed the actual value into the Name box, but by using the reference, you can change input values in the data table, and then both the chart and the chart legend will update automatically.

To replace each series name with the unit price:

1. Click **Series2** in the Series list box, click the **Name** text box, click the **Collapse dialog box** button 🔲, click cell **G14**, and then press the **Enter** key.

2. Click **Series3**, click the **Name** text box, click the **Collapse dialog box** button 🔲, click cell **H14**, and press the **Enter** key.

3. Click **Series4**, click the **Name** text box, click the **Collapse dialog box** button 🔲, click cell **I14**, and press the **Enter** key.

4. Click **Series5**, click the **Name** text box, click the **Collapse dialog box** button 🔲, click cell **J14**, and press the **Enter** key.

5. Scroll to and click **Series6**, click the **Name** text box, click the **Collapse dialog box** button 🔲, click cell **K14**, press the **Enter** key, and then click outside the Name box. See Figure 9-25. Each series name has been replaced by the unit price in both the series box and in the legend.

Figure 9-25 ◀
Labeling
series names

name of each
series comes from
cell reference

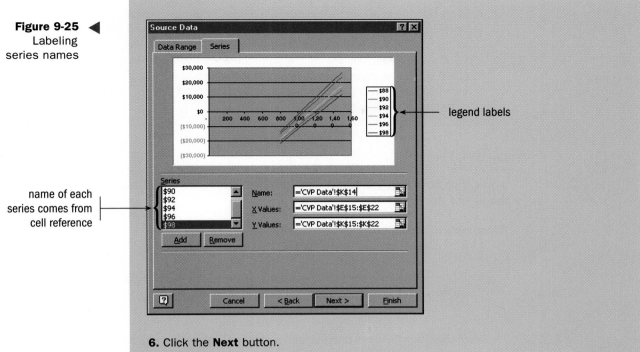

legend labels

6. Click the **Next** button.

Now you'll use the Chart Wizard to add the chart title and axes titles.

To complete the chart of two-variable table values:

1. Click the **Chart title** text box, type **Revenue for each unit price** and then press the **Tab** key.

2. In the Value (X) Axis text box, type **Units Sold** and then press the **Tab** key.

3. In the Value (Y) Axis text box, type **Revenue** and click the **Next** button.

4. Click the **As new sheet** button, type **Revenue for Different Prices**, and click the **Finish** button. Figure 9-26 displays the completed chart of revenue.

Figure 9-26 ◀
Chart of
revenue
for varying
unit prices

break-even point

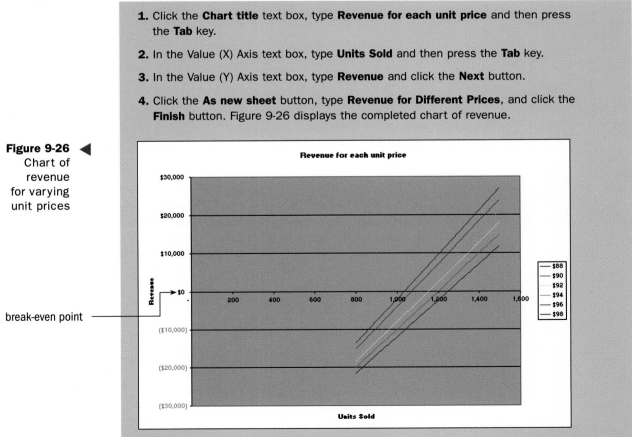

By viewing the chart, Anne can quickly see how different prices for the Professional will affect the relationship between operating income and units sold. At the lowest price of $88, the region will break even at slightly above 1,200 units. At the highest price of $98, the break-even point is just above 1,000 units. The graph also makes it clear that at a level of 1,500 units, a $10 decrease in the price of the Professional could create a drop of about $15,000 in monthly operating income.

This information will help Anne plan her marketing strategy for the Professional to effectively compete with Street-Wise. Anne will take these figures and study them for a while. For now your job is finished. Save your changes to the Break-even Analysis workbook and print your work.

To complete your work:

1. Save your changes, and print the CVP data worksheet and the CVP chart.

2. Click the **Title Sheet** sheet tab so the next user sees the Title sheet when this workbook is opened, and close the workbook.

Anne thanks you for supplying her with the information she needs.

Quick Check

1 Define CVP analysis.

2 What is the difference between variable, fixed, and mixed expenses?

3 What is a data table?

4 What is an input cell? What is a result cell?

5 What is the break-even point?

6 What is a one-variable data table?

7 What is a two-variable data table?

8 How many result cells can you display with a one-variable data table? How many with a two-variable table?

In this session, you have learned about the principles of cost-volume-profit relationships, including the break-even point. You have created a one-variable data table that calculates the results of changing the price variable, and a two-variable data table to see the results of changing both the price and units sold variables. In the next session, you'll learn how to analyze outcomes when more than one or two input cells vary.

In this session you'll use the Excel Scenario Manager to see the effect of changing several input cells on several result cells. You'll learn how to edit and save your scenarios and to print scenario reports.

Using Scenario Manager

Anne has looked over your figures and discussed them with the regional managers. They would like to look at several different options for reducing cost and/or increasing sales to deal with the new competition from Street-Wise. They have settled on four pricing and expense options, and have estimated what they believe to be reasonable sales figures under each option. Figure 9-27 displays the current situation and three other options.

Figure 9-27 ◀
Four pricing
and expense
options

Option	Conditions
Status Quo	■ Units sold = 900 ■ Unit price = $99 ■ Material cost per unit = $25 ■ Advertisement expense = $5000 ■ Administrative expense = $5000
Low Cost	■ Units sold = 1400 ■ Unit price = $85 ■ Material cost per unit = $22 ■ Advertisement expense = $5000 ■ Administrative expense = $2500
Competitive	■ Units sold = 1300 ■ Unit price = $90 ■ Material cost per unit = $22 ■ Advertisement expense = $8000 ■ Administrative expense = $2500
High Cost	■ Units sold = 1000 ■ Unit price = $95 ■ Material cost per unit = $22 ■ Advertisement expense = $5000 ■ Administrative expense = $2500

The **Status Quo** option would keep things as they are at Davis Blades. Management feels that sales could drop from 1200 units per month to 900 units, given the increased competition from Street-Wise. Under the **Low Cost** option, Davis Blades would reduce the price of the Professional from $99 to $85—$5 less than the Street-Wise price. At the same time, the company would try to reduce its per unit cost of materials from $25 to $22, and would cut administrative overhead (a part of fixed costs) from $5,000 a month to $2,500. The managers feel that reducing the price of the Professional would cause an increase in sales to 1400 units per month.

Under the **Competitive** option, Davis Blades would reduce the cost of the Professional to $90 to compete directly with the Street-Wise price of $89. Davis Blades would try to reduce the per-unit cost of materials from $25 to $22 per unit, and would increase the advertising budget from $5,000 per month to $8,000. At the same time, it would reduce administrative costs to $2,500. Under this option, the company assumes that sales would increase to 1300 units per month.

Finally, the **High Cost** option assumes that Davis Blades would reduce the cost of the Professional to $95 while reducing administrative overhead to $2,500. The company would try to reduce the per-unit cost of materials to $22. This option assumes a decrease in sales from 1200 to 1000 units per month.

Anne wants you to use Excel to evaluate all of these options and create a report summarizing them. She is interested in knowing the revenue that would be generated, the total monthly expenses, and the region's monthly operating income from sales of the Professional under each option.

You quickly see that you can't generate such a report using a data table, since Anne has asked you to work with more than two input cells. To deal with problems with more than two input cells, you have to create scenarios. A **scenario** is a set of values entered into a worksheet that describes different situations, like the options that Davis Blades created in Figure 9-27. Instead of creating workbooks for each possible situation, or entering values every time you want to perform a what-if analysis, you set up these situations as scenarios using Excel's **Scenario Manager**. Once you have saved the scenarios, you can view them and work with them any time you want. You'll use Scenario Manager to create the four scenarios that Anne has outlined for you. As you did with data tables, you'll begin by naming the input and result cells.

First though, open the Davis workbook and save it as Scenario Report.

To open the workbook and display the data:

1. If you took a break after the last session, make sure that Excel is running, and make sure your Student Disk is in the appropriate drive.

2. Open the workbook named **Davis** in the Tutorial.09 folder on your Student Disk, and save it as **Scenario Report** in the Tutorial.09 folder on your Student Disk.

3. Enter **Scenario Report** in cell B3, your name in cell B4, and the date in cell B5.

4. Click the **CVP Data** tab.

Now you're ready to create the range names you need.

Naming Input and Result Cells

Before using Scenario Manager, you should assign range names to all the input and result cells that you intend to use in your scenarios. As you'll see later, the range names will automatically appear in Scenario Manager's dialog boxes and reports. Though not a requirement, range names make it easier for you to work with your scenarios and for other people to understand your scenario reports.

You can quickly create range names for the values in the Davis Blades workbook using the Excel Names Create feature. This feature allows you to automatically assign names to cells containing values from the cells' labels. The Monthly Income Statement contains labels on the left in column B and values on the right in column C. The Names Create feature will assign, for example, the range name Units_Sold to cell C3, because that is the entry to its left. Use this feature to assign range names to the values in column C.

To create range names for the values in the table:

1. Select the range **B3:C21**.

2. Click **Insert** on the menu bar, point to **Name**, and click **Create**.

3. Make sure the Left column check box is the only check box selected, and then click the **OK** button.

4. Click cell **A2** to deselect the range.

Now that you have entered the range names in the workbook, you are ready to start defining the scenarios using Scenario Manager.

Defining Scenarios

To create the first scenario, you start Scenario Manager and enter a name for the scenario.

DEFINING A NEW SCENARIO

- Click Tools and then click Scenarios to start the Scenario Manager.
- Click the Add button to add a new scenario.
- Enter a name for your scenario.
- Define the Changing cells in the scenario.
- Insert a comment describing the scenario.
- Click the OK button and then enter values for each Changing cell in the scenario.

You'll enter the Status Quo scenario first.

To start Scenario Manger and add a new scenario:

1. Click **Tools** on the menu bar, and then click **Scenarios**. The Scenario Manager dialog box opens. See Figure 9-28.

 Figure 9-28 ◄ Scenario Manager

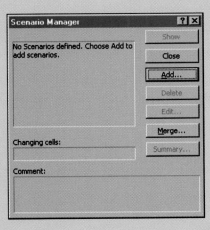

2. Click the **Add** button to add a new scenario to the workbook. The Add Scenario dialog box opens.

3. To name the first scenario you'll create, type **Status Quo** in the Scenario name box, and then press the **Tab** key.

Next you'll specify the input cells you want to use for this scenario. Scenario Manager refers to input cells as **changing cells** because these are the worksheet cells whose values you want to change. Changing cells can be located anywhere on the worksheet. You can type in the names or locations of changing cells, but it's usually easier to select them with the mouse. To select nonadjacent changing cells, hold down the Ctrl key as you click each cell. In the Status Quo scenario, the values that will change are units sold, price per unit, material cost per unit, and the fixed expenses of advertising and administration.

To specify the changing cells in a scenario:

1. With the Changing cells box selected, click the **Collapse dialog box** button 🖳, and select the range **C3:C4** on the worksheet.

2. Press and hold down the **Ctrl** key and click cell **C8**, the Material Cost per Unit.

3. With the Ctrl key still pressed, select the range **C16:C17**, the fixed costs.

4. Release the Ctrl key and press the **Enter** key. The cell range, $C$3:$C$4,$C$8,$C$16:$C$17, should appear in the Changing cells box. Now that you have entered the changing cells, you'll document the scenario with the assumptions that apply to it. That way, other users will know how this scenario relates to the current situation.

5. Press the **Tab** key and type **Projected income assuming current prices and a drop in monthly sales.** in the Comment box. See Figure 9-29.

Figure 9-29
Specifying
changing cells
for Status
Quo scenario

range of cells
that change in
Anne's scenarios

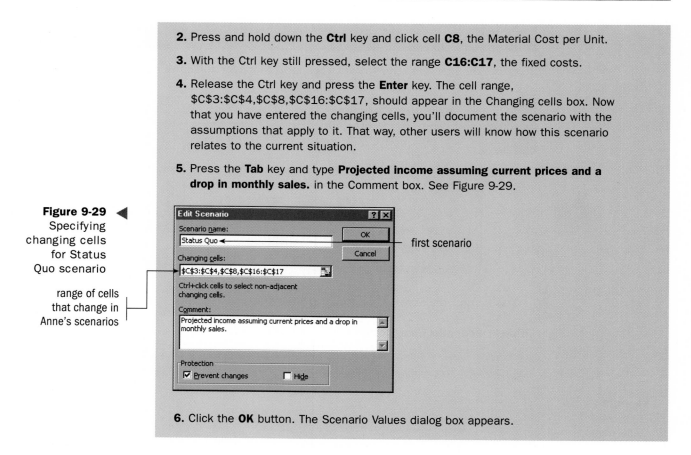

first scenario

6. Click the **OK** button. The Scenario Values dialog box appears.

So far you've specified the location of the changing cells. Now you need to enter the values you want to test under this scenario. With the Status Quo scenario, most of the values will be unchanged from the current workbook, except that management anticipates a decline in monthly sales from 1200 units to 900 units.

To specify values for the changing cells in the scenario:

1. In the Units_Sold box, type **900**. The rest of the values in the Scenarios Values dialog box remain the same. See Figure 9-30.

Figure 9-30
Specifying
values for
changing cells
for Status
Quo scenario

range names identify
changing cells

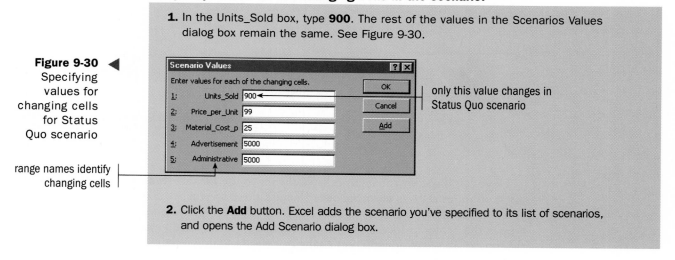

only this value changes in
Status Quo scenario

2. Click the **Add** button. Excel adds the scenario you've specified to its list of scenarios, and opens the Add Scenario dialog box.

In Figure 9-30, note that Excel uses the range names you've created to identify each input cell in the Scenario Values dialog box. This makes it easier for you to correctly enter scenario information. Note also that because you clicked the Add button rather than the OK button, you are returned to the Add Scenario dialog box and can proceed to add Anne's remaining scenarios.

To add the three remaining scenarios:

1. Type **Low Cost** in the Scenario name box, and then press the **Tab** key twice.

2. Type **Projected income assuming $85 price and a rise in sales.** and click the **OK** button.

3. Enter the following Low Cost values in the Scenarios Values dialog box:

    1400 in the Units_Sold box

    85 in the Price_per_Unit box

    22 in the Material_cost box

    5000 in the Advertisement box

    2500 in the Administrative box

4. Click the **Add** button, type **Competitive** in the Scenario name box, and then press the **Tab** key twice.

5. Type **Projected income assuming $90 price and a slight rise in sales.** and click the **OK** button.

6. Enter the following values in the Scenarios Values dialog box:

    1300 in the Units_Sold box

    90 in the Price_per_Unit box

    22 in the Material_cost box

    8000 in the Advertisement box

    2500 in the Administrative box

7. Click the **Add** button, type **High Cost** in the Scenario name box and then press the **Tab** key twice.

8. Type **Projected income assuming $95 price and a slight decline in sales.** and click the **OK** button.

9. Enter the following values in the Scenarios Values dialog box:

    1000 in the Units_Sold box

    95 in the Price_per_Unit box

    22 in the Material_cost box

    5000 in the Advertisement box

    2500 in the Administrative box

10. Click the **OK** button. Figure 9-31 shows all four scenarios listed in the Scenario Manager dialog box.

Figure 9-31 ◄
List of four
scenarios

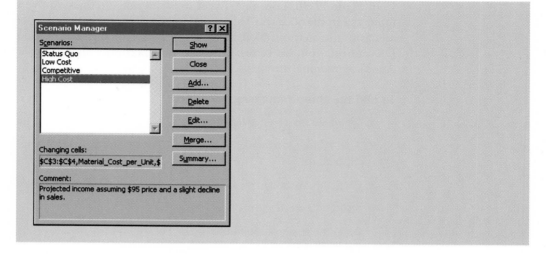

Your scenarios are entered and you are ready to view the effect of each scenario.

Viewing Scenarios

Now that you have entered the four scenarios, you can view the impact each scenario has on operating income by selecting the scenario and clicking the Show button or by double-clicking the scenario name.

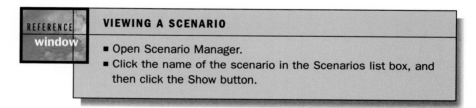

REFERENCE
window

VIEWING A SCENARIO

■ Open Scenario Manager.
■ Click the name of the scenario in the Scenarios list box, and then click the Show button.

You'll preview the effect of each scenario on operating income.

To view each scenario:

1. Click **Status Quo** in the Scenarios list box, and click the **Show** button. Before you can actually view the scenario you've just selected, you need to close the Scenario Manager.

2. Click the **Close** button to close Scenario Manager dialog box. Figure 9-32 shows the income statement assuming the Status Quo scenario.

   TROUBLE? Don't worry that only a portion of Figure 9-32 appears on your screen.

Figure 9-32 ◀
Status Quo
scenario

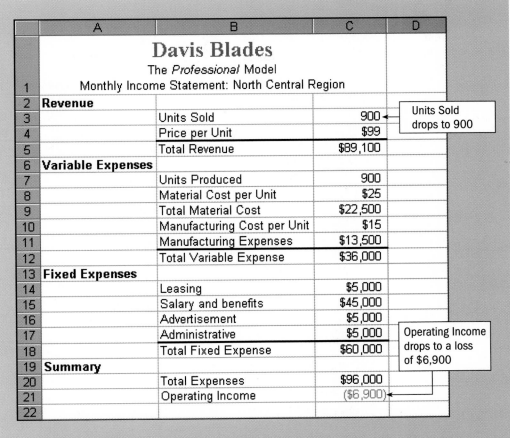

	A	B	C	D
1		**Davis Blades** The *Professional* Model Monthly Income Statement: North Central Region		
2	**Revenue**			
3		Units Sold	900 ◀	Units Sold drops to 900
4		Price per Unit	$99	
5		Total Revenue	$89,100	
6	**Variable Expenses**			
7		Units Produced	900	
8		Material Cost per Unit	$25	
9		Total Material Cost	$22,500	
10		Manufacturing Cost per Unit	$15	
11		Manufacturing Expenses	$13,500	
12		Total Variable Expense	$36,000	
13	**Fixed Expenses**			
14		Leasing	$5,000	
15		Salary and benefits	$45,000	
16		Advertisement	$5,000	
17		Administrative	$5,000	Operating Income drops to a loss of $6,900
18		Total Fixed Expense	$60,000	
19	**Summary**			
20		Total Expenses	$96,000	
21		Operating Income	($6,900) ◀	
22				

Excel has automatically changed the first input cell, Units Sold to 900. The operating income is recalculated in the scenario to be an operating loss of $6,900,
as you can see in cell C21.

To view the other scenarios, you'll reopen Scenario Manager.

To view the remaining scenarios:

1. Click **Tools** on the menu bar, and then click **Scenarios**.

2. Double-click **Low Cost**.

3. Click the **Close** button. Figure 9-33 shows the workbook for the Low Cost scenario.

Figure 9-33 ◄
Low Cost
scenario

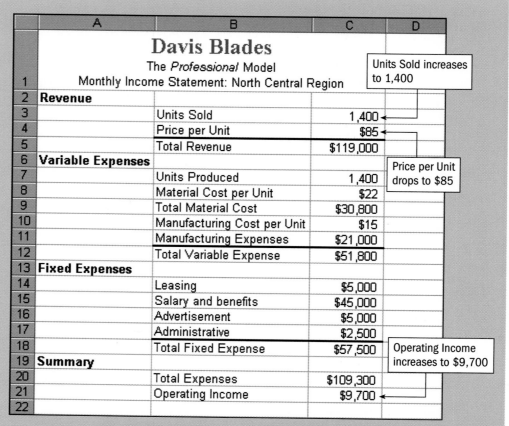

	A	B	C	D
1	**Davis Blades** The *Professional* Model Monthly Income Statement: North Central Region			
2	**Revenue**			
3		Units Sold	1,400	
4		Price per Unit	$85	
5		Total Revenue	$119,000	
6	**Variable Expenses**			
7		Units Produced	1,400	
8		Material Cost per Unit	$22	
9		Total Material Cost	$30,800	
10		Manufacturing Cost per Unit	$15	
11		Manufacturing Expenses	$21,000	
12		Total Variable Expense	$51,800	
13	**Fixed Expenses**			
14		Leasing	$5,000	
15		Salary and benefits	$45,000	
16		Advertisement	$5,000	
17		Administrative	$2,500	
18		Total Fixed Expense	$57,500	
19	**Summary**			
20		Total Expenses	$109,300	
21		Operating Income	$9,700	
22				

Callouts in Figure 9-33: Units Sold increases to 1,400 — Price per Unit drops to $85 — Operating Income increases to $9,700

4. Repeat Steps 1 through 3 for the Competitive scenario. Figure 9-34 shows the Competitive scenario.

Figure 9-34 ◄
Competitive
scenario

	A	B	C	D
1	**Davis Blades** The *Professional* Model Monthly Income Statement: North Central Region			
2	**Revenue**			
3		Units Sold	1,300	
4		Price per Unit	$90	
5		Total Revenue	$117,000	
6	**Variable Expenses**			
7		Units Produced	1,300	
8		Material Cost per Unit	$22	
9		Total Material Cost	$28,600	
10		Manufacturing Cost per Unit	$15	
11		Manufacturing Expenses	$19,500	
12		Total Variable Expense	$48,100	
13	**Fixed Expenses**			
14		Leasing	$5,000	
15		Salary and benefits	$45,000	
16		Advertisement	$8,000	
17		Administrative	$2,500	
18		Total Fixed Expense	$60,500	
19	**Summary**			
20		Total Expenses	$108,600	
21		Operating Income	$8,400	
22				

Callout in Figure 9-34: Operating Income is $8,400

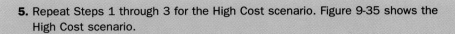

5. Repeat Steps 1 through 3 for the High Cost scenario. Figure 9-35 shows the High Cost scenario.

Figure 9-35 ◀
High Cost
scenario

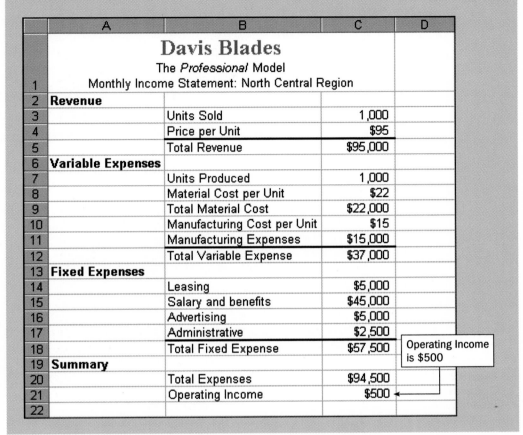

	A	B	C	D
1		**Davis Blades** The *Professional* Model Monthly Income Statement: North Central Region		
2	**Revenue**			
3		Units Sold	1,000	
4		Price per Unit	$95	
5		Total Revenue	$95,000	
6	**Variable Expenses**			
7		Units Produced	1,000	
8		Material Cost per Unit	$22	
9		Total Material Cost	$22,000	
10		Manufacturing Cost per Unit	$15	
11		Manufacturing Expenses	$15,000	
12		Total Variable Expense	$37,000	
13	**Fixed Expenses**			
14		Leasing	$5,000	
15		Salary and benefits	$45,000	
16		Advertising	$5,000	
17		Administrative	$2,500	
18		Total Fixed Expense	$57,500	
19	**Summary**			
20		Total Expenses	$94,500	
21		Operating Income	$500 ◀	
22				

Operating Income is $500

As you look over the four scenarios you can draw several conclusions. The Status Quo scenario assumes a sales volume drop to 900 units per month and produces an operating loss of $6,900. However, the Low Cost scenario indicates that by lowering prices, reducing overhead, and increasing sales, the region's monthly operating income could be a positive $9,700. This is close to the operating income of $8,400 shown in the Competitive scenario (Figure 9-34). Finally, the monthly operating income in the High Cost scenario is only $500, as shown in Figure 9-35. At this point, the most attractive scenarios seem to be the ones in which Davis Blades drops prices and increases sales. Of course, these scenarios assume that the sales will increase and that Davis Blades will be able to successfully control its overhead.

You present the scenario results to Anne, who evaluates the impact of each strategy on monthly operating income. After some thought, she decides she would like you to modify the High Cost scenario, this time assuming that sales will fall to only 1100 units per month in her region. To do this, you'll edit the scenario.

Editing Scenarios

Once you have created a scenario, it's easy to make changes so you can examine variations of given sets of assumptions. The scenario results will automatically update to reflect the new information.

EDITING A SCENARIO

- Open Scenario Manager.
- Click the scenario name from the Scenarios list box, and click the Edit button.
- Enter a new cell range for the Changing cells if necessary, and click the OK button.
- Enter new values for the Changing cells.
- Click the OK button and click the Show button to show the results of the edited scenario.

You return to the worksheet to modify the Units Sold value in the High Cost scenario.

To edit the High Cost scenario:

1. Click **Tools** on the menu bar, and then click **Scenarios**.

2. In the Scenarios list box, click **High Cost** and then click the **Edit** button.

3. Click the **OK** button to accept the cell range for the changing cells.

4. In the Units_Sold box, type **1100** and then click the **OK** button.

5. Click the **Show** button and then click the **Close** button. The Income Statement showing the values for the High Cost scenario with the new Units Sold value appears. See Figure 9-36.

Figure 9-36 ◄
Edited High Cost scenario

	A	B	C	D
1		**Davis Blades** The *Professional* Model Monthly Income Statement: North Central Region		
2	**Revenue**			
3		Units Sold	1,100	← edited value
4		Price per Unit	$95	
5		Total Revenue	$104,500	
6	**Variable Expenses**			
7		Units Produced	1,100	
8		Material Cost per Unit	$22	
9		Total Material Cost	$24,200	
10		Manufacturing Cost per Unit	$15	
11		Manufacturing Expenses	$16,500	
12		Total Variable Expense	$40,700	
13	**Fixed Expenses**			
14		Leasing	$5,000	
15		Salary and benefits	$45,000	
16		Advertisement	$5,000	
17		Administrative	$2,500	
18		Total Fixed Expense	$57,500	
19	**Summary**			
20		Total Expenses	$98,200	
21		Operating Income	$6,300	← Operating Income rises
22				

Monthly operating income from sales of the Professional rises to $6,300 under this revised scenario. So the High Cost scenario might be more attractive to Anne if she were confident that they could sell more units.

While the scenarios help you make important business decisions, it can be time consuming to compare the results of each scenario. Anne still will want to have a table of scenario values that she can hold in her hand and show to others. You could type the results of each scenario into a table for Anne, or you can save yourself time by having Scenario Manager generate a formatted report automatically.

Creating a Scenario Summary Report

A scenario summary report is a useful tool for those making business decisions based on scenario results. Rather than listing all the cells on the Income Statement, the summary report lists only the changing cells, or input values, and the result cells for each scenario. The report's tabular layout makes it easy to compare the results of each scenario, and the automatic formatting makes it useful for reports and meetings.

CREATING A SCENARIO SUMMARY REPORT

- Open the Scenario Manager.
- Click the Summary button.
- Click the Scenario summary option button.
- Enter the cell range for the Results cells of the scenario.
- Click the OK button and view the Scenario Summary worksheet.

In creating the report, you can identify which cells are the result cells. Anne is most interested in the monthly revenue, total monthly expenses, and monthly operating income under each scenario. These values are located in cells C5, C20 and C21, so she will specify these values as the results in the summary report.

To create the scenario summary report:

1. Click **Tools** on the menu bar, and then click **Scenarios**.

2. Click the **Summary** button. The Scenario Summary dialog box opens, allowing you to create a Scenario Summary or a Scenario Pivot Table.

3. Verify that the **Scenario summary** option button is selected. Now enter the result cells representing revenue, expenses, and operating income.

4. Type **C5,C20:C21** in the Result cells box. See Figure 9-37.

Figure 9-37 ◀
Preparing a
Scenario
Summary
report

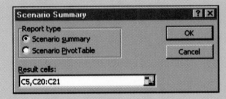

5. Click the **OK** button. Excel creates the Scenario Summary worksheet shown in Figure 9-38. You might have to scroll to see the entire report.

Figure 9-38 ◀
Scenario
Summary
report

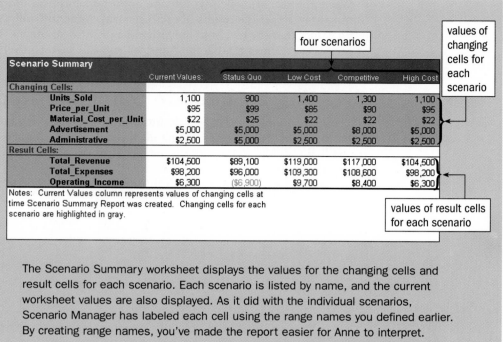

The Scenario Summary worksheet displays the values for the changing cells and result cells for each scenario. Each scenario is listed by name, and the current worksheet values are also displayed. As it did with the individual scenarios, Scenario Manager has labeled each cell using the range names you defined earlier. By creating range names, you've made the report easier for Anne to interpret.

You've completed your work for Anne, so print the Scenario Summary report before closing it and exiting Excel.

To complete your work:

1. Print the Scenario Summary report.

2. Click the **Title Sheet** tab, so the next user sees the title sheet when this workbook is opened.

3. Save the workbook and close Excel.

You hand in your Scenario Summary report. Anne will look it over, discuss it with other managers, and get back to you if she needs any additional scenario results. Based on your findings, it is clear that Davis Blades will have to change some of its operating practices in the North Central region. It will probably have to cut the price of the Professional model and find ways to reduce expenses.

Quick Check

1 What is an advantage of scenarios over data tables?

2 What should you do before starting Scenario Manager in order to make the reports you generate easier to interpret?

3 What are changing cells?

4 What are result cells? Where do you define result cells in Scenario Manager?

5 How do you display a scenario?

6 How do you create a scenario summary report?

Excel

In this tutorial, you have created one- and two-variable data tables. You've seen how to use Excel to easily investigate different scenarios for Davis Blades. You've learned how to use Excel to explore cost-volume-profit relationships and to display the results in the form of a report. Davis Blades will use these results to try and remain competitive in a changing marketplace.

Tutorial Assignments

Anne is considering using the Low Cost scenario you analyzed for her. She would like some more information before recommending that course of action. She would like to know what would happen to the region's operating income if the monthly sales of the Professional were 1000, 1100, 1200, 1300, 1400, or 1500 units. She would like you to place this information in a one-variable data table.

She would also like you to create a two-variable data table that includes the values from the one-variable data table and reports the operating income for unit prices of $85 through $89. Finally, she is not sure that the region can cut the material cost per unit to $22 or monthly administrative expenses to $2500. She would like you to report on a new scenario, called "Low Cost 2" where:

- Units Sold = 1,400
- Unit Price = $87
- Material Cost per Unit = $24
- Advertising expense = $5000
- Administrative expense = $4000

To report on Anne's scenarios:

1. If necessary, start Excel and make sure your Student Disk is in the appropriate drive. Open the LowCost workbook in the TAssign folder for Tutorial 9 and save it as Low Cost Scenario 2.

2. On the Title Sheet worksheet, enter your name, the date, and the new workbook name.

3. Go to the CVP Data worksheet and in cell E4, enter a formula referencing the value in cell C3 (Units Sold) and in cell F4, a formula referencing the value in cell C21 (Operating Income).

4. In cells E5:E10, enter the values 1000, 1100, 1200, 1300, 1400, and 1500.

5. Select the range E4:F10 and create a one-variable data table with cell C3 as the input cell. Add descriptive labels to the data table. Can the region still show a profit from the Professional if the monthly sales volume is 1200 units?

6. Create a chart sheet titled Income Chart, and chart operating income against units sold. Label the axes appropriately.

7. Copy the unit sales values in the range E5:E10 to the range E14:E19. Enter the unit price values $85 through $89 in one-dollar increments in the range F13:J13.

8. In cell E13, type a formula referencing the Operating Income value in cell C21.

9. Select the range E13:J19 and create a two-variable data table. Format cell E13 to display the text "Units Sold." Add the label Price Per Unit across the cells F12 to J12. What combination of units sold and unit price will result in an operating income of $1300 per month?

10. Using the Name Create command, create names for values in column C based on the labels in column B.

11. Using Scenario Manager, create a scenario titled "Low Cost 2" using the values outlined above.

12. Create a scenario summary report.

13. Save your workbook on your Student Disk.

14. Print the Scenario Summary report and the worksheet containing the one-variable and two-variable data tables.

Case Problems

1. Calculating the Break-Even Point for HomeEd Videos You can calculate the break-even point for cost-volume-profit relationships if you know the total fixed expense and the profit per unit. The break-even point is calculated as:

Break-Even Point = Total Fixed Expenses /(Price per Unit – Unit Variable Expense)

You work at HomeEd Videos, a company that makes educational videos for home instruction. Cindy Webber, the sales manager for HomeEd Videos, wants you to look at how changing the price per unit will affect the company's break-even point. To perform a CVP analysis, do the following:

1. If necessary, start Excel and make sure your Student Disk is in the appropriate drive. Open the HomeEd workbook in the Cases folder for Tutorial 9 and save it as HomeEd Analysis.

2. Enter the new workbook name, your name, and the date on the Title Sheet worksheet.

3. In cell C20 of the Sales worksheet, enter the break-even formula, =C15/(C4-C8). How many units per month must HomeEd videos sell to break even?

4. In range E2:F14, create a one-variable data table that will use the unit price value as the input cell and the break-even value as the result cell. Enter the text "Unit Price" in cell E2 and Break Even in cell F2. Enter references to the current values in cells E3:F3. Use unit prices of $20 to $30 in increments of $1 as the input values in your data table.

5. Format the values in F4:F14 with the format found in C20 (use the Format Painter button on the Standard toolbar).

6. Create a chart sheet named Break-Even, and chart unit price against the break-even point. Label the axes appropriately.

7. Among the unit prices in the one-variable data table, what price should HomeEd Videos set if it wants to sell less than 1300 units and still break even?

Cindy asks you to repeat the analysis, this time with a two-variable data table, assuming that the cost of producing each video is $4, $5, $6, or $7 per unit.

8. In cell E16, enter a formula referencing the break-even value in C20.

9. Copy the Unit Expense values from the range E4:E14 into the range E17:E27.

10. Enter the Unit Cost values $4, $5, $6, and $7 into the range F16:I16.

11. Select the range E16:I27 and create a two-variable data table using the Unit Cost as the Row Input cell and the Unit Expense as the Column Input cell.

12. Format the values in the range F17:I27 with the format found in C20.

13. Format cell E16 to display the label "Break-Even."

14. If the number of units produced each month by HomeEd video is about 1300, what combinations of unit price and unit cost will result in the company breaking even? In general, how great of a markup over the unit cost of each video must the company use in order to break even?

15. Print the worksheet containing the one and two-variable data tables.

16. Save your changes and close the HomeEd Analysis workbook.

2. Sales Mix at Fine Prints Inc. When a company sells more than one product, it must produce and sell the right combination of products in order to maximize its profits. This combination is called the "sales mix," and is an important factor in determining CVP relationships. At Fine Prints Inc., the manager, Mark Davis, is selling posters for the upcoming Summer Olympic games. He has three styles of posters: regular, fine, and matted. Mark wants you to determine how sales mix affects the cost-volume-profit relationship. At present Mark produces and sells about 500 copies of the Olympics prints in the following proportions: regular – 40%, fine – 30%, and matted – 30%. Mark wants you to explore what would happen to the operating income and the break-even point if the sales mix were as follows:

Current	Units Sold=500, Regular = 40%, Fine = 30%, Matted = 30%
Even	Units Sold=500, Regular = 33.3%, Fine = 33.3%, Matted = 33.3%
Regular	Units Sold=500, Regular = 50%, Fine = 25%, Matted = 25%
Fine	Units Sold=500, Regular = 25%, Fine = 50%, Matted = 25%
Matted	Units Sold=500, Regular = 25%, Fine = 25%, Matted = 50%

Do the following:

1. If necessary, start Excel and make sure your Student Disk is in the appropriate drive. Open the Prints workbook in the Cases folder for Tutorial 9 and save it as Sales Mix.

2. Enter the new workbook name, your name, and the date in the Title Sheet worksheet.

3. Give the Total Prints Sold value in cell C4 the range name "Units_Sold." Use the Create Names command to create names for the Percent of Sales values found in the D6:F6 range of the Sales worksheet.

4. Using Scenario Manager, create the five scenarios listed above. The changing cells in each scenario are the percent of sales values found in the D6:F6 range and the Units Sold value found in cell C4. Add a description of each scenario.

5. Use the Names Create command to create names for the outcome values in the range C20:C21.

6. Create a Scenario Summary report for the five scenarios. Include the operating income and the break-even point in the scenario summary report.

7. Print the scenario summary report in landscape orientation.

8. Analyze the report. Which sales mix results in the highest operating income and the lowest break-even point? Based on this, which of the three print types is the most profitable to the company?

9. Save your changes and close the Sales Mix workbook.

3. Calculating the Present Value of an Investment When companies plan expenditures for upgrading equipment or adding new products, they hope that the expenditure will produce additional revenue and profit. Given that that they could invest their money elsewhere, companies need to determine if the income generated by capital improvements gives them a desirable rate of return on the investment. One way to do this is to calculate the **present value** of the expenditure based on its anticipated earnings in the future. The present value expresses the worth of the investment in today's dollars. If the present value is greater than the initial investment, the investment is profitable. If not, the company may want to consider investing in other vehicles that are more likely to produce the desired rate of return.

You work with Allan Williams, owner of the Bread House bakery. Allan has $50,000 to invest and is considering using it to upgrade the bakery's kitchen. The cost of the upgrade is $50,000. Allan expects that the new kitchen will result in increased efficiency and productivity, which will be worth about $15,000 a year for the next five years. Allan wants to know how this level of increased revenue compares to other investments which could yield returns of 10 to 16% a year. If the level is equal to or above the return rate of other investments, he will proceed with the renovation.

A workbook calculating the net present value of Allan's proposed kitchen upgrade has been placed in the Bakery workbook in the Cases folder for Tutorial 9 on your Student Disk. The workbook shows the present value of upgrading the equipment, based on the assumptions that 1) the renovation will increase revenue by $15,000 per year, and considering that 2) Allan would like to see at least a 12% return on his $50,000 investment.

Allan would like you to use this workbook to calculate the value of upgrading the bakery for return rates other than 12%, such as rates between 10% and 16%.

Allan is also not sure that the upgrade will generate the type of extra revenue he is expecting. He wants you to calculate the present value of his investment assuming that the bakery upgrade yields the revenue shown in the following scenarios:

Low Initial Income	Desired Rate of Return = 12%
	Year 1 = $5000
	Year 2 = $10,000
	Year 3 = $15,000
	Year 4 = $25,000
	Year 5 = $35,000
Early Income	Desired Rate of Return = 12%
	Year 1 = $25,000
	Year 2 = $20,000
	Year 3 = $15,000
	Year 4 = $10,000
	Year 5 = $5000
Steadily Growing Income	Desired Rate of Return = 12%
	Year 1 = $10,000
	Year 2 = $12,000
	Year 3 = $14,000
	Year 4 = $16,000
	Year 5 = $20,000

What is the present value of the purchase under each of these scenarios? To answer Allan's questions, complete the following:

1. If necessary, start Excel and make sure your Student Disk is in the appropriate drive. Open the Bakery workbook in the Cases folder for Tutorial 9 on your Student Disk and save it as Bakery Analysis.

2. Enter the new workbook name, your name, and the date in the Title Sheet worksheet.

3. In the Present Value worksheet, create in the cell range F6:G13, a one-variable data table that identifies cell B4, the desired rate of return as the input cell and the net present value in cell D14 as the result cell. Use the following input values in the data table: 10%, 11%, 12%, 13%, 14%, 15%, and 16%.

4. Label the data table appropriately.

5. Analyze the table and determine at what rate of return the investment in the equipment is no longer as profitable. In other words, under what conditions is the present value of the upgrade worth less than $50,000? If Allan can get a 16% yearly rate by investing his money elsewhere, should he do so?

6. Use the Define Names dialog box to create names for each of the values in B7:B11, B4, and D14.

7. Use Scenario Manger to create the three scenarios that Allan has outlined for you. Do any of the scenarios show a negative net present value for the kitchen upgrade?

8. Create a scenario summary report based on your three scenarios. What would you tell Allan regarding the value of the kitchen upgrade versus investing the $50,000 elsewhere? Are there some situations that Allan should watch out for given that he wants his upgrade to be financially successful?

9. Print out your scenario summary reports, data table, and analysis of the results.

4. Starting a New Business Ray and Debbie Chen are considering opening a new restaurant. Both are experienced in cooking and in restaurant management. The restaurant they intend to lease has a maximum of eight tables, each of which can seat four people. Debbie has drawn up the following expense estimates:

Variable Expense

Average cost of food, including preparation	$8 per meal

Fixed Expenses

Salaries and Benefits	$50,000 per year
Rent (property and equipment)	$30,000 per year
Cleaning and upkeep	$3600 per year
Utilities	$9600 per year
Phone	$2400 per year
Advertising	$3600 per year
Miscellaneous overhead	$1800 per year

Debbie is trying to determine, on average, how much she should charge per meal and how many meals she should serve per night in order for the restaurant to show a profit. Debbie is assuming that the restaurant will be open 360 nights per year, and that the average price charged per meal will range from $20 to $30. She assumes that the restaurant will serve an average of 10 to 30 people per night. Ray and Debbie believe that the restaurant should show an operating income of $80,000 per year in order for them to risk the venture. They would like your help in analyzing the situation.

Your analysis should include the following:

1. The Chen workbook that you create and save in the Cases folder for Tutorial 9 on your Student Disk.

2. A worksheet showing the operating income under the assumption that the price per meal is $25 and the number of meals served each night is 20 and the number of meals produced is to the number meals served.

3. A one-variable data table showing the revenue, total expenses and operating income under the assumption that the price of each meal is $25 and that 10 to 30 people (in increments of 2) are served each night.

4. A CVP chart based on your one-variable data table.

5. An analysis of your results, answering the question "How many people should be served on average each night to show an operating income of $80,000 per year?"

6. A two-variable data table assuming that 10 to 30 people are served each night and that the average price per meal is $20, $22, $24, $26, $28 or $30.

7. An analysis that determines how many people on average must be served each night before the restaurant starts showing a profit based on the results of the two-variable data table.

8. The results of the following possible scenarios:

    Low Cost
    Price per meal = $22
    Cost of preparing meal = $7
    Avg. meals per day = 26
    Yearly salaries and benefits = $40,000
    Medium Cost
    Price per meal = $26
    Cost of preparing meal = $8
    Avg. meals per day = 24
    Yearly salaries and benefits = $45,000
    High Cost
    Price per meal = $28
    Cost of preparing meal = $9
    Avg. meals per day = 22
    Yearly salaries and benefits = $55,000

9. A scenario summary report for each of three scenarios displaying the total revenue, total expenses and operating income under each scenario. Make sure that you create range names for the appropriate values.

10. When finished with these tasks, save your workbook, print the scenario summary reports in landscape orientation, as well as your worksheets.

Using Solver for Complex Problems

Determining the Most Profitable Product Mix for Appliance Mart Superstore

OBJECTIVES

In this tutorial you will:

▤ Formulate a problem

▤ Perform what-if analyses

▤ Try to solve a problem using trial and error

▤ Use Goal Seek to automate the trial-and-error process

▤ Use Solver to find the best solution

▤ Create an answer report

CASE

Appliance Mart Superstore, Inc.

Jordan Maki is the general manager of the Appliance Mart Superstore in Boulder, Colorado. Appliance Mart has been in business for 25 years and is one of the biggest appliance dealers in Boulder County. The company specializes in laundry and kitchen appliances, including washers, dryers, dishwashers, refrigerators, stoves, and microwave ovens. Like all large appliance dealers, one of the managers' biggest problems is deciding how much inventory they should keep in their warehouse. They like to take advantage of special manufacturer price reductions, but they have a limited amount of warehouse space. They regularly must determine the most efficient and profitable combination of products (or "product mix") to keep on hand, given this limited amount of space.

One of Jordan's largest suppliers, GoldStar Corporation, just advertised special dealer pricing on selected models of GoldStar stoves, refrigerators, and microwave ovens. The Coldpoint, a refrigerator that usually costs $935 wholesale, is now on sale to dealers for $875. The Breakdale stove, which usually costs $450 wholesale, is $420. And the popular Quickcook microwave oven, which usually costs $220 wholesale, is now $195. Jordan thinks this looks like a great opportunity to stock up on some fast-moving merchandise and to increase profits.

Jordan asks you to recommend how many refrigerators they should order to take advantage of the special GoldStar pricing. You return to your desk to consider the problem and realize that you'll need more information in order to make a recommendation based on sound inventory-management principles. You begin to make a list of the information you need.

In this tutorial, you'll plan and create the workbook that will calculate the best combination of appliances that Jordan should buy. You'll consider the dealer cost and customer price for each type of appliance, and enter cost and profit formulas. Then you'll use a trial-and-error process to try to determine how many refrigerators will produce the most profit. Then you'll use an Excel feature that automates the trial-and-error process. You'll then move on to a more complex problem: finding the correct mix of refrigerators, stoves, and microwaves to order, given limits imposed by such factors as budget, warehouse space, and the number of orders Jordan has already received from customers. Finally, you'll use Excel to create a report that summarizes your analysis.

SESSION

10.1

In this session you will plan and create the refrigerator order workbook, perform a what-if analysis, seek a solution by trial and error, and use the Excel Goal Seek command. With the skills you learn in this session, you will be able to use Excel to find answers to questions by experimenting with different sets of circumstances.

Planning the Worksheet

Begin by assembling the information you have and using it to plan the structure of your worksheet. You know that the Coldpoint refrigerator usually costs Appliance Mart $935 wholesale and that it is now $875. However, you also need to know the retail price of the refrigerator to calculate the total profit Appliance Mart will make from selling the refrigerators from this order.

Next, you need to know if there are any customer orders for the Coldpoint refrigerator. If there are, you should recommend to Jordan that he order at least the number of refrigerators required to fill the customer orders.

You also need to know if there is a limitation on Appliance Mart's warehouse space that might affect the maximum number of refrigerators Jordan could order. If warehouse space is limited, you need to know the size of each refrigerator so you can determine how many would fit into the available space. Finally, you wonder if Jordan has placed a limit on the funds available for the GoldStar order. Although he did not mention a limit, you guess that he probably has one in mind.

You begin to gather the information you need. The sales manager tells you that each Coldpoint refrigerator has a retail price of $1250 and that there are six existing customer orders. From the inventory manager you learn that each of these apartment-sized Coldpoints requires 25 cubic feet of storage space.

You can't determine the warehouse space limitation yet, because the warehouse manager is at lunch. In addition, you can't track down Jordan to ask him his spending limit for the GoldStar order. While you wait for this additional information, you start working on an Excel worksheet that could help you analyze inventory purchase decisions. You develop the worksheet plan shown in Figure 10-1. Then, you make the sketch for the order worksheet shown in Figure 10-2.

Figure 10-1 ◀
Worksheet plan

Worksheet Plan for GoldStar Order

My Goal:
Calculate how many Coldpoint refrigerators to order from GoldStar.

What results do I want to see?
The total cost of the order.
The total warehouse space required for the refrigerators.
The amount of profit from selling all the refrigerators on the order.

What information do I need?
The wholesale cost of each GoldStar refrigerator.
The retail price of each GoldStar refrigerator.
The number of customer orders for GoldStar refrigerators.
The amount of warehouse space available (in cubic feet).
The size (in cubic feet) of each GoldStar refrigerator.
The maximum amount of funds available for the order.

What calculations will I perform?
profit per unit = unit retail price − unit wholesale cost
total cost = unit wholesale cost * quantity to order
total profit = profit per unit * quantity to order
total cubic feet = cubic ft. per unit * quantity to order

Figure 10-2 ◀
Worksheet
sketch

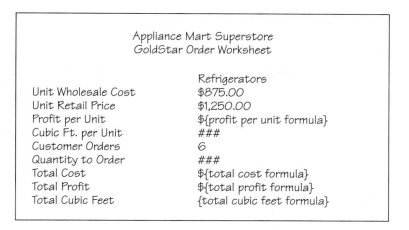

Appliance Mart Superstore
GoldStar Order Worksheet

	Refrigerators
Unit Wholesale Cost	$875.00
Unit Retail Price	$1,250.00
Profit per Unit	${profit per unit formula}
Cubic Ft. per Unit	###
Customer Orders	6
Quantity to Order	###
Total Cost	${total cost formula}
Total Profit	${total profit formula}
Total Cubic Feet	{total cubic feet formula}

Creating the Order Worksheet

Begin by launching Excel.

To launch Excel and organize the desktop:

1. Start Excel as usual, make sure your Student Disk is in the appropriate disk drive, and make sure the Microsoft Excel and Book1 windows are maximized.

Start by entering information on the content and purpose of the workbook on a Title sheet.

2. Rename Sheet1 **Title Sheet**. Enter the information shown in Figure 10-3, with your name in cell B4 and the date in cell B5.

3. Format the titles as shown in Figure 10-3

enlarge column width   type your name here   type the date here

Figure 10-3 ◀
Refrigerator
Order Title
Sheet

16 point bold red title

bold labels

rename the worksheet

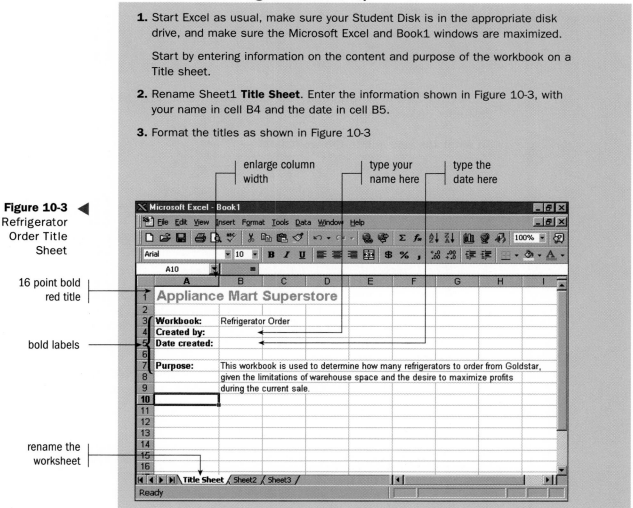

With the Title Sheet worksheet finished, you'll now enter titles and labels for the worksheet that you'll use to determine how many refrigerators to order.

To enter the worksheet titles and labels:

1. Click the **Sheet2** tab.

2. Enter the titles and formats in Figure 10-4.

3. Resize column A to accommodate the longest label (aside from the two title lines) in the worksheet.

4. Rename Sheet2 **Orders**.

Figure 10-4 ◄
Order worksheet

16 point bold red title

red italics

bold labels

rename worksheet

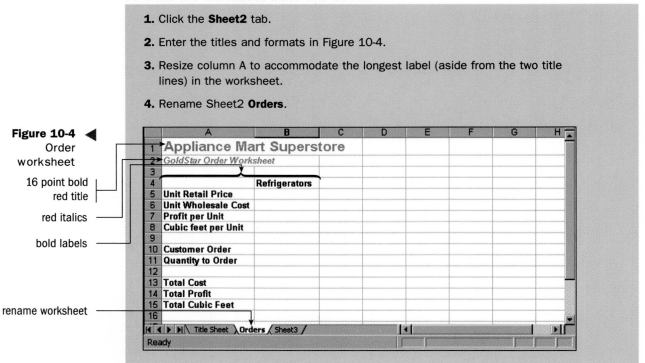

	A	B	C	D	E	F	G	H
1	Appliance Mart Superstore							
2	GoldStar Order Worksheet							
3								
4		Refrigerators						
5	Unit Retail Price							
6	Unit Wholesale Cost							
7	Profit per Unit							
8	Cubic feet per Unit							
9								
10	Customer Order							
11	Quantity to Order							
12								
13	Total Cost							
14	Total Profit							
15	Total Cubic Feet							
16								

Title Sheet \ Orders / Sheet3 /

Ready

Next, enter the information you know about cost, price, size, and the number of customer orders on the worksheet.

To enter the values into the worksheet:

1. In cell B5, enter **1250** to specify the unit retail price.

2. In cell B6, enter **875** to specify the unit wholesale cost.

3. In cell B8, enter **25** to specify the cubic feet per unit.

4. In cell B10, enter **6** to specify the number of orders Appliance Mart has already received from customers for this model.

Now that you've entered descriptive information about the Coldpoint refrigerator, you are ready to enter the formulas you'll use in the worksheet. The first formula on your planning sheet calculates the profit per unit, that is, how much money Appliance Mart will make on each Coldpoint refrigerator. The profit on a refrigerator unit is the retail price minus the wholesale cost:

Profit Per Unit = Unit Retail Price - Unit Wholesale Cost

On your worksheet, the unit retail price is in cell B5, and the unit wholesale cost from GoldStar is in cell B6. You'll enter this formula in cell B7.

To enter the formula for profit per unit:

1. In cell B7, enter the formula **=B5-B6**. The formula result 375 appears in cell B7.

Next, in cell B13 you'll enter the formula to calculate the total cost of the order:
*Total Cost = Unit Wholesale Cost * Quantity to Order*
After you enter this formula, you expect to see a zero as the result, because on the current worksheet the value for Quantity to Order is blank, or zero, and 875 multiplied by 0 is 0.

To enter the formula for total cost:

1. In cell B13, enter the formula **=B6*B11**. A zero appears in cell B13.

The formula for total profit that you'll enter in cell B14 is:
*Total Profit =Profit Per Unit * Quantity to Order*
You expect this formula to display a zero as the result until you enter a value for Quantity to Order.

To enter the formula for total profit:

1. In cell B14, enter the formula **=B7*B11**. A zero appears in cell B14.

In cell B15, you'll enter the formula that calculates total cubic feet:
*Total Cubic Feet = Cubic ft. per Unit * Quantity to Order*
As with the results of the two previous formulas, you expect this formula to display a zero as the result until you enter a value other than zero for Quantity to Order.

To enter the formula for total cubic feet:

1. In cell B15, enter the formula **=B8*B11**. A zero appears in cell B15.

Finally, you'll format the values and formulas you've entered into the worksheet. Because the refrigerators are priced in whole dollar amounts, you'll use the currency format with no decimal places. You can format the currency cells by selecting non-adjacent ranges that contain currency amounts, and then using the Format menu to apply the currency format.

To format the currency amounts and save the workbook:

1. Use the Format Cells dialog box to format the values in range **B5:B7** and in cells **B13** and **B14**. Apply the currency style with no decimal places, and show negative numbers in black, within parentheses.

Figure 10-5 shows the formatted data.

Figure 10-5 ◀
Orders
worksheet
with values,
formulas,
and formats

currency formats

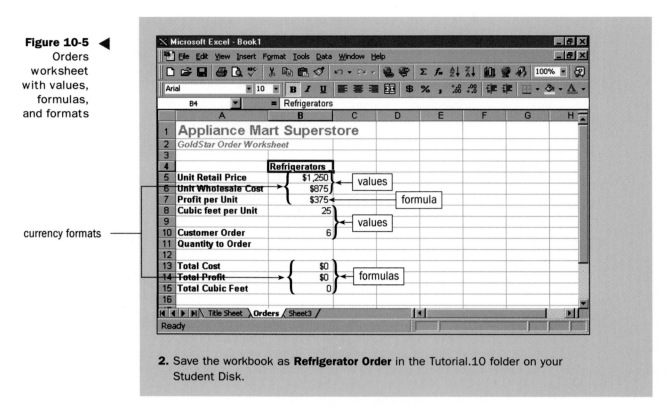

2. Save the workbook as **Refrigerator Order** in the Tutorial.10 folder on your Student Disk.

Now that you have set up the worksheet, you are ready to examine the problem and see how Excel can help you solve it.

Finding a Solution

You have completed the labels and formulas, but you have not yet received a call from the warehouse manager, so you don't know how much warehouse space is available. While waiting for the call, you enter some values for the quantity to order to see how much profit Appliance Mart could potentially make when it sells the GoldStar refrigerators. By inserting some hypothetical numbers into your worksheet, you'll start to get a feel for the cost of the purchase, as well as the impact on warehouse space, and potential profit for the company. Your goal is to balance the desire for high profits, the amount of money the company wants to invest in stock, and warehouse space limitations for the duration of the sale.

You know that there are customer orders for six GoldStar refrigerators, so you first want to determine the total cost, the total profit, and the total cubic feet for an order of six refrigerators. But you also know that Appliance Mart usually keeps at least 20 Coldpoint refrigerators in stock. So you want to know what the cost, profit, and space requirement would be for an order of 20 refrigerators as well. To see the results under both of these scenarios, enter order values of 6 and 20 into cell B11 of the Orders worksheet.

To calculate cost, profit, and cubic feet for 6 and 20 refrigerators:

1. Enter **6** in cell B11.

The cost of ordering 6 refrigerators is $5,250 and the total profit is $2,250. The space required for storing 6 refrigerators is 150 cubic feet. Now examine the results with an order of 20 refrigerators.

2. Enter **20** in cell B11.

The total cost of the order has increased to $17,500 that results in a profit of $7,500. The space requirements have grown to 500 cubic feet.

Figure 10-6 compares the results for both orders.

Excel

Figure 10-6 ◀
Impact of order
quantities of 6
and 20 on cost,
profit, and
space

values assuming
that 6 refrigerators
are ordered

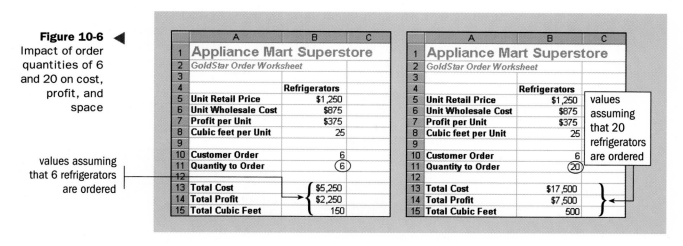

While profits are obviously much higher with 20 refrigerators, you are not sure if Jordan will approve an order for $17,500. You call him, and he says that he would like to keep the cost of the order down to about $15,000. Soon after you talk to Jordan, you receive a call from the warehouse manager who says that he has about 1,000 cubic feet of space for the refrigerators. Given these limitations, how many refrigerators should you order?

Finding Solutions by Trial and Error

When you used your worksheet for the what-if analyses, you were interested in the results for the total cost, the total profit, and the total cubic feet, but you were not concerned with any limits that might affect these results. Now you know that there are two limiting factors: Jordan does not want to spend more than $15,000 on the order, and the refrigerators on the order cannot take up more than 1,000 cubic feet of warehouse space. You decide to modify the worksheet plan's "goal" and "results" sections to reflect these limiting factors, as shown in Figure 10-7.

Figure 10-7 ◀
Revised
worksheet
plan

The revised worksheet plan

Worksheet Plan for GoldStar Order

My Goal:
Calculate how many Coldpoint refrigerators to order from GoldStar
without exceeding cost and space limits.

What results do I want to see?
The total cost of the order does not exceed $15,000.
The total warehouse space required for the refrigerators does not
exceed 1,000 cubic feet.
The amount of profit from selling all the refrigerators in this order.

What information do I need?
The wholesale cost of each GoldStar refrigerator.
The retail price of each GoldStar refrigerator.
The number of customer orders for GoldStar refrigerators.
The amount of warehouse space available (in cubic feet).
The size (in cubic feet) of each GoldStar refrigerator.
The maximum amount of funds available for the order.

What calculations will I perform?
profit per unit = unit retail price − unit wholesale cost
total cost = unit wholesale cost * quantity to order
total profit = profit per unit * quantity to order
total cubic feet = cubic ft. per unit * quantity to order

You now have a particular solution you are trying to reach. You want the value for the total cost in cell B13 to be as close to $15,000 as possible without exceeding that number, at the same time you must also make sure the value for total cubic feet in cell B15 does not exceed 1,000. You decide to adjust the value for Quantity to Order in cell B11 until the value for total cost in cell B13 is close to $15,000. This strategy is referred to as **trial and error** because you "try" different entries and they result in "errors" (solutions that are not optimal) until you enter the value that produces the result you want.

To determine the number of units by trial and error:

1. Enter **10** in cell B11.

   This order would cost $8,750 and take up 250 cubic feet of storage. It appears that you could order more than 10 units without exceeding the available funds and storage space. Now try a higher quantity.

2. Enter **15** in cell B11.

   Cell B13 displays $13,125. You could order more than 15 units and not exceed the two limitations.

3. Enter **17** in cell B11.

   The total cost for 17 units is $14,875.

With the total cost only $125 less than the $15,000 limit, you recognize that 17 is the maximum number of refrigerators Jordan can purchase with the available funds. Only 425 cubic feet are required for the 17 refrigerators, so the units will fit in the warehouse.

Just as you arrive at this solution, Jordan calls to tell you that GoldStar has announced an additional discount on Coldpoint refrigerators purchased for this sale. With this additional discount, the wholesale cost of each Coldpoint refrigerator is only $850. Jordan also tells you that because of this price reduction, he has decided to allocate a total of $18,000 for the refrigerator order. He asks you to determine the maximum number of units that he can purchase at the new price.

You begin by changing the value for unit wholesale cost in cell B6.

To enter the new refrigerator price:

1. Enter **850** in cell B6.

The value for total cost in cell B13 changes to $14,450, which is well below the new order limit of $18,000.

You could start the trial-and-error process again, but there is an Excel feature called Goal Seek that will help you find a solution to the new problem much more quickly.

Finding Solutions with Goal Seek

The Excel **Goal Seek** command automates the trial-and-error process of changing one cell to make another cell display a specified result. Goal Seek uses a different approach from traditional what-if analysis, where you change the *input values* in worksheet cells, and then Excel uses these values to calculate formula results. With Goal Seek, you specify the *results* you want a formula to display, and Excel changes the input values that the formula uses. Figure 10-8 illustrates the difference between a what-if analysis and a goal seek.

Excel

You enter a value…

Figure 10-8 ◄
What-if analysis
and Goal Seek

…and Excel calculates the result.

…and Excel calculates the value
needed to reach that result.

Suppose you want to purchase some audio CDs that cost $12 each. You can ask the what-if question, "*What* would it cost *if* I buy 15 CDs?" In Figure 10-8 the what-if analysis is shown on the left. If you were to place this data in Excel, you would quickly write a formula to calculate what it would cost you to purchase 15 CDs.

The Goal Seek example on the right in Figure 10-8 shows a different approach to the problem: If you have $216 to spend on CDs, how many can you purchase? You could use the Goal Seek capability to determine the answer, 18. Unlike traditional what-if analysis, Goal Seek starts with the end result (the formula) and determines what value you should use to reach a desired answer.

REFERENCE window

USING GOAL SEEK

- Set up the worksheet with labels, formulas, and values.
- Click Tools, and then click Goal Seek to display the Goal Seek dialog box.
- In the Set cell box, enter the cell where you want to display the result, which should contain a formula.
- Click the To value box, and then type the value you want to see as the result.
- In the By changing cell box, enter the cell that Excel can change to produce the result.
- Click the OK button.

You can use Goal Seek to solve your refrigerator problem. As you know, this problem has two limiting factors. First, the total cost of the order is limited to a maximum of $18,000. Second, the space required is limited to a maximum of 1,000 cubic feet. So, in fact, you have two goal seeking questions: One is "How many refrigerators can I order with $18,000?" and the other is "How many refrigerators can I order to fill up 1,000 cubic foot space?"

You can't do both goal seeking problems at the same time. Therefore, you decide to solve the goal-seeking problem for cost first. By first observing the cost factor and then the space factor, you can determine which one is the limiting factor and specifying the maximum number of refrigerators you can order, without spending too much money or overstocking the warehouse.

To set up the first goal seek, you first identify two cells in your worksheet: the result cell and the changing cell. The **result cell** is the cell containing your goal, which in this case is cell B13—the total cost of the order. The **changing cell** is the cell whose value is changed in order to reach your goal. In this case, the changing cell is B11, the number of refrigerators in the order.

What about the limitation on warehouse space? Excel will not consider this factor as it seeks a result for the problem. So after Excel solves the problem, you will need to manually confirm that the space limitation was not exceeded. You are ready to try the Goal Seek command.

To use Goal Seek to determine the number of refrigerators you can order for $18,000:

1. Click **Tools** on the menu bar, and then click **Goal Seek** to display the Goal Seek dialog box.

2. Move the Goal Seek dialog box so it doesn't hide any of the labels or values on your worksheet

3. With the Set cell box active, click cell **B13** to indicate the cell whose value you want to set.

4. Click the **To value** box, and then type **18000** to indicate that the total cost in cell B13 cannot exceed $18,000.

5. Click the **By changing cell** box, and then click cell **B11** to indicate that Goal Seek should change the order quantity in cell B11 to arrive at the result. The dialog box should look like Figure 10-9.

Figure 10-9 ◀
Completed Goal
Seek dialog box

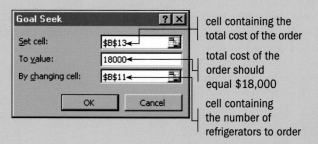

cell containing the
total cost of the order

total cost of the
order should
equal $18,000

cell containing
the number of
refrigerators to order

6. Click the **OK** button to seek the goal.

The Goal Seek Status dialog box, shown in Figure 10-10, indicates that Goal Seek has found a solution.

Figure 10-10 ◀
Goal Seek's
solution

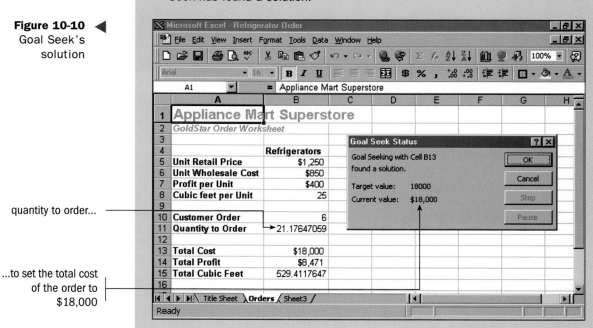

quantity to order...

...to set the total cost
of the order to
$18,000

You'll close the dialog box and examine the solution Goal Seek has entered on the worksheet.

7. Click the **OK** button to continue.

Goal Seek determined that an order for 21.17647 refrigerators would use up the entire $18,000 that Jordan has allotted for the purchase. Since you cannot order a fraction of a refrigerator, you'll round this number down to 21 and manually change it in the worksheet.

To change the number of refrigerators in the order:

1. Enter **21** in cell B11, which contains the number of refrigerators to order.

Before going further, look at cell B15 to check the total cubic feet needed to store the 21 refrigerators. The total space required is 525 cubic feet, well below the 1,000 cubic feet available in the warehouse.

So you have some additional space in the warehouse. How many refrigerators can you order before filling up that space? Find out this answer by formulating the second goal seeking problem.

To use Goal Seek to determine the number of refrigerators that will fit in a 1000 cubic foot space:

1. Click **Tools** on the menu bar, and then click **Goal Seek** to display the Goal Seek dialog box.

2. Click cell **B15** to set (enter) the cell containing the total cubic feet available.

3. Type **1000** in the To Value box to set the total cubic feet value to 1000, and then press the **Tab** key.

4. Click cell **B11** to make the Quantity to Order cell the changing cell.

5. Click the **OK** button.

The Goal Seek Status dialog box indicates that Goal Seek has found a solution.

6. Click the **OK** button.

Figure 10-11 shows that you can order 40 refrigerators to fill the 1000 cubic feet the warehouse allotted to you.

Figure 10-11 ◀
Goal Seek
solution to fill
up warehouse
space

The number of
refrigerators needed...

...exceeds the
18,000 purchasing
allowance...

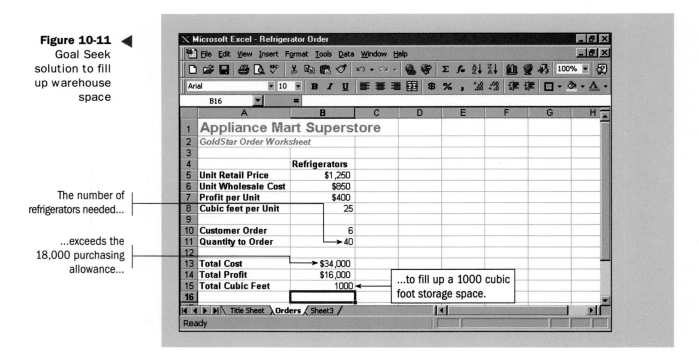

In looking over your results, you observe the cost of purchasing 40 refrigerators. The total cost, $34,000, almost doubles the amount Jordan said you could spend. You've found your limiting factor. In this case, it's not the space in the warehouse that will determine how many refrigerators you can buy; it's the total cost allowed for the purchase. Under the restriction set by Jordan, you can purchase up to 21 refrigerators, but no more. You'll enter 21 as the quantity to order in your workbook and then close the workbook and show Jordan your results.

To save, print, and close the Refrigerator Order workbook:

1. Enter **21** as the quanity to order in cell B11.

2. Delete any empty worksheets in the workbook.

3. Press **Ctrl + Home** to return to cell A1, and then click the **Title Sheet** tab so that the next time the worksheet is opened, the information on the Title Sheet will appear.

4. Save the workbook, and then print the worksheet and close the workbook.

Goal Seek has given you a solution to the ordering problem, and you expect that Jordan will be pleased when he learns how Appliance Mart can best benefit from the GoldStar sale.

Quick **Check**

1. Describe the trial-and-error process.

2. What is a limitation of the trial-and-error process?

3. Describe the difference between a what-if analysis and a goal seek.

4. Identify a typical business problem that you could solve using Goal Seek.

5. Define the following terms:

Changing cell

Resulting cell

6. Name the three components of the Goal Seek command.

Excel

In this session, you've planned and created a workbook that calculates the number of refrigerators that Appliance Mart should order, using both trial and error and Goal Seek. While Goal Seek is a useful tool in solving problems like these, you'll need to learn to solve more complex inventory problems, which you'll do in the next session.

SESSION

10.2

In this session you will work with more complex problems that involve changing two or more parameters to arrive at the "best" solution. To do this you'll work with a useful Excel add-in called Solver.

Exploring More Complex Problems

Jordan stops by to see how you are doing, so you show him the worksheet. Jordan is so pleased with the work you have done that he asks you to take charge of the entire GoldStar order. He explains that GoldStar has great prices on Breakdale stoves and Quickcook microwave ovens, in addition to refrigerators. He wants you to determine the most profitable mix of refrigerators, stoves, and microwave ovens to order. He gives you a total budget of $50,000 for the order.

You check with the sales manager and learn that Appliance Mart has customer orders for 14 Breakdale stoves and 19 Quickcook microwave ovens. You realize that your solution must take into account the customer orders for six refrigerators, as well as the orders for the 14 stoves and 19 microwave ovens. Next, you call the warehouse and learn that the products for the entire order must fit in 1,300 cubic feet of storage space. Your task is to find the best combination of refrigerators, stoves and microwaves that will meet the purchasing budget and also fit within the warehouse space allotted to you. You'll find an answer to this complex problem using Excel.

A revised worksheet containing columns for stoves and microwaves is stored on your Student Disk as GoldStar. First, open and resave the file.

To open and resave the revised workbook:

1. If you took a break after the last session, make sure Excel is running, open the **GoldStar** workbook in the Tutorial.10 folder on your Student Disk, and save it as **Appliance Order**.

2. On the Title Sheet worksheet, type **Appliance Order** in cell B3.

3. Type your name in cell B4 and the date in cell B5.

4. Click the **Orders** tab to display the worksheet showing price, cost, and order information for all three types of appliances. So far, only the number of appliances needed to meet customer orders has been entered. See Figure 10-12.

Figure 10-12 ◄
Appliance Order
workbook

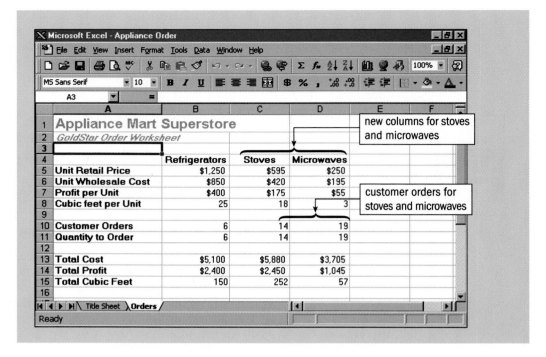

Notice that the worksheet has a column for stoves and a column for microwave ovens, each with the same format as the refrigerator column. There are also cells for the unit wholesale cost, the unit retail price, and the customer orders for each product.

You need to calculate the total order cost, the total order profit, and the total space required for all of the refrigerators, stoves, and microwave ovens on the order. To do this, you'll add a new column to the table that sums these values over all three appliances.

To add a column for total orders:

1. In cell E4, enter **ALL APPLIANCES**.

2. Select the range **E10:E11**, and then press and hold down the **Ctrl** key and select the range **E13:E15**.

3. Click the **AutoSum** button Σ on the Standard toolbar.

   Excel automatically sums the values in columns B through D and places the result in column E.

4. Select the range **D13:D15**.

5. Click the **Format Painter** button on the Standard toolbar, and click cell **E13**.

6. Apply the bold format to the contents of the range **E4:E15**.

7. Enlarge the width of column E to fit the column title.

8. Click cell **A3**.

   Figure 10-13 displays the revised Goldstar Order worksheet.

Figure 10-13 ◀
Totals for all
appliances

refrigerators generate
the most profit
per unit

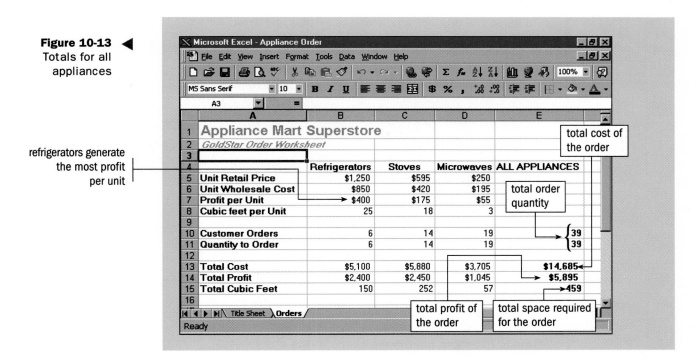

The total cost of the GoldStar order that would just meet customer orders is $14,685, the total profit from all appliances is $5,895, and the space required to store the order is 459 cubic feet.

Formulating the Problem

You need to determine the mixture of refrigerators, stoves, and microwave ovens that will generate the greatest profit, assuming all units are sold. The total order cost cannot exceed $50,000, and the total space required cannot exceed 1,300 cubic feet.

You might consider using Goal Seek to determine how many of each appliance you should order. However, Goal Seek is too limited for this task, because it can change the contents of only one cell to find the solution. To determine how many of each appliance to order, three cells must change: cell B11, which contains the number of refrigerators to order; cell C11, which contains the number of stoves to order; and cell D11, which contains the number of microwave ovens to order. First you'll try solving the problem by trial and error.

Solving Complex Problems Using Trial and Error

Since it appears that Goal Seek won't work, you consider using trial and error to solve the problem manually. At first, this seems easy. Your worksheet currently shows the result of ordering 6 refrigerators, 14 stoves, and 19 microwave ovens. The cost of this order would be $14,685 and the appliances would take up 459 cubic feet of storage space. If you place this order, you would not use the entire $50,000 or fill the storage space, so you can order additional appliances. But should you order more stoves, refrigerators, or microwave ovens?

You can see from the values in cells B7, C7, and D7 that refrigerators generate the greatest profit, so you consider purchasing as many refrigerators as space and funds permit, and then purchase stoves and microwave ovens to use up the remaining money and storage space. Try to manually solve the problem of what product mix will provide the most profit, while still meeting the total order cost and space limitations. You start by ordering 50 refrigerators.

To solve the product mix problem by trial and error:

1. In cell B11, enter **50**.

   The total order cost is $52,085 and the total space required is 1,559. There is not enough money or storage space for 50 refrigerators, so you try a smaller number.

2. Enter **40** in cell B11.

   The total order cost is $43,585 and the total space required is 1309. There is not quite enough space to store 40 refrigerators, so again you try a smaller number.

3. Enter **39** in cell B11.

   The total order cost is $42,735 and the total space required is 1284. There is sufficient money and space to order 39 units. The total profit from selling the appliances on this order would be $19,095.

You see that there is quite a bit of money left, but only 16 cubic feet of storage space. Microwave ovens require 3 cubic feet of space, so you decide to purchase five more microwave ovens to use up the remaining space and some of the remaining money.

To add five more microwave ovens to the order:

1. Enter **24** in cell D11.

   The total order profit increases to $19,370 with a total order cost of $43,710 and a total space requirement of 1,299 cubic feet.

You look at the worksheet and wonder if this is really the best answer. You used just about all of the available storage space but you still have over $6,000 left. What would happen if you had ordered more microwave ovens and fewer refrigerators?

Test the effect of ordering only 35 refrigerators and as many microwave ovens as you can purchase with the remaining money.

To test the effect of ordering more microwave ovens instead of refrigerators:

1. Reduce the number of refrigerators by entering **35** in cell B11. Next, increase the number of microwaves.

2. Enter **50** in cell D11.

   The total profit drops to $19,200, but the order would require only 1,277 cubic feet, leaving 23 cubic feet of remaining space. Since each microwave requires 3 cubic feet of storage, there seems to be room for seven more microwave ovens.

3. Enter **57** in cell D11.

   Total profit increases to $19,585.

This is the best solution yet. It yields a profit of $19,585, compared to $19,370 for the previous solution. But there are so many combinations. It could take hours or even days to try them all. You explain the problem to Jordan, who suggests that you try the Solver feature in Excel. He explains that Solver calculates solutions to what-if scenarios just like this one.

Solving Complex Problems Using Solver

Solver is an Excel add-in, or a program that you can install on your computer to add extra capabilities. Solver automatically calculates a maximum or minimum value of a cell by changing other cells that are "connected" to it by a formula.

When you use Solver, you must identify a target cell, the adjustable or changing cells, and the constraints that apply to your problem. A **target cell** is a cell that you want to maximize, minimize, or change to a specific value, such as the total profit from the appliance order. An **adjustable cell** is a cell that Excel changes to produce the desired result in the target cell. This could be the number of refrigerators to order. Finally, a **constraint** is a value that limits the way the problem is solved. One of your constraints is that you have to fit the appliance into the warehouse space allotted to you. You specify the target cell, changing cells, and constraints using the Solver Parameters dialog box. The settings you make in this dialog box are called the problem's **parameters**.

Setting Up Solver to Find a Solution

You examine the worksheet and determine that the target cell on your order worksheet is cell E14. This cell displays the total profit that will result from selling all the appliances on the order. You want Excel to produce a solution that maximizes the value in this cell.

The changing cells—the cells Excel can change to reach the solution—are cells B11, C11, and D11, the same cells that you changed when you tried to solve the problem manually. These cells contain the quantity to order for each appliance.

The two major constraints for this problem are the $50,000 spending limit and the 1,300-cubic-foot space limit. Next you'll set up the parameters to solve this problem using Solver.

REFERENCE
window

USING SOLVER

- Create a worksheet that contains the labels, values, and formulas for the problem you want to solve.
- Click Tools, and then click Solver to display the Solver parameters dialog box.
- The Set Target Cell box must contain the cell reference for the target cell, the cell you want to maximize, minimize, or set to a certain value.
- In the By Changing Cells box, list the cells that Excel can change to arrive at the solution.
- Use the Add button to add constraints that limit the changes Solver can make to the values in the cells.
- Click the Solve button to generate a solution.
- Click the OK button to return to the worksheet.

First, display the Solver Parameters dialog box, where you'll specify the target cell, changing cells, and constraints.

To set up the target cell and changing cells in Solver:

1. Click **Tools** on the menu bar, and then click **Solver**. Drag the Solver dialog box to display as much of the Orders worksheet as you can. See Figure 10-14.

Figure 10-14 ◀
Solver
Parameters
dialog box

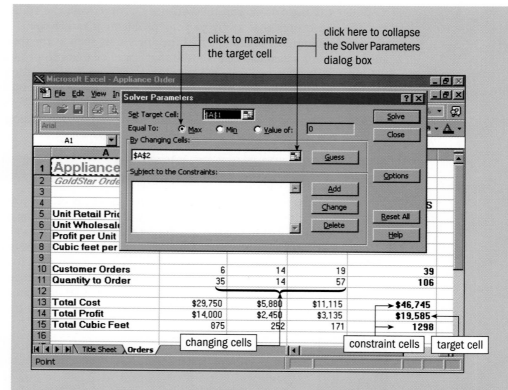

click to maximize
the target cell

click here to collapse
the Solver Parameters
dialog box

changing cells

constraint cells   target cell

TROUBLE? If you don't see Solver on the Tools menu, it might not be installed on your system. Click Tools on the menu bar, click Add-Ins, and select the Solver Add-In from the list. If you don't see the Solver add-in listed, you will have to install it from the Excel installation disks or CD. Ask your instructor or technical support person for more information.

To specify the target cell, you'll reduce the dialog box and point to the cells you want to include, which is easier and more accurate than typing them.

2. Click the **Collapse Dialog Box** button [icon] next to the Set Target Cell text box. The dialog box becomes reduced in size, showing only the target cell reference, and letting you see more worksheet cells.

3. Click cell **E14** to specify Total Profit as the target cell.

   E14 should now be entered in the Set Target Cell box.

4. Press the **Enter** key to restore the Solver Parameters dialog box to its original size.

5. Click the **Max** option button to indicate that you want Solver to maximize the total order profit.

6. In the By Changing Cells section, click the **Collapse Dialog Box** button [icon] to reduce the Solver Parameters dialog box again.

7. Select cells **B11** through **D11**, and then press the **Enter** key to specify that the quantities to order for each appliance are the changing cells.

Now that you have identified the target and changing cells, identify the other parameters for Solver by entering the two constraints. The first constraint is that the total order cost (in cell E13) must be less than or equal to $50,000, which can be expressed as E13 <= 50000. The second constraint is that the total space required (in cell E15) must be less than or equal to 1,300 cubic feet, which can be expressed as E15<=1300. You can either type these equations or select the cell references with your mouse. Since these are just single-cell references, you'll type them in.

To enter the constraints in Solver:

1. Click the **Subject to the Constraints** box, and then click the **Add** button to display the Add Constraint dialog box.

2. Type **E13** in the Cell Reference box to specify the Total Order Cost cell.

3. Click the **Constraint** list arrow in the middle of the Add Constraint dialog box, and then click the **<=** option from the list.

4. Click the **Constraint** box, and then type **50000** to indicate the spending limit.

   You have entered the first constraint, E13 <= 50000. See Figure 10-15.

Figure 10-15
Add Constraint
dialog box

cell with total cost
of the order

click to select the
comparison operator

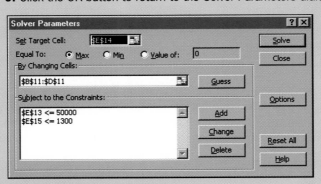

total order value must
be <=50,000

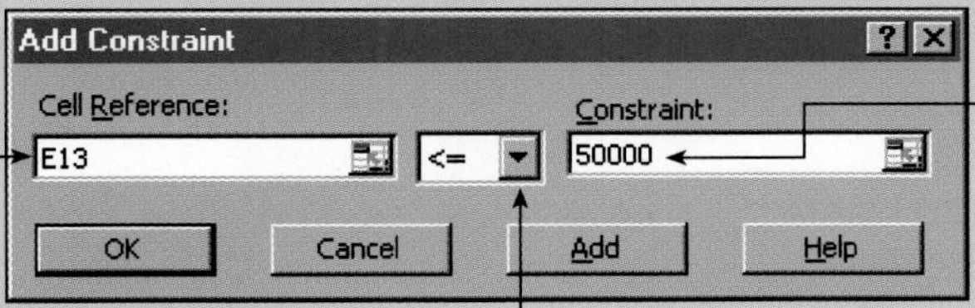

Next you need to add a second constraint this time to limit the total cubic feet in cell E15 to 1300.

5. Click the **Add** button. Solve stores the first constraint, and clears the dialog box so you can add another one.

6. Type **E15** in the Cell Reference box to specify the total cubic feet.

7. Make sure that the **<=** option is still selected from the comparison list.

8. Click the **Constraint** box, and then type **1300**, the maximum for total cubic feet.

   You have entered the second constraint, E15 <= 1300.

9. Click the OK button to return to the Solver Parameters dialog box. See Figure 10-16.

Figure 10-16
Setting the
target cell,
changing
cells, and
constraints

The two constraints you entered are listed in the Subject to the Constraints list.

TROUBLE? If the constraints on your screen are not the same as those in Figure 10-16, do one of the following: Select a constraint, click the Change button if you need to change the cell references in a constraint; click the Add button if you need to add a constraint; or click the Delete button if you need to delete a constraint.

Now that you have specified the target cell, changing cells, and constraints, you are ready to have Solver look for a solution to the problem.

To generate the solution using Solver:

1. Click the **Solve** button.

In the status bar, you can see Solver rapidly "trying out" solutions. After a short time, the Solver Results dialog box appears and displays the message, "Solver has converged to the current solution. All constraints are satisfied." See Figure 10-17.

Figure 10-17 ◀
Solver results

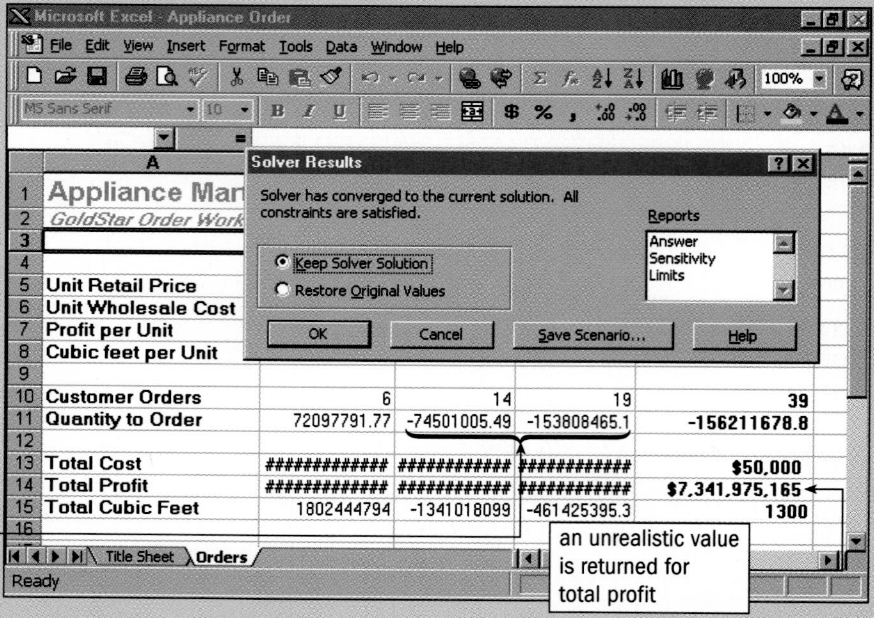

Solver has
determined you
should order negative
amounts of stoves
and microwaves

an unrealistic value
is returned for
total profit

TROUBLE? If you see the message, "The Set Target Cell Values do not Converge" in the Show Trial Solutions dialog box, click the Stop button. When the Solver Results dialog box appears, continue with the following steps. If you see any other message in the Solver Results dialog box, simply continue with the steps.

2. If necessary, drag the dialog box out of the way to view the values Solver has produced so far as a solution to the problem.

You see that something is clearly wrong. In the current trial solution, Solver recommends ordering a very large number of refrigerators and large negative numbers of stoves and microwave ovens. This results in an enormous profit for the company but, of course, you can't order a negative number of items. You can solve this problem by adding additional constraints.

Inserting Additional Constraints

You need additional constraints for your analysis to take into account the fact that you need to order at least enough refrigerators, stoves, and microwaves to cover customer demands. First, though, you need to remove the values Solver placed in the worksheet and add some additional constraints.

To remove the current values from the target cells:

1. Click the **Restore Original Values** option button in the Solver Results dialog box.

2. Click the **OK** button to close the Solver dialog box.

Solver restores the original values to the worksheet.

To allow Solver to produce a realistic solution that reflects all the circumstances, you will specify the following additional constraints:

- The number of refrigerators to order in cell B11 must be greater than or equal to the customer orders for refrigerators in cell B10; in Solver terms, the constraint would be B11>=B10.

- The number of stoves to order in cell C11 must be greater than or equal to the customer orders for stoves in cell B14, or C11>=C10.

- The number of microwave ovens to order in cell D11 must be greater than or equal to the customer orders for microwave ovens in cell D10, or D11>=D10.

These constraints will also prevent Solver from ordering negative quantities because the order quantities are greater than zero. Now add these three additional constraints to the Solver parameters.

To add a constraint forcing Solver to order enough refrigerators to fill customer orders:

1. Click **Tools** on the menu bar, and then click **Solver**.

2. Click the **Add** button.

3. Click the **Cell Reference** box, and then type **B11**.

4. Click the **Constraint** list arrow in the middle of the Add Constraint dialog box, and then click the **>=** option in the list.

5. Click the **Constraint** box, and then type **B10**.

   This indicates that the quantity to order must always be greater than or equal to the customer orders.

6. Click the **Add** button.

Next, you add a constraint forcing Solver to order enough stoves to fill customer orders.

To add the constraint that C11>=C10:

1. Type **C11** in the Cell Reference box.

2. Click the **Constraint** list arrow in the middle of the Add Constraint dialog box, and then click the **>=** option in the list.

3. Type **C10** in the Constraint box.

   This constraint specifies that the quantity of stoves to order from GoldStar must always be greater than or equal to the quantity of customer orders for stoves.

4. Click the **Add** button.

Finally add a constraint forcing Solver to order enough microwave ovens to fill customer orders.

To add the constraint that D11>=D10:

1. Type **D11** in the Cell Reference box.

2. Click the **Constraint** list arrow in the middle of the Add Constraint dialog box, and then click the **>=** option in the list.

3. Type **D10** in the Constraint box.

The new constraint specifies that the quantity of microwave ovens to order must always be greater than or equal to the customer orders for microwaves.

4. Click the **OK** button.

The revised values are shown in the Subject to the Constraints box as displayed in Figure 10-18.

Figure 10-18 ◀
Additional constraints in the Solver Parameters dialog box

new constraints ────

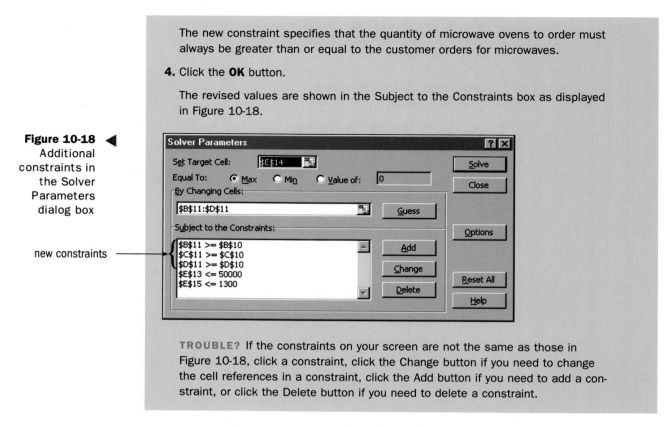

TROUBLE? If the constraints on your screen are not the same as those in Figure 10-18, click a constraint, click the Change button if you need to change the cell references in a constraint, click the Add button if you need to add a constraint, or click the Delete button if you need to delete a constraint.

Now, have Solver try again to find a solution, this time using the new set of constraints.

To activate Solver:

1. Click the **Solve** button.

This time the Solver dialog box message says, "Solver found a solution. All constraints and optimality conditions are satisfied."

The solution is shown in Figure 10-19.

Figure 10-19 ◀
Solver's second solution

order quantities are not integers ────

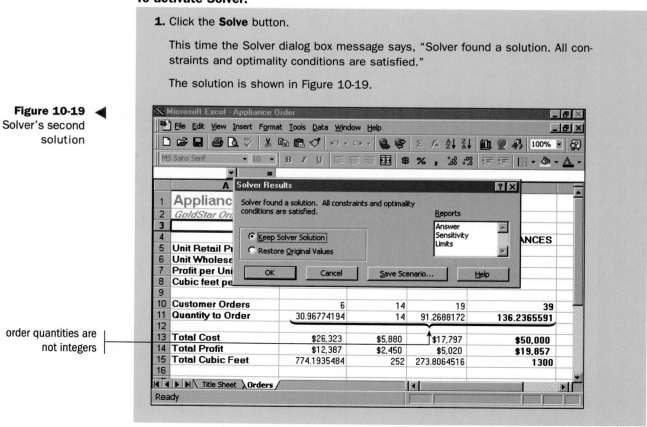

This solution is better. Solver did not order negative quantities, and you can see in row 11 that it did recommend ordering enough of each item to cover the customer orders shown in row 10. However, you notice yet another problem. Solver has ordered 30.96774194 refrigerators and 91.2688172 microwave ovens. Since you can only order whole units, you need another constraint to have Solver order non-fractional unit quantities: the integer constraint.

Inserting an Integer Constraint

In addition to constraints based on values or on the contents of other cells, you can have Solver recommend only integer values, commonly called "whole numbers," in the cells it changes to reach the solution. This is particularly important in a situation like your appliance order, where you can't order part of an appliance. You need to specify that adjustable cells B11, C11, and D11 must contain integer values.

To specify integers in cells B11, C11, and D11:

1. Click the **Restore Original Values** option button, and then click the **OK** button.

2. Click **Tools** on the menu bar, and then click **Solver**.

3. Click the **Add** button.

4. Click the **Cell Reference Collapse Dialog Box** button 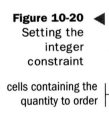 to reduce the size of the Add Constraints dialog box.

5. Drag the pointer to outline cells **B11** through **D11**, and then release the mouse button.

6. Press the **Enter** key to restore the Add Constraints dialog box to its original size.

7. Click the **Constraint** list arrow in the middle of the Add Constraint dialog box, and then click **int**.

   The word "integer" appears in the Constraint box, as shown in Figure 10-20.

Figure 10-20 ◀
Setting the integer constraint

cells containing the quantity to order

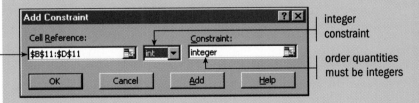

integer constraint

order quantities must be integers

8. Click the **OK** button.

9. Click the **Solve** button in the Solver Parameters dialog box.

   Solver returns a message stating that it has found a solution.

10. Click the **OK** button.

    Solver's solution is shown in Figure 10-21.

Figure 10-21 ◀
Solver's third
solution

all but $25 of the
purchasing budget
will be spent

positive integers

all allotted storage
space is used

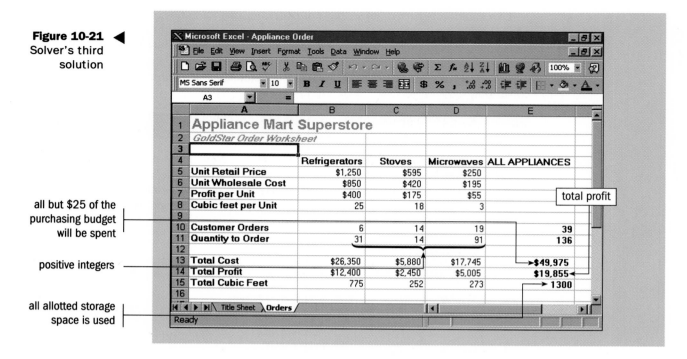

Solver indicates that you should order 31 refrigerators, 14 stoves, and 91 microwave ovens. This solution uses all but $25 of the available funds and all of the available storage space. It also generates a total profit of $19,855. Note that this might not be the ultimate solution because Solver tries a limited number of combinations in its search for a solution. There is a small chance that the best solution might not be found. However, with all storage space used and only $25 left, you are fairly certain that this solution must be very close to the optimal solution.

You've come up with an excellent solution to the problem of maximizing profits while staying within Jordan's budget and within the space allotted to you by the warehouse manager. You are ready to start preparing your report for Jordan. You can do this in Excel by creating an answer report.

Creating an Answer Report

How do you evaluate and report the solution that Solver produced? Solver can create three different reports—an answer report, a sensitivity report, and a limits report.

The **answer report** is the most useful of the three, because it summarizes the results of a successful solution by displaying information about the target cell, changing cells, and constraints. This report includes the original and final values for the target and changing cells, as well as the constraint formulas.

The **sensitivity** and **limits reports** are used primarily in science and engineering environments when the user wants to investigate the mathematical aspects of the Solver solution. These reports allow you to quantify the reliability of the solution. However, you can't use these reports when your problem contains integer constraints, so you will create only an answer report for your inventory solution.

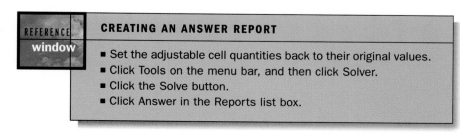

REFERENCE
window

CREATING AN ANSWER REPORT

- Set the adjustable cell quantities back to their original values.
- Click Tools on the menu bar, and then click Solver.
- Click the Solve button.
- Click Answer in the Reports list box.

You decide to create an answer report as part of the final written report you'll give Jordan about your analysis.

An answer report provides information on the process used to go from the original values to the final solution. To make sure that the answer report includes information on the entire process, you'll set the quantities to order back to their original values, and then solve the problem again and generate the answer report. You only need to change the values for refrigerators and microwave ovens because the current value for the quantity of stoves to order, 14, is the same as the original value.

To set the quantity to order back to the original values for refrigerators and microwave ovens:

1. In cell B11, enter **6**, the original quantity that you had in this cell.

2. In cell D11, enter **19**, the original quantity that you had in this cell.

Now you'll use Solver to solve the problem again, but this time you'll create an answer report.

To solve the problem again and create an answer report:

1. Click **Tools** on the menu bar, and then click **Solver**. Your original parameters, changing cells, and constraints remain as you set them earlier.

2. Click the **Solve** button.

After a few seconds the Solver Results dialog box appears. You can now create the answer report.

3. Click **Answer** in the Reports list box. Make sure the Keep Solver Solution option button is selected this time. See Figure 10-22.

Figure 10-22 ◄
Creating an answer report

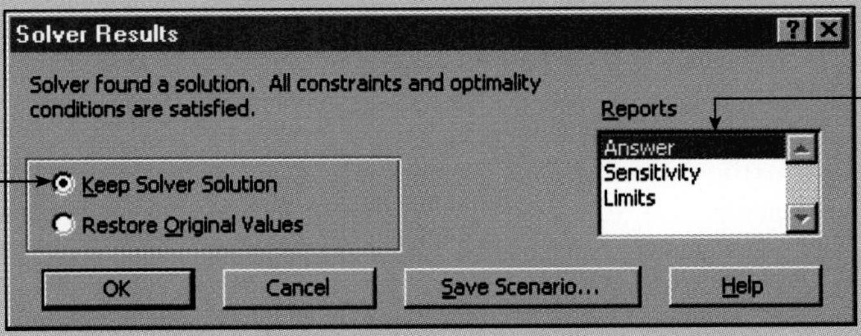

this time you'll keep the solution

click to create an answer report

4. Click the **OK** button to save the answer report.

Solver places the answer report in a separate sheet called "Answer Report 1."

The first time you create an answer report for a problem, Excel names it Answer Report 1. It calls the second report Answer Report 2, and so on. You decide to view the answer report.

To examine the answer report:

1. Click the **Answer Report 1** tab.

Figure 10-23 shows the answer report for the solution Solver just produced.

Figure 10-23 ◀
Answer report

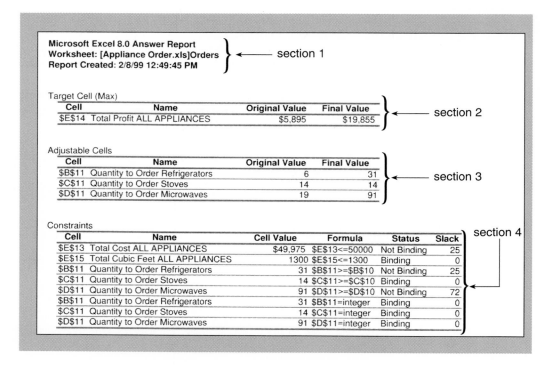

The answer report is divided into four sections. The first section includes titles, which indicate that this is an Excel answer report created from the Orders sheet in the Appliance Order workbook. The second section displays information about the target cell, in this case Total Profit, including its location, the cell label, and the cell's original value and final values.

The third section displays information about the changing cells, which the report calls Adjustable Cells. This section of the report shows the location, column and row label, the original value, and the final value of each cell. The column and row labels from the worksheet are joined to form the cell name in the answer report. For example, on the worksheet, Quantity to Order is the row label and Refrigerators is the column label, so cell B11 is called Quantity to Order Refrigerators in the answer report.

The fourth section of the report displays information about the constraints. In addition to the location, name, and value of each constraint, this section shows the constraint formulas. The second column from the right shows the status of each constraint. The status of Total Cost ALL APPLIANCES, Quantity to Order Refrigerators, and Quantity to Order Microwaves is listed as "Not Binding." **Not Binding** means that these constraints were not limiting factors in the solution. The status of the other constraints is listed as "Binding." **Binding** means that the final value in these cells was equal to the constraint value. For example, the Total Cubic Feet ALL APPLIANCES constraint was E15 <=1300. In the solution, cell E15 is 1300, which is at the maximum limit of the constraint, so this was a binding constraint in the solution.

The last column on the right shows the slack for each constraint. The **slack** is the difference between the value in the cell and the value at the limit of the constraint. For example, the constraint for the Total Cost ALL APPLIANCES was $50,000. In the solution the total order cost was $49,975. The difference, or slack, between these two numbers is $25. Binding constraints show a slack of zero. Constraints listed as not binding show the difference between the constraint limit and the final value.

You decide to add a header as additional documentation, and then print the answer report.

To add a header and print the answer report:

1. Click the **Print Preview** button 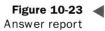 on the Standard toolbar.

2. Click the **Setup** button to display the Page Setup dialog box, and then click the **Header/Footer** tab.

3. Click **Custom Header** to display the Header dialog box.

4. Delete any headers displayed in the Left or Center Section, and then enter you name in the **Right Section** and press the **spacebar** to separate your name from the date.

5. Click the **Date** button . The code for the date appears.

6. Press the **spacebar**, and then click the **Filename** button . The filename code appears. Don't be concerned if "&[File]" appears on a separate line. See Figure 10-24.

Figure 10-24 ◄
Completed
Header
dialog box

7. Click the **OK** button to return to the Page Setup dialog box.

8. Click the **OK** button to return to the Print Preview window.

9. Click the **Print** button on the Print Preview toolbar to open the Print dialog box.

10. Click the **OK** button to print the report.

Next, you'll print the Orders worksheet.

To save and print the Orders worksheet:

1. Click the **Orders** tab.

2. Click the **Print Preview** button on the Standard toolbar.

3. Click the **Setup** button and format the printout so that it prints in landscape mode on a single page, with the gridlines turned off. The header should be the same as the one used in the printout for the answer report.

4. Click the **OK** button to return to the Print Preview window.

5. Click the **Print** button and then click the **OK** button to print the worksheet. You printout should look like Figure 10-25.

Figure 10-25 ◀
Final printed
worksheet

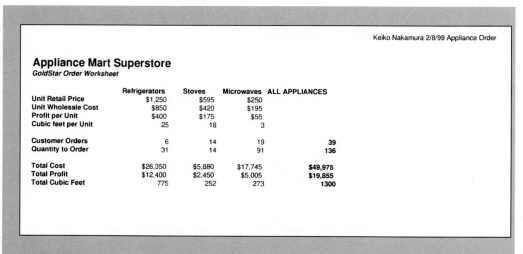

Keiko Nakamura 2/8/99 Appliance Order

Appliance Mart Superstore
GoldStar Order Worksheet

	Refrigerators	Stoves	Microwaves	ALL APPLIANCES
Unit Retail Price	$1,250	$595	$250	
Unit Wholesale Cost	$850	$420	$195	
Profit per Unit	$400	$175	$55	
Cubic feet per Unit	25	18	3	
Customer Orders	6	14	19	39
Quantity to Order	31	14	91	136
Total Cost	$26,350	$5,880	$17,745	$49,975
Total Profit	$12,400	$2,450	$5,005	$19,855
Total Cubic Feet	775	252	273	1300

Examine the printed worksheet and answer report to make sure they contain the correct information.

6. Save and close the workbook, and exit Excel.

You can now take the printed reports to Jordan. He'll be pleased that you used one of Excel's more powerful features to determine how best to order appliances that fit your budget and space constraints.

Quick **Check**

1 In your own words, describe Excel Solver.

2 Under what circumstances would you use Solver rather than Goal Seek or trial and error?

3 Define the following terms:

target cell

constraint

4 What should you do if Solver returns an erroneous solution (such as negative product orders) to your problem?

5 What should you do if you do not want Solver to produce fractional numbers as the solution?

6 What is an answer report?

7 Define the following terms:

Not Binding constraint

Binding constraint

slack

8 Why should you reset your worksheet back to its original values before generating an answer report?

In this tutorial, you formulated a problem that had several parameters and constraints, and attempted to solve it using both trial and error and Solver. Solver proved to be the fastest and most effective way of solving this type of problem. Then you generated an answer report to help you evaluate the Solver solution to your inventory problem.

Tutorial Assignments

Jordan was impressed with your report that told him the best "mix" of product to buy. Now, in addition to refrigerators, stoves, and microwave ovens, GoldStar has offered Appliance Mart Superstore special pricing on dryers. GoldStar dryers are available for $215 and require 11 cubic feet of storage space; the retail price is $385. There are five orders for GoldStar dryers at this time, and the sales manager thinks they will sell very well. Given funds of $75,000 and a storage space limit of 1,500 cubic feet for all the items on the order, Jordon would like you to perform a similar analysis to help him decide what mix of products he should order.

Do the following:

1. If necessary, start Excel, and open the Dryers workbook in the TAssign folder for Tutorial 10 and save it as "Dryer Order."

2. Enter the new workbook name, "Dryer Order" in cell B4, and enter your name and the date in cells B5 and B6.

3. Go to the Orders worksheet, insert a new column between column D and column E and enter the heading Dryers in the new cell E4.

4. Enter the wholesale unit price of a dryer in the new cell E5 and the retail cost of a dryer in cell E6.

5. Enter the formula in cell E7 to calculate the profit for a dryer.

6. Enter the cubic feet of storage required for a dryer in cell E8.

7. Enter 5 for the customer orders and the quantity to order.

8. Copy the formulas from the range D13:D15 to the range E13:E15.

9. Activate Solver and adjust the changing cells to $B$11:$E$11.

10. Change the integer constraint so all of the units sold must be integers.

11. Add a constraint so the quantity of dryers to order is greater than or equal to customer orders for dryers.

12. Change the constraint that limits the total order cost from $50,000 to $75,000.

13. Change the storage space constraint that limits total space required to 1500.

14. Use Solver to solve the problem and produce an answer report.

15. Replace the default headers on the worksheet and on the answer report so they contain your name, the date, and the filename.

16. Preview the worksheet and the answer report, and give it a professional appearance by using font styles, shaded fills, and/or other formatting features.

17. Save the modified workbook.

18. Print the worksheet and the answer report.

19. Print the formulas for the worksheet.

Case Problems

1. Ordering Products for a Furniture Sale at Home Furnishings WareHouse Bruce Hsu is the assistant manager at Home Furnishings WareHouse, a retail furniture outlet. One of Home Furnishings WareHouse's suppliers is having a sales promotion featuring special prices on couches and chairs. Bruce has been asked to determine the mix of products that will generate the greatest profit within the limits of the available funds and display space. Bruce can spend up to $60,000 on the order, and display space is limited to 1,300 square feet. There are no customer orders for either couches or chairs, but the sales manager doesn't want Bruce to order more than 15 chairs.

Bruce has created a worksheet for this problem and has made several attempts to determine the solution manually. Bruce has asked you to help him use Solver to find the best solution. Do the following:

1. If necessary, start Excel, and then open the Couches workbook in the Cases folder for Tutorial 10. Save it in the same folder as Furniture Order. Maximize the worksheet window, and then enter the new workbook name, your name, and the date on the Title sheet.

2. Click the Orders tab, and then set up the Solver parameters for this problem using the following hints:
   a. The target cell contains the value for total order profit. Solver should attempt to maximize this cell.
   b. The changing cells contain the quantities of couches and chairs to order.
   c. The total order cost cannot exceed $60,000.
   d. The total space required must be less than or equal to 1300.
   e. You cannot order more than 15 chairs.
   f. You must order couches and chairs in whole units.
   g. You must order a positive number of couches and chairs.

3. Use Solver to produce a solution, and then create an answer report.

4. Format the worksheet to give it a professional appearance.

5. Preview the worksheet and make any necessary formatting changes.

6. Save the workbook, and then preview and print the worksheet including the answer report.

2. Manufacturing Pontoon Boats at Robbins Pontoon Incorporated Mike Chignell is the assistant to the director of manufacturing at Robbins Pontoon Incorporated. Robbins manufactures four different models of pontoon boats: All Purpose, Camping, Utility, and Fishing. Each of the four models is built on the same boat frame. A topside assembly is attached to the frame to create each model.

Robbins currently has 135 boat frames in stock and a limited number of the four different topside assemblies. Mike wants you to determine the mix of models that will generate the greatest profit, given the available frames and topside assemblies. You'll have to make sure he manufactures enough of each model to fill the customer orders. Do the following:

1. If necessary, start Excel, open the Pontoon workbook in the Cases folder for Tutorial 10 on your Student Disk, and save it in the same folder as Pontoon Boat Order. Maximize the worksheet window, and then enter the new worksheet name, your name, and the date on the Title sheet.

2. Click the Orders tab, and then set up the Solver parameters for this problem using the following hints:
   a. You want to maximize the total profit from all models of pontoon boats by changing the quantity to make of each boat model.
   b. The optimal solution should include the following limits:
      - You cannot make more boats than you have available assemblies for each type.
      - You have to satisfy the customer orders for each boat type.
      - The total number of boats you make cannot exceed the total number of available frames.
      - Make only complete boats.

3. Use Solver to produce a solution and generate an answer report.

4. Modify the answer report worksheet so it contains your name, the date, and the filename.

5. Format the worksheet to give it a professional appearance.

6. Preview the printout and make any formatting changes necessary for a professional appearance.

7. Save the completed workbook, and then preview and print the completed worksheet.

3. Scheduling Employees at Chipster's Pizza Lisa Avner is the assistant manager at Chipster's Pizza, a popular pizza place located in Cedar Falls, Iowa. Chipster's is open every day from 5:00 PM to 1:00 AM. Friday and Saturday are the busiest nights; Sunday and Wednesday nights are moderately busy; Monday, Tuesday, and Thursday are the slowest nights.

Lisa is responsible for devising a schedule that provides enough employees to meet the usual demand, without scheduling more employees than are needed for each shift. All of Chipster's employees work five consecutive days, and then have two days off. This means Lisa can schedule employees for seven different shifts—the Sunday through Thursday shift, the Monday through Friday shift, the Tuesday through Saturday shift, and so forth.

Lisa has created a worksheet showing the number of employees scheduled for each of the seven shifts, the total hours scheduled for each day, the hours needed for each day, and the difference between the hours scheduled and the hours needed. Lisa has asked you to help her find the schedule that will result in enough employee hours to meet the daily demand without scheduling excess hours.

Do the following:

1. If necessary, start Excel, and open the Pizza workbook in the Cases folder for Tutorial 10. Save it on your Student Disk as Chipster Employee Schedule in the same folder. Maximize the worksheet window, and then enter the new workbook name, your name, and the date on the Title sheet.

2. Click the Schedule tab. The worksheet shows the current schedule. Cell B13 displays the current total of 560 scheduled hours. Cell B14 displays the current total of 448 needed hours. Cell B15 displays the current total of 112 excess scheduled hours.

3. Set up the Solver parameters to find a solution to the scheduling problem using the following parameters:
   a. Minimize the total difference between total hours worked and hours needed so that you don't over-schedule employees.
   b. Minimize the difference between hours worked and hours needed by modifying the number of shifts for each schedule.
   c. Use the following constraints:
      ■ You must have at least as many total hours worked over the entire schedule as total hours needed.
      ■ You must have a positive number of workers for each shift.
      ■ Workers must be scheduled for an entire shift.
      ■ You must schedule enough workers so the difference between the total hours worked each day and the total hours needed each day is greater than or equal to zero.

4. Use Solver to produce a solution and create an answer report.

5. Modify the headers on the worksheet and the answer report so they contain your name, the date, and the filename.

6. Save the workbook.

7. Preview and print the worksheet and the answer report.

4. Furniture Purchasing at Southland Furniture Eve Bowman is the manager of Southland Furniture store, and she is planning a New Year's Day sale. The store has only 75 square feet of space available to display and stock this merchandise. During the sale, each folding table costs $5, retails for $11, and takes up two square feet of space. Each chair costs $4, retails for $9, and takes up one square foot of space. The maximum amount allocated for purchasing the tables and chairs for the sale is $280. Eve doesn't think she can sell more than 40 chairs, but the demand for tables is virtually unlimited. Eve has asked you to help her determine how many tables and chairs she should purchase in order to make the most profit. Complete the following:

1. What is the goal in this problem?

2. Which element of the problem would you specify for the changing cells if you used Solver to find a solution to this problem?

3. List the constraints for this problem.

4. Enter the information into a worksheet in Excel, including a title sheet and data on total cost, total profit, and total space.

5. Save the workbook as Southland Furniture in the Cases folder for Tutorial 10 on your Student Disk.

6. Using Solver, determine how many folding tables and folding chairs should be purchased to maximize profits.

7. Create an answer report, detailing the parameters of the problem and the optimal solution.

8. Modify the headers on the worksheet and the answer report so they contain your name, the date, and the filename.

9. Save the workbook, and then preview and print the worksheet and the answer report.

Importing Data into Excel

Working with a Stock Portfolio for Davis & Larson

In this tutorial you will:

- Import data from a text file into an Excel workbook

- Retrieve data from a database using the Query Wizard

- Retrieve data from multiple database tables

- Retrieve data from a database into a pivot table

- Retrieve stock market data from the World Wide Web

- Use hyperlinks to view information on the World Wide Web

LAB

Databases

Davis & Larson

CASE Davis & Larson is a brokerage firm based in Chicago. Founded by Charles Davis and Maria Larson, the company has provided financial planning and investment services to Chicago-area corporations and individuals for the last 15 years. As part of its investment services business, the company advises clients on its investment portfolios, so it needs to have a variety of stock market information available at all times. Like all brokerage firms, the company is connected to many financial and investment information services. The investment counselors at the company must have access to current financial data and reports, but they also must be able to examine information on long-term trends in the market.

Some of this information comes from Excel workbooks, but other information is stored in specialized financial packages and statistical programs. In addition, the company maintains a database with detailed financial information about a variety of stocks, bonds, and funds. Company employees also have access to the Internet to receive up-to-the-minute market reports. Since much of the information the counselors need comes from outside the company, they must retrieve information in order to analyze it and make decisions.

Kelly Watkins is an investment counselor at Davis & Larson. She wants you to help her manage the different types of data available to her as she works on the Sunrise Fund, one of the company's most important stock portfolios. Since Kelly prefers to work with financial data using Excel, she wants you to retrieve the data for her and place it into an Excel workbook.

SESSION

11.1

In this session, you'll use the Excel Text Import Wizard to retrieve data from a text file. You'll select columns of data for retrieval and specify the format of the incoming data. You'll learn about basic database concepts, and about how to retrieve information from a database using the Query Wizard. Finally, you'll learn how to create retrieval criteria so you can retrieve only the information you want.

Planning Data Needs at Davis & Larson

In her job as an investment counselor at Davis & Larson, Kelly Watkins needs to help her clients plan their investment strategies. To do her job well, Kelly needs to look at the market from a variety of angles. She needs to examine long-term trends to help her clients understand the benefits of creating a long-term investment strategy. She also needs to see market performance for recent months in order to analyze current trends. Finally, she needs to be able to assess the daily mood of the market by regularly viewing up-to-the-minute reports.

The information that Kelly needs to do her job comes from a variety of sources. As shown in Figure 11-1, long-term and historical stock information from the company's old record-keeping system has been retrieved from other financial software packages and placed in text files that are accessible to all counselors. The company stores its current market information in databases, which is where Kelly gets information on recent trends. Finally, Kelly can access current market reports electronically from the Internet.

Figure 11-1 ◀
Kelly's data
sources

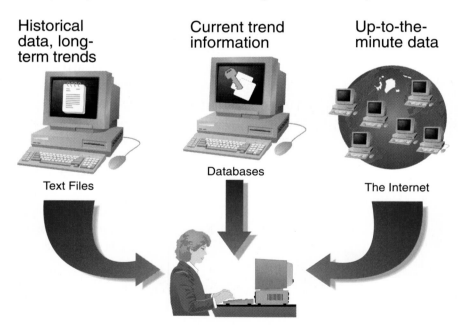

Historical data, long-term trends

Current trend information

Up-to-the-minute data

Text Files

Databases

The Internet

Kelly is responsible for tracking the performance of one of the company's investment vehicles called the Sunrise Fund. The Sunrise Fund is composed of 21 different stocks on the New York Stock Exchange (NYSE), and it is one of Davis & Larson's oldest and most successful funds. Kelly would like to have a single Excel workbook that summarizes essential information about the Sunrise Fund. She wants the workbook to include historical information describing: a) how the fund has performed over the past few years; b) more recent information on the fund's performance in the last year as well as the last few days; and c) up-to-the-minute reports on the fund's current status.

Kelly has written up a plan for the workbook that she wants you to create, shown in Figure 11-2.

Excel

Figure 11-2 ◄
Kelly's plan for
the Sunrise
Fund workbook

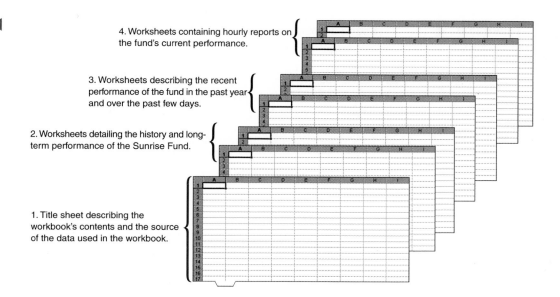

4. Worksheets containing hourly reports on the fund's current performance.

3. Worksheets describing the recent performance of the fund in the past year and over the past few days.

2. Worksheets detailing the history and long-term performance of the Sunrise Fund.

1. Title sheet describing the workbook's contents and the source of the data used in the workbook.

Once she has these three types of information in her Excel workbook, Kelly will use Excel tools to analyze the data.

Locating and organizing the different types of data Kelly wants in the workbook will be challenging, since you will have to bring in data from three different sources. You quickly see that you're going to have to master the techniques of retrieving information from each of them.

You'll begin by retrieving the first piece of information she needs, the Sunrise Fund's historical data. After talking with a few coworkers, you manage to locate a text file containing daily values for the fund over the last three years. You'll import this text file to Excel.

Working with Text Files

A **text file** contains only text and numbers, without any formulas, graphics, special fonts, or formatted text that you would find in a file saved in a spreadsheet program format. Text files are one of the simplest and most widely used methods of storing data because most software programs can both save and retrieve data in a text file format. For example, Excel can open a text file into a worksheet, where you can then format it as your would any data. Excel can also save a worksheet as a text file, preserving only the data, without any of the formats applied to it. In addition, many different types of computers can read text files. So although text files contain only raw, unformatted data, they are very useful in situations where you want to share data with others. There are several types of text file formats, which you'll learn in the next section.

Text File Formats

Since a text file doesn't contain formatting codes to give it structure, there must be some other way of making it understandable to a program that will read it. If a text file contains only numbers, how will the importing program know where one column of numbers ends and another begins? When you import or create a text file, you have to know how that data is organized within the file. One way to structure text files is to use a **delimiter**, which is a symbol, usually a space, a comma, or a tab, that separates one column of data from another. The delimiter tells a program that reads it where columns begin and end. Text that is separated by delimiters is called **delimited text**. Figure 11-3 shows three examples of the same stock market data delimited by spaces, commas, and tabs.

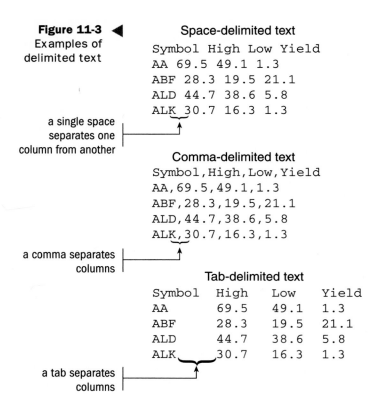

Figure 11-3 ◀
Examples of
delimited text

Space-delimited text

a single space
separates one
column from another

a comma separates
columns

a tab separates
columns

In each example there are four columns of data: Symbol, High, Low, and Yield. In the first example, a space separates the columns. The second example shows the same data, except that a comma separates each data column. In the third example, a tab separates the columns. As you can see, columns in delimited text files are not always vertically aligned as they would be in a spreadsheet, but this is not a problem for a program that reads and recognizes the delimiter. A tab delimiter is often the best way of separating text columns, since tab-delimited text can include spaces or commas within each column.

In addition to delimited text, you can also organize data with a fixed width file. In a **fixed width** text file, each column will start at a same location in the file. For example, the first column would start at the first space in the file; the second column will start at the 10th space, and so forth. Figure 11-4 shows columns arranged in a fixed width format. As you can see, all the columns line up visually, because each one must start at the same location.

Figure 11-4 ◀
An example of
fixed width text

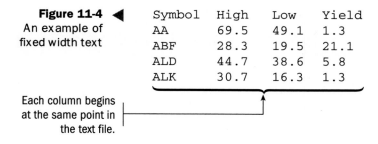

Each column begins
at the same point in
the text file.

When Excel starts to open a text file, it automatically starts the **Text Import Wizard** to determine whether the data is in a fixed width format or a delimited format—and if it's delimited, what delimiter is used. If necessary, you can also intervene and tell it how to interpret the text file.

Excel

REFERENCE
window

IMPORTING A TEXT FILE WITH THE TEXT IMPORT WIZARD

- Click File and then click Open.
- In the Open dialog box, in the Files of type list box, click Text Files.
- In the file list window, click the name of the text file you want to import, and then click the Open button.
- In the Text Import Wizard - Step 1 of 3 dialog box, choose the Delimited or Fixed width data type option, and set the Start import at row value.
- In the Text Import Wizard - Step 2 of 3 dialog box, do one of the following: If the text file is delimited, check the appropriate delimiter symbol. If the text file is fixed width, click, double-click, or drag the vertical column break lines to indicate where columns begin and end.
- In the Text Import Wizard - Step 3 of 3 dialog box, choose a Column data format option that specifies the format for each incoming column, or click the Do not import Column (Skip) option button to omit a specific column from the import.
- Click the Finish button.

Having seen some of the issues involved in using a text file, you are ready to import the file containing the Sunrise Fund's historical data.

Starting the Text Import Wizard

The text file that Kelly wants you to import into Excel is stored in the file named History.txt. The .txt filename extension identifies it as a text file. (Some other common text filename extensions are .dat, .prn, or .csv.) The person who gave you the text file didn't tell you anything about its structure, but you can easily determine that using the Text Import Wizard. You'll begin by opening the text file, which is similar to opening an Excel workbook, except that in the Open dialog box, you need to tell Excel to display text filenames in the file list. By default, Excel will display only Excel files unless you indicate you want to see other types of files.

To open the History text file:

1. Start Excel as usual, and make sure your Student Disk is in the appropriate drive.

2. Click **File** on the menu bar and then click **Open**.

3. In the Look in list box, locate the Tutor11 folder on your Student Disk.

4. Click the **Files of type** list arrow (near the bottom of the dialog box) and then click **Text Files**. The names of all text files in that folder now appear.

5. Click **History** in the File List window, and click the **Open** button.

Excel starts the Text Import Wizard, as shown in Figure 11-5.

Figure 11-5
Text Import
Wizard -
Step 1 of 3
dialog box

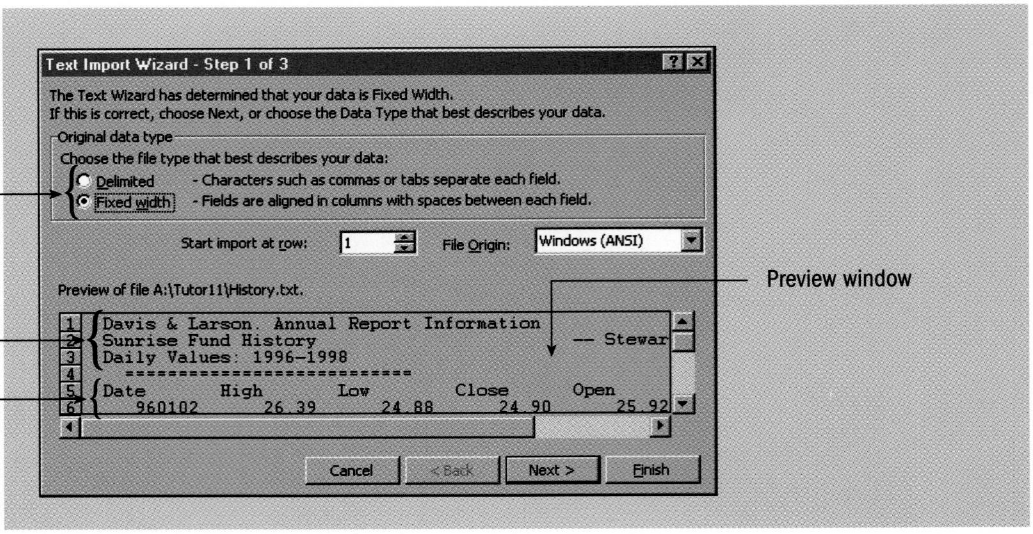

types of text files

title lines

start of data
to be imported

In the Original data type section, the Fixed width option button is already selected. This means that the Text Import Wizard has determined that the data is arranged in fixed width format. By looking in the Preview window, you can see that the first line of data (in row 6) does look like a fixed width file, so you won't want to change the Text Import Wizard's recommendation.

There are five columns of data in the text file: Date, High, Low, Close, and Open, corresponding to the date, the fund's high and low values on that date, and the fund's opening and closing values. The Preview window also shows that the first four lines, or rows, of the text file contain titles and lines describing the contents of the file. You want to import only the data, not the title lines, so you'll indicate the row at which you want to begin the import process, called the starting row.

Specifying the Starting Row

By default, the Text Import Wizard will start importing text with the first row of the file. Since you're only interested in retrieving the data and not the title lines, you will have the Text Import Wizard skip the first three lines of the file. You do this by specifying a new starting row for the import. You want it to start with the fifth row, which contains the labels for each column of numbers.

To specify the starting row or line number of the text file:

1. Click the **Start import at row** spin up arrow to change the value to **5**.

   The Preview window now displays only the data from the text file, without the rows of descriptive text.

   TROUBLE? Don't be concerned if the Preview window doesn't change quickly; it might take a few seconds before the window updates.

2. Click the **Next** button to display the Text Import Wizard - Step 2 of 3 dialog box. See Figure 11-6.

Figure 11-6 ◀
Text Import
Wizard -
Step 2 of 3
dialog box

misplaced
column break

missing
column break

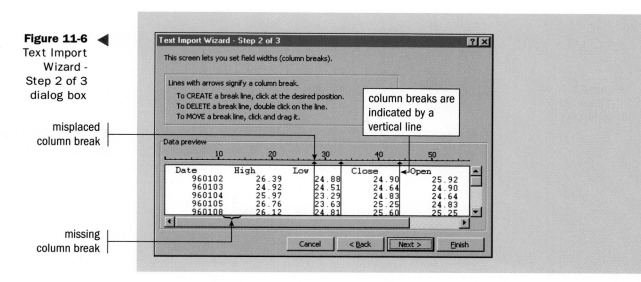

Having specified the starting row for the text file, you'll add column breaks and edit those automatically inserted by the Text Import Wizard, so the imported text will be imported correctly.

Editing Column Breaks

In order for a fixed width text file to import correctly into Excel, there must be some way for the Text Import Wizard to know where each column begins and ends. The point at which one column ends and another begins is called a **column break**. In a delimited file, the delimiter automatically determines the column break. In a fixed width file, the Wizard tries to determine the location of the column breaks for you, and places vertical lines in the Data preview window at its best guess at column locations. Sometimes the Wizard's attempt to define the number and location of columns is not exactly right, so you should always check it, and edit the columns if necessary. Figure 11-6 shows the columns that the Wizard has proposed for your text file. Unfortunately, the Wizard has not inserted a column break between the Date and the High columns. In addition, the column break between the High and Low column is too far to the right, cutting off the title for the Low column. Clearly, you'll have to revise the Text Import Wizard's choice of column breaks.

You insert a new column break by clicking the position in the Data preview window where you want the break to appear. If a break is in the wrong position, you click and drag it to a new location in the Data preview window. Finally, you can delete an extra column break by double-clicking it. You'll use these techniques to modify the column breaks for the History text file.

To edit the Text Import Wizard's column breaks:

1. Click in the space directly after the end of the Date column and to the left of the High column title.

   A vertical line appears, representing a new column break.

2. Click the second column break in the Data preview window, and drag it so it is immediately to the left of the Low column title.

   TROUBLE? Don't be concerned if your column breaks are not all immediately to the right of each data column. They can be off by a space or two. As long as the lines separate the columns and titles, Excel will import the data correctly.

Figure 11-7 shows the Data preview window with the column breaks in the correct locations. When it imports this text file, Excel will now place each column into a separate column in the worksheet.

Figure 11-7 ◄
Revised
column breaks

column breaks are in
the correct positions

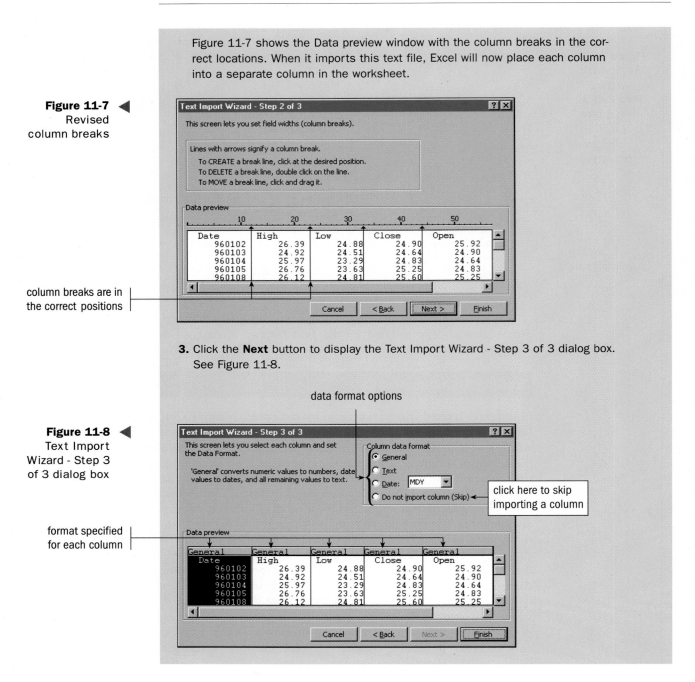

3. Click the **Next** button to display the Text Import Wizard - Step 3 of 3 dialog box. See Figure 11-8.

data format options

Figure 11-8 ◄
Text Import
Wizard - Step 3
of 3 dialog box

click here to skip
importing a column

format specified
for each column

Now you'll tell Excel how you want to format each column of the NYSE data.

Formatting and Trimming Incoming Data

The third and final step of the Text Import Wizard allows you to format the data in each column. Unless you specify a format, Excel will use a General format for all columns, which means that the Import Wizard tries to determine which columns contain text, numbers, or dates.

If you're worried that the Import Wizard will misinterpret the format of a column, you can specify the format yourself in this dialog box, before the column is imported. In addition to specifying the data format, you can also indicate which columns you do not want to import at all. Eliminating columns is useful when there are only a few items you want to import from a large text file containing many columns.

Excel

As you look over the Data preview window shown in Figure 11-8, you note that the Date column displays the year first, followed by the month and the day with no separators. This is an unusual date format, so you'll want to see that the Text Import Wizard correctly interprets these values by making sure they're formatted as dates, not in the General format.

In addition, to reduce the amount of data in the workbook, you decide not to import the daily opening value of the Sunrise Fund, since it's the same as the closing value from the previous day. You'll therefore only import the date and the high, low, and close values of the fund for each day.

To specify a Date format and remove the Open column:

1. Make sure that the first column is selected in the Data preview window. Now you'll assign the correct date format.

2. In the Column data format section, click the **Date** option button.

3. Click the **Date** list arrow, and click **YMD** from the list of date formats.

   Although the data appears unchanged, the column heading changes from General to YMD, indicating that Excel will interpret the values in this column as dates formatted with the year first, followed by the month and day. Now you'll omit the Open column from the import.

4. In the Data preview window, click anywhere in the **Open** column to select it.

5. Click the **Do not import column (Skip)** option button.

   The column format for the Open column changes to Skip Column, indicating that Excel will not import it.

6. Click the **Finish** button.

   Excel retrieves the data from the text file and places it into a new workbook.

7. Name the new worksheet History Table.

8. Format the worksheet to show the high, low, and close values with two decimal places, and the column titles boldface and centered. See Figure 11-9.

Figure 11-9 ◄
Sunrise Fund data as it appears in the Excel workbook

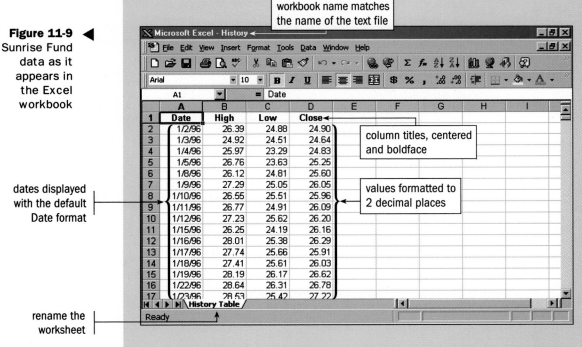

workbook name matches the name of the text file

column titles, centered and boldface

values formatted to 2 decimal places

dates displayed with the default Date format

rename the worksheet

Excel displays the Date column in the default month/day/year format, and all the columns were imported except the Open column.

Now that you've imported the historical data on the Sunrise Fund, you can use an Excel custom chart to create a traditional high-low-close chart.

To create a high-low-close chart for the fund data:

1. Select the range **A1:D756**, click **Insert** on the menu bar, and then click **Chart** to display the Chart Wizard - Step 1 of 4 - Chart Type dialog box.

2. Click **Stock** in the Chart type list box, and click the **High-Low-Close** chart type as shown in Figure 11-10.

Figure 11-10 ◄
Choosing one of the custom Stock charts

click to create a High-Low-Close chart

click to display Stock charts

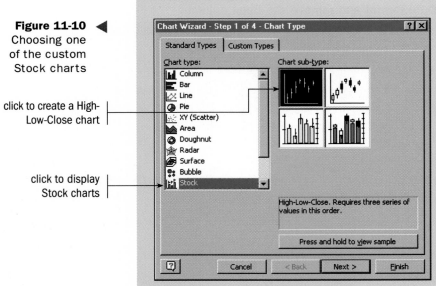

3. Click the **Next** button twice to display the Chart Wizard - Step 3 of 4 - Chart Type dialog box.

4. Click the **Titles** tab, if necessary, and enter the chart title **Sunrise Fund: 1996-1998**, the Category (X) axis title **Date** and the Value (Y) axis title **Fund Value**.

5. Click the **Legend** tab, click the **Show legend** check box to deselect this option and remove the legend from the chart, and then click the **Next** button to display the fourth and final Chart Wizard dialog box.

6. Place the chart on a new worksheet named **History Chart**, and then click the **Finish** button.

Figure 11-11 shows the Sunrise Fund value from 1996 through 1998.

Excel

Figure 11-11 ◀
Chart of the
fund's
performance
from 1996-
1998

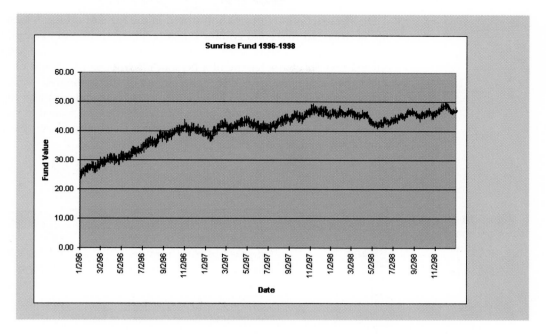

You've successfully imported the fixed width text file containing the Sunrise Fund's performance over the past three years into an Excel workbook and created a High-Low-Close stock chart. Kelly will find the chart useful in interpreting the fund's behavior over the past few years. In the Case Problems at the end of this tutorial, you'll learn how to import a delimited file using the Text Import Wizard.

Before you add more data to Kelly's workbook, you should save your file as Sunrise Fund to your Student Disk. However, you'll have to specify that you want to save the file as an Excel workbook, or Excel will automatically save it as a text file (since the original file you opened was a text file).

To save the imported Sunrise Fund data as an Excel workbook:

1. Click the **History Table** sheet tab.

2. Click **File** on the menu bar, and click **Save As**.

3. Click the **Save as type** list arrow, and click **Microsoft Excel Workbook**.

4. Type **Sunrise Fund** in the File name text box.

5. Save the workbook in the Tutor11 folder on your Student Disk.

Kelly is pleased with the progress you've made in locating the text file and importing it into Excel. Now that she has the historical stock information she needs, she wants you to insert some current data from the company's databases.

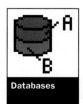

Databases

Databases and Queries

As in many financial firms, much of the information Davis and Larson analysts work with is stored in databases. A **database** is a program that stores and retrieves large amounts of data and creates reports describing that data. There are many database programs available, including Microsoft® Access, Borland dBASE®, Borland Paradox®, and Microsoft FoxPro. Excel can retrieve data from most database programs. At Davis and Larson, information on the stocks in the Sunrise Fund is stored in the Sunrise database.

Databases contain information stored in the form of tables. A **table** is a collection of data that is stored in rows and columns. Figure 11-12 shows an example of one database table Kelly wants you to work with. Each column of the table, called a **field**, stores information about a specific characteristic of a person, place, or thing. In this example, the middle field, called the Company field, stores the names of the companies whose stock is part of the Sunrise portfolio. Each row of the table, called a **record**, displays the collection of characteristics of a particular person, place, or thing. The first record in the table in Figure 11-12 displays stock information for the Aluminum Company of America, which has the ticker symbol AA, and belongs to the group of industrial stocks.

column or field

Figure 11-12
A database
table

row or record

Ticker Symbol	Company	Category
AA	Aluminum Company of America	INDUSTRIALS
ABF	Airborne Freight Corporation	TRANSPORTATION
AEP	American Electric Power Company, Inc.	UTILITIES
CRR	CONRAIL Inc.	TRANSPORTATION
CX	Centerior Energy Corporation	UTILITIES
ED	Consolidated Edison Company of New Y	UTILITIES
EK	Eastman Kodak Company	INDUSTRIALS
GM	General Motors Corporation	INDUSTRIALS
LUV	Southwest Airlines Co.	TRANSPORTATION
NMK	Niagara Mohawk Power Corporation	UTILITIES
R	Ryder System, Inc.	TRANSPORTATION
T	AT&T Corp.	INDUSTRIALS
TX	Texaco Inc.	INDUSTRIALS
UCM	Unicom Corporation	UTILITIES
UNP	Union Pacific Corporation	TRANSPORTATION

The Sunrise database has four such tables: Company, Long Term Performance, Recent Performance, and Stock Info. Figure 11-13 describes the contents of each table.

Figure 11-13
Sunrise
database table
names and
descriptions

Table Name	Description
Company	Data about each company in the fund and the percent of the fund that is allocated to purchasing stocks for that company.
Long Term Performance	Summarizes the performance over the last 52 weeks for each stock, recording the high and low values over that period of time, and its volatility.
Recent Performance	Daily high, low, closing, and volume values for each stock in the portfolio over the last five days.
Stock Info	Description of each stock including the yield, dividend amount and date, earnings per share, and the number of outstanding shares.

With several tables in a database, you need some way of relating information in one table to information in another. You relate tables to one another by using **common fields**, which are the fields that are the same in each table. As shown in Figure 11-14, both the Company table and the Stock Info table contain the Ticker Symbol field, so Ticker Symbol is a common field in this database.

Figure 11-14 ◀
Combining
tables based on
a common field

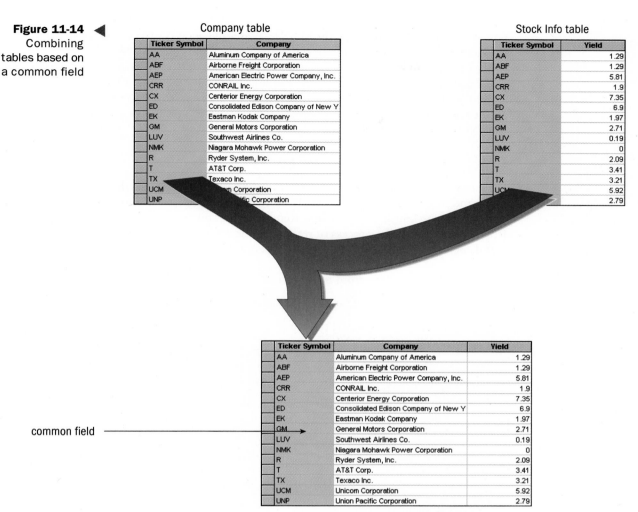

Company table

Ticker Symbol	Company
AA	Aluminum Company of America
ABF	Airborne Freight Corporation
AEP	American Electric Power Company, Inc.
CRR	CONRAIL Inc.
CX	Centerior Energy Corporation
ED	Consolidated Edison Company of New Y
EK	Eastman Kodak Company
GM	General Motors Corporation
LUV	Southwest Airlines Co.
NMK	Niagara Mohawk Power Corporation
R	Ryder System, Inc.
T	AT&T Corp.
TX	Texaco Inc.
UCM	m Corporation
UNP	fic Corporation

Stock Info table

Ticker Symbol	Yield
AA	1.29
ABF	1.29
AEP	5.81
CRR	1.9
CX	7.35
ED	6.9
EK	1.97
GM	2.71
LUV	0.19
NMK	0
R	2.09
T	3.41
TX	3.21
UCM	5.92
	2.79

common field ⟶

Ticker Symbol	Company	Yield
AA	Aluminum Company of America	1.29
ABF	Airborne Freight Corporation	1.29
AEP	American Electric Power Company, Inc.	5.81
CRR	CONRAIL Inc.	1.9
CX	Centerior Energy Corporation	7.35
ED	Consolidated Edison Company of New Y	6.9
EK	Eastman Kodak Company	1.97
GM	General Motors Corporation	2.71
LUV	Southwest Airlines Co.	0.19
NMK	Niagara Mohawk Power Corporation	0
R	Ryder System, Inc.	2.09
T	AT&T Corp.	3.41
TX	Texaco Inc.	3.21
UCM	Unicom Corporation	5.92
UNP	Union Pacific Corporation	2.79

combined table

When you want to retrieve information from two tables, like the Company table and the Stock Info table, Excel matches the value of the ticker symbol in one table with the value of the ticker symbol in the other. Because the ticker symbol values match, you can create a new table that contains information about both the company and the stock itself. Without common fields, there would be no way of matching the company information from one table with the yield information from the other.

A large database can have many tables and each table can have several fields and thousands of records, so you need a way to choose only the information that you most want to see. When you want to look only at specific information from a database, you create a query. A **query** is a question you ask about the data in the database. In response to your query, the database finds the records and fields that meet the requirements of your question, and then **extracts**, or reads only that data and places it in a separate table. A query might ask something like, "What are the names of all the stocks in the portfolio, and what are their corresponding ticker symbols?" To answer this question, you would submit the query to the database in a form that the database can read. The database would then extract the relevant information and create a table of all the stocks and their symbols.

When you query a database, you might want to extract only selected records. In this case, your query would contain **criteria**, which are conditions you set to limit the number of records the database extracts. A criterion tells Excel to extract only those records that match certain conditions. For example, you might want to know the names and ticker symbols of only the top five performing stocks from the past three months. In submitting the query to the database, you would include this criterion to limit the information returned to only the top five performing stocks from that time period in the portfolio.

In a query, you can also specify how you want the data to appear. If you want the names and ticker symbols of the top ten performing stocks arranged alphabetically by ticker symbol, you can include that in your query definition.

Extracting just the information you need from a database to answer a particular question might seem like a daunting task, but Excel provides the Query Wizard, which greatly simplifies the task of creating and running your queries. You'll use the Query Wizard to extract data from Davis and Larson's database, and to add the next set of worksheets to Kelly's Sunrise Fund workbook.

Using the Query Wizard

Kelly next wants you to add a worksheet to the workbook that lists the stocks in the Sunrise Fund and describes their performance in the last year. As you'll remember from the worksheet plan, you can get this current trend information from the company database called Sunrise. You'll start the process of retrieving this information with the Excel Get Data command. Before doing that, you'll have to insert a new worksheet into the workbook.

To start retrieving data from an external source:

1. Insert a new worksheet at the beginning of the workbook and name it **Portfolio**.

   Now you are ready to start the process of retrieving the stock information into this worksheet.

2. Click **Data** on the menu bar, point to **Get External Data**, and click **Create New Query**.

   Excel opens the Choose Data Source dialog box, as shown in Figure 11-15.

   TROUBLE? If the Get External Data or Create New Query commands are not available, you may have to install Microsoft Query from your installation disk. See online help, your instructor, or lab manager for more information.

Figure 11-15 ◀
Choose Data
Source
dialog box

your dialog box
may display other
data sources

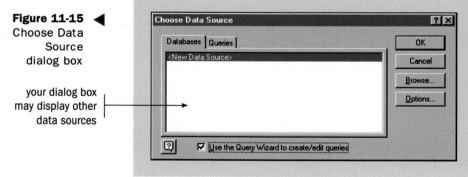

Now you are ready to specify the company database as your data source.

Defining a Data Source

A **data source** is any file that contains the data that you want to retrieve. Data sources can be databases, text files, or other Excel workbooks. Before you open a data source with the Query Wizard, you first have to define the data source.

When you **define** a data source you have to do three things: 1) You have to give the data source a name that will identify it to Excel; 2) You have to choose a driver for the data source. The **driver** translates information between the data source and Excel. Unless the data source is another Excel workbook, the source most likely stores data in a different way than Excel does. The function of the driver is to make sure that no data is lost in the retrieval. 3) Finally, you have to specify the location of the data source, whether it is on your floppy disk, on your hard disk, or on the computer network. The location of the data is also part of the data source's definition.

In some situations, you might have to enter additional information in your data source's definition. For example, if your data source is a database that is password-protected, you may have to specify the password before you can use the data source.

REFERENCE window

DEFINING A DATA SOURCE

- Click Data, point to Get External Data, and click Create New Query.
- Click <New Data Source> and click the OK button.
- Enter the name for the new data source, and select the driver type corresponding to the data source format.
- Click the Connect button and then click the Select button.
- Specify the location of the new data source.
- Click the OK button twice.

The company database from which you'll extract data is named Sunrise, and is located in the Tutor11 folder of your Student Disk. It's an Access database, so you'll use the Access driver when you define your data source.

To define a data source:

1. Make sure that <New Data Source> is selected on the Databases tab and that the Use the Query Wizard to create/edit queries check box is selected (if not, click it to select it), and then click the **OK** button. A dialog box asks you to give a name to your data source. You'll name it Sunrise Fund.

2. Type **Sunrise Fund** and press the **Tab** key.

   Next, you'll define the type of driver this data source uses.

3. Click the list arrow after #2, and then click **Microsoft Access Driver (*.mdb)** from the list of database drivers.

   Now that you've specified the type of database, you'll connect Excel to the specific Access database from which you want to retrieve data.

4. Click the **Connect** button. The ODBC Microsoft Access 97 Set up dialog box opens.

5. Click the **Select** button to display the Select Database dialog box.

6. Locate the Tutor11 folder on your Student Disk in the Directories list box, click **Sunrise.mdb** in the Name Database list box, as shown in Figure 11-16, and then click the **OK** button.

Figure 11-16 ◄
Location of the
Sunrise
database

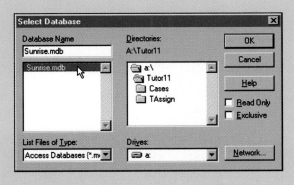

7. Click the **OK** button to close the ODBC Microsoft Access 97 Setup dialog box.

The completed Create New Data Source dialog box appears. See Figure 11-17.

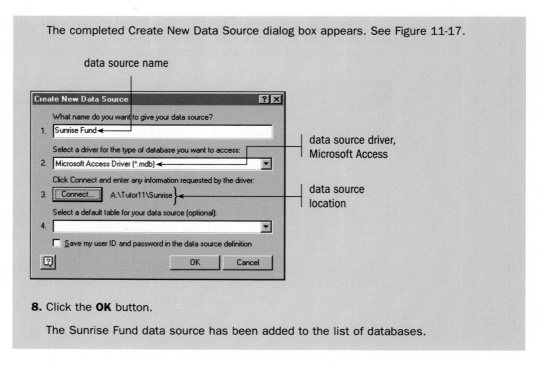

Figure 11-17 ◄
Definition of the
Sunrise Fund
data source

data source name

data source driver,
Microsoft Access

data source
location

8. Click the **OK** button.

The Sunrise Fund data source has been added to the list of databases.

Now that you have defined the data source, you are ready to create a query to extract data from it.

Choosing Tables and Columns

The next step in retrieving data from the Sunrise database is to choose the table and fields (columns) that you want to include in the query. The Query Wizard lets you "peek" inside the database so that you can preview the structure of the database and its contents.

To view a list of the tables and columns in the Sunrise database:

1. Make sure that the Use the Query Wizard check box at the bottom of the Choose Data Source dialog box is selected.

2. Click **Sunrise Fund** in the list of databases, and then click the **OK** button.

The Query Wizard starts and displays the four tables in the Sunrise database. See Figure 11-18.

Move button

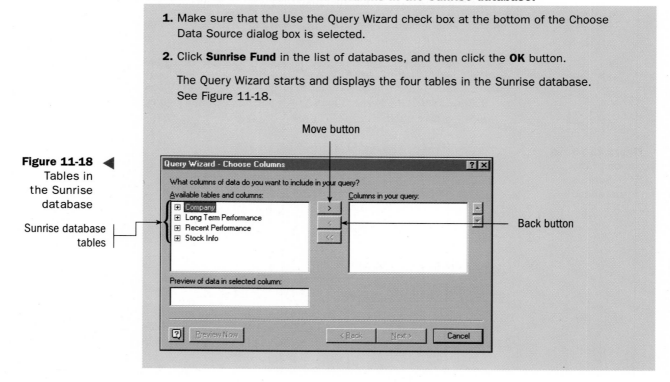

Figure 11-18 ◄
Tables in
the Sunrise
database

Sunrise database
tables

Back button

3. Click the plus sign ⊞ in front of the Company table name.

The Available tables and columns list box expands to display the columns (or fields) in the Company table. See Figure 11-19.

Figure 11-19 ◀
Fields in the
Company table

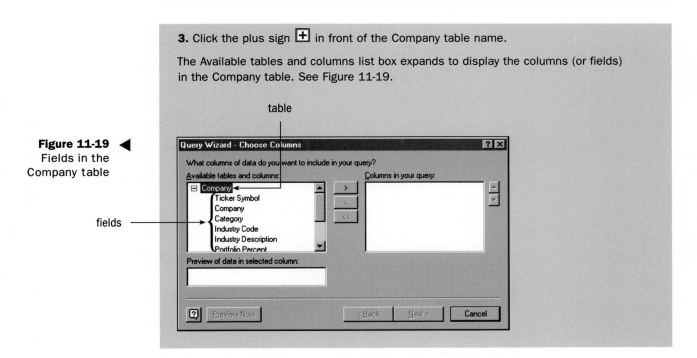

You're not sure what fields Kelly wants to place into the worksheet. You contact her and she indicates that she would like to include the ticker symbol, the company, and the portfolio percent from the Company table. The portfolio percent, you learn, is the percentage of the portfolio that is invested in each particular stock. Kelly also wants the Year High and Year Low fields from the Long Term Performance table so that she can tell what the high and low points in the previous year has been for each stock in the portfolio. Since the two tables share Ticker Symbol as a common field, you'll select data from both tables with the Query Wizard.

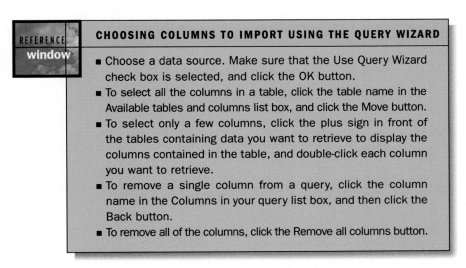

REFERENCE
window

CHOOSING COLUMNS TO IMPORT USING THE QUERY WIZARD

■ Choose a data source. Make sure that the Use Query Wizard check box is selected, and click the OK button.
■ To select all the columns in a table, click the table name in the Available tables and columns list box, and click the Move button.
■ To select only a few columns, click the plus sign in front of the tables containing data you want to retrieve to display the columns contained in the table, and double-click each column you want to retrieve.
■ To remove a single column from a query, click the column name in the Columns in your query list box, and then click the Back button.
■ To remove all of the columns, click the Remove all columns button.

To select fields, you can click the field name and click the Move button ⬛▸, or you can simply double-click the field name, and Excel will automatically move it to the list of selected columns in your query.

To select the columns you want to import into Excel:

1. Click **Ticker Symbol** in the Available tables and columns list box, and then click the **Move** button ⬛▸.

Ticker Symbol moves to the Columns in your query of the Query Wizard - Choose Columns dialog box, indicating that it will be included in your query. You'll continue selecting the remaining columns that Kelly wants to view by using the alternative method of double clicking.

2. Double-click **Company**.

3. Double-click **Portfolio Percent**.

Next you'll open the Long Term Performance table and select the other fields you need.

4. Scroll down and click the plus sign ⊞ in front of the Long Term Performance table name.

5. Double-click **Year High** and then double-click **Year Low**.

The five fields that Kelly wants should now be selected. See Figure 11- 20.

Figure 11-20 ◄
Fields selected
for the query

fields not included
in the query

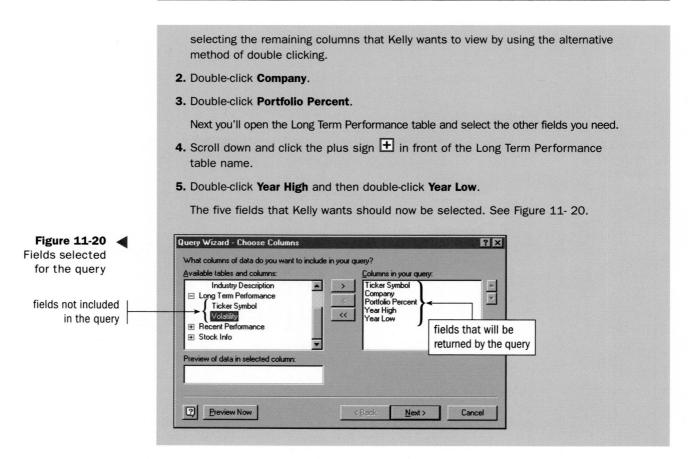

You can preview the contents of each field in the table by selecting it (either in the left pane or the right pane of the Choose Columns dialog box) and then clicking the Preview Now button. You decide to preview the contents of the Company field to get an idea of the types of entries it contains.

To preview the contents of the Company field:

1. Click **Company** in the Columns in your query list box.

2. Click the **Preview Now** button.

Some of the values in this column display in the Preview of data in selected column list box. See Figure 11- 21.

Figure 11-21 ◄
Preview of the
Company field

preview of company
field data

click to preview a
selected field

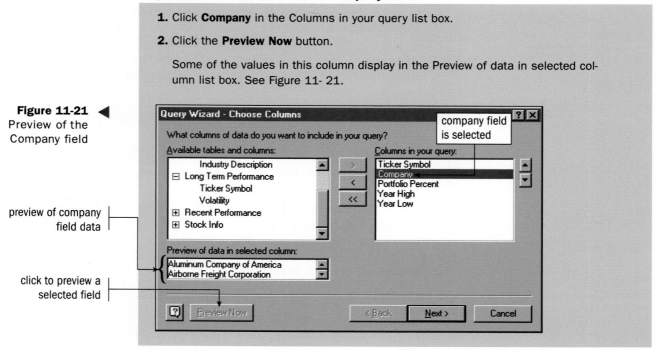

> **3.** Click the **Next** button to display the Query Wizard - Filter Data dialog box.

Now that you have selected the five columns for your Portfolio worksheet, you next have to determine whether to retrieve all of the records in the database or only records that satisfy particular criteria.

Filtering and Sorting Data

In discussing the issue with Kelly, she indicates that she would like you to retrieve information on all the stocks. However, she thinks she will want you to filter the incoming data at selected times. You decide to examine the filtering capabilities of the Query Wizard to get familiar with them.

When you **filter** data, you specify which records you want to retrieve. In this query, you can filter the data to remove particular stocks or to retrieve only those stocks that perform at a certain level.

REFERENCE
window

FILTERING DATA IN A QUERY

- Start the Query Wizard, select the columns to include in your query, and click the Next button to display the Query Wizard - Filter Data dialog box.
- In the Column to filter list box, click a column you want to include in your filter.
- In the Only include rows where list box, select a comparison type.
- Select a value for the comparison in the adjacent list box that displays values.
- Specify any additional comparisons for the selected column.

To see how the data filter works, you'll create a filter that will retrieve stock information only for stocks from the Eastman Kodak Company and the Unicom Corporation.

To create a filter:

> **1.** Click **Company** in the Column to filter list box.
>
> On the right side of the Query Wizard - Filter Data dialog box, there are two columns of list boxes. The column on the left specifies the type of comparison you want to make in the filter, such as "equals," "greater than," or "less than." In the column on the right, you enter a value for the comparison. You'll use these two list boxes to have the query retrieve the Eastman Kodak stock.
>
> **2.** Click the list arrow in the first row of the left column, and then click **equals**.
>
> **3.** Click the list box in the first row of the right column, and then click **Eastman Kodak Company**.
>
> Next, you'll add a second set of conditions so that the query includes either the Eastman Kodak Company *or* the Unicom Corporation.
>
> **4.** Click the **Or** option button.
>
> Now that you have completed the first row and indicated that you want to include another filter, the second row of list boxes becomes available.
>
> **5.** Click the list arrow in the second row of the left column, and then click **equals**.
>
> **6.** In the right column of the second row, click **Unicom Corporation** from the list box.

Figure 11-22 shows the completed Filter Data dialog box.

Figure 11-22 ◄
Entering a
data filter

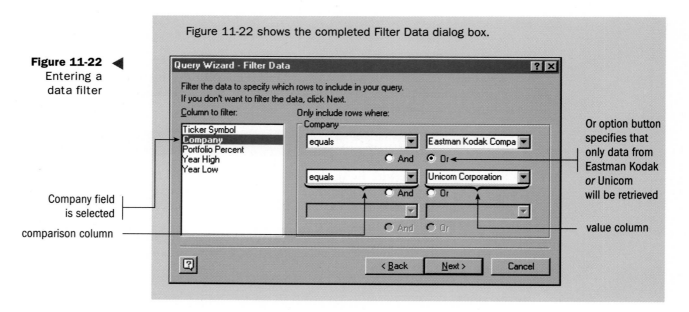

Company field
is selected

comparison column

Or option button
specifies that
only data from
Eastman Kodak
or Unicom
will be retrieved

value column

The filter you created will retrieve only those records for Eastman Kodak *or* for Unicom. The Query Wizard will not retrieve stock information for other companies in the Sunrise Fund. While only three rows of criteria are shown in the Filter Data dialog box, additional rows would be added if you inserted additional requirements to your filter. However, since Kelly wants information on all the companies in the portfolio, you'll now remove the data filters you just created.

To remove a filter:

1. Click the comparison list box in the second row of the left column, and click the blank space at the top of the list.

2. Repeat for the comparison list box in the first row.

   The filters are removed from the query. You can proceed to the next step of the Query Wizard.

3. Click the **Next** button.

So far, you've identified the fields you want to retrieve, and you've had a chance to filter out any records. In the last part of creating your query, you specify whether you want the data sorted in a particular order.

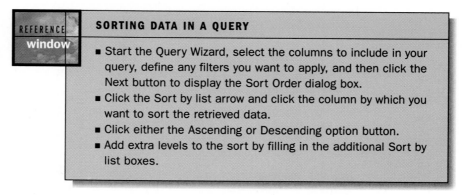

REFERENCE
window

SORTING DATA IN A QUERY

■ Start the Query Wizard, select the columns to include in your query, define any filters you want to apply, and then click the Next button to display the Sort Order dialog box.
■ Click the Sort by list arrow and click the column by which you want to sort the retrieved data.
■ Click either the Ascending or Descending option button.
■ Add extra levels to the sort by filling in the additional Sort by list boxes.

Kelly has indicated that she would like to have the portfolio displayed starting with the stocks in which the Sunrise Fund has the largest capital investment, and proceeding down to the stocks with the smallest capital investment. The Portfolio Percent field tells you how much of the fund is invested in each stock, so you should sort the data by the values in that field in descending order (from highest percentage to lowest).

To sort the data by company name:

1. Click the **Sort by** list arrow, and click **Portfolio Percent**.

2. Click the **Descending** option button.

3. Click the **Next** button to display the final Query Wizard dialog box.

You have finished defining your query. You could run the query now and get the information that Kelly has requested, but you should first save your query.

Saving Your Queries

When you save a query, you are actually placing the query choices you've made into a file. You can open the file later and run the query, saving you the trouble of redefining it. You can also share the query with others who might want to extract the same type of information. Query files can be stored in any folder you choose. The default folder for queries is the Queries folder, which is a subfolder of Microsoft Office. Saving the query file to this folder has some advantages. If you are running Excel on a network, you can make the query file accessible to other network users. Also, query files in this folder will appear on the Queries tab of the Choose Data Source dialog box (see Figure 11-15), giving you quick and easy access to your saved queries. In this case, however, you'll save your query to your Student Disk, because you may not have access to your Queries folder. After saving a query as a file, you automatically return to the last dialog box of the Query Wizard, where you can then retrieve the data from the database into your workbook.

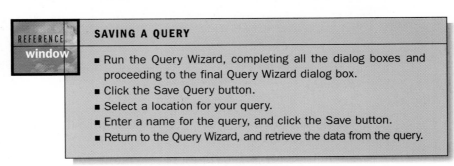

REFERENCE window

SAVING A QUERY

- Run the Query Wizard, completing all the dialog boxes and proceeding to the final Query Wizard dialog box.
- Click the Save Query button.
- Select a location for your query.
- Enter a name for the query, and click the Save button.
- Return to the Query Wizard, and retrieve the data from the query.

You decide to save your query with the name "Sunrise Portfolio," because it displays a list of stocks in the Sunrise Fund, and place it on your Student Disk.

To save a query:

1. Click the **Save Query** button.

2. Open the **Tutor11** folder on your Student Disk.

3. Enter **Sunrise Portfolio** in the File name text box.

   The file type for query files is (*.dqy), meaning that your saved query files will have the .dqy extension.

4. Click the **Save** button.

Now that you have saved your query, you have two options. You can return (import) the data to your Excel workbook, or you can further refine the query with Microsoft Query. Microsoft Query is a program included on your installation disk, with several tools that allow you to create more complex queries. You can use Excel online help if you want to explore Microsoft Query on your own. For now, you can retrieve the portfolio data to the Sunrise Fund workbook.

To retrieve the data from the Sunrise database:

1. Click the **Return Data to Microsoft Excel** option button.

2. Click the **Finish** button. A dialog box asks you where you want to place the imported data.

3. Click cell **A3** in the workbook to insert the retrieved data into the worksheet, starting at that cell.

4. Click the **OK** button.

Excel retrieves the data from the Sunrise database and inserts it into the current worksheet. Excel also displays the External Data toolbar, which lets you perform several common tasks with your data; you'll use it in the next session. See Figure 11-23.

Figure 11-23 ◄
Portfolio data retrieved into the Sunrise Fund workbook

External Data toolbar

fields from the query

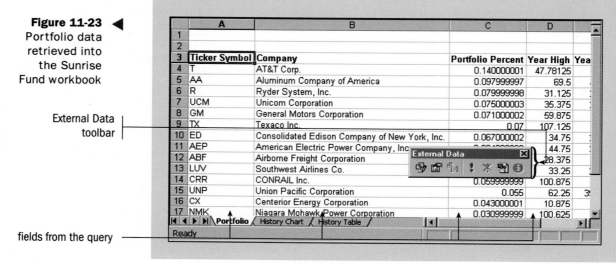

Before closing and saving your workbook, you should add a title and then format the portfolio information.

To format the Portfolio worksheet:

1. Type **Sunrise Fund Portfolio** in cell A1. Format it in 16-point boldface type, and center it across the first four columns of the worksheet.

2. Apply the Percent format to the values in the Portfolio Percent column, and display the percentages with two decimal places.

3. Change the name of the Portfolio Percent column to **Percent**, and reduce the column width to 7 points. Now format the Year High and Year Low values to show fractional values instead of decimal values.

4. Select the range **D4:E18**, click Format on the menu bar, and then click **Cells**.

5. Click the Number tab, click **Fraction** in the list of format categories, and then click **Up to three digits (312/943)** in the type list.

6. Click the **OK** button, and if necessary widen the columns to 11 points to show all the values with fractions.

7. Press **Ctrl + Home**.

Figure 11-24 shows the contents of the formatted Portfolio worksheet.

Excel

Figure 11-24 ◀
The formatted
Portfolio
worksheet

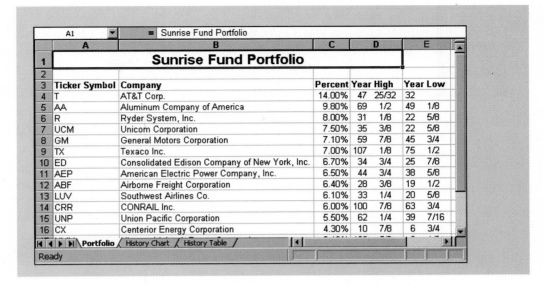

A1	▼	=	Sunrise Fund Portfolio			
	A	**B**	**C**	**D**	**E**	
1		**Sunrise Fund Portfolio**				
2						
3	Ticker Symbol	Company	Percent	Year High	Year Low	
4	T	AT&T Corp.	14.00%	47 25/32	32	
5	AA	Aluminum Company of America	9.80%	69 1/2	49 1/8	
6	R	Ryder System, Inc.	8.00%	31 1/8	22 5/8	
7	UCM	Unicom Corporation	7.50%	35 3/8	22 5/8	
8	GM	General Motors Corporation	7.10%	59 7/8	45 3/4	
9	TX	Texaco Inc.	7.00%	107 1/8	75 1/2	
10	ED	Consolidated Edison Company of New York, Inc.	6.70%	34 3/4	25 7/8	
11	AEP	American Electric Power Company, Inc.	6.50%	44 3/4	38 5/8	
12	ABF	Airborne Freight Corporation	6.40%	28 3/8	19 1/2	
13	LUV	Southwest Airlines Co.	6.10%	33 1/4	20 5/8	
14	CRR	CONRAIL Inc.	6.00%	100 7/8	63 3/4	
15	UNP	Union Pacific Corporation	5.50%	62 1/4	39 7/16	
16	CX	Centerior Energy Corporation	4.30%	10 7/8	6 3/4	

◀◀ ▶ ▶▶ \ **Portfolio** / History Chart / History Table /

Ready

Looking at the contents of the portfolio, you can quickly see that 14% of the fund is invested in the AT&T Corporation and that the value of that stock has ranged from a high of 47 $^{25}/_{32}$ points to a low of 32 points. This worksheet will be very helpful to Kelly in working with the stocks in the Sunrise Fund portfolio.

Print the Portfolio worksheet, and then save and close your workbook.

To print and save the Sunrise Fund data:

1. Print the Portfolio worksheet (not the History Table worksheet).

2. Save the workbook.

You'll show Kelly the progress you've made in importing the data from the company database. If she is satisfied with it, you'll move on to importing data from external databases.

Quick **Check**

1 What is the difference between a fixed width and a delimited text file?

2 Name three delimiters that can separate data in a delimited text file.

3 How do you insert column breaks when importing a text file using the Text Import Wizard?

4 Define the following terms:
   a. database
   b. table
   c. field
   d. record

5 What is a common field?

6 What is a query?

7 What are criteria?

8 What is a data source? What are three of the characteristics you specify when defining a data source?

Kelly thanks you for your work. She will work with the newly imported Sunrise Fund Portfolio and see if it meets her needs. In the next session, you'll add more current information about the Sunrise Fund stocks to your workbook. You'll learn how to refresh data, edit your queries, and how to control the way Excel retrieves data from its data sources. You'll then see how to import data into pivot tables.

In this session, you'll learn how to edit and rerun your queries to retrieve new data. You'll see how to modify the properties of your existing queries. Finally, you'll learn how to use pivot tables to summarize the data in your database.

Working with External Data and Queries

In the last session, you learned two ways to bring data into Excel: by importing a text file and by importing data from a database. Importing data from a database has several advantages over importing from a text file. Using queries, you can control which records you import into your workbook. More importantly, by retrieving data from a database, you can easily refresh, or update, the data in your workbooks when the data source itself is updated.

Refreshing External Data

When you retrieved the portfolio data for Kelly in the last session, you did more than insert the data into the Excel workbook. By defining a data source, you also gave Excel information about where to go to find updated information for your workbook. Davis & Larson are constantly updating their databases, and it's important for Kelly to be able to view the most up-to-date information on the Sunrise Fund so that she can offer accurate and timely advice to her clients.

Excel allows you to keep your data current by refreshing the data in your queries. When you **refresh** a query, Excel retrieves the most current data from the data source, using the query definition you've already created.

REFERENCE window	**REFRESHING EXTERNAL DATA**
	■ Click a cell in the range that contains the external data, and click the Refresh button on the External Data toolbar.
	or
	■ If your workbook contains several external data ranges, click the Refresh All button on the External Data toolbar to refresh all the external data in the workbook.

You've explained the concept of refreshing data to Kelly. She wants you to show her how to refresh the information in the Sunrise Fund workbook so she can make sure she has the most current version of the database information. To refresh the imported data, you select a cell from the range containing the data and use the Refresh command.

To refresh the portfolio data:

1. If you took a break at the end of the last session, make sure Excel is running, and open the **Sunrise Fund** workbook in the Tutor11 folder on your Student Disk.

2. Click cell **A3** in the Portfolio worksheet.

   Although you've selected cell A3 here, you can select any cell in the data range when you refresh your data.

3. Click the **Refresh Data** button on the External Data toolbar.

   TROUBLE? If the External Data toolbar is not visible, click View on the menu bar, point to Toolbars, and click External Data to display the toolbar.

Excel goes to the Sunrise database and retrieves the current information from the database back into the workbook. The contents of this workbook doesn't change, because the Sunrise database has not been modified since you last saved the Sunrise Fund workbook.

Having seen how the refresh command works, Kelly wonders if there are any other ways to control how and when Excel refreshes external data.

Setting External Data Properties

Kelly likes the fact that she can refresh her external data so quickly and easily, but she has a couple of concerns. She worries that she may forget to refresh the data each time she opens her workbook and she prefers to have Excel automatically refresh the data. On the other hand, there are times when she wants some of her workbooks to contain a "snapshot" of the data as it exists at a particular moment in time. In that case, her needs are just the opposite—she doesn't want the data refreshed at all.

You can meet both of these requirements by modifying the properties of the query. By modifying the query properties, you can:

- Remove the underlying external data query, freezing the data so that it cannot be refreshed.

- Require that the user enter a password before the data is refreshed, thus keeping other users from updating the data without permission.

- Run the query in the background, so you can work on other portions of the workbook as you wait for the data to be retrieved; this is helpful if you are retrieving large amounts of data.

- Refresh the data automatically whenever the workbook is reopened.

- Specify how new data from the external data source is added when the size of the external data range changes. You can insert new cells and delete unused cells, insert an entire row and clear unused cells, or replace existing cells with new data.

- Automatically copy formulas into adjacent columns, preserving them as the size of the external data range expands into new columns after refreshing.

As you can see, Excel gives you a great deal of flexibility as to how and when you refresh your external data.

REFERENCE window	**SETTING PROPERTIES FOR EXTERNAL DATA**
	- Click a cell in the data range containing the external data. - Click the Data Range Properties button on the External Data toolbar. - Select the external data properties that you want. - Click the OK button.

Because she frequently consults her database files as she advises her clients on stock market trends, Kelly decides that she would like to have the query refreshed automatically whenever she opens the Sunrise Fund workbook.

To set properties for the Industrial Stocks external data:

1. Click the **Data Range Properties** button 🖭 on the External Data toolbar.

2. Click the **Refresh data on file open** check box to select this option.

   Clicking this check box also makes the Remove External Data Before Saving check box appear. Clicking this option causes Excel to remove the data that you've retrieved from the workbook before closing the workbook. The advantage of using this option is that it makes the size of the workbook relatively small when it's not in use. Then, when you reopen the workbook, Excel automatically retrieves the data and puts it back in its proper place. You tell Kelly about this option, but she decides to keep the data in the workbook at all times.

   The completed External Data Range Properties dialog box appears, as shown in Figure 11-25.

Figure 11-25 ◀
Properties of
a query

Excel's internal name
for the query

click to refresh the
data when the
workbook is opened

click to remove the
data when the
workbook is closed

options to control how
Excel places the
retrieved data into
the workbook

External Data Range Properties
Name: ExternalData1
Query definition
☑ Save query definition
☑ Save password
Refresh control
☑ Enable background refresh
☑ Refresh data on file open
☐ Remove external data from worksheet before saving
Data layout
☑ Include field names   ☑ Autoformat data
☐ Include row numbers   ☑ Import HTML table(s) only
If the number of rows in the data range changes upon refresh:
◉ Insert cells for new data, delete unused cells
○ Insert entire rows for new data, clear unused cells
○ Overwrite existing cells with new data, clear unused cells
☐ Fill down formulas in columns adjacent to data
OK   Cancel

3. Click the **OK** button.

From now on, whenever Kelly opens this workbook, Excel will automatically refresh the data. Kelly now asks you how she can modify the query that you performed earlier, in case she needs to import additional information.

Editing a Query

Once you've created a query, you can go back and modify the query's definition using the Query Wizard. By editing the query, you can add new columns to your worksheet, change the sort order options, or specify a filter.

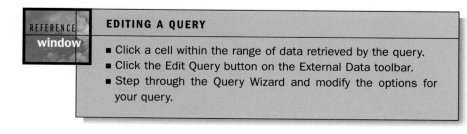

REFERENCE
window

EDITING A QUERY

- Click a cell within the range of data retrieved by the query.
- Click the Edit Query button on the External Data toolbar.
- Step through the Query Wizard and modify the options for your query.

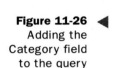

Kelly has reviewed the contents of the Portfolio worksheet. She would like you to include categories for each stock: industrials, transportation, and utilities. She would like to know how the fund is distributed over these kinds of classifications. She would also like to have the data sorted by stock category, and within each stock category by descending order of portfolio percentage. You can add the Category column to the Portfolio worksheet and modify the sort order by editing the query.

To edit the query:

1. Click the **Edit Query** button on the Get External Data toolbar.

    The Query Wizard starts and displays the Query Wizard - Choose Columns dialog box. First, you'll add the Category column.

2. Click the plus box in front of the Company table, and double-click **Category**.

    Category is added to the list of columns in the query. See Figure 11-26.

Figure 11-26 ◄
Adding the
Category field
to the query

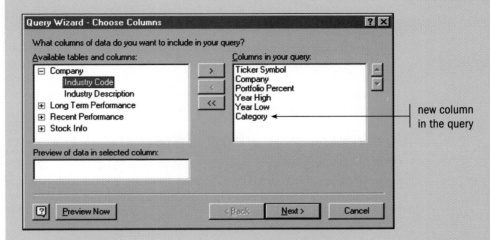

new column
in the query

3. Click the **Next** button twice to go to the Query Wizard - Sort Order dialog box, where you'll enter the two sorting criteria.

4. Click **Category** in the Sort by list box, and then click the **Ascending** button.

5. Click **Portfolio Percent** in the Then by list box, and then click the **Descending** option button.

6. Click the **Next** button and then click the **Finish** button to retrieve the data.

    By retrieving the data, you've overwritten the Percent column title because, by default, the Query field is set to retrieve names along with the data. But you can retype this title now.

7. Enter **Percent** in cell C3, and reduce the column width to 7 points.

    Figure 11-27 displays the contents of the Portfolio worksheet with the newly added Category column and the sort order changed.

Figure 11-27
Revised
Portfolio
worksheet

data sorted by stock
category, and within
each category by
portfolio percentage

new category column

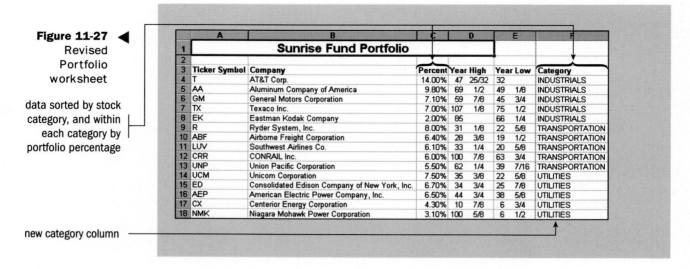

	A	B	C	D		E		F
1		Sunrise Fund Portfolio						
2								
3	Ticker Symbol	Company	Percent	Year High		Year Low		Category
4	T	AT&T Corp.	14.00%	47	25/32	32		INDUSTRIALS
5	AA	Aluminum Company of America	9.80%	69	1/2	49	1/8	INDUSTRIALS
6	GM	General Motors Corporation	7.10%	59	7/8	45	3/4	INDUSTRIALS
7	TX	Texaco Inc.	7.00%	107	1/8	75	1/2	INDUSTRIALS
8	EK	Eastman Kodak Company	2.00%	85		66	1/4	INDUSTRIALS
9	R	Ryder System, Inc.	8.00%	31	1/8	22	5/8	TRANSPORTATION
10	ABF	Airborne Freight Corporation	6.40%	28	3/8	19	1/2	TRANSPORTATION
11	LUV	Southwest Airlines Co.	6.10%	33	1/4	20	5/8	TRANSPORTATION
12	CRR	CONRAIL Inc.	6.00%	100	7/8	63	3/4	TRANSPORTATION
13	UNP	Union Pacific Corporation	5.50%	62	1/4	39	7/16	TRANSPORTATION
14	UCM	Unicom Corporation	7.50%	35	3/8	22	5/8	UTILITIES
15	ED	Consolidated Edison Company of New York, Inc.	6.70%	34	3/4	25	7/8	UTILITIES
16	AEP	American Electric Power Company, Inc.	6.50%	44	3/4	38	5/8	UTILITIES
17	CX	Centerior Energy Corporation	4.30%	10	7/8	6	3/4	UTILITIES
18	NMK	Niagara Mohawk Power Corporation	3.10%	100	5/8	6	1/2	UTILITIES

In reviewing the category values, you note that the fund is comprised of 15 stocks with 5 industrials, 5 transportation stocks, and 5 utilities. The fund is therefore well balanced across the three categories. Kelly is satisfied with the appearance of the Portfolio worksheet. The next thing she wants you to insert into the workbook is the most recent performance of the 15 stocks in the Sunrise Fund.

Creating a Pivot Table from External Data

Kelly and you discuss how the worksheet with the recent stock performance data should appear. She wants data for each stock to look like the sample table shown in Figure 11-28 for the Eastman Kodak stock. The table displays the high, low, close, and volume figures for each day for the past five market days.

Figure 11-28
Eastman Kodak
data from the
Recent
Performance
table

market date

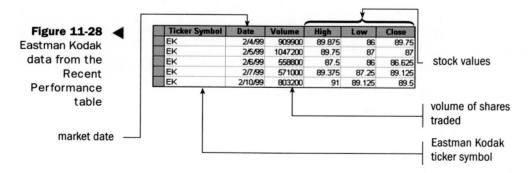

Ticker Symbol	Date	Volume	High	Low	Close
EK	2/4/99	909900	89.875	86	89.75
EK	2/5/99	1047200	89.75	87	87
EK	2/6/99	558800	87.5	86	86.625
EK	2/7/99	571000	89.375	87.25	89.125
EK	2/10/99	803200	91	89.125	89.5

stock values

volume of shares
traded

Eastman Kodak
ticker symbol

Kelly would also like the worksheet page to include a Volume-High-Low-Close chart shown in Figure 11-29, so that she can visually track each stock's recent history.

Excel

low value   high value   closing value

Figure 11-29
Eastman Kodak
Volume-High-
Low-Close
chart

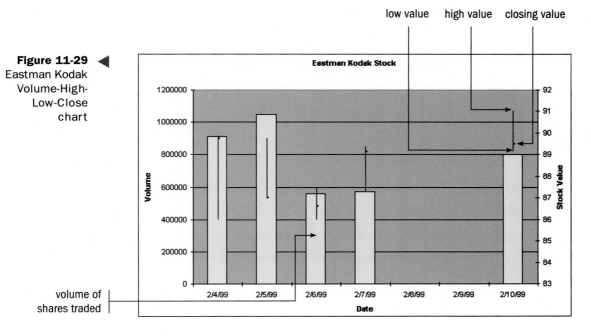

volume of
shares traded

As you review the table, you wonder how best to display the results in the workbook. You could have 15 worksheets—one for each stock in the fund, displaying the table of values and an accompanying chart. Kelly vetoes the idea, thinking that it would be too cumbersome to navigate through 15 worksheet pages. Besides, she argues, at some point she wants to create similar workbooks for other funds that might have hundreds of stocks in their portfolios.

A second option occurs to you. You can create a pivot table that will display market values from the past five days. By using the page feature of the pivot table, you can include a list box that Kelly can use to display the values for only the stock that she is interested in. As Kelly clicks a different stock from the page's list box, a new table and chart will be created. Figure 11-30 shows a preview of what you intend to create.

Figure 11-30
The pivot table
and chart you
plan to create

Page area of the pivot
table contains a drop-
down list box you can
use to select stocks

embedded stock
chart

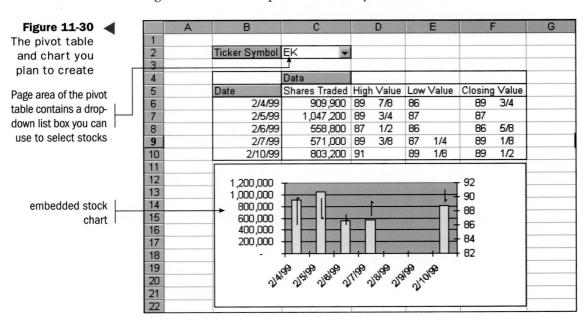

One advantage of this approach is that you can place the recent performance data on a single worksheet. A second advantage is that the pivot table can use data that's stored in databases or other external files. This means that you won't have to insert the entire contents of the Recent Performance table to display recent performance values. You can let the pivot table retrieve only those values for each stock when needed.

REFERENCE window	RETRIEVING EXTERNAL DATA INTO A PIVOT TABLE
	■ Click Data and then click Pivot Table Report to start the PivotTable Wizard.
	■ In the Pivot Table Wizard - Step 1 of 4 dialog box, click the External Data Source option button, and click the Next button to display the second dialog box.
	■ Click the Get Data button to display the third dialog box.
	■ Select a data source and click the OK button.
	■ Use the Query Wizard to define your query and retrieve the data into the pivot table.
	■ Complete the final PivotTable Wizard dialog box.

To start creating a worksheet containing recent performance results, you will insert a new sheet in the workbook and start the PivotTable Wizard.

To start creating the pivot table:

1. Insert a new sheet after the Portfolio worksheet and name it **Recent Results**.

2. Click **Data** on the menu bar, and click **Pivot Table Report**. Step 1 of the PivotTable Wizard dialog box asks for the type of data you want to import.

3. Click the **External data source** option button, and click the **Next** button to display the PivotTable Wizard - Step 2 of 4 dialog box. You use this dialog box to indicate where your data is stored.

4. Click the **Get Data** button to display the Choose Data Source dialog box. Here you select the data source.

5. Click **Sunrise Fund** and click the **OK** button.

Now you indicate the columns that you want to include in the table. You want to retrieve the ticker symbol of each stock, the volume of shares traded, the daily high and low of the stock, and the closing value. All these fields are located in the Recent Performance table. Once you've selected the columns for the table, you can go through the rest of the Query Wizard without specifying any filters or sorting. You're only interested in the complete and unfiltered recent performance data.

To enter the query for the pivot table:

1. Click **Recent Performance** and click the **Move** button [>].

   The Query Wizard selects all of the fields in the table, which is want you want. Clicking the table name followed by the Move button is a useful shortcut if you know that you want to select all table fields.

2. Click the **Next** button three times to reach the final dialog box in the Query Wizard.

3. Click the **Finish** button.

   You are returned to the PivotTable Wizard - Step 2 of 4 dialog box. The comment, "Data fields have been retrieved" now appears next to the Get Data button.

You're finished with the query and the PivotTable Wizard has retrieved the data. You'll next design the layout for your pivot table.

To design the pivot table's layout:

1. Click the **Next** button to display the PivotTable Wizard - Step 3 of 4 dialog box.

   First, you'll place the Ticker Symbol field in the Page area of the pivot table. This will create the list box you saw in Figure 11-30.

2. Drag the **Ticker Symbol** button to the Page area of the pivot table diagram.

   Next, place the Date field in the Row area of the pivot table.

3. Drag the **Date** button to the Row area of the sample pivot table.

   Finally, you'll place the volume and stock values in the data section of the pivot table. You'll need to be careful to put the fields in the correct order. The Volume-High-Low-Close chart that you'll create later expects to find the volume values in the first column, followed by the high value, low value, and closing values.

4. Drag the **Volume** button to the Data section, followed by the **High** button, **Low** button and **Close** button.

   Figure 11- 31 displays the layout of the pivot table.

Figure 11-31 ◀
Layout of your
pivot table

Column area ⟶

Page area ⟶

Row area ⟶

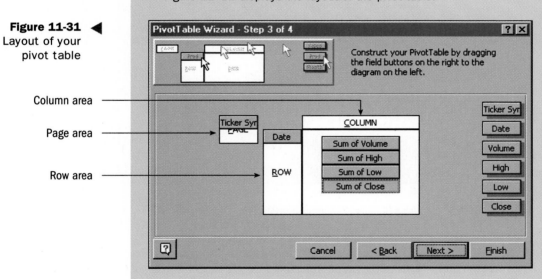

TROUBLE? If your layout does not match the one shown in Figure 11-31, drag the buttons until the positions match the ones shown in the figure.

Notice that the Data area labels say "Sum of" before the name of each field. This is a little misleading, because there is only one value of these items for each stock on each day, so the pivot table will show a "sum" of only one record. Although the table will display individual volume and stock values, you should change these labels to avoid confusing others who might interpret them as the sum of many such values. You can also specify the format for these values.

To change the labels and enter the number format for the data values of the table:

1. Double-click the **Sum of Volume** button in the Data area of the pivot table to open the PivotTable Field dialog box.

2. Type **Shares Traded** in the Name text box.

3. Click the **Number** button to open the Format Cells dialog box, and click **Number** in the Category list box.

4. Format the Shares Traded field with a **1000 separator** and display **0** decimal places.

5. Click the **OK** button twice to return to the third PivotTable Wizard dialog box.

   Now, change the title and format of the Sum of High value.

6. Double-click the **Sum of High** button in the Data area and type **High Value** in the Name text box.

7. Click the **Number** button, and then select the **Up to three digits (312/943)** Fraction format.

8. Click the **OK** button twice to return to the PivotTable Wizard, and rename the two remaining data values **Low Value** and **Closing Value**. Format each with the three-digit Fraction format.

   See Figure 11-32 for the revised pivot table layout.

Figure 11-32 ◀
Revised layout
of the pivot
table

new data
value names

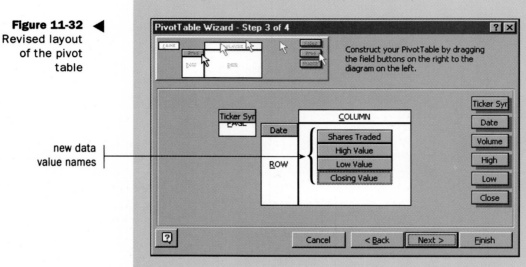

9. Click the **Next** button to display the PivotTable Wizard - Step 4 of 4 dialog box.

You're almost finished creating the pivot table. Your last task is to remove the summary column and row from the pivot table, specify the location for the table, and modify its layout.

To finish the pivot table:

1. Click the **Options** button.

2. Click the **Grand totals for columns** and **Grand totals for rows** check boxes to deselect these options, and then click the **OK** button.

3. Click the **Finish** button. An initial version of the pivot table appears. See Figure 11-33.

Excel

Figure 11-33 ◀
Initial
appearance of
the pivot table

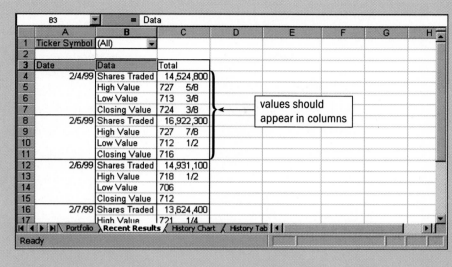

As you can see, in this initial pivot table, the stock values appear in rows.
According to your plan, they should appear in columns. To change the orientation
of the data, move the Data button located in cell B3 to the right.

4. Click the **Data** button in cell B3, drag the Data button over to cell **C3**, and then
release the mouse button.

By moving the Data button, you change the orientation of the data results from
rows to columns. See Figure 11-34 for the final version of the pivot table.

Figure 11-34 ◀
Final version of
the pivot table

values now appear
in columns

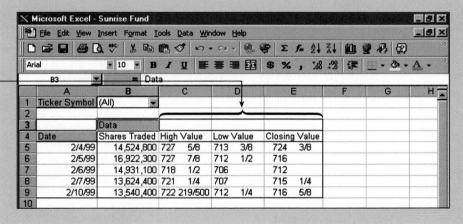

By clicking the Ticker Symbol list arrow, you can quickly view the daily values from
the last five days for any stock in the portfolio. Try this now.

To use the pivot table to display 5-day market values for a stock:

1. Click the **Ticker Symbol** list arrow in cell B1, and click **AA** in the list.

The stock values for Alcoa Aluminum for the last five days display, replacing the
prior values in the pivot table.

2. Click the list arrow again and select **GM**.

The General Motors values appear.

Using the pivot table makes it easy to retrieve summary information like this from the Sunrise database.

To augment the worksheet, you add a Volume-High-Low-Close chart.

To create the Volume-High-Low-Close chart:

1. Click cell **A3** to select the table.

2. Click **Insert** on the menu bar, and then click **Chart**.

3. Click **Stock** in the Chart type list box, and click the **Volume-High-Low-Close** chart type.

4. Click the **Next** button twice to display the Chart Wizard - Step 3 of 4 dialog box.

5. Remove the legend from the chart. Do not enter any text for chart titles.

6. Click the **Finish** button.

7. Drag the chart underneath the stock market table, and resize it to fit under the pivot table as necessary. See Figure 11-35.

Figure 11-35
Stock market table and chart for General Motors stock

General Motors ticker symbol

Volume-High-Low-Close chart

shares traded

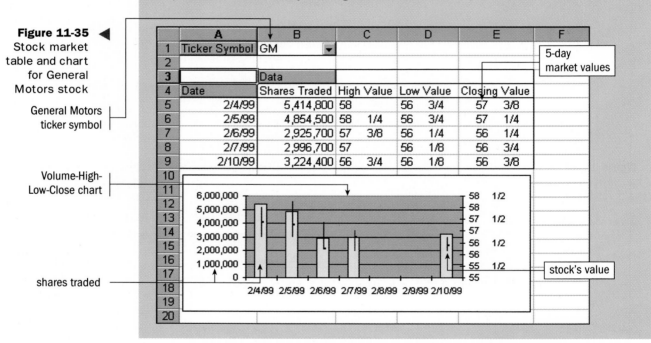

You show Kelly the Recent Results worksheet. She likes working with the pivot table to retrieve values from the Sunrise database quickly and easily. Kelly will experiment with the workbook and get back to you later with any changes she wants you to make. For now you can close the workbook.

To save the Sunrise Fund workbook:

1. Click the **Portfolio** worksheet so that this is the first worksheet you'll see the next time you open the workbook.

2. Save the workbook.

Quick Check

1. How do you refresh external data and what does refreshing do?

2. How would you set up your external data so that it refreshes automatically whenever the workbook is opened?

3. How do you edit a query?

4. How do you format stock market data to display 3.25 as 3¼?

5. How do you create a pivot table based on an external data source?

6. What is the advantage of using external data in a pivot table rather than importing data into the workbook and creating a pivot table from the imported data?

In this session, you've learned some techniques to increase the power and flexibility of your database queries. You've seen how to control the properties of your query and how to edit them. You've used queries to create pivot tables to summarize data from your database. In the next session, you'll learn how to retrieve the most current data Kelly needs from the World Wide Web.

SESSION

11.3

In this session you'll learn about some the basic principles of the Internet and the World Wide Web. You'll learn how to run Web queries to retrieve data from the World Wide Web and place the data into your Excel workbooks. Also you'll see how to activate a hyperlink within your Excel documents to display a Web page in your Web browser.

Web Queries

While text files and databases contain a wealth of information that Kelly and her colleagues at Davis & Larson will be able to use in their everyday work, the Internet has become an increasingly important source of financial information. The **Internet** is a worldwide collection of interconnected computer networks. The computers on the Internet contain information on a variety of subjects, from sports and history to financial reports. One way users access materials on the Internet is through the World Wide Web. The **World Wide Web**, often called just the "Web," is a graphical interface to the Internet that allows users to access different information sources by clicking a button. These information sources are displayed in **Web pages**, which are documents containing text, graphics, video, sound, and other elements.

To use the World Wide Web, you need to have a computer that can access the Internet, either through a direct connection in a campus or business computer lab, or with a dial-up connection using your computer's modem and the phone lines. You also need a Web browser. A **Web browser** is a program that displays Web pages. Microsoft Office 97 comes with the Internet Explorer Web browser. Netscape Navigator™ is another popular browser. If you're not sure whether your computer is capable of connecting to, and retrieving information from, the World Wide Web, ask your instructor or technical support person before proceeding with the steps in this session.

Once you have the hardware and software you need to use the World Wide Web, you can start retrieving data into your Excel workbooks using the Excel Web query feature. A **Web query** operates like the queries you created earlier in this tutorial: It connects to the World Wide Web, retrieves data requested by the user, and places it in the active workbook.

To help you access data from the Web, Excel has supplied four Web query files. These files are similar to the query file you created and saved on your Student Disk earlier in this tutorial, except that they define how to retrieve data from a page on the Web rather than from a database.

Kelly knows that there is a huge amount of stock information available on the Web, and she wants you to make her Sunrise Fund workbook capable of retrieving current values on all of the stocks in the Sunrise portfolio.

Retrieving Multiple Stock Quotes

There are 15 stocks in the Sunrise Fund and Kelly wants to be able to view current information on all of them. One of the Web query files Excel supplies is the Multiple Stock Quotes query. It allows you to enter up to 20 ticker symbols, and then it retrieves current market values of those stocks and places the information into a table in the workbook. This seems to be just what Kelly wants, so you reopen the Sunrise Fund workbook and begin creating a worksheet with values imported from a Web query.

To open the Sunrise Fund workbook:

1. If you took a break after the last session, make sure Excel is running, and open the Sunrise Fund workbook in the Tutor11 folder on your Student Disk.

2. Insert a new worksheet directly to the right of the Portfolio worksheet and name it **Current Values**.

You'll place the Web query results in this worksheet.

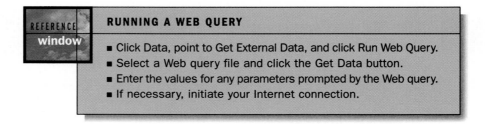

REFERENCE window

RUNNING A WEB QUERY

- Click Data, point to Get External Data, and click Run Web Query.
- Select a Web query file and click the Get Data button.
- Enter the values for any parameters prompted by the Web query.
- If necessary, initiate your Internet connection.

With the worksheet created, you'll now run the Multiple Stock Quotes Web query.

To run the Multiple Stock Quotes Web query:

1. Click **Data** on the menu bar, point to **Get External Data**, and then click **Run Web Query**.

   The list of Web query files appears, as shown in Figure 11-36.

Figure 11-36 ◀
List of built-in
Web queries

Web queries provided
by Excel

Multiple Stock
Quotes query

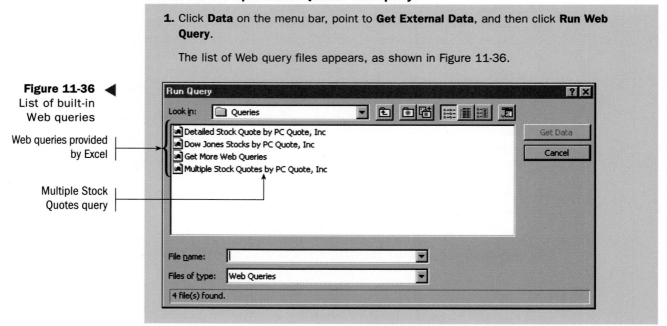

2. Click **Multiple Stock Quotes by PC Quote, Inc**, and then click the **Get Data** button.

Excel displays a dialog box in which you can specify the parameters for your query. If you click the OK button now, Excel will then prompt you for the ticker symbols of the stocks you want to see. You can also have Excel retrieve the ticker symbols from a cell range in the workbook. Since you've already retrieved this information and placed it in the Portfolio worksheet, you'll choose that option and save yourself some typing.

3. Click the **Parameters** button.

4. Click the **Get the Value from the following cell** option button.

Now you'll select the cell range containing the ticker symbols.

5. Click the **Collapse Dialog Box** button ⬜ and select the range **A4:A18** on the Portfolio worksheet.

6. Click the **Expand Dialog Box** button ⬜ to restore the Parameters dialog box.

7. Click the **OK** button twice to initiate your Web query.

Depending on the speed of your Internet connection, it might take a few seconds or up to a minute to retrieve current stock quotes from the Web. Once you are connected and the query is processed, Excel displays the data in the table format shown in Figure 11-37.

Figure 11-37 ◀
Multiple Stock
Quotes query
results

stocks in the Sunrise
Fund portfolio

current market values

the time the market
values were recorded

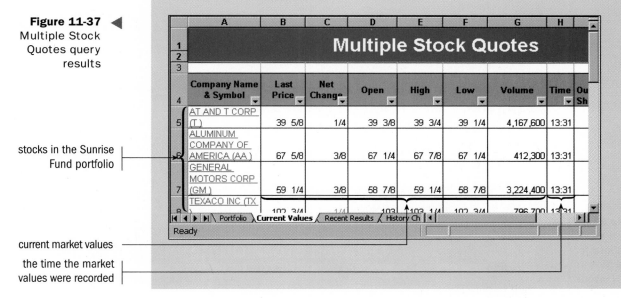

You show the results of the Web query to Kelly. Based on this information, she has a good idea how the stocks of the Sunrise Fund are doing today. Kelly is happy that it is so easy to retrieve timely information from the Web into her Excel workbooks. You point out to her that the stock quotes returned from the Web query are twenty minutes old; paid subscribers to the PC Quote service can receive up-to-the-minute stock information. She asks you how she would update stock quotes during a normal workday. You tell her she can refresh a Web query in much the same way she would refresh external data.

Refreshing a Web Query

Kelly can easily refresh the information in her workbook at any time. When you direct Excel to refresh Web data, Excel reconnects to the Web page supplying the data. To show Kelly how this works, you decide to refresh the Multiple Stock Quotes query.

To refresh the Multiple Stock Quotes query:

1. Click the **Refresh** button ⏷ on the External Data toolbar.

2. If necessary, click the **Connect** button in the Dial-up Networking dialog box.

Excel connects the Web site again and retrieves the latest information on the stocks.

Retrieving Detailed Stock Quotes

Kelly likes the prospect of using a Web query to keep her workbook current. She asks you whether she can get more detailed information on a particular stock, including information on the time of the last sale of the stock and the size of the last sale. You tell her that she can retrieve this information using a Detailed Stock query. Kelly asks you to add this query to another sheet in the workbook and use it to receive detailed stock information on General Motors stock.

To retrieve a detailed stock quote:

1. Insert a new worksheet named **Detailed Quote**, and place it after the Current Values worksheet.

2. Click **Data** on the menu bar, point to **Get External Data**, and click **Run Web Query**.

3. Click **Detailed Stock Quote by PC Quote, Inc**, and click the **Get Data** button.

4. Click the **OK** button to place the quote information in cell A1 of the current worksheet.

You are prompted for the ticker symbol of the stock. The ticker symbol for General Motors stock is GM.

5. Type **GM** and click the **OK** button.

6. Click the **Connect** button to start your network dial-up connection, if requested.

After a few seconds, the Web query retrieves the detailed stock quote values for General Motors. See Figure 11-38.

Figure 11-38 ◀
Detailed stock
quote for
General Motors
stock

time of stock quote ——

current stock
information

	A	B	C	D
1				
2	**Detailed Stock Quote**			
3	GENERAL MOTORS CORP (GM)			
4	Price Data		Fundamental Data	
5	Last Sale	59 1/4	52 Week High	63 3/4
6	Net Change	- 1/4	52 Week Low	45 3/4
7	Exchange	New York	Volatility	22
8	Time of Last Sale	13:45	Ex-Dividend Date	02/04/99
9	Size of Last Sale	600	Dividend Amount	0.5
10	Bid		Dividend Frequency	Quarterly
11	Ask		Earnings per Share	$6.08
12	Size of Bid & Ask	0x0	P/E Ratio	9.74
13	Open	59 1/2	Yield	3.37
14	High	59 1/2	Shares Outstanding	755,968
15	Low	59	Market Cap.	$44,791,104
16	Volume	4,854,500	Percent Change	0.42%

Portfolio / Current Values \ **Detailed Quote** / Recent Re

Ready

Looking over the detailed stock quote information, Kelly sees that the time of the last sale of GM stock was at 13:45, or 1:45 in the afternoon. The size of the last sale was 600 shares. So far today, GM stock has fallen a quarter of a point from its opening value of 59½.

You tell Kelly that she can refresh this Web query as well. When she refreshes it, she'll be prompted again for the ticker symbol of the stock she wants to see. She can use this particular worksheet to get detailed stock quotes on any stock in the Sunrise Fund by simply refreshing the query and entering a different ticker symbol.

Using Hyperlinks

In looking over the results of the Web query in the Current Values worksheet, Kelly notices that the company name and ticker symbol values in column A are all underlined in blue. Underlined blue text, in Excel and in many other programs, usually means that the text in the cell is hypertext. **Hypertext** consists of words that are connected to related information; when you click the text, the related information is retrieved and displayed. Hypertext shows you information not in a linear fashion, like a book that you would read straight from the front cover to the back cover, but rather through a set of associations linking common ideas and topics. Think of reading an encyclopedia in which an article on Einstein refers you to other articles on relativity and physics. With an encyclopedia, you still have to get up and manually locate the articles. But with hypertext, you simply click on a word, phrase, or picture, called a **link** or **hyperlink**, and the computer takes you directly to the related material. The Excel Help system you've used to learn about Excel is a hypertext document in which clicking symbols or underlined words "jumps" you to related material or displays a definition. The World Wide Web applies this principle to information on a larger scale involving information stored on thousands of computers around the world.

Clicking a hypertext entry in a worksheet will activate your computer's Web browser to display the Web page associated with that entry. Kelly will find this feature useful when she wants more detailed information about a particular stock in the Sunrise Fund. She can even use a hyperlink to access the Web page of each of the stocks in the portfolio. You decide to demonstrate this feature by activating the hyperlink associated with AT&T.

To activate a hyperlink:

1. Click the **Current Values** sheet tab.

2. Position your mouse pointer over the AT&T hyperlink in cell A5. The pointer changes to 🖑.

   TROUBLE? If AT&T hyperlink does not appear in your table, choose a different hyperlink and continue with the remaining steps.

3. Click the mouse button.

   Excel starts your default Web browser and displays the Web page shown in Figure 11-39. (You will have to scroll to see the table shown in Figure 11-39.)

   TROUBLE? The numeric values of the Web page you retrieve will be different from the one shown in Figure 11-39, because the figures change rapidly over time. Also, if you are using a different Web browser, such as Netscape, you might notice some other differences as well. If you can't get the links to work, talk to your instructor or lab support person.

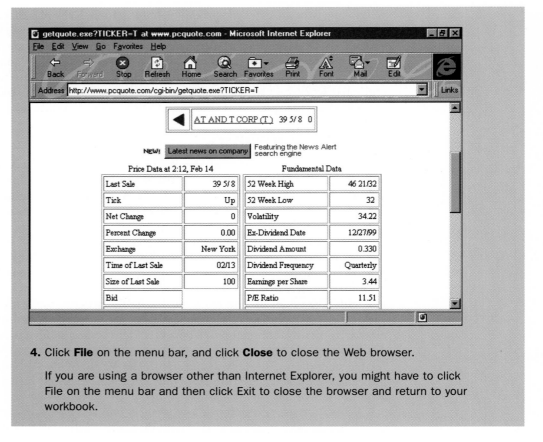

Figure 11-39 ◀
Web page for
AT&T stock

4. Click **File** on the menu bar, and click **Close** to close the Web browser.

If you are using a browser other than Internet Explorer, you might have to click File on the menu bar and then click Exit to close the browser and return to your workbook.

By using hypertext, you've discovered another way of viewing data from within your Excel workbook. This is something that Kelly can use often when she needs to view additional information about her stocks.

You've completed your job of retrieving data into Excel. You've seen how easy it is to retrieve data from text files using the Text Import Wizard and how flexible the Query Wizard is in allowing you to choose the records and fields you want to display. Using Web queries, you can retrieve up-to-the-minute stock information and refresh that data any time you want.

Your final task is to provide the Sunrise Fund workbook with accurate documentation.

Documenting Your Data Sources

Before you close the Sunrise Fund workbook, you should add a title sheet that describes the different data sources you used in creating the workbook. Documenting your work is particularly important when you workbook relies on outside sources for its data. By viewing the contents of your title sheet, other users can view the sources of your data, its timeliness, and its accuracy. They can also use the information to retrieve this data themselves.

To insert a title sheet into a workbook:

1. Insert a new worksheet named **Title Sheet** into the Sunrise Fund workbook, and place it at the beginning of the workbook.

2. Enter the information shown in Figure 11-40 into your title sheet.

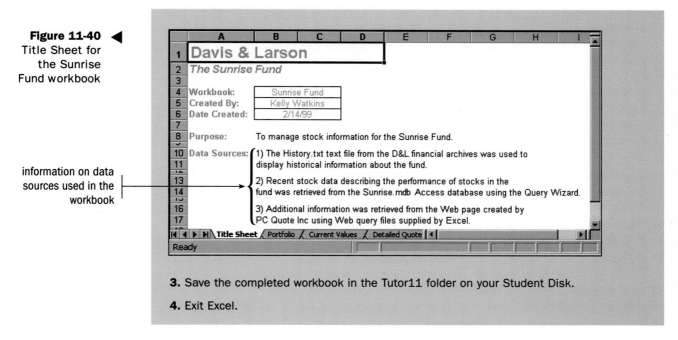

Figure 11-40 ◀
Title Sheet for
the Sunrise
Fund workbook

information on data
sources used in the
workbook

3. Save the completed workbook in the Tutor11 folder on your Student Disk.

4. Exit Excel.

You're finished with the Sunrise Fund workbook. Kelly appreciates the work you've done. By tapping into a variety of data sources, you've created a document for her that she can use to get current information on the fund as well as examine long-term and short-term data to look for important trends. She expects to find many ways to incorporate this wealth of new information into her daily work as an investment counselor at Davis and Larson.

Quick Check

1 What are the Internet and the World Wide Web?

2 What is a Web query?

3 What is a Web browser?

4 What do you need to have before you run a Web query?

5 How do you update the data values in a Web query?

6 What is hypertext? What are hyperlinks?

In this tutorial, you have imported a text file, and used the Query Wizard to import database information into Excel. You have created a pivot table from an external database, and used Web queries and hyperlinks to retrieve current stock information. Finally, you have documented your workbook to help others who may use it in the future.

Tutorial Assignments

Kelly Watkins has had a chance to work with some of the data you've retrieved for her. She would like you to create a new workbook that analyzes the performance of the stocks in the Sunrise database by the three NYSE categories: the industrials, the transportation stocks, and the utilities.

She has a text file that contains the daily indexes of these subgroups for 1995. First she wants you to import the text file into the Excel workbook. Then she would like you to create a table of yield and P/E ratio values for the stocks in the Sunrise database, sorted by category. Your next task will be to create a table and chart that displays the average closing values of the industrial, transportation, and utility stocks in the Sunrise Fund over the past five days. She wants the data in a pivot table in which she can click a Category list box and view the corresponding table and chart for that category (industrial, transportation, or utility). Finally, she would like a worksheet that displays a table of current Dow Jones Stock quote data retrieved from the Web.

To create Kelly's workbook, do the following:

1. If necessary, start Excel, and make sure your Student Disk is in the appropriate drive. Open the text file NYA95 in the TAssign folder for Tutorial 11 on your Student Disk. Adjust break lines as necessary.

2. Using the Text Import Wizard, choose the appropriate columns to import, ignoring the first three lines of the text file. Adjust break lines as necessary.

3. Format the date column in YMD format. Do not import data from the Finance column into the workbook.

4. Save the workbook as NYSE Index Analysis in the TAssign folder for Tutorial 11 on your Student Disk. Be sure to save it in Excel format.

5. Insert a new sheet named Yield and PE Values into the workbook.

6. Use the Query Wizard to retrieve the following fields and tables from the Sunrise Fund data source.
   Ticker Symbol and Category fields from the Company table
   Yield and P/E Ratios from the Stock Info table

7. Sort these values by the Category field, and place them in the new worksheet.

8. Insert a worksheet named Recent Index Performance into the workbook.

9. Create a pivot table in the worksheet that displays the average closing value for each stock category over the last five days. Organize the pivot table as follows:

   - In the Page area of the pivot table, display the Category field taken from the Company table.

   - In the Row area, display the Date field taken from the Recent Performance table.

   - In the Data area, insert the Average of the Closing value from the Recent Performance table.

10. Create a line chart of the data in the pivot table.

11. Verify that your line chart changes as you change values in the Category list box.

12. Add a new sheet to the workbook named Dow Jones.

13. Using the Web query, Dow Jones Stocks by PC Quote, Inc, retrieve stock and category data from the Web and insert it into the Dow Jones worksheet.

14. Add a title sheet to the beginning of your workbook, describing the source of the data used in the workbook. Include your name, the workbook name, and the current date in the title sheet.

15. Print a copy of the workbook, but on the NYA95 worksheet, print only the first 25 rows.

Case Problems

1. Retrieving Invoice Data for a Freelance Programmer Kevin Perkins is a freelance programmer who manages most of his financial data in a budget program. Occasionally though, Kevin needs to export his data into Excel to analyze his data and produce reports. His budget program does not allow him to save his data as an Excel workbook, but he can export it as a comma-delimited text file. Kevin has created a text file named Invoice.txt containing invoice records from the last month and a half, and he needs your help in retrieving the data and placing it into Excel. To help Kevin retrieve the data, do the following:

1. If necessary, start Excel and make sure your Student Disk is in the appropriate drive. Open the Invoice.txt file in the Cases folder for Tutorial 11.

2. Select the Delimited option button in the first step of the Text Import Wizard.

3. Choose Comma as the delimiter symbol in the second step of the Text Import Wizard.

4. Format the Date column in MDY format.

5. Do not import the Hours and the Hourly Rate columns.

6. Using the Pivot Table Wizard, create a pivot table on a new sheet, showing the total amount that Kevin has charged on his invoices, broken down by Project and then by Project Category.

7. Analyze the results. On which project has he made the most money in the recent months? Does he make more money with hourly-rate charges or with a flat fee?

8. Name the sheet containing the pivot table Invoice Report in landscape orientation.

9. Print the Invoice worksheet and the Invoice Report worksheet.

10. Save your workbook in Excel format as Invoice Data in the Cases folder for Tutorial 11 on your Student Disk.

2. Retrieving Parts Information at EZ Net Robert Crawford has just started working as the parts inventory manager at EZ Net, one of the leading suppliers of computer network cards and devices. He's responsible for managing the parts inventory. The company uses an Access database to store information on the parts that it uses and the vendors that supply the parts.

The database, named EZNet, contains three tables: Orders, Parts, and Vendors. The Orders table records information on the parts orders the company places with vendors. The Parts table contains descriptive information on each part. The Vendors table records descriptive information on each vendor. Common fields link each table with another.

EZ Net purchases its parts from many different vendors. Robert wants to retrieve the contents of the three tables into an Excel workbook so that he can examine which vendors are responsible for which parts. He also wants to create a table that will tabulate the number of parts broken down by part number and vendor. He's asked you to help him perform these tasks. To help Robert retrieve the table contents, do the following:

1. If necessary, start Excel and create a data source to the EZNet database located in the Cases folder for Tutorial 11 on your Student Disk. Name the data source EZNet.

2. Using the Query Wizard, retrieve the contents of the Orders, Parts, and Vendors tables and place them in three separate worksheets in your workbooks.

3. Name the three worksheets Orders, Parts, and Vendors.

4. Add a fourth worksheet to your workbook.

5. Using the Pivot Table Wizard, retrieve the following fields from the EZNet database:
   Quantity from the Orders table
   Description from the Parts table
   Name from the Vendors table

6. Using the Pivot Table Wizard, place the name of the vendor in the row section, the description of the part in the column section, and the sum of quantity in the data section of the table.

7. Name the worksheet containing the pivot table Parts Summary.

8. Write a paragraph analyzing the table you created. Which vendor supplies most of the parts to EZNet? Which one supplies the least?

9. Print the four worksheets in the workbook in landscape orientation.

10. Save the workbook as Inventory Data in the Cases folder for Tutorial 11 on your Student Disk.

3. Retrieving Sales Information at EuroArts EuroArts, located in Ste. Genevieve, Missouri, sells reproductions of European art to American interior design companies and to homeowners by mail order. Jeanne Domremy is the finance manager who prepares quarterly reports on the company's products and sales. The company is interested in increasing its sales to the home market, so she's particularly interested in information on sales and products intended for home use. She's asked you to help retrieve some product and sales information from the company database into an Excel workbook.

The company data is stored in an Access database named Arts. The database has five tables: Catalog, Customer, Orders, Item, and Staff. Each table shares a common field with at least one other table in the database. The Catalog table stores information about products in the company's catalog. The Customer table records personal information about people who have bought products from EuroArt. The Orders table contains information about each order, including the date, who placed the order, and who recorded the transaction. The Item table records the items purchased in each order. Finally, the Staff table contains information about the sales personnel who take the orders.

Jeanne wants the following information:

- What items in the current catalog are of interest to homeowners? She would like the list to include the catalog ID #, product category, product type, product description, and price. She wants the list sorted by descending order of price.

- How many units have been sold recently, of what kind, and where? She wants a pivot table that shows items sold by region versus product type.

To find the information Jeanne needs, do the following:

1. If necessary, start Excel, make sure your Student Disk is in the appropriate drive, and open a blank workbook.

2. Create a new data source for the Arts database located in the Cases folder for Tutorial 11 on your Student Disk, and name it EuroArts.

3. Start the Query Wizard (make sure you have the Use Query Wizard check box selected when you try to open the EuroArts data source.)

4. Select all the fields in the Catalog table.

5. In the Query Wizard's Filter Data dialog box, limit the query to only those records whose Category value equals Home or Multiple.

6. Sort the query in descending order of price and retrieve the data.

7. Print the worksheet containing the catalog list, and then save the workbook as Home Catalog in the Cases folder for Tutorial 11 on your Student Disk.

Excel

8. Open a new blank workbook, and start the Pivot Table Wizard.

9. Access the Arts data source and select the following fields from the following tables:
Order_ID# and Region from the Orders table
Item_ID# and Quantity from the Item table
Type from the Catalog table

10. Do not add any criteria to the query, but return to the Pivot Table Wizard.

11. Place Region in the Column area of the table, Type in the Row area of the table, and Sum of Quantity in the Data area of the pivot table.

12. Print the worksheet containing the resulting pivot table, and then save the workbook as Regional Sales in the Cases folder for Tutorial 11 on your Student Disk.

4. Retrieving and Running a Web Query at Brooks & Beckman Henry Sanchez is a financial consultant at Brooks & Beckman. He would like to use the Excel Web query feature to retrieve timely financial data. Unfortunately, he's not interested in the market queries supplied with Excel. Instead, he would like to retrieve current information on currency exchange rates and place them into his Excel workbooks.

Fortunately, Excel includes a Web query to retrieve additional Web queries. He asks you to help him find a Web query to retrieve currency exchange rates, and then to run that Web query to create a workbook containing exchange rate information. To retrieve the currency data that Henry needs, do the following:

1. If necessary, start Excel, and make sure your Student Disk is in the appropriate drive. Open a blank workbook and run the Web query titled Get More Web Queries.

2. Save the results of your query into a workbook named Web Query Data. Insert a title sheet at the beginning of the workbook containing the workbook name, your name, and the date. Save the workbook in the Cases folder for Tutorial 11 on your Student Disk.

3. Use the hyperlinks in the worksheet to retrieve the Web query for the CNN Currencies Web query.

4. Save the Web query on your Student Disk.

5. Use the CNN Currencies Web query to retrieve the latest currency information, and place that information on a new sheet named Currency Data in your Web Query Data workbook.

6. Save the query on your Student Disk, and print the Currency Data worksheet.

Lab Assignments

Databases

These Lab Assignments are designed to accompany the interactive Course Lab called Databases. To start the Databases Lab, click the Start button on the Windows 95 taskbar, point to Programs, point to Course Labs, point to New Perspectives Applications, and click Databases. If you do not see Course Labs on your Programs menu, see your instructor or technical support person.

Databases The Databases Lab demonstrates the essential concepts of file and database management systems. You will use the Lab to search, sort, and report the data contained in a file of classic books.

1. Click the Steps button to review basic database terminology and to learn how

to manipulate the classic books database. As you proceed through the Steps, answer all of the Quick Check questions that appear. After you complete the Steps, you will see a Quick Check summary report. Follow the instructions on the screen to print this report.

2. Click the Explore button. Make sure you can apply basic database terminology to describe the classic books database by answering the following questions:
   a. How many records does the file contain?
   b. How many fields does each record contain?
   c. What are the contents of the Catalog # field for the book written by Margaret Mitchell?
   d. What are the contents of the Title field for the record with Thoreau in the Author field?
   e. Which field has been used to sort the records?

3. Manipulate the database as necessary to answer the following questions:
   a. When the books are sorted by title, what is the first record in the file?
   b. Use the Search button to search for all the books in the West location. How many do you find?
   c. Use the Search button to search for all the books in the Main location that are checked in. What do you find?

4. Use the Report button to print out a report that groups the books by Status and sorts by title. On your report, circle the four field names. Put a box around the summary statistics showing which books are currently checked in and which books are currently checked out.

Enhancing Excel with Visual Basic

Creating a Customized Application for the Imageon Shareholders' Convention

OBJECTIVES

In this tutorial you will:

- Create macros using the macro recorder

- Assign a macro to a button

- View macro code in the Visual Basic Editor

- Learn about the features of the Visual Basic Editor

- Write a macro with the Visual Basic Editor

- Learn basic concepts and principles of the Visual Basic programming language

- Write an interactive macro that asks the user for input

- Modify a macro so it responds to different user input

CASE

Imageon Inc.

Imageon, Inc. is a mid-sized manufacturer of high-quality computer imaging products, including scanners, copiers, and laser printers. Located in Seattle, Washington, Imageon was founded in 1989. The company has grown rapidly since then, and is now a leader in the computer imaging market.

The company is planning to hold its annual shareholders' conference next month, and you're assisting the convention coordinator, Steve Howard, in preparing materials for the convention. The materials will focus on building shareholders' confidence in Imageon by emphasizing the company's success over the last several years. Steve feels that past shareholder conventions have given attendees more printed information than necessary. This year he wants to set up an information center called a **kiosk** in the convention hall lobby, with computers that shareholders can use to display company information. Specifically, he wants the shareholders to be able to display and view financial tables and charts describing the company's performance over the last few fiscal years. Most of the tables and charts are in Excel workbooks. Steve cautions you that many of the shareholders are not experienced Excel users, so he wants you to make it as easy as possible for them to work with the various Excel files.

You are already familiar with some basic Excel macros, and know that Excel includes a programming language called Visual Basic, a very powerful and easy-to-use tool that helps you create more complex macros. You suggest adding user-friendly macros to the workbooks to help the shareholders view tables and charts easily and quickly. These more sophisticated macros can help you customize the way users interact with a workbook. You can even have a workbook perform alternate tasks based on different user responses. You decide to explore how you can use Visual Basic to create an easy-to-use system for the convention kiosk. The conference is next month, so you don't have much time to prepare.

SESSION

12.1

In this session, you'll review how to create a macro using the Excel macro recorder and how to assign that macro to a button in the workbook. After creating the macro, you'll view the macro code in the Visual Basic Editor. You'll learn about some of the features of the editor, and you'll use it to create a second macro based on the first one you recorded.

Planning Your Macros

You sit down with Steve to review the contents of one of the workbooks he wants to place on the computer in the kiosk. The Imageon workbook, shown in Figure 12-1, includes reports that show the financial performance of the company over the past four years.

Figure 12-1 ◀
Contents of the
Imageon
workbook

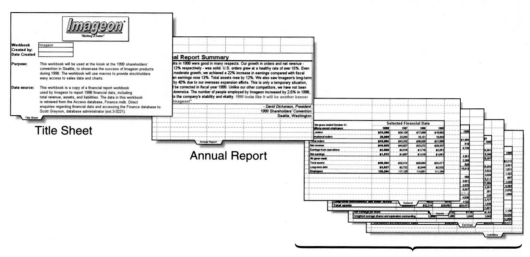

Title Sheet

Annual Report

Financial Reports

The workbook contains six worksheets: a title sheet, a sheet containing a message from the company president, and four sheets of financial reports. Steve doesn't want the shareholders to have to click each tab in the workbook to locate the report they want to view. Since users might not know Excel, it would be ideal if they only had to click self-explanatory buttons on the screen that would immediately display a particular sheet. Steve wants you to use Excel to create an application that would make this possible.

You look into the matter, and discover that you can create what Steve needs by creating a **customized application**, a program that uses Excel macros written in the Visual Basic programming language to perform a specific task. You learn that creating a customized application is a five-step planning process:

1. **Define your needs.**
   Write a short statement describing what tasks you want your customized application to perform. Can you perform any of the tasks using built-in Excel features instead? If so, what limitations of these features are you trying to overcome?

2. **Decide on the application's appearance.**
   How will the application appear to the end user? Will you ask the user to supply information in response to a dialog box? If so, what type of message will the dialog box display? What limitations, if any, will you put on what the user enters?

3. **Use the macro recorder.**
   If some of the tasks can be performed within Excel, consider using the macro recorder to record them as macros. You can then use the macro that the recorder creates as a building block to help form a larger application, and as a springboard to better understand Visual Basic.

4. **Modify the macros.**

Once you've created the foundation of your macros with the macro recorder, edit the code to meet your needs. You can take advantage of the Visual Basic online Help feature as you enter new code and modify existing statements. You can use Visual Basic to create dialog boxes to make your workbook more flexible and easier to use.

5. **Finalize the appearance of the application.**

Evaluate the appearance of the workbook containing your application. What elements of the Excel document window will you keep, which ones will you remove, and which will you modify? Will you want screen elements like sheet tabs, or row and column headers visible to the user? What do you want the menu bar to look like? Will you create a customized toolbar?

You decide to apply the planning process to Steve's proposal. By defining Steve's needs, you know that the application he has in mind is a simple one. He wants users to easily access certain worksheets from the workbook by clicking self-explanatory buttons. While you can, of course, display an Excel worksheet by clicking its tab, Steve sees a couple of limitations in this method. First, shareholders who have never used Excel might not know about this method for displaying worksheets. Secondly, even if they did know it, there are several worksheets in the workbook, and not all of the worksheet tabs would be immediately visible. Users could easily overlook some of the worksheets. In this situation, a macro would be very useful in helping shareholders find all the information they need quickly and easily.

How should this customized application appear to the user? Imageon sales representatives will staff the kiosk, but they will be busy talking with shareholders, and won't have much time to help attendees use the computers. So the **interface,** the way the program communicates to the user, needs to be self-explanatory. It should not overwhelm the user with choices, but it should concisely display the available options. Steve thinks the shareholders will want to view either the annual report summary or one of the financial worksheets. He sketches out a diagram like the one shown in Figure 12-2 that shows how he wants the application to appear.

Figure 12-2 ◀
The custom
application
that Steve is
planning

click on-screen
buttons to view
worksheets

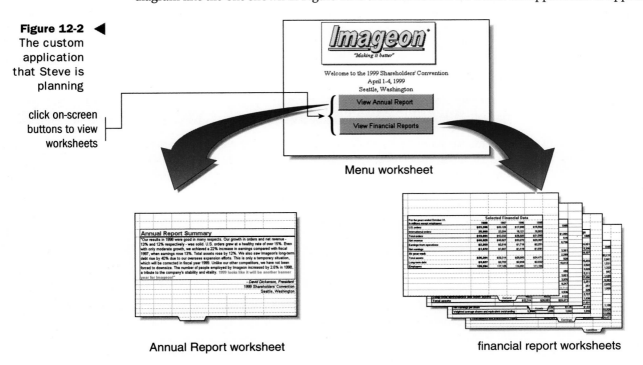

Menu worksheet

Annual Report worksheet

financial report worksheets

Now that you know what tasks you want the application to perform and how you want the interface to look, you are ready to start using the macro recorder to lay the foundation for your customized application. The Imageon workbook that contains the Annual Report summary and the financial reports that Steve wants displayed has been stored on your Student Disk. You'll open the workbook now.

To open the Imageon workbook:

1. Start Excel as usual, and make sure your Student Disk is in the appropriate drive. Open the **Imageon** workbook in the Tutorial.12 folder on your Student Disk, and save it as **Kiosk 1**.

2. Enter **Kiosk 1** in the Workbook box in cell B7, the date on the Title Sheet worksheet, and then enter your name.

Take a moment to become familiar with the contents of the workbook. Steve has added a menu worksheet that contains the Imageon logo and a welcome message that the convention goers will see. On this worksheet, you'll add the buttons they'll click to display the Annual Report and the financial reports. After the Menu worksheet, the Annual Report worksheet contains a message from company president, David Dickerson, summarizing the company's 1998 annual report. After the Annual Report worksheet, four financial worksheets give information on the company's general fiscal state as well as its earnings, assets, and liabilities for the last four years. Once you know what the workbook contains, you're ready to start programming your macros.

Creating and Running a Simple Macro

The fastest way to create macros is to use the Excel macro recorder. As you saw earlier, you record a macro by turning on the recorder, performing a set of tasks, and then turning off the recorder when you're finished. The recorder saves the steps you performed, and users can rerun the macro any time to perform the same tasks. Then, since users need an easy way to run your macro, you can assign it to a button, so that whenever the user clicks the button, your macro will run.

You'll record a macro that takes users to the Annual Report worksheet. Then you'll use a tool on the Forms toolbar to create a button with the text "View Annual Report Summary" that users can click to display the Annual Report worksheet.

Using the Macro Recorder

The macro you'll record will be a simple one: It will display the Annual Report worksheet and then select cell A1, to make sure that the entire annual report summary appears in the document window. You'll name this macro "Annual_Report."

To start recording the Annual Report macro:

1. Click **Tools** on the menu bar, point to **Macro**, and click **Record New Macro**. Now you'll name the macro, using a name with an underscore character, since macro names cannot contains spaces.

2. Type **Annual_Report** in the Macro name text box.

3. Make sure that This Workbook is selected in the Store macro in list box since this macro will only be used in the current workbook. Now document the macro.

4. In the Description text box, replace the existing text with the following: **This macro displays the Annual Report worksheet**. See Figure 12-3 for the completed Record Macro dialog box.

Figure 12-3 ◄
Record Macro
dialog box

name of macro ─────

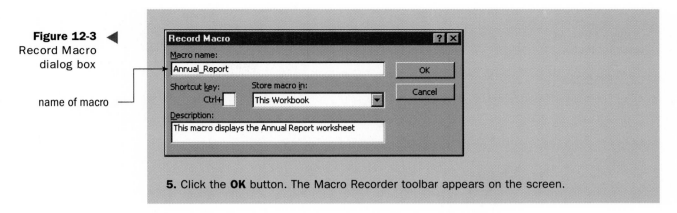

5. Click the **OK** button. The Macro Recorder toolbar appears on the screen.

With the Macro Recorder active, you'll go through the steps of selecting the Annual Report worksheet, clicking cell A1, and then turning off the recorder when you're finished.

To record the Annual_Report macro:

1. Click the **Annual Report** sheet tab.

2. Click cell **A1**.

3. Click the **Stop Recording** button ■ on the Macro Recorder toolbar.

Before going further with the macro, you should run it and verify that it works correctly.

To test the Annual_Report macro:

1. Click the **Menu** sheet tab.

2. Click **Tools** on the menu bar, point to **Macro**, and click **Macros** to open the Macro dialog box.

3. Click **Annual_Report** in the Macro Name list box, and click the **Run** button.

The Annual Report worksheet appears in the document window with cell A1 selected.

TROUBLE? If the Annual_Report macro does not display the Annual Report worksheet, go back to the Macro name list box, and click the Delete button to delete it. Then use the Macro Recorder to record the macro again.

Now you know the macro runs correctly. Since you don't want users to have to use the Tools menu to run your macro, you'll place a button on the Menu worksheet and assign the button to the macro you created. Then you'll place the text "View Annual Report Summary" on the button so users know they can simply click the button to view the Annual Report worksheet.

Assigning a Macro to a Button

To create a button on the worksheet and assign a macro to it, you first display the Forms toolbar. This toolbar contains several tools that help you create the interface that makes your macros easy to use.

To display the Forms toolbar:

1. Click the **Menu** sheet tab to return to the Menu worksheet.

2. Click **View** on the menu bar, point to **Toolbars**, and click **Forms**.

The Forms toolbar appears. See Figure 12-4.

Figure 12-4 ◄
Forms toolbar

Button tool ─

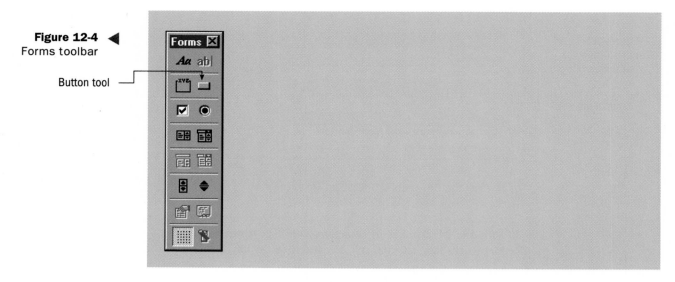

Now you'll use the Button tool to place a button on the worksheet. After you create the button, Excel will automatically ask you for a macro to assign to it. You'll specify the Annual_Report macro that you just created with the Macro Recorder.

To create the View Annual Report button:

1. Click the **Button** tool ▭ on the Forms toolbar.

   When you move the pointer over the worksheet, the pointer changes to +.

2. Drag the pointer over the range **D10:F11**, and then release the mouse button. A button appears, and you are asked to name the macro you want to assign to it.

3. Click **Annual_Report** from the list of macros, and then click the **OK** button. Now you'll enter the text that will appear on the button.

4. Type **View Annual Report Summary** and click cell **A1**.

5. Click the **Close** box ☒ on the Forms toolbar to close it.

   The Menu worksheet appears with the new button. See Figure 12-5.

Figure 12-5 ◄
Menu
worksheet with
the View
Annual Report
button

click to view the
Annual Report
worksheet

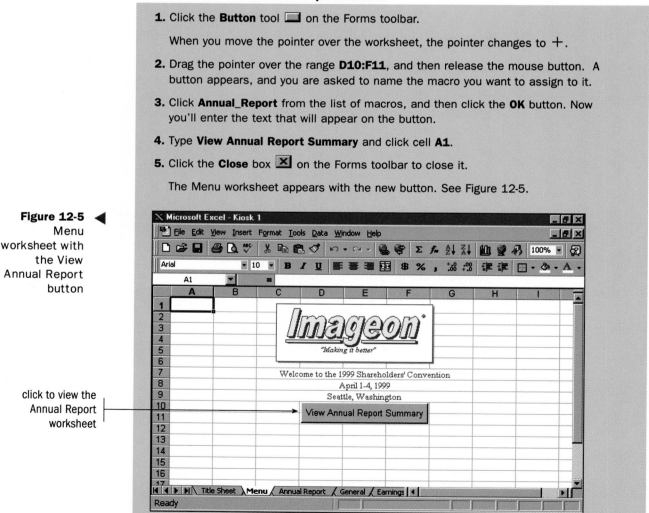

To make sure that the button and macro work properly, you should test them.

To test the View Annual Report Summary button:

1. Move the mouse pointer over the button so that the pointer changes to , and then click the button.

   The Annual Report worksheet appears with cell A1 selected.

Having created and tested your first macro in this workbook, you are ready to examine the macro code to see how it works. By examining the code, you can learn some of the techniques you'll need to create new and more sophisticated macros. To look at the code, you'll use the Visual Basic Editor.

Starting the Visual Basic Editor

All Excel macros are written in a programming language called **Visual Basic** (or **Visual Basic for Applications**, also called **VBA**). All the Microsoft Office programs (Excel, Word, Access, and PowerPoint) use this programming language, so when you master the art of writing macros in Excel, you have a firm foundation for writing macros in the other Office products.

To edit the macros you've created with the Macro Recorder, you need to use the **Visual Basic Editor**. The editor is an application that allows you to edit your macros, create customized dialog boxes, and modify the contents of your Excel workbook. You use the Visual Basic Editor whether you are creating macros in Excel, Word, Access, or PowerPoint.

REFERENCE window	STARTING THE VISUAL BASIC EDITOR
	■ Click Tools and point to Macro.
	■ Click Visual Basic Editor to start (or click Macros to open the Macro dialog box, select the name of the macro you want to edit, and then click the Edit button).

You can open the Visual Basic Editor directly, or by editing a macro you've created using the Macro Recorder. You'll open the Annual_Report macro, which will automatically open the editor.

To start the Visual Basic Editor:

1. Click **Tools** on the menu bar, point to **Macro**, and click **Macros**.

2. Click **Annual_Report** in the Macro Name list box, and click the **Edit** button.

   The Visual Basic Editor opens. See Figure 12-6.

Figure 12-6 ◀
Visual Basic
Editor

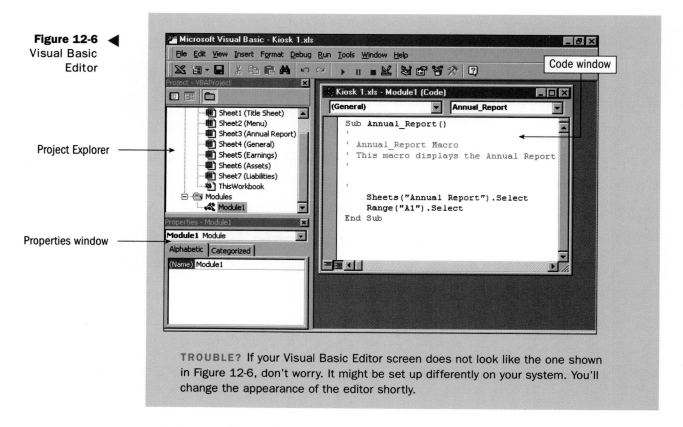

TROUBLE? If your Visual Basic Editor screen does not look like the one shown in Figure 12-6, don't worry. It might be set up differently on your system. You'll change the appearance of the editor shortly.

Before you begin editing the Annual_Report macro, take a moment to become familiar with the main features of Visual Basic Editor.

Elements of the Visual Basic Editor

When the Visual Basic Editor opens, it displays three windows: the Project Explorer, the Properties window, and the Code window. You can use these windows to look at the structure and content of your workbooks, as well as any macros you've created. You might see other windows, depending on how the editor was installed on your system. To start learning about the different features of the editor, you'll begin with a clean slate by closing these windows and reopening them one at a time.

To clear the Visual Basic Editor window:

1. Click the **Close** box ⊠ on each window in the Microsoft Visual Basic Kiosk 1.xls window.

The Visual Basic Editor window is now clear.

Now you are ready to examine each element of the Visual Basic Editor. You'll start with the Project Explorer.

The Project Explorer

One important use of the Visual Basic Editor is the management of your projects. A **project** is a collection of macros, worksheets, forms for data entry, and other items that make up the customized application you're trying to create. You manage your projects with the Project Explorer. The **Project Explorer** is a window in the editor that displays a hierarchical list of all currently opened projects and their contents.

The Project Explorer window is **dockable**, meaning that you can drag it to the edge of the screen, and it will always remain on top of an other window. Docking a window is useful when you want the contents of that window always in view, but it can also take up valuable screen space. In this case, you'll make the Project Explorer undockable to make it easier to view the other windows in the editor.

REFERENCE window	**VIEWING WINDOWS IN THE VISUAL BASIC EDITOR** ■ Click View and click the name of the window you want to view. ■ To make a window undockable, right-click the window's title bar, and deselect Dockable from the shortcut menu. ■ To make a window dockable again, click Tools and click Options. In the Options dialog box, click the Docking tab, and click to select the check box corresponding to the window you want to dock.

To begin viewing your shareholders' project in the editor, you'll first display the Project Explorer, and undock it if it isn't already undocked.

To view and undock the Project Explorer:

1. Click **View** on the menu bar, and then click **Project Explorer**. The Project Explorer window opens, with Project - VBAProject in its title bar.

2. Right-click the title bar of the Project Explorer, and deselect **Dockable** from the shortcut menu.

   TROUBLE? If you don't see a shortcut menu when you right-click the title bar, Project Explorer is already undocked, and you can continue with the tutorial.

   Figure 12-7 shows the contents of the undocked Project Explorer for the Kiosk 1 workbook.

Figure 12-7 ◀
Contents of the Project Explorer

project name

objects folder

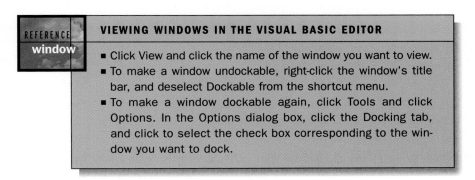

workbook name

worksheets in the workbook

the workbook itself is an object

Like Windows Explorer, the Project Explorer arranges your project components hierarchically. At the top of the hierarchy is the project itself. In this case, the name of the project is "VBAProject," the default name the editor assigns to new projects. The name of the workbook containing the project follows in parentheses. Within your project are various items called objects. An **object** is an element of a custom application, such as a worksheet, a cell, a chart, a form, or a report. In Visual Basic, just about anything can be an object; the VBAProject is itself an object. As you can see in Figure 12-7, the Project

Explorer has placed the worksheets in the current workbook, as well as the current workbook itself, in a folder called Microsoft Excel Objects.

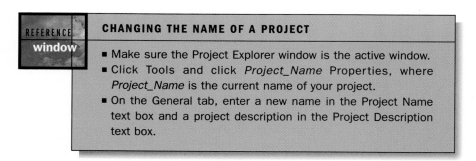

REFERENCE window

CHANGING THE NAME OF A PROJECT

- Make sure the Project Explorer window is the active window.
- Click Tools and click *Project_Name* Properties, where *Project_Name* is the current name of your project.
- On the General tab, enter a new name in the Project Name text box and a project description in the Project Description text box.

Since the default name VBAProject isn't very descriptive, you'll change it to something more informative for future users of the workbook. You can change the name and enter a description of the project in the Project Properties dialog box.

To change the name of your project:

1. Click the title bar of the Project Explorer window to activate it.

2. Click **Tools** on the menu bar, and then click **VBAProject Properties**. Since project names cannot include spaces, you'll use an underscore to separate the two words.

3. Type **Shareholders_Convention** in the Project Name text box, and then press the **Tab** key.

4. In the Project Description text box, type **Macros that aid users in viewing information at the 1999 convention**. See Figure 12-8.

Figure 12-8 ◄
Completed VBAProject-Project Properties dialog box

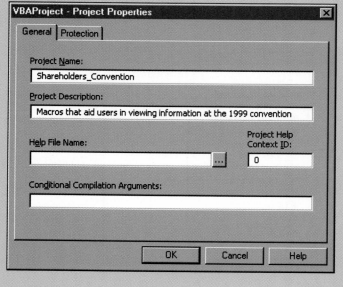

5. Click the **OK** button.

The Project Explorer window displays the new project name. See Figure 12-9.

Figure 12-9 ◄
The revised
Project
Explorer
window

new project name ──

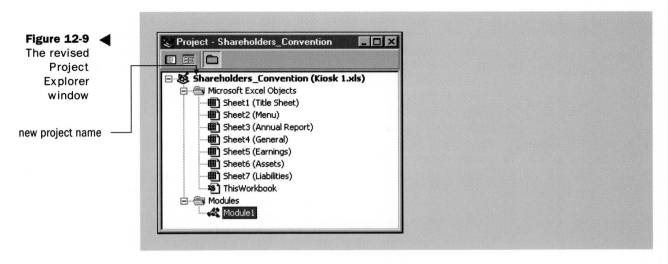

Now that you've seen how the Project Explorer gives you an overview of your project, you'll view objects in more detail in the Properties window.

The Properties Window

When you entered the name and description of your project, you were actually modifying two of its properties. A **property** is an attribute of an object that defines one of its characteristics, such as its name, size, color, or location on the screen. All objects have properties. The **Properties window** lists the properties for the object that is selected in the Project Explorer. You'll display the Properties window now, and removing the docking feature if the window is docked.

To view and undock the Properties window:

1. Click **View** on the menu bar, and then click **Properties Window**. The Properties window opens.

2. Right-click the title bar of the Properties window, and deselect **Dockable** from the shortcut menu. The Properties window undocks from the menu bar and appears as a window in the Visual Basic Editor display area. See Figure 12-10.

Figure 12-10 ◄
Properties
window

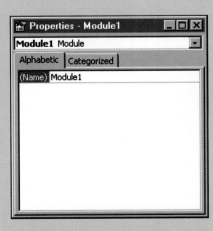

TROUBLE? If you don't see a shortcut menu when you right-click the title bar, the Properties window is already undocked, and you can continue with the tutorial.

In the Properties window, you can change the name of a worksheet, the width of a worksheet's columns, and whether or not the worksheet is visible to the user. As shown in Figure 12-10, you can view properties alphabetically and by category by clicking the Alphabetic and Categorized tabs at the top.

To see how the Properties window works, you decide to change the name of the Menu worksheet in the workbook to "Main Menu." You could do this from within Excel, but changing it here will give you some practice in using the Project Explorer and the Properties window.

To change the name of the Menu worksheet:

1. Click **Sheet2 (Menu)** in the Project Explorer window.

   The contents of the Properties window immediately change to show the properties of the Menu worksheet.

2. Click the **Alphabetic** tab in the Properties window, if necessary.

3. If necessary, scroll down to the bottom of the window, and then select **Menu** in the right column of the window in the Name row.

4. Type **Main Menu** and press the **Enter** key.

   The name of the worksheet displayed in the Project Explorer window changes to Main Menu. See Figure 12-11. The next time you return to the Kiosk 1 workbook, you will find that the worksheet name has been changed there as well.

Figure 12-11 ◀
Using the Properties window to change a worksheet name

Sheet2 is selected in the Project Explorer

list of properties

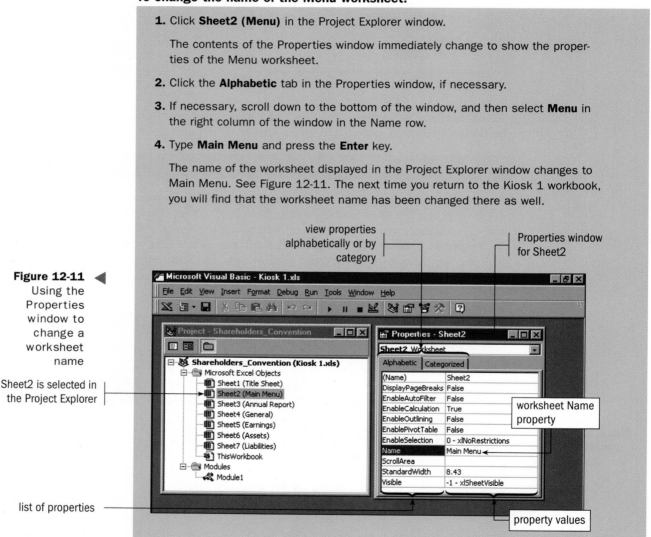

There can be many properties listed in the Properties window. The meaning of some of them will be very clear (such as the Name property), while others will not be as readily understandable. If you need more information about a particular property in the Property window, you can use Visual Basic online Help. You'll use online Help now to learn more about one of the properties of the Main Menu worksheet.

To view information on a property:

1. Click **StandardWidth** in the list of properties.

2. Press the **F1** key.

The Help window shown in Figure 12-12 appears with the information that the StandardWidth property returns or sets the standard (default) width of all the columns in the worksheet. So if you want to change the default width of the columns in the Main Menu worksheet, you would change the value for this property.

TROUBLE? If the Visual Basic Editor fails to display the Help topic, the Visual Basic Help files might not be installed. See your instructor or technical support person.

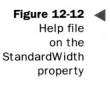

Figure 12-12
Help file
on the
StandardWidth
property

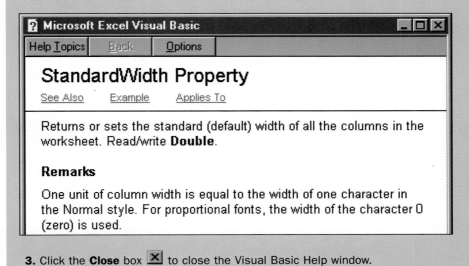

3. Click the **Close** box ☒ to close the Visual Basic Help window.

In the Visual Basic Editor, if you are not sure what a button, command, or object does, you can get information on it by selecting it and pressing the F1 key. You can display online Help either when you are in the Properties window or when you're writing and viewing Visual Basic code.

Now that you're familiar with the Project Explorer and Properties windows, you'll learn about modules, one of the most important parts of the Project Explorer.

Modules

When you viewed your project in the Project Explorer, you might have noticed the folder at the bottom of the object list called Modules. A **module** is a collection of macros. You might use several modules in a single project to group macros according to the type of tasks they perform. For example, you might group all the macros that handle printing tasks in one module, and the macros that format worksheets in another. When you recorded the Annual_Report macro, the Visual Basic Editor created a module and assigned it the default name "Module1."

You can give your module a name that better describes the type of macros it will contain. You decide to change the name of Module1 to "Report_Macros."

To change the name of a macro module:

1. Click **Module1** in the Project Explorer window.

2. Click the Properties window title bar to make the window active, and then double-click **Module1** in the (Name) row, type **Report_Macros**, and press the **Enter** key.

   The name of the module in the Project Explorer window and the Properties window changes to Report_Macros. See Figure 12-13.

Figure 12-13 ◄
Changing the
name of a
project module

folder containing the
project modules

Report_Macros
module

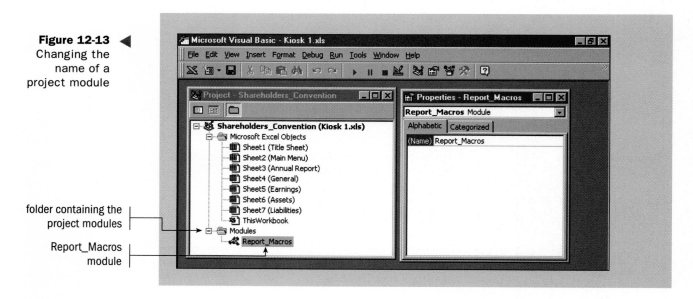

Having seen a little of the structure of your project and how to modify its properties, you're ready to start looking at the macro you created for your Shareholders_Convention project. You'll view the macro in the Code window.

The Code Window

When you want to view the contents of the macros in your project modules, you use the **Code window**. The Code window displays the Visual Basic macro code associated with any item in the Project Explorer. You saw the Code window when you first opened the Visual Basic Editor. You'll reopen it now.

To view the Code window:

1. Click **View** on the menu bar, and click **Code**.

Figure 12-14 shows the contents of the Code window for the Report_Macros module.

Figure 12-14 ◄
Viewing the
Code window

Code window

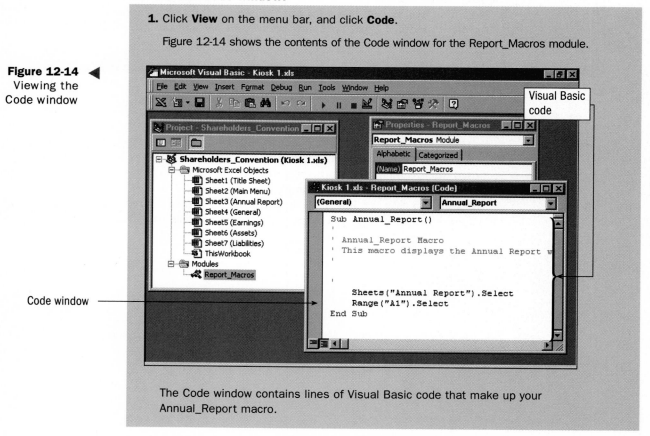

The Code window contains lines of Visual Basic code that make up your Annual_Report macro.

Now that you've viewed the Code window, you can use it to look closely at the contents of your macro. To understand the code, you'll first need to learn about Visual Basic procedures.

Working with Visual Basic Sub Procedures

A macro in Visual Basic is called a **procedure**. Visual Basic supports three kinds of procedures: sub procedures, function procedures, and property procedures. A **sub procedure** performs an action on your project or workbook, such as formatting a cell or displaying a chart. A **function procedure** returns a value. You would use a function procedure if you wanted to create a customized function to use in your worksheets. A **property procedure** is a more advanced subject, used when you want to create customized properties for the objects in your project.

Because your project deals with displaying different worksheets within the Kiosk workbook, which are all actions, you'll be creating only sub procedures.

Introducing Sub Procedures

In order to write a sub procedure, you'll have to know a few basic rules of Visual Basic syntax. **Syntax** refers to the set of rules specifying how you must enter certain commands so that Visual Basic will interpret them correctly, much like grammatical syntax rules make our sentences understandable to others. If you use improper syntax, Excel will not be able to run your macro, or it might run it incorrectly. The general syntax for a Visual Basic sub procedure is:

```
Sub Procedure_Name( )

        <Visual Basic commands and comments>

End Sub
```

Here, *Procedure_Name* is the name of the sub procedure or macro, such as Annual_Report. The parentheses after the procedure name can contain any information passed to the procedure, in the same way a function does. Many of the procedures you'll write will not require any information in the parentheses, but the parentheses are required anyway.

After the first Sub line, you enter either commands that perform certain tasks, or comments that document the procedure's use. The End Sub command is always the last line in a sub procedure. To see an example of a sub procedure, look at the Annual_Report macro you created earlier. Figure 12-15 shows the Visual Basic code for the Annual_Report macro. The name of the macro, Annual_Report, is also the name of the procedure, and appears in the first line of the sub procedure. Below that, the sub procedure displays the comments you entered in the Macro Recorder dialog box. All comments begin with an apostrophe and are usually displayed in green text. After the comments, the procedure lists the Visual Basic commands needed to first select and display the Annual Report worksheet, and then to select cell A1 on that worksheet. The "End Sub" line signals the end of the Annual_Report sub procedure.

Figure 12-15 ◄
Annual_Report
sub procedure

procedure name ⎯

comments ⎯

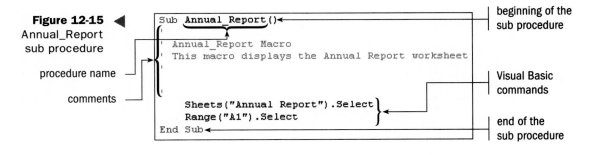

```
Sub Annual_Report()                              ┤← beginning of the
                                                        sub procedure
' Annual_Report Macro
' This macro displays the Annual Report worksheet

    Sheets("Annual Report").Select               ┤← Visual Basic
    Range("A1").Select                                  commands
End Sub ◄                                         ┤← end of the
                                                        sub procedure
```

If you want more information about sub procedures or about any of the commands in the Annual_Report macro, you can open online Help the same way you did earlier in the Properties window.

To view additional information about sub procedures:

1. Select the word **Sub** in the first line of the Annual_Report macro.

2. Press the **F1** key.

   The Visual Basic Editor displays a Help window with additional information on sub procedures and the Sub statement.

3. Read the Help text, and then click the **Close** box ☒ to close the Visual Basic Help window.

You can use to the F1 key to get help on most of the commands in the macros that you create with the Macro Recorder.

Now that you are familiar with the structure of your Annual_Report macro, you'll create another, similar one using copy and paste.

Creating a Sub Procedure Using Copy and Paste

The Annual_Report macro you created takes users from the Main Menu sheet to the Annual Report worksheet. But once they use your macro, they will need another sub procedure that will take them back to the Main Menu worksheet. This code will be very similar to the Annual_Report sub procedure. Without learning the details of Visual Basic commands in the Annual_Report macro (you'll do that in the next session), you can copy the macro lines and adapt them to create the new macro. You'll begin by adding a new sub procedure to the Report_Macros module, and then copying and pasting the code from the Annual_Report sub procedure into it. You'll then edit that macro, replacing the occurrences of Annual Report with Main Menu.

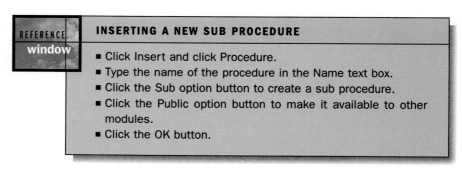

REFERENCE window

INSERTING A NEW SUB PROCEDURE

- Click Insert and click Procedure.
- Type the name of the procedure in the Name text box.
- Click the Sub option button to create a sub procedure.
- Click the Public option button to make it available to other modules.
- Click the OK button.

You'll call the new sub procedure Main_Menu. You'll start the new sub procedure by using the Insert Procedure command.

To insert a new procedure into the Code window:

1. Click the title bar of the Code window to activate it.

2. Click **Insert** on the menu bar, and then click **Procedure**. The Add Procedure dialog box opens, where you'll enter the name and type of procedure you're creating.

3. Type **Main_Menu** in the Name text box to assign a title to the macro. See Figure 12-16

Figure 12-16 ◄
Inserting a new
procedure into
a module

select to create a
sub procedure

select to make the
procedure available
to all modules
in the project

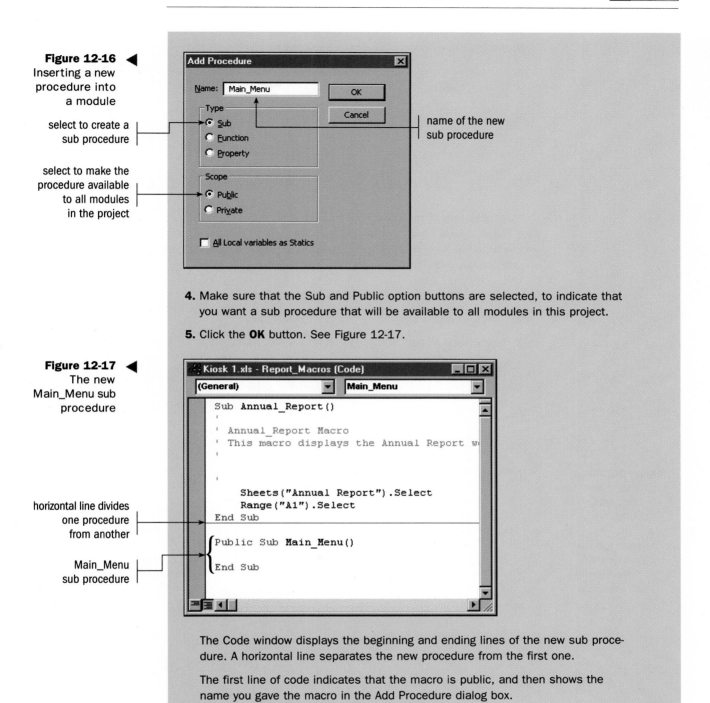

name of the new
sub procedure

4. Make sure that the Sub and Public option buttons are selected, to indicate that you want a sub procedure that will be available to all modules in this project.

5. Click the **OK** button. See Figure 12-17.

Figure 12-17 ◄
The new
Main_Menu sub
procedure

horizontal line divides
one procedure
from another

Main_Menu
sub procedure

The Code window displays the beginning and ending lines of the new sub procedure. A horizontal line separates the new procedure from the first one.

The first line of code indicates that the macro is public, and then shows the name you gave the macro in the Add Procedure dialog box.

With the new procedure created, you are ready to copy the Visual Basic code from the Annual_Report Sub Procedure into the Main_Menu Sub Procedure. You add, delete, and replace text in the Code window the same way you do in a word processor.

To copy and paste the Visual Basic code:

1. Scroll up the Code window until you can see the entire Annual_Report macro.

2. Select the code *between* the Sub procedure line and the End Sub line, including the comments. Do *not* include either the Sub procedure line or the End Sub line in your selection.

3. Click the **Copy** button 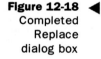 on the Standard toolbar.

4. Scroll down and click the blank line in the middle of the Main_Menu sub procedure.

5. Click the **Paste** button 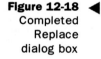 on the Standard toolbar.

The Visual Basic code is pasted into the Main_Menu sub procedure.

TROUBLE? You might want to enlarge the Code window to make it easier to copy, paste, and view your Visual Basic code.

Your next task is to replace the occurrences of "Annual Report" and "Annual_Report" with "Main Menu" and "Main_Menu." You can do this by selecting the old text and typing over it with the new text, or you can use the editor's Replace command to replace all the occurrences at once. You'll use the Replace command.

To replace text in the Main_Menu sub procedure:

1. Click **Edit** on the menu bar, and then click **Replace**.

2. Type **Annual Report** in the Find What text box, and then press the **Tab** key.

3. Type **Main Menu** in the Replace With text box.

4. In the Search section, click the **Current Procedure** option button to replace only the occurrences of the words "Annual Report" in the current procedure (not in the entire module or project).

Figure 12-18 displays the completed Replace dialog box.

Figure 12-18 ◀
Completed
Replace
dialog box

select to replace
occurrences within
the current
sub procedure

5. Click the **Replace All** button.

Excel indicates that two occurrences of the words "Annual Report" have been replaced.

6. Click the **OK** button.

TROUBLE? If the message says that four occurrences have been replaced, you have accidentally changed all the occurrences in the module. To restore the changed occurrences, click the Undo button.

Now replace the occurrences of the word "Annual_Report."

7. Type **Annual_Report** in the Find What text box, press the **Tab** key, and then type **Main_Menu** in the Replace With text box.

8. Click the **Current Procedure** option button and click the **Replace All** button.

One occurrence of the word "Annual_Report" is replaced.

9. Click the **OK** button, and then click the **Cancel** button to close the Replace dialog box.

Figure 12-19 displays the Main_Menu sub procedure after the text replacement.

Figure 12-19 ◄
The completed
Main_Main
sub procedure

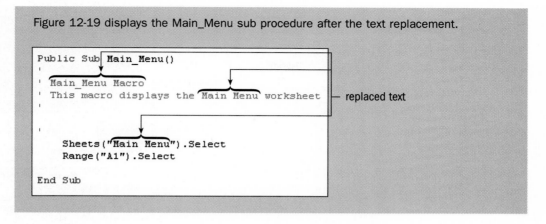

```
Public Sub Main_Menu()
'
' Main_Menu Macro
' This macro displays the Main Menu worksheet        ── replaced text
'
'
    Sheets("Main Menu").Select
    Range("A1").Select

End Sub
```

Using copy, paste, find, and replace, you've created a new procedure in the Shareholders_Convention project. Because you've replaced the name "Annual Report" with "Main Menu," this new procedure should display the contents of the Main Menu worksheet when you run it. You decide to return to Excel and test the new macro. In Excel, you'll assign this procedure to a button on the Annual Report worksheet, and run the macro by clicking the button.

To close the Visual Basic Editor and return to Excel:

1. Click **File** on the menu bar, and then click **Close and Return to Microsoft Excel**.

   The Visual Basic Editor closes, and the Annual Report worksheet appears. Notice that the second worksheet in the workbook has been changed to Main Menu, which you changed from the Project Explorer window of the Visual Basic Editor.

Now using the techniques you used earlier, you'll add a button to the Annual Report worksheet and assign the newly-created Main_Menu macro to it.

To create the Main Menu button:

1. If necessary, click the **Annual Report** worksheet tab to display the worksheet.

2. Click **View** on the menu bar, point to **Toolbars**, and then click **Forms**.

3. Click the **Button** tool 🔲 on the Forms toolbar, and drag the pointer over the range **E1:G2**, and then release the mouse button. The new button appears and the Assign Macro dialog box opens.

4. Click **Main_Menu** in the Macro Name list box, and click the **OK** button. Now you'll enter the text that will display on the button.

5. Type **Return to the Main Menu** and click cell **A1**.

6. Click the **Close** box 🗵 on the Forms toolbar to close it.

   The Return to the Main Menu button appears on the Annual Report sheet. See Figure 12-20.

Figure 12-20 ◄
The Main Menu
button placed
on the Annual
Report
worksheet

click to view the Main
Menu worksheet

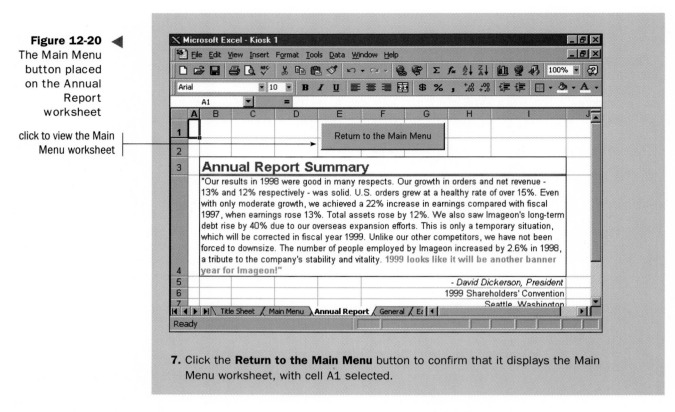

7. Click the **Return to the Main Menu** button to confirm that it displays the Main
Menu worksheet, with cell A1 selected.

So far, you've added two macros to the Kiosk workbook: one using the Macro Recorder
and the other using the Visual Basic Editor. You can use the Visual Basic Editor to add
other procedures to the workbook to display the remaining worksheets. Before proceeding
though, you decide to save the workbook and show it to Steve to discuss your progress and
get his comments.

To save your changes:

1. Click the **Title Sheet** sheet tab so that the next time you open this worksheet,
the Title Sheet is displayed.

2. Press **Ctrl + Home** to return to cell A1, and save the workbook.

Quick Check

1   What are five basic steps you should follow in planning and creating your customized
application?

2   Describe what each of the following is used for:
    a. the Project Explorer
    b. the Properties window
    c. the Code window

3   Define the following terms:
    a. project
    b. object
    c. property
    d. module
    e. syntax

4 How would you get help on a particular property listed in the Properties window?

5 What are the three types of procedures in Visual Basic?

6 Describe the syntax of a sub procedure.

7 Why would a project contain several modules?

In this session, you have begun to create the workbook that will make it easy for Imageon stockholders to view company financial information at the annual shareholders' conference. You have created a simple macro using the Macro Recorder and attached the macro to a button you placed on a worksheet. You've opened the Visual Basic Editor and learned about some of the editor's features. You've also been introduced to the Visual Basic programming language and have created your first Visual Basic sub procedure by copying and pasting code from one procedure into another. In the next session, you'll learn more about the Visual Basic programming language. You'll see how the Visual Basic Editor helps you write your own procedures, and you'll learn how to create a sub procedure that asks the user for information.

SESSION

12.2

In this session, you'll learn about the fundamentals of the Visual Basic programming language. You'll learn how the Visual Basic Editor can help you learn about Visual Basic and enter Visual Basic code. Finally, you'll learn how to create a macro that prompts the user for information and uses that information to determine what tasks the macro should perform.

Introducing Visual Basic

You've completed the first stage of the Kiosk workbook application, in which users can easily move back and forth between the Main Menu and Annual Report sheets. To unlock the power of Visual Basic and the Visual Basic Editor, you'll learn more about the elements and structure of the Visual Basic language. There are four terms you should know to understand Visual Basic: objects, properties, methods, and variables. After you learn the meaning of each term, you'll apply this knowledge to the Visual Basic commands you created in the Annual_Report macro. Then you'll use it as a basis for creating more sophisticated procedures.

Objects

Visual Basic is an **object oriented programming language**, which means that it performs tasks by manipulating objects. An object can be almost anything in Excel, from a single cell or worksheet to the Excel application itself. Each object has an **object name**. Figure 12-21 lists some of the objects often used in writing Visual Basic programs.

Figure 12-21 ◀
Objects and
their Visual
Basic object
names

Object	Visual Basic Object Name
A cell in a worksheet	Range
A worksheet in a workbook	Worksheet
A workbook	Workbook
The Microsoft Excel Application	Application
A chart in the workbook	Chart
A Visual Basic project	VBProject

Objects are commonly grouped into collections, which are themselves objects, called **collection objects**. For example, a sheet in your workbook is an object, as is the collection of all the sheets in the workbook. Some of the object collections and their object names that you'll use frequently in your Visual Basic programs are shown in Figure 12-22.

Figure 12-22 ◀
Object
collections

Object Collection	Visual Basic Object Name
The chart sheets in the workbook	Charts
The worksheets in the workbook	Worksheets
Sheets of any kind in the workbook	Sheets
Currently open workbooks	Workbooks
Currently open projects	VBProjects

When you want to refer to a particular object in a collection, you use either the name of the object or its position in the collection. For example, in the Kiosk 1 workbook, the second worksheet is the Main Menu worksheet. If you wrote a Visual Basic program that modified that object, you could refer to it as Worksheets("Main Menu"), which refers to the name of the object within the collection of worksheets. Or you could call it Worksheets(2), where 2 refers to its position as the second sheet in the collection of Worksheets.

Most of your Visual Basic programs modify objects. You modify objects either by changing the object's properties or by applying a method to the object; you'll learn more about properties and methods in the next sections.

Properties

Properties are the attributes that distinguish an object, such as its name, and whether it's active, visible, or selected. In the last session, you used the Project Explorer and the Properties window to change the value of some of the properties in your project. For example, you changed the Name property of the Menu worksheet object to "Main_Menu." Figure 12-23 displays some Visual Basic objects and the properties associated with them.

Figure 12-23
Objects
and their
properties

Object	Properties	Description
Range	Formula Name Value	The formula entered into a cell The name assigned to the cell range The value entered into a cell
Worksheet	Name Visible	The name of the worksheet Whether the worksheet is hidden or not
Workbook	HasPassword Name Saved	Whether the workbook is password protected The name of the workbook Whether the workbook has been saved
Sheets	Count	The number of sheets of any kind in the workbook
Application	ActiveCell ActiveSheet ActiveWorkbook Selection	The cell that is active in the worksheet The sheet currently active in the workbook The workbook that is currently active within Excel The selected object

This list is only a sampling of the vast number of objects and properties available to you in Visual Basic programs.

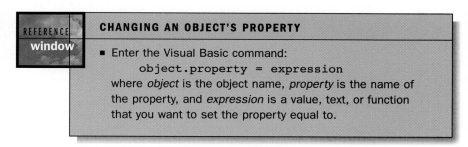

REFERENCE
window

CHANGING AN OBJECT'S PROPERTY

■ Enter the Visual Basic command:
    `object.property = expression`
where *object* is the object name, *property* is the name of
the property, and *expression* is a value, text, or function
that you want to set the property equal to.

To change the property of an object, you use the following syntax, or structure, in your Visual Basic command:

`object.property = expression`

In this case, *object* is the object name, *property* is the name of the property, and *expression* is a value that you want to assign to the property. Here are three examples of Visual Basic statements that use this syntax.

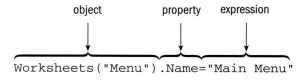

object   property   expression

```
Worksheets("Menu").Name="Main Menu"

Range("A1").Value=23

Range("A5").Formula="=SUM(A1:A4)"
```

The first example changes the Name property of the Menu worksheet object to "Main Menu." You did this in the last session when you changed the name of the worksheet using the Properties window. This is how you would write the command in Visual Basic. The second example shows how you would change the value property of the cell A1 object to the value 23. The third example shows how you would assign a formula property to the range A5 object. This command enters the formula that calculates the sum of cells A1:A4 in cell A5.

You can also use an object property statement to turn a property on or off, as in the following Visual Basic command:

```
Sheets("Title Sheet").Visible = False
```

This command hides the Title Sheet from the user by making the Visible property "False" (that is, hidden). To make the Title Sheet visible again, you would use this command:

```
Sheets("Title Sheet").Visible = True
```

Properties are one way to define objects; another way to define them is with methods.

Methods

A **method** is an action that can be performed on an object. For example, one of the things you can do to a workbook is close it, so "Close" is a method that goes with the Workbook object. Figure 12-24 shows some of the objects and methods used in Visual Basic.

Figure 12-24 ◄
Objects and
their methods

Object	Methods	Description
Range	Clear Copy Merge	Clears all formulas and values in the range Copies values of the range into the Clipboard Merges the cells in the range
Worksheet	Delete Select	Deletes the worksheet Selects (and displays) the worksheet
Workbook	Close Protect Save	Closes the workbook Protects the workbook Saves the workbook
Chart	Copy Select Delete	Copies the chart Selects the chart Deletes the chart
Charts	Select	Selects chart sheets in the workbook
Worksheets	Select	Selects worksheets in the workbook

REFERENCE
window

APPLYING A METHOD TO AN OBJECT

■ Enter the Visual Basic command:
     `object.method`
  where *object* is the object name and *method* is the method
  you want to apply.

The syntax for applying a method to an object is:

```
object.method
```

Here, *object* is the name of the object, and *method* is the method that you want to apply. Following are three examples of methods applied to objects:

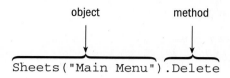

```
Sheets("Main Menu").Delete
```

```
Range("A1:B10").Clear
```

```
Workbooks("Kiosk 1").Save
```

The first example shows the command you would type to delete the Main Menu worksheet. In the second example, the Clear method is applied to the cells in the A1:B10 range to remove any values or formulas inserted there. The third example saves changes in the Kiosk 1 workbook.

Some methods require a **parameter**, a piece of information that controls how the method is applied. For example, one parameter of the SaveAs method is the filename assigned to the workbook being saved. The value that the user enters for the parameter is the **parameter value**. Some methods require more than one parameter value. The syntax for methods that require parameters is:

```
object.method(parameter values)
```

Here are some examples of methods that require parameter values:

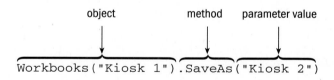

```
Workbooks("Kiosk 1").SaveAs("Kiosk 2")
```

```
Range("A1").AddComment("Total Assets")
```

```
Workbooks("Kiosk 2").Protect("Glencoe")
```

The first example shows how to apply the SaveAs method to a Workbook object called Kiosk 1 in order to save it under a new name, Kiosk 2. In the second example, the AddComment method is applied to cell A1. The parameter value used with the AddComment method is the comment text "Total Assets." This command adds the comment "Total Assets" to cell A1. In the third example, a Protect method is applied to the Kiosk 2 workbook, which includes the parameter value "Glencoe"—the password under which the workbook is protected.

With what you've learned about how Visual Basic works with objects, properties, and methods, you can now interpret the Annual_Report sub procedure you created in the last session. Recall that the two lines of the macro were:

```
Sheets("Annual Report").Select
```

```
Range("A1").Select
```

This Annual_Report procedure is an example of applying the Select method to a series of objects. The first line applies the Select method to the Annual Report worksheet, a member of the Sheets object collection. The second line applies the Select method to the Range object, cell A1. The effect of the two lines of code is to first select the Annual Report worksheet (and display it in the document window) and then to select cell A1 on the sheet.

Now that you've been introduced to objects, properties, and methods, the last major area you'll explore is variables.

Variables

Occasionally you will want your Visual Basic procedures to retrieve and store information. You do this with variables. A **variable** is a named storage location containing data that you can retrieve and modify while the program is running. Every variable is identified by a **variable name**. For example, you could create a variable named "Workforce" and use it to store the total number of people employed by Imageon. You could create a variable named "Company" and use it to store the company's name. You could also create a variable named "Wbook" and use it to store the name of the currently open workbook. All of these items are considered variables because they can change, or assume different values, over time.

The Visual Basic syntax for storing data in a variable is:

```
variable = expression
```

Here, *variable* is the name of the variable that will store the information and *expression* is a value, text, a function, or a property. Some sample Visual Basic statements that use variables are:

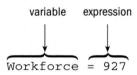

```
Workforce = 927

Sheetname = "Main Menu"

Assets = Range("B22").Value
```

In the first example, the variable "Workforce" is assigned the value 927. In the second example, the text "Main Menu" is stored in the variable called Sheetname. In the last example, the value entered in cell B22 is retrieved and stored in the Assets variable. This last example shows how you would retrieve data from an object's property and store it in a variable. The object in this expression is the Range object, cell B22, and the property is the Value property.

Once you've created a variable and given it a value, you can assign that value to an object's property. This is one of the more common tasks in a Visual Basic program. Earlier you changed the name of the Menu worksheet to "Main Menu." You could also do this using a variable as shown in the following set of Visual Basic steps:

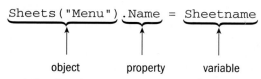

```
    variable          expression
       │                 │
       ↓                 ↓
Sheetname  =  "Main Menu"


Sheets("Menu").Name  =  Sheetname
        ↑        ↑            ↑
        │        │            │
      object  property     variable
```

The first line stores the text string "Main Menu" in the variable Sheetname, and the second line inserts that text into the Name property of the Menu worksheet.

You've finished reviewing some of the basic concepts of the Visual Basic programming language. Now you'll put these principles to work by enhancing the macros in the Kiosk 1 workbook.

Retrieving Information from the User

Steve has looked over your first version of the Kiosk workbook. He's pleased with what he's seen so far. In this version of the workbook, he wants you to provide a button that will let users display one of the workbook's financial worksheets. The four worksheets in the Kiosk workbook are described in Figure 12-25.

Figure 12-25 ◀
Financial
reports in the
Kiosk 2
workbook

Worksheet Name	Description
General	Table of general financial data
Earnings	Table of earnings and net revenue
Assets	Table of current and long-term company assets
Liabilities	Table of liabilities and long-term debts

Steve hopes to add more financial reports and charts to the workbook before the convention, and he doesn't want to clutter the main menu with buttons for each worksheet. So he wants you to create a single button that prompts the user for the name of the worksheet, and then acts on that information to display the appropriate sheet. Steve's plan for the macro is shown in Figure 12-26.

To create a procedure like this, you'll need a Visual Basic command that prompts users for information and stores the information they type in a variable for later use in the program.

To practice what you've learned about Visual Basic, you'll create that procedure from scratch, using only the Code window in the Visual Basic Editor. This will also give you a chance to see how the Visual Basic Editor helps you write error-free code.

First, you'll open the Kiosk workbook. In other tutorials in this book, you revised previously saved versions of a workbook using the same workbook name. When you're working with Visual Basic, however, it's a good idea to save later versions of your workbook under a new name. Then you can easily repeat a session, without having to redo all the steps in the tutorial. Here, you'll resave the Kiosk1 workbook from the last session as Kiosk 2.

Figure 12-26 ◀
Steve's
plan for the
Financial_Reports
macro

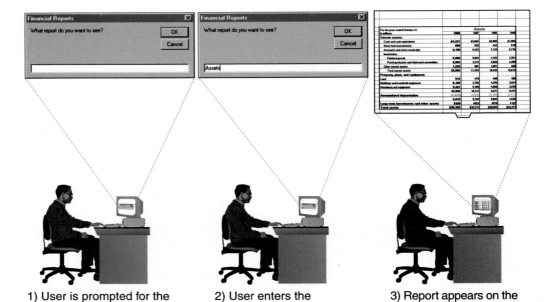

1) User is prompted for the name of a financial report.

2) User enters the report name.

3) Report appears on the computer monitor.

To open and save the Kiosk 1 workbook:

1. If you took a break after the last session, make sure Excel is running and that the Kiosk 1 workbook is open.

2. If you are reopening the workbook, and you see a dialog box about macros, click the **Enable Macros** button.

   TROUBLE? Some viruses work within macros and attack Excel workbooks. This message informs you of the existence of these kinds of viruses. If you open a workbook that you are *sure* does not contain macros, but you see this message anyway, the file *may* have been infected with a macro virus. If this happens, you should avoid opening the workbook and contact either the person who sent you the workbook or your technical support person for ways of removing the virus. If your macro does contain macros, and it has come to you from a trustworthy source, click the Enable Macros button.

3. Save the workbook as **Kiosk 2** in the Tutorial.12 folder on your Student Disk.

4. Enter **Kiosk 2** in the Workbook box in cell B7 of the Title Sheet worksheet.

First you'll create a new procedure called Financial_Reports, and then document the procedure using comment lines.

To open the Visual Basic Editor and start a new procedure:

1. Click **Tools** on the menu bar, point to **Macro**, and click **Visual Basic Editor**.

   The Visual Basic Editor opens with the same windows you worked with at the end of Session 1.

2. Click the Code window title bar to activate it, click **Insert** on the menu bar, and click **Procedure**.

3. Type **Financial_Reports** in the Name text box. Since you want to create a sub procedure that will be available to all modules in this project, make sure that the Sub and Public option buttons are selected, and then click the **OK** button.

Before attempting to write any code, you should first enter comments about what the Financial_Reports procedure does and how to use it. These comments will document your application so anyone else modifying it can easily learn its purpose. The Macro Recorder did this for you automatically in the last session.

To add comments to the Financial_Reports macro:

1. Click the **Maximize** box ▢ to maximize the Code window in the Visual Basic Editor display area.

2. If it is not already selected, click the blank line between the Public Sub statement and the End Sub statement.

3. Type **'Financial_Reports Macro** and press the **Enter** key. Like all comment lines, the comment text appears in green type.

    TROUBLE? Be sure to start the line with the apostrophe, or else Visual Basic will not interpret the line as a comment. Do not type an apostrophe at the end of the line. If you get an error message that Visual Basic expected a particular statement, you most likely forgot to type the starting apostrophe.

4. Continue entering the following comment lines in the Code window. Notice that the first and the fourth lines contain only apostrophes, which create blank lines in your comments.

    ```
    '

    'This macro prompts the user to enter a worksheet name.

    'The macro then opens the worksheet with that name in

    'the workbook.

    '

    'For use at the 1999 Shareholders' Convention
    ```

5. Press the **Enter** key after the last comment line.

    Figure 12-27 shows the Financial_Reports macro with the comments you have entered.

Figure 12-27 ◄
Comments in the
Financial_Reports
sub procedure

comments begin with
an apostrophe

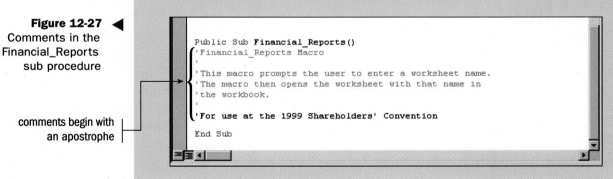

Now that you have entered the comments, you are ready to enter a command that displays a dialog box, asks the user for information, and stores that information in a variable. To do this, you'll need to use the InputBox function.

Entering the InputBox Function

As part of your macro, you want the Imageon stockholders to see a dialog box that asks them to type in the name of the financial statement that they want to see. When you want an easy way to prompt the user for information, you can create an input box by inserting the InputBox function into your Visual Basic program. A function in Visual Basic has the same syntax and purpose as a function you enter in a worksheet cell. The syntax for the InputBox function is:

```
InputBox(Prompt,Title)
```

Here, *Prompt* is the message you want to appear in the input box, and *Title* is the text that appears in the title bar of the input box. Figure 12-28 displays the relationship between the InputBox function and the input box that Visual Basic will display to the user.

```
InputBox("Enter your down payment", "Mortgage Analysis")
```

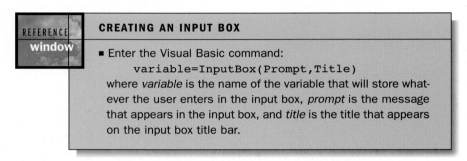

Figure 12-28 ◀
The InputBox function

Because InputBox is a function, it returns a value. In this case, the returned value is whatever value or text the user enters in the dialog box. In your Financial_Reports sub procedure, you'll store the user input in a variable named "Sheetname."

REFERENCE **window**

CREATING AN INPUT BOX

- Enter the Visual Basic command:
    ```
    variable=InputBox(Prompt,Title)
    ```
  where *variable* is the name of the variable that will store whatever the user enters in the input box, *prompt* is the message that appears in the input box, and *title* is the title that appears on the input box title bar.

Try entering the InputBox function into your procedure now. When you do, you'll see how the Visual Basic Editor helps you use the correct syntax as you type.

To enter the InputBox function:

1. Type **Sheetname=InputBox(** *but do not press the Enter key.*

   As soon as you type the opening parenthesis, the editor displays the syntax of the InputBox function. See Figure 12-29.

Figure 12-29 ◀
Visual Basic provides help for the InputBox function

optional parameters indicated by brackets

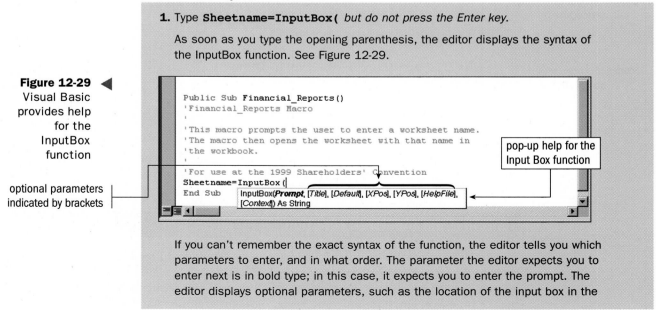

If you can't remember the exact syntax of the function, the editor tells you which parameters to enter, and in what order. The parameter the editor expects you to enter next is in bold type; in this case, it expects you to enter the prompt. The editor displays optional parameters, such as the location of the input box in the document window, in brackets. You won't be using the location parameter in your InputBox function. Continue entering the InputBox function, starting with the Prompt parameter enclosed in quotation marks. Your prompt will contain the names of the four worksheets; you want the user to type one of these names.

2. Type **"Type General, Earnings, Assets, or Liabilities"**, *but do not press the Enter key*.

As you finish entering the prompt in the input box, the Visual Basic Editor bolds the next parameter it is expecting, the Title parameter. This parameter is enclosed in brackets, so it's an optional parameter. You'll enter a title anyway to provide extra information to the user.

3. Press the **Spacebar**, type **"Name of Report")** and then press the **Enter** key to complete the line.

TROUBLE? If you receive an error message and the line appears in red after you press the Enter key, you made a typing mistake in entering the command. Review the line you typed and compare it to the instructions above; verify that you typed everything correctly, including the quotation marks and the ending parenthesis.

So far, you have entered the InputBox function into your procedure, including a variable called Sheetname that will store the information the user types. Now you are ready to finish the macro. In the next line, you'll insert a command to select the worksheet specified in the Sheetname variable. To do this, you will use the Select method with a Sheets object. The Visual Basic Editor will again help you with the syntax.

To enter the Visual Basic line that selects a worksheet:

1. Type **Sheets(**

The editor recognizes that you've entered the name for an object collection and displays information indicating that it's now expecting a value such as the name of a worksheet or a number indicating its place in the order of sheets (1, 2, 3, etc.). You'll enter the sheet name, using the Sheetname variable.

2. Type **Sheetname).Select** and then press the **Enter** key.

TROUBLE? If you get a message that reads "Compile Error: Expected: End of statement," you might have forgotten to type the period before "Select." Check your typing carefully.

Finally, enter the line telling Excel to select cell A1 in the worksheet. Once again, be prepared to take advantage of some of the editor's helpful hints.

To select the A1 cell:

1. Type **Range(**

The editor displays a pop-up box, indicating that it expects you to enter a cell reference.

2. Type **"A1")**.

After you type the period at the end of the statement, the editor displays a list of all of the properties or methods associated with a Range object. Properties are identified by the 🖾 icon, while methods are indicated with the ⬛ icon. You can select the property or method directly from the pop-up list box to enter it into your program.

3. Press the **S** key to display the Select method. See Figure 12-30.

Figure 12-30 ◀
Select a
property or
method from
the list box

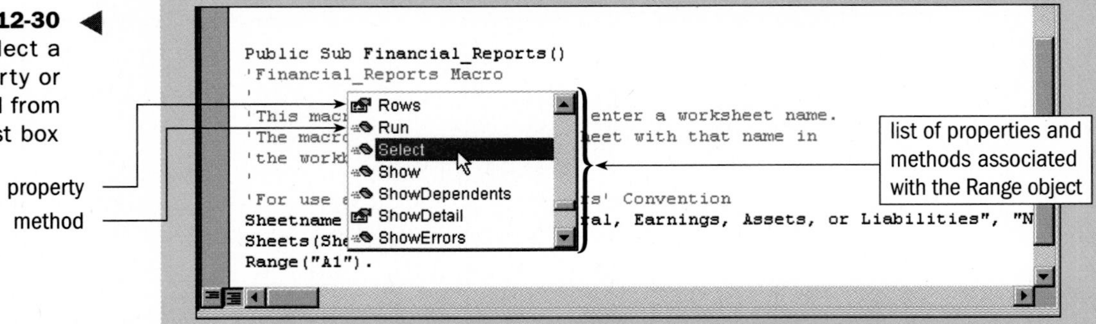

property

method

```
Public Sub Financial_Reports()
'Financial_Reports Macro
'
'This macr    📑 Rows            enter a worksheet name.
'The macr    ➡ Run             eet with that name in
'the workl    ➡ Select
                ➡ Show
'For use      ➡ ShowDependents   s' Convention
Sheetname     📑 ShowDetail      al, Earnings, Assets, or Liabilities", "N
Sheets(She    ➡ ShowErrors
Range("A1").
```

list of properties and
methods associated
with the Range object

4. Double-click the **Select** method.

The Select method is automatically appended to the Range object you entered.

5. Press the **Down Arrow** ↓ key to complete the line.

Figure 12-31 shows the completed Financial_Reports sub procedure.

Figure 12-31 ◀
The completed
Financial_Reports
sub procedure

```
Public Sub Financial_Reports()
'Financial_Reports Macro
'
'This macro prompts the user to enter a worksheet name.
'The macro then opens the worksheet with that name in
'the workbook.
'
'For use at the 1999 Shareholders' Convention
Sheetname = InputBox("Type General, Earnings, Assets, or Liabilities", "Name of Report")
Sheets(Sheetname).Select
Range("A1").Select
End Sub
```

You've finished entering the Financial_Reports macro, including selecting the sheet that the user enters, and selecting cell A1 on that sheet. Now you'll create a button that will activate the macro, and then test your macro and input box by using them in the worksheet.

Using the Input Box

To test your new macro, you'll return to the Kiosk 2 workbook and add a new button to the Main Menu worksheet that activates the Financial_Reports sub procedure.

To create the View Financial Reports button:

1. Click **File** on the menu bar, and click **Close and Return to Microsoft Excel**.

2. Click the **Main Menu** sheet tab. Now you'll add the button that will activate your macro.

3. Display the Forms toolbar and use the Button tool 🔲 to create a button in range **D12:F13**. The Assign Macro dialog box appears.

4. Click **Financial_Reports** in the Macro Name list box, and then click the **OK** button. Now you'll enter the text for the button.

5. Type **View Financial Reports** and click cell **A1**.

6. Click the **Close** box 🗙 on the Forms toolbar.

Figure 12-32 shows the new button on your Main Menu worksheet

Figure 12-32 ◀
The View
Financial
Reports button

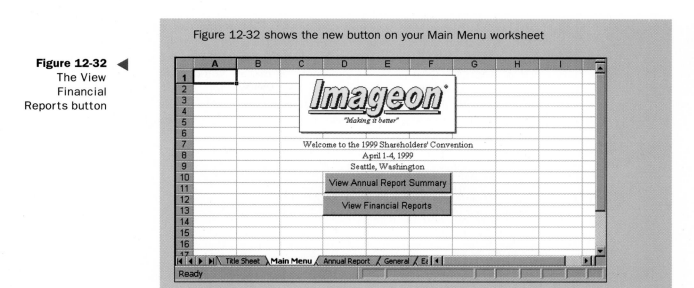

Now you'll test your macro by using it to display Imageon general financial data from 1995 through 1998.

To display the General worksheet:

1. Click the **View Financial Reports** button on the Main Menu worksheet. The dialog box you created in your macro appears, asking you to enter the name of the sheet you want to see.

2. Type **General** in the Name of Report input box. See Figure 12-33.

Figure 12-33 ◀
The View
Financial
Reports
input box

title

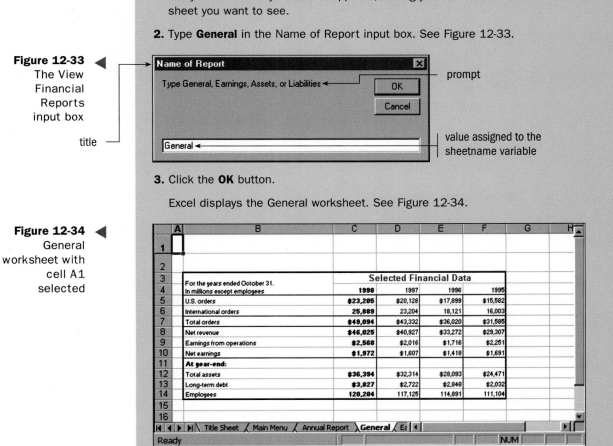

prompt

value assigned to the
sheetname variable

3. Click the **OK** button.

Excel displays the General worksheet. See Figure 12-34.

Figure 12-34 ◀
General
worksheet with
cell A1
selected

The macro works as you hoped it would. By entering the name of one of the four reports, the user can view the worksheet for that report. Your final task is to create buttons on each of the financial report worksheets that will take the user back to the Main Menu worksheet. Rather than recreating that button, you can copy and paste the button you created in the last session. Copying a button not only copies the button's image, but also copies the macro assigned to it. You'll try this now by pasting the "Return to Main Menu" button on the General worksheet and then on the remaining worksheets.

To copy and paste the Return to Main Menu button:

1. Click the **Annual Report** sheet tab.

2. Right-click the **Return to Main Menu** button.

3. Click **Copy** from the shortcut menu.

4. Click cell **A1** to deselect the button.

5. Click the **General** sheet tab.

6. Click the **Paste** button 📋 on the Standard toolbar, and click cell **A1** to deselect the button.

7. Click the **Return to Main Menu** button to test it. The Main Menu worksheet should appear.

8. Paste the button into the other three financial report worksheets. Since you've already copied the button image, you do not have to recopy it. Each time you paste the button, deselect the pasted button by clicking cell A1.

9. Test your macro buttons by verifying that you can open each of the financial worksheets and return to the Main Menu from each one.

   TROUBLE? If you type the name of one of the financial worksheets incorrectly, or click Cancel and receive a Runtime error or Subscript Out of Range error when trying to run the Financial_Reports macro, click the End button in the dialog box. You'll learn how to deal with problems of this kind in the next session.

You're finished working on the Financial_Reports macro for now. Save the Kiosk 2 workbook.

To save your changes:

1. Click the **Title Sheet** sheet.

2. Save the workbook.

You'll show Steve what you've accomplished and then get his recommendations on what to do next.

Quick Check

1. Define the following terms:
   a. object-oriented programming language
   b. collection object
   c. method
   d. parameter
   e. variable

2 What Visual Basic command would you enter to change the name of the Assets worksheet to "Assets Table"? Hint: The object name is Sheets("Assets") and the name of the worksheet is contained in the Name property.

3 What Visual Basic command would you enter to select the Assets worksheet?

4 What Visual Basic command would you enter to store the name of the Assets worksheet in a variable named "Sheetname"?

5 How do you enter comments into your Visual Basic procedures?

6 What are optional parameters and how are they displayed in the Visual Basic Editor's pop-up help?

7 What Visual Basic command would you enter to display an input box containing the prompt "Enter your last name", the text "Log In" in the title bar, and then save whatever the user entered into a variable named "Lastname"?

In this session, you've learned some of the fundamentals of Visual Basic and how to work with selected objects, properties, and methods. You've learned about variables and how to use them in your Visual Basic programs. You've created an input box that convention attendees will use to display the financial worksheets. In the next session, you'll learn how to create procedures called control structures that "make decisions" based on the type of information the attendees enter. Finally, you'll learn how to create message boxes that will give attendees information describing what they should enter.

SESSION

12.3

In this session, you'll learn about control structures that cause your macros to operate differently under different conditions. You'll learn how to create message boxes that give the user directions for using your macros. Finally, you'll learn how to print your macros so that you can review them when you're not in front of your computer.

Introducing Control Structures

You've shown Steve the Kiosk 2 workbook that you completed in the last session. He was very impressed. He clicked on the View Financial Reports button and was able to quickly bring up the General financial report table. In response to the input box you created, he entered "Assets" and was able to view the Assets table. Unfortunately, when he tried to view the Liabilities table, he mistyped it as 'Libelities" and was confronted with the dialog box shown in Figure 12-35.

Figure 12-35 ◄
The error message Steve sees after his typing mistake

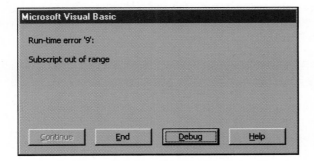

What happened? There was no worksheet named "Libelities" in the Kiosk 2 workbook, and when the Financial_Reports macro tried to select that worksheet, it failed to find it, and displayed the dialog box shown in Figure 12-35. This is the last thing Steve wants to see happen at the shareholders' convention. He asks you if you can revise the macro so that it checks the user-entered value to make sure it is one of the four financial worksheets in the Kiosk workbook.

To do this, you have to create a control structure. A **control structure** is a series of commands that evaluates conditions in your program, and then directs the program to perform certain actions based on the status of those conditions. Figure 12-36 shows the kind of control structure that Steve has in mind for the Financial_Reports macro.

Figure 12-36 ◀
Differerent
conditions that
might arise
when running
the Financial_
Reports macro

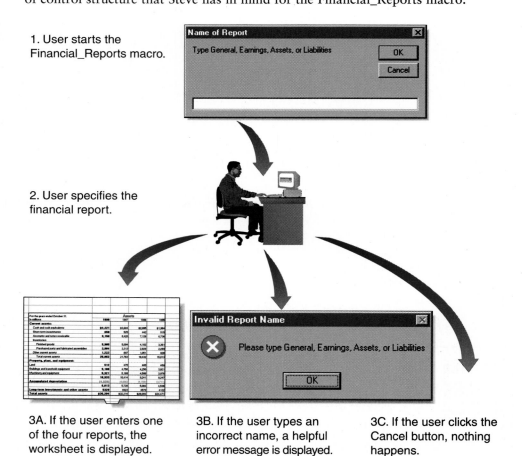

1. User starts the Financial_Reports macro.

2. User specifies the financial report.

3A. If the user enters one of the four reports, the worksheet is displayed.

3B. If the user types an incorrect name, a helpful error message is displayed.

3C. If the user clicks the Cancel button, nothing happens.

In this control structure, the user will start the Financial_Reports macro by clicking the View Financial Reports button on the Main Menu worksheet of the Imageon workbook. The procedure will first ask for the name of the financial report, and then evaluate whatever the user enters. If the user enters one of the four worksheet names containing financial data, the program selects and displays that worksheet. However, if the user does not enter one of the four worksheet names, the program displays a message, telling the user what the acceptable entries are. If the user clicks the Cancel button instead of entering the name of a report, the input box closes and redisplays the Main Menu worksheet.

To adjust your macro to handle all three of these situations, you'll need to create a Visual Basic If-Then-Else control structure.

Using the If-Then-Else Control Structure

The most commonly used control structure in Visual Basic is the If-Then-Else control structure. In this structure, Visual Basic evaluates some conditions. IF those conditions are true, THEN Visual Basic runs a set of commands, or ELSE it will run a different set of commands. The syntax for an If-Then-Else control structure is:

```
If <Condition> Then

        <Visual Basic statements>

Else

        <Visual Basic statements>

End If
```

Figure 12-37 shows an example of an If-Then-Else control structure that evaluates financial data to approve or deny a loan application.

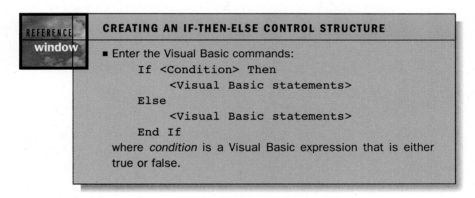

Figure 12-37 ◄
An example of
an If-Then-Else
control
structure

condition: Is the amount of savings greater than $20,000?

```
If Savings > 20000 Then

        Range("B10").Value="Loan Approved"
```
statement that is run if the condition is true

```
Else

        Range("B10").Value="Loan Denied"
```
statement that is run if the condition is false

IF the user enters a savings figure that is greater than $20,000, THEN the loan is approved, otherwise (ELSE) it is denied. The control structure evaluates the value of a variable named Savings and, based on the condition of that variable, enters the appropriate text in cell B10.

This macro can respond to only two possible conditions: the user has above $20,000 in savings, or below $20,000 in savings.

REFERENCE
window

CREATING AN IF-THEN-ELSE CONTROL STRUCTURE

■ Enter the Visual Basic commands:
```
        If <Condition> Then
                <Visual Basic statements>
        Else
                <Visual Basic statements>
        End If
```
where *condition* is a Visual Basic expression that is either true or false.

If your control structure has more than two conditions, you may want to use an If-Then-ElseIf control structure. The syntax for this control structure in Visual Basic is:

```
If <Condition> Then

        <Visual Basic statements>

ElseIf <condition 2> Then

        <Visual Basic statements>

ElseIf <condition 3> Then

        <Visual Basic statements>

End If
```

In order to cover all possible conditions, control structures can have an unlimited number of conditions. Figure 12-38 shows an example of Visual Basic code using multiple conditions in a control structure that evaluates whether or not a user qualifies for a loan. In this example, there are three conditions. The person applying for the loan could have more than $20,000 in savings, or she could have more than $15,000, or she could have less than $15,000. There are three conditions, and based on which of these conditions is true, the text "Loan Approved", "Loan Pending", or "Loan Denied" is entered into cell B10.

Figure 12-38 ◀
An example of an If-Then-ElseIf control structure

statement that is run if the savings are greater than $15,000, but not greater than $20,000

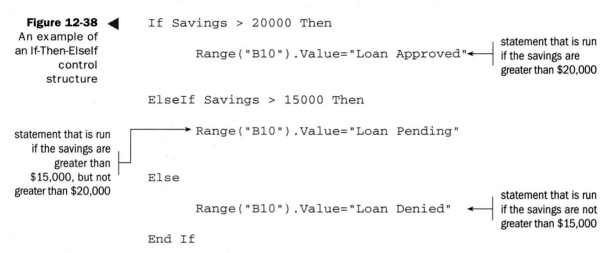

```
If Savings > 20000 Then

        Range("B10").Value="Loan Approved"◀─── statement that is run
                                               if the savings are
                                               greater than $20,000

ElseIf Savings > 15000 Then

     ──▶ Range("B10").Value="Loan Pending"

Else

        Range("B10").Value="Loan Denied" ◀─── statement that is run
                                              if the savings are not
                                              greater than $15,000
End If
```

The first If-then statement and the last Else statement are the same as the ones in Figure 12-37. The second statement handles the third possible condition, where the user has more than $15,000 but not more than $20,000 in savings.

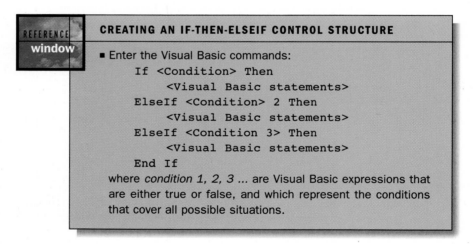

REFERENCE window

CREATING AN IF-THEN-ELSEIF CONTROL STRUCTURE

- Enter the Visual Basic commands:
```
        If <Condition> Then
            <Visual Basic statements>
        ElseIf <Condition> 2 Then
            <Visual Basic statements>
        ElseIf <Condition 3> Then
            <Visual Basic statements>
        End If
```
where *condition 1, 2, 3 ...* are Visual Basic expressions that are either true or false, and which represent the conditions that cover all possible situations.

When control structures evaluate conditions, they determine how a value compares to another value. To do this, the condition statement uses comparison and logical operators.

Comparison and Logical Operators

When you enter conditions in your Visual Basic control structure, you will usually be comparing one value to another. You saw an example of this in Figure 12-38 where the value of the Savings variable was compared to the values $20,000 and $15,000. The > symbol used in that example is a **comparison operator**, because you use it to compare values or expressions within a condition. If the comparison is true, then Visual Basic performs the tasks in the lines that follow. If the comparison is not true, then it performs another task. Figure 12-39 shows some of the comparison operators you'll frequently use in your Visual Basic control structures.

Figure 12-39 ◄
Comparison
operators

Comparison Operator	Description
>	Greater than
<	Less than
>=	Greater than or equal to
<=	Less than or equal to
=	Equal to
<>	Not equal to
Is	Compares whether one object is the same as another

Another type of operator that you'll use in writing conditions for your control structures are logical operators. **Logical operators** are used to combine expressions within a condition. The most commonly used logical operators are the AND and OR operators. You
use the **AND** operator when you want both expressions to be true before the procedure
acts upon them, while the **OR** operator requires only one of the conditions to be true.
Figure 12-40 shows an example of a condition that uses the AND logical operator.

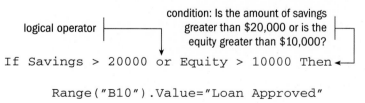

Figure 12-40 ◄
An example of
a condition
using the AND
logical operator

```
logical operator
                                                    condition: Is the amount
                                                    of savings greater than
If Savings > 20000 and Credit="Good" Then ◄─      $20,000? and the credit
                                                    rating "Good"?
        Range("B10").Value="Loan Approved"

Else

        Range("B10").Value="Loan Denied"

End If
```

In this example, the text "Loan Approved" will be placed in cell B10 only if the Savings
variable has a value greater than 20,000 AND the Credit variable has the value
"GOOD". Otherwise, the value placed in cell B10 is "Loan Denied". Figure 12-41 shows
an example of a condition that uses the OR logical operator.

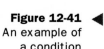

Figure 12-41 ◄
An example of
a condition
using the OR
logical operator

```
                          condition: Is the amount of savings
logical operator          greater than $20,000 or is the
                          equity greater than $10,000?
If Savings > 20000 or Equity > 10000 Then ◄─

        Range("B10").Value="Loan Approved"

Else

        Range("B10").Value="Loan Denied"

End If
```

In this example, the loan is approved if either the Savings variable is greater than
20,000 or the value of the equity in a home mortgage is greater than 10,000.

As you continue to learn Visual Basic, you'll discover that it supports other control structures. These include the **For-Next control structure**, which allows you to repeat a series of commands a set number of times, and the **Do-While control structure**, which repeats a series of commands as long as a particular condition is true. For the Financial_Reports macro, however, you will need only the If-Then-ElseIf control structure.

Writing an If-Then-ElseIf Control Structure

You are ready to write the If-Then-Else control structure needed to make the Financial_Reports macro work under all possible conditions. You can reopen the Kiosk 2 workbook now and save it as Kiosk 3.

To open the Kiosk 2 workbook:

1. If you took a break after the last session, make sure Excel is running, and that the Kiosk 2 workbook is open.

2. If you are reopening the workbook, click the **Enable Macros** button when prompted by Excel.

3. Save the workbook as Kiosk 3 in the Tutorial.12 folder on your Student Disk, and update the workbook name on the Title Sheet.

Before you start revising the Financial Reports sub procedure, review the various conditions that you have to account for in the macro. When the dialog box asks the user to enter a report name, there are three possible outcomes. These are:

1. The user enters a valid financial report name.

2. The user enters an invalid financial report name.

3. The user clicks the Cancel button.

Because you have three conditions to account for, you will have to include an If-Then-ElseIf control structure. Also, you'll have to account for the fact that the first condition (that the user enters a valid name for the report) has four possible answers, and therefore that condition will need to contain several expressions. You will have to link the four possibilities with an OR logical operator, so that if the user enters any one of the four allowed report names, the procedure will then display the appropriate worksheet.

Now that you understand the conditions your macro needs to account for, you are ready to start editing the Financial_Reports macro.

To edit the Financial_Reports macro:

1. Click **Tools** on the menu bar, point to **Macro**, and click **Macros**.

2. Click **Financial_Reports** in the Macro Name list box, and click the **Edit** button.

   The Visual Basic Editor opens with the Code window still maximized and displaying the Financial_Reports sub procedure.

The first line you'll add to the macro will include the IF statements that test the condition of whether the user has entered one of the four valid report names.

To enter the first condition in the If-Then-ElseIf control structure:

1. Click the beginning of the line `Sheets(Sheetname).Select` and press the **Enter** key to place a blank line above it.

2. Press the ↑ key to move the insertion point into the new blank line.

3. Type `If Sheetname="General" or Sheetname="Earnings" or Sheetname="Assets" or Sheetname="Liabilities" Then`

4. Press the ↓ key twice to go the end of the line that selects cell A1.

The next line of the macro (`Sheets(Sheetname).Select`) selects the worksheet the user typed, which was stored in the Sheetname variable. The next line, `Range("A1").Select`, selects cell A1. So if the user has entered one of the four correct names, the program will then select and display one of the four financial report worksheets, and select cell A1 on that sheet.

In the next part of the control structure, you'll account for the two remaining possibilities: the user has entered the wrong name in the input box, or by clicking the Cancel box has not entered any value. You'll first determine whether a value was entered into the input box, and if so, display an error message that an incorrect name was entered.

To enter the second condition in the If-Then-ElseIf control structure:

1. Press the **Enter** key to insert a new blank line before the End Sub line.

Now you'll enter a condition using<>, which is a "not equal to" operator, and " " which represents nothing, or no user text entered. It tests whether the Sheetname variable is "not equal to" nothing. In other words, as long as something was entered into the input box, this condition will be true.

2. Type `ElseIf Sheetname <>"" Then` and press the **Enter** key.

TROUBLE? If you see a Compile error after you press the Enter key, click the OK button and check to make sure you have typed spaces in the correct places in the statement, and that you have capitalized the words correctly.

Now you'll enter the comment line placeholder that you'll replace later on.

3. Type `'Display an error message` and press the **Enter** key.

This is the comment line that you'll be replacing later on.

So far you've accounted for two conditions: first, if the user has entered one of the four correct report names and then, if not, whether the user entered anything at all. The only remaining condition is that the user has clicked the Cancel button, and the Sheetname variable therefore has no value. If this happens, you want the procedure to end without doing anything at all, so you simply end the If-Then-ElseIf structure and the Financial_Reports sub procedure. This will close the input box without performing any task in the workbook.

To finish If-Then-ElseIf control structure:

1. Type **End If** and press the ↓ key.

2. To make the program code easier to read, indent the lines between the If, ElseIf and End If statements by pressing the **Tab** key at the beginning of those lines.

To review how this control structure works (and how your code should appear) see Figure 12-42. As you can see from the figure, this control structure has covered all possible conditions.

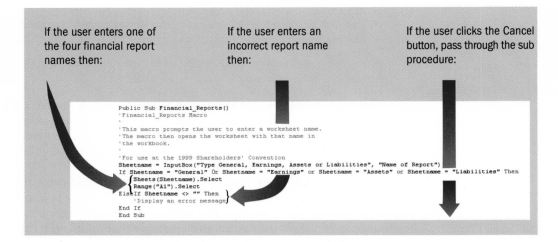

Figure 12-42 ◀
The If-Then-
ElseIf code for
the
Financial_Reports
sub procedure

Your next step is to replace the placeholder comment with a command that displays an error message in a dialog box when the user enters an incorrect name. To do this, you'll use the MsgBox (message box) function.

Creating a Message Box

To create a message box, you use the MsgBox function, which is similar to the InputBox function you used in the last session, except that it does not contain a text box for the user to enter values. You would use a message box for situations where you simply want to inform the user and have them click the OK button. The user does not type in any text. The syntax for the MsgBox function is:

```
MsgBox(Prompt,Buttons,Title)
```

As in the InputBox function, *prompt* is the message in the dialog box, and *title* is the text that appears in the title bar. The *Buttons* parameter specifies the kind of buttons that appear in the message box, as well as the style of the message box itself. There are several options you can choose for the Buttons parameter, a few of which are shown in Figure 12-43.

Figure 12-43 ◀
Button
parameter
values and the
resulting
message boxes

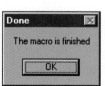

Button = vbOKOnly

Button = vbCritical

Button = vbOKCancel

Button = vbInformation

Some button styles merely inform, some ask a question, and others provide an alert to a problem of some kind. You don't have to learn the names of these different buttons and message styles; the Visual Basic Editor will provide popup help as it did when you wrote the InputBox function in the last session.

REFERENCE
window

CREATING A MESSAGE BOX

- Enter the Visual Basic command:

  ```
  variable=MsgBox(Prompt,Buttons,Title)
  ```

  where *variable* is the name of the variable that will store which-ever button the user clicks in the message box, *prompt* is the message that appears in the message box, *Buttons* indicates the button and message window style of the message box, and *Title* is the title that appears on the message box title bar.

Since the MsgBox function is a function, it returns a value that Visual Basic expects you to assign to a variable. The returned value indicates which message box button the user clicked. That might seem strange to you if you're creating a message box with only one button, since it's no mystery which button the user will click and there's no need to store that information in a variable. However message boxes are also used in situations where the user has to chose between two options, in which case you might build a control structure around which button was pressed. So you'll still assign the value returned to a variable, even though there's only one possible value it could have.

In the Financial_Reports macro, you'll assign the results of the message box function to a variable named "Warning." The Warning variable doesn't do anything, but Visual Basic requires it to comply with the syntax of the MsgBox function.

To enter the MsgBox function:

1. Select the comment line you entered as a placeholder in the previous set of steps, and press the **Delete** key.

2. Type **Warning=MsgBox(**

   The Visual Basic Editor displays the syntax for the MsgBox function, with the word "Prompt" bolded. You'll first enter the prompt or message that you want to show the user.

3. Type **"Please type General, Earnings, Assets, or Liabilities",**

   After typing the comma, the editor displays a pop-up list box showing all the possible button styles.

4. Double-click **vbCritical** from the pop-up list box, and then type **,** (a comma).

   The next parameter you need to enter is the text for the message box title bar.

5. Type **"Invalid Report Name")** and press the ↓ key. See Figure 12-44.

   TROUBLE? If you see an error message that reads "Compile error - expected list separator or)," you may have forgotten to type the closing parenthesis. Go back and type it now, and then press the ↓ key. There a few other optional parameters for the message box function, but you don't need to enter them.

Figure 12-44 ◀
The completed
Financial_
Reports macro

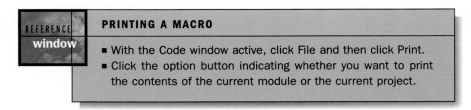

```
Public Sub Financial_Reports()
'Financial_Reports Macro
'
'This macro prompts the user to enter a worksheet name.
'The macro then opens the worksheet with that name in
'the workbook.
'
'For use at the 1999 Shareholders' Convention
Sheetname = InputBox("Type General, Earnings, Assets or Liabilities", "Name of Report")
If Sheetname = "General" Or Sheetname = "Earnings" Or Sheetname = "Assets" Or Sheetname = "Liabilities" Then
    Sheets(Sheetname).Select
    Range("A1").Select
ElseIf Sheetname <> "" Then
    Warning = MsgBox("Please type General, Earnings, Assets or Liabilities", vbCritical, "Invalid Report Name")
End If
End Sub
```

You've finished the Financial_Reports macro. You only need to print a hard copy of the macros in your module, close the Visual Basic Editor, and test the macros. If the macros work, you'll then modify a few elements of the workbook to make it ready for use at the convention.

REFERENCE
window

PRINTING A MACRO

- With the Code window active, click File and then click Print.
- Click the option button indicating whether you want to print the contents of the current module or the current project.

Before you print your macro, be sure to save it.

To print and test your macros:

1. Click the **Save** button 🖫 on the Standard toolbar.

   Excel saves the current version of the Kiosk workbook along with the macros it contains.

2. Click **File** on the menu bar, and then click **Print**.

3. Make sure that the Current Module option button is selected, and then click the **OK** button.

4. Click **File** on the menu bar, and then click **Close and Return to Microsoft Excel**.

5. Click the **Main Menu** sheet tab.

6. Click the **View Financial Reports** button. The dialog box you created asks you to name a report. First, test how the macro responds to an incorrect entry.

7. Type **Libelities** (the spelling mistake that Steve made earlier) and click the **OK** button.

   Excel displays the message box shown in Figure 12-45.

Figure 12-45 ◀
The error
message box
you created in
Visual Basic

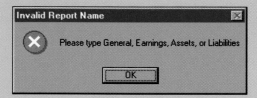

Invalid Report Name

Please type General, Earnings, Assets, or Liabilities

OK

TROUBLE? If you get an error message from Excel when running your macro, compare the printout of your macro with the one shown in Figure 12-44, and then return to the editor to correct any typing mistakes.

8. Click the **OK** button.

Now you'll test the situation where you enter nothing and click Cancel.

To test the macro with no user input:

1. Click the **View Financial Reports** button again, and then click the **Cancel** button.

You should be returned to the Main Menu worksheet without seeing the message box.

2. Click the **View Financial Reports** button one last time.

3. Type **Liabilities** (spelling it correctly this time) and click the **OK** button.

The Liabilities worksheet is displayed.

TROUBLE? If the Liabilities worksheet is not displayed, check your typing. The worksheet name should begin with a capital "L".

4. Click the **Return to Main Menu** button on the worksheet to display the Main Menu worksheet.

The macro now appears to work properly. You contact Steve to show him the new features of the macro and to ask him if there are any more changes he wants you to make.

Finishing Your Customized Application

When you are finished creating your macros, you will want to think about other aspects of your workbook. Will users be allowed to change any of the values in the worksheets? What elements of the document window do you want them to see? Do you want them to see the toolbars or menu commands? Which, if any, of the worksheets do you want to hide from them?

You discuss these issues with Steve. Steve looks over the Kiosk workbook and suggests that you make the following changes:

1. Protect the contents of all the worksheets so they can't be changed by one of the convention attendees.

2. Hide the Title Sheet worksheet.

3. Remove all gridlines, row and column headers, and scroll bars from each of the financial report worksheets.

4. Hide the sheet tabs so that all users are forced to use the macro buttons that you created.

5. Hide the formula bar, status bar, and any toolbars in the document window.

You'll begin by protecting the worksheets in the workbook, which you have to do one at a time.

To protect the Title Sheet:

1. Click the **Title Sheet** sheet tab.

2. Click **Tools** on the menu bar, point to **Protection**, and click **Protect Sheet** to open the Protect Sheet dialog box.

3. Make sure that the Contents, Objects, and Scenarios check boxes are selected.

If you want to add a password so that other users can't unprotect the sheet, you could enter one now in the Password text box. For now though, protect the sheet without a password and leave the Password text box blank.

4. Click the **OK** button.

5. Repeat these steps for the remaining six worksheets in the workbook.

Now that the sheets have been protected from unwanted changes, you will hide the Title Sheet from the user.

To hide the Title Sheet:

1. Click the **Title Sheet** worksheet tab.

2. Click **Format** on the menu bar, point to **Sheet**, and click **Hide**.

   The Title Sheet is now hidden from view.

Finally, you'll group the remaining worksheets in the Kiosk workbook and hide their tabs, as well as the Standard toolbar, using the Options command on the Tools menu.

To modify the appearance of the remaining worksheets:

1. Click the **Main Menu** sheet tab, press and hold down the **Shift** key and click the **Liabilities** sheet tab to group the remaining sheets in the workbook.

2. Click **Tools** on the menu bar, and click **Options**.

3. Click the **View** tab, if necessary.

4. Deselect the following check boxes.

   Formula bar

   Status bar

   Gridlines

   Row & column headers

   Horizontal scroll bar

   Vertical scroll bar

   Sheet tabs

5. Click the **OK** button.

6. Click **View** on the menu bar, point to **Toolbars**, and click **Standard** to hide the Standard toolbar.

7. Repeat this process to hide the remaining toolbars.

   Figure 12-46 shows your Main Menu worksheet without the gridlines, scroll bars, row and column headers, or sheet tabs.

Figure 12-46 ◀
The final appearance of the Main Menu

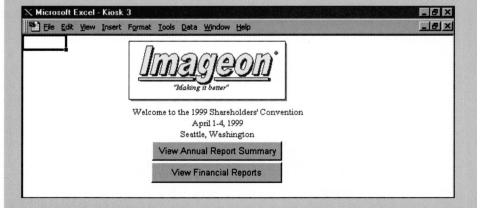

8. Test the operation of your workbook, verifying that the macro buttons display the financial tables they're supposed to.

You show Steve the final product. He's pleased with the appearance of the workbook. He may suggest some changes later, but for now, you can save the workbook.

To save your changes:

1. Click **File** on the menu bar, and click **Close**. Click the **Yes** button when prompted to save your changes.

   The formula bar, status bar and toolbars are still hidden after you close the Kiosk 3 workbook. Restore them now and then exit Excel.

2. Click **View** on the menu bar, and click **Formula Bar**.

3. Click **View** again and click **Status Bar**.

4. Click **View** once more, point to **Toolbars**, and click **Standard**.

5. Redisplay the Formatting toolbar and any other toolbars you normally use, using the same process.

6. Exit Excel.

Steve is very pleased with your work, and looks forward to using your workbook at the shareholders' meeting. He feels that your Excel workbook is user-friendly, and that it will help shareholders find the information they want easily, even if they aren't familiar with Excel. This will then free up the convention staff for more substantive discussions with the shareholders.

Quick Check

1. What is a control structure and why might you need one in your Visual Basic procedure?

2. Define the following terms:
   a. comparison operator
   b. logical operator

3. What is the syntax of the If-Then-Else control structure?

4. What control structure would you use if you had multiple conditions from which to choose?

5. Other than the If-Then-Else and If-Then-ElseIf control structures, name two other control structures supported by Visual Basic.

6. What is the syntax of the MsgBox function?

7. What command would you enter to display a message box with the following elements: The text "File Status" in the title bar, the message "File Saved", and a single OK button in the dialog box.

You've completed your customized application. You've seen how you can write Visual Basic macros that prompt users for information and evaluate the information they enter. You've seen some of the basic features of the Visual Basic Editor and you've observed how the editor can assist you in writing and interpreting the Visual Basic language. The shareholders' convention is still a month away—plenty of time for you to learn more about the powerful capabilities of the Visual Basic Editor and the Visual Basic language.

Tutorial Assignments

Steve has worked with the Kiosk 3 workbook you completed in the tutorial. He has added four chart sheets to the workbook. He would like to have you create another button on the Main Menu worksheet with the caption "View Financial Charts." When the user clicks this button, an input box will appear asking for the name of the chart. There are four names the user can enter: Orders, Revenue, Total Assets, and Debt. Steve wants you to put in the usual error control structure so that if the user types an incorrect name, or clicks the Cancel button, the sub procedure can respond to it properly. To create Steve's custom application, do the following:

1. If necessary, start Excel, and make sure your Student Disk is in the appropriate drive. Open the Imageon workbook in the TAssign folder for Tutorial 12, and save it as Kiosk 4.

2. Enter the new workbook name, your name, and the date in the Title Sheet worksheet.

3. Use the Macro Recorder to record the act of clicking the Orders chart sheet, but do not select any object within the chart sheet. Name the macro you've recorded "Show_Charts" and include the description "This macro displays financial charts from the Kiosk workbook".

4. Start the Visual Basic Editor. Rename the project "Imageon_Convention" and rename Module1 "Charts_Macros".

5. Edit the Show_Charts macro in the Code window, and create an input box that will prompt the user for the name of the chart sheet they want to view. Name the variable that stores this information as "Chartname". Make the prompt of the input box read, "Enter the chart you want to view: Orders, Net Revenue, Total Assets, or Debt". Let the title bar of the input box read "View Financial Chart".

6. Replace the occurrence of the "Orders" worksheet in the macro with the Chartname variable.

7. Create a control structure for the Show_Charts macro that tests whether the user has entered one of the four chart sheet names. If the user has not entered one of the four allowed names, have the macro display a message box with the text "Please enter: Orders, Net Revenue, Total Assets, or Debt". The title bar of the message box should read "No Chart Found". Use the vbInformation button style for the message box.

8. Use the Print command in the Visual Basic Editor to print the contents of your current module.

9. Return to Excel and create a macro button on the Main Menu worksheet with the Show_Charts macro attached to it. Name the macro button "View Financial Charts".

10. Copy and paste the "Return to Main Menu" button on each of the four chart sheets.

11. Test your macros and verify that they work properly.

12. Remove gridlines, sheet tabs, column and row headers, toolbars, the status bar, and the formula bar from the Kiosk 4 workbook.

13. Save your file in the TAssign folder for Tutorial 12 on your Student Disk.

14. Close the Kiosk 4 workbook, and restore the sheet tabs, gridlines, and other window features to your Excel window.

Case Problems

1. Creating a Print Macro at Casey's Flowers Barbara Twain works in the finance department of Casey's Flowers, a nationwide distributor of flowers and greeting cards. Part of Barbara's job is to create and print the company's financial statements.

Barbara has entered the statements in an Excel workbook in three worksheets: Finance, Income, and Balance, representing the financial summary, income statement, and balance sheet.

The workbook also has a Title Sheet in which Barbara would like to place macros to quickly print any sheet in the workbook. The macro would display an input box and prompt Barbara for the name of the report she wants to print. It will also check to see that she's entered one of three financial worksheets in the workbook. She's asked you for some help in creating her macro.

1. If necessary, start Excel, open the Casey workbook in the Cases folder for Tutorial 12 on your Student Disk and save it as Casey Print Macro.

2. Enter the new workbook name, your name, and the date on the Title Sheet worksheet.

3. Using the Macro Recorder, record a macro named Print_Macro in which you click the Finance sheet tab, print the worksheet, and then return to the Title Sheet worksheet, selecting cell A1.

4. Edit the Print_Macro sub procedure in the Visual Basic Editor. Add an input box to the macro in which the user is prompted to "Enter sheet to print." Give the input box the title "Print a financial report." Save whatever the user enters in the input box into a variable named "Sheetname".

5. Use the Edit and Replace command to replace the occurrence of the word "Finance" (including the quotation marks) with the word Sheetname.

6. Add an If-Then-ElseIf control structure that checks to see whether the user has entered either Finance, Income, or Balance. If the wrong name is entered, have the procedure display a message box informing them of the error. Use the Exclamation style for the message box and button. If they've pressed the Cancel button in your input box, have the procedure end without doing anything.

7. Place a button on your Title Sheet worksheet that runs the macro when the user clicks it.

8. When the macro runs, it flickers as it goes through the process of selecting a sheet, printing it, and reselecting the Title Sheet worksheet. One of the properties of the Excel application is screen updating. Return to the Visual Basic Editor to continue editing the Print_Macro sub procedure. Enter a new line at the beginning of the procedure (directly after the Sub Print_Macro statement) to turn off screen updating for the Application object. Turn screen updating back on in the last line of the macro before the End Sub statement. *Hint*: You have to enter a Visual Basic statement that turns the ScreenUpdating property of the Application object on and off.

9. Print your Print_Macro sub procedure.

10. Save the workbook.

2. Creating a Break-Even Function for Brakdale Skis Clyde Mason analyzes monthly sales figures at Brakdale Skis, a manufacturer of cross-country skis in Green Bay, Wisconsin. One of the most important pieces of information he looks at each month is the break-even point for the company. The break-even point is the point at which sales revenue equals the total fixed and variable expenses of producing the product (for a full discussion of break-even analysis, see Tutorial 9.) The break-even point is equal to:

Total Fixed Expenses / (Average Unit Price - Average Unit Cost)

Clyde uses this function so frequently that he wishes Excel included it in its list of financial functions. He asks you to help him create a customized function named "breakeven" that would calculate the break-even point when given the total fixed expense, unit price, and unit cost.

To create a customized function, you have to create a function procedure in the Visual Basic Editor. The syntax for a Function procedure is:

```
Function Function_Name(Parameters)

    <Visual Basic Statements>

    Function_Name=Expression

End Function
```

Here, *Function_Name* is the name of your function. Note that it is listed twice, once in the first line in the macro where the name of the function is declared, and then later when it gets its value from an expression in the last line of the procedure before the End Function statement. The *parameters* are the list of variables, separated by a comma, that are used in calculating the function. Clyde's break-even function has three variables: Fixed_Expense, Unit_Price, and Unit_Cost. To create Clyde's break-even function, do the following:

1. If necessary, start Excel, and open the Brakdale workbook in the Cases folder for Tutorial 12 on your Student Disk, and save it as Brakdale Break-even.

2. On the Title Sheet, enter the new workbook name, your name, and the date.

3. Open the Visual Basic Editor.

4. Use the Insert Module command on the menu bar to insert a new module in the project.

5. Use the Insert Procedure command to insert a public function procedure into the module you just created. Name the function "breakeven".

6. In the set of parentheses on the first line of breakeven function, enter the list of parameters to be used in the function, separated by commas.

7. Insert a line into the function procedure that calculates the value of breakeven, in terms of the three parameters you entered into the function breakeven line.

8. Save your work and print a copy of your function procedure.

9. Exit the Visual Basic Editor and return to the Brakdale Break-even workbook.

10. In cell C17 of the Break-even worksheet, use the Function Wizard to enter your new customized function. Look for the function in the User-Defined category of functions provided by the Function Wizard.

11. Using your breakeven function, determine how many units per month Brakdale Skis must sell to break even. Label the cell appropriately. Save the file.

3. Viewing Stock Information at Larson and Davis Victoria D'Allesandro at the investment company of Larson and Davis has created a workbook with information on 26 different industrial stocks. She wants to make this worksheet available to some of her coworkers and clients. There is a list of the stocks at the front of the workbook. Victoria wants you to create a macro that will allow users to click the ticker symbol from the list of stocks, press a key, such as Ctrl + t, and then have the macro display the worksheet for that stock in the workbook. You suggest using an input box, but with 26 ticker symbols, the prompt for the box would be very long.

The macro you create will use an Excel object with the object name "ActiveCell." The ActiveCell object is simply the cell that happens to be currently selected in the workbook. The macro will then extract whatever value has been entered into the active cell and then open a worksheet thats name is equal to that value.

Victoria also wants the user to be able to go back to the list of stocks by pressing a single key or key a combination.

Finally, you should modify the workbook's appearance. Remove the column and row headings, the sheet tabs, a status bar, and a formula bar. To create Victoria's customized application, do the following:

1. If necessary, start Excel, open the Stocks workbook in the Cases folder for Tutorial 12 on your Student Disk, and save it as Stock Information Macro.

2. On the Title Sheet worksheet, enter the new workbook name, your name, and the date.

3. Use the Macro Recorder to create two new macros: one named Stock_Info that displays the AA worksheet, selecting cell C2 in the process, and the other named Stock_List that displays the Stock List worksheet, selecting cell A1. Within the Macro Recorder dialog box, assign the keyboard combination Ctrl + t to the Stock_Info macro and Ctrl + m to the Stock_List macro.

4. Edit the Stock_Info macro in the Visual Basic Editor, adding a line at the beginning of the macro that retrieves the value from the active cell and stores it in a variable named "Stockname". Edit the macro further so that it opens the worksheet referenced by the Stockname variable.

5. Print the macros in your module.

6. Test your macro by clicking a ticker symbol in the Stock List worksheet and pressing Ctrl + t. Verify that the macro displays the worksheet for that stock. Also test that pressing Ctrl + m takes the user back to the Stock List worksheet.

7. Group the sheets of the workbook together and hide the row and column headers, the worksheet tabs, and the scrollbars.

8. Save the changes to your workbook, with the Stock List worksheet as the active sheet.

4. Creating a Title Sheet at BG Software Sally Crawford works at BG Software, a company that produces educational software for children. Sally uses Excel workbooks to track product plans, schedules, marketing, and sales. Sally knows that title sheets are an important element of an Excel workbook. They allow others who look at the workbook to quickly see its purpose and contents. The steps Sally takes to create the title sheets are always the same from workbook to workbook. She could save herself valuable time if she had a macro that automated the process of creating a title sheet, prompting her for the information it needs.

Figure 12-47 shows the general form of Sally's title sheet.

Figure 12-47 ◀

	A	B	C	D	E
1	BG Software				
2					
3					
4	Workbook:				
5	Created by:				
6	Date:				
7					
8	Purpose:				
9					

Only cells A1, A4-A6, and A8 of this sheet will remain constant for each workbook. Sally would like the macro that generates the title sheet to always include those elements in the proper locations. She would also like to have a dialog box that prompts her for this information:

Workbook name	to place in cell B4
User name	to place in cell B5
Date	to place in cell B6
Purpose	to place in cell B8

Sally asks you to write such a macro for her. To create Sally's macro, do the following:

1. If necessary, start Excel, and create a new workbook with the name Title Sheet Macro in the Cases folder for Tutorial 12 on your Student Disk.

2. Use the Macro Recorder to record the steps you take to create the title sheet, using a mock workbook name, user name, and date. Include a step to format the width of column A to 20 points and to bold the title, "BG Software," in cell A1.

3. Edit the macro you create with the Macro Recorder, replacing the mock names you entered with variables whose values are entered by the user via an input box.

4. Print a copy of your macro.

5. Go through the macro line by line and using Excel online Help, write a short description of what each line in the macro does. Identify any objects, properties or methods in your sub procedure.

6. Save and test your macro and verify that it works properly.

Answers to Quick Check Questions

SESSION 8.1

1 Right-click the sheet tab of the active sheet, click Insert on the Shortcut menu, click the Worksheet icon in the Insert dialog box, then click the OK button; click the sheet tab of the newly created worksheet, then drag it to the right of the previously active sheet.

2 A worksheet group is a collection of worksheets that have all been selected for editing and formatting.

3 Select the worksheet group by either pressing and holding down the Ctrl key and clicking the sheet tabs of each worksheet in the group, or if the worksheets occupy a contiguous range in the workbook, click the first sheet tab in the range, press and hold down the Shift key and click the sheet tab of the last sheet in the range. Deselect a worksheet group by either clicking the sheet tab of a worksheet not in the group or right-clicking one of the sheet tabs in the group and clicking Ungroup Sheets on the Shortcut menu.

4 Create a worksheet group consisting of the range of worksheets. In the first worksheet in the group, select the text and formulas you want to copy and click Edit, click Fill, then click Across Worksheets. Click whether you want to copy the contents, formulas, or both, then click the OK button.

5 the sheet range and the cell range

6 'Section 1'!A1:A10

7 Sheet1:Sheet10!A1:A10

SESSION 8.2

1 A template is a workbook that contains specific content and formatting that you can use as a model for other similar workbooks.

2 Click File, click Save As, click Template in the Save as type list box, then click the Save button.

3 Templates folder (a subfolder of the Microsoft Office folder)

4 The template used in creating the blank workbook you first see when starting a new Excel session

5 Create a subfolder in the Templates folder, then move the template file into it.

6 A user can modify the contents of a workbook based on a template without changing the template file itself. The next time a workbook is created based on the template, it is opened with all the original properties intact.

SESSION 8.3

1 'D:\Reports\[Product Report]Sales Info'!A1:A10

2 It includes both the location and the name of the workbook.

3 Click Edit, then click Links.

4 A lookup table is a table in which rows and columns of information are organized into separate categories. The lookup value is the value that indicates in which category your looking. The categories for the lookup table are usually located in the table's first row or column and are called compare values.

5 VLOOKUP and HLOOKUP

6 The range_lookup value is a parameter in the VLOOKUP and HLOOKUP functions that tell Excel whether to look for an exact match in a lookup table. A value of TRUE means that Excel does not have to find an exact match.

SESSION 9.1

1 CVP analysis expresses the relationship between a product's expenses (cost), its volume (units sold), and the resulting profit.

2 Variable expenses increase in directly relation to the number of units produced. Fixed expenses remain constant regardless of production. Mixed expenses are fixed expenses, which are somewhat susceptible to increases in production to cause an increase in their value.

3 a table that shows the results of several what-if analyses

4 An input cell is the cell in the table whose value you are interested in changing. The result cell is the cell containing the results you're interested in viewing.

5 the point at which total expenses equal total revenue

6 a data table with a single column or row of input values

7 a data table that uses two sets of input values, one in the first row of the table and the other in the first column

8 You can display an unlimited number of result values with the one-variable data table, but only one result value with the two variable-data table.

SESSION 9.2

1 Scenarios allow you to perform what-if analyses with more than one input cell.

2 assign range names to the cells

3 cells whose values you are changing in the scenario

4 Result cells display the output you're interested in. You define result cells when creating scenario summary reports.

5 Click Tools, click Scenarios, then click the scenario name in the list of available scenarios.

6 Click the Summary button in the Scenario Manager dialog box, click the Scenario Summary option button, then click the OK button.

SESSION 10.1

1 a hit-and-miss strategy where you try different values, attempting to find the optimal solution

2 With several variables to consider, you might never hit upon the best solution.

3 In a what-if analysis, you change the input cell to observe the value in the result cell. In a goal seek, you define a value you want to obtain for the result cell, and then determine what input value is required in the input cell.

4 One example is: "How should I change the price of my product to reach a desired level of profit?"

5 The changing cell is the cell in the goal seek that you want to modify. The result cell is the cell in a goal seek that contains the value you want to match.

6 the location of the changing cell, the location of the result cell, and the value you want to see in the result cell

SESSION 10.2

1 Solver is an Excel add-in that calculates solutions to what-if scenarios based on adjustable cells and constraints. Adjustable cells are cells whose value Solver can change to reach the optimal result; constraints are limits placed on Solver in changing the values of the adjustable cells.

2 when you have too many variables in the worksheet that must be maximized, minimized, or that must reach a specific value in the result cell

3 The target cell is the cell that is maximized, minimized or set a specific value. A constraint is a limitation placed on a cell in the worksheet when Solver is run.

4 Click the Restore Original Values option button to set the worksheet back to the state it was in before you ran Solver.

5 Use an integer constraint on the target cell.

6 A report that includes information about the target cell, changing cell, and constraints. The report includes the original and final values for these cells.

7 A Not Binding constraint is a constraint that was not a limiting factor in the Solver solution. A Binding constraint was a limiting factor. Slack is the difference between the value of the constraining cell and the limiting value of the constraint.

8 so that the answer report will include information on the entire Solver process, from the original values through to its final solution

SESSION 11.1

1 A fixed width text file places all columns in the same location in the file, while a delimited text file uses a special character to separate one column from another.

2 A space, a comma, or a tab

3 Click the location in the Data preview window of the Text Import Wizard where you want the column break to appear.

4 a. A database is a program that stores and retrieves large amounts of data, and that creates reports describing that data.
b. A table is a collection of data that is stored in rows and columns.
c. A field stores information about a specific characteristic for a person, place or thing.
d. A record is a row of the table that displays the collection of characteristics for a particular person, place, or thing.

5 A common field is a field that is shared by two or more tables and is used to combine records from those tables.

6 A query is a question you ask about the data in the database.

7 Criteria are conditions you set to limit the number of records the database extracts.

8 A data source is any file that contains the data that you want to retrieve. Data sources can be databases, text files, or other Excel workbooks. To define a data source you must specify the name of the data source, its location, and the type of driver to use in accessing data from it.

SESSION 11.2

1 Click the Refresh Data Button on the External Data toolbar. Refreshing data causes Excel to go back to the data source and retrieve the data using the query you created.

2 With a selected cell in the data range containing the external data, click the Data Range Properties button on the External Data toolbar, and select the Refresh data on the File Open check box.

3 Click the Edit Query button on the External Data toolbar.

4 Format the data using the Fraction format category and specifying one of the format types in that category.

5 Start the PivotTable Wizard and click the External data source option button in the first step.

6 It keeps the size of the workbook small.

SESSION 11.3

1 The Internet is a worldwide collection of interconnected computer networks. The World Wide Web is a graphical interface to the Internet that allows user to access different information sources by clicking a button.

2 a query that retrieves data from the Internet, placing it into your Excel workbook

3 a program that retrieves and displays Web pages from the World Wide Web

4 an Internet connection, a Web browser, and Web query file

5 Click the Refresh button on the External Data toolbar.

6 Hypertext is text that is linked to related material so that when the text is clicked or otherwise activated, the related material is retrieved and displayed. A hyperlink is a word, phrase, or graphic that, when clicked or activated, "jumps" the user to another document or information source.

SESSION 12.1

1 Define your needs; decide on the application's appearance; use the Macro Recorder to create the initial Visual Basic code for the macros; modify the Visual Basic code; and finalize the appearance of your application.

2 a. The Project Explorer gives a hierarchical view of the objects in your project.
b. The Properties window gives you a view of the properties of the individual objects.
c. The Code window displays the Visual Basic code for your project's macros.

3 a. A project is a collection of macros, worksheets, forms for data entry, and other items that make up the customized application you're trying to create.
b. An object is an element of an application, such as a worksheet, a cell, a chart, a form, or a report.
c. A property is an attribute of an object that defines one of its characteristics, such as its name, size, color, or location on the screen.
d. A module is a collection of macros.
e. Syntax refers to the set rules specifying how you must enter certain commands.

4 Select the property and press the F1 key.

5 sub, function, and property

6 Sub Procedure_Name( )

<Visual Basic commands and comments>

End Sub

7 to organize macros based on their content or purpose

SESSION 12.2

1 a. An object-oriented programming language performs tasks by manipulating objects.
b. A collection object is an object that is composed of a group of other objects.
c. A method is an action that can be performed on an object.
d. A parameter a piece of information that controls how the method or function is used.
e. A variable is a named storage location containing data that you can retrieve and modify as the program is running.

2 Sheets("Assets").Name="Assets Table"

3 Sheets("Assets").Select

4 Sheetname = Sheets("Assets").Name

5 Type an apostrophe at the beginning of the line.

6 Optional parameters are parameters in methods or functions that are not required for the method or function to work. They are displayed within brackets.

7 Lastname=InputBox("Enter your last name","Log In")

SESSION 12.3

1 A control structure is a series of commands that evaluates conditions in your program, and then directs the program to perform certain actions based on the status of those conditions.

2 a. A comparison operator is a word or symbol that is used to compare values or expressions within a condition.
   b. A logical operator is used to combine expressions within a condition.

3 If <Condition> Then

   <Visual Basic Statements>

   Else

   <Visual Basic Statements>

   End If

4 the If-Then-ElseIf control structure

5 the For-Next and the Do-While control structures

6 MsgBox(Prompt,Buttons,Title)

7 MsgBox("File Saved",vbOKOnly,"File Status")

Sales Invoicing for Island Dreamz Shoppe

OBJECTIVES

In this case you will:

- Create a template worksheet

- Format a worksheet to improve its appearance

- Enhance a worksheet with varied fonts and borders

- Embed a graphic object in a worksheet

- Protect worksheet cells

- Use TODAY, IF, and VLOOKUP functions

- Create and edit a print macro

Island Dreamz Shoppe

CASE

Like many entrepreneurs, Nicole Richardson discovered the old-fashioned way to make money: choose something you like to do, keep costs low and quality high, and make teamwork a priority. This principle led to the success of her Island Dreamz Shoppe, a gift gallery featuring crafts of artists from the Caribbean whose jewelry, paintings, and embroidered giftware capture the spirit of the islands.

Since the gallery opened two years ago, business has been brisk. Responding to requests from many of her customers, Nicole expanded her business to include mail orders. When customers visit the Shoppe, Nicole gives them a catalog to take home. Many customers find it more convenient to order items after they return home than to cram extra gifts into an already overstuffed suitcase.

On a good day, Nicole receives about a dozen phone calls from customers who want to place orders. With so few calls, she doesn't need a full-blown order-entry system, but she would like to automate her invoice preparation. She decides to create an Excel template for her sales invoices. After she creates the template, all she needs to do is enter data for each order and print the invoice.

Nicole recently completed a paper invoice for an order from Rachel Nottingham, shown in Figure AC-1. Using this invoice as a model for the labels, formulas, and format that she wants to use in her template worksheet, Nicole prepares her planning analysis sheet (Figure AC-2). The calculations she needs in the template include the current date, the unit price of each item ordered times the quantity ordered (the extended price), the total amount for all items, the sales tax, the shipping cost, and the total amount of the order.

Figure AC-1 ◄
Island Dreamz
Shoppe sales
invoice

Island Dreamz Shoppe
1001 Anchor Cove
Montego Bay, Jamaica, B.W.I.

Date	24-Nov-99
Invoice No	1097

Name: Rachel Nottingham
Address: 2741 Landsdowne Road
City: Victoria, BC   Postal Code: V8R 3P6
Country: Canada

Item #	Description	Quantity	Unit Price	Extended Price
21	Summer Beach Scene	3	$25.00	$75.00
27	Sea Scape Watch	2	36.00	72.00
47	Spanish Ducat Key Chain	1	12.00	12.00
63	Raindrop Crew Neck T-shirt	2	14.00	28.00
67	Stone-washed Twill Jacket	3	54.00	162.00

		Total Sale	$349.00
		Sales Tax	24.43
		Shipping	25.00

Payment Method			TOTAL	$398.43
	Check			
	Visa			
X	MasterCard			
	Discover			
	American Express			
Credit Card #	4799123456789000	Expiration	03/99	

Thank you for your order!

Figure AC-2 ◄
Nicole's
planning
analysis
sheet

Planning Analysis Sheet

<u>My goal</u>:

Develop a template worksheet for preparing sales invoices

<u>What results do I want to see?</u>

A sales invoice for each order

<u>What information do I need?</u>

Customer name and address
Item number and quantity to be shipped
Lookup description in product table ❶
Lookup unit price for item in product table ❷
Method of payment

<u>What calculations will I perform?</u>

1. Extended price ❸ = quantity * unit price
2. Total sale ❹ = sum of extended price
3. Sales tax ❺ = total sale * 7%
4. Shipping ❻ = if total sale is less than $200 then $15, otherwise $25
5. Total ❼ = total sale + sales tax + shipping

Using her planning analysis sheet and the original paper invoice, Nicole sketches the template she wants to create using Excel (Figure AC-3). For each item ordered, she plans to enter the item number, description, quantity, and unit price. She wants Excel to do the calculations described in her Planning Analysis Sheet (Figure AC-2). The circled numbers are guides to help you relate Nicole's sketch to the required calculations.

Figure AC-3 ◀
Nicole's sketch
of her template
worksheet

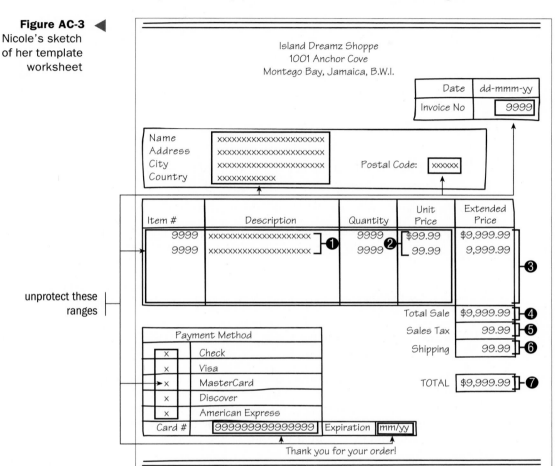

Nicole also sketches a table that lists the items Island Dreamz sells (Figure AC-4). The table includes the number, description, and unit price of each product.

Figure AC-4 ◀
Island Dreamz
product table

Item #	Description	Unit Price
21	Summer Beach Scene	25.00
27	Sea Scape Watch	36.00
31	Victorian Walking Stick	28.00
47	Spanish Ducat Key Chain	12.00
63	Raindrop Crew Neck T-shirt	14.00
67	Stone-washed Twill Jacket	54.00
78	Island Can Coolers	6.00

Nicole has asked you to help her create the invoice worksheet. To create the sales invoice worksheet, do the following:

1. Create the sales invoice for Island Dreamz by entering the labels for the invoice worksheet. Adjust column widths as necessary. Label placement should correspond to Nicole's sketch but does not need to match it exactly. Include a title sheet in the sales invoice workbook to document the purpose and content of the workbook.

2. Enter the calculations specified in Figure AC-2 in the worksheet. Use the TODAY function to enter the date.

3. Format the cells as shown in Figure AC-1. Also note that the first cell in the Unit Price and Extended Price columns is formatted differently than the rest of the cells in those columns.

4. Add fonts and borders as shown in Figure AC-1. Save your sales invoice workbook as Island Dreamz Invoice.

5. Embed the Logo.bmp file in the Tutorial.add folder on your Student Disk at the top of the invoice as shown in Figure AC-1.

6. Name the invoice sheet with the sales information Invoice.

7. Use the Macro Recorder to create a macro that prints the Invoice worksheet. Add a button at the bottom of the Invoice worksheet to run the macro.

8. Apply protection as indicated in Figure AC-3 so that only those cells in which data is entered can be changed. Protect the worksheet. Make sure you remember the password. Before entering any data, save the revised worksheet.

9. Test the operation of the worksheet by entering data for the order shown in Figure AC-1. Note how the values in the Extended Price column are calculated automatically as you enter the data. Use the macro to print this invoice.

10. Choose additional fonts and borders to enhance the appearance of Nicole's invoice. Explain why you selected these characteristics. Delete the data for Rachel's order, and then save the workbook as Island Dreamz Invoice 2. Test the operation of the worksheet with realistic data values. Print your enhanced worksheet, and then close it without saving the data you entered.

11. Open the Island Dreamz Invoice 2 workbook again and turn off the protection so you can modify the workbook. Insert a new sheet after the Invoice sheet and name it Product. Create a product table that contains the product information shown in Figure AC-4. Excluding the column titles, give this table the range name Products. Print a copy of this worksheet.

12. Nicole wants Excel to automatically look up the description and unit price in the product table when an item number is entered in the worksheet. If fewer than eight items are entered in the worksheet, the Item # in the unused lines should be left blank and the Description, Unit Price, and Extended Price columns in that row should also remain blank. To do this, combine the IF and VLOOKUP functions in the Description and Unit Price cells, and the IF function in the Extended Price cell. The IF function tests for an empty cell in the Item # column by testing whether the empty cell is equal to two successive quotation marks (""). If the cell is empty, the Description and Unit Price cells are left blank by setting the value of those cells to the same set of quotation marks. If the Item # is not blank, then the IF function uses the VLOOKUP function in the Description and Unit Price cells and the item number to obtain the appropriate information from the product table. The Extended Price cell is calculated as shown in Figure AC-2 and Figure AC-3, using the IF function to insert a blank value if no Item # is entered. Place the appropriate formulas in the Description, Unit Price, and Extended Price cells. Test the worksheet with at least two orders; use a different number of items each time. Save the workbook as Island Dreamz Invoice 3. Use the print macro to print these invoices.

13. Remove the data. Protect the Description and Unit Price cells. Activate the worksheet protection. Test the worksheet with realistic data. Save the workbook as Island Dreamz Invoice 4 in template format.

14. Write instructions for operating Nicole's sales invoice worksheet.

15. Nicole wants to include an order form with her catalog that a customer can complete and return to Island Dreamz. Design this catalog order form. For ideas, you might want to research orders forms in catalogs you have received. Create the form using Excel. Save the workbook as Island Dreamz Invoice 5 in Excel workbook format, and then print a copy of the blank order form.

16. Arrange and clearly identify the printouts and answers for all problems in this case.

Performance Reporting for Boston Scientific

In this case you will:

- Create and use a multiple sheet workbook

- Enhance worksheets with formatting

- Consolidate worksheet files

- Link worksheets

- Create macros for displaying and printing sheets

- Edit your macros so they prompt the user for information and check user input

- Create charts from summary data

- Use Microsoft Word as a destination application

CASE

Boston Scientific[1]

Boston Scientific is on the cutting edge of medical cost reduction. The company develops and manufactures catheters and other products that are used as alternatives to traditional surgery. As described by CEO Peter Nicholas: "We were one of the first companies to articulate the concept of less invasive procedures." Less invasive procedures are possible because current medical imaging techniques let physicians see inside the body and manipulate instruments through a natural opening or a tiny incision. Boston Scientific aggressively markets its products for these medical procedures. For example, a traditional coronary bypass operation often costs $50,000 to $70,000, including the hospital stay and weeks of recovery time. By contrast, clearing a clogged artery with one of Boston Scientific's catheters, which is inserted under the skin of a patient's arm, takes just a few hours and costs around $12,000.

Although many of Boston Scientific's products are expensive relative to the cost of a scalpel, they enable a patient to leave the hospital much sooner and avoid huge hospital bills. For this reason, Boston Scientific's products are popular and sales continue to increase rapidly. Another important element in its growth is the company's ability to leverage technology across its four largely autonomous divisions: Medi-Tech (radiology), Mansfield (cardiology), Microvasive Endoscopy (gastroenterology), and Microvasive Urology.

[1]Adapted from *Fortune*, "Boston Scientific," April 5, 1993, p. 97.

Willow Shire joined Boston Scientific last year as a junior accountant. Her responsibilities include preparing the quarterly performance report that consolidates the financial results for the four divisions. Willow created a template for reporting quarterly financial results, a copy of which was sent to and completed by the controller of each division. Willow just received the workbook files from the four divisions. She now needs to prepare the consolidated statement of operation summarizing the division results, and she has asked you to help her. To help Willow prepare the statement, do the following:

1. Open the Boston workbook from the Tutorial.add folder on your Student Disk and review the sheets for each division: Urology (Microvasive Urology), Mansfield (Mansfield), Endoscopy (Microvasive Endoscopy), and Meditech (Medi-Tech).

2. Add a consolidation sheet named All. Insert formulas in the consolidation worksheet that add the division results to determine the corporation total. Copy the format from one of the division worksheets and paste the format into the consolidation worksheet. Insert a title sheet describing the purpose and contents of the workbook, and enhance its appearance using special fonts and formatting. Save the workbook as Boston Scientific.

3. Create a worksheet named Earnings that displays the operating Earnings for each division by quarter. Insert a column titled Total that displays each division's overall earnings for the year.

4. Create a chart sheet containing a stacked column chart that compares the operating earnings for each division by quarter. Name the chart sheet Column Chart.

5. Create a chart sheet containing a pie chart that compares the operating earnings for the year (the value in the Total column from the Earnings worksheet) for the four divisions. Name the chart sheet Pie Chart. Save the workbook as Boston Scientific 2.

6. Use the Macro Recorder to record a macro that displays the All worksheet, and selects cell A1. Name the macro Show_Report. Edit the macro in the Visual Basic Editor so that it prompts the user for the name of the sheet to view and then displays that worksheet. Include an If-Then-Else control structure to detect errors. If the user enters an incorrect name, the macro should display a message box informing the user of the error.

7. Insert a new worksheet after the Title Sheet worksheet named Menu. Place a macro button named "View Report" on the Menu worksheet that runs the Show_Report macro when clicked. Add the title "Boston Scientific" to the Menu worksheet and include text describing the purpose of the worksheet.

8. Create a second macro named Show_Chart that displays one of the two charts in the workbook. Include the necessary code to prompt the user for the name of the chart and to check the user's input, informing the user of any errors. Create a button named "View Chart" on the Menu worksheet that runs the Show_Chart macro.

9. Create a third macro, named Print_Sheet, to print a sheet from the workbook. Have the macro prompt the user for the name of the sheet, check the validity of the user's response, and tell the user if a mistake was made. Add a button "Print Sheet" to the Menu worksheet that runs this macro.

10. Print the sheets in the workbook using the Print_Sheet macro and test the other macros you created.

11. Open the Visual Basic Editor and print the macros you created.

12. On the Title Sheet worksheet, write instructions on how to work with the consolidation workbook. Assume that the user knows how to start and run Excel, but not how to consolidate data. Save the workbook as Boston Scientific 3.

13. What else could Willow include in the Boston Scientific 3 to make it more useful? Explain your answer.

14. Start Microsoft Word and create a memo to Mr. Nicholas that includes the chart from Step 4. This memo should include your summary of the results displayed in the chart. Embed the chart in the memo. Save the document as Boston Scientific Report. Print the document with the embedded chart.

15. Willow needs a summary report that contains the product sales and operating earnings data for all quarters and the annual total. She wants the report to list the product sales and operating earnings by division, as well as a corporate total. Prepare a sketch of this report. Create the report as a separate workbook file. Use appropriate fonts and borders to enhance your report. Use file linking to obtain the necessary data values from each of the individual division workbook files. Include a title sheet that documents the contents and purpose of the workbook. Save the workbook as Boston Scientific 4. Print the workbook.

16. Revise your memo from Step 13 by adding the summary report from Step 14 as a table. The memo should now include both the chart from Step 4 and the summary table from Step 14. Save the document as Boston Scientific Final Report, and then print the document.

17. Organize and clearly identify the printouts and answers for all the problems in this case.

Negotiating Salaries for the National Basketball Association

CASE

National Basketball Association

When Dr. James Naismith nailed a peach basket to a pole, he could not possibly have envisioned the popularity of the sport that he founded. Since those early days of peach baskets and volleyballs, basketball has become one of the most popular sports in the world—especially in America.

The National Basketball Association (NBA) is home to some of the world's greatest athletes. The popularity of the NBA soared in the 1980s, thanks to players like Michael Jordan, Julius Erving, "Magic" Johnson, and Larry Bird. This popularity resulted in larger attendance at games, larger television viewing audiences, and an increase in advertising sponsorships that, in turn, led to increased player salaries. While growing up, Troy Jackson wanted to be a professional basketball player. However, during his senior year of college, Troy had reconstructive knee surgery, ending his chances of ever playing competitive basketball. But Troy was still determined to make it to the NBA one way or another. Upon graduation, he was offered a job in the NBA head offices in New York, working on the staff of Commissioner David Stern.

Commission Stern and his staff are concerned with the large number of player salaries being decided through arbitration. Salary arbitration is the process of negotiating a contract when both sides cannot agree to a specific dollar amount. The arbitration process is conducted through an independent third party who listens to arguments from both sides and then makes a final determination about the terms of the contract. During the past several years, the number of contracts decided through arbitration has more than tripled. To help the NBA head office keep track of these arbitration cases, Troy suggests developing a list of the information shown in Figure AC-5.

Figure AC-5 ◀
Data definition
for salary
arbitration
database

Field Name	Description
Player	Name of player involved in arbitration
Position	Position player plays (guard, center, forward)
Team	Name of team that is involved in arbitration
Player Bid	Amount that player is asking for
Team Bid	Amount that team is willing to pay
Settle	Amount that arbitrator feels is "fair"

The commissioner agrees that this would be useful in overseeing salaries being decided through arbitration. Commissioner Stern asks Troy to list all the players who have gone through arbitration during the past three years, and Troy has asked for your help. To help Troy create the list, do the following:

1. Develop a planning analysis sheet in preparation for creating, modifying, and manipulating the list. Use your planning analysis sheet to develop your Excel solution.

2. Create a list using the data definitions in Figure AC-5. Insert the field names in the same order as specified in the figure. Include an appropriate title centered at the top of your worksheet. Bold and underline the field names. Name the worksheet Arbitration. Insert a title sheet at the beginning of the workbook that documents the workbook's purpose.

3. Add the records in Figure AC-6 to the Arbitration worksheet. Save the workbook as NBA Salaries.

Figure AC-6 ◀
Records
for salary
arbitration
database

Player	Position	Team	Player Bid	Team Bid	Settle
Miller, Sam	Guard	Indiana	4450000	3850000	4270000
Smith, Kim	Forward	New York	2350000	1580000	2200000
Powers, Sam	Center	Seattle	2450000	2100000	2390000
Gilmore, Kevin	Forward	Boston	2650000	1950000	1960000

4. Open the Players workbook from the Tutorial.add folder on your Student Disk and view its contents. This workbook contains a list of players and teams who entered into arbitration over the last six years. Make NBA Salaries your active workbook. Combine the contents of the Players workbook with the contents of the Arbitration worksheet you created in Step 2. Save the combined workbook as NBA Salaries 2. Preview and print the Arbitration worksheet.

5. Assign a range name to the list and the fields in the list. Which ranges did you name and why?

6. Add a row two rows below the player list that contains the averages for the three salary fields. Use functions and range names to calculate these averages. Save the workbook as NBA Salaries 3. Print the Arbitration worksheet.

7. Create three filtered lists: one for each of the guards, forwards, and centers. Copy each list and arrange it in alphabetical order by player on a separate sheet. Name each sheet for the appropriate player position. Place an appropriate title above the list. Below each list, add formulas that average the salary fields for that list.

8. Create a pivot table on a separate sheet that calculates the averages for each position. This table should compare the average player bid, team bid, and settle price. Based on the table, create a column chart that displays the values on a chart sheet named Column Chart. Include the appropriate headings, labels, and legends on the chart. Save the workbook as NBA Salaries 4.

9. Create three macros. One macro should sort the entire contents of the Arbitration worksheet by player and then print it. The second should sort each of the three lists (guards, forwards, and centers) by team and player and then print these reports. The final macro should print the column chart. Open the Visual Basic Editor and insert comments into the macro describing what each line does. Print the contents of the module that contains these macros.

10. Troy wants to update the player records in the workbook. Use a data form to change the data for Brett Thompson to these values:

Player Bid	2250000
Team Bid	1710000
Settle	1990000

    Were all averages updated? Was the Forwards list updated? If not, update this list.

11. Troy needs to add a new player to the list. Use a data form to enter the following data:

Player	Wiley, Bill
Position	Guard
Team	Washington
Player Bid	1550000
Team Bid	1200000
Settle	1310000

    Save the workbook as NBA Salaries 5. Print the list using the print macro. Were all averages updated? If not, which ones were not updated? If necessary, make the required revisions to the average formulas.

12. To make the workbook easier to use, add a Menu worksheet after the Title Sheet worksheet. Insert buttons on the worksheet to run the macros you created. Test the macro buttons to verify that they work properly.

13. Create a fourth filtered list from the Arbitration worksheet based on your own criteria. Explain why you selected this filter. Copy the list and place it on a separate worksheet. Use an appropriate title for this worksheet. Print the new list.

14. Revise the Title Sheet to reflect the changes to the workbook. Include instructions for using this workbook. Assume that the user knows how to start and run Excel but not how to use Excel's data forms. Save the workbook as NBA Salaries Final.

15. What else could you include in the workbook to make it more useful, and how would it improve it?

16. Organize and clearly identify the printouts and answers for all the problems for the case.

Managing Tours for Executive Travel Services

CASE

Executive Travel Services

Executive Travel Services (ETS) of San Diego is a travel agency that specializes in selling packaged tours to business executives from Fortune 500 companies. Tom Williams, a retired executive from a Fortune 500 company, started ETS in 1982. As an executive, Tom often wished he could socialize with other top executives in an informal setting for several days. Acting on his idea, Tom founded ETS. ETS books tours that last from one to three weeks. The tours' design lets executives enjoy a variety of activities while becoming acquainted with one another.

In the last several months, the number of executives requesting tours has nearly doubled. ETS accidentally overbooked several of its more popular tours, such as the Orient Express. Tom discussed the overbooking problem with Melissa Merron, a recently hired travel associate. They agreed that an Excel list could be used to develop a tour management system that would provide them with the necessary information to avoid overbooking problems in the future. Melissa worked with Tom and the other ETS associates to develop the field definitions shown in Figure AC-7.

Figure AC-7
Data definition
for Tours
database

Field Name	Description
Tour	Tour name
Month	Month tour is scheduled to start
Type	Type of tour: Fish, Golf, Photo, or Relax
Sold	Number of seats sold for tour
Open	Number of seats still open for sale
Price	Price of tour

Melissa used Excel to set up the list. Tom would like her to make several changes to improve the operation of the tour management system. To help Melissa improve her list, complete the following:

1. Develop a planning analysis sheet in preparation for creating, modifying, and operating the tour management system. Use your planning analysis sheet to develop your Excel solution.

2. Open the Travel workbook from the Tutorial.add folder on your Student Disk. Review the Tours list on the Travel worksheet. Examine the named ranges. What is missing from the list?

3. Add the appropriate field names in the order they are listed in Figure AC-7. Center and bold each field name. Create range names for each field in the list.

4. Enhance the appearance of the report title and subtitle:

   ■ Bold both titles.

   ■ Italicize the subtitle.

   ■ Increase the point size of the title to 14 points.

   Add any other formatting that you feel is appropriate to give the workbook a professional appearance. Print the Tours database. Save the workbook as Executive Travel.

5. Sort the list by the Month field. Preview and print the sorted list.

6. Create a macro named Sort_Data to do the sort described in Step 5. Add a button to the worksheet to run the macro.

7. Open the Visual Basic Editor and edit the Sort_Data macro so that it prompts the user for the name of the first field by which to sort the data. Include code that will validate the user's response (it must be one of the six field names shown in Figure AC-7) and display a helpful message if the user enters a wrong field name. Print your macro. Return to the workbook and save it as Executive Travel 2.

8. Tom wants to know how much revenue the tour produces. Add a Total Revenue field to the list, and place it immediately to the right of the Price field. Total revenue for a tour is calculated as the number of seats sold for a tour multiplied by the price charged for the tour. In a cell in the worksheet, add a formula, using range names, to sum the total revenue for all tours. Place the formula in a cell that will not be in the way of additional records that may be added to the list. Print the worksheet and then save the workbook as Executive Travel 3.

9. Filter the Tours list to produce a report of all golf tours priced at less than $1,000. Adjust column widths as needed. Sort the list in ascending order by price. Print the list.

10. At the beginning of the workbook, insert a title sheet that documents the workbook's contents. Save the workbook as Executive Travel 4.

11. Open the Travel2 workbook, ETS's projected income statement. What is missing from the income statement? How can you solve this problem?

12. Using a linking formula, include the total revenue for all tours from the Tours list in ETS's projected income statement. Add a title sheet to this workbook.

13. Add a rental expense of $12,000 in a new row inserted immediately below administrative expense. What is the net income for ETS? Save the workbook as Executive Travel 5.

14. Based on the expected revenue from the Tours list and considering the added rental expense, what commission rate could ETS pay and still realize a net income of $15,000?

15. Develop high-cost and low-cost scenarios for expenses. Create at least two ranges for these scenarios. Select appropriate expense items and/or key assumptions to include in the scenarios. Print a report with each scenario, and circle the values used for each. Save the workbook as Executive Travel 6. Write a summary comparing the scenarios.

16. Formulate a two-variable data table by selecting the input cells and the range of values to be examined for each cell. Explain why you selected these inputs. Create the data table. Save the workbook as Executive Travel 7. Print the data table.

17. Produce a chart on a chart sheet based on the data table in Step 16. Include appropriate titles and legends. Save the workbook as Executive Travel 8, and print the chart sheet. Review the results from the data table and chart, and write a summary that explains these results.

18. Start Word and create a memo to Tom that includes the table you created in the projected income statement and the results of your scenarios. Print the document and save it as Executive Travel 9.

19. What other information could Melissa produce for either the Tours list or the projected income statement? How would these reports support the ETS management's decision-making?

20. Arrange and clearly identify the printouts and answers for all problems in this case.

Microsoft Excel 97 **Index**

If you are using this text as part of our Custom Edition Program, you will find entries in the Index and Task Reference that do not apply to your custom tutorials.

Windows 95 Brief **Task Reference**

If you are using this text as part of our Custom Edition Program you will find entries in the Index and Task Reference that do not apply to your custom tutorials.

Windows 95 Brief **Task Reference**

TASK	PAGE #	RECOMMENDED METHOD
Program, quit	WIN95 10	Click ☒ or Alt+F4
Program, start	WIN95 9	Click the Start button, point to Programs, point to the program option, click the program
Radio button, de-select	WIN95 21	Click a different radio button
Radio button, select	WIN95 21	Click the radio button
Start menu, display	WIN95 9	Ctrl+Esc
Student data disk, create	WIN95 41	Click 🔲Start, click Programs, CTI Win95, Windows 95 Brief, Make Windows 95 Student Disk, press Enter
Text, select	WIN95 34	Drag the pointer over the text
Tooltip, display	WIN95 19	Position pointer over the tool
Window, change size	WIN95 17	Drag ▨
Window, close	WIN95 10	Click ☒ or Ctrl+F4
Window, maximize	WIN95 17	Click ☐
Window, minimize	WIN95 15	Click ▬
Window, move	WIN95 17	Drag the title bar
Window, redisplay	WIN95 16	Click the taskbar button
Window, restore	WIN95 16	Click 🗗
Window, switch	WIN95 12	Click the taskbar button of the program, or Alt+Tab
Windows 95, shut down	WIN95 12	Click 🔲Start, click Shut Down, Click Yes
Windows 95, start	WIN95 5	Turn on the computer

Microsoft Excel 97 **Task Reference**

TASK	PAGE #	RECOMMENDED METHOD
3-D cell reference, create	E 8.18	(When entering a function into a worksheet cell) select a sheet or sheet range, then select the cell range within those worksheets.
AutoComplete, use	E 1.15	To accept Excel's AutoComplete suggestion, press Enter. Otherwise, continue typing a new label.
AutoFill, create series	E 7.20	Enter the first or first two values in a series. Select this range. Click and drag the fill handle over cells you want the series to fill.
AutoFilter	E 5.16	Click any cell in list. Click Data, point to Filter, then click AutoFilter. Click list arrow in column that contains the data you want to filter, then select the value you want to filter on.
AutoFilter, custom	E 5.19	Click any cell in list. Click Data, point to Filter, then click AutoFilter. Click list arrow in column that contains the data you want to filter. Click Custom, then enter the criteria in Custom AutoFilter dialog box.
AutoFormat, use	E 2.29	Select the cells to format, click Format, then click AutoFormat. Select desired format from Table Format list, then click OK.
AutoSum button, use	E 2.9	Click the cell where you want the sum to appear. Click [Σ]. Make sure the range address in the formula is the same as the range you want to sum.
Border, apply	E 3.20	See Reference Window: Adding a Border.
Cancel action		Press Esc, or click [↶].
Cell contents, clear	E 1.28	Select the cells you want to clear, then press Delete.
Cell contents, copy using Copy command	E 2.15	Select the cell or range you want to copy, then click [⧉].
Cell contents, copy using fill handle	E 2.11	Click cell(s) with data or label to copy, then click and drag the fill handle to outline the cell(s) to which the data is to be copied.
Cell reference types, edit	E 2.14	Double-click cell containing formula to be edited. Move insertion point to part of cell reference to be changed, then press F4 until reference is correct, and then press Enter.
Chart title, add or edit	E 4.15 E 4.19	Select the chart. Click Chart, and then click Chart Options. In the Titles tab, click one of the title text boxes, then type the desired title.
Chart, activate	E 4.11	Click anywhere within the chart border. Same as selecting.
Chart, add data labels	E 4.16	Select the chart, then select a single data marker for the series. Click Chart, click Chart Options, then click Data Labels. Select the type of data label you want, then click OK.
Chart, adjust size	E 4.11	Select the chart and drag selection handles.
Chart, apply a pattern to a data marker	E 4.18	See Reference Window: Selecting a Pattern for a Data Marker.
Chart, apply a texture	E 4.28	Click Format Chart Area on Chart toolbar, click Patterns tab, click the Fill Effects button, and then click the Texture tab. Select the desired texture.

Microsoft Excel 97 **Task Reference**

TASK	PAGE #	RECOMMENDED METHOD
Chart, create	E 4.6	Select data to be charted. Click , then complete the steps in the Chart Wizard dialog boxes.
Chart, use picture	E 4.31	Create column or bar chart. Select all columns/bars to be filled with picture, then click Insert, point to Picture, then click From File. Select picture from Insert Picture dialog box, then click OK.
Chart, delete data series	E 4.13	Select the chart, select the data series, then press Delete.
Chart, explode pie slice	E 4.25	Select the pie chart, then click the slice to explode. Drag the selected slice away from center of pie.
Chart, format labels	E 4.27	Select chart labels, then use Formatting toolbar to change font type, size, and style.
Chart, move	E 4.11	Select the chart and drag it to a new location.
Chart, rotate a 3-D chart	E 4.26	Select a 3-D chart. Click Chart, then click 3-D View. Type the values you want in the Rotation and Elevation boxes.
Chart, select	E 4.11	Click anywhere within the chart border. Same as activating.
Chart, update	E 4.12	Enter new values in worksheet. Chart link to data is automatically updated.
Chart Wizard, start	E 4.6	Click .
Clipboard contents, paste into a range	E 2.15	Click .
Code Window, view the	E 12.14	Start Visual Basic Editor. Click View and Code.
Colors, apply to a range of cells	E 3.23	See Reference Window: Applying Patterns and Color.
Column width, change	E 2.24	See Reference Window: Changing Column Width.
Conditional formatting	E 5.21	Select the cells you want to format. Click Format, then click Conditional Formatting. Specify the condition(s) in the Conditional Formatting dialog box. Click the Format button and select the formatting to apply if condition is true.
Copy formula, use copy-and-paste method	E 2.15	Select the cell with the formula to be copied, click , click the cell you want the formula copied to, then click .
Data, validation	E 7.6	Select the cell for data validation. Click Data, then click Validation. Use the tabs in the Data Validation dialog box to specify validation parameters (Settings tab), the input message (Input Message tab), and the error alert message (Error Alert tab).
Data form, add record	E 5.11	Click any cell in list, click Data, then click Form. Click New button, type values for new record, then click Close.
Data form, search	E 5.13	Click any cell in list, click Data, then click Form. Click Criteria button, enter criteria, then click Find Next.

Microsoft Excel 97 **Task Reference**

TASK	PAGE #	RECOMMENDED METHOD
Data form, delete record	E 5.14	Click any cell in list, click Data, then click Form. Click Criteria button, enter criteria, then click Find Next. After finding record to delete, click Delete button.
Data source, define a	E 11.14	Click Data, point to Get External Data and click Create New Query. Click <New Data Source> and click OK. Specify name, driver type and location of data source.
Delimited text files, import	E 11.5	Open text file. Click Delimited option button in Step 1 of Text Import Wizard and specify delimiter in Step 2.
Embed, object	E 6.15	In Excel, select object and click Copy button. Switch to another program and open document. Select location where document will appear and click Edit, click Paste Special. Click the Paste option button, click Microsoft Excel worksheet Object, then click OK.
Excel, exit	E 1.32	Click File, then click Exit, or click Excel Close button.
Excel, start	E 1.5	Click the Start button, then point to Programs, if necessary click Microsoft Office, and then click Microsoft Excel.
Fixed width text files, create column breaks for	E 11.7	Open text file. In Step 2 of Text Import Wizard, click spot in the Preview window where you want column breaks to appear.
Fixed width text files, import	E 11.5	Open text file. Click Fixed Width option button in Step 1 of Text Import Wizard and specify column breaks in Step 2.
Fixed width text files, move a column break in	E 11.7	Open text file. In Step 2 of Text Import Wizard, click column break and drag it to new location in Preview window.
Fixed width text files, remove column breaks from	E 11.7	Open text file. In Step 2 of Text Import Wizard, double-click column break line to delete.
Font, select	E 3.17	Select the cell or range you want to format. Click Format, click Cells, and then click the Font tab. Select the desired Font from the Font list box.
Font, select size	E 3.17	Select the cell or range you want to format. Click Format, click Cells, and then click the Font tab. Click the Font Size list arrow, then click the desired font size.
Footer, add	E 2.34	In the Print Preview window, click Setup, then click the Header/Footer tab in the Page Setup dialog box. Click the Footer list arrow to choose a preset footer, or click Custom Footer and edit the existing footer in the Footer dialog box.
Format, bold	E 3.16	Select the cell or range you want to format, then click **B**, which toggles on and off.
Format, center text across columns	E 3.15	Select the cell or range with text to center. Click Format, click Cells, then click the Alignment tab. Click the Horizontal Text alignment arrow and select Center Across Selection.

Microsoft Excel 97 **Task Reference**

TASK	PAGE #	RECOMMENDED METHOD
Format, comma	E 3.10	Select the cell or range of cells you want to format, then click [button].
Format, copy	E 3.9	Select the cell or range of cells with the format you want to copy. Click [button], then select the cell or the range of cells you want to format.
Format, currency	E 3.6	Select the cell or range of cells you want to format. Click Format, then click Cells. Click the Number tab, click Currency in the Category box, then click the desired options.
Format, italic	E 3.17	Select the cell or range you want to format, then click [button] which toggles on and off.
Format, indent text	E 3.15	Select the cell or range you want to indent. Click [button].
Format, center in cell	E 3.13	Select the cell or range you want to format. Click [button], which toggles on and off.
Format, font	E 3.16	Select the cell or range you want to format. Click the Font arrow and select the desired font.
Format, percent	E 3.11	Select the cell or range of cells you want to format, then click [button].
Formats, enter into several worksheets	E 8.15	Group worksheets to be formatted and format worksheet group. Ungroup worksheets when finished.
Format, wrap text	E 3.13	Select the cell or cells you want to format. Click Format, click Cells, then click the Alignment tab. Click Wrap Text check box.
Formula, enter	E 1.17	Click the cell where you want the result to appear. Type = and then type the rest of the formula. For formulas that include cell references, type the cell reference or select each cell using the mouse or arrow keys. When the formula is complete, press Enter.
Formulas, display	E 2.37	Click Tools, then click Options. Click the View tab, then click the Formulas check box.
Formulas, enter in several worksheets	E 8.11	Group worksheets to contain formulas. Enter formulas into grouped sheets. Ungroup the worksheets.
Freeze rows and columns	E 5.6	Select the cell below and right of row or column you want to freeze. Click Window, then click Freeze Panes.
Function, enter	E 2.21	Type = to begin the function. Type the name of the function in either upper-case or lowercase letters, followed by an opening parenthesis (. Type the range of cells you want to calculate using the function, separating the first and last cells in the range with a colon, as in B9:B15, or drag the pointer to outline the cells you want to calculate. See also Paste Function button, activate.
Goal Seek, use	E 10.8	Click Tools and Goal Seek. Enter cell containing the goal in Set Cell box and intended value in To Value box. Enter cell that should be changed to reach that goal in By Changing Cell box.
Gridlines, add or remove	E 3.31	Click Tools, click Options, then click View. Click Gridlines check box.

Microsoft Excel 97 **Task Reference**

TASK	PAGE #	RECOMMENDED METHOD
Header, add	E 2.34	In the Print Preview window, click Setup, then click the Header/Footer tab in the Page Setup dialog box. Click the Header list arrow to select a preset header, or click the Custom Header button to edit the existing header in the Header dialog box.
Help, activate	E 1.26	See Reference Window: Using the Office Assistant, and Figure 1-23.
Hyperlinks, insert	E 6.33	Select text or graphic to serve as hyperlink, then click Insert Hyperlink button. Click the Browse button, select the file you want to link to, and then click OK.

If-Then-Else control structure, Visual Basic syntax for create a	E 12.36	If <Condition> Then
		<Visual Basic Statements>
		Else
		<Visual Basic Statements>
		End If

If-Then-ElseIf control structure, Visual Basic syntax for create a	E 12.40	If <Condition 1> Then
		<Visual Basic Statements>
		ElseIf <Condition 2> Then
		<Visual Basic Statements>
		ElseIf <Condition 2> Then
		<Visual Basic Statements>
		End If

Input Box, Visual Basic syntax for creating	E 12.29	variable = InputBox(Prompt, Title)
Labels, enter	E 1.15	Select cell, then type text you want in cell.
Link, objects	E 6.10	In Excel, select object and click Copy button. Switch to another program and open document. Select location where document will appear and click Edit, and then click Paste Special. Click the Paste Link option button, click Microsoft Excel Worksheet Object, then click OK.
Link, update	E 6.13	In Excel, edit data. Switch to other program to view changes in destination document.
Linked Workbook, open	E 8.36	Click Edit, click Links, click name of workbook from list of links and click Open.
Linked workbook, retrieve data from	E 8.37	Click Edit, click Links, click name of workbook from list of links and click Update Now.
Links, view list of	E 8.35	Click Edit and Links from Excel menu bar.
Lookup Tables, create	E 8.38	Create a table on a worksheet. Insert compare values in first row or column of table. Insert values to be retrieved in rows or columns that follow.
Macro, assign shortcut key	E 7.34	Click Tools, point to Macro, click Macros. Select name of macro, click Options, enter shortcut key letter in Shortcut key text box, click OK.
Macro, assign to button	E 7.39	See Reference Window: Assigning a Macro to a Button Object in a Worksheet.
Macros, assign to a button	E 12.5	Display Forms toolbar. Click button tool and draw button image on worksheet. Click the macro name in Macros list box that appears and type text that describes the button's purpose on the button image.

Microsoft Excel 97 **Task Reference**

TASK	PAGE #	RECOMMENDED METHOD
Macros, edit	E 12.18	Click Tools, point to Macro and click Macros. Click macro name in list box and click Edit.
Macros, print	E 12.44	Open Code Window in Visual Basic Editor. Click File and Print. Specify current module or project, click OK.
Macros, record	E 12.4	Click Tools, point to Macro and click Record New Macro. Enter name and description for macro. Perform macro actions, then click ■ on the Macro toolbar.
Macro, recording	E 7.36	Click Tools, point to Macro, then click Record New Macro. In Record New Macro dialog box, enter a descriptive name in the Macro Name box, select location where you want to store macro, assign a shortcut key, then click OK. Perform the tasks in the macro. Click ■.
Macro, run from Tools menu	E 7.33	Click Tools, then click Macro. Select the name of macro you want to run, then click Run button.
Macro, run using shortcut key	E 7.34	Press Ctrl + shortcut key.
Message box, Visual Basic syntax for creating a	E 12.42	variable = MsgBox(Prompt, Buttons, Title)
Methods, Visual Basic syntax for applying a	E 12.24	object.method
Natural language formula	E 5.23	Use column headers and row labels in place of cell references to build formulas.
Non-adjacent ranges, select	E 4.22	Click the first cell or range of cells to select, then press and hold the Ctrl key as you select the other cell or range of cells to be selected. Release the Ctrl key when all non-adjacent ranges are highlighted.
Numbers, enter	E 1.16	Select the cell, then type the number.
One-Variable Data Table, create	E 9.10	Set up One-Variable Data Table structure, click Data and Table. Enter cell reference for input cell in Row Input Cell box or Column Input Cell box.
Page Break, insert	E 5.28	Click row selector button where you want to start new page. Click Insert, then click Page Break.
Page Break, remove	E 5.28	Click row where you want new page to start. Click Insert, then click Remove Page Break.
Paste, graphic object	E 6.8	Select cell where you want to place object. Click Insert, point to Picture, then click From File. Select object, then click Insert.
Paste Function button, activate	E 2.19	See Reference Window: Using the Paste Function button.
Patterns, apply to a range of cells	E 3.23	See Reference Window: Applying Patterns and Color.
PivotTable, create	E 5.30	Select any cell in list. Click Data, then click PivotTable Report. Identify source, location, layout of data, and placement of pivot table.

Microsoft Excel 97 **Task Reference**

Microsoft Excel 97 **Task Reference**

TASK	PAGE #	RECOMMENDED METHOD
Range, highlight	E 1.18 E 1.28	Position pointer on the first cell of the range. Press and hold the mouse button and drag the mouse through the cells you want, then release the mouse button.
Range, move	E 2.27	Select the cell or range of cells you want to move. Place the mouse pointer over any edge of the selected range until the pointer changes to an arrow. Click and drag the outline of the range to the new worksheet location.
Range, nonadjacent	E 4.22	See Non-adjacent ranges, select.
Range, select	E 1.18 E 1.28	See Range, highlight.
Range name, defining	E 7.12	Select the cell or range you want to name. Click Insert, point to Name, then click Define. Type the name in Name in Workbook box, then click Close.
Row or column, delete	E 2.25	Click the heading(s) of the row(s) or column(s) you want to delete, click Edit, then click Delete.
Row or column, insert	E 2.25	Click any cell in the row/column above which you want to insert the new row/column. Click Insert and then click Rows/Columns. Above the selected range, Excel inserts one row/column for every row/column in the highlighted range.
Scenario Reports, create	E 9.35	Click Tools and Scenarios to open Scenario Manager. Click Summary. Click Scenario Summary option button and specify the result cells and click OK.
Scenarios, create	E 9.25	Click Tools and Scenarios. Click Add and entera scenario name. Specify Changing cells.
Scenarios, edit	E 9.33	Click Tools and Scenarios. Click scenario name and click Edit.
Scenarios, view	E 9.30	Click Tools and Scenarios. Click scenario name and click Show.
Sheet tab, rename	E 2.16	Double-click the sheet tab then type the new sheet name.
Sheet, activate	E 1.11	Click the sheet tab for the desired sheet.
Shortcut menu, activate	E 3.24	Select the cells or objects to which you want to apply the command, click the right mouse button, then select the command you want.
Solver, add constraints to	E 10.19	Start Solver and click Add. Specify constraint cell or cells and type of constraint.
Solver, add integer constraints to	E 10.23	Start Solver and click Add. In the Add Constraint dialog box, select INT from Constraint list arrow.
Solver, create an Answer Report for	E 10.24	Start Solver and click Solve. Click Answer in Reports list box after solver finds solution.
Solver, set a target cell for	E 10.17	Start Solver and specify cell reference for the target cell and whether Solver should minimize, maximize, or set the cell to a specific value.
Solver, start	E 10.17	Make sure that Solver add-in is installed. Click Tools then click Solver.
Sort, single sort field	E 5.7	Select any cell in column you want to sort by. Click [A↓] or [Z↓] on Standard toolbar.

Microsoft Excel 97 **Task Reference**

TASK	PAGE #	RECOMMENDED METHOD
Sort, more than one sort field	E 5.9	Select any cell in list. Click Data, then click Sort. Specify sort fields and sort order, then click OK.
Spell check	E 2.23	Click cell A1, then click [icon].
Sub procedure, insert	E 12.16	Click Insert and Procedure from the Visual Basic Editor menu bar. Type procedure name, click Sub and Public option. Click OK.
Subtotals, insert	E 5.25	Sort the list on column you want to subtotal. Select any cell in list, then click Data, then click Subtotals. Specify the criteria for subtotals, click OK.
Templates, create	E 8.28	Create a workbook. Click File and Save As. Enter template filename and select Template from Save As Type drop-down list box.
Templates, open	E 8.26	Click File and New. Double-click icon of the template you want to open.
Text box, add	E 3.27	Click [icon] on the Drawing toolbar. Position pointer where text box is to appear, then click and drag to outline desired size and shape. Type comment in text box.
Text files, import	E 11.5	Click File and Open and select Text Files from Files of Type list box. Locate text file and click Open. Complete the steps of Text Import wizard.
Text files, remove columns from	E 11.8	Open text file. In Step 3 of Text Import wizard, click column and click the Do Not Import Column (skip) option button.
Text files, specify the starting row for	E 11.6	Open text file, click Starting Row list arrow in Step 1 of Text Import wizard.
Text Import Wizard, start	E 11.5	Open a text file.
Toolbar, add or remove	E 3.25	Click any toolbar with right mouse button. Click the name of the toolbar you want to use/remove from the shortcut menu.
Two-Variable Data Table, create	E 9.16	Set up Two-Variable Data Table structure, click Data and Table from menu bar. In the Row Input Cell box enter input cell corresponding to row of input values. In Column Input Cell box enter input cell corresponding to column of input values
Undo button, activate	E 2.26	Click [icon].
Visual Basic Editor, start	E 12.7	Click Tools, point to Macro and click Visual Basic Editor.
Web page, converting worksheet	E 6.37	Select range you want to convert, click File, then click Save As HTML. Specify the information using the Internet Assistant Wizard.
Web Query, refresh a	E 11.37	Click a cell in external data range. Click [icon] on External Data toolbar.
Web Query, run a	E 11.35	Click Data, point to Get External Data and click Run Web Query. Select Web query file and click Get Data. Enter any values when prompted.
WordArt, embedding	E 6.7	Click [icon], then click [icon]. Select WordArt style, enter the text, specify font, then click OK.

Microsoft Excel 97 **Task Reference**

TASK	PAGE #	RECOMMENDED METHOD
Workbook, open	E 1.11	Click 📂 (or click File, then click Open). Make sure the Look in box displays the name of the folder containing the workbook you want to open. Click the name of the workbook you want to open, then click Open.
Workbook, save with a new name	E 1.21	Click File then click Save As. Change the workbook name as necessary. Specify the folder in which to save workbook in the Save in box. Click Save.
Workbook, save with same name	E 1.21	Click 💾.
Worksheet, close	E 1.31	Click File, then click Close, or click the worksheet Close button.
Worksheet, delete	E 7.28	Click sheet tab of sheet you want to delete. Click Edit, click Delete Sheet, then click OK.
Worksheet, print	E 1.29	Click 🖨 to print without adjusting any print options. Use the Print command on the File menu to adjust options.
Worksheets, consolidate	E 8.18	Create a summary sheet, insert 3-D cell references to consolidate data from other sheets in workbook.
Worksheets, group	E 8:9	For a range of sheets, click sheet tab of the first worksheet in range, hold down Shift and click tab of last sheet in range. To select sheets not in a range, hold down Control and click tabs of each sheet in group.
Worksheets, insert	E 8.8	Right-click tab of a worksheet in workbook and click Insert from Shortcut menu. Double-click Worksheet icon in dialog box.
Worksheets, move	E 8.7	Click worksheet tab and drag tab along the row of sheet tabs, drop at desired location.
Worksheets, Ungroup	E 8.11	Click sheet tab of a sheet not in group, or right-click the tab of a sheet in group and click Ungroup Sheets from Shortcut menu.